KIERKEGAARD'S

CONCLUDING UNSCIENTIFIC POSTSCRIPT

KIERKEGAARD'S
CONCLUDING UNSCIENTIFIC
POSTSCRIPT

Translated from the Danish by

DAVID F. SWENSON
PROFESSOR OF PHILOSOPHY AT THE UNIVERSITY OF MINNESOTA

Completed after his death
and provided with Introduction and Notes by

WALTER LOWRIE

PRINCETON
PRINCETON UNIVERSITY PRESS
FOR AMERICAN-SCANDINAVIAN FOUNDATION

Dedicated to the Memory of
Professor Frederick J. E. Woodbridge
a Great Teacher

FOREWORD

THIS publication of the concluding *Unscientific Postscript* by Søren Kierkegaard, marks not only the first English translation of the greatest work of the Danish thinker, but it also marks the last work of its translator, whose devotion to Kierkegaard began with his accidental discovery of this same work in a public library nearly forty years ago. As a young graduate student in philosophy, not wholly oriented in his thought, he chanced upon this volume in the original Danish. He took it home with him, and in the course of the next twenty-four hours devoured it. That discovery marked a crisis in his intellectual and spiritual development: he had found a philosopher who could guide him in his thinking, one with whom he had many things in common—a talent for dialectic, a feeling for literary expression, and, above all, a burning passion for intellectual honesty. Nothing else ever exerted so profound an influence upon him as did the writings of Kierkegaard in whose thought he was to saturate himself for the rest of his life. Indeed, for a time he was forced to lay this reading aside in order to free himself from too close an adherence to Kierkegaard's style. But always Kierkegaard was a living force to him, and I think it doubtful whether a student ever passed through his classes without hearing him allude not once but many times to some phase of Kierkegaard's thought.

Not for many years did he trust himself to attempt to translate for publication any of Kierkegaard's works. So keen was his sensitivity for the delicate nuances of Kierkegaard's literary expression, that he was his own most severe critic in his attempt to reproduce in English not merely Kierkegaard's thought but his unique poetic style, and never did he attain a form that fully satisfied him.

For many years, his was a lone voice crying in the wilderness, for though Kierkegaard's works had long been known in Germany and France, even his name was practically unknown to English-speaking people. Then some eight years ago Dr. Walter Lowrie of Princeton, burning with a dynamic enthusiasm for the Kierkegaardian literature, returned to this country, and began his crusade for an English edition of Kierkegaard's works. Under this stimulus, and encouraged by the co-operation of one more aggressively active than himself, Mr. Swenson completed his translation of the *Philosophical Fragments,* and then took up in earnest the translation of the *Postscript*. This he felt to be peculiarly his task, since the *Fragments* and the *Postscript* constitute Kierkegaard's chief contributions to philosophical thought. Perhaps, too, he felt that he was discharging a debt of gratitude in the translation of the work which had initiated him into Kierkegaard's thought. Unfortunately, owing to ill health and the press of academic duties, along with his excessive meticulousness already alluded to, he was not able to complete it, and died leaving about one-sixth of it unfinished.

Dr. Lowrie at once most generously volunteered to complete the translation and supervise its publication. For this I owe him a debt of gratitude which words but poorly express. I know, however, that for him his best reward is the consciousness that he, more than any other one man, has ensured the publication in English of nearly all of the more important works of Søren Kierkegaard.

I also wish to thank Mr. Brandt of Princeton University Press for his very sympathetic cooperation in making this publication possible, to acknowledge gratefully the conspicuous aid received from the American-Scandinavian Foundation, and to express to Miss Hanna Astrup Larsen, Literary Secretary of the Foundation, and to Professor Robert Herndon Fife of Columbia University, my appreciation of their diligence in reading the proofs.

LILLIAN MARVIN SWENSON

EDITOR'S PREFACE

BESIDES a sense of personal loss at the death of David F. Swenson on February 11, 1940, I felt dismay that he had left unfinished his translation of the *Unscientific Postscript*. I had longed to see it published among the first of Kierkegaard's works in English. In the spring of 1935 it did not seem exorbitant to hope that it might be ready for the printer by the end of that year. For in March I learned from Professor Swenson that he had years before "done about two thirds of a rough translation." In 1937/38 he took a sabbatical leave from his university for the sake of finishing this work. Yet after all it was not finished —partly because Professor Swenson was already incapacitated by the illness which eventually resulted in his death; but also because he aimed at a degree of perfection which hardly can be reached by a translator. At one time he expressed to me his suspicion that perhaps, as in the translation of Kant's philosophy, it might require the cooperation of many scholars during several generations before the translation of Kierkegaard's terminology could be definitely settled. I hailed with joy this new apprehension, which promised a speedy conclusion of the work, and in the words of Luther I urged him to "sin boldly."

But already (as is now apparent) high blood pressure was rendering it doubly difficult for him to make the thousand decisions involved in a meticulous translation. He died leaving the translation unfinished. Fortunately, it was more nearly finished than I had hoped. In asking me to complete the work, Mrs. Swenson furnished me with a carefully rewritten copy of the manuscript. My part therefore is reduced to small proportions. Besides furnishing the Introduction and the Notes in the Appendix, I have only had to translate the last 77 pages of the text, and pages 152-67 which had been accidentally omitted in the translation of the earlier part. Emphatically, this book is Dr. Swenson's. Even in the part for which I am responsible, I have been scrupulous not to use the terms I prefer but the locutions he had chosen.

This compliance is not irksome to me, because of the veneration I feel for Professor Swenson as a philosophic thinker and as a man—more expressly as a Christian man. From the moment when I first ventured upon the dubious task of trying to make Kierkegaard and his works known and appreciated in England and America, Professor Swenson has been my firm support. Although he was younger than I, he was far better acquainted with Danish, and far more profoundly versed in the thought of Kierkegaard, with which he had been passionately occupied for more than thirty years. I have recently been reviewing the letters exchanged with Professor Swenson in the course of barely five years. Including copies of my letters, there are one hundred and forty-two of them, for the most part long letters, carefully thought out. On this account I am the more vividly conscious of the great debt I owe him. I am impressed at seeing how much give and take there is in these letters. That is to say: I was well aware how much he had to give; but, as he was a severe critic, I am surprised now to note, on reviewing the whole correspondence, how much "take" there was. The cause of Kierkegaard has suffered by the death of David Swenson a very serious setback, and that at a time when our collaborators in England are immobilized by the war.

There was only one point where I was disposed to balk in following Swenson. I had fiercely combatted, both by letter and by word of mouth, his use of the word "reason" as the translation of *Forstand*—instead of "understanding." I have been rereading one of his long letters, in which he marshalled many arguments for his choice. He persisted in using it in his translation of the *Fragments,* and, as he had given me no inkling of a change of mind, I had no doubt that he would use it in the *Postscript.* But I was not put to this test, for I was relieved to see that in this manuscript he has invariably used "understanding." I mention the fact because I am sure he would have remarked upon this change had he lived to write the Preface.

I have read this work, first in German and then in Danish, I cannot say how many times; and now when I have reread it in Professor Swenson's translation, first in the manuscript and then in the printer's proof, I am profoundly impressed by the accuracy and lucidity of his rendering. And it has style. It is worthy of Kierkegaard, and surely it will last as an impressive memorial of Swenson. For this is not only a big book, it is a book difficult to understand, and without understanding it thoroughly it would not be possible to translate it adequately. I wonder if any great book in a foreign tongue has ever in the first instance been so adequately translated as this.

It is not by accident that, while I was engaged in translating the religious works, Professor Swenson assumed responsibility for the *Fragments* and the *Postscript;* nor was this division of labor due solely to the consideration that it needed a philosopher to deal with the works which are incomparably the most important for philosophy as well as for theology; it was determined also by the fact that for Swenson personally the *Postscript* had a decided religious value. He told me that, when as a young man he was beginning his career as assistant professor, knowing all the views philosophers have entertained, but having nothing to support him except the faith his mother had taught him as a child, he happened to be attracted by the quaint name of a book, "Concluding Unscientific Postscript to the Philosophical Fragments." He took it home, read it all that night and all the next day, with the profoundest emotion; and in this book he found support for his stalwart Christian life.

The late Professor Eduard Geismar of Copenhagen related to me an experience which was in every respect similar, except that his mental excitement was so great that the physician felt compelled to prohibit him from reading anything of Kierkegaard's for a year. When that year was over he devoted his life to enforcing the lessons he had learnt from S. K. The last labor in this behalf was the lecture tour in the United States which Professor Swenson and I engineered.

Probably none of the reviewers of this translation will be so profoundly moved. Yet this may not be ascribed to any fault in the translation, for Kierkegaard reported three years later that only sixty copies of this book had been sold and that it had nowhere been reviewed (X^6B 114, p. 146). In Germany, however, it has had an incalculable influence upon theology, and a new philosophy, the so-called Existential Philosophy, has been prompted by it. Perhaps it will make its way slowly in England and America. It is in fact a very big book; and yet no great work on philosophy or theology, if we except the Dialogues of Plato, has been written with so much wit, with so much art; and many may find pleasure in reading it, even though they have no previous acquaintance with these austere disciplines.

It is another question whether they will understand it. Doubtless many will feel the need of a commentary or of an ample introduction. Would that Swenson had lived to write it! I shall not attempt to do here what he might have done. As I have said, this is already a big book, therefore I propose to make the introduction as short as possible. I regard it only as an orientation. A few quotations from S. K.'s Works and from his Papers suffice to determine the place of this book among his writings. An adequate discussion of the problems involved in this book would require a separate volume. Such a discussion ought to be separate, for it is only fair that in this volume S. K. should be allowed to speak for himself.

As usual, I would express my obligations to Dr. Lange, the only surviving editor of the Danish edition of S. K.'s Collected Works, for permission to make use of many of the notes which I place in the Appendix and indicate in the text by small arabic numerals. The notes of the Danish edition have been gradually accumulated. In some respects they are inadequate, in others they seem to me redundant. Only occasionally have I furnished a translation of Latin and Greek words, and still more rarely have I indicated the source of the very numerous Biblical quotations and allusions. But if this proves to be what the age demands, it can be supplied in a subsequent edition. Professor Swenson has in many instances preferred to follow Kierkegaard's rather singular punctuation, which was criticized in his day and defended by him as an aid to reading aloud.

Princeton
March 10, 1941

                                                    WALTER LOWRIE

INTRODUCTION BY THE EDITOR

THIS, as I remarked in the Preface, is so big a book that between its covers no room is left for an adequate introduction. It might be said, on the other hand, that this book is so big and so important, and withal so complicated, that more than any other it requires an introduction. But this means that the introduction, if there is to be any, must be outside of these covers. The only competent introduction at present available is contained in the *Kierkegaard Studien* of Professor Emanuel Hirsch (1930-33), pp. 729-827.

Here I propose to provide only the most necessary hints for the preliminary orientation of the reader.

The title, as S. K. first conceived it (VI B 88), was as follows:

Logical Problems
by
Johannes Climacus
edited by
S. Kierkegaard.

Later he proposed (VI B 98):

Concluding [simple] Postscript
to the
Philosophical Fragments
by
Johannes Climacus

edited by
S. Kierkegaard.

In the title actually used, the word "unscientific" may be misleading, and it must be interpreted by the word "simple," which S. K. occasionally used even after the book was printed with its present title.

In the title, the word "concluding" has emphatic significance. It indicates S. K.'s intention of terminating here his literary work. He says in his Journal (VII A 4, Feb. 7, 1846), "My idea is to give up being an author (which I can only be altogether or not at all) and prepare myself to be a pastor." This was a serious resolution, which many times was reaffirmed in the Journal (cf. VII A 221, Jan. 20, 1847), and it was a natural course for him to take, seeing that as a Candidate in Theology he had prepared himself for this career. But it was not exactly to a career he was looking forward: he proposed to retire to a country parsonage and remain there for the rest of his life. He had been compelled to become an author because his experience with Regina had made him a poet. The first three of his pseudonymous books were written for "her." But he was born a philosopher, and he felt a potent urge to say what he says in the *Fragments* and in the *Postscript*. His resolution to conclude with the *Postscript* proves how great an importance he attached to this work. In his Journal he gave thanks to God that he had been enabled to say adequately what he wanted to say.

However, this resolution was not carried out. The moment he was free from preoccupation with this great work, having sent the manuscript to the printer, he wrote the challenge to the *Corsair* which brought down upon him a deluge of ridicule which prompted him to stay at his post. If he were then to give up writing and retire to a country cure, it would be interpreted, he thought, as a cowardly retreat.

So it came about that the *Postscript,* instead of being his concluding work, proved to be, as two years later he viewed it in retrospect when writing *The Point of View* (pp. 13, 41 *f.*, 97 *f.*), the central point of his whole authorship. It was central, as he remarked at that time, even with respect to the total bulk of the works which preceded and followed it. In relation to the immense production of the year 1848, it was no longer central in that material sense, but it remained "the turning point." In the passages referred to above, S. K. says: "The *Concluding Postscript* is not an aesthetic work, but neither is it religious; hence, it is by a pseudonym, though I adjoin my name as editor, as I did not do in the case of any purely aesthetic work. The *Concluding Postscript,* as I have already said, constitutes the turning point in my whole work as an author. It presents the 'problem,' that of becoming a Christian. Having assumed responsibility for the whole pseudonymous aesthetic work as a description of *one* way a person may take to become a Christian (viz. *away* from the aesthetic so as to become a Christian), it undertakes to describe the other (viz. *away* from Speculation, etc. so as to become a Christian)." Thus the *Postscript,* so far from being the conclusion of S. K.'s work as an author, is the starting point for the serious religious books which followed it, and it deals dialectically with the problems which underlie the Edifying Discourses approximately contemporary with it. Inasmuch as I have been engaged in translating the serious religious works of 1848, which find their definition and dialectical support in the *Postscript,* I have been very eager to see this work published in English, and am more than willing now to take a hand in producing it.

The second word in the strange title which S. K. bestowed upon this book is far too significant to be ignored. It is the word "unscientific." The Danish word is substantially the same as the German *wissenschaft-lich* and is used with the same latitude. S. K. was inclined to satirize "the professor" in all the forms he assumed, he was against pedantry of all sorts. A glance at the Table of Contents is enough to reveal that in this book all accepted rules for the composition of a philosophic treatise are defied. It mingles together a little of everything, a little about history, a good deal about "speculation" and metaphysics, "something about Lessing," more than a little psychology, still more about religion and about Christianity in particular, the most subtle and abstract definitions alternating with poetical prose, and the whole of it spiced with the condiment of humor. I remember that in one of his letters to me, Professor Swenson remarked with some sense of dismay that he knew of no author who so swiftly and thoroughly altered his style. In English we have no other word to translate *uvidenskabelig* but "unscientific." The reference of this word is narrower, and yet it does not misrepresent the meaning of the title. For it was principally against the natural sciences S. K. inveighed—notwithstanding that in his youth, although he was nominally a student of theology, he proposed to devote his life to the study of the natural sciences. The year this book was written (1846) he made the following entry in his Journal (VII A 186, cf. 187-200, and for the year 1853, X^5 A 73):

"Almost everything that nowadays flourishes most conspicuously under the name of science (especially as natural science) is not really science but curiosity. *In the end all corruption will come about as a consequence of the natural sciences.* . . . But such a scientific method becomes especially dangerous and pernicious when it would encroach also upon the sphere of spirit. Let it deal with plants and animals and stars in that way; but to deal with the human spirit in that way is blasphemy, which only weakens ethical and religious passion. Even the act of eating is more reasonable than speculating with a microscope upon the functions of digestion. . . . A dreadful sophistry spreads microscopically and tele-scopically into tomes, and yet in the last resort produces nothing, quali-tatively understood, though it does, to be sure, cheat men out of the simple, profound and passionate wonder which gives impetus to the ethical. . . . *The only thing certain is the ethical-religious.*"

Science, he says, by pretending to explain the "miracle" of qualitative change, only throws dust in our eyes. In so far as it succeeds in persuading men that it is just on the point of explaining everything, it suffocates faith, depriving us of the air we must breathe or die, defrauding us not only of the wonder which is the starting point of religion, but of "the possibility" which makes spiritual life possible. About the ultimate effects of science he makes prognostications which in our day we must recognize as veridical.

The choice of the pseudonym, Johannes Climacus, is interesting and important. It may be a matter of only curious interest that S. K. found this name applied to a Greek monk who was celebrated as the author of a book entitled "The Ladder of Heaven." S. K. adopted it as a denomination for himself when in 1842 he started to write a polemic against the followers of Descartes, entitled *Johannes Climacus; or, De omnibus dubitandum est* (IV B 1, pp. 103-82). This work was left unfinished—perhaps because he began to realize that the real adversary was Hegel, perhaps only because he was diverted by the urge to write two more books for Regina. But when, with the *Fragments,* he returned again to philosophy, Johannes Climacus appears again as his pseudonym. A glance at the earlier work, which was in large part autobiographical (see my *Kierkegaard,* pp. 29 *ff.*), will make it evident that this was S. K.'s most personal pseudonym. Whereas each of the other pseudonyms may be taken to represent one or another side of S. K.'s character, or a possibility which he discovered in himself, Johannes was neither more nor less than the young man Kierkegaard as he was in his twenty-fifth year, before his conversion in 1838, a young man thoroughly informed about Christianity, who had meditated profoundly upon its dialectical positions, was attracted to it like a moth to the candle, but, still critical, unresolved as yet to make the leap of faith. Hence, Climacus affirms emphatically that he is not a Christian. It is true he gives himself out to be thirty years of age (about the same age as S. K. when he wrote this book), but this merely signifies that he was far more developed intellectually than was S. K. at the time of his conversion. S. K. was a Christian before he wrote the *Postscript,* yet on looking back upon it he acknowledged that it was "a deliberation." By this I understand him to mean that until he had stated to himself in the sharpest form the paradoxical implications of the Christian faith, he could not be said to have accepted them. Only when he had surely appropriated these positions did he presume to call them his own; hence, in his Edifying Discourses, even at this time, he essayed to give expression only (as he affirms) to religion in the sphere of immanence, which in this work he distinguishes as "religion A."

Another leap was required of him before he could reach "religion B," that is to say, Christianity in its distinctive form as a paradoxical religion. I do not say a *second* leap, for a leap had already been involved in the passage from the aesthetical to the ethical. And when the final leap had been made, S. K. was by no means at the end of his path; he was still struggling to "become a Christian," that is, to become existentially what he was. At this stage, when he personally was confronted by the obligation of a disciple to imitate Christ, and by his writings was confronting others with this serious challenge, his pseudonym was still a Climacus, but now a very different figure, called Anti-Climacus, who, instead of saying that he was not yet a Christian, proclaims himself a Christian in a superlative degree.

Johannes Climacus, as author of the *Fragments,* promised a sequel, which was to clothe in their historical costume the abstract problems presented in the earlier book. The *Postscript* obviously does much more than this. So much would be accomplished by the mere statement by Climacus that he was talking about Christianity. But why was the sequel so slow in coming? There is no answer to this query—unless one is content with the observation that in S. K.'s mind many and various thoughts were teeming and demanding utterance. A psychological study, *The Concept of Dread,* was published only four days later than the *Fragments,* and along with that a rollicking book of humor entitled *Prefaces;* the *Four Edifying Discourses* followed, then *Three Discourses on Imagined Occasions,* which were intended to "accompany" the *Stages on Life's Way,* which appeared on April 30, 1845, as a repetition, in a certain sense, of *Either-Or,* and thus a reversion to the earlier category, the aesthetic.

The most positive aid to orientation in this work is the observation that the theme of the whole is expressed in the problem of Johannes Climacus, "How am *I* to become a Christian?"

When the problem is stated in this way, the response of theology must be altered at every point, for hitherto it has been formulated in answer to the objective question, "What is Christianity?"

And when the problem is stated in this subjective way, it is natural and necessary that this book should deal at great length, as it does in the earlier part, with the question, "What is truth?" That is where Lessing comes in. Also it will seem natural, if not necessary, that Climacus should reply: "Subjectivity is the truth."

The Christian therefore has to renounce the comfort of calm assurance bolstered upon objective proofs, and must be content with a fighting certainty. He constantly lies over a depth of seventy thousand fathoms.

What renders faith perpetually uneasy (i.e. what insures that it shall always remain faith and not become knowledge) is the paradox and the possibility of the offense. In its extremest expression, the paradox is the God-Man, the fact that a man's relation to his eternal blessedness is dependent upon something historical, something moreover which, by its very nature, cannot become historical. But this is the apex. Below that, every thought of God is paradoxical to an "exister." Thus the unknowable God was a paradox for Socrates. S. K.'s thought is akin to the *coincidentia oppositorum* and the *docta ignorantia* of Nicholas of Cues.

The reader will not fail to observe that, in S. K.'s language, "to exist" does not mean simply "to be." The difference becomes clear when the etymological meaning is stressed. *Ex-sistere* means to stand out from. Heidegger in his Existential Philosophy strives to render the essential thought by *in-der-Welt-sein,* and by *Da-sein,* thus indicating the *thereness,* the concretion of the *ego* in relation to its environment and its task. In our tongue we might express S. K.'s meaning well enough in some instances by the word "life," as when he says that Christianity is not essentially a doctrine but an existential communication. We are familiar with Coleridge's word to the same effect, "not a doctrine but a life." Unfortunately it is not possible in an English translation to limit the use of the word "existence" exclusively to this sense, as a rendering of the Danish *Existenz;* it has to be used also in the more generic sense of coming into being, as a translation of the Danish *Tilværelse* or *bliven til,* since our language has no equivalent for the German *Dasein.*

But in addition to this concise positive orientation, a negative orientation may be needed, especially the warning which Professor Hirsch utters against treading the well-worn paths of German misinterpretation. The *Postscript* does present an either-or; but the alternative is *not*: the ethical and religion of immediacy/*or* Christianity in its most paradoxical form. From the very first S. K.'s either/or was: either the aesthetical/or the ethical and the religious. The only difference now is that he has learned to discriminate between "religion A" and "religion B." But with this he has no notion of discarding the former. It goes without saying that the religion of immanence and of immediacy which he continued to

expound in his Edifying Discourses meant for him true religion. He
often asserted that immediacy is the element of religion, without which
it cannot live. Therefore he posited "a new immediacy after reflection."
Even of the aesthetic he says that when one passes over to the ethical
sphere this is "not abolished but dethroned." But of "religion A" he
never would have said that it was dethroned when one had reached
"religion B." Nor would he have said this of the ethical. The most extravagant of Léon Chestov's misinterpretations of Kierkegaard is the
affirmation that he triumphantly repudiated the ethical. The ethical always implied for S. K. a God-relationship. It is significant that in his
delimitation of the "spheres" or stages, the ethical culminated in repentance, just as the aesthetic culminated in despair, and both of these positions are divided only by a line from the religious—only a line, but a line
which one can cross only by a leap. The either/or of the *Postscript* is defined by Hirsch substantially in these terms: *either* aesthetic immediacy,
whether it be eudaemonistic search for pleasure, or despair, or religious
or metaphysical self-explanation/*or* the ethical along with the religion of
immanence and immediacy and (as its culmination) Christianity apprehended as paradox. All of these latter terms belong emphatically on the
same side of the alternative. This means that S. K.'s ideal was truly humane. He conceived that only through repentance (the sense of guilt)
and through religious faith (including the paradoxical faith in the forgiveness of sin) does man become truly a man.

The reader will observe with how much care the "existence spheres"
are defined in this work, which carries out more accurately the classification begun in the *Stages*. Here for the first time we find a clear determination of the position of irony as the *confinium* of the aesthetical,
and of humor as the *confinium* of the ethical. This is, at least, interesting,
for never before had these problems been dealt with, or even envisaged.
However, the reader may wonder whether it was worth while devoting
so much space in this book to the delimitation of the spheres. But evidently this was a question of considerable importance not only to Climacus but to Kierkegaard, who in *The Book on Adler* found frequent
use for these categories. If to the reader all this seems of little importance,
it is all the more important that he should be warned not to dismiss the
subject hastily and so fall into a misunderstanding which is only too
naturally suggested by the title of the *Stages*. For the word "stage"
seems to imply that with each advance the preceding stage is definitely
left behind. But even in the *Stages,* Climacus spoke more commonly of

the "spheres" of existence, and it is evident that the spheres overlap and penetrate one another.

S. K. seized the opportunity offered by this "concluding" book to explain through the mouth of Johannes Climacus the purport of all his previous pseudonymous works. To us this interpretation is very valuable, but it does not go far enough, because S. K. was not yet ready to concede that his method of "indirect communication" was condemned by the fact that an explanation was needed. Hence the thing had to be done over again two years later in *The Point of View*. S. K., who had so much to say against reviews and reviewers, felt naturally some embarrassment in "reviewing" his own works, and in one of his papers he offers his pseudonyms an apology for reviewing works which were cast in the form of "double reflection" and so rendered inaccessible to the objective scrutiny of a reviewer.

But this long passage about the pseudonymous works is far from being an intrusion in this book. It was appropriate that when he was pointing out "the other way of becoming a Christian" (i.e. by abandoning Speculation), he should recall the first way, which he had indicated in the earlier works (i.e. away from the aesthetical); for this new way could not be supposed to supersede the first, both were necessary, and by this passage S. K. intimates that his whole effort from the beginning had been the same, namely, to point out the way to become a Christian.

In this passage S. K. virtually, though in an indirect fashion, assumed responsibility for all the pseudonymous works, since every one knew that they were his. Hirsch calls this a "retraction"; but it was a retraction only in the sense that *The Point of View* was a retraction when it asserted that from the first he was not an aesthetical writer.

The direct and explicit declaration that he was the author of all of the pseudonymous works, that is, the "First and Last Declaration" appended to this book, was an afterthought. It was not sent to the printer till after the rest of the manuscript had been delivered, and it was sent with instructions to print it in smaller type and without numeration of the pages. It was to be regarded, he said, as a "dust-cover."

Rather than prolong the Introduction, I have put in the appended notes a few quotations which show that S. K., polemical as he was, was at the same time dialectical enough to appreciate highly the qualities and talents of the men in this book whom he singles out for attack: Hegel, Martensen and Grundtvig. Essentially his polemic here was directed, not against these men (Martensen, for example, was not mentioned by name), but against Speculation. He was always courageous enough to shoot at the most shining marks, and his polemic was the more effective for the fact that it was sharply directed against the most distinguished representatives of the positions which he denounced. It may need to be remarked that this work possesses perennial importance because essentially it contends not merely against a system of thought which has had its day (the Hegelian philosophy), but against a way of thinking which is still prevalent and still finds in Hegel its most brilliant exponent.

This book is full of humorous gibes against J. L. Heiberg, who was recognized as *arbiter elegantiarum* in the Danish literary circles of that time, and with whom S. K. always stood on the best of terms. Heiberg, although he professed to be a Hegelian, did not seriously represent any position which S. K. felt called upon to attack. Although at the very moment when the *Postscript* was published, S. K. found himself in conflict with Goldschmidt, the editor of the *Corsair,* it may be said that there was no one in Copenhagen who more highly appreciated this young man's talents or had so sincere a liking for him. His last polemic was directed against Mynster, the deceased Primate of Denmark, and one of the greatest contemporary figures in that land—who also was the man whom S. K. had admired above all others. It was a case of disappointed love.

WALTER LOWRIE

CONCLUDING UNSCIENTIFIC POSTSCRIPT TO THE PHILOSOPHICAL FRAGMENTS

A Mimic-Pathetic-Dialectic Composition
An Existential Contribution

By

JOHANNES CLIMACUS

Responsible for Publication:

S. KIERKEGAARD

Copenhagen
1846
[Feb. 27]

'Αλλὰ δή γ', ὦ Σώκρατες, τί οἴει ταῦτ' εἶναι ξυνά-
παντα; κνίσματα τοί ἐστι καὶ περιτμήματα τῶν
λόγων, ὅπερ ἄρτι ἔλεγον, κατὰ βραχὺ διῃρημένα.

HIPPIAS MAJOR §304 A.

But really, Socrates, what do you think this all amounts to? It is
really scrapings and parings of systematic thought, as I said a while
ago, divided into bits.

PREFACE

SELDOM perhaps has a literary enterprise been more favored by fortune, or had a reception more in accordance with the author's wishes, than was the case with my *Philosophical Fragments*.[1] Hesitant and reserved as it is my custom to be in connection with every form of self-appraisal, I dare nevertheless affirm one thing, and that with confidence, about the fate of the little book: it has created no sensation, absolutely none. Undisturbed, and in compliance with his own motto: "Better well hung than ill wed,"[2] the well-hung author has been left hanging. No one has asked him, not even in jest, for whom or for what purpose he hung. Better so, better well hung than by an unfortunate marriage to be brought into systematic relationship with all the world.

In view of the character of the book, I had indeed hoped for some such reception. But in view of the seething ferment of the times, the incessant forebodings of prophets, seers, and philosophers, I feared lest through some misunderstanding this hope might be doomed to disappointment. Even the most insignificant of travellers runs a risk of misunderstanding if he happens to arrive at a town when all the inhabitants are in a state of tense and varied expectancy: some with cannons planted, fuses lighted, fireworks and transparencies at hand; some with the town hall festively decorated, reception committee on its feet, speakers ready; some with note-books open, pens dripping with ink, minds yearning for systematic instruction; all and sundry awaiting the arrival of the promised hero *incognito*. Under such circumstances a mistake is always possible, and literary misunderstandings of this nature belong to the order of the day.

Thank heaven, therefore, that nothing of the kind occurred. The book was permitted to enter the world unnoticed, without fuss or fury, without shedding of ink or blood. It was neither reviewed nor mentioned anywhere. No learned outcry was raised to mislead the expectant multitude; no shouts of warning from our literary sentinels served to put the reading public on its guard; everything happened with due decency and decorum. As the enterprise itself was free from every tincture of magic, so fate preserved it from false alarms.[3] The author is thus *qua* author in the happy situation of owing nothing to anybody—I refer to critics, reviewers, middlemen, appraisers, and the like, these tailors of the literary world, who make the man and help the author cut a figure. They place the reader at the proper standpoint, and it is by their art and aid that a book may eventually amount to something. But then it is with these benefactors as it is with tailors generally, according to Baggesen's words:[1] "Their art makes the man but their bills slay him." One comes to owe them everything; and one cannot even discharge the debt by writing a new book, for the new book, if it has any significance, will again owe this to the critical assistance of these benefactors.

Encouraged in this manner by fortune's favor, I now propose to carry on with my project. Without let or hindrance from the outside, with no overhasty concern for what the times demand, following solely my own inner impulse, I shall proceed to knead the thoughts, so to speak, until in my opinion the dough is a good one. Aristotle remarks somewhere[2] that it was the custom in his day to prescribe the ridiculous rule for the narrative that its movement should be rapid. He goes on to say: "Surely it is fitting here to cite the answer once given to a man who was kneading dough and asked if he should make the dough hard or soft: 'Is it not then possible to make it good?'" The one thing I am afraid of is a sensation, particularly if it registers approval. The age is liberal, broad-minded, and philosophical; the sacred claims of personal liberty have everywhere a host of appreciated and applauded spokesmen. Nevertheless, it seems to me that the case is not always apprehended in a sufficiently dialectical manner; for otherwise the strenuous exertions of the elect would scarcely be rewarded with noisy acclaim, huzzahs at midnight, torchlight processions, and other similar encroachments upon the liberty of the person.

It would seem to be a reasonable presumption that everyone should in lawful things be permitted to do as he likes. An infringement of liberty occurs only when one person attempts to bind another to perform some definite action. An expression of disapproval is hence always permissible, since it does not seek to impose any obligation upon the other. If the crowd brings a man a *pereat,* it does not interfere with his personal freedom. No response on his part is necessary, no obligation has been imposed. He is free to lounge indolently in his apartment, to smoke his cigar, to bury himself in his thoughts, to jest with his sweetheart, to take his ease in dressing-gown and slippers, to turn over for another hour of sleep. He may even absent himself altogether, since his personal presence is by no means necessary. Not so, however, if he happens to be waited upon by a torchlight procession of his admirers. If the hero of such a demonstration is absent, he must instantly be summoned; if he has just lit a fragrant cigar, he must toss it aside; if he has retired for the night, he must be roused from his slumbers; and there is scarcely time for a hurried dive into coat and trousers before he must out bareheaded under the open sky to make a speech.

What holds true for persons of prominence in connection with popular demonstration, holds true also for us lesser folk in our lesser circumstances. A literary attack, for example, constitutes no infringement upon the personal freedom of an author. It must be regarded as a matter of course that the privilege of expressing an opinion should be open to everyone. As for the object of such an attack, he is still free to go on with his work, to fill up his pipe, to leave the attack unread, and so forth. But an expression of approval is by no means so innocuous. The critical judgment which excludes a writer from the realm of literature does not limit his sphere of action; but the criticism which assigns him a definite place within, may well be cause for apprehension. A passer-by who laughs at you does not place you under obligation; rather he becomes your debtor, in so far as he owes to you the opportunity to enjoy a laugh. Here each remains free to pursue his own way, unhampered by binding and intrusive friendships. A passer-by who stares at you defiantly, as much as to intimate that you are not worthy of a bow or greeting, does not oblige you to do anything; he rather relieves you of the necessity of tipping your hat. An admirer on the other hand, is not so easily disposed of. His tender assiduities soon become so many burdens laid upon the object of his admiration, and before the latter has an inkling of what is taking place, he finds himself groaning under heavy taxes and assessments, though he began by being the most independent of men. If an author borrows an idea from some other author without naming his source, and proceeds perhaps to make a perverted use of the borrowed idea, this is by no means an intrusion. But if he names his author, perhaps even with admiration, as the source of the perverted idea, he creates a most embarrassing situation.

To speak dialectically, it is not the negative which constitutes an encroachment, but the positive. How strange! Just as it was reserved for the liberty-loving states of the American Union to invent the most cruel of punishments, that of enforced silence,[5] so it was reserved for our liberal and broad-minded age to invent the most illiberal of all vexations: torchlight processions by night, popular demonstrations thrice a day, nine hurrahs for the great, and similar lesser vexations for us lesser folk. The social principle is precisely the illiberal principle.

The present offering is again a *piece, proprio Marte, proprio stipendio, propriis auspiciis.*[6] The author is an independent proprietor in so far as he holds in fee simple the fragment that he owns; but otherwise he is as far from having a retinue of bond-servants as he is from being a serf in his own person. He hopes that fortune will again smile upon his enterprise, and above all that the tragi-comic predicament may be averted from him and his book, that some deeply earnest seer or jesting wag takes it upon himself to persuade the public that there is something in it, and thereupon runs away and leaves the author in the lurch, after the fashion of "the peasant boy in pawn."

                                                                    J. C.

TABLE OF CONTENTS

INTRODUCTION

YOU will perhaps remember, dear reader, that near the end of the *Philosophical Fragments* there appeared a certain remark which might look like the promise of a sequel. Viewed as a promise, indeed, the remark in question ("if I ever write a sequel") was in the highest degree tentative, and at the farthest possible remove from a solemn engagement. I have therefore never felt myself bound by this promise, though it was from the beginning my intention to fulfill it, and the necessary materials were already at hand when the promise was made. In so far the promise might well have been launched with great solemnity, *in optima forma*. But it would have been an inconsistency to publish a piece of such a character that it was incapable of creating a sensation, and wished for none, and then at the end of it to introduce a solemn promise, which, if anything, is calculated to arouse a sensation, and would doubtless also in this case have caused a tremendous flurry. You must have had occasion to notice how these things come about. An author publishes a big book; it has scarcely been out a week before he falls into conversation with a reader. The reader asks politely, sympathetically, and in a very glow of longing, if he does not soon intend to write another book. The author is enchanted: to think of having a reader who so quickly works his way through a big book, and in spite of the labor and the toil preserves his zest undimmed! Alas for the poor deluded author! In the further course of the conversation, the benevolently interested reader, the same who so longingly awaits the new book, admits that he has not read the published book, and that he will probably never find the time to do so. But he had heard some talk in a social gathering about a new book by the same author, and he has become greatly interested in arriving at certainty on the point. Or an author publishes a book, and fondly imagines that he will have a month's respite until the critics have had time to read it. But what happens? Three days after publication there appears in the press a breathless shriek, something in the way of a literary notice; at the close of the article there is a promise that the writer will furnish a critical review later. This outcry creates a tremendous sensation, though the book itself is gradually forgotten, and the critical review never makes its appearance. Two years later, the book being mentioned casually in a conversational group, a well-informed person recalls it to the memory of the forgetful by identifying it as the book that so-and-so reviewed. This is the way in which a promise satisfies the demand of the times. First it creates a tremendous sensation, and two years later the promiser even enjoys the honor of having fulfilled it. For a promise is interesting; but if the promiser fulfills his promise he only injures himself, for a fulfillment is not interesting.

As for my own "promise," its vague and tentative form was by no means accidental. In the strict sense of the word it was not a promise at all, since the fulfillment was given in the piece itself. When a task is capable of being divided into an easier and a harder part, the proper procedure for a promising author is to begin with the easier part, and then to promise the harder part as a sequel. Such a promise is serious, and well worthy of acceptance. More frivolous is the procedure of an author who completes the harder part first, and then promises the easier part as a sequel. And this is especially the case if the sequel is such that any attentive reader of the first part, provided he has the necessary equipment of culture, can write the second part for himself, should he think it worth his while.

So in the case of the *Philosophical Fragments*. The sequel was to be devoted to the task of investing the problem in historical costume. The problem itself, if indeed there was anything difficult in connection with the whole matter, was the difficult part; the historical costume is easy enough. With no desire to offend, it is nevertheless my opinion that not every divinity student would have been able to formulate the problem with a dialectical precision equalling that given it in the *Fragments*. It is also my opinion that not every divinity student, after having read the piece, would be able to lay it aside and proceed to formulate the problem with a dialectical clarity equal to that achieved in the *Fragments*. But as for the historical costume, I am convinced that every divinity student (and I am not sure that this conviction could flatter anyone) would be able to furnish it—provided he can reproduce the fearless dialectical positions and movements involved.

Such being the nature of the promise, it seems quite suitable that its fulfillment should be relegated to a *Postscript*. The author can scarcely be charged with having indulged in the feminine practice of saying the most important thing (if there is anything important in connection with the whole matter) as an after-thought, in a note at the end. Essentially, there is no sequel. In another sense, the sequel might become endlessly voluminous, in proportion to the learning and erudition of whoever might undertake to invest the problem in its historical costume. All honor to learning and scholarship, all praise to the man who can control the material detail, organizing it with the authority of genuine insight, with the reliability that comes from acquaintance with the original sources. But the life of the problem is nevertheless in the dialectical issue. If the presentation of the problem fails in dialectical clarity, while exceptional learning and great acumen are expended upon the details, it becomes only increasingly difficult for the dialectically interested inquirer to find his way about. In connection with this problem there have been produced undeniably, many excellent works of thorough scholarship, revealing both critical acumen and powers of organization, on the part of men for whom the present author feels a deep respect, and whose guidance he could wish that he might have been able to follow in his student years with greater talent than he had at his disposal. But there came a time when he believed himself to have discovered, with mingled feelings of admiration for the distinguished authorities and of dejection over his own isolated doubting situation, that in spite of the meritorious labors of the scholars, the problem was not being advanced but retarded.

If a naked dialectical analysis reveals that no approximation to faith is possible, that an attempt to construct a quantitative approach to faith is a misunderstanding, and that any appearance of success in this endeavor is an illusion; if it is seen to be a temptation for the believer to concern himself with such considerations, a temptation to be resisted with all his strength, lest he succeed (by giving way to a temptation, and hence by the most signal failure) in transforming faith into something else, into a certainty of an entirely different order, replacing its passionate conviction by those probabilities and guarantees which he rejected in the beginning when he made the leap of faith, the qualitative transition from non-belief to belief—if this be true, then everyone who so understands the problem, in so far as he is not wholly unfamiliar with scientific scholarship or bereft of willingness to learn, must feel the difficulty of his position, when his admiration for the scholars teaches him to think humbly of his own insignificance in comparison with their distinguished learning and acumen and well-merited fame, so that he returns to them repeatedly, seeking the fault in himself, until he is finally compelled to acknowledge dejectedly that he is in the right. The spirit of dialectical fearlessness is not so easily acquired; and the sense of isolation which remains despite the conviction of right, the sadness of the parting from admired and trustworthy authorities, is the line of demarcation which marks the threshold of its acquirement.

The relation between the dialectician and the considerations usually presented by way of an introduction, is analogous to the relation between the dialectician and the eloquence of the orator. The orator demands to be heard, and asks to be allowed to develop his ideas in a connected manner; and since he hopes to learn, the dialectician gladly consents. But the orator has rare gifts, and a great understanding of the human passions; he knows how to make effective use of the imagination for purposes of delineation; and he commands the resources of fear and terror for use in the critical moment of decision. He speaks, and carries the listener with him. The hearer loses himself in engrossed attention, his admiration for the distinguished speaker filling his soul with an almost feminine devotion; he feels his heart beat, his soul is stirred. Now the orator brings to bear all his resources of earnestness and pathos; he bids every objection keep silence, and brings the case before the throne of the Almighty. He asks if there is anyone who dares deny in sincerity before God what only the most ignorant and erring wretch could bring himself to deny. And then, in gentler mood, he adds an admonition not to yield to doubt, explaining that it is not the temptation, but the yielding to it which is so terrible. He comforts the anxious soul, and rescues it from fear as a mother reassures her child with tender caresses. But the poor dialectician goes home with a heavy heart. He sees indeed that the problem was not even presented, much less solved; but he has not yet acquired the strength to withstand the force of eloquence. With the unhappy love of admiration he understands that there must be a tremendous justification also in the force of eloquence.

When the dialectician has finally emancipated himself from the domination of the orator, the systematic philosopher confronts him. He says with speculative emphasis: "Not until we have reached the end of our exposition will everything become clear." Here it will therefore be necessary to wait long and patiently before venturing to raise a dialectical doubt. True, the dialectician is amazed to hear the same philosopher admit that the System[1] is not yet completed. Alas! everything will be made clear at the end, but the end is not yet there. However, the dialectician has not gained the necessary dialectical fearlessness, or this admission would soon teach him to smile in irony at such a proposal, where the prestidigitator has made so sure of a loophole. For it is ridiculous to treat everything as if the System were complete, and then to say at the end, that the conclusion is lacking. If the conclusion is lacking at the end, it is also lacking in the beginning, and this should therefore have been said in the beginning. A house may be spoken of as finished even if it lacks a minor detail, a bell-pull or the like; but in a scientific structure the absence of the conclusion has retroactive power to make the beginning doubtful and hypothetical, which is to say: unsystematic. So at least from the standpoint of dialectical fearlessness. But our dialectician has not yet acquired it. Hence he refrains in youthful modesty from drawing any conclusion respecting the absence of a conclusion—and begins the study, hoping that the labor will bear fruit. He plunges into the reading, and is quite overwhelmed with astonishment; admiration holds him captive, and he yields himself to the superior mind. He reads and reads and understands in part; but above all he sets his hope upon the clarifying light which the conclusion will throw upon the whole. And he finishes the book, but has not found the problem presented. And yet the young dialectician has with all the enthusiasm of youth put his trust in the famous man; like a maiden with but a single wish, to be loved by the beloved, so he has but one desire—to become a thinker. And, alas! the famous man has it in his power to decide his fate; for if he does not understand him, the youth is rejected, and his one desire must suffer shipwreck. Hence he does not yet dare to confide in anyone else, so as to initiate him into his misfortune, his disgrace, the fact that he cannot understand the famous man. So he begins again from the beginning. He translates all the more important passages into his mother-tongue, to be sure that he understands them and has not overlooked anything, and thereby overlooked something about the problem; for it does not seem possible to him that there should be absolutely nothing about that. He learns much of it by heart; he makes an outline of the argument, which he takes with him everywhere so as to ponder it in odd moments; he tears up his notes and writes new ones—what will a man not do to realize his heart's single desire! He comes to the end of the book a second time, but finds himself no nearer the problem. So he buys a new copy of the same book, in order not to be disturbed by the discouraging memories of past failures; he moves to a distant place, so as to begin with fresh vigor—and then? Well, he perseveres in this manner until at last he acquires the true dialectical fearlessness. And then? Then he learns to give unto Caesar his due, and to the famous philosopher his admiration; but he also learns to hold fast to his problem, in spite of all notabilities.

The scholarly introduction draws the attention away from the problem by its erudition, and makes it seem as if the problem were posed at the moment when the scholarly inquiry reaches its maximum. That is to say, it seems as if the learned and critical striving toward its own ideal of perfection, were identical with the movement toward the problem. The rhetorical address serves to distract by intimidating the dialectician. The systematic tendency promises everything and keeps nothing. In none of these three ways does the problem come to light, least of all in the systematic. The System presupposes faith as something given—and this in a system that is supposed to be without presuppositions! It presupposes further that faith has an interest in understanding itself otherwise than through the preservation of its passion, which is a presupposition (for a system supposed to be without presuppositions), and a presupposition insulting to faith, proving definitely that faith was never given to the System. The presupposition of the System that faith is given, resolves itself into a delusion in which the System has deceived itself into thinking that it knew what faith was.

The problem posed and formulated in the piece, but without pretense of solving it, was as follows: *Is an historical point of departure possible for an eternal consciousness; how can such a point of departure have any other than a mere historical interest; is it possible to base an eternal happiness upon historical knowledge?*[2] In the book itself the following passage is found:[3] "It is well known that Christianity is the only historical phenomenon which in spite of the historical, nay, precisely by means of it, has offered itself to the individual as a point of departure for his eternal consciousness, has assumed to interest him in another than the merely historical sense, has proposed to base his eternal happiness on his relationship to something historical." Thus the historical costume is Christianity. The problem is thus relevant to Christianity. Less problematically, in the form of a dissertation, it might be viewed as involving the apologetic presuppositions for faith, the approximations leading toward faith, the quantitative introduction to the decision of faith. That which accordingly would have to be treated would be a multitude of considerations, which are, or were, once dealt with by theologians in an introductory discipline, in the introduction to dogmatics, and in apologetics.

But in order to avoid confusion, it is at once necessary to recall that our treatment of the problem does not raise the question of the truth of Christianity. It merely deals with the question of the individual's relationship to Christianity. It has nothing whatever to do with the systematic zeal of the personally indifferent individual to arrange the truths of Christianity in paragraphs; it deals with the concern of the infinitely interested individual for his own relationship to such a doctrine. To put it as simply as possible, using myself by way of illustration: I, Johannes Climacus, born in this city and now thirty years old, a common ordinary human being like most people, assume that there awaits me a highest good, an eternal happiness, in the same sense that such a good awaits a servant-girl or a professor. I have heard that Christianity proposes itself as a condition for the acquirement of this good, and now I ask how I may establish a proper relationship to this doctrine. "What extraordinary presumption," I seem to hear a thinker say, "what egotistical vanity to dare lay so much stress upon one's own petty self in this theocentric age, in the speculatively significant nineteenth century, which is entirely immersed in the great problems of universal history." I shudder at the reproof; and if I had·not already hardened myself against a number of fearful things, I would no doubt slink quietly away, like a dog with his tail between his legs. But my conscience is quite clear in this matter; it is not I who have become so presumptuous of my own accord, but it is Christianity itself which compels me to ask the question in this manner. It puts quite an extraordinary emphasis upon my own petty self, and upon every other self however petty, in that it proposes to endow each self with an eternal happiness, provided a proper relationship is established.

Without having understood Christianity, since I merely present the problem, I have still understood enough to apprehend that it proposes to bestow an eternal happiness upon the individual man, thus presuming an infinite interest in his eternal happiness as *conditio sine qua non;* an interest by virtue of which the individual hates father and mother, and thus doubtless also snaps his fingers at speculative systems and outlines of universal history. Although I am only an outsider, I have at least understood so much, that the only unpardonable offense against the majesty of Christianity is for the individual to take his relationship to it for granted, treating it as a matter of course. However unassuming it may seem to permit oneself this kind of a relationship to Christianity, Christianity judges it as insolence. I must therefore respectfully decline the assistance of all the theocentric helpers and helpers' helpers, in so far as they propose to help me into Christianity on such a basis. Then I rather prefer to remain where I am, with my infinite interest, with the problem, with the possibility.

It is not entirely impossible that one who is infinitely interested in his eternal happiness may sometime come into possession of it. But it is surely quite impossible for one who has lost a sensibility for it (and this can scarcely be anything else than the infinite interest), ever to enjoy an eternal happiness. If the sense for it is once lost, it may perhaps be impossible to recover it. The foolish virgins had lost the infinite passion of expectation. And so their lamps were extinguished. Then came the cry: The bridegroom cometh. Thereupon they run to the market-place to buy new oil for themselves, hoping to begin all over again, letting bygones be bygones. And so it was, to be sure, everything was forgotten. The door was shut against them, and they were left outside; when they knocked for admittance, the bridegroom said: "I do not know you." This was no mere quip in which the bridegroom indulged, but the sober truth; for they had made themselves strangers, in the spiritual sense of the word, through having lost the infinite passion.

The objective problem consists of an inquiry into the truth of Christianity. The subjective problem concerns the relationship of the individual to Christianity. To put it quite simply: How may I, Johannes Climacus, participate in the happiness promised by Christianity? The problem concerns myself alone; partly because, if it is properly posed, it will concern everyone else in the same manner; and partly because all the others already have faith as something given, as a triviality of little value, or as a triviality which amounts to something only when tricked out with a few proofs. So that the posing of the problem cannot be regarded as presumption on my part, but only as a special kind of madness.

In order to make my problem clear I shall first present the objective problem, and show how this is dealt with. In this manner the historical will receive its just due. Then I shall proceed to present the subjective problem. This is at bottom more than the promised sequel, which proposed to invest the problem in its historical costume; since the historical costume is given merely by citing the one word: Christianity. The first part of what follows is then the promised sequel; the second part is a new attempt of the same general tenor as the *Fragments,* a new approach to the problem of that piece.

BOOK ONE

THE OBJECTIVE PROBLEM CONCERNING
THE TRUTH OF CHRISTIANITY

INTRODUCTORY REMARKS CONCERNING
THE OBJECTIVE PROBLEM

FROM an objective standpoint Christianity is a *res in facto posita,* whose truth it is proposed to investigate in a purely objective manner, for the accommodating subject is much too objective not to leave himself out; or perhaps he even unhesitatingly counts himself in, as one who possesses faith as a matter of course. The truth in this objective sense may mean, first, the historical truth; second, the philosophical truth. Viewed as historical, the truth of Christianity must be determined through a critical examination of the various sources, and so forth; in short, in the same manner that historical truth generally is determined. When the question of the philosophical truth is raised, the object is to determine the relationship of the doctrine thus historically given and verified, to the eternal truth.

The inquiring, speculating, and knowing subject thus raises a question of truth. But he does not raise the question of a subjective truth, the truth of appropriation and assimilation. The inquiring subject is indeed interested; but he is not infinitely and personally and passionately interested on behalf of his own eternal happiness for his relationship to this truth. Far be it from the objective subject to display such presumption, such vanity of spirit.

The inquiring subject must be in one or the other of two situations. *Either* he is in faith convinced of the truth of Christianity, and in faith assured of his own relationship to it; in which case he cannot be infinitely interested in all the rest, since faith itself is the infinite interest in Christianity, and since every other interest may readily come to constitute a temptation. *Or* the inquirer is, on the other hand, not in an attitude of faith, but objectively in an attitude of contemplation, and hence not infinitely interested in the determination of the question.

So much here at the outset, by way of calling attention to a consideration to be developed in Part II, namely, that the problem cannot in this manner decisively arise; which means that it does not arise at all, since decisiveness is of the essence of the problem. Let the inquiring scholar labor with incessant zeal, even to the extent of shortening his life in the enthusiastic service of science; let the speculative philosopher be sparing neither of time nor of diligence; they are none the less not interested infinitely, personally and passionately, nor could they wish to be. On the contrary, they will seek to cultivate an attitude of objectivity and disinterestedness. And as for the relationship of the subject to the truth when he comes to know it, the assumption is that if only the truth is brought to light, its appropriation is a relatively unimportant matter, something which follows as a matter of course. And in any case, what happens to the individual is in the last analysis a matter of indifference. Herein lies the lofty equanimity of the scholar, and the comic thoughtlessness of his parrot-like echo.

CHAPTER I

THE HISTORICAL POINT OF VIEW

WHEN Christianity is viewed from the standpoint of its historical documentation, it becomes necessary to secure an entirely trustworthy account of what the Christian doctrine really is. If the inquirer were infinitely interested in behalf of his relationship to the doctrine he would at once despair; for nothing is more readily evident than that the greatest attainable certainty with respect to anything historical is merely an *approximation*. And an approximation, when viewed as a basis for an eternal happiness, is wholly inadequate, since the incommensurability makes a result impossible. But the interest of the inquiring subject being merely historical (whether he also has an infinite interest in Christianity in his capacity as believer, in which case the whole enterprise might readily come to involve him in several contradictions; or whether he stands aloof, yet without any passionate negative decision *qua* unbeliever), he begins upon the tremendous task of research, adding new contributions of his own, and continuing thus until his seventieth year. Just two weeks before his death he looks forward to the publication of a new work, which it is hoped will throw light upon one entire side of the inquiry. Such an objective temper is an epigram, unless its antithesis be an epigram over it, over the restless concern of the infinitely interested subject, who surely needs to have such a question answered, related as it is to his eternal happiness. And in any case he will not upon any consideration dare to relinquish his interest until the last moment.

When one raises the historical question of the truth of Christianity, or of what is and is not Christian truth, the Scriptures at once present themselves as documents of decisive significance. The historical inquiry therefore first concentrates upon the Bible.

§ I. THE HOLY SCRIPTURES

Here it is necessary for the scholar to secure the maximum of dependability; for me, on the contrary, it is of importance not to make a display of learning, or to betray the fact that I have none. In the interest of my problem it is more important to have it understood and remembered that even with the most stupendous learning and persistence in research, and even if all the brains of all the critics were concentrated in one, it would still be impossible to obtain anything more than an approximation; and that an approximation is essentially incommensurable with an infinite personal interest in an eternal happiness.*

When the Scriptures are viewed as a court of last resort for determining what is and is not Christian doctrine, it becomes necessary to make sure of the Scriptures historically and critically.†

In this connection there are a number of topics that come up for consideration: the canonicity of the individual books, their authenticity, their integrity, the trustworthiness of their authors; and a dogmatic guaranty is posited: Inspiration.‡ When one thinks of the labors which the English have devoted to digging the tunnel under the Thames,[1] the tremendous expenditure of energy involved, and then how a little accident may for a long time obstruct the entire enterprise, one will be able to form a fitting conception of this critical undertaking as a whole. How much time, what great industry, what splendid talents, what distinguished scholarship have been requisitioned from generation to generation in order to bring this miracle to pass. And yet a little dialectical

* In seizing upon this contradiction, the *Philosophical Fragments* posed or presented the problem in the following manner: Christianity is something historical, in relation to which the best knowledge attainable is merely an approximation, the most masterly historical elucidation is only the most masterly "as good as," an almost; and yet it proposes *qua* historical, and precisely by means of the historical, to have decisive significance for a man's eternal happiness. It goes without saying that the little merit of the piece consisted merely in posing the problem, and in disentangling it from all prating and speculative attempts at explanation, which serve indeed to explain that their authors have no notion of what it is all about.

† Even so it is impossible to exclude dialectics. A single generation, or perhaps two, might succeed in maintaining itself undisturbed in the presumption that a barrier had been found which is the end of the world and of dialectics: that is no use. Thus it was for a long time believed that one could keep dialectics away from faith, by saying that its conviction rested upon the basis of authority. If the believer was asked about his faith, i.e. if he was dialectically challenged, he would declare with a certain easy air of confidence that he neither could nor needed to give any account of it, since his trust reposed in others, in the authority of the saints, and so forth. This is an illusion. For the dialectician has merely to shift his point of attack, so as to ask him, i.e. challenge him dialectically to explain, what authority is, and why he regards just these as authorities. He is then not questioned about the faith he has on the basis of his confidence in these authorities, but about the faith he has in these authorities.

‡ The incommensurability between inspiration and critical inquiries is analogous to the incommensurability between an eternal happiness and critical considerations; for inspiration is solely an object of faith. Or is it because the books are inspired that the critical zeal is so great? In that case, the believer who believes that the books are inspired does not know the identity of the books he believes to be inspired. Or does inspiration follow as a consequence of the critical inquiry, so that when criticism has done its work it has also demonstrated that the books are inspired? In that case, one will never be in a position to accept their inspiration, since the critical labors yield in their maximum only an approximation.

doubt touching the presuppositions may suddenly arise, sufficient for a long time to unsettle the whole, closing the subterranean way to Christianity which one has attempted to construct objectively and scientifically, instead of letting the problem remain subjective, as it is.

One sometimes hears uneducated or half educated people, or conceited geniuses, speak with contempt of the labor of criticism devoted to ancient writings; one hears them foolishly deride the learned scholar's careful scrutiny of the most insignificant detail, which is precisely the glory of the scholar, namely, that he considers nothing insignificant that bears upon his science. No, philological scholarship is absolutely within its rights, and the present author yields to none in profound respect for that which science consecrates. But the scholarly critical theology makes no such clear and definite impression upon the mind; its entire procedure suffers from a certain conscious or unconscious ambiguity. It constantly seems as if this labor of criticism were suddenly about to yield a result for faith, issue in something relevant to faith. Here lies the difficulty. When a philologist prepares an edition of one of Cicero's writings, for example, and performs his task with great acumen, the scholarly apparatus held in beautiful subservience to the control of the spirit; when his ingenuity and his familiarity with the period, gained through formidable industry, combine with his instinct for discovery to overcome obstacles, preparing a clear way for the meaning through the obscure maze of the readings, and so forth—then it is quite safe to yield oneself in whole-hearted admiration. For when he has finished, nothing follows except the wholly admirable result that an ancient writing has now through his skill and competence received its most accurate possible form. But by no means that I should now base my eternal happiness on this work; for in relation to my eternal happiness, his astonishing acumen seems, I must admit, inadequate. Aye, I confess that my admiration for him would be not glad but despondent, if I thought he had any such thing in mind. But this is precisely how the learned theologian goes to work; when he has completed his task (and until then he keeps us in suspense, but holds this prospect before us) he draws the conclusion: *ergo,* now you can base your eternal happiness on these writings.

Anyone who posits inspiration, as a believer does, must consistently consider every critical deliberation, whether for or against, as a misdirection, a temptation for the spirit. And anyone who plunges into these critical inquiries without being a believer, cannot possibly intend to have inspiration emerge as a result. Who then really has any interest in the whole inquiry?

But the contradiction remains unnoticed because the mode of approach is purely objective; and then indeed the contradiction is no longer there. The inquirer forgets what he has up his sleeve, except in so far as he occasionally stimulates and encourages himself lyrically by referring to it; or indulges in lyrical polemics with the aid of eloquence. But let an individual approach this enterprise, let him propose in infinite personal passion to attach his eternal happiness to the result: he will readily perceive that there is no result, and that none is to be expected; and the contradiction will bring him to despair. Luther's rejection of the Epistle of James[2] will alone suffice. In relation to an eternal happiness, and an infinite passionate interest in its behalf (in which latter alone the former can exist), an iota is of importance, of infinite importance; or rather, despair over the contradiction involved will teach him that there is no possibility of getting through along this road.

The years pass, but the situation remains unchanged. One generation after another departs from the scene, new difficulties arise and are overcome, and new difficulties again arise. Each generation inherits from its predecessor the illusion that the method is quite impeccable, but the learned scholars have not yet succeeded . . . and so forth. All of them seem to find themselves becoming more and more objective. The infinite personal passionate interest of the subject (which is, in the first instance, the potentiality of faith, and in the next, faith itself, as the form for an eternal happiness, and thereupon an eternal happiness itself) vanishes more and more, because the decision is postponed, and postponed as following directly upon the result of the learned inquiry. That is to say, the problem does not arise; we have become so objective as no longer to have an eternal happiness. For an eternal happiness is rooted in the infinite personal passionate interest, which the individual renounces in order to become objective, defrauded of his interest by the predominating objectivity. With the assistance of the clergy, who occasionally display learning, the laity get an inkling of how the land lies. The "community of believers" becomes at last a mere courtesy title; for the laity become objective merely by looking at the clergy, and expect a tremendously significant result, and so on. Now a hostile critic rushes forward to attack Christianity. He is precisely as well oriented as the scholarly critics and the dilettante laity. He attacks a book of the Bible, or a suite of books. Instantly the learned rescue corps rushes in to defend; and so it goes on indefinitely.

Wessel said that he always seeks to avoid a crowd, and so it is doubtless imprudent for the author of a little piece to intervene in this dispute, with a respectful request for a hearing on behalf of a few dialectical considerations: he will be as welcome as a dog in a game of bowls. Nor is there much of anything that a stark naked dialectician can do in such a learned dispute, where in spite of all learning and talent *pro* and *contra,* it is, in the last analysis, dialectically uncertain what the dispute is about. If it is purely a philological controversy, let us honor learning and talent with the admiration they deserve; but in that case the dispute is no concern of faith. If the disputants have something up their sleeves, let us have it brought out, so that we can think it through with dialectical deliberation. Whoever defends the Bible in the interest of faith must have made it clear to himself whether, if he succeeds beyond expectation, there could from all his labor ensue anything at all with respect to faith, lest he should come to stick fast in the parenthesis of his labor, and forget, over the difficulties of scholarship, the decisive dialectical *claudatur.* Whoever attacks the Bible must also have sought a clear understanding of whether, if the attack succeeds beyond all measure, anything else would follow than the philological result, or at most a victory *ex concessis,* where it must be noted that everything may be lost in another manner, provided, namely, the mutual underlying agreement is a phantom.

In order therefore that the dialectical issue be accorded the significance it deserves, and that we may think the thoughts through without disturbing irrelevancies, let us first assume the one and then the other.

I assume, accordingly, that the critics have succeeded in proving about the Bible everything that any learned theologian in his happiest moment has ever wished to prove about the Bible. These books and no others belong to the canon; they are authentic; they are integral; their authors are trustworthy—one may well say, that it is as if every letter were inspired. More than this it is impossible to say, for inspiration is an object of faith and subject to a qualitative dialectic; it is incapable of being reached by a quantitative approximation. Furthermore, there is not a trace of contradiction in the sacred writings. For let us be careful in formulating our hypothesis; if so much as a single hint in this direction is admitted the parenthesis again begins, and the critical philological occupation-complex will again lead us astray on bypaths. In general, all that is needed to make the question simple and easy is the exercise of a

certain dietetic circumspection, the renunciation of every learned inter-
polation or subordinate consideration, which in a trice might degenerate
into a century-long parenthesis. Perhaps this is after all not so easy, and
just as our human life runs into danger everywhere, so a dialectical exposition runs everywhere into the danger of slipping into a parenthesis.
The same principle holds in smaller things as in greater; and in general,
what makes it so tiresome to listen as third party to an argumentative
dispute, is the fact that usually by the second round the dispute has already run into a parenthesis, and now moves in this perverse direction
more and more passionately away from the point at issue. This failing
may be utilized as a sort of fencing feint, for the purpose of testing out
an opponent, to determine whether he is a real master of the dialectical
parade, or a mere parenthesis-hound who leaps into a gallop whenever
the parenthetical suggests itself. How often has it not happened that an
entire human life has from early youth moved only in parentheses! But
I break off these moralizing reflections, looking toward the promotion
of the common welfare, by which I have sought to atone somewhat for
my lack of historico-critical competence.

Well then, everything being assumed in order with respect to the
Scriptures—what follows? Has anyone who previously did not have
faith been brought a single step nearer to its acquisition? No, not a single
step. Faith does not result simply from a scientific inquiry; it does not
come directly at all. On the contrary, in this objectivity one tends to lose
that infinite personal interestedness in passion which is the condition of
faith, the *ubique et nusquam* in which faith can come into being. Has
anyone who previously had faith gained anything with respect to its
strength and power? No, not in the least. Rather is it the case that in this
voluminous knowledge, this certainty that lurks at the door of faith and
threatens to devour it, he is in so dangerous a situation that he will need
to put forth much effort in great fear and trembling, lest he fall a victim
to the temptation to confuse knowledge with faith. While faith has
hitherto had a profitable schoolmaster in the existing uncertainty, it
would have in the new certainty its most dangerous enemy. For if passion is eliminated, faith no longer exists, and certainty and passion do not
go together. Whoever believes that there is a God and an over-ruling
providence finds it easier to preserve his faith, easier to acquire something that definitely is faith and not an illusion, in an imperfect world
where passion is kept alive, than in an absolutely perfect world. In such

a world faith is in fact unthinkable. Hence also the teaching that faith is abolished in eternity.

How fortunate then that this wishful hypothesis, this beautiful dream of critical theology, is an impossibility, because even the most perfect realization would still remain an approximation. And again how fortunate for the critics that the fault is by no means in them! If all the angels in heaven were to put their heads together, they could still bring to pass only an approximation, because an approximation is the only certainty attainable for historical knowledge—but also an inadequate basis for an eternal happiness.

I assume now the opposite, that the opponents have succeeded in proving what they desire about the Scriptures, with a certainty transcending the most ardent wish of the most passionate hostility—what then? Have the opponents thereby abolished Christianity? By no means. Has the believer been harmed? By no means, not in the least. Has the opponent made good a right to be relieved of responsibility for not being a believer? By no means. Because these books are not written by these authors, are not authentic, are not in an integral condition, are not inspired (though this cannot be disproved, since it is an object of faith), it does not follow that these authors have not existed; and above all, it does not follow that Christ has not existed. In so far, the believer is equally free to assume it; equally free, let us note this well, for if he had assumed it by virtue of any proof, he would have been on the verge of giving up his faith. If matters ever come to this pass, the believer will have some share of guilt, in so far as he has himself invited this procedure, and begun to play into the hands of unbelief by proposing to demonstrate.

Here is the crux of the matter, and I come back to the case of the learned theology. For whose sake is it that the proof is sought? Faith does not need it; aye, it must even regard the proof as its enemy. But when faith begins to feel embarrassed and ashamed, like a young woman for whom her love is no longer sufficient, but who secretly feels ashamed of her lover and must therefore have it established that there is something remarkable about him—when faith thus begins to lose its passion, when faith begins to cease to be faith, then a proof becomes necessary so as to command respect from the side of unbelief. And as for the rhetorical stupidities that have been perpetrated by clergymen in connection with this matter, through a confusion of the categories—alas, let us not speak of them. The vanity of faith (a modern substitute: How can they believe who receive honor one of another, John 5:44) naturally will not and cannot bear the martyrdom of faith; and the note of genuine faith is today perhaps the rarest note struck in the pulpit oratory of Europe. Speculative philosophy has understood everything, everything, everything. But the clergyman, nevertheless, holds himself a little in check; he admits that he has not yet understood everything, he admits that he is still striving. Poor man, what a confusion of the categories! "If there is anyone who has understood everything," he says, "then I confess (alas, he feels ashamed, and does not perceive that he ought to use irony against the others) that I have not understood it all, and that I cannot prove everything; we humbler folk (alas, he feels his humility in a very wrong place) must be content with faith." Poor, misunderstood, highest passion "faith," to have to be content with such a champion! Poor chap of a clergyman, that you do not know what you are talking about! Poor unlearned Peter Ericksen,[3] on the other hand, who cannot quite make out about science, but who has faith; for he really has it, the faith which transformed fishermen into apostles, the faith which removes mountains —when one has it!

When the question is treated in an objective manner it becomes impossible for the subject to face the decision with passion, least of all with an infinitely interested passion. It is a self-contradiction and therefore comical, to be infinitely interested in that which in its maximum still always remains an approximation. If in spite of this, passion is nevertheless imported, we get fanaticism. For an infinitely interested passion every iota will be of infinite value.* The fault is not in the infinitely interested passion, but in the fact that its object has become an approximation-object.

The objective mode of approach to the problem persists from generation to generation precisely because the individuals, the contemplative individuals, become more and more objective, less and less possessed by an infinite passionate interest. Supposing that we continue in this manner to prove and seek the proof of the truth of Christianity, the remarkable phenomenon would finally emerge, that just when the proof for its truth had become completely realized, it would have ceased to exist as a present fact. It would then have become so completely an historical phenomenon as to be something entirely past, whose truth, i.e. whose

* Herewith the objective standpoint is reduced to absurdity, and the subjective standpoint simultaneously posited. For if one were to ask why then the least iota is of infinite importance, the answer can only be: because the subject is infinitely interested. But this discloses the subject's infinite interest as the decisive factor.

historical truth, had finally been brought to a satisfactory determination. In this way perhaps the anxious prophecy of Luke 18:8, might be fulfilled: Nevertheless when the Son of Man cometh, shall he find faith on the earth?

The more objective the contemplative inquirer, the less he bases an eternal happiness, i.e. his eternal happiness, upon his relationship to the inquiry; since there can be no question of an eternal happiness except for the passionately and infinitely interested subject. Objectively, the contemplative inquirer, whether learned scholar or dilettante member of the laity, understands himself in the following farewell words, as he faces the final end: When I was a young man, such and such books were in doubt; now their genuineness has been demonstrated, but then again a doubt has recently been raised about certain books which have never before been under suspicion. But there will doubtless soon arise a scholar who will . . . and so forth.

The accommodating and objective subject holds himself aloof, displaying an applauded heroism. He is completely at your service, and ready to accept the truth as soon as it is brought to light. But the goal toward which he strives is far distant, undeniably so, since an approximation can continue indefinitely; and while the grass grows under his feet the inquirer dies, his mind at rest, for he was objective. It is not without reason that you have been praised, O wonderful objectivity, for you can do all things; not even the firmest believer has ever been so certain of his eternal happiness, and above all of not losing it, as the objective subject! Unless this objective and accommodating temper should perhaps be in the wrong place, so that it is possibly unchristian; in that case, it would naturally be a little dubious to have arrived at the truth of Christianity in this manner. Christianity is spirit, spirit is inwardness, inwardness is subjectivity, subjectivity is essentially passion, and in its maximum an infinite, personal, passionate interest in one's eternal happiness.

As soon as subjectivity is eliminated, and passion eliminated from subjectivity, and the infinite interest eliminated from passion, there is in general no decision at all, either in this problem or in any other. All decisiveness, all essential decisiveness, is rooted in subjectivity. A contemplative spirit, and this is what the objective subject is, feels nowhere any infinite need of a decision, and sees no decision anywhere. This is the *falsum* that is inherent in all objectivity; and this is the significance of mediation as the mode of transition in the continuous process, where nothing is fixed and where nothing is infinitely decided; because the movement turns back upon itself and again turns back, so that the movement becomes chimerical, and the philosopher is wise only after the event.* There are indeed, in the objective sense, results everywhere, a

* The scepticism that is inherent in the Hegelian philosophy, in spite of its much advertised positivity, may be understood in the light of this consideration. According to Hegel,[4] truth is the continuing world-process. Each generation, each stage of this process, is valid; and yet it is only a moment of the truth. Unless we here allow ourselves to introduce a dash of charlatanry, which helps out by assuming that the generation in which Professor Hegel lived, or the generation which after him plays the rôle of *Imprimatur*,[5] is the last generation, we are all in a state of sceptical uncertainty. The passionate question of truth does not even arise, since philosophy has begun by tricking the individuals into becoming objective. The positive Hegelian truth is as illusory as happiness was in paganism. The individual could not know whether he was happy until all was at an end,[6] and so here: only the next following generation can know what the truth was in the preceding generation. The great secret of the System—but this had better be kept among ourselves, like the secret the Hegelians are supposed to share privately—is pretty much the same as the sophism of Protagoras,[7] that everything is relative; except that here, everything is relative in the continuing world-process. But this cannot help any living individual; and if he happens to know an anecdote in Plutarch's *Moralia*[8] about a certain Lacedaemonian by name of Eudamidas, he will doubtless be reminded of it. When Eudamidas saw the aged Xenocrates and his disciples in the Academy, engaged in seeking for the truth, he asked: "Who is this old man?" And when he was told that Xenocrates was a wise man, one of those occupied in the search for virtue, he cried: "But when does he then propose to use it?"

It is presumably the witchery of this ever continuing process which has inspired the misunderstanding that one must be a devil of a fellow in philosophy in order to emancipate himself from Hegel. But this is by no means the case. All that is needed is sound common sense, a fund of humor, and a little Greek ataraxy. Outside the *Logic*, and partly also within the same, because of a certain ambiguous light which Hegel has not cared to exclude, Hegel and Hegelianism constitute an essay in the comical. Blessed Hegel has presumably by this time found his master in Socrates; and the latter has doubtless found something to laugh at, if Hegel otherwise remains the same. There Socrates will have found a man worth conversing with, and especially well worth asking the typically Socratic question: whether he knows anything or not. It will be remembered that Socrates proposed to ask this question of the shades in Hades.[9] Socrates must have suffered a very great change in his nature if he permitted himself to be impressed in the slightest degree by the recitation of a series of paragraphs, and the promise that everything will become clear at the end.

Perhaps I may in this note find a suitable place for something I have to complain about. In the recently published biography of Poul Møller,[10] there is found only a single passage which conveys any notion of his attitude towards Hegel during the last years of his life. The respected editor has doubtless been determined to this reserve by a loyal and affectionate regard for the deceased, an anxious concern for what certain people might say, and what a speculative and almost Hegelian public might judge. And yet, it is possible that the editor, precisely when he thought to act in a spirit of affectionate regard for the deceased, has instead injured his memory. More remarkable than many an aphorism included in the printed collection, and quite as noteworthy as many a youthful trait that the careful and sensitive biographer has preserved for us in a beautiful and worthy setting, is the fact that Poul Møller, while everything here at home bore the Hegelian stamp, judged quite differently; that at first he spoke of Hegel almost with indignation, until at last the sound good humor that was his nature taught him to smile, especially at the Hegelian school; or, to recall Poul Møller still more clearly to mind, right heartily to laugh. For who that has been enamored of Poul Møller can have forgotten his humor; who that has known him can have forgotten his laughter, which did one good even when it was not entirely clear what it was he laughed at; for his distraction of mind was sometimes very confusing.

superfluity of results. But there is no decisive result anywhere. This is quite as it should be, since decisiveness inheres in subjectivity alone, essentially in its passion, and maximally in the personal passion which is infinitely interested in an eternal happiness.

§ 2. THE CHURCH

The protection against the intrusion of dialectics which the Catholic Church deems itself to have in the visible presence of the Pope, we shall here leave out from consideration.* But it has come about also within Protestantism, that after having given up the Bible as the certain recourse for determining Christian doctrine, resort has been had to the Church. Though attacks are still being levelled against the Bible, and though learned theologians are engaged in defending it linguistically and critically, this entire procedure is to a certain extent antiquated. And above all, precisely because of the increasing objectivity, the decisive conclusions with respect to faith are no longer there in the background. The letter-fanaticism of a bygone age, which nevertheless had passion, has vanished. That it had passion was its merit. In another sense it was comical; and just as the age of chivalry really comes to a close with Don Quixote (for the comic interpretation is always the concluding one), so a poet might still bring to consciousness that the age of the letter-theology is past, by immortalizing comically such an unhappy slave of the letter in his tragi-comic romanticism. For wherever there is passion there is also romance; and anyone who has flexibility of mind and a sensitiveness for passion, and has not merely learned by rote to know what poetry is, will be able to see in such a figure a beautiful *Schwärmerei*. It is as when a loving maiden embroiders the artfully wrought setting of the gospel in which she reads the happiness of her love, or counts the letters

---

 * The infinite reflection in which alone the concern of the subject for his eternal happiness can realize itself, has in general one distinguishing mark: the omnipresence of the dialectical. Let it be a word, a proposition, a book, a man, a fellowship, or whatever you please: as soon as it is proposed to make it serve as limit, in such a way that the limit is not itself again dialectical, we have superstition and narrowness of spirit. There always lurks some such concern in a man, at the same time indolent and anxious, a wish to lay hold of something so really fixed that it can exclude all dialectics; but this desire is an expression of cowardice, and is deceitfulness toward the divine. Even the most certain of all things, a revelation, *eo ipso* becomes dialectical whenever I attempt to appropriate it; even the most fixed of things, an infinite negative resolve, the infinite form for God's presence in the individual, at once becomes dialectical. As soon as I take the dialectical away, I become superstitious, and attempt to cheat God of each moment's strenuous reacquisition of that which has once been acquired. But it is far more comfortable to be objective, and superstitious, and boastful about it, proclaiming thoughtlessness as wisdom.

in the note she has received from her lover. But if the poet has a feeling for the romantic, he will also see the comic.

Such a figure would undoubtedly be laughed at, but it is another question with what right; for the fact that the entire age has become passionless constitutes no justification for its laughter. The ludicrousness of the zealot consisted in the fact that his infinite passion had attached itself to a mistaken object (an approximation-object); the good in him was that he had passion.

This change in tactics, the letting go of the Bible and laying hold of the Church, is even a Danish idea. However, I cannot bring myself either to rejoice personally on the score of a fellow-countryman over this "matchless discovery"[1] (so the idea is officially called in the camp of the ingenious discoverer and his admirers), or to consider it desirable for the authorities to proclaim a *Te Deum* of all the people in devout thanksgiving for the matchless discovery. It is better, and for me, at least, indescribably easy, to let Grundtvig keep what belongs to him: the matchless discovery. It was indeed hinted at one time, especially when a similar little movement began in Germany with Delbrück[2] and others, that it was really Lessing to whom Grundtvig owed the idea, without however owing him its matchlessness; so that Grundtvig's merit would consist in having transformed a little Socratic doubt[3] presented problematically with fine dialectical skill, with genial acumen and rare sceptical expertness, into an eternal, matchless, historic, absolute, trumpet-tongued and sun-clear truth. But even supposing there were a relationship from the side of Pastor Grundtvig—which I do not by any means assume, since the matchless discovery bears the unmistakable stamp of Grundtvigian originality—it would still be unjust to call it a loan from Lessing, since there is not in the entire Grundtvigian exposition of the idea the least feature reminiscent of Lessing, or anything which that great master of the understanding could without a matchless resignation claim as his property. Had it been intimated that the clever and dialectical Magister Lindberg, the talented chief advocate and defender of the matchless discovery, possibly owed something to Lessing, the suggestion would have been more plausible. In any case the discovery owes much to Lindberg's talent, in so far as it was by his efforts that the discovery took on form, was constrained to assume a dialectical structure, became less afflicted with hiatus,[4] less matchless—and more accessible to common sense.

Grundtvig had rightly perceived that the Bible could not hold out against the encroaching doubt; but he had not perceived that the reason was that both attack and defense were involved in an approximation-process which in its everlastingly continued striving is dialectically incommensurable with an infinite decision, such as that on which an eternal happiness is based. Since he had no dialectical consciousness of this principle, it could only have been by a stroke of pure chance that he would really escape the presuppositions within which the Bible theory has its great merit, its venerable scientific significance. But a stroke of chance is unthinkable in connection with the dialectical. In so far it was more probable that in formulating the Church theory he would come to remain within the same presuppositions. The application of abusive epithets to the Bible, by which at one time he actually offended the older generation of Lutherans, abusive epithets and autocratic decrees instead of thoughts, can naturally satisfy only admiring worshippers, but will of course give immense satisfaction to them. Everyone else readily perceives that when thought is absent from the noisy discourse, it is thoughtlessness that runs riot in the licentious expressions.

Just as in the preceding paragraph it was the Bible which was to decide objectively what is Christianity and what is not, so now it is the Church that is to serve as the certain objective recourse. More specifically, it is the living word in the Church, the confession of faith, and the word in connection with the sacraments.

First it is clear that the problem is dealt with objectively. The obliging, immediate, wholly unreflective subject is naïvely convinced that if only the objective truth stands fast, the subject will be ready and willing to attach himself to it. Here we see at once the youthfulness (of which the aged Grundtvig is so proud) which has no suspicion of the subtle little Socratic secret: that the point is precisely the relationship of the subject. If truth is spirit, it is an inward transformation, a realization of inwardness; it is not an immediate and extremely free-and-easy relationship between an immediate consciousness and a sum of propositions, even if this relationship, to make confusion worse confounded, is called by the name which stands for the most decisive expression for subjectivity: faith. The unreflected personality is always directed outward, toward something over against it, in endeavor toward the objective. The Socratic secret, which must be preserved in Christianity unless the latter is to be an infinite backward step, and which in Christianity receives an intensification, by means of a more profound inwardness which makes it infinite, is that the movement of the spirit is inward, that the truth is the subject's transformation in himself. The prophetic genius who envisages so matchless a future for Greece,[5] is not expertly familiar with the Greek spirit. The study of Greek scepticism is much to be recommended. There one may learn thoroughly what it will always require time and exercise and discipline to understand (a narrow way for freedom of speech!), that the certainty of sense perception, to say nothing of historical certainty, is uncertainty, is only an approximation; and that the positive and immediate relationship to it is the negative.

The first dialectical difficulty with the Bible is that it is an historical document; so that as soon as we make it our standard for the determination of Christian truth, there begins an introductory approximation-process, and the subject is involved in a parenthesis whose conclusion is everlastingly prospective. The New Testament is a document out of the past, and is thus historical in the stricter sense. Just this is what serves to beguile the inquirer, tending to prevent him from making the problem subjective, and encouraging him to treat it objectively, in consequence of which it fails altogether to arise. The *Philosophical Fragments* directed itself to this difficulty in Chapters IV and V, and dealt with it by abolishing the difference between the contemporary disciple and the disciple of the last generation, assumed to be separated by the interval of 1800 years. This is of importance lest the problem, the contradiction that God has existed in human form, be confused with the history of the problem, i.e. with the *summa summarum* of 1800 years of opinion, and so forth.

In this experimental manner, the *Fragments* set the problem forth in relief. The difficulty with the New Testament as a document belonging to the past appears now to be obviated in the case of the Church, which of course exists in the present.

On this point Grundtvig's theory has merit. Especially has it been developed by Lindberg with competent juristic precision, that the Church eliminates all the proving and demonstrating that was necessary in connection with the Bible because it was something past, while the Church exists as a present reality. To demand that it prove its existence, says Lindberg quite correctly, is nonsense, like asking a living man to prove that he exists.* In this matter Lindberg is wholly in the right; and

---

* The reason for this, formulated dialectically-metaphysically, is that existence itself is superior to any demonstration for existence, and hence it is in the given case stupid to ask for proof. Conversely, the inference from essence to existence is a leap.

he deserves credit for the steadfastness and clarifying sureness of grasp by which he knows how to hold something fast.

So then the Church exists; and from the Church as something present, as contemporaneous with the inquirer (by which there is secured for the problem the equality of contemporaneity), one may learn what is essential to Christianity; for this is what the Church professes.

Quite right. But not even Lindberg has been able to confine the issue to this point; and I prefer to deal with a dialectician, leaving Grundtvig in possession of all the incomparable. After it has been asserted of the Church that it exists, and that one may learn from the Church what Christianity is, it is further asserted of this Church, the present Church, that it is the Apostolic Church, the same Church which has persisted for eighteen centuries. The predicate: Christian, is thus more than a present predicate. When predicated of the present it implies a past, and thus involves a historicity in quite the same sense as the Bible. The only historical factuality which is superior to proof is contemporaneous existence; every determination of pastness requires proof. Thus if someone were to say to a man: prove that you exist, the other will answer quite properly that the demand is nonsense. But if he says on the other hand: "I who now exist had an existence over four hundred years ago as essentially the same person," the other man has a right to reply: "Here a proof is needed." It is very strange that so experienced a dialectician as Lindberg, whose competence to formulate an issue sharply has been well documented, should have failed to notice this.

The moment we make use of the living word to urge the continued existence of the Church through past centuries, the issue is brought back to precisely the same point where it was in the Bible theory. The objections are in the same case as the Kobold: a man moves to get away from it—the Kobold also moves. Sometimes an illusion will momentarily prevail. By suddenly shifting the plan of campaign, when one is at the same time fortunate enough to have no one attack the new line of defense, a genius like Grundtvig may readily find himself blissfully convinced that all is now well, with the help of his matchless discovery. But let the Church theory endure attack as the Bible theory has had to endure it; let the whole swarm of possible objections arise to seek its life: what then? Then we shall here again consistently find that an introductory discipline becomes necessary; for every other procedure would nullify the Church theory itself, and transfer the problem to the realm of the subjective where it properly belongs, though the objective Grundtvig does not think so. This discipline would have the task of proving the primitive character of the confession of faith, its identity of meaning everywhere and in every moment through eighteen centuries (where criticism will stumble on difficulties that the Bible theory never knew*); and so again there will be a nosing about in ancient documents. The living word cannot help us. To be sure, neither will it help to set this forth before Grundtvig, which is therefore done here not hopefully, but rather without any sort of hope.

The living word declares the existence of the Church. Quite right; even Satan himself cannot take this away from anyone. But the living word does not suffice to declare that the Church has been in existence for eighteen centuries, that it is essentially the same, that it has persisted in a wholly unaltered form, and so forth; so much even a youth in dialectics can perceive. There corresponds to the immediate indemonstrable existence of the contemporaneous present, a living word as expression for existence. But as little as pastness is indemonstrable, i.e. superior to proof, so little can the living word be made to correspond with pastness, seeing that the predicate *living,* indicates merely an immediate present. A Grundtvigian anathema over those who cannot understand the saving or decisive power of the living word with respect to the category of historical pastness—a living word of the dead!—proves neither that Grundtvig thinks, nor that his opponents do not think.

It is precisely Magister Lindberg, who has too clear a head to be content year out and year in to sound the alarm, who has given this turn to the matter. When at one time there arose a dispute as to whether it was more correct to say: "I believe in a Christian Church," or, "I believe in the existence of a Christian Church," he himself had recourse to ancient books[6] in order to show when the incorrect variant crept in. There is naturally nothing else to be done, unless a new renunciation is added to the Christian confession of faith, namely the renunciation of all genuine thinking in relation to the matchless discovery, and the Abracadabra of the living word.†

* In the interest of caution I must here again refer to the dialectical situation. It is perhaps not unthinkable that one who had sufficient imagination to sense the voluminous difficulties here involved, might wish to say: "No, then the Bible theory is to be preferred." But let us not in distraction of mind forget that this more or less, this easier or harder, is merely a difference within the essential difficulty of an approximation, so that in spite of all such differences the incommensurability for the determination of an eternal happiness remains equally intact.

† No one whose imagination is to some degree sensitive will wish to deny, if he happens to remember this polemic, that Lindberg's procedure was quite vividly reminiscent of a worried

In this way the approximation-process again begins; the parenthesis is launched, and no one can say when it will end; for it is and always remains only an approximation, and this has the remarkable property of being able to continue indefinitely.

The advantage the Church theory was supposed to have over the Bible theory, consisted in its supposed elimination of the subsequent-historical, thus making the historical identical with the present. But this merit immediately vanishes as soon as the more specific determinations of the theory make their appearance.

The other things that have been said now and then about the advantages of the confession of faith over the Bible as a bulwark against attack, are tolerably obscure. That the Bible is a big book and the articles of the confession only a few propositions, is an illusory comfort, valid only for people who have not learned that wealth of thought is not always proportionate to volume of words. And the opponents need only to shift the point of attack, directing it to the articles of the confession, when everything will be in full cry as before. If opponents can resort to exegesis of the New Testament for the purpose of supporting a denial of the personality of the Holy Spirit, they can just as easily make use of the variation in the reading of the confession, which Lindberg has himself discussed exegetically:[7] whether we should read the Spirit of Holiness or the Holy Spirit. This but by way of an example; for it goes without saying that it is impossible in the case of historical problems to reach an objective decision so certain that no doubt could disturb it. This also serves to show that the problem ought to be put subjectively, and that it is precisely a misunderstanding to seek an objective assurance, thereby avoiding the risk in which passion chooses and continues to live, reaffirming its choice. It would also have been a tremendous injustice if any later generation were enabled safely, that is objectively, to enter Christianity, and thus secure a share in that which the first generation had bought in the extremity of subjectivity and its peril, and which it had repeatedly reacquired in the same peril, throughout a long life.

If anyone were to say that the briefer declaration is easier to hold fast and harder to attack, he conceals something, namely, how many thoughts there are contained in the briefer declaration. In so far another

Biblical exegete's erudite exertions. Anything sophistical in Lindberg's procedure, however, I have never been able to detect; provided, as is right and reasonable, one does not presume to judge infallibly the secrets of the heart, with which sort of judgment Lindberg has always been pursued.[8]

might with equal justice say that the more detailed statement (when as *in casu* both derive from the same authors, here the Apostles) is clearer, and thus easier to hold fast and more difficult to attack. But everything that can be said in this direction, *pro et contra,* is again only approximation-scepticism.

The Church theory has been quite sufficiently praised as being objective, a word which in our age is an *amende honorable* by which thinkers and prophets imagine that they are saying something big to one another. Sad to say, however, in the strict scientific disciplines where objectivity is a requisite, there it is seldom met with; for a scholar equipped with a thorough first-hand acquaintance with his field, is a great rarity. In relation to Christianity, on the other hand, objectivity is a most unfortunate category; he who has an objective Christianity and none other, is *eo ipso* a pagan, for Christianity is precisely an affair of spirit, and so of subjectivity, and so of inwardness. That the Church theory is objective, I shall not seek to deny; on the contrary, I shall show it to be such by the following consideration. When I place an individual who is passionately and infinitely interested in his eternal happiness, in relation to this theory, so that he proposes to base his happiness upon it, he becomes a comic figure. He does not become comical because he is infinitely and passionately interested, this being precisely the good in him; but he becomes comical because the objectivity of the Church theory is incommensurable with his interest. If the historical aspect of the confession is urged as decisive (that it derives from the Apostles, and so forth), then each iota must be infinitely stressed; and since a conclusion can be reached only *approximando,* the individual will be involved in the contradiction of attaching, i.e. of trying to attach, and yet not being able to attach his eternal happiness to it, because the approximation is never completed. From this again it follows that the individual will never in all eternity attach his eternal happiness to the theory, but only a less passionate something. If we all agreed to use the confession of faith instead of the Scriptures, psychological phenomena would arise in this field quite analogous to the fanaticism of the anxious Biblical exegete. The individual is tragic on account of his passion, and comical because he attaches it to an approximation.

If one accentuates the sacrament of baptism,[9] so as to base one's eternal happiness on the actual performance of the rite in one's own case, one becomes again a comic figure. Not because the infinitely interested passion is comic, far from it, it is precisely worthy of all honor; but because its object is only an approximation-object. We all rest in the conviction that we are baptized; but if baptism is to be decisive, and infinitely decisive, for my eternal happiness, then I must ask for certainty. And so must everyone else who has not found an objective bliss, and put passion behind him as mere child's play; and such a man has no eternal happiness for which to seek a basis, so that he can well afford to base it upon very little. Alas, the misfortune is: with respect to an historical fact, I can obtain only an approximation. My father has told me so, the church records attest it, I have a certificate,* and so forth. Oh, yes, my mind is at rest. But let a man have passion enough to understand the significance of an eternal happiness, and then let him try to attach it to the fact that he is baptized: he will despair. If the Church theory really exercised any influence, and if we had not all become so objective, it would in this manner have led directly to adult baptism, or to the repetition of the baptismal rite as in the case of the Lord's Supper, simply in order to make sure.

Precisely because Grundtvig, as a poet, is tossed about and stirred tumultuously in immediate passion, which is precisely his glory as a poet, he feels a need, and feels it in the immediate sense quite profoundly, to have something certain to cling to, and so keep the dialectical at a distance. But such a need is only a craving for a superstitious security; for as was said above, every limit that is intended to keep the dialectical away, is *eo ipso* superstition. Precisely because Grundtvig is stirred in immediate passion, he is no stranger to doubts and temptations. With respect to these, one finds a short cut, by depending upon something magical; and so one has plenty of time to occupy himself with world-history. But it is just here that we have the contradiction: with respect to one's own life and its problems, to take refuge in something magical, and then to be so busily engaged with the whole of human history. When tests and temptations assail dialectically, and when the victory is also always dialectically construed, a man will always have enough to do with himself. To be sure, in that case he will not be in a position to fascinate all human kind by the blissful enchantment of matchless visions.

Whether in addition it is not unchristian, respecting one's eternal happiness to rest in the assurance that one has been baptized, just as the Jews appealed to circumcision, and to their being the children of Abra-

---

* Who knows whether Pastor Grundtvig assumes that there is also a living word which proves that I am baptized?

ham, as the decisive proof for the validity of the God-relationship, and so to rest not in a free spiritual relationship to God (and then we are in the subjectivity-theory, where the real religious categories belong, where everyone has merely to save himself and finds in this a sufficient task, because the salvation becomes more difficult and more intensive in inwardness, the more significant the personality; where playing the rôle of world-historic genius and *extraordinarius* admitted to fraternize with God as spectator of universal history, is the equivalent of what frivolity is in the moral sphere) but in an external event, keeping doubts away by means of this magic rite of baptism,* not interpenetrating it with faith—this is something I shall not take it upon myself to decide. I have everywhere no opinion of my own, but merely seek to bring the problem to light experimentally.

As far as the Bible theory is concerned, the present author, even if he became still more convinced of the dialectical misdirection that lurks within it, will never be able to remember otherwise than with gratitude and admiration its distinguished achievements within the presupposition, the rare and thorough scholarship exhibited in its writings, the beneficent total impression made by a movement expressed in a literature, with whose entire compass the present author is far from arrogating to himself an unusual scholarly acquaintance. As for Grundtvig's theory, the author does not precisely feel any great amount of pain in the moment of parting, nor any special sense of isolation at being in disagreement with this thinker. No one could wish to have Grundtvig for an ally who desires to know definitely where he is, and does not wish to be

* When it is said that the reassuring thing in connection with baptism over against all temptations to doubt, is that in this sacrament God does something to us, the idea is naturally only an illusion, in so far as it is by this means intended to keep dialectics away. The dialectical returns at once with the appropriation of this thought, its inward assimilation. Every genius, including the greatest that has ever lived, has to expend all his powers exclusively upon this matter of appropriation, the transformation of inwardness and its actualization in himself. But people wish to be rid of doubts once for all. In the moment of temptation, therefore, faith does not lay hold of God, but is reduced to a belief that one has really been baptized. If there were not lurking here under the surface considerable quantities of sham and pretence, there would long ago have emerged psychologically remarkable manifestations of concern, over how to get certainty that one has really been baptized. Were it only a matter of say ten thousand dollars at stake, the case would scarcely be permitted to stand with the kind of certainty we all now have that we are baptized.

where there is an alarm, especially when the alarm itself is only the more specific determination of where one is. As for Magister Lindberg, he is a man of so many scholarly attainments, he is so experienced a dialectician, that it must always be a great gain to have him on one's side; as an opponent he will always be capable of making the combat difficult—but also satisfying—because he is a trained fencer who sends his strokes home, and does not slay so absolutely but that the survivor readily convinces himself that it is not he who is slain, but rather one or another tremendous absolute. It has always seemed to me an injustice that while Pastor Grundtvig enjoys a certain annual tribute of admiration and *accidentalia* from the worshipping party membership, Magister Lindberg has had to stand in the shade. And yet it is in truth something definite, and something that can in truth be said about Lindberg, that he has a good head on his shoulders; it is on the other hand extremely doubtful what in truth it all means when it is said that Grundtvig is seer, bard, skald, prophet, endowed with a well-nigh matchless insight into world history, and with an eye for the profound.

§ 3. THE PROOF OF THE CENTURIES

The problem is posed objectively. The self-adequate subject thinks as follows: "Let the truth of Christianity only be made clear and certain, and there need be no fear that I shall not prove myself ready and willing to accept it, and that quite as a matter of course." The difficulty is, that the truth of Christianity has, in consequence of its paradoxical form,* something in common with the nettle: the self-adequate subject merely succeeds in stinging himself, when he seeks thus to lay hold of it without further ado. Or rather—for since this is a spiritual relationship, the stinging can be understood only metaphorically—he does not lay hold of it at all; he grasps its objective truth so objectively as to remain himself outside.

The argument cannot really be treated in a strictly dialectical manner at all, for at the very outset it transforms itself into an hypothesis. And an hypothesis may become more probable by maintaining itself against objections for three thousand years, but it does not on that account become an eternal truth, adequately decisive for one's eternal happiness. Has not Mohammedanism persisted for twelve hundred years? The guaranty of the eighteen centuries, the circumstance that Christianity

---

* Compare on this point the *Fragments*.

has interpenetrated all the relations of life, has transformed the world, and so forth—all this assurance is nothing but a deceptive snare in which the resolving and choosing subject is held captive, lost in the wilderness of the parenthesis. Eighteen centuries have no greater demonstrative force than a single day, in relation to an eternal truth which is to decide my eternal happiness. But the eighteen centuries, and all the countless things which in that connection may be narrated and asserted and repeated, have contrariwise a power to distract the mind, and serve that purpose admirably. Every man is by nature designed to become a thinker —honor and praise to the God who created man in his own image! God cannot be held responsible if habit, and routine, and want of passion, and affectation, and gossiping with friends and neighbors, little by little ruin most men, so that they become thoughtless—and base their eternal happiness on this, that, and the other; not perceiving that what they say about their eternal happiness is an affectation, precisely because it is passionless, which is also the reason why it can be so beautifully supported by arguments as slender as toothpicks.

This argument can therefore be presented only in a rhetorical form.* True eloquence is indeed rare, and true eloquence would doubtless hesitate to use such an argument; perhaps this is the reason why it is so often heard. In its best form the argument refrains from dialectics (for it is only the bunglers who begin with the dialectical, and later on resort to rhetoric); it seeks merely to impress. The speaker isolates the deliberating or doubting subject from all connection with others. He confronts the poor sinner with innumerable hosts of past generations, with millions upon millions, and then says to him: "Now dare you be so insolent as to deny the truth? Dare you really imagine that you are in possession of the truth, and that the eighteen centuries, the innumerable generations of men, millions upon millions, have lived their lives in error? O wretched solitary man, do you dare thus to plunge all these many millions, all mankind indeed, into destruction? Behold, they arise from their graves, they pass as if in review before my thought, these generations upon generations of believers, whose minds found rest in the truth of Christianity. Their glances condemn you, O insolent rebel, until the separation of the judgment day snatches you from their sight, because you were weighed and found wanting, were thrown into the outer dark-

* Perhaps most fittingly with an undertone of humor, as when Jean Paul says[1] that, even if all other arguments for the truth of Christianity were disproved or abandoned, one argument would still remain intact, namely, that Christianity has existed for eighteen centuries.

ness, far from eternal bliss, etc., etc." Behind the tremendous barrage of the many millions the cowardly speaker sometimes trembles in his boots when he uses the argument, because he dimly feels that there is a contradiction in his whole procedure.

But he cannot do the sinner any harm. Such a rhetorical shower-bath from the height of eighteen centuries is very stimulating. The speaker performs a service, if not precisely in the way intended, by separating the subject out for himself over against other men—ah, and this is a great service, for only a very few are able to do this for themselves. And yet it is experience in this situation which constitutes an absolute condition for entering Christianity. The eighteen centuries ought precisely to inspire fear. As proof *pro* they are in the moment of decision worth precisely nothing to the individual subject; but as fear-inspiring *contra* they are excellent. The only question is whether the rhetorician will succeed in getting the poor sinner under the shower-bath. For he does him an injustice, since the sinner neither affirms nor denies the truth of Christianity, but is concerned solely for his relationship to it. As the Icelander in the story said to the king: "It is too much, your majesty"; so the sinner might say: "It is too much, right reverend sir, why all these many millions? It makes my head swim in such a confusion, that I know neither in nor out." As noted above, it is Christianity itself which stresses so tremendously the significance of the individual subject. It desires to deal with the individual, and with the individual alone; and so with every other individual. In so far it is an unchristian use of the eighteen centuries to employ them for the purpose either of enticing or of threatening the individual to embrace Christianity. He will none the less never become a Christian in that manner; and if he does become a Christian, it will be a matter of indifference whether he has the eighteen centuries for him or against him.

The principle here indicated has often enough been stressed in the exposition given in the *Fragments,* namely, that no direct or immediate transition to Christianity exists. All who in this manner propose to give the individual a rhetorical push into Christianity, or perhaps even to help him by administering a beating, all these are deceivers—nay, they know not what they do.

CHAPTER II

THE SPECULATIVE POINT OF VIEW

FROM the speculative standpoint, Christianity is viewed as an historical phenomenon. The problem of its truth therefore becomes the problem of so interpenetrating it with thought, that Christianity at last reveals itself as the eternal truth.

The speculative approach to the problem is characterized by one excellent trait: it has no presuppositions. It proceeds from nothing, it assumes nothing as given, it begs no postulates. Here then we may be sure of avoiding such presuppositions as were met with in the preceding.

And yet, something is after all assumed: Christianity is assumed as given. Alas and alack! philosophy is altogether too polite. How strange is the way of the world! Once it was at the risk of his life that a man dared to profess himself a Christian; now it is to make oneself suspect to venture to doubt that one is a Christian. Especially when this doubt does not mean that the individual launches a violent attack against Christianity with a view to abolishing it; for in that case it would perhaps be admitted that there was something in it. But if a man were to say quite simply and unassumingly, that he was concerned for himself, lest perhaps he had no right to call himself a Christian, he would indeed not suffer persecution or be put to death, but he would be smothered in angry glances, and people would say: "How tiresome to make such a fuss about nothing at all; why can't he behave like the rest of us, who are all Christians? It is just as it is with F. F., who refuses to wear a hat on his head like others, but insists on dressing differently." And if he happened to be married, his wife would say to him: "Dear husband of mine, how can you get such notions into your head? How can you doubt that you are a Christian? Are you not a Dane, and does not the geography say that the Lutheran form of the Christian religion is the ruling religion in Denmark? For you are surely not a Jew, nor are you a Mohammedan; what then can you be if not a Christian? It is a thousand years since paganism was driven out of Denmark, so I know you are not a pagan. Do you not perform your duties at the office like a conscientious civil servant; are you not a good citizen of a Christian nation, a Lutheran Christian state? So then of course you must be a Christian."

We have become so objective, it seems, that even the wife of a civil servant argues to the particular individual from the totality, from the state, from the community-idea, from the scientific standpoint of geography. It is so much a matter of course that the individual is a Christian, a believer and so forth, that it is frivolous to make a fuss about it, or to be such a crotcheteer. Since it is always unpleasant to have to admit the lack of something that everyone has as a matter of course, and which therefore properly gets a sort of special significance only when someone is stupid enough to betray his defect, what wonder then that no one admits it? In the case of what amounts to something, presupposing skill or aptitude or the like, it is easier to make an admission. But the more insignificant the matter, insignificant, namely, because we are all in possession of it, the more it is stupid and in bad taste to make the admission. And this is the modern category for any sign of concern lest one should not be a Christian: it is in bad taste. *Ergo,* we are all Christians.

But perhaps philosophy will say: "These are popular and simple reflections, which theologues and popularizing philosophers are fit to expound; but speculative philosophy has nothing to do with such things." How terrible to be excluded from the superior wisdom of speculative philosophy! But it seems strange to me that people are always talking of philosophy or speculation as if it were a man, or as if a man were speculative philosophy. It is speculative philosophy that does everything, that doubts everything, and so forth. The philosopher, on the other hand, has become too objective to talk about himself; he does not say that he doubts everything, but that speculative philosophy does, and that he makes this affirmation about speculative philosophy. Further than this he refuses to commit himself—in case of private inquiry. But is it not then possible to agree to be human beings? Socrates says[1] that when we posit flute-playing we must also posit a flute-player; and so if we posit speculative philosophy we must also assume the existence of a philosopher, or of several philosophers. Therefore, dear man and most worthy philosopher, I may surely venture to approach you at least in terms of subjective address: "What view do you take of Christianity? That is to say, are you or are you not a Christian? The question is not whether you have advanced beyond Christianity, but only whether you are a Christian. Unless indeed an advance beyond Christianity means for a speculative philosopher the ceasing to be what he was, a veritable achievement *à la* Munchausen, possible perhaps for speculative philosophy, an entity which I do not pretend to understand; but surely impossible for the speculative philosopher *qua* human being."

The speculative philosopher, unless he is as objective as the wife of our civil servant, proposes to contemplate Christianity from the philosophical standpoint. It is a matter of indifference to him whether anyone accepts it or not; such anxieties are left to theologues and laymen—and also surely to those who really are Christians, and who are by no means indifferent as to whether they are Christians or not. The philosopher contemplates Christianity for the sake of interpenetrating it with his speculative thought; aye, with his genuinely speculative thought. But suppose this whole proceeding were a chimera, a sheer impossibility; suppose that Christianity is subjectivity, an inner transformation, an actualization of inwardness, and that only two kinds of people can know anything about it: those who with an infinite passionate interest in an eternal happiness base this their happiness upon their believing relationship to Christianity, and those who with an opposite passion, but in passion, reject it—the happy and the unhappy lovers. Suppose that an objective indifference can therefore learn nothing at all. Only the like is understood by the like, and the old principle: *quidquid cognoscitur, per modum cognoscentis cognoscitur,*[2] must be so expanded as to make room for a mode of knowing in which the knower fails to know anything at all, or has all his knowledge reduced to an illusion. In the case of a kind of observation where it is requisite that the observer should be in a specific condition, it naturally follows that if he is not in this condition, he will observe nothing. He may, of course, attempt to deceive by saying that he is in this condition without being so; but when fortunately he himself avers that he is not in this condition, he deceives nobody.

Now if Christianity is essentially something objective, it is necessary for the observer to be objective. But if Christianity is essentially subjectivity, it is a mistake for the observer to be objective. In every case where the object of knowledge is the very inwardness of the subjectivity of the individual, it is necessary for the knower to be in a corresponding condition. But the utmost tension of human subjectivity finds its expression in the infinite passionate interest in an eternal happiness. Even in the case of earthly love it is a necessary requirement for a would-be observer, that he should know the inwardness of love. But here the interest is not so great as it is in the case of an eternal happiness, because all love is affected by illusion, and hence has a quasi-objective aspect, which makes it possible to speak of something like an experience at second-hand. But when love is interpenetrated with a God-relationship, this imperfection of illusion disappears, together with the remaining semblance of objectivity; and now it holds true that one not in this condition can gain nothing by all his efforts to observe. In the infinite passionate interest for his eternal happiness, the subject is in a state of the utmost tension, in the very extremity of subjectivity, not indeed where there is no object, which is the imperfect and undialectical distinction, but where God is negatively present in the subject; whose mode of subjectivity becomes, by virtue of this interest, the form for an eternal happiness.

The speculative philosopher views Christianity as an historical phenomenon. But suppose Christianity is nothing of the kind. "How stupid," I think I hear someone say, "what an extraordinary hankering after originality to say such a thing, especially now, when philosophy has arrived at an understanding of the necessity of the historical." Aye, indeed, what is it not given philosophy to understand! But if a philosopher were to assert that he had understood the necessity of an historical phenomenon, I would ask him to give a moment's attention to the critical considerations that were quite simply presented in the *Fragments,* in the "Interlude" between Chapters IV and V. To this little essay I must for the present refer; I shall always be willing to make it the point of departure for further dialectical developments, whenever I am so fortunate as to have a philosopher before me, a human being, for I dare not argue with speculative philosophy.

And now this extraordinary hankering after originality! Let us consider an analogy. Take husband and wife: their marriage expresses itself clearly in terms of external fact, and constitutes a phenomenon in existence, just as Christianity has stamped its impress upon life on the larger stage of the world's history. But their wedded love is no historical phenomenon. The phenomenal is here in itself the insignificant, and it receives significance for husband and wife only through their love; but otherwise considered, i.e. objectively, the phenomenal is a deception. And so also with Christianity. Is this then so original? To be sure, over against the Hegelian principle,[3] that the external is the internal and the internal the external, it is highly original. But it would be a case of still greater originality if the Hegelian axiom were not only admired by contemporaries, but also had retroactive power to abolish, in historical retrospect, the distinction between the visible and the invisible Church. The invisible Church is no historical phenomenon; it cannot be observed objectively at all, since it exists only in the subjectivity of the individuals. Alas, my originality does not seem to be so very great after all; in spite of all my hankering, of which however I am not conscious, I say only what every schoolboy knows, though he may not be able to express himself quite so clearly. And this is a trait which the schoolboy shares with great philosophers, only that the schoolboy is still too immature, the great philosopher over-mature.

That the speculative point of view is objective I do not deny. On the contrary, and in order to give a further demonstration of this fact, I shall here again repeat the experiment of placing a subject who is in passion infinitely concerned for his eternal happiness, in relation to speculative philosophy; when it will become evident that the speculative point of view is objective, from the fact that the so interested subject becomes comical. He does not become comical because he is infinitely interested; on the other hand, everyone who is not infinitely and passionately interested, but tries nevertheless to make people believe that he has an interest in his eternal happiness, is a comic figure. No, the comical inheres precisely in the incommensurability between his interest and the speculative objectivity.

If the speculative philosopher is at the same time a believer, as is also affirmed, he must long ago have perceived that philosophy can never acquire the same significance for him as faith. It is precisely as a believer that he is infinitely interested in his eternal happiness, and it is in faith that he is assured of it. (It should be noted that this assurance is the sort of assurance that can be had in faith, i.e. not an assurance once for all, but a daily acquisition of the sure spirit of faith through the infinite personal passionate interest.) And he does not base his eternal happiness upon his philosophical speculations. Rather, he associates circumspectly with philosophy, lest it lure him away from the certainty of faith (which has in every moment the infinite dialectic of uncertainty present with it) so as to rest in an indifferent objective knowledge. This is the simple dialectical analysis of the situation. If, therefore, he says that he bases his eternal happiness on his speculation, he contradicts himself and becomes comical, because philosophy in its objectivity is wholly indifferent to his and my and your eternal happiness. An eternal happiness inheres precisely in the recessive self-feeling of the subject, acquired through his utmost exertion. And besides contradicting himself, such a philosopher lies, with respect to his pretensions to be a believer.

Or the speculative philosopher is not a believer. In this case, he is of course not comical, since he does not raise the question of his eternal happiness at all. The comical appears only when the subject with an infinite passionate interest tries to attach his eternal happiness to philosophical speculation. But the speculative philosopher does not pose the problem of which we speak; for precisely as a speculative philosopher he becomes too objective to concern himself about an eternal happiness.

Let me here say merely a word, in case any one misunderstands many of my expressions, to make it clear that it is he who wishes to misunderstand me, and that I am without responsibility. All honor to philosophy, all praise to everyone who brings a genuine devotion to its service. To deny the value of speculation (though one might wish that the money-changers in the forecourts of the temple could be banished as profane) would be, in my opinion, to prostitute oneself. It would be particularly stupid in one whose own energies are for the most part, and in proportion to aptitude and opportunity, consecrated to its service; especially stupid in one who admires the Greeks. For he must know that Aristotle, in treating of what happiness is,[4] identifies the highest happiness with the joys of thought, recalling in this connection the blessed pastime of the eternal gods in speculation. And he must furthermore have some conception of, and respect for, the fearless enthusiasm of the philosophical scholar, his persistent devotion to the service of the Idea. But for the speculating philosopher the question of his personal eternal happiness cannot arise; precisely because his task consists in getting more and more away from himself so as to become objective, thus vanishing from himself and becoming what might be called the contemplative energy of philosophy itself. This sort of thing I am quite conversant with myself. But the blessed gods, those great prototypes for the speculative philosopher, were not concerned for their eternal happiness; and so the problem did not at all arise in paganism. But to treat Christianity in the same manner is simply to invite confusion. Since man is a synthesis of the temporal and the eternal, the happiness that the speculative philosopher may enjoy will be an illusion, in that he desires in time to be merely eternal. Herein lies the error of the speculative philosopher. Higher than this speculative happiness, therefore, is the infinite passionate interest in a personal eternal happiness. It is higher because it is truer, because it definitely expresses the synthesis.

So understood (and in a certain sense it would not need to be shown that the infinite interest in one's eternal happiness is higher, since the point is merely that it is what we here inquire about), the comical will readily become apparent in the emergence of the contradiction. The subject is in passion infinitely interested in his eternal happiness, and is now supposed to receive assistance from speculation, i.e. by himself philosophizing. But in order to philosophize he must proceed in precisely the opposite direction, giving himself up and losing himself in objectivity, thus vanishing from himself. The incommensurability thus confronting him will wholly prevent him from beginning, and will throw a comic illumination upon every assurance that he has gained anything in this manner. This is, from the opposite side, quite the same as what was said in the preceding about an observer's relationship to Christianity. Christianity does not lend itself to objective observation, precisely because it proposes to intensify subjectivity to the utmost; and when the subject has thus put himself in the right attitude, he cannot attach his eternal happiness to speculative philosophy.

This contradiction between the subject who is in passion infinitely interested, and philosophical speculation viewed as something that might assist him, I shall permit myself to illustrate by means of an image from the sensible world. In sawing wood it is important not to press down too hard on the saw; the lighter the pressure exerted by the sawyer, the better the saw operates. If a man were to press down with all his strength, he would no longer be able to saw at all. In the same way it is necessary for the philosopher to make himself objectively light; but everyone who is in passion infinitely interested in his eternal happiness makes himself subjectively as heavy as possible. Precisely for this reason he prevents himself from speculating. Now if Christianity requires this interest in the individual subject (which is the assumption, since this is the point on which the problem turns), it is easy to see that he cannot find what he seeks in speculation. This can also be expressed by saying that speculative philosophy does not permit the problem to arise at all; and it follows that all its pretense of answering the problem constitutes only a mystification.

BOOK TWO

THE SUBJECTIVE PROBLEM

THE RELATION OF THE SUBJECT TO THE TRUTH
OF CHRISTIANITY
THE PROBLEM OF BECOMING A CHRISTIAN

Part One
Something About Lessing

CHAPTER I

AN EXPRESSION OF GRATITUDE

IF A poor thinker who is a private practitioner, a cultivator of speculative eccentricities, occupying like a poverty-stricken lodger a garret at the top of a vast building, sat there in his little refuge, held captive in what seemed to him difficult thoughts; if, without being able to understand how or why, he began to conceive a dim suspicion that there was something wrong with the foundations; if, whenever he looked out of the little garret window, he saw shudderingly only busy and redoubled exertions to beautify or enlarge the structure, so that after having seen and shuddered he collapsed in utter exhaustion, feeling as a spider who in some narrow nook has managed to eke out a precarious existence since the last house-cleaning, and now senses anxiously the coming storm; if whenever he communicated his doubts to someone he perceived that his speech, because of its departure from the prevailing fashion, was regarded as the bizarre and threadbare costume of some unfortunate derelict—if, I say, such a privately practising thinker and speculative crotcheteer were suddenly to make the acquaintance of a man whose renown did not indeed directly insure for him the validity of his thoughts (for the poor lodger was not quite so objective as to be able without more ado to draw the converse conclusion from renown to truth), but whose fame was nevertheless like a smile of fortune in the midst of his loneliness, when he found one or two of his difficult thoughts touched upon by the famous man: ah, what joy, what festivity in the little garret chamber, when the poor lodger took comfort to himself from the glorious memory of the renowned thinker, when his own thinking began to breathe courage, the difficulties began to take on form, and hope finally sprang into being—the hope of understanding himself; that is to say, the hope first of understanding the nature of the difficulty, and then perhaps of being able to overcome it! For with respect to the understanding of difficulties, the principle that Peter the

Deacon[1] wrongly desires to incorporate into the order of ecclesiastical preferment, namely, "first the deacon," really applies: first comes the understanding of the difficulty, and then it will be in order to explain it—if one can.

Well, then, in jest and in earnest: forgive, illustrious Lessing, this expression of a romantic gratitude, forgive its jesting form! It is indeed kept at a respectful distance, quite unintrusive and wholly personal, free from the bluster of the world-historic and the violence of the systematic. If it is not strictly true, this is because it is all too romantic; for which the jesting tone seeks to make amends. And this jesting tone has also its deeper ground in the opposition involved in the relationship: on the one hand, one who evokes doubts experimentally, without explaining why he does it; on the other hand, one who experimentally seeks to make the religious stand out in its supernatural proportions, without explaining why he does it.

This expression of gratitude does not relate to what is ordinarily, and I assume also rightly, admired in Lessing. To admire in this manner I scarcely seem to myself warranted. My admiration does not have to do with Lessing as a scholar, nor relate to what appeals to me as a brilliant myth: that he was a librarian; it does not have to do with what seems well-nigh an epigram: that he was the soul in a library, that he held possession of an enormous learning in an almost omnipresent autopsy, a gigantic apparatus kept under the control of thought and obedient to every hint of the spirit, pledged to the service of the Idea. It does not have to do with Lessing as a poet, nor relate to his mastery in the construction of the dramatic sentence, his psychological power in poetic revelation of the secrets of the mind, his hitherto unexcelled gift of dramatic dialogue, which in his hands moves freely and unembarrassed in an easy conversational tone, though heavily freighted with thought. It does not have to do with Lessing as an aesthetician, nor relate to that line of demarcation which at his command (quite otherwise authoritative than a papal bull) was drawn between poetry and the formative arts; nor does it relate to that wealth of aesthetic observation which was his, and which continues to suffice even in our own age. Nor, again, does it have to do with Lessing as sage; nor does it relate to that genial wisdom which was his, and which modestly concealed itself in the unpretentious dress of the fable.

No, my admiration has to do with something else, something such that its very nature makes it impossible to admire it directly, or establish through one's admiration any immediate relationship with Lessing; for his merit consists precisely in his having prevented it. I refer to the fact that he religiously shut himself up within the isolation of his own subjectivity; that he did not permit himself to be deceived into becoming world-historic and systematic with respect to the religious, but understood and knew how to hold fast to the understanding that the religious concerned Lessing, and Lessing alone, just as it concerns every other human being in the same manner; understood that he had infinitely to do with God, and nothing, nothing to do with any man directly. This is my theme, the object of my gratitude—now if I could only be sure that Lessing really does exemplify this principle! And if I could be sure, Lessing would have the right to say to me: "You have nothing to thank me for." Ah, if I could only be sure! In vain would I try to break through Lessing's defenses with the assaults and with the persuasiveness of my admiration; in vain would I beg, threaten, bluster; Lessing has seized upon that Archimedean point of the religious life, which does not precisely enable one to move the world, but which it needs an energy of cosmic proportions to discover, when you have Lessing's presuppositions. Ah, if I could only be sure!

But now to his result! Has Lessing accepted Christianity or has he rejected it, has he defended it or has he attacked it—in order that I too may adopt the same conclusion, in reliance upon him, this man who had poetic imagination enough to make himself at any moment contemporary with the event that occurred now 1812 years ago, and that in so primitive a manner as to exclude every historical illusion, every perverse objective falsification. Aye, take Lessing there! No, he had the sceptical ataraxy and the religious sensibility necessary in order to become aware of the category of the religious. If anyone wishes to deny this, I demand that the question be submitted to a vote. Well, then, to his result! Wonderful Lessing, he has no result, none whatever; there is no trace of any result. Verily, no father confessor to whom a secret has been intrusted, no maiden who has pledged herself and her love to silence and becomes immortal through keeping her pledge, no man who takes every explanation of his life with him into the grave, no one, no one could carry himself more circumspectly than Lessing, while achieving the still more difficult task of keeping silent though speaking. Not Satan himself, as third party, can say anything definite about it as third party. As for God, he is never a third party when he is present in the religious consciousness; this is precisely the secret of the religious consciousness.

The world has perhaps always suffered from a dearth of what might be called essential individualities, men of decisive subjectivity, men artistically interpenetrated with reflection, self-thinking men, as distinct from town-criers and docents. The more objective the world becomes, the more subjectivity tends to be submerged in objectivity, the greater the difficulties besetting the religious categories, which lie precisely in subjectivity. Hence, the tendency to become world-historical, scientific, and objective, with respect to the religious, constitutes well-nigh an irreligious exaggeration. But I have not brought Lessing forward here for the sake of having someone to appeal to; even to wish to be so subjective as to appeal to another's subjectivity is an attempt to become objective, the first step toward obtaining a majority in one's favor, and toward transforming one's God-relationship into a speculation on the basis of probabilities, and of fellowship, and of support from the other shareholders in the enterprise.

In connection with this task of becoming essentially subjective, it is necessary to take into account the scope of the reflective presuppositions that the subject has to interpenetrate, the weight of the objectivity he has to throw off; and how infinite a conception he has of the significance of this change (the change from objectivity to subjectivity), its responsibility and its limits. If such considerations posit a requirement that restricts to a very few the number of personalities that can come in question; aye, even if it seemed to me that Lessing stood alone, it is again not for the sake of appealing to him that I here bring him forward. (But oh, that one dared appeal to him, that one might place himself in an immediate relationship to him, for then one would surely be helped!)

It also occurs to me that such an appeal would be questionable for still another reason, in that, by means of such an appeal, I would have contradicted myself, and nullified my entire position. If the subject has not worked himself through and out of his objectivity, every appeal to another individual will be merely a misunderstanding. And if he has so won his way through, he will, as subjective, doubtless know all about his own course, and the dialectical presuppositions in which and in accordance with which he has his religious existence. The course of development of the religious subject has the remarkable trait that it comes into being for the individual and closes behind him. And why should not the divinity know how to set a value upon itself! Wherever there is something extraordinary and valuable to be seen, there is indeed always a crowd, but the owner generally takes care to permit a view of it only to one at a time—the crowd, the mass, the mob, the world-historical tumult is left outside. And the divinity surely has the most precious of all treasures; but it also knows how to make itself secure, in a fashion quite different from the means available to all earthly care-takers, so as to prevent anyone from slipping in world-historically, objectively, scientifically, under cover of the crowd.

Whoever understands this will presumably also wish to express it in his mode of life; although the same behavior may in one person be insolence, and in another true religious courage, no objective determination of this being possible. Now, whether or not Lessing has achieved this greatness; whether, humbling himself under the divine, and loving the human, he has come to the assistance of the divinity by expressing his God-relationship also in his relationship to others, lest he should incur the meaningless consequence of having his own God-relationship for himself, but occasioning another to have his God-relationship only through him,—who can tell with certainty? If I knew with certainty, I could appeal to him; and if I could appeal to him and be justified in so doing, it would be certain that Lessing had failed to do it.

To be sure, Lessing has long since been left behind; he is merely a vanishing little way-station on the systematic railway of world-history. To attach oneself to him is to condemn oneself, and to justify every contemporary in passing the objective judgment that one so doing has proved himself incapable of keeping up with the times, now that travel goes by train; so that the entire art of keeping up with the times consists in jumping into the first coach that comes along, leaving it to the world-historic process to carry one on. To recall Lessing is an act of desperation; for it makes it certain that it is all up with one, and that one has been left far, far behind, if it so happens that Lessing has said something of what one wishes to say. Of course, it might be the case, either that what Lessing had said was true (when it would seem to be a little questionable to run away from it so fast, with the speed of a railway train), or else that people had neglected to take the time to understand Lessing, who always cleverly knew how to withdraw himself, keeping his dialectical insight, and his subjectivity within it, away from every officious transportation-process which seeks to divert it into the hands of some merely external possessor.

But when I have hardened myself sufficiently against all this scorn and all these temptations, the worst remains behind: suppose that Lessing has deceived me! That man Lessing surely was an egoist! With respect to the religious, he always had something that he kept to himself, something which he did indeed give utterance to, but in so artful a manner that it could not be repeated after him directly and by rote; something which always remained the same while it constantly changed its form; something which was not stereotyped for insertion in a systematic formulary, but which the trained dialectical gymnast produces and changes and produces again, the same and yet not the same.

It was really malicious of Lessing thus always to be changing the lettering in connection with the dialectical, just as when a mathematician confuses a student who has not fixed his attention mathematically on the proof, but contented himself with a bowing acquaintance that judges by the lettering. It was a shame of Lessing thus to place all those who are so infinitely willing to swear in *verba magistri,* in the embarrassing position of never being able, in relation to him, to assume the only attitude natural to them, namely, the attitude of taking oath. It was a shame that he did not say outright: "I attack Christianity," so that the swearers could say: "We take our oath on the same"; or that he did not say outright: "I defend Christianity," so that the swearers could say: "We take our oath on the same." It was indeed a sad misuse of his dialectical skill, so to bring it about that they must needs swear falsely (since they had to swear); partly when they swore that what he now said was the same as what he said before, because the form and investiture were the same; partly when they swore that what he now said was not the same, because the form and investiture were different: like the traveller who recognized under oath in an innocent man the robber who had despoiled him, failing to know the robber because he only recognized his wig, and hence should surely have restricted himself to taking oath that he recognized the wig. No indeed, Lessing was no serious man. His entire mode of communication is without earnestness, being lacking in that true dependability which suffices for others, namely, those who always think in the wake of someone else, though without thoughtfulness.

And now his style! This polemic tone, which every instant has unlimited leisure to indulge in a witticism, and that even in a period of ferment; for according to an old newspaper I have found, the age was then precisely as now in such a ferment of change that the world has never seen the like. This stylist equanimity, which develops a simile in minutest detail, as if the literary expression had a value in itself, as if peace and safety reigned; and that although perhaps the printer's devil and world-history and all mankind stood waiting for him to have it finished. This systematic slackness, which refuses to obey the paragraphic norm. This mingling of jest and earnest, which makes it impossible for a third party to know which is which—unless indeed the third party knows it by himself. This artfulness, which perhaps even sometimes puts a false emphasis upon the indifferent, so that the initiated may precisely in this manner best grasp the dialectically decisive point, while the heretics[2] get nothing to run with. This form of his, so completely an expression of his individuality, spontaneously and refreshingly cutting its own path, not dying away in a mosaic of catchwords and authorized phrases and contemporary slogans, which in quotation marks give evidence that the writer keeps up with the times, while Lessing on the other hand confides to the reader *sub rosa* that he keeps up with the thought. This adroitness in teasingly using his own ego, almost like Socrates, excusing himself from all fellowship; or rather, insuring himself against fellowship in relation to all that truth, whose chief feature it is, that one must be alone about it; not wishing to have others with him for the sake of the triumph, since there is here no triumph to win, unless indeed one thinks of the infinite, where the triumph consists in becoming nothing before God; not wishing to have other men about him when struggling in the deadly perils of solitary thought, since it is just this solitariness which is the way.

Does all this betoken a serious mind? Is it a mark of earnestness so to treat all in essentially the same manner, only varying the form, not only evading the stupid attempts of fanatics to enroll him in the service of positive social ends, but also eluding their presumptuous attempts to exclude him; refusing to be impressed even by Jacobi's enthusiastic eloquence, and remaining unmoved by Lavater's amiable and simple-minded concern for his soul? Is his manner of departing this life such as befits an earnest man, seeing that his last words[3] were as mysterious as all the rest,* so that the noble Jacobi dares not vouch for his soul's

* Hegel is also supposed to have died with the words upon his lips, that there was only one man who had understood him, and he had misunderstood him; and when Hegel has done the same it might serve to reflect some credit upon Lessing to have done it also. But alas, there was a great difference. Hegel's statement reveals at once the defect of a direct form, and hence is quite inadequate as an expression for such a misunderstanding, giving sufficient evidence that Hegel has not existed artistically in the elusive form of a double reflection. In

salvation, which Jacobi was serious enough to concern himself about—almost as much as about his own? Is this earnestness? Aye, let those decide the point who are so earnest that they cannot understand jest. They ought to be competent judges, unless it should happen to be the case that one cannot understand earnest without understanding jest, which according to Plutarch's *Moralia* was the view of that earnest Roman, Cato Uticensis, who demonstrated the dialectical reciprocity of jest and earnest.[4] But when Lessing is thus proved to have been no earnest man, what hope is there for one who renounces such weighty values as the world-historical and contemporary system-making, in order to attach himself to Lessing?

So difficult is it to approach Lessing on the religious side. If I were to set about expounding the several ideas, patteringly referring them to him directly, dutifully enclosing him in my admiring embrace as one to whom I owed everything, he would perhaps smilingly withdraw, leaving me in the lurch, an object of ridicule. If I were to suppress the mention of his name in connection with these ideas, loudly proclaiming myself the happy author of the matchless discovery, of which no one had ever before thought, then that πολυμήτις Όδμσσευς,[5] if I imagined him present, would doubtless lay his hand on my shoulder, saying in an ambiguously admiring tone: "*Darin haben Sie recht, wenn ich das gewusst hätte.*" And then I should understand, if no one else, that he had the best of me.

the second place, Hegel's mode of communication in the entire series of seventeen volumes is direct communication; so that if he has not found anyone to understand him, it is all the worse for him. It would be quite a different thing in the case of Socrates, for example, who had planned his entire form of communication to the end of being misunderstood. Regarded as a dramatic *replique* by Hegel in the hour of death, this saying is best interpreted as an attack of absent-mindedness, a piece of thoughtlessness on the part of a man who, now in death, attempts to walk paths he has never frequented in life. If Hegel as a thinker is *sui generis,* then there is no one with whom he can be compared; and if there should perhaps exist a parallel somewhere, one thing is certain: he has absolutely nothing in common with Socrates.

CHAPTER II

THESES POSSIBLY OR ACTUALLY ATTRIBUTABLE TO LESSING

WITHOUT presuming to appeal to Lessing or daring to cite him definitely as my authority, without pledging anyone because of Lessing's fame dutifully to understand or profess to understand that which brings him into embarrassing connection with my obscurity, which is doubtless as repellent as Lessing's fame is attractive, I now propose to set forth what, in spite of all, I refer to Lessing, although uncertain whether he would acknowledge it. I could almost be tempted to insist, teasingly and in reckless abandon, that Lessing has affirmed these theses, if not directly; I could wish, in still another mood, to thank him for them sentimentally and with admiration; I could sometimes wish to refer them to him with proud reserve and deep self-feeling, simply as a matter of generosity; and again, I entertain at times the fear that it may prove impertinent or embarrassing to bring these things into connection with his name.

Aye, one seldom finds an author who is so pleasant to have to do with as Lessing. And how comes it to be so? Because, I think, he is so sure of himself. All this trivial and comfortable intercourse between a distinguished man and one less distinguished: that the one is genius and master, the other pupil, messenger, slave and so forth, is here excluded. Even if I strove with might and main to become Lessing's disciple, I could not, for Lessing has prevented it. Just as he himself is free, so I imagine that he desires to make everyone else free in relation to himself. He begs to be excused the exhalations and *gaucheries* of the disciple, fearing to be made ridiculous through repetitioners who reproduce what is said like a prattling echo.

§ I. THE SUBJECTIVE EXISTING THINKER HAS REGARD TO THE DIALECTICS OF THE PROCESS OF COMMUNICATION

While objective thought is indifferent to the thinking subject and his existence, the subjective thinker is as an existing individual essentially interested in his own thinking, existing as he does in his thought. His thinking has therefore a different type of reflection, namely the reflection of inwardness, of possession, by virtue of which it belongs to the thinking subject and to no one else. While objective thought translates everything into results, and helps all mankind to cheat, by copying these off and reciting them by rote, subjective thought puts everything in process and omits the result; partly because this belongs to him who has the way, and partly because as an existing individual he is constantly in process of coming to be, which holds true of every human being who has not permitted himself to be deceived into becoming objective, inhumanly identifying himself with speculative philosophy in the abstract.

The reflection of inwardness gives to the subjective thinker a double reflection. In thinking, he thinks the universal; but as existing in this thought and as assimilating it in his inwardness, he becomes more and more subjectively isolated.

The difference between subjective and objective thinking must express itself also in the form of communication suitable to each.* That is to say, the subjective thinker will from the beginning have his attention called to the requirement that this form should embody artistically as much of reflection as he himself has when existing in his thought. In

* A double reflection is implicit in the very idea of communication. Communication assumes that the subject who exists in the isolation of his inwardness, and who desires through this inwardness to express the life of eternity, where sociality and fellowship is unthinkable, because the existential category of movement, and with it also all essential communication, is here unthinkable, since everyone must be assumed essentially to possess all, nevertheless wishes to impart himself; and hence desires at one and the same time to have his thinking in the inwardness of his subjective existence, and yet also to put himself into communication with others. This contradiction cannot possibly (except for thoughtlessness, for which indeed all things are possible) find expression in a direct form. That a subject who exists in this manner might wish to impart himself is not so difficult to understand. A lover, for example, whose inwardness is his love, may very well wish to communicate; but he will not wish to communicate himself directly, precisely because the inwardness of his love is for him essential. Essentially occupied constantly in acquiring and reacquiring the inwardness of love, he has no result, and is never finished. But he may nevertheless wish to communicate, although he can never use a direct form, because such a form presupposes results and finality. So, too, in the case of a God-relationship. Precisely because he himself is constantly in process of becoming inwardly or in inwardness, the religious individual can never use direct communication, the movement in him being the precise opposite of that presupposed in direct communication. Direct communication presupposes certainty; but certainty is impossible for anyone in process of becoming, and the semblance of certainty constitutes for such an individual a deception. Thus, to make use of an erotic relationship, if a loving maiden were to long for the wedding day on account of the assured certainty that it would give her; if she desired to install herself as wife in a legal security, exchanging maidenly longing for wifely yawning, her lover would have the right to complain of her unfaithfulness, and that although she loved no one else; because she had lost the Idea constitutive of the inwardness of love, and did not really love him. And it is this which characterizes all essential faithlessness in the erotic relationship; loving another is accidental.

an artistic manner, please note; for the secret does not lie in a direct assertion of the double reflection; such a direct expression of it is precisely a contradiction.

Ordinary communication between man and man is wholly immediate, because men in general exist immediately. When one man sets forth something and another acknowledges the same, word for word, it is taken for granted that they are in agreement, and that they have understood one another. Precisely because the speaker has not noticed the reduplication requisite to a thinking mode of existence, he also remains unaware of the double reflection involved in the process of communication. Hence he does not suspect that an agreement of this nature may be the grossest kind of misunderstanding. Nor does he suspect that, just as the subjective existing thinker has made himself free through the reduplication given his reflection, so the secret of all communication consists precisely in emancipating the recipient, and that for this reason he must not communicate himself directly; aye, that it is even irreligious to do so. This last holds true the more the subjective is of the essence of the matter, and hence applies first and foremost in the religious sphere; unless indeed the author of the communication is God himself, or dares appeal to the miraculous authority of an apostle, but is merely a human being, and at the same time in favor of having a meaning in what he says and does.

The subjective religious thinker, who in order to become such must have apprehended the doubleness characteristic of existence, readily perceives that a direct mode of communication is an attempt to defraud God, possibly depriving him of the worship of another human being in truth. He sees also that it is a fraud practised upon himself, as if he had ceased to be an existing individual; and an attempt to defraud the recipient of the communication, who possibly acquires a merely relative God-relationship; and moreover, that it is a fraud which brings him into contradiction with his entire thought. It would again be a contradiction to assert this directly, because in spite of the double reflection in the content, the form would be direct.

To demand of a thinker that he should contradict his entire thought and view of life in the form which he gives to his communication; to offer him the consolation that he will in this way succeed in accomplishing something; to persuade him that no one will bother his head about such a peccadillo, aye, that no one will even notice it in these objective times, since so extreme a consistency is accounted a trifling thing, to which no systematic hireling pays any attention,—all this is good advice, and quite cheap to boot. Suppose thus, that it happened to be the view of life of a religiously existing subject, that no man ought to have any disciple, that having disciples is an act of treason to God and man; suppose he also happened to be a little stupid (for if something more than honesty is required to make one's way through the world, it is always necessary to be stupid in order to have a real success, and in order to be thoroughly understood by many), and asserted this principle directly, with pathos and unction: what would happen? Why then he would be understood; and he would soon have applications from at least ten candidates, offering to preach this doctrine, in return merely for a free shave once a week. That is to say, he would in further confirmation of his doctrine have experienced the peculiar good fortune of obtaining disciples to accept and disseminate this doctrine of not having any disciples.

Objective thinking is wholly indifferent to subjectivity, and hence also to inwardness and appropriation; its mode of communication is therefore direct. It goes without saying that it need not on that account be at all easy. But it is direct, and lacks the elusiveness and the art of a double reflection, the godly and humane solicitude in communicating itself, which belongs to subjective thinking. It can be understood directly and be recited by rote. Objective thinking is hence conscious only of itself, and is not in the strict sense of the word a form of communication at all,* at least not an artistic form, in so far as artistry would always demand a reflection within the recipient, and an awareness of the form of the communication in relation to the recipient's possible misunderstanding. Objective thinking† is, like most human beings, so touchingly kind and communicative. It imparts itself without further ado, and, at the most, takes refuge in assurances respecting its own truth, in recommendations as to its trustworthiness, and in promises that all men will some time accept it—it is so certain. Or perhaps rather

---

* So it is always in the case of the negative: where it is unconsciously present it transforms positivity into negativity. Here it transforms a supposed communication into an illusion, because the negative factor in the communication is not reflected upon, but the communication is conceived simply and solely as positive. In the elusiveness of a double reflection, the negative element in the process of communication is reflected upon; hence this type of communication, which seems in comparison with the other to be no communication, is precisely communication.

† It must always be remembered that I speak of the religious, in which sphere objective thinking, when it ranks as highest, is precisely irreligious. But wherever objective thinking is within its rights, its direct form of communication is also in order, precisely because it is not supposed to have anything to do with subjectivity.

so uncertain; for the assurances and the recommendations and the promises, which are presumably for the sake of the others who are asked to accept it, may also be for the sake of the teacher, who feels the need of the security and dependability afforded by being in a majority. If his contemporaries deprive him of this consolation, he makes a draft on the future—so certain is he. This type of certainty has something in common with that independence, which in independence of the world needs the world as witness to its independence, to feel sure that it really is independent.

The form of a communication must be distinguished from its expression. When the thought has found its suitable expression in the word, which is realized by means of a first reflection, there follows a second reflection, concerned with the relation between the communication and the author of it, and reflecting the author's own existential relationship to the Idea. Let us yet again cite a few examples; for we have plenty of time, since what I write is not the expected last paragraph which will complete the System. Suppose that someone wished to communicate the following conviction: Truth is inwardness; there is no objective truth, but the truth consists in personal appropriation.* Suppose him to display great zeal and enthusiasm for the propagation of this truth, since if people could only be made to listen to it they would of course be saved; suppose he announced it on all possible occasions, and succeeded in moving not only those who perspire easily, but also the hard-boiled temperaments: what then? Why then, there would doubtless be found a few laborers, who had hitherto stood idle in the market-place, and only after hearing this call went to work in the vineyard—engaging themselves to proclaim this doctrine to all. And then what? Then he would have contradicted himself still further, as he had contradicted himself from the beginning; for the zeal and enthusiasm which he directed toward the end of getting it said and heard, was in itself a misunderstanding. The matter of prime importance was, of course, that he should be understood; the inwardness of the understanding would consist precisely in each individual coming to understand it by himself. Now he had even succeeded in obtaining town criers of inwardness, and a town crier of inwardness is quite a re-

* I say only "suppose"; and in this form I have the right to posit both what is most certain and what is most absurd. For even the certain is not posited as certain, but only as a supposition, to throw light on the relationship involved; and even the absurd is not posited essentially, but only hypothetically, in order to illustrate the consequence of the relationship.

markable species of animal. Really to communicate such a conviction would require both art and self-control: self-control to understand inwardly that the God-relationship of the individual man is the thing of prime importance, and that the busy intermeddling of third parties constitutes lack of inwardness, and an excess of amiable stupidity; art enough to vary inexhaustibly the doubly reflected form of the communication, just as the inwardness itself is inexhaustible. The greater the artistry, the greater the inwardness. If the author of the communication had much art, he could even afford to say that he was using art, certain of being able in the next moment to insure the inwardness of his communication, because he was infinitely concerned for the preservation of his own inwardness; it is this concern which saves the individual from every form of slovenly positivity.

Suppose a man wished to communicate the conviction that it is not the truth but the way which is the truth, i.e. that the truth exists only in the process of becoming, in the process of appropriation, and hence that there is no result. Suppose he were a philanthropic soul who simply had to proclaim this to all and sundry; suppose he hit upon the excellent short cut of communicating it in a direct form through the newspapers, thus winning masses of adherents, while the artistic way would in spite of his utmost exertions have left it undetermined whether he had helped anyone or not: what then? Why then his principle would have turned out to be precisely a result. Suppose someone wished to communicate the conviction that all receiving consists in producing; suppose he repeated it so often that this sentence even came to be used as a model of handwriting in copy-books: then he would certainly have had his principle confirmed. Suppose a man wished to communicate the conviction that the God-relationship of the individual is a secret. Suppose he were what we are accustomed to call a kindly soul, who loved others so much that he simply could not keep this to himself; suppose he nevertheless had sense enough to feel a little of the contradiction involved in communicating it directly, and hence told it to others only under a pledge of secrecy: what then? Then he must either have assumed that the disciple was wiser than his teacher, so that he could really keep the secret while the teacher could not (beautiful satire upon being a teacher!); or he must have become so overwhelmed with the bliss of galimatias that he did not notice the contradiction.

There is something so strange about these kind souls; their emotions are so deeply stirred that they simply cannot keep anything to themselves. And it is also so vain of them to believe that some other human being needs their help in his God-relationship, as if God were unable to help himself and the human being immediately concerned. But it is a somewhat strenuous exertion to hold fast the thought that one is nothing before God, and that all one's exertion is but a jest. It requires a discipline of the spirit to honor every human being, so as not to venture directly to meddle with his God-relationship; partly because there is enough to think about in connection with one's own, and partly because God is no friend of impertinences.

Wherever the subjective is of importance in knowledge, and where appropriation thus constitutes the crux of the matter, the process of communication is a work of art, and doubly reflected. Its very first form is precisely the subtle principle that the personalities must be held devoutly apart from one another, and not permitted to fuse or coagulate into objectivity. It is at this point that objectivity and subjectivity part from one another.

Ordinary communication, like objective thinking in general, has no secrets; only a doubly reflected subjective thinking has them. That is to say, the entire essential content of subjective thought is essentially secret, because it cannot be directly communicated. This is the meaning of the secrecy. The fact that the knowledge in question does not lend itself to direct utterance, because its essential feature consists of the appropriation, makes it a secret for everyone who is not in the same way doubly reflected within himself. And the fact that this is the essential form of such truth, makes it impossible to express it in any other manner.* Hence when anyone proposes to communicate such truth directly, he proves his stupidity; and if anyone else demands this of him, he too shows that he is stupid. Over against such an elusive and artistic communication of truth, the customary human stupidity will always raise the cry that it is egoism. And when stupidity at length prevails, and the communication becomes direct, stupidity will have gained so much, that the author of the communication will have become equally stupid with the pretended recipient.

* If there were living in our age a man who had been subjectively developed, so as to become conscious of the art of communication, he would be bound to experience the most precious of drolleries, and the most comic of situations. He would have the door shut in his face, as one incapable of being objective; until finally a kind-hearted objective fellow, a systematic sort of chap, would take pity on him, and help him partly into the paragraphs. For what was once considered to be an impossibility, namely, to paint Mars in the armor that made him invisible, would now succeed extremely well; indeed, what is still more strange, it would have a partial success.

A distinction may be drawn between a secret which is essentially a secret, and one which is so only accidentally. For example, what was said at a secret meeting of the ministry is an accidental secret as long as it is not made public; for it is in itself such as to be directly understandable as soon as it is revealed. It is an accidental secret, because no one yet knows it, or what will happen a year from now; but when it has happened, it will be capable of being directly understood. On the other hand, when Socrates isolated himself from every external relationship by making an appeal to his *daemon*, and assumed, as I suppose, that everyone must do the same, such a view of life is essentially a secret, or constitutes an essential secret, because it cannot be communicated directly. The most that Socrates could do was to help another negatively, by a maieutic artistry, to achieve the same view. Everything subjective, which through its dialectical inwardness eludes a direct form of expression, is an essential secret.

Such a form of communication corresponds to and reflects in all its inexhaustible artistry, the existing subject's own relationship to the Idea. In order to throw light on this point experimentally, without deciding whether anyone has actually been existentially conscious of it or not, I shall, in the following, indicate the nature of the existential situation.

§ 2. THE EXISTING SUBJECTIVE THINKER IS IN HIS EXISTENTIAL RELATION TO THE TRUTH AS NEGATIVE AS HE IS POSITIVE; HE HAS AS MUCH HUMOR AS HE HAS ESSENTIAL PATHOS, AND HE IS CONSTANTLY IN PROCESS OF BECOMING, I.E. HE IS ALWAYS STRIVING

Since the existing subject is occupied in existing (and this is the common lot of all men, except those who are objective, and have pure being to be in), it follows that he is in process of becoming. And just as the form of his communication ought to be in essential conformity with his mode of existence, so his thought must correspond to the structure of existence. Now everyone is familiar with the dialectic of becoming, through Hegel. Whatever is in process of becoming is in a state of alternation between being and non-being (a somewhat obscure determination, however, inasmuch as being must also constitute the continuity necessary to the alternation); later it is described as a synthesis of the negative and the positive.

In these times much is heard about the negative, and about negative thinkers. In this connection we are often enough compelled to listen to the preachments of the positive, and to the public thanks they offer up

ATTRIBUTABLE TO LESSING 75

to God and Hegel that they are not like these negative ones, but have become positive. The positive in the sphere of thought comes under the head of certainty in sense-perception, in historical knowledge, and in speculative results. But all this positiveness is sheer falsity. The certainty afforded by sense-perception is a deception, as one may learn from a study of the Greek sceptics, and from the entire treatment of this subject in the writings of modern idealism, which is very instructive. The positiveness of historical knowledge is illusory, since it is approximation-knowledge; the speculative result is a delusion. For all this positive knowledge fails to express the situation of the knowing subject in existence. It concerns rather a fictitious objective subject, and to confuse oneself with such a subject is to be duped. Every subject is an existing subject, which should receive an essential expression in all his knowledge. Particularly, it must be expressed through the prevention of an illusory finality, whether in perceptual certainty, or in historical knowledge, or in illusory speculative results. In historical knowledge, the subject learns a great deal about the world, but nothing about himself. He moves constantly in a sphere of approximation-knowledge, in his supposed positivity deluding himself with the semblance of certainty; but certainty can be had only in the infinite, where he cannot as an existing subject remain, but only repeatedly arrive. Nothing historical can become infinitely certain for me except the fact of my own existence (which again cannot become infinitely certain for any other individual, who has infinite certainty only of his own existence), and this is not something historical. The speculative result is in so far illusory, as the existing subject proposes *qua* thinker to abstract from the fact that he is occupied in existing, in order to be *sub specie aeterni*.[1]

Negative thinkers therefore always have one advantage, in that they have something positive, being aware of the negative element in existence; the positive have nothing at all, since they are deceived. Precisely because the negative is present in existence, and present everywhere (for existence is a constant process of becoming), it is necessary to become aware of its presence continuously, as the only safeguard against it. In relying upon a positive security the subject is merely deceived.

The negativity that pervades existence, or rather, the negativity of the existing subject, which should be essentially reflected in his thinking in an adequate form, has its ground in the subject's synthesis: that he is an existing infinite spirit. The infinite and eternal is the only certainty, but as being in the subject it is in existence; and the first expression for this, is its elusiveness, and this tremendous contradiction, that the eternal becomes, that it comes into being.

Hence it is necessary for the thinking of the existing subject to have a form in which this can be reflected. If the subject says this in direct utterance, he says something untrue; for in direct utterance the elusiveness is omitted. This makes the form of the communication confusing, as when the tongue of an epileptic pronounces the wrong word, though the speaker who gives a direct utterance to the negativity of existence may not notice the contradiction as clearly as the epileptic. Let us take an example. The existing subject is eternal, but *qua* existing temporal. The elusiveness of the infinite now expresses itself through the possibility of death at any moment. All positive security is thus rendered suspect. If I am not aware of this in every moment, my positive confidence in life becomes mere childishness, in spite of its having become speculative, strutting superior in the systematic buskins. But if I do become conscious of it, this infinite thought is so infinite as to threaten to transform my existence into a vanishing nothing. Now how does the existing subject reflect this characteristic of his thinking existence? That existence is thus constituted, all men know; but the positive know it positively, i.e. they do not know it at all—but then to be sure they are so busily occupied with world-history. Once a year on a solemn occasion this thought grips them, and now they enunciate the principle of uncertainty in the form of assurances. But the fact that they perceive the uncertainty of life only once in a while on a solemn occasion, betrays the fact that they are very positive; and the circumstance that they say it in the form of dependable assurances shows that even while they are saying it they do not know what they say, for which reason they are also capable of forgetting it again the next moment.

In connection with such negative principles, an elusive form of communication is the only adequate one; because a direct form of communication is based upon the security of social continuity, while the elusiveness of existence isolates me whenever I apprehend it. Everyone who is conscious of this and is content to be human, everyone who has the strength and imperturbability to refuse to become a dupe, in order to be allowed to prate about universal history, admired by the like-minded but mocked by existence, will avoid a direct form of statement. We all know that Socrates was an idler, who concerned himself neither with world-history nor with astronomy. Diogenes[2] tells us how he gave up the study of the latter science; and when he later sometimes stood

still and gazed into space,[3] I cannot assume, though not otherwise attempting to decide what he was doing, that he was engaged in star-gaz-
ing. But he had plenty of time and the needful singularity to devote
himself to the simply human, which concern is strangely enough regarded as singular in human beings; while it is not at all deemed singular to occupy oneself with world-history. From an excellent article in
Fyenske Tidsskrift[4] I learn that Socrates is supposed to have been somewhat ironical. It was really high time that this was said; and now that
the disclosure has been made, I am in a position to appeal to this article
for confirmation when I myself assume something similar. The irony
of Socrates makes use, and that precisely when he wishes to bring out
the infinite, makes use, among other things, of a form of speech which
sounds in the first instance like the speech of a madman. Just as existence is treacherous, so also is the speech of Socrates, perhaps (I say perhaps, for I am not so wise a man as the positive author in *Fyenske Tidsskrift*) in order to prevent getting on his hands a moved and believing
listener, who would proceed to appropriate positively the proposition
that existence is negative. This is something that no one can understand
who is able to speak only in a direct form; and it is also something it
cannot help saying once for all, since its secret is that it must be present
everywhere in the thought and in its reflection, just as it is present everywhere in existence. In so far, it is quite in order not to be understood,
for in that manner one is at least secure against misunderstanding. Thus
when Socrates says somewhere[5] that it is a strange mode of behavior on
the part of the skipper who has just safely transported you from Greece
to Italy, calmly to walk back and forth on the beach after his arrival,
accepting his pay as if he had done a good deed, although it is impossible for him to know whether he has rendered his passengers a genuine
service, or whether it might not have been better for them to have lost
their lives at sea—he speaks quite like a madman.* One or another of
those present may even have thought him mad, for, according to Plato
and Alcibiades,[6] there was an opinion abroad that he was at least a bit
peculiar ($\check{\alpha}\tau o\pi o\varsigma$) ; others may perhaps have thought it a droll turn
of speech. But Socrates had at the same time a little tryst with the Idea,
with the Socratic ignorance. If he has conceived infinity in the form of
ignorance, he must indeed have this conception with him everywhere.

---

* If one of our contemporaries were to speak in this manner, everyone would doubtless
perceive that he was a madman. But the positive know, and know positively, that Socrates was
a wise man, that this is quite certain: *ergo*.

Such matters do not occupy the attention of a *Privatdocent*.[7] He does it once a year in § 14 with pathos, and it is well for him that he does not do it otherwise; supposing he has a wife and children and excellent prospects—but no reason to fear the loss of them.

The subjective existing thinker who has the infinite in his soul has it always, and for this reason his form is always negative. When it is the case that he actually reflects existentially the structure of existence in his own existence, he will always be precisely as negative as he is positive; for his positiveness consists in the continuous realization of the inwardness through which he becomes conscious of the negative. Among so-called negative thinkers, there are some who after having had a glimpse of the negative have relapsed into positiveness, and now go out into the world like town criers, to advertise, prescribe and offer for sale their beatific negative wisdom—and of course, a result can quite well be announced through the town crier, just like herring from Holstein, and the like. These town criers of negativity are not much wiser than the positive thinkers, and it is inconsistent of the latter to be so wroth with them, since they are essentially positive. They are not existing thinkers; once upon a time perhaps they were, until they found their result; but from that moment they no longer existed as thinkers, but as town criers and auctioneers.

But the genuine subjective existing thinker is always as negative as he is positive, and *vice versa*. He continues to be such as long as he exists, not once for all in a chimerical mediation. His mode of communication is made to conform, lest through being too extraordinarily communicative he should succeed in transforming a learner's existence into something different from what a human existence in general has any right to be. He is conscious of the negativity of the infinite in existence, and he constantly keeps the wound of the negative open, which in the bodily realm is sometimes the condition for a cure. The others let the wound heal over and become positive; that is to say, they are deceived. In his mode of communication he expresses the same principle. He is therefore never a teacher but a learner; and since he is always just as negative as he is positive, he is always striving.

To be sure, in this manner, such a subjective thinker misses something; he does not enjoy life in the customary positive and comfortable manner. For most men, when they have arrived at a certain point in their search for truth, life takes on a change. They marry, and they acquire a certain position, in consequence of which they feel that they must in all honor have something finished, that they must have results. For regard for the opinions of men bids them have a result; what reverence for the divinity might dictate is less frequently regarded. And so they come to think of themselves as really finished, or feel obliged to think so out of deference to custom and convention; or now and then they sigh and complain, because there are so many things that keep them from striving. What an affront to God, if the sigh seeks Him! What an affront to God, if the sigh is only, so to speak, from regard for custom and convention! What a contradiction to sigh, because one's immersion in the effort to grasp the lower makes it impossible to seek the higher; instead of ceasing to sigh, and ceasing to grasp the lower! And so they occupy themselves now and then with a little striving, but this is only the parsimonious marginal note for a text long since complete. Living in this manner, one is relieved of the necessity of becoming executively aware of the strenuous difficulties which the simplest of propositions about existing *qua* human-being involves; while on the other hand, as positive thinker, one knows all about world-history, and is fully initiated into the secrets of providence.

An existing individual is constantly in process of becoming; the actual existing subjective thinker constantly reproduces this existential situation in his thoughts, and translates all his thinking into terms of process. It is with the subjective thinker as it is with a writer and his style; for he only has a style who never has anything finished, but "moves the waters of the language" every time he begins, so that the most common expression comes into being for him with the freshness of a new birth.

Thus constantly to be in process of becoming is the elusiveness that pertains to the infinite in existence. It is enough to bring a sensuous man to despair, for one always feels a need to have something finished and complete; but this desire does not come from the good, but needs to be renounced. The incessant becoming generates the uncertainty of the earthly life, where everything is uncertain. Every human being knows this, and at times gives it expression, especially on solemn occasions, and then not without tears and perspiration. He says it directly and stirs the emotions, both his and other people's—and shows in action what was already evident from the form of his utterance, that he does not understand what he says.*

---

* What serves to mark the thoroughly cultivated personality is the degree to which the thinking in which he has his daily life has a dialectical character. To have one's daily life in the decisive dialectic of the infinite, and yet continue to live: this is both the art of life and

Lucian[8] lets Charon in the underworld tell the following story. A man in the upper world stood talking with one of his friends, whom he invited to dine with him, promising him a rare dish. The friend expressed his thanks. Then the man said: "But now you must be sure to come." "You can count on me quite definitely," said the invited guest. So they parted; and as he walked away, a tile fell down from a roof and killed the prospective guest. And Charon adds the comment: "Is not that something to laugh yourself to death over?" Suppose now that the invited guest had been a speaker, who a moment before had moved himself and others by discoursing on the uncertainties of life! For so men speak: in one moment they know everything, and in the next moment they do not know it. And this is the reason it is regarded as folly and singularity to bother one's head about it, and to attend to the difficulties; because everyone knows it. But what everyone does not know, so that it counts as differential knowledge, that is a glorious thing to be concerned with. What everyone knows on the other hand, so that the difference is merely the trivial one of *how* it is known, that is a waste of effort to be concerned about—for one cannot possibly become self-important through knowing it. Suppose the invited guest of Lucian's story had answered his host out of a consciousness of uncertainty, what then? Then his reply would not have been so extremely unlike the speech of a madman, though many might not have noticed anything; for this sort of thing can be said so elusively that only a man himself familiar with such thoughts will notice it. And such an one will not deem it madness, nor is it madness; for while the jesting phrase winds its way drolly through the rest of the conversation, the speaker may privately have a rendezvous with the Deity, who is present as soon as the uncertainty of all things is thought infinitely. For this reason one who really has an eye for the Deity can see Him everywhere; while he who sees Him only on extraordinary occasions does not really see Him, but is superstitiously the dupe of a phantom vision.

its difficulty. Most men have complacent categories for their daily use, and resort to the categories of the infinite only upon solemn occasions; that is to say, they do not really have them. But to make use of the dialectic of the infinite in one's daily life, and to exist in this dialectic, is naturally the highest degree of strenuousness; and strenuous exertion is again needed to prevent the exercise from deceitfully luring one away from existence, instead of providing a training in existence. It is a well-known fact that a cannonade tends to deafen one to other sounds; but it is also a fact that persistence in enduring it may enable one to hear every word of a conversation as clearly as when all is still. Such is also the experience of one who leads an existence as spirit, intensified by reflection.

That the subjective existing thinker is as positive as he is negative, can also be expressed by saying that he is as sensitive to the comic as to the pathetic. As men ordinarily live, the comic and the pathetic are divided, so that one person has the one and another person has the other, one person a little more of the one, another, a little less. But for anyone who exists in a double reflection, the proportions are equal: as much of the pathetic, so much also of the comic. The equality in the relationship provides a mutual security, each guaranteeing the soundness of the other. The pathos which is not secured by the presence of the comic is illusion; the comic spirit that is not made secure by the presence of pathos is immature. Only one who himself produces this will understand it, otherwise not. What Socrates said about the voyage across the water[9] sounds wholly like a jest, and yet it was an expression for the highest earnestness. If it were to be regarded merely in the light of a jest, many might be willing to follow; if regarded as sheer earnest, many an easily perspiring individual would doubtless be emotionally stirred. But suppose Socrates did not at all understand it in this one-sided manner. It would sound like jesting, if a prospective guest were to say on receiving the invitation: "You can count on me, I shall certainly come; but I must make an exception for the contingency that a tile happens to blow down from a roof, and kills me; for in that case I cannot come." But it might at the same time also be the highest earnestness; and the speaker, though jesting with men, might exist before God.

Suppose a young woman were expecting the arrival of her lover by the ship to which Socrates refers; suppose she ran down to the harbor and found Socrates there, and took occasion to ask him, in all the glow of her passion, for news of her lover. Suppose instead of answering her directly, the old wag said: "Aye, the skipper walks back and forth on the beach, jingling the money he has received from the passengers in his pocket; and that although he does not know for certain whether it might not have been better for the passengers to have perished in the waves": what then? If she were a clever little damsel she would perceive that Socrates had told her, in a fashion, that her lover had arrived safely; and as soon as she was assured of this, what then? Why then she would laugh at Socrates and his queer speech. For she was not so silly as to entertain any uncertainty about how splendid it was that her lover had come. To be sure, such a little damsel is attuned in spirit only to a tryst with her lover, in erotic embrace on the safe shore; she is too undeveloped for a Socratic rendezvous with the divinity in the Idea, on the boundless ocean of uncertainty.

But now let us suppose that the clever little maid had been confirmed, what then? Why then she would have had precisely the same knowledge as Socrates—the only difference being in the manner of it. Yet Socrates had presumably shaped his entire life in accordance with this distinction, and in his seventieth year was still engaged in so disciplining himself as to understand with greater and greater inwardness what a lass of sixteen summers already knows. For he was not as one who knows Hebrew, and thus is in a position to say to the maiden: "There is something you do not know, and you must understand that it takes a long time to learn it." He was not as one who could carve in stone, which the damsel would readily understand that she could not do, and would know how to admire. No, he knew no more than she. What wonder then that he was so indifferent to the approach of death; the poor fellow had presumably come to see that his life was wasted, and that it was now too late for him to begin to learn what only the distinguished know. What wonder then that he made absolutely no fuss about his death, as if the State were to lose in him something it could never replace. Alas, he has perhaps thought something like this: "Had I only been a professor of Hebrew, or a sculptor, or a solo dancer, to say nothing of being a world-historic genius bestowing beatific blessings on all mankind, then how could the State have recovered from the loss of my presence among them, and how could its citizens ever have learned to know what I could tell them! But as it is, no question will ever be raised about me; for what I know, everybody knows." What a jester this fellow Socrates was, to indulge himself in such frivolity about Hebrew, and the art of the sculptor, and the ballet, and the beatific benefits of world-history; and to be so deeply concerned, on the other hand, about the divinity, that although he had disciplined himself unremittingly through a long life (as a solo dancer dancing to the honor of God), he nevertheless looked forward with diffidence to the divine test, fearful lest he should be found wanting. What shall we call that?

The relative difference which exists for the immediate consciousness between the comic and the tragic, vanishes in the doubly reflected consciousness where the difference becomes infinite, thereby positing their identity. The comic expression for worship is therefore just as reverent, religiously, as its pathetic expression. What lies at the root of both the comic and the tragic in this connection, is the discrepancy, the contradiction, between the infinite and the finite, the eternal and that which becomes. A pathos which excludes the comic is therefore a misunderstanding, is not pathos at all. The subjective existing thinker is as bifrontal as existence itself. When viewed from a direction looking toward the Idea, the apprehension of the discrepancy is pathos; when viewed with the Idea behind one, the apprehension is comic. When the subjective existing thinker turns his face toward the Idea, his apprehension of the discrepancy is pathetic; when he turns his back to the Idea and lets this throw a light from behind over the same discrepancy, the apprehension is in terms of the comic. If I have not exhausted the comic to its entire depth, I do not have the pathos of the infinite; if I have the pathos of the infinite, I have at once also the comic.

Prayer expresses the highest pathos of the infinite,* and yet it is comical,† precisely because it is, in its inwardness, incommensurable for every external expression; especially when one conforms to the scriptural injunction to anoint the head and wash the face while fasting. The comic is here present in a two-fold manner. The obnoxious form of it would be illustrated if a robust fellow stepped forward to pray, and to signify the inwardness of his prayer proceeded to writhe in a series of athletic contortions instructive for an artist studying the musculature of the arm, especially if the speaker obliged by rolling up his sleeves. The

* The Socratic gaze is also an expression for the highest pathos, and hence also comical, and in the same degree. Let us try an experiment. Socrates stands and gazes into empty space. Two individuals pass by, one of whom says to the other: "What is that man doing?" The first man answers: "Nothing." Let us suppose, however, that one of them has a little more notion of inwardness, and gives to Socrates' behavior a religious expression, saying: "He immerses himself in the divine, he prays." But does he make any use of words, or is he perhaps voluble in prayer? No, Socrates has understood his God-relationship in such a manner that he dared not say anything at all, from fear of indulging in foolish prattle, and from fear of having a mistaken wish fulfilled, of which examples are supposed to have existed. As for instance when the oracle[10] informed a man that all his sons would acquire fame and distinction, and the anxious father said: "And then I suppose they will all come to an unfortunate end?" The oracle replied: "This too will be granted you." For the oracle was consistent enough to suppose that whoever consults it is a petitioner; whence the use of the word, granted—a sad irony for the anxious father.

Socrates does absolutely nothing. He does not even speak to God inwardly, and yet he realizes the highest of human actions. Socrates has doubtless himself been aware of this, and has known how to emphasize the comic aspect. Magister Kierkegaard, however, to judge from his dissertation,[11] has scarcely understood it. He mentions this negative attitude of Socrates toward prayer, citing the dialogue *Alcibiades II*; but as might be expected from a positive candidate in theology of our own day, he cannot refrain from instructing Socrates in a note that this negativity is only to a certain extent true.

† I am not here speaking of the comical by accident, as when a man praying, holds his hat before his face, and does not notice that the hat has nothing left but the rim, so that another person accidentally comes to see him face to face.

inwardness of prayer, and its inexpressible sighs, are not commensurable for the muscular. The true form of the comic is, that the infinite may move within a man, and no one, no one be able to discover it through anything appearing outwardly. In connection with the incessant becoming of existence, the comic and the pathetic aspects of prayer are simultaneously present in its repetition; for precisely its infinite inwardness would seem to make a repetition impossible, and hence the repetition is both something to smile at and to grieve over.

Just as the subjective existing thinker himself exists in this manner, so the mode of his communication reflects it; and hence it is impossible for anyone to appropriate his pathos directly. Like the comic parts of the romantic drama, the comic winds its way through Lessing's exposition; perhaps sometimes in the wrong place, perhaps so, perhaps not, for I cannot say with certainty. *Hauptpastor* Goetze[12] is a highly *ergötzlich* figure, whom Lessing has preserved comically for immortality by making him inseparable from his exposition. All this is indeed disturbing; for one cannot repose the same secure confidence in Lessing as in those who in genuine speculative seriousness make all things of a piece, and so have everything finished.

The principle that the existing subjective thinker is constantly occupied in striving, does not mean that he has, in the finite sense, a goal toward which he strives, and that he would be finished when he had reached this goal. No, he strives infinitely, is constantly in process of becoming. And this, his striving, is safeguarded by his constantly being just as negative as he is positive, and by his having as much essential humor as essential pathos; which has its ground in the fact that he is an existing individual, and reflects this in his thinking. This process of becoming is the thinker's own existence; from which it is indeed possible to make abstraction, but only thoughtlessly, in order to become objective. How far the subjective thinker has come along this road, whether a long distance or a short one, makes no essential difference. This is indeed only a finitely relative comparison; but as long as he is an existing individual, he is in process of becoming.

Existence itself, the act of existing, is a striving, and is both pathetic and comic in the same degree. It is pathetic because the striving is infinite; that is, it is directed toward the infinite, being an actualization of infinitude, a transformation which involves the highest pathos. It is comic, because such a striving involves a self-contradiction. Viewed pathetically, a single second has infinite value; viewed comically, ten thousand years are but a trifle, like yesterday when it is gone. And yet, the time in which the existing individual lives, consists of just such parts. If one were to say simply and directly that ten thousand years are but a trifle, many a fool would give his assent, and find it wisdom; but he forgets the other, that a second has infinite value. When it is asserted that a second has infinite value, one or another will possibly hesitate to yield his assent, and find it easier to understand that ten thousand years have an infinite value. And yet, the one is quite as hard to understand as the other, provided merely we take time to understand what there is to be understood; or else are in another manner so infinitely seized by the thought that there is no time to waste, not a second, that a second really acquires infinite value.

This characteristic of existence recalls the Greek conception of Eros, as found in the *Symposium,* and which Plutarch in his work on Isis and Osiris (§ 57) interprets correctly. The parallel he draws between Isis, Osiris and Typhon does not interest me; but when Plutarch reminds us that Hesiod has assumed Chaos, Earth, Tartarus, and Love as cosmic principles, it is quite proper in this connection to recall Plato. For Love is here evidently taken as identical with existence, or that, by virtue of which, life is lived in its entirety, the life which is a synthesis of the infinite and the finite. According to Plato, Wealth and Poverty conceived Eros, whose nature partook of both. But what is existence? Existence is the child that is born of the infinite and the finite, the eternal and the temporal, and is therefore a constant striving. This was Socrates' meaning. It is for this reason that Love is constantly striving; or to say the same thing in other words, the thinking subject is an existing individual. It is only systematists and objective philosophers who have ceased to be human beings, and have become speculative philosophy in the abstract, an entity which belongs in the realm of pure being. The Socratic principle is naturally not to be understood in a finite sense, about a continued and incessant striving toward a goal without reaching it. No, but however much the subject has the infinite within himself, through being an existing individual, he is in process of becoming.

The thinker who can forget in all his thinking also to think that he is an existing individual, will never explain life. He merely makes an attempt to cease to be a human being, in order to become a book or an objective something, which is possible only for a Munchausen. It is not denied that objective thought has validity; but in connection with all thinking where subjectivity must be accentuated, it is a misunderstanding. If a man occupied himself, all his life through, solely with logic, he would nevertheless not become logic; he must therefore himself exist in different categories. Now if he finds that this is not worth thinking about, the choice must be his responsibility. But it will scarcely be pleasant for him to learn, that existence itself mocks everyone who is engaged in becoming purely objective.

§ 3. LESSING HAS SAID[1] THAT ACCIDENTAL HISTORICAL TRUTHS CAN NEVER SERVE AS PROOFS FOR ETERNAL TRUTHS OF THE REASON; AND THAT THE TRANSITION BY WHICH IT IS PROPOSED TO BASE AN ETERNAL TRUTH UPON HISTORICAL TESTIMONY IS A LEAP

The considerations which will be brought forward under this head and the following, are more definitely referrible to Lessing, in so far as there are utterances of his which may be quoted directly. But yet again, not with any simple certainty; for Lessing is not dogmatic but subjectively evasive, showing no wish to pledge anyone to the acceptance of his view for his sake, and in no way seeking to help others establish a direct relationship in continuity with him. It is possible that Lessing has understood that such things cannot be communicated directly; at any rate his procedure can be explained in this manner, and the explanation is possibly the right one: I say only possibly.

I shall now consider somewhat in detail the two propositions cited above, and proceed to relate them to the problem of the *Fragments*: Is it possible to base an eternal happiness on historical knowledge? But first I wish to find room here for a remark which may serve to show how deceptive the thinking of men usually is, like the reading of the schoolboy, who "pretends to read his lesson, but does not read at all."[2] When two thoughts stand to one another in an inseparable relation, so that if anyone is able to think the one, he is *eo ipso* able to think the other, it often happens that an opinion passes from mouth to mouth, from generation to generation, which holds it easy to think the one thought, while an opposite opinion makes it difficult to think the other, and even establishes a habit of scepticism with respect to it. And yet the true dialectical situation is, that anyone who can think the one thought can *eo ipso* think the other, and indeed has *eo ipso* thought the other— provided he has thought the one. I refer to the *quasi*-dogma of eternal punishment.

The problem presented in the *Fragments* was: How can something of an historical nature be decisive for an eternal happiness? When we

say "decisive," we say *eo ipso* that when the happiness is decided, the unhappiness is also decided, either as posited or as excluded. The first is supposed to be easy to understand, every systematic philosopher has thought it, every believer, and we are all believers; it is as easy as falling off a log to get an historical point of departure for one's eternal happiness, and to get it thought. In the midst of all this safety and security, the question of an eternal unhappiness comes up, as decided by means of an historical point of departure in time. Ah, that, we find, is a difficult question; we cannot quite make up our minds about it, we agree to let it stand as something that may on occasion be appropriate to the popular form of address, but is undecided—alas, alack, and so it is in fact decided; nothing is easier—provided the first question is decided. Miraculous human thoughtfulness—who can look into your thoughtful eyes without a solemn sense of exaltation! Here then we have the result of the continued thoughtfulness: The one thought is understood, and the other is left alone, i.e. not understood; and yet this one and that other are, aye, it is embarrassing to say it, they are one and the same.*
If time and a relationship in time to an historical phenomenon can be decisive for an eternal happiness, it can be *eo ipso* decisive for an eternal unhappiness. But human thoughtfulness proceeds in quite a different fashion. An eternal happiness is in fact an eternal presupposition from behind, immanently, for every individual. As eternal, the individual is higher than time, and therefore always has his eternal happiness behind him. That is to say, only an eternal happiness is thinkable, an eternal unhappiness is absolutely unthinkable. This is philosophically entirely in order. Now comes Christianity and posits the disjunction: either an eternal happiness or an eternal unhappiness, the decision to be in time. What does human thoughtfulness do? It does not take cognizance of the fact, as did the *Fragments,* that this is a hard saying, and the proposal to think it, pretty well the most difficult proposal that can be made; it does not do what in the first instance can be done, it does not even formulate the problem. No, it has recourse to a little lying, and now everything becomes quite easy. It takes the first half of the disjunction: either an eternal happiness, and understands by it the principle of immanence, which precisely excludes the disjunction; and so it pretends to

* In so far the *Fragments* might just as well have posed the opposite, and made that the problem: How can something historical become decisive for an eternal unhappiness? In that case human thoughtfulness would no doubt have discovered that it was something worth raising a question about, since it is a question that could not even be answered.

have thought the whole problem. Then when it comes upon the second half of the disjunction it balks, and declares that it cannot think it; which is to give itself the lie, and to accuse itself of not having thought the first half. The paradoxical character of Christianity consists in its constant use of time and the historical in relation to the eternal; all thinking is rooted in the principle of immanence; now what does human thoughtfulness do? It thinks the principle of immanence, pretends that this is the first half of the disjunction, and so it has thought Christianity.*

Now for Lessing. The passage is found in a little essay: *Ueber den Beweis des Geistes und der Kraft*. Lessing opposes what I would call an attempt to create a quantitative transition to a qualitative decision. He attacks the direct transition from historical trustworthiness to the determination of an eternal happiness. He does not deny, for he knows how to make concessions so as to make the categories stand out more clearly, that the accounts of miracles and prophecies found in the Scriptures are as reliable as other historical testimony, as reliable as historical testimony in general is capable of being. "But now, seeing that they are only so reliable, why is it proposed to make a use of them that demands an infinitely greater reliability?" This is because it is proposed to base on them the acceptance of a doctrine that conditions an eternal happiness, and so to base on them an eternal happiness. Lessing is willing like all others to believe that an Alexander who conquered all Asia has existed; "But who would risk, on the basis of this belief, something of such great and lasting significance that its loss would be irreparable?"

It is always the transition, the simple and direct transition, from the reliability of an historical account to an eternal decision, against which Lessing opposes himself. Hence he adopts the position of drawing a distinction between historical testimony relating to miracles and prophecies, and contemporaneity with such things. This distinction is one to which the *Fragments*[3] addressed itself, in bringing about contemporaneity through the use of an imaginative experiment, and thus eliminating what was called the subsequent-historical. Lessing says that from the historical accounts, i.e. from their admitted reliability, no conclusion can be drawn; but if he had been contemporary with the mir-

---

* The proofs by which a devout orthodoxy has sought to safeguard the dogma of eternal punishment must be regarded as a misunderstanding. Nevertheless, its procedure is by no means the same in kind with that of speculative philosophy; for since it really lies itself in the disjunction, every proof is superfluous.

acles and the prophecies it would have helped him.* Well informed as Lessing always is, he therefore protests against a partially misleading quotation from Origen, cited for the purpose of putting in relief this proof for the truth of Christianity, by adding the closing words of the quotation, which shows that Origen assumed that miracles still happened in his own age, and ascribed to these contemporary miracles a like demonstrative power with those of which he reads.

Since Lessing has assumed this position over against a given form of argumentation, he has no occasion to deal with the further dialectical problem of whether contemporaneity could be of the slightest assistance, whether it could contribute anything more than an *occasion,* which rôle, historical testimony could also fill. Lessing seems to assume the contrary. Perhaps this is merely an appearance, created for the purpose of giving his polemic *ex concessis* a greater degrée of dialectical clarity over against a particular opponent. The *Fragments* sought to show, on the contrary, that contemporaneity is of no avail; because there can in all eternity be no direct transition from the historical to the eternal, whether the historical is contemporary or not. So to single out the contemporary generation for special favor would also be a boundless injustice against those who came after, an injustice and a distinction much more reprehensible than the one between Jews and Greeks, circumcised and uncircumcised, which Christianity has abolished.

Lessing has himself compressed his problem into the following thesis, which he has singled out for special emphasis: *"zufällige Geschichtswahrheiten können der Beweis von nothwendigen Vernunftwahrheiten nie werden."*† There is here a difficulty about the adjective *zufällige.* It is misleading, since it might seem to lead to the absolute distinction between accidental and essential historical truths, a distinction which is merely a subdivision. If in spite of the identity of the higher predicate: historical, the distinction here is made absolute, it might seem to follow that in relation to essential historical truths a direct transition is realizable. I might here allow myself to become excited, and to say: "It is impossible that Lessing should be so inconsistent, *ergo"*

* However, the reader may perhaps remember here what was expounded in the *Fragments,*4 about the impossibility of being contemporary, in the immediate sense, with a paradox; and about the vanishing character of the distinction between a contemporary disciple and one of a subsequent generation.

† In relation to this way of putting the matter, it is clear enough that the *Fragments* † really oppose Lessing, in so far as he has posited an advantage on the side of contemporaneity. It is in the denial of this advantage that the real dialectical problem lies; and therewith the solution of Lessing's problem also receives a different significance.

—and my excitement would undoubtedly convince many. However, I shall restrict myself to a polite perhaps, which makes the assumption that Lessing has concealed everything in the adjective: accidental, but said only a part, so that "accidental" is not here a relatively-distinguishing predicate, but a genus-predicate: historical truths, which as such are accidental. If not, we have here the whole misunderstanding which again and again crops up in recent philosophy: to let the eternal become historical without further ado, and to pretend to an understanding of the necessity of the historical.* Everything that becomes historical is accidental or contingent; it is precisely through coming into being, and thus becoming historical, that it has its moment of contingency, for contingency is precisely one factor in all becoming. Here again we have the root of the incommensurability that subsists between an historical truth and an eternal decision.

Understood in this manner, the transition by which something historical and the relationship to it becomes decisive for an eternal happiness, is $\mu\epsilon\tau\acute{\alpha}\beta\alpha\sigma\iota\varsigma$ $\epsilon\grave{\iota}\varsigma$ $\ddot{\alpha}\lambda\lambda o$ $\gamma\acute{\epsilon}\nu o\varsigma$,[5] a leap, both for a contemporary and for a member of some later generation. Lessing even says, "If this is not what it is, then I do not understand what Aristotle has meant by it." It is a leap, and this is also the word that Lessing has used about it, within the accidental limitation indicated by the application of an illusory distinction between contemporaneity and non-contemporaneity. His words are as follows: *"Das, das ist der garstige breite Graben, über den ich nicht kommen kann, so oft und ernstlich ich auch den Sprung versucht habe."* It is possible that the word *Sprung* is merely a stylistic phrase, and that perhaps it is for this reason that the metaphor is expanded for the imagination by adding the predicate *breit;* as if the least leap did not have the characteristic of making the chasm infinitely wide; as if it were not equally difficult for one who absolutely cannot leap whether the chasm is wide or narrow; as if it were not the passionate dialectical abhorrence for the leap which makes the chasm so infinitely wide, just as Lady Macbeth's passion makes the blood spot so infinite that not all the waters of the ocean can wash it away.[6] Possibly also it is a bit of cunning on Lessing's part to make use of the word *ernstlich;* for in connection with a leap, especially when the metaphor

---

* Concerning this piece of systematic legerdemain the reader will perhaps remember what was expounded in the Interlude of the *Fragments,* that nothing comes into being by necessity, because becoming and necessity contradict one another; and that still less, therefore, does anything become necessary by coming into being. The one thing that it is impossible to become, is to become necessary; because the necessary is always presupposed as being.

is developed for the imagination, the reference to earnestness is droll enough, because it stands in no relation, or in a comic relation, to the leap; for it is not externally the width of the chasm which prevents the leap, but internally the dialectical passion which makes the chasm infinitely wide. To have been very near doing something has in itself a comic aspect; but to have been very near making the leap is absolutely nothing, because the leap is the category of decision. And now to have tried with the utmost earnestness to make the leap—aye, that man Lessing is indeed a wag; for it is no doubt rather with the utmost earnestness that he has endeavored to make the chasm wide: does it not seem as if he were making fun of people? Yet it is well known that it is also possible to make fun of people in another and more favored manner, in connection with the leap: you shut your eyes, you seize yourself by the neck à la Munchausen, and then—and then you stand on the other side, on the other side of sound common sense, in the promised land of systematic philosophy.

This expression, the leap, is connected with Lessing's name also in another manner. In general, it is seldom that any thinker of modern times reminds us of the beautiful Greek mode of philosophizing, by genially concentrating himself and his reflection relative to a certain question in a single brief happily chosen sentence;[7] but Lessing reminds us vividly of the Greeks. His knowledge is not a learned hodge-podge and genuinely speculative mediation of what Peter and Paul, geniuses and *Privatdocents,* have thought and written; his merit does not consist in stringing all these splendors together on the string of the historicising method. No, Lessing has something for himself, something briefly and simply told. Just as one may call many a Greek thinker to mind by mentioning his watchword instead of citing his name, so Lessing has also left behind him such a last word. These "last words" of Lessing, it will be remembered, gave occasion for quite a little scribbling at one time. The noble and enthusiastic Jacobi, who often speaks with amiable sympathy of the need of being understood by other thinkers, of how desirable it is to be in agreement with others, was the father confessor to whose lot it fell to preserve Lessing's last words. To be sure, it was no easy thing to essay the rôle of confessor for an ironical personality like Lessing, and Jacobi has had to suffer much: undeservedly, in so far as he has been unjustly criticized; deservedly, in so far as Lessing had by no means sent for him in the capacity of father confessor, still less requested him to make the conversation public, and least of all asked him to put the pathetic accent in the wrong place.

There is something extremely poetical in the entire situation: two such markedly developed personalities as Lessing and Jacobi in conversation with one another. The inexhaustible spokesman for enthusiasm as observer, and the subtle Lessing as catechumen. Jacobi takes it upon himself to examine Lessing, to find out how things really stand with him. What happens? To his horror he discovers that Lessing is at bottom a Spinozist. The enthusiastic Jacobi ventures upon extreme measures, and proposes to him the only saving *salto mortale*.

Here I must pause a moment; it might seem as if it were Jacobi that finally became the discoverer of the leap. Yet it must be noted in the first place, that Jacobi has no clear notion of where the leap essentially belongs. His *salto mortale* is, in the first instance, only the subjectifying act as over against Spinoza's objectivity, not the transition from the eternal to the historical. In the next place, he is not dialectically clear about the leap, so as to understand that it cannot be taught or communicated directly, precisely because it is an act of isolation, which leaves it to the individual to decide, respecting that which cannot be thought, whether he will resolve believingly to accept it by virtue of the absurdity. Jacobi proposes, by a resort to eloquence, to give assistance in making the leap. But this is a contradiction; and all forms of instigation or impulsion constitute precisely an obstacle to the making of the leap in reality, which must not be confused with the assurance that one has made it. Assuming that Jacobi has himself made the leap, let us suppose that he persuades by his eloquence a learner, so that the latter wishes to make it: in that case the learner acquires a direct relationship to Jacobi, and so does not make the leap for himself. The direct relationship between man and man is naturally far easier, satisfies the sympathies and the urgencies of the self far more quickly, and apparently more securely. It is directly understandable, and dispenses with the dialectic of the infinite, which is required if one is to preserve oneself in infinite resignation and infinite enthusiasm in the sympathy of the infinite. The secret of this sympathy is precisely the renunciation of the delusion that one man is not the equal of another in his God-relationship, whereby the supposed teacher becomes a learner who attends to himself, and all instruction is transformed into a divine jest, because every human being is taught essentially only by God.

In relation to Lessing, the desire of Jacobi is merely to secure fellowship in making the leap; his eloquence is that of one who is in love with Lessing, and it is for this reason that it is so important to him to have Lessing with him. The dialectical weakness of his position is here at once evident: the eloquent orator, the everlastingly convinced personality, feels in himself the strength and energy to win others for his conviction; that is to say, he is so uncertain as to need the assent of others in behalf of his enthusiastic conviction. In general, the enthusiastic personality who cannot, in relation to every human being, express his enthusiasm in a contrasting form, is not the stronger but the weaker party, and has only the strength of a woman, which is weakness. Jacobi did not know how to discipline himself artistically, so as to be content existentially to express the Idea. The restraint of that personal isolation which is posited precisely in the leap, cannot restrain Jacobi; he must betray something. He bubbles over in an eloquence which in ardor and content and lyrical ebullience sometimes ranks with Shakespeare, but which nevertheless is directed to the end of helping others into a direct relationship with the speaker; or as *in casu,* intended to win for him the consolation that Lessing agrees with him.

Now further. When Jacobi accordingly discovers to his horror that Lessing is a Spinozist, he proceeds to speak out of his entire conviction. He wants to take Lessing by storm. Lessing replies: *"Gut, sehr gut, ich kann das alles auch gebrauchen; aber ich kann nicht dasselbe damit machen. Ueberhaupt gefällt mir Ihr salto mortale gar nicht uebel, und ich begreife wie ein Mann von kopf auf diese Art kopf unten machen kann, um von der Stelle zu kommen; nehmen Sie mich mit, wenn es angeht."** Here Lessing's irony beautifully reveals itself, since he is presumably aware that when one is to leap, one must be alone about it, and hence also alone about understanding its impossibility. One cannot help admiring his urbanity, and his affectionate predilection for Jacobi, and the conversational art which so politely says: *"nehmen Sie mich mit— wenn es angeht."* Jacobi speaks further: *"Wenn Sie nur auf die elastische Stelle treten wollen die mich fortschwingt, so geht es von selbst."* This is in general rather well said; but there is the incorrectness about it that he seems inclined to transform the leap into something objective, and to interpret the act of the leap in analogy with finding the Archimedean point, for example. The merit of the answer consists in his not

---

* Cf. Jacobi, *Works,* Vol. IV, sec. 1, p. 74.

asking for a direct relationship or a direct fellowship in making the leap.

Then we come to Lessing's last words: *"Auch dazu gehört schon ein Sprung, den ich meinen alten Beinen und meinem schweren Kopf nicht mehr zumuten darf."* Here Lessing expresses himself ironically, through the use he makes of the dialectical, while the last phrase has the true Socratic coloring: speaking of meat and drink, doctors, pack animals, and the like, *item* his old legs and his heavy head.[8] Although, as we have frequently remarked, the leap is itself the decision, Jacobi proposes to make something like a transition to it. The eloquent Jacobi wishes to lure Lessing on: "There is nothing very complicated about it," he says, "it is not at all difficult, you merely step out on the spring-board —and the leap comes automatically." This is a very good example of the well-intentioned deceptiveness of eloquence. It is as if one were to recommend being put to death by the guillotine, saying: "It is a very easy matter, forsooth; you simply lay your head down on a block, somebody pulls a string, the axe falls—and the thing is done." But suppose that being executed was precisely what one did not wish; and so also with the leap. When one is indisposed to make the leap, so indisposed that this passion makes the chasm infinitely wide, then the most ingenious contrivance for the purpose will help one not at all. Lessing sees very clearly that the leap, as being decisive, is subject to a qualitative dialectic, and permits no approximating transition. His answer is therefore a jest. It is very far from being dogmatic; it is entirely correct dialectically, and it is personally evasive. Instead of hurriedly discovering the principle of mediation, he makes use of his old legs and his heavy head. To be sure, anyone who has young legs and a light head can doubtless leap.

In this manner is rounded out the psychological contrast between Lessing and Jacobi. Lessing rests in himself, feels no need of fellowship; hence he parries ironically, and slips away from Jacobi on his old legs— which are not good enough to leap with. He makes no attempt to persuade Jacobi that the leap does not exist.* But Jacobi is self-seeking, despite all his enthusiasm for others, and the fact that he is so anxious to persuade Lessing is precisely an expression for his need. The fact that

---

* It was fortunate for Lessing that he did not live in our not less serious than genuinely speculative-doctrinaire nineteenth century. He would then perhaps have to undergo the humiliation of having some extremely earnest man, one who certainly did not understand jests or jesting, propose in all seriousness to have Lessing sent back to school again, to be taught earnestness by the parish priest.[9]

he presses Lessing so hard, shows that he needs Lessing—in order to get his help in playing with propositions,[10] a game that Jacobi was especially fond of.

From what passed between Jacobi and Mendelssohn through Emilie (Reimarus),[11] respecting Jacobi's relationship to Lessing, one may in general obtain some conception of how inexhaustible Lessing has been, and with what Greek abandon he jested dialectically with Jacobi, whom he so highly esteemed otherwise. Jacobi thus relates that Lessing once said to him, *"mit halbem Lächeln"*: *"er selbst wäre vielleicht das höchste Wesen, und gegenwärtig in dem Zustande der äussersten Contraktion."** No wonder that Lessing was declared to be a pantheist. And yet the jest is so evident (though it need not on that account be merely a jest), and becomes particularly excellent in a later reference to the same remark. For when Lessing and Jacobi were dining with Gleim, and it began to rain, which Gleim deplored, since they had planned to visit the garden after dinner, Lessing said to Jacobi, presumably again *"mit halbem Lächeln"*: *"Jacobi, Sie wissen, das thue ich vielleicht."*

Mendelssohn, who also has expressed himself in these matters, has indicated quite correctly the lyrical culmination of thought in the leap. In seeking to transcend itself lyrically, thought† wills the discovery of the paradoxical. This presentiment of thought is a synthesis of jest and earnest, and here all the Christian categories are to be found. Outside this point, every dogmatic determination is a philosophical theorem which has entered into the heart of man, and is to be thought immanently. The last thing that human thinking can will to do, is to will to transcend itself in the paradoxical. And Christianity is precisely the paradoxical. Mendelssohn says: *"Zweifeln, ob es nicht etwas giebt, das nicht nur alle Begriffe übersteigt, sondern völlig ausser dem Begriffe liegt, dieses nenne ich einen Sprung ueber sich selbst hinaus."* Men-

---

* Dialectically, this confusion is not so easily solved. In the *Fragments*[12] I have sought to show how it arises, recalling how the self-knowledge of Socrates suffered shipwreck on the curious circumstance that he did not know definitely whether he was a human being, or a more composite animal than Typhon.

† It goes without saying that I speak merely of thinking as it is in the subjective existing thinker; I have never been able to understand how a man could become Speculation, the objective speculation and pure being. A man may indeed become many things in the world, as the German rime says:

> Rich man, poor man, beggar man, thief,
> Doctor, lawyer, merchant, chief.

So far I can understand the Germans. A man may become a thinker or a blockhead; but to become Speculation . . . is the most inconceivable of all miracles.

delssohn of course begs to be excused, and knows neither how to make jest or earnest of it.*

This is about all there is to say concerning Lessing's relation to the leap. It is not in itself very much, and it is not entirely clear dialectically what Lessing has proposed to make of it. It is not even clear whether there may not be a pathetic note in the style of the above passage cited from his writings, and a Socratic jesting note in the conversation with Jacobi; or whether these two contrasting moods proceed from and are borne by one and the same categorical thought of the leap. For me the little that is found in Lessing has had its significance. I had read *Fear and Trembling,* by Johannes *de silentio,* before I came to read the volume of Lessing cited above. In that work I had noted how the leap, according to the author's view, becomes as the decision κατ᾽ ἐξοχήν precisely decisive for the Christian categories and for every dogmatic determination. And this is something that cannot be attained either by means of the intellectual intuition of Schelling, or by what Hegel, dismissing Schelling's concept with disdain, proposes to substitute for it, namely, the Method. For the leap is neither more nor less than the most decisive protest possible against the inverse procedure of the Method. According to *Fear and Trembling,* all Christianity is rooted in the paradoxical, whether one accepts it as a believer, or rejects it precisely because it is paradoxical. Aye, it lies in fear and trembling, which are the desperate categories of Christianity, and of the leap. In reading Lessing afterwards, the matter did not indeed become any clearer, because it is so very little that Lessing has to say; but it was at any rate an encouragement, to find that Lessing had had his attention called to it. It is unfortunate that he has not himself chosen to pursue the thought further. But then, he did not happen to have the mediation-principle to deal with, this deified and divine mediation, which performs and has performed miracles, transforming individual human beings into speculative philosophy in the abstract—and which has completely bewitched Christianity. All honor to mediation! It may doubtless assist human beings also in another manner, just as, presumably, it has helped the author of *Fear and Trembling* to seek the desperate way out represented by the leap. Christianity was also a desperate way out when it first came into the world, and in all ages remains such; because it is a desperate way out for everyone who really accepts it. A once fiery and spirited steed may come to lose its mettle and pride of carriage when it is held for hire and

* Cf. Jacobi, *Werke,* IV, p. 110.

ridden by every bungler. But in the world of the spirit, sluggishness never gains the victory; it always loses, and remains outside. Whether Johannes *de silentio* has had his attention called to the leap by reading Lessing, I shall not attempt to say.

§ 4. LESSING HAS SAID THAT, IF GOD HELD ALL TRUTH IN HIS RIGHT HAND, AND IN HIS LEFT HAND HELD THE LIFELONG PURSUIT OF IT, HE WOULD CHOOSE THE LEFT HAND

Lessing's words are:[1] *"Wenn Gott in seiner Rechten alle Wahrheit, und in seiner Linken den einzigen immer regen Trieb nach Wahrheit, obschon mit dem Zusatze mich immer und ewig zu irren, verschlossen hielte, und spräche zu mir: wähle! Ich fiele ihm mit Demuth in seine Linke und sagte: Vater, gieb! die reine Wahrheit ist ja doch nur für dich allein!"* When Lessing wrote these words the System was presumably not finished; alas! and now Lessing is dead. Were he living in these times, now that the System is almost finished, or at least under construction, and will be finished by next Sunday: believe me, Lessing would have stretched out both his hands to lay hold of it. He would not have had the leisure, nor the manners, nor the exuberance, thus in jest as if to play odd and even with God, and in earnest to choose the left hand. But then, the System also has more to offer than God had in both hands; this very moment it has more, to say nothing of next Sunday, when it is quite certain to be finished.

The quoted words are found in a little essay (*Eine Duplik,* 1778) occasioned by a devout man's defence of the story of the Resurrection against the attack made upon it in the *Selections* that Lessing had had published. It will be remembered that people simply could not understand what Lessing's purpose was in publishing these fragments. Not even the high learning of *Hauptpastor* Goetze sufficed him to determine just what passage in the Apocalypse applied to Lessing, aye, was fulfilled in him. In so far Lessing has curiously enough compelled men, in their relation to him, to accept his own principle. Although even in those times there were results and finalities to spare, nobody was quite able to squeeze the life out of Lessing, and pack him away embalmed in a paragraph of universal history. A riddle he was, and a riddle he remained. If anyone were now to attempt to bring him forward again, he would get no further with him.

Here first an assurance respecting my own humble person. I shall be as willing as the next man to fall down in worship before the System, if only I can manage to set eyes on it. Hitherto I have had no success; and though I have young legs, I am almost weary from running back and forth between Herod and Pilate. Once or twice I have been on the verge of bending the knee. But at the last moment, when I already had my handkerchief spread on the ground, to avoid soiling my trousers, and I made a trusting appeal to one of the initiated who stood by: "Tell me now sincerely, is it entirely finished; for if so I will kneel down before it, even at the risk of ruining a pair of trousers (for on account of the heavy traffic to and fro, the road has become quite muddy),"—I always received the same answer: "No, it is not yet quite finished." And so there was another postponement—of the System, and of my homage.

System and finality are pretty much one and the same, so much so that if the system is not finished, there is no system. I have already in another place called the reader's attention to the consideration, that a system which is not quite finished is an hypothesis; while on the other hand to speak of a half-finished system is nonsense. If anyone says that this is merely a dispute about words, and that the systematic philosophers themselves say that the System is not finished, I would merely ask, why then do they call it a system? Why in general do they make use of equivocal language? When they publish their epitomes they say nothing about anything being lacking. Thus they lead their readers to suppose that everything is complete, unless they write for those better informed than they are themselves, which would doubtless seem unthinkable to systematists. But if someone makes a gesture as if to touch the structure anywhere, out comes the master builder. He is an extremely pleasant gentleman, exhibiting a courteous and friendly manner to visitors. He says: "Aye, it is true that we are still under construction, and that the System is not finished." But did he not know about this beforehand? Did he not know it when he sent out his inviting prospectus promising happiness to all mankind? If he did, why did he not say so? That is to say, why did he not refrain from calling the proffered fragment a system? For here we have it again: a fragment of a system is nonsense. A persistent striving to realize a system is on the other hand still a striving; and a striving, aye, a persistent striving, is precisely what Lessing talks about. And surely not a striving for nothing! On the contrary, Lessing speaks of a striving for truth, and he uses a remarkable phrase about it: *den einzigen immer regen Trieb*. This word *einzig* can scarcely be understood otherwise than as equivalent to infinite, in the same sense as that having one thought and one thought only is higher than having many thoughts. So it seems that these two, Lessing and the systematist, both talk about a persistent striving; only that Lessing is stupid or honest enough to call it a persistent striving, while the systematist is clever or dishonest enough to call it the System. What would be thought in other connections, about such a difference in language? When Agent Behrend[2] had lost a silk umbrella he advertised for it, and described it in the advertisement as a cotton one; for, thought he, if I call it a silk umbrella, the finder will be more strongly tempted to keep it. So also thinks, in all probability, the systematist: "If on the title-page and in the announcements I call my production a persistent striving for the truth, alas! who will buy it or admire me? But if I call it the System, the Absolute System, everyone will surely want to buy the System"—if only the difficulty did not remain, that what the systematist sells is not the System.

Let us then proceed, but let us not try to deceive one another. I, Johannes Climacus, am a human being, neither more nor less; and I assume that anyone I may have the honor to engage in conversation with, is also a human being. If he presumes to be speculative philosophy in the abstract, pure speculative thought, I must renounce the effort to speak with him; for in that case he instantly vanishes from my sight, and from the feeble sight of every mortal.

And so we shall here posit and expound two theses: (A), a logical system is possible; (B), an existential system is impossible.

A. A logical system is possible.

(α) In the construction of a logical system, it is necessary first and foremost to take care not to include in it anything which is subject to an existential dialectic, anything which is, only because it exists or has existed, and not simply because it is. From this it follows quite simply that Hegel's unparalleled discovery, the subject of so unparalleled an admiration, namely, the introduction of movement into logic, is a sheer confusion of logical science; to say nothing of the absence, on every other page, of even so much as an effort on Hegel's part to persuade the reader that it is there.* And it is surely strange to make movement

---

* The frivolity with which systematists concede that Hegel has perhaps not been successful in introducing movement everywhere in logic, about as when a huckster thinks that a couple of oranges more or less is nothing to worry about when the purchase is a large one—this farcical complaisance is naturally an expression of contempt for Hegel, which not even his most violent antagonist has permitted himself. There have of course been logical attempts made before Hegel, but in his case the Method is supposed to be everything. For Hegel himself, and for everyone who is sufficiently alert intellectually to sense what it means to have willed

fundamental in a sphere where movement is unthinkable; and to make movement explain logic, when as a matter of fact logic cannot explain movement. On this point I am so fortunate as to be in a position to refer the reader to a man whose thinking is sound, who is happily schooled in Greek philosophy—rare trait in these times! and who has known how to emancipate himself and his thought from every obsequious and slavish relationship to Hegel, from whose fame all seek to profit, if not otherwise, then by transcending him, i.e. by pretending to have assimilated him and made him a subordinate moment in one's thought; but who has preferred to rest content with Aristotle and with himself. I refer to Trendelenburg in his *Logische Untersuchungen*. His merit consists among other things in having apprehended movement as the inexplicable presupposition and common factor of thinking and being, and as their continued reciprocity. I cannot here make any attempt to show how his view is related to the Greeks and to Aristotle, or to what, strangely enough, in a certain popular sense, has a certain likeness to the terms of his exposition: a little passage in Plutarch's work on Isis and Osiris. I am by no means of the opinion that the Hegelian philosophy has been without beneficial influence on Trendelenburg. But the fortunate thing about him is, that he has perceived that it will not do merely to tinker with Hegel's thought-structure, so as to introduce a few improvements; or to transcend him and so forth—a dishonest device by which many a bungler in our age seeks to appropriate Hegel's celebrity to himself, fraternizing with him like a lazzarone. But sober-minded as a Greek thinker, without promising everything or pretending to shower blessings on all mankind, Trendelenburg nevertheless gives his reader much, and cheers the heart of one who needed his guidance in studying the Greeks.

Nothing must then be incorporated in a logical system that has any relation to existence, that is not indifferent to existence. The infinite preponderance which the logical as the objective has over all thinking, is again limited by the fact that seen subjectively it is an hypothesis, pre-

something great, the fact that the fundamental principle supposed to underlie and interpenetrate the whole is not present at this point or that, cannot be a matter of indifference, as when a huckster and his customer squabble over whether there is a little under- or over-weight Hegel has staked all on this question of the Method. But a method has the remarkable trait of being nothing in the abstract; it is precisely in the application or execution that it is a method. Where it is unapplied, it is not the method, and if there is no other method, then there is no method at all. Let admirers of Hegel keep to themselves the privilege of making him out to be a bungler; an opponent will always know how to hold him in honor, as one who has willed something great, though without having achieved it.

cisely because it is indifferent to existence in the sense of actuality. This double aspect of the logical distinguishes it from the mathematical, which has no relationship at all either to or from existence, but simply has objectivity—not objectivity and the hypothetical together—as the synthesis and the contradiction in which the logical is negatively related to existence.

Nor may the logical system be a mystification, an exhibition of ventriloquism, by which the content of reality is underhandedly and surreptitiously produced; an exhibition in which the logical thought suddenly gives a start, and finds what the Herr Professor or the licentiate has had up his sleeve. A stricter judgment would be possible on this point if it were determined in what sense the categories constitute an abridgement of existence, whether logical thought is abstract after existence or abstract without any relation to existence. This is a question I could wish to treat a little more fully in another connection; and even if the problem were not in all respects satisfactorily solved, it is always something to have raised the question.

(β) The dialectic of the beginning must be made clear. This, its almost amusing character, that the beginning is, and again is not,[3] just because it is the beginning—this true dialectical remark has long enough served as a sort of game played in good Hegelian society.

The System, so it is said, begins with the immediate;[4] in lieu of being dialectical, some are even oratorical enough to say that it begins with the most immediate of all, although precisely the comparative reflection here involved might prove dangerous to the beginning.* The System begins with the immediate, and hence without any presuppositions, and hence absolutely; the beginning of the System is an absolute beginning. This is quite correct, and has also been sufficiently admired. But before making a beginning with the System, why is it that the second, equally, aye, precisely equally important question has not been raised, taken understandingly to heart, and had its clear implications respected: *How does the System begin with the immediate? That is to say, does it begin with it immediately?* The answer to this question must be an unconditional negative. If the System is presumed to come after existence, by

* It would take too much space here to show how. Very often the care and trouble taken in such matters proves to have been wasted; for after taking great pains to set forth an objection sharply, one is apt to learn from a philosopher's reply that the misunderstanding was not rooted in any inability to understand the divine philosophy, but in having persuaded oneself to think that it really meant something—instead of merely being loose thinking concealed behind pretentious expressions.

which a confusion with an existential system may be occasioned, then the System is of course *ex post facto,* and so does not begin immediately with the immediacy with which existence began; although in another sense it may be said that existence did not begin with the immediate, since the immediate never is as such, but is transcended as soon as it is. The beginning which begins with the immediate *is thus itself reached by means of a process of reflection.*

Here is the difficulty. For unless, in disingenuousness or in thoughtlessness or in breathless haste to get the System finished, we let this one thought slip away from us, it is, in all its simplicity, sufficient to decide that no existential system is possible; and that no logical system may boast of an absolute beginning, since such a beginning, like pure being, is a pure chimera.

When it is impossible to begin immediately with the immediate, which would be to think as by accident or miracle, and therefore not to think, and it is necessary to reach the beginning through a process of reflection, let us quite simply ask (alas! here I must apprehend being stood in a corner for my simplicity, since everyone can understand my question—and must therefore feel embarrassed over my display of popular knowledge): How do I put an end to the reflection which was set up in order to reach the beginning here in question? Reflection has the remarkable property of being infinite. But to say that it is infinite is equivalent, in any case, to saying that it cannot be stopped by itself; because in attempting to stop itself it must use itself, and is thus stopped in the same way that a disease is cured when it is allowed to choose its own treatment, which is to say that it waxes and thrives. But perhaps the infinity thus characterizing reflection is the bad infinite (*das schlechte Unendlichkeit*)?[5] In that case we shall naturally soon have finished with our process of reflection, for the bad infinite is supposed to be something so contemptible that it must at all odds be renounced, the sooner the better. But may I not ask in this connection, if it is permitted to offer a question, How does it happen that Hegel himself and all Hegelians, who are otherwise supposed to be dialecticians, become angry at this point, angry as Dutchmen? Or is "bad" a logical determination? From whence does such a predicate find its way into logic? How does it happen that derision, and contempt, and measures of intimidation, are pressed into service as legitimate means of getting forward in logic, so that the consent of the reader is secured for an absolute beginning, because he is afraid of what acquaintances and neighbors

will think of him if he does not agree to its validity? Is not "bad" an
ethical category?* What is the implication involved in speaking of a
bad infinite? The implication is, that I hold some person responsible for
refusing to end the reflective process. And this means, does it not, that
I require him to do something? But as a genuinely speculative philosopher I assume, on the contrary, that reflection ends itself. If that is the
case, why do I make any demand upon the thinker? And what is it
that I require of him? I ask him for a resolve. And in so doing, I do
well, for in no other way can the process of reflection be halted. But
a philosopher is never justified, on the other hand, in playing tricks on
people, asserting one moment that the reflective process halts itself and
comes to an end in an absolute beginning; and the next moment proceeding to mock a man whose only fault is that he is stupid enough to
believe the first assertion, mocking him, so as to help him to arrive in
this manner at an absolute beginning, which hence seems to be achieved
in two different ways. But if a resolution of the will is required to end
the preliminary process of reflection, the presuppositionless character of
the System is renounced. Only when reflection comes to a halt can a
beginning be made, and reflection can be halted only by something else,
and this something else is something quite different from the logical,
being a resolution of the will. Only when the beginning, which puts an
end to the process of reflection, is a radical breach of such a nature that
the absolute beginning breaks through the continued infinite reflection,
then only is the beginning without presuppositions. But when the
breach is effected by breaking off the process of reflection arbitrarily, so
as to make a beginning possible, then the beginning so made cannot be
absolute; for it has come into being through a μετάβασις εἰς ἄλλο
γένος.

When a beginning with the immediate is arrived at by means of a
preliminary reflection, the term "immediate" must evidently mean
something else than it usually does. Hegelian logicians have quite
rightly perceived this, and they therefore define this "immediate," with
which logic begins, as the most abstract content remaining after an
exhaustive reflection. To this definition there can be no objection, but
it is certainly objectionable not to respect the implications of what is
thus asserted; for this definition says indirectly that there is no absolute

* And if not ethical, it is in any case an aesthetic category, as when Plutarch says that some
have assumed a single world because they feared that they would otherwise have an infinite
and troublesome infinity of worlds on their hands. εὐθὺς ἀδρίστου καὶ χαλεπῆς ἀπειρίας ὑπολαμ-
βανούσης. *De defectu oraculorum,* xxii.

beginning. "How so," I think I hear someone say, "when we have abstracted from everything, is there then not, etc., etc.?" Aye, to be sure—
when we have abstracted from everything. Why can we not remember
to be human beings? This act of abstraction, like the preceding act of
reflection, is infinite. How then does it come to an end—and it is only
when . . . that . . . Let us try an experiment in thought. Suppose the
infinite act of abstraction to be *in actu*. However, the beginning is not
identical with the act of abstraction, but comes afterwards. With what
do I begin, now that I have abstracted from everything? Ah, here an
Hegelian will perhaps fall on my breast, overcome by deep emotion,
blissfully stammering the answer: with nothing. Very well, but now I
must offer my second question: *How* do I begin with nothing? Unless
in fact the infinite act of abstraction is one of those tricks of legerdemain
which may readily be performed two at a time; if, on the contrary, it is
the most strenuous of all acts of thought, what then? Why then of
course, all my strength is required to hold it fast. If I let slip any part
of my strength, I no longer abstract from everything. And if under such
circumstances I make a beginning, I do not begin with nothing; precisely because I did not abstract from everything when I began. That is
to say, if it is at all possible for a human being to abstract from everything in his thinking, it is at any rate impossible for him to do more,
since if this act does not transcend human power, it absolutely exhausts
it. To grow weary of the act of abstracting, and thus to arrive at a beginning, is an explanation of the sort valid only for costermongers, who do
not take a little discrepancy so seriously.

This expression—beginning with nothing—quite irrespective of its
relation to the previous infinite act of abstraction, is in itself deceptive.
This "beginning with nothing" is in fact neither more nor less than a
new phrase for the dialectic of the beginning. The beginning is, and
again is not, precisely because it is the beginning—this is something
which can also be expressed by saying that the beginning begins with
nothing. It is only a new expression, and does not carry us a single step
forward. In the one case I merely think a beginning in the abstract; in
the second case I think of the relation which this same equally abstract
beginning has to a something with which it begins. And now it appears,
quite properly, that this something, aye, the only something which
could correspond to such a beginning, is nothing. But this constitutes
only a tautological variation of the second of the above propositions:
the beginning is not. The beginning is not, and the beginning begins

with nothing, are wholly identical propositions; and we have not advanced a single step.

What if instead of talking or dreaming about an absolute beginning, we talked about a leap. To be content with a "mostly," an "as good as," a "you could almost say that," a "when you sleep on it until tomorrow, you can easily say that," suffices merely to betray a kinship with Trop,[6] who, little by little, reached the point of assuming that almost having passed his examinations, was the same as having passed them. We all laugh at this; but when philosophers reason in the same manner, in the kingdom of the truth and in the sanctuary of science, then it is good philosophy, genuine speculative philosophy. Lessing was no speculative philosopher; hence he assumed the opposite, namely, that an infinitesimal difference makes the chasm infinitely wide, because it is the presence of the leap itself that makes the chasm infinitely wide.

It is strange that Hegelians, who know in logic that reflection comes to an end of itself, and that a universal doubt changes over into its opposite by itself (a true sailor's yarn, i.e. truly a sailor's yarn), in daily life, on the other hand, when they are pleasant people, when they are like all the rest of us (except, as I am always willing and ready to admit, that they are more talented and more learned and so forth) know that reflection can be halted only by a leap. Let us dwell a little on this point. When the subject does not put an end to his reflection, he is made infinite in reflection, i.e. he does not arrive at a decision.* In so running wild in his reflection the individual becomes essentially objective, and loses more and more the decisiveness that inheres in subjectivity, its return back into itself. And yet it is assumed that reflection can be halted objectively, though the truth is the precise contrary; objectively it is not to be stopped, and when it is halted subjectively it does not stop itself, but it is the subject who stops it.

Take an example. As soon as Rötscher, who in his book on Aristophanes[7] professes to understand the necessity of the transitions found in the world-process, and who has presumably also understood how in logic, reflection works its way through to an absolute beginning—as soon as Rötscher sets himself the task of explaining Hamlet,[8] he knows that reflection can be halted only by means of a resolve. He does not assume—shall I say strangely enough?—strangely enough, Rötscher

---

* The reader will perhaps remember what has been said in the preceding: When the case becomes an objective one, the problem of an eternal happiness cannot arise, because such a happiness inheres precisely in subjectivity and its decisiveness.

does not assume that Hamlet finally came to an absolute beginning simply by continuing to reflect. But in logic he assumes—shall I say strangely enough?—strangely enough, in logic Rötscher presumably assumes that reflection works itself through by itself, so as to come to a stop at an absolute beginning. This is something I cannot understand, and it troubles me not to be able to understand it, precisely because I admire Rötscher's talent, his classical culture, and his tasteful and yet primitive grasp of psychological phenomena.

That which has here been said about the beginning of a logical system (for the fact that the same considerations show the impossibility of an existential system will be further developed under B) is very plain and simple; I feel almost embarrassed to say it, or I feel embarrassed to be obliged to say it, embarrassed on account of my situation, that the poor author of a little piece, who would rather kneel in worship before the System, should be compelled to say something of this kind. An argument to the same purport might also be presented in a different manner, as a consequence of which one or another reader might be impressed, in that the method of presentation chose to recall specifically the philosophical controversies of a recent past.[9] The question would then turn on the significance of Hegel's *Phaenomenologie* for the System: whether it is an Introduction, whether it remains outside the System, and if it is an Introduction, whether it is again incorporated within the System; furthermore, whether Hegel does not have to his credit the astonishing achievement of not only having written the System, but of having written two, aye, three Systems, which must always require a matchless systematic talent, but which nevertheless seems to be the case, since the System is finished more than once; and so forth. All this has at bottom been said often enough. But it has also been said in a confusing manner: a big book has been written about it, which first says everything that Hegel has said, and thereupon takes cognizance of this or that later contribution—all of which serves only to distract the attention, and involves in a distracting voluminousness that which can be said quite briefly.

(γ) In order to throw some light on the nature of logic, it might be desirable to orient oneself psychologically in the state of mind of anyone who thinks the logical—so as to determine what kind of a dying away from the self is involved, and how far the imagination plays a rôle in this connection. This is again a simple and very unassuming remark, but for all that possibly quite true, and by no means superfluous.

A philosopher has gradually come to be so fantastic a being, that scarcely the most extravagant fancy has ever invented anything so fabulous. In general, how does the empirical ego stand related to the pure ego, the I-am-I? Anyone who is ambitious to become a philosopher would naturally like to have a little information on this point, and above all, cannot wish to become ridiculous by being transformed, *ein zwei drei kokolorum,* into speculative philosophy in the abstract. If the logical thinker is at the same time human enough not to forget that he is an existing individual, even if he completes the system, all the fantasticalness and charlatanry will gradually disappear. Granted that it would require an eminent logical talent to reconstruct Hegel's *Logic,* it needs only sound common sense in one who once enthusiastically believed in the great achievement that Hegel professed, and proved his enthusiasm by believing it, and his enthusiasms for Hegel by believing it of him—it needs only sound common sense for such an one to see that Hegel has in many places dealt indefensibly, not with costermongers who never believe the half of what a man says, but with enthusiastic youth who believed him. Even if such a youth has not been exceptionally gifted, when he has had enthusiasm enough to despair of himself in the moment of difficulty, rather than give up Hegel—when such a youth comes to himself, he has a right to demand that laughter should destroy in Hegel what laughter has a just claim upon. And such a youth has honored Hegel more highly than many a follower, who in deceptive asides sometimes makes Hegel everything, and sometimes a mere triviality.

B. An existential system is impossible.

An existential system cannot be formulated. Does this mean that no such system exists? By no means; nor is this implied in our assertion. Reality itself is a system—for God; but it cannot be a system for any existing spirit. System and finality correspond to one another, but existence is precisely the opposite of finality. It may be seen, from a purely abstract point of view, that system and existence are incapable of being thought together; because in order to think existence at all, systematic thought must think it as abrogated, and hence as not existing. Existence separates, and holds the various moments of existence discretely apart; the systematic thought consists of the finality which brings them together.

In reality we are likely to encounter a deception, an illusion. This was dealt with in the *Fragments,* and to this treatment I must here refer. It will be found in the Interlude, in the discussion of the question whether the past is more necessary than the future. Whenever a particular existence has been relegated to the past, it is complete, has acquired finality, and is in so far subject to a systematic apprehension. Quite right—but for whom is it so subject? Anyone who is himself an existing individual cannot gain this finality outside existence which corresponds to the eternity into which the past has entered. If a thinker is so absent-minded as to forget that he is an existing individual, still, absent-mindedness and speculation are not precisely the same thing. On the contrary, the fact that the thinker is an existing individual signifies that existence imposes its own requirement upon him. And if he is a great individual, it may signify that his own contemporary existence may, when it comes to be past, have the validity of finality for the systematic thinker. But who is this systematic thinker? Aye, it is he who is outside of existence and yet in existence, who is in his eternity forever complete, and yet includes all existence within himself—it is God. Why the deception? Because the world has stood now for six thousand years, does not existence have the same claim upon the existing individual as always? And this claim is, not that he should be a contemplative spirit in imagination, but an existing spirit in reality. All understanding comes after the fact. Now, while the existing individual undoubtedly comes after the preceding six thousand years, if we assume that he spends his life in arriving at a systematic understanding of these, the strangely ironical consequence would follow, that he could have no understanding of himself in his existence, because he had no existence, and thus had nothing which required to be understood afterwards. Such a thinker would either have to be God, or a fantastic *quodlibet*. Everyone doubtless perceives the immorality of such a situation, and doubtless also perceives that it is quite in order, as another author[1] has said respecting the Hegelian system, that we owe to Hegel the completion of the System, the Absolute System—without the inclusion of an Ethics.[2] Let us smile if we will at the ethico-religious extravaganzas of the Middle Ages in asceticism and the like; but let us above all not forget, that the speculative low-comedy extravagance of assuming to be an I-am-I, and nevertheless *qua* human being often so Philistine a character that no man of enthusiasm could endure to live such a life—is equally ridiculous.

Respecting the impossibility of an existential system, let us then ask quite simply, as a Greek youth might have asked his teacher (and if the superlative wisdom can explain everything, but cannot answer a simple question, it is clear that the world is out of joint): "Who is to write or complete such a system?" Surely a human being; unless we propose again to begin using the strange mode of speech which assumes that a human being becomes speculative philosophy in the abstract, or becomes the identity of subject and object. So then, a human being—and surely a living human being, i.e. an existing individual. Or if the speculative thought which brings the systems to light is the joint effort of different thinkers: in what last concluding thought does this fellowship finally realize itself, how does it reach the light of day? Surely through some human being? And how are the individual participants related to the joint effort, what are the categories which mediate between the individual and world-process, and who is it again who strings them all together on the systematic thread? Is he a human being, or is he speculative philosophy in the abstract? But if he is a human being, then he is also an existing individual. Two ways, in general, are open for an existing individual: *Either* he can do his utmost to forget that he is an existing individual, by which he becomes a comic figure, since existence has the remarkable trait of compelling an existing individual to exist whether he wills it or not. (The comical contradiction in willing to be what one is not, as when a man wills to be a bird, is not more comical than the contradiction of not willing to be what one is, as *in casu* an existing individual; just as the language finds it comical that a man forgets his name, which does not so much mean forgetting a designation, as it means forgetting the distinctive essence of one's being.) *Or* he can concentrate his entire energy upon the fact that he is an existing individual. It is from this side, in the first instance, that objection must be made to modern philosophy; not that it has a mistaken presupposition, but that it has a comical presupposition, occasioned by its having forgotten, in a sort of world-historical absent-mindedness, what it means to be a human being. Not indeed, what it means to be a human being in general; for this is the sort of thing that one might even induce a speculative philosopher to agree to; but what it means that you and I and he are human beings, each one for himself.

The existing individual who concentrates all his attention upon the circumstance that he is an existing individual, will welcome these words of Lessing about a persistent striving, as a beautiful saying. To be sure, it did not indeed win for its author an immortal fame, because it is very simple; but every thoughtful individual must needs confirm its truth. The existing individual who forgets that he is an existing individual, will become more and more absent-minded; and as people sometimes embody the fruits of their leisure moments in books, so we may venture to expect as the fruit of his absent-mindedness the expected existential system—well, perhaps not all of us, but only those who are almost as absent-minded as he is. While the Hegelian philosophy goes on and becomes an existential system in sheer distraction of mind, and what is more, is finished—without having an Ethics (where existence properly belongs), the more simple philosophy which is propounded by an existing individual for existing individuals, will more especially emphasize the ethical.

As soon as it is remembered that philosophizing does not consist in addressing fantastic beings in fantastic language, but that those to whom the philosopher addresses himself are human beings; so that we have not to determine fantastically *in abstracto* whether a persistent striving is something lower than the systematic finality, or *vice versa,* but that the question is what existing human beings, in so far as they are existing beings, must needs be content with: then it will be evident that the ideal of a persistent striving is the only view of life that does not carry with it an inevitable disillusionment. Even if a man has attained to the highest, the repetition by which life receives content (if one is to escape retrogression or avoid becoming fantastic) will again constitute a persistent striving; because here again finality is moved further on, and postponed. It is with this view of life as it is with the Platonic interpretation of love[3] as a want; and the principle that not only he is in want who desires something he does not have, but also he who desires the continued possession of what he has. In a speculative-fantastic sense we have a positive finality in the System, and in an aesthetic-fantastic sense we have one in the fifth act of the drama. But this sort of finality is valid only for fantastic beings.

The ideal of a persistent striving expresses the existing subject's ethical view of life. It must therefore not be understood in a metaphysical sense, nor indeed is there any individual who exists metaphysically. One might thus by way of misunderstanding set up an antithesis between finality and the persistent striving for truth. But this is merely a misunderstanding in this sphere. In the ethical sense, on the contrary, the persistent striving represents the consciousness of being an existing individual; the constant learning[4] is the expression for the incessant realization, in no moment complete as long as the subject is in existence; the subject is aware of this fact, and hence is not deceived. But Greek philosophy always had a relation to Ethics. Hence it was not imagined that the principle of always being a learner was a great discovery, or the enthusiastic enterprise of a particular distinguished individual; for it was neither more nor less than the realization that a human being is an existing individual, which it constitutes no great merit to be aware of, but which it is thoughtless to forget.

So-called pantheistic systems have often been characterized and challenged in the assertion that they abrogate the distinction between good and evil, and destroy freedom. Perhaps one would express oneself quite as definitely, if one said that every such system fantastically dissipates the concept *existence*. But we ought to say this not merely of pantheistic systems; it would be more to the point to show that every system must be pantheistic precisely on account of its finality. Existence must be revoked in the eternal before the system can round itself out; there must be no existing remainder, not even such a little minikin as the existing Herr Professor who writes the system. But this is not the way in which the problem is usually dealt with. No, pantheistic systems are attacked, partly in tumultuous aphorisms which again and again promise a new system; and partly by way of scraping together something supposed to be a system, and inserting in it a special paragraph in which it is laid down that the concept *existence,* or actuality, is intended to be especially emphasized. That such a paragraph is a mockery of the entire system, that instead of being a paragraph in a system it is an absolute protest against the system, makes no difference to busy systematists. If the concept of existence is really to be stressed, this cannot be given a direct expression as a paragraph in a system; all direct swearing and oath-supported assurances serve only to make the topsy-turvy profession of the paragraph more and more ridiculous. An actual emphasis on existence must be expressed in an essential form; in view of the elusiveness of existence, such a form will have to be an indirect form, namely, the absence of a system. But this again must not degenerate into an asseverating formula, for the indirect character of the expression will constantly demand renewal and rejuvenation in the form. In the case of committee reports, it may be quite in order to incorporate in the report a dissenting opinion; but an existential system which includes the dissenting opinion as a paragraph in its own logical structure, is a curious monstrosity. What wonder that the System continues to sustain its life as a going concern. In general, objections are haughtily ignored; if a particular objection seems to attract a little attention, the systematic entrepreneurs engage a copyist to copy off the objection, which there-upon is incorporated in the System; and when the book is bound the System is complete.

The systematic Idea is the identity of subject and object, the unity of thought and being. Existence, on the other hand, is their separation. It does not by any means follow that existence is thoughtless; but it has brought about, and brings about, a separation between subject and object, thought and being. In the objective sense, thought is understood as being pure thought; this corresponds in an equally abstract-objective sense to its object, which object is therefore the thought itself, and the truth becomes the correspondence of thought with itself. This objective thought has no relation to the existing subject; and while we are always confronted with the difficult question of how the existing subject slips into this objectivity, where subjectivity is merely pure abstract subjectivity (which again is an objective determination, not signifying any existing human being), it is certain that the existing subjectivity tends more and more to evaporate. And finally, if it is possible for a human being to become anything of the sort, and it is merely something of which at most he becomes aware through the imagination, he becomes the pure abstract conscious participation in and knowledge of this pure relationship between thought and being, this pure identity; aye, this tautology, because this being which is ascribed to the thinker does not signify that he is, but only that he is engaged in thinking.

The existing subject, on the other hand, is engaged in existing, which is indeed the case with every human being. Let us therefore not deal unjustly with the objective tendency, by calling it an ungodly and pan-theistic self-deification; but let us rather view it as an essay in the comical. For the notion that from now on until the end of the world nothing could be said except what proposed a further improvement in an almost completed system, is merely a systematic consequence for systematists.

By beginning at once to use ethical categories in criticism of the objective tendency, one does it an injustice, and fails to make contact with it, because one has nothing in common with what is under attack. But by remaining in the metaphysical sphere, one is enabled to use the comical, which also lies in the metaphysical, so as to bring such a transfigured professor to book. If a dancer could leap very high, we would admire him. But if he tried to give the impression that he could fly, let laughter single him out for suitable punishment; even though it might be true that he could leap as high as any dancer ever had done. Leaping is the accomplishment of a being essentially earthly, one who respects the earth's gravitational force, since the leaping is only momentary. But flying carries a suggestion of being emancipated from telluric conditions, a privilege reserved for winged creatures, and perhaps also shared by the inhabitants of the moon—and there perhaps the System will first find its true readers.

Being an individual man is a thing that has been abolished, and every speculative philosopher confuses himself with humanity at large; whereby he becomes something infinitely great, and at the same time nothing at all. He confounds himself with humanity in sheer distraction of mind, just as the opposition press uses the royal "we," and sailors say: "devil take me!" But when a man has indulged in oaths for a long time, he returns at last to the simple utterance, because all swearing is self-nugatory; and when one discovers that every street urchin can say "we," one perceives that it means a little more, after all, to be a particular individual. And when one finds that every cellar-dweller can play the game of being humanity, one learns at last, that being purely and simply a human being is a more significant thing than playing the society game in this fashion. And one thing more. When a cellar-dweller plays this game everyone thinks it ridiculous; and yet it is equally ridiculous for the greatest man in the world to do it. And one may very well permit oneself to laugh at him for this, while still entertaining a just and proper respect for his talents and his learning, and so forth.

Part Two

How the Subjectivity of the Individual must be Qualified in Order that the Problem may Exist for him

CHAPTER I

THE TASK OF BECOMING SUBJECTIVE

THE CONCLUSION THAT WOULD BE FORCED UPON ETHICS IF THE ATTAINMENT OF SUBJECTIVITY WERE NOT THE HIGHEST TASK CONFRONTING A HUMAN BEING— CONSIDERATIONS LEFT OUT OF ACCOUNT IN CONNECTION WITH THE CLOSER UN- DERSTANDING OF THIS—EXAMPLES OF THINKING DIRECTED TOWARDS BECOMING SUBJECTIVE

OBJECTIVELY we consider only the matter at issue, subjectively we have regard to the subject and his subjectivity; and behold, precisely this subjectivity is the matter at issue. This must constantly be borne in mind, namely, that the subjective problem is not something about an objective issue, but is the subjectivity itself. For since the problem in question poses a decision, and since all decisiveness, as shown above, inheres in subjectivity, it is essential that every trace of an objective issue should be eliminated. If any such trace remains, it is at once a sign that the subject seeks to shirk something of the pain and crisis of the decision; that is, he seeks to make the problem to some degree objective. If the Introduction still awaits the appearance of another work before bringing the matter up for judgment, if the System still lacks a paragraph, if the speaker has still another argument up his sleeve, it follows that the decision is postponed. Hence we do not here raise the question of the truth of Christianity in the sense that when this has been determined, the subject is assumed ready and willing to accept it. No, the question is as to the mode of the subject's acceptance; and it must be regarded as an illusion rooted in the demoralization which remains ignorant of the subjective nature of the decision, or as an evasion springing from the disingenuousness which seeks to shirk the decision by an objective mode of approach, wherein there can in all eternity be no decision, to assume that the transition from something objective to the subjective acceptance is a direct transition, following upon the objective deliberation as a matter of course. On the contrary, the subjective acceptance is precisely the decisive factor; and an objective acceptance of Christianity (*sit venia verbo*) is paganism or thoughtlessness.

Christianity proposes to endow the individual with an eternal happiness, a good which is not distributed wholesale, but only to one individual at a time. Though Christianity assumes that there inheres in the subjectivity of the individual, as being the potentiality of the appropriation of this good, the possibility for its acceptance, it does not assume that the subjectivity is immediately ready for such acceptance, or even has, without further ado, a real conception of the significance of such a good. The development or transformation of the individual's subjectivity, its infinite concentration in itself over against the conception of an eternal happiness, that highest good of the infinite—this constitutes the developed potentiality of the primary potentiality which subjectivity as such presents. In this way Christianity protests every form of objectivity; it desires that the subject should be infinitely concerned about himself. It is subjectivity that Christianity is concerned with, and it is only in subjectivity that its truth exists, if it exists at all; objectively, Christianity has absolutely no existence. If its truth happens to be in only a single subject, it exists in him alone; and there is greater Christian joy in heaven over this one individual than over universal history and the System, which as objective entities are incommensurable for that which is Christian.

It is commonly assumed that no art or skill is required in order to be subjective. To be sure, every human being is a bit of a subject, in a sense. But now to strive to become what one already is: who would take the pains to waste his time on such a task, involving the greatest imaginable degree of resignation? Quite so. But for this very reason alone it is a very difficult task, the most difficult of all tasks in fact, precisely because every human being has a strong natural bent and passion to become something more and different. And so it is with all such apparently insignificant tasks, precisely their seeming insignificance makes them infinitely difficult. In such cases the task itself is not directly alluring, so as to support the aspiring individual; instead, it works against him, and it needs an infinite effort on his part merely to discover that his task lies here, that this is his task—an effort from which he is otherwise relieved. To think about the simple things of life, about what the plain man also knows after a fashion, is extremely forbidding; for the differential distinction attainable even through the utmost possible exertion is by no means obvious to the sensual man. No indeed, thinking about the high-falutin is very much more attractive and glorious.

When one overlooks this little distinction, humoristic from the Socratic standpoint and infinitely anxious from the Christian, between being something like a subject so called, and being a subject, or becoming one, or being what one is through having become what one is: then it becomes wisdom, the admired wisdom of our own age, that it is the task of the subject increasingly to divest himself of his subjectivity in order to become more and more objective. It is easy to see what this guidance understands by being a subject of a sort. It understands by it quite rightly the accidental, the angular, the selfish, the eccentric, and so forth, all of which every human being can have enough of. Nor does Christianity deny that such things should be gotten rid of; it has never been a friend of loutishness. But the difference is, that philosophy teaches that the way is to become objective, while Christianity teaches that the way is to become subjective, i.e. to become a subject in truth. Lest this should seem a mere dispute about words, let me say that Christianity wishes to intensify passion to its highest pitch; but passion is subjectivity, and does not exist objectively.

In a curiously indirect and satirical manner it is often enough incul-cated, though men refuse to heed the instruction, that the guidance of philosophy in this matter is misguidance. While we are all subjects of a sort, and labor to become objective, in which endeavor many succeed bestially enough, Poesy goes about anxiously seeking its object. In spite of our all being subjects, Poesy must be content with a very sparing selection it can use; and yet it is precisely subjectivity that Poesy must have. Why then does it not take the very first that comes to hand, from among our estimable circle? Alas, he will not do; and if his only ambi-tion is to become objective he will never do. This would seem to signify that there might after all be something quite special about being a sub-ject. Why have a few become immortal as enthusiastic lovers, a few as high-minded heroes, and so forth, if all men in every generation are such as a matter of course, merely by virtue of being subjects in the im-mediate sense? And yet, being a lover, a hero, and so forth, is precisely a prerogative of subjectivity; for one does not become a hero or a lover objectively. And now the clergy! Why does the religious address re-peatedly return to the revered remembrance of a select circle of devout men and women, why does the clergyman not take the very first that comes to hand from our esteemed circle, and make him our pattern: are we not all subjects of a sort? And yet, devoutness inheres in subjectivity, and no one ever becomes devout objectively.

Love is a determination of subjectivity, and yet real lovers are very rare. We do indeed say, about as when we speak of everyone being a subject of a sort: There went a pair of lovers, there goes another pair; last Sunday the banns were published for sixteen couples; there are in Storm Street a couple of lovers who cannot live peaceably together. But when Poesy explains love in terms of its own lofty and festive conception, the honored name which it brings forward to exemplify the ideal sometimes carries us several centuries back in time; while the speech of daily life makes us as humoristic as funeral sermons generally, according to which every moment sees the burial of a hero. Is this merely a *chicane* on the part of Poesy, which is otherwise a friendly power, seeking to console us by uplifting our spirits in the intuition of what is excellent? And what sort of excellence? Why, to be sure, the excellence of subjectivity. So then it would seem that there must be something distinguished about being subjective.

Faith is the highest passion in the sphere of human subjectivity. But take note merely of what the clergy say, concerning how rarely it is found in the community of believers. For this phrase, the community of believers, is used in about the same manner as being subjects of a sort. Now pause a moment, and do not be so ironical as to ask further how rare, perhaps, faith is among the clergy! But this complaint, is it merely a cunning device on the part of the clergy, who have consecrated their lives to the care of our souls, by uplifting us in the spirit of devotion, while the soul's longing goes out to the transfigured ones—but to which transfigured ones? Why, to be sure, to those who proved that they were possessed of faith. But faith inheres in subjectivity, and so there must after all be something distinguished about subjectivity.

The objective tendency, which proposes to make everyone an observer, and in its maximum to transform him into so objective an observer that he becomes almost a ghost, scarcely to be distinguished from the tremendous spirit of the historical past—this tendency naturally refuses to know or listen to anything except what stands in relation to itself. If one is so fortunate as to be of service within the given presupposition, by contributing one or another item of information concerning a tribe perhaps hitherto unknown, which is to be provided with a flag and given a place in the paragraph parade; if one is competent

within the given presupposition to assign China[1] a place different from
the one it has hitherto occupied in the systematic procession,—in that
case one is made welcome. But everything else is divinity-school prattle.
For it is regarded as a settled thing, that the objective tendency in
direction of intellectual contemplation, is, in the newer linguistic usage,
the *ethical* answer to the question of what I *ethically* have to do; and
the task assigned to the contemplative nineteenth century is world history. The objective tendency is the way and the truth; the ethical is,
becoming an observer! That the individual must become an observer,
is the *ethical* answer to the problem of life—or else one is compelled to
assume that there is no ethical question at all, and in so far no ethical
answer.

Let us here in all simplicity seek to bring clearly before our minds a
little subjective doubt with respect to the tendency toward objectivity.
Just as the *Fragments*[2] called attention to an introductory consideration,
which might suitably be reflected upon before proceeding to exhibit in
the concrete the world-historic progress of the Idea, so I now propose to
dwell a bit upon a little introductory consideration bearing upon the
objective tendency. The question I would ask is this: *What conclusion
would inevitably force itself upon Ethics, if the becoming a subject were
not the highest task confronting a human being?* And to what conclusion would Ethics be forced? Aye, it would, of course, be driven to
despair. But what does the System care about that? It is consistent
enough not to include an Ethic in its systematic scheme.

The Idea of a universal history tends to a greater and greater systematic concentration of everything. A Sophist has said that he could
carry the whole world in a nutshell, and this is what modern surveys of
world history seem to realize: the survey becomes more and more com-
pendious. It is not my intention to show how comical this is, but rather
to try to make it clear, through the elaboration of several different
thoughts all leading to the same end, what objection Ethics and the
ethical have to raise against this entire order of things. For in our age
it is not merely an individual scholar or thinker here and there who
concerns himself with universal history; the whole age loudly demands
it. Nevertheless, Ethics and the ethical, as constituting the essential anchorage for all individual existence, have an indefeasible claim upon
every existing individual; so indefeasible a claim, that whatever a man
may accomplish in the world, even to the most astonishing of achievements, it is none the less quite dubious in its significance, unless the in-

dividual has been ethically clear when he made his choice, has ethically clarified his choice to himself. The ethical quality is jealous for its own integrity, and is quite unimpressed by the most astounding quantity.

It is for this reason that Ethics looks upon all world-historical knowledge with a degree of suspicion, because it may so easily become a snare, a demoralizing aesthetic diversion for the knowing subject, in so far as the distinction between what does or does not have historical significance obeys a quantitative dialectic. As a consequence of this fact, the absolute ethical distinction between good and evil tends for the historical survey to be neutralized in the aesthetic-metaphysical determination of the great and significant, to which category the bad has equal admittance with the good. In the case of what has world-historic significance, another set of factors plays an essential rôle, factors which do not obey an ethical dialectic: accidents, circumstances, the play of forces entering into the historic totality that modifyingly incorporates the deed of the individual so as to transform it into something that does not directly belong to him. Neither by willing the good with all his strength, nor by satanic obduracy in willing what is evil, can a human being be assured of historical significance. Even in the case of misfortune the principle holds, that it is necessary to be fortunate in order that one's misfortune may obtain world-historical significance. How then does an individual acquire historical significance? By means of what from the ethical point of view is accidental. But Ethics regards as unethical the transition by which an individual renounces the ethical quality in order to try his fortune, longingly, wishingly, and so forth, in the quantitative and non-ethical.

An age or an individual may be immoral in many different ways. It is also a form of immorality, or at any rate constitutes a temptation, for an individual to practise too assiduous an intercourse with the historical, since this may readily lead him to crave world-historical significance when the time comes for him to act for himself. Through an absorption in constant contemplation of the accidental, of that *accessorium* through which historical figures become historical, one may easily be misled into confusing this with the ethical; and instead of concerning oneself infinitely with the ethical, one may existentially be betrayed into developing an unwholesome, frivolous and cowardly concern for the accidental. This is possibly the reason why the contemporary age is seized with discontent when it confronts the necessity of action, because it has been spoiled by the habit of contemplation; and from this proceed, perhaps,

the many sterile attempts to count for more than one by socially club-
bing together, hoping thus numerically to overawe the spirit of history.
Demoralized by too assiduous an absorption in world-historical considerations, people no longer have any will for anything except what is
world-historically significant, no concern for anything but the accidental, the world-historical outcome, instead of concerning themselves
solely with the essential, the inner spirit, the ethical, freedom.

The constant intercourse with the world-historical tends in fact to
make the individual unfit for action. The true ethical enthusiasm consists in willing to the utmost limits of one's powers, but at the same time
being so uplifted in divine jest as never to think about the accomplishment. As soon as the will begins to look right and left for results, the
individual begins to become immoral. The energy of the will is slack-
ened; or it is abnormally developed in the direction of an unwholesome
and unethical craving, greedy for reward, and even if it accomplishes
what is great, it does not do so ethically: the individual demands something else than the ethical itself. A truly great ethical personality would
seek to realize his life in the following manner. He would strive to develop himself with the utmost exertion of his powers; in so doing he
would perhaps produce great effects in the external world. But this
would not seriously engage his attention, for he would know that the
external result is not in his power, and hence that it has no significance
for him, either *pro* or *contra*. He would therefore *choose* to remain in
ignorance of what he had accomplished, in order that his striving might
not be retarded by a preoccupation with the external, and lest he fall
into the temptation which proceeds from it. For what a logician chiefly
fears, namely a fallacy, a μετάβασις εἰς ἄλλο γένος, that the ethicist
fears quite as profoundly, namely a conclusion or transition from the
ethical to something non-ethical. He would therefore keep himself in
ignorance of his accomplishment by a resolution of the will; and even
in the hour of death he would will not to know that his life had any
other significance than that he had ethically striven to further the development of his own self. If then the power that rules the world should
so shape the circumstances that he became a world-historic figure: aye,
that would be a question he would first ask jestingly in eternity, for
there only is there time for carefree and frivolous questions.

If a human being cannot become a world-historic figure through himself, by the exercise of his freedom, by willing the good—and this is impossible because it is merely possible, i.e. perhaps possible, i.e. dependent

upon something else—then it is unethical to be concerned about it. And when, instead of forsaking this concern and emancipating himself from its temptation, a man dresses it up in sacred habiliments, asserting that it is for the sake of benefiting other people, then he is immoral, and seeks slyly to slip the thought into his dealings with God, that God needs him just a little. But this is stupidity, for God needs no man. It would otherwise be a highly embarrassing thing to be a creator, if the result was that the creator came to depend upon the creature. On the contrary, God may require everything of every human being, everything and for nothing. For every human being is an unprofitable servant, and the human being who is inspired by ethical enthusiasm differs from others only in knowing this, and in hating and abhorring every form of deception.

When a polemic temperament comes into conflict with his contemporaries, and endures everything, but at the same time raises the cry that the generations to come, the verdict of history, will reveal that he speaks the truth, then men believe that this is evidence for his enthusiasm. Ah, no, he is only a little shrewder than the people who are altogether stupid; instead of choosing money and the prettiest maiden and the like, he chooses world-historic significance: aye, such a man doubtless well knows what he chooses. But in relation to God and the ethical he is a deceitful lover; he, too, is one of those for whom Judas became the guide (Acts 1:16); he too sells his God-relationship, if not for money. And while he may perhaps contrive to reform an entire generation through his zeal and teaching, he nevertheless confounds existence as much as in him lies, because his own existential form is not adequate to his doctrine, and because by making an exception of himself, he establishes a teleology which makes existence meaningless.

A king or a philosopher may perhaps be well served, in the finite sense, by some clever talent who safeguards the king's power, and establishes the philosopher's doctrine, and binds all in obedience under the sway of the king or the philosopher, although he is himself not a good subject or a loyal follower. But in relation to God this is pretty stupid. The deceitful lover who refuses to be faithful as lover, but is willing to be loyal in the capacity of world-historical entrepreneur, is not faithful unto the last. He refuses to understand that there is nothing between him and God except the ethical; he refuses to understand that God, without injustice, and without denying his nature which is love, might create a man equipped with unexampled powers, set him down

in a solitary place, and say to him: "Do you now live through and experience the human in unparallelled intensity; labor so that half the
effort might suffice to transform an entire contemporary generation.
But you and I, we are to be alone about all this; your efforts are to have
no significance whatever for any other human being. And yet, you understand, you are to will the ethical, and you are to be enthusiastic in
your striving, because this is the highest." The deceitful lover does not
understand this, and much less is he capable of understanding the next:
when a genuinely inspired ethical personality, earnestly stirred, lifts
himself into the sacred sportiveness of the divine madness,[3] saying: "Let
me be as if created for a whim, this is the jest; and yet I propose to will
the ethical with all my strength, with utmost exertion, this is earnest;
and I propose to will absolutely nothing else. O insignificant significance, O sportive earnestness, O blessed fear and trembling! It is a
blessed thing to be able to satisfy the divine requirement, smiling at the
demands of the age; it is blessed even to despair of being able to satisfy
the divine requirement, provided one does not for all that let go of
God!" Only such a personality is ethical. But such a personality has also
understood that the world-historical is a composite of factors, not directly commensurable for the ethical.

The longer he lives, and the more the activities of the existing individual involve him in the warp and woof of life, the more difficult
becomes the task of separating the ethical from the external; and the
more readily may the metaphysical principle seem to be confirmed, that
the outward is the inward, the inward the outward,[4] the one wholly
commensurable with the other. But this is precisely the temptation to
be met and conquered; and hence the ethical becomes day by day increasingly difficult, in so far as the ethical precisely consists in that true
hypertension of the infinite in the spirit of man, which constitutes the
beginning, where it is therefore also most clearly apparent.

Let us imagine an individual who stands at the beginning of life. Let
us say that he resolves to devote his entire life to a pursuit of the truth,
and to the realization of the insight attained. In the moment of forming
this resolution he accordingly makes renunciation of everything, including the craving for world-historic significance. But now, when little
by little such significance comes to him as the fruit of his labor—but this
it never does. If and when it comes, it is Providence that superimposes
it upon his ethical striving within himself, and so it is not the fruit of
his labor. It is an item *pro*, which fully as much as every item *contra*,

must be regarded as a temptation. And it is the most dangerous of all temptations; many a glorious beginning, launched with the spiritual hypertension of the infinite, has become enervated in what for the fallen individual is an effeminate and self-indulgent embrace.

But let us go back to the beginning. With the true ethical hypertension of the infinite, the individual resigns everything. In fables and stories of adventure there is mention made of a lamp, called the wonderful; when it is rubbed, a spirit appears. Jest! But freedom is the true wonderful lamp; when a man rubs it with ethical passion, God comes into being for him. And behold, the spirit of the lamp is a servant; so wish for it then, all ye whose spirit is a wish! But whoever rubs the wonderful lamp of freedom becomes himself a servant—the Spirit is Lord. This is the beginning. Let us now see if it is possible to add something else to the ethical. The resolved individual then says: "I will—but at the same time I also will to have world-historic significance—but." There is then a "but"—and the Spirit vanishes, because the lamp of freedom has not been rightly rubbed, and the beginning is not realized. But if the beginning has been made, if it has been properly launched, every "but" must again be renounced in the sequel, even if existence does everything in the most ingratiating and alluring manner, to force it upon one.

Or the resolved individual says: "I will this, but I also will that my efforts should prove to be of benefit to other men; for let me tell you, I am a very benevolent fellow, and anxious to do good to others, even to the extent of improving the whole human race." Even if the Spirit were to appear when the lamp is rubbed in this manner, methinks it would gather itself together in wrath, and say to him: "Stupid man! Do I not exist, I who am omnipotent? And if the human beings whom I have created and numbered, even as I have numbered the hairs of your head, were innumerable as the sands of the sea, could I not help each one just as I help you? Presumptuous man! Have you any right to demand aught of me? But I have every right to demand all. Do you possess anything of your own, whereof you might give to me? Or is it not the fact, that even when you do your utmost you merely give me back my own, and that sometimes perhaps in paltry enough fashion?"

So then, here is where the beginner stands; the least trace of a "but" and the beginning has gone wrong. But if it is so with the beginning, the rest of the way must be in complete conformity therewith. If then our beginner has made a good beginning, and if he has also accomplished what is fitted to excite astonishment; if the entire contemporary generation owed him much, and offered him the reward of its gratitude, —the test of his faithfulness is nevertheless his ability to understand in a spirit of jest what actually is jest. The earnestness of it all is his own inner life; the jest is, that it pleases God to attach this significance to his striving, he who is nothing but an unprofitable servant.

When a mirage lays hold of a man, and by its magic of transformation shows him to the wondering observer in supernatural proportions, is that any merit attaching to the man himself? And so also when Providence so shapes affairs that the inner striving in a human being magically reflects itself in the world-historical shadow-play, is this his merit? I think that the true ethicist, if such a thing happened to him, when he talked about it would mockingly recall the case of Don Quixote. He would say that just as this knight, perhaps in recompense for having desired world-historic significance, was pursued by a jinx who ruined everything, so he, too, must have a jinx that plays a game with him in the converse sense—for only stupid schoolmasters and equally stupid geniuses make the mistake of thinking that it is they who do it, and proceed to forget themselves over their great importance in history.

Whoever cannot understand this is stupid; and if anyone dares to contradict me, I propose to make him ridiculous, by virtue of the power I happen this moment to have in comic characterization. More than this I refuse to say; for it might please Providence to take this power away from me this very day, and perhaps give it to another, merely to test me. It might please Providence to let me do the work, but so to shape things that the gratitude of my contemporaries was bestowed upon a barber's apprentice, as if he had done it. This I cannot know, I know only that it is my task to cling to the ethical, making absolutely no demands, but continuing to find my enthusiasm in the ethical relationship to God, which might very well subsist, and perhaps become still more intimate, if such a gift were taken away from me. It might therefore have been more prudent to have said nothing beforehand, lest I should all the more become an object of mockery if I fail. But the ethical never raises questions of prudence, it merely requires understanding sufficient to discover the danger—in order to brave it confidently; which seems indeed very stupid. O wonderful power, the power that is in the ethical! Suppose a king were to say to his enemies: "Obey my commands; if not, tremble before my scepter, whose sway shall be terrible over you—unless it should please Providence this very day to take my throne away from me, and to select a swineherd as my successor!" Why is this "if" so rarely heard, this "unless," the last part of the discourse, which is the ethical truth? For true it is, and the art consists merely in being enthusiastic, as another author has said:[5] to be joyful in lying above a depth of seventy thousand fathoms. And whoever has himself existentially understood life in this manner, will not mistake the significance of the world-historical; it is only the dim vision of speculative philosophy that confuses this *compositum* with something entirely different, about which the philosopher is profoundly wise after the event.

It has indeed been said, that *die Weltgeschichte ist das Weltgericht,*[6] and the word "judgment" here seems to present a claim that the saying expresses an ethical view of life. For God it may perhaps be so; because he has in his eternal consciousness the medium which alone provides the needed commensurability between outer and inner. But the human spirit cannot see the world-historical in this manner, even when we abstract from difficulties and objections which I do not wish to dwell upon here in detail, in order not to distract attention from the ethical. I propose merely to indicate them, touching upon them as far as possible in a spirit of concession, in order not to focus attention too exclusively upon them.

(a) We must abstract from the consideration already touched upon in the preceding, that *access to the realm of the historical is subject to a quantitative dialectic, so that whatever has historical significance has passed through this dialectic.* It is possible that such a distinction does not exist for omniscience; but this cannot carry any comfort for the finite spirit, since (I scarcely dare say aloud what I mean, it will not do in the history-conscious nineteenth century; but perhaps I may venture to whisper it into the ear of the systematic philosopher) there is a difference between King Solomon and Jørgen the hatmaker—but do not repeat my words. For God, the apprehension of the historical is interpenetrated by His knowledge of the inmost secrets of conscience, alike in the greatest and in the humblest. If a human being seeks to occupy this standpoint he is a fool; if he refrains from such an attempt, he will have to content himself with a survey of the more prominent items, and this is precisely what makes the quantitative the deciding factor in the selection. That the ethical is present in the historical process, as it is everywhere where God is, is not on this account denied. But it is denied that the finite spirit can see it there in truth; and it must be reckoned a piece of presumption to attempt to see it there, a reckless venture which may readily end by the observer losing the ethical in himself.

For the study of the ethical, every man is assigned to himself. His own self is as material for this study more than sufficient; aye, this is the only place where *he* can study it with any assurance of certainty. Even another human being with whom he lives can reveal himself to his observation only through the external; and in so far the interpretation is necessarily affected with ambiguities. But the more complicated the externality in which the ethical inwardness is reflected, the more difficult becomes the problem of observation, until it finally loses its way in something quite different, namely, in the aesthetic. The apprehension of the historical process therefore readily becomes a half poetic contemplative astonishment, rather than a sober ethical perspicuity. It becomes more and more difficult even for a judge to find a clear way through the mazes of his case, the more significant the parties involved. And yet the judge does not have the responsibility of passing an ethical judgment, but merely a legal one, where guilt and innocence are subject to a dialectic which takes a quantitative account of the greater or the lesser in the circumstances, and is partly determined by an accidental reference to the consequences. There is a far wider scope for confusion in connection with the contemplation of the world-process, where it often seems as if good and evil were subject to a quantitative dialectic, and that there is a certain magnitude of crime and cunning, affecting millions of individuals and entire peoples, where the ethical becomes as shy and diffident as a sparrow in a dance of cranes.

But again and again to be absorbed in this everlasting quantification is harmful to the observer, who may easily lose the chaste purity of the ethical, which dismisses the quantitative infinitely with a sacred contempt, though to the sensuous man it is his eyes' delight, and to the sophistical man, his fig-leaf.

The ethical as the absolute is infinitely valid in itself, and does not need to be tricked out with accessories to help it make a better showing. But the world-historical is precisely such a dubious *accessorium* (when it is not the eye of omniscience, but the eye of a human being which is to penetrate it). In the world-historical view, the ethical, like nature in the words of the poet,[1] serves *knechtisch dem Gesetz der Schwere;* for the quantitative differentials also constitute a depressing weight. The more simplified the ethical, the more perspicuous does it become. It is therefore not the case, as men deceitfully try to delude themselves into believing, that the ethical is more clearly evident in human history, where millions are involved, than in one's own poor little life. On the contrary, precisely the reverse is true, and it is more clearly apparent in one's own life, precisely because one does not here so easily mistake the meaning of the material and quantitative embodiment. The ethical is the inwardness of the spirit, and hence the smaller the circumstances in which it is apprehended, provided it really is apprehended in its infinitude, the more clearly it is perceived; while whoever needs the world-historical accessories in order, as he thinks, the better to see it, proves thereby precisely that he is ethically immature. Whoever does not apprehend the eternal validity of the ethical, even if it concerned him alone in all the world, does not really apprehend the ethical; for the fact that it concerns all men is in a certain sense wholly irrelevant to him, except as a shadow which accompanies the ethical clarity in which he has his life. It is with the apprehension of the ethical as it is with arithmetical calculation—one learns best how to reckon in abstract numbers; for when one begins with denominate numbers, the interest may readily come to be shifted to something else. In universal history we reckon with denominate magnitudes, and with tremendous denominations, magnitudes that, by virtue of their manifold variety, manifoldly move the manifold in the observer. This quantitative process is greatly to the taste of the sensuous man; and hence it is the case, to recall once more the simile and the unlikeness involved in it, that it is here by no means the beginner who reckons in abstract numbers, but that it is contrariwise a mark of ethical maturity to renounce that which one perhaps aspires to both early and naturally: the reckoning with world-historic magnitudes. As a noble Greek has said, namely Empedocles, as reported by Plutarch, that one ought to fast from evil ($\nu\eta\sigma\tau\epsilon\acute{\upsilon}\epsilon\iota\upsilon$ $\kappa\alpha\kappa\acute{o}\tau\eta\tau\sigma\varsigma$),[2] so also it is a mark of the true ethical apprehension of the ethical, that it is fasting and sober. It is an important ethical principle not to lust after the banquet table of the world-historical, nor to seek intoxication in the astounding. But this abstinence is again ethically understood the most divine of all enjoyments, the refreshment of eternity unto the strengthening of the heart. On the other hand, from the point of view of the historical, a man may easily be tempted to assume that when he is an insignificant individual, it has no infinite significance if he errs; and when he is a great man, that the magnitude of the circumstances may transmute the error into something good.

But even if the contemplative individual is not demoralized in this fashion, nevertheless, when the ethical is confused with the world-historical, so that it becomes essentially different when it has to do with millions from when it has to do with one, another confusion readily arises: namely, that the ethical first finds its concrete embodiment in the world-historical, and becomes in this form a task for the living. The ethical is thus not the primitive, the most primitive of all that the individual has within him, but rather an abstraction from the world-historical experience. We contemplate universal history, and seem to see that every age has its own moral substance. We become objectively puffed up, and, though existing individuals, we refuse to be content with the so-called subjective-ethical. No, the now living generation, while still in the midst of its allotted span of life, desires to discover its own world-historical moral idea, and to act out of a consciousness of this. Alas, what will not the Germans do for money—and the Danes do afterwards, when the Germans have done it first!

In relation to the past, the illusion which forgets to distinguish, and partly cannot know, what belongs to the individual and what belongs to that objective order of things which is the spirit of world-history, is easily accounted for. But in relation to the generation now living, and in relation to each particular member of it, to let the ethical become something which it needs a prophet to discover, a man with a world-historical outlook upon world-history—that is indeed a rare and ingeniously comical conceit. Happy nineteenth century! If no such prophet arises, we can all enjoy a holiday, for in that case no one knows what the ethical is. It is already droll enough that the ethical is so lightly regarded that instruction in it is by preference left to divinity students and village schoolmasters; it is ridiculous enough for one to say that the ethical has not yet been found, but still has to be discovered. And yet, it would not be a wholly insane notion if he meant that it was to be discovered by means of the self-penetration of the individual in himself and his God-relationship. But that a prophet should be needed for the purpose, a world-historical swashbuckler, who by means of a deep eye and a blue eye, by means of a knowledge of universal history, perhaps also by reading coffee grounds and laying out the cards, is to discover the ethical; that is to say (for this is the modern catchword of the demoralized ethic), what it is the age demands: this is in a double manner to create a confusion for which the lover of laughter must always be deeply indebted to the wise men of our time. It is ludicrous that something like this should be the ethical; it is ludicrous that a seer is to discover it by inspecting world-history, where it is so difficult to see; and, finally, it is ludicrous that the constant intercourse with the world-historical has generated this consequence from itself. What the most stupid human being, deriving his instruction from a reformatory, can understand, has with the assistance of the professorial wisdom been transformed and improved so as to become this genuinely speculative profundity. Alas, while the speculative and worshipful Herr Professor is engaged in explaining the whole of existence, he has in distraction forgotten his own name: namely, that he is a human being, not a fantastic three-eighths of a paragraph. He completes the System, and in a final paragraph announces that he proposes to discover the ethical, which this generation, and therein he and I, is pledged to realize—because it has not yet been discovered! What has not yet been discovered: the ethical, or, what the age demands? Alas, the ethical is an old discovery; but I am readily disposed to believe that it has not yet been learned what the age demands, in spite of the many satisfactory and highly respectable, but still always promising, attempts in galimatias.

If someone were now to say that this is a caviling exaggeration, that the world-historical philosophers gladly permit divinity students and village schoolmasters to give instruction in the popular ethic, and that they have no objection if especially the lower classes seek to live in accordance with it, but that the world-historical interest merely points to higher and far greater tasks; then this reply suffices to prove that it was no caviling exaggeration at all, for if the other is the higher, let us begin upon it, the sooner the better; but the misfortune is, that it has doubtless not yet been discovered. And as for the far greater tasks, let us talk quite simply about them, as neighbor speaks with neighbor in the evening dusk. The general assertion that the task is far greater is not enough; only if it became clear that the dividend for the individual participant became greater, would it carry encouragement to a sensible man. Out in the country, where peace dwells under the shade of the leafy canopy, when, according to the amiable king's pious wish,[3] the little family sits down to dinner with a fowl on the table, and there is a plentiful sufficiency for the few: is then this dinner not a rich abundance compared with the great dinner where indeed an entire ox was set forth, but where the participants were so numerous that there was scarcely a mouthful for each one? Or where an individual, who in the ordinary course loves silence, secretly finds the mysterious way to the solitude of some forsaken human being, and here finds time and place for the brief word which nevertheless is so indescribably cheering and refreshing: does not such a speaker produce an equally great effect, or rather one infinitely greater, than the admired orator who is rewarded with tumultuous applause—and why? Because he uses the catchword which the multitude likes to hear, and hence not because he spoke wisely, for the noise was so deafening that one could not hear clearly what he said; but because he made use of a phrase that every dunderhead can say, and hence not because he was a speaker, but a bellows-blower.

The speculative distraction must be explained psychologically solely as the result of the constant intercourse with world-history, with the past. Instead of closely attending to himself, as one who lives in the present and faces the future, so that he may in this manner be enabled to reproduce psychologically the individual moment which is only one factor among others in the world-historical, the philosopher mixes everything up together in a conglomerate, and attempts to anticipate his own pastness—to help him to act; although it would seem tolerably easy to understand that when an individual has once become a thing of the past, he must already have acted.

Only by closely attending to myself, can I arrive at an understanding of how an historical personality must have conducted himself while he lived; and only so do I understand him, when in my understanding I preserve him alive, not in the fashion of children, who smash the watch to pieces in order to find out what makes it run, or in the fashion of speculative philosophy, which transforms the historical personality into something different in order to understand him. But I cannot, by apprehending him as dead, learn from him what it means to live; that I must experience by myself. And therefore I must first understand myself, and not conversely; I must not allow myself after first having misunderstood him, to proceed now to use this misunderstanding to help me misunderstand myself, as if I, too, were already dead. The historical personality has presumably while living helped himself with the subjective ethic, and then Providence has added the world-historical significance, if he gets any.*

* One of the most distinguished and significant of all world-historical figures, is surely Socrates. How was it with him? Let the System, now that it is afterwards, understand his necessity, the necessity of his coming into existence, of his mother being a midwife; the necessity of his father having been advised by an oracle[4] to leave the child to his own devices, and never to subject him to any restraint (curious life, when viewed as exemplifying a necessary method); the necessity of his being married, and precisely to Xanthippe; the necessity of his

There is a class of people who have quite rightly perceived this, although they are otherwise far from hitting the truth, since they go to the opposite extreme. These are the mockers and the unbelievers, who hold that the whole of human history hinges upon pure trivialities, upon "a glass of water."[5] Speculative philosophy represents the opposite position, since after depriving him of his soul, it attempts to transform the historical individual into a metaphysical determination, a sort of categorical designation for the relation between cause and effect, immanently conceived. Both are in error; the mocker does man an injustice, the speculative philosopher does God an injustice. From the standpoint of world-history, the individual subject is indeed unimportant; but then it must be remembered that the world-historical is an extraneous addition. Ethically, the individual subject is infinitely important. Take any human passion whatever, and let it come into contact with the ethical in the individual: this will ethically have great significance, historically perhaps none at all, perhaps again a great one; for the world-historical comes into being through what is ethically a perhaps. Now while this relationship between passion and the ethical absorbs the existing individual to the utmost (this is what the mocker calls nothing, and what speculative philosophy speculatively overlooks, with the assistance of an immanent mode of apprehension), the power that governs the world creates perhaps for this individual an environment in which his life is reflected, by means of which he obtains a far-reaching world-historical significance. He does not have this significance, but Providence adds it to him. The mocker laughs, and says: "All this hinges

being condemned by a majority of just three votes[6]—for here everything is necessary; and it is lucky for the System that it has to do only with the dead, since it must be intolerable for a living individual to be understood in this manner. But let us now also look to see, less systematically and more simply, how he conducted himself while he lived, when he went about in public places and mocked the Sophists; when he was a human being, and, even in the most ridiculous situation that has been preserved for posterity (cf. *Antoninus philosophus—ad se ipsum*, XI, 28), when, because Xanthippe had taken his clothes and left the house, he threw a pelt around him and appeared thus clad in the market-place to the great amusement of his friends, still in this situation remained a human being, and not nearly so ridiculous in his pelt as he later became in the System, where he appears fantastically draped in the rich systematic trappings of a paragraph. Did Socrates go about talking of what the age demands, did he apprehend the ethical as something to be discovered, or which had been discovered by a prophet with a world-historical outlook, òr as something to be determined by an appeal to the ballot box? No, Socrates was concerned only with himself, and could not even count to five when it was a question of counting votes (Xenophon)[7]; he was unfitted for participation in any task where several were required, to say nothing of where it was necessary to have a world-historical mob. He attended to himself—and then Providence proceeds to add world-historical significance to his ironical self-contentment. It is too bad that we have heard nothing from him for the last two thousand years—God only knows what he thinks about the System.

on wounded pride," i.e. on nothing. But this is not true; for wounded pride in its relationship to the ethical is ethically by no means indifferent, nor is it a nothing; and the world-historical is something quite heterogeneous, which does not immediately or directly follow. For speculative philosophy, everything is of a piece. It has won its victory over the mocker and the unbeliever, not by saving the ethical out from the world-historical, but by indiscriminately sweeping everything together, under the viewpoint of a declamatory immanence-theory. But the mockery takes its revenge; it is so far from being excluded that it rather seems as if speculative philosophy had shut itself in with it, so ridiculous has it become. Its distraction of mind is also revenged, when speculative philosophy proposes in Ethics to have a living individual act by virtue of a theory of immanence, i.e. to act by inaction; for the point of view of immanence exists only for contemplation, essentially and in truth only for God, and as an illusion for worshipful professors and their friends and relatives.

But if it is thus venturesome to have aught to do with the contemplation of the world-historical, perhaps the objection is simply an expression of slackness and cowardice, always at hand to put a damper on enthusiasm, here seeking to hinder the lofty flight of the world-historical philosophers, who understand very well the risks they take, but therefore also dare. By no means. If anything in the world can teach a man to venture, it is the ethical, which teaches to venture everything for nothing, to risk everything, and therefore also to renounce the flattery of the world-historical in order to become as nothing. No, the objection is confident precisely because it is ethical; it asserts that the ethical is the absolute, and in all eternity the highest, and that it is not every daring venture which is half the battle, since there is also a daring venture where much is lost.

Besides, a daring venture is surely not merely a high-sounding phrase or a bold ejaculation, but a toilsome labor; a daring venture is not a tumultuous shriek, however reckless, but a quiet consecration which makes sure of nothing beforehand, but risks everything. Therefore, says the ethical, dare, dare to renounce everything, including this loftily pretentious and yet delusive intercourse with world-historical contemplation; dare to become nothing at all, to become a particular individual, of whom God requires everything, without your being relieved of the necessity of being enthusiastic: behold, that is the venture! But then you will also have gained that God cannot in all eternity get rid of you, for only in the ethical is your eternal consciousness: behold, that is the reward! To be a particular individual is world-historically absolutely nothing, infinitely nothing—and yet, this is the only true and highest significance of a human being, so much higher as to make every other significance illusory; not in and for itself, but always illusory if supposed to be the highest.

(b)   We shall have to abstract from the fact that *knowledge of the world-historical is, as a cognitive act, an approximation,* subject to the dialectic involved in every conflict between the ideal and the empirical, a dialectic which threatens every moment to prevent a beginning, and after a beginning has been made threatens every moment a revolt against this beginning.* The historical material is infinite, and the imposition of a limit must therefore in one way or another be arbitrary. Although the historical material belongs to the past, it is as subject for cognition not complete; it is constantly coming into being through new observations and inquiries, new discoveries are constantly brought to light, compelling not only additions but also revisions. Just as improvements in the instruments of observation facilitate new discoveries in the natural sciences, so every improvement in the methods of critical inquiry will in the same manner affect the world-historical material.

How I wish that I might in this connection reveal learning! Oh, that I could show how the authorized and yet *valore intrinseco* tolerably dubious Hegelian arrangement of the historical process is guilty of arbitrariness and omissions; how China ought to be assigned to another place,† and a new paragraph provided for a recently discovered tribe in

---

* Even if everything had to be conceded to Hegel, there is one introductory question which he has not answered: the significance, namely, of the fact that the apprehension of the world-historical is an approximation-process. It is true that he has spoken deprecatingly of Schelling's intellectual intuition,[1] which is in Schelling the expression for the beginning; he has said himself, and it has often been repeated, that his merit consists in the Method. But he has never told us how the Method is related to the intellectual intuition, or whether a *leap* is not here again required. Concerning the Method and its beginning we have nothing but the constant assertion that it is necessary to begin upon it and with it. But if such a beginning is to be something more than a mere arbitrary conceit, there must have been a preliminary reflection; and in this preceding reflection the introductory problem is rooted.

† It is not yet quite clear where China finds its place in the world-historical process, where every *Privatdocent* from day before yesterday finds clearly and definitely an ample space. All *Privatdocents* are in fact included, and as soon as the Method reaches our own times, everything goes as if it were greased, and there is room for us all. The Method has room for only one Chinese thinker, but not a single German *Privatdocent* is excluded, especially no Prussian, since whoever has the cross makes the sign for himself first. But of course, the System is not yet quite complete; perhaps it anticipates being able soon to appropriate the toilsome labor of some genuine scientist, incorporating it in its own *ein zwei drei* form, by having one or two additional Chinamen presented to it. Such is the Method; at present it is of course a little embarrassing to have only one Chinaman[2] when there are so many Germans.

Monomotapa; that I could show how the Hegelian method looks almost like sheer tomfoolery when applied to a lesser detail,—in that case
I might satisfy one or another reader. Essentially the interest would be
focused upon the arrangement of the world-historical; what I said
about Monomotapa[3] struck home, just as Jeronimus was struck by what
the schoolmaster in Holberg's *Christmas Eve*[4] says about the bird Phoe-
nix which is found in Arabia. But for anyone to regard the entire world-
historical interest, except when it seeks in true philological-scientific
disinterestedness to apprehend lovingly some historical phenomenon for
its own sake, solely as a matter of knowledge, when it speculatively proposes to assist in confounding the ethical task which confronts the particular individual with the task which the world-historical sets for the
race, and still more when this interest seeks to make itself everyman's
concern—then to regard this interest as an immoral and neurasthenic
exhibition of curiosity, will doubtless be interpreted as an abominable
ethical narrow-mindedness.

Only a very limited intelligence, or someone who cunningly wishes
to guard himself against feeling impressed, could here assume that I am
in this objection playing the rôle of a vandal, seeking to violate the
sacred security of the precincts of science, and to have the cattle let loose;
or that I am a lazzarone, placing myself at the head of a herd of newspaper readers and balloting idlers, in order to rob the modest scholar of
his lawful possessions, earned by the employment of his happy gifts in
resigned toil. Verily, there are many, many, who possess more than I do
in the realm of the mind; but there is no one who more proudly and
gratefully believes that in this realm there prevails an eternal security of
property rights, that the idlers remain outside. But when a generation *en
masse* proposes to dabble in universal history; when demoralized by
this, as one is demoralized by playing the lottery, it rejects the highest
of human tasks; when speculative philosophy is no longer disinterested,
but creates a double confusion, first by overleaping the ethical, and then
by proposing a world-historical something as the ethical task for the
individuals—then it is due to science itself that something be said about
it. No, all honor to the pursuits of science, and all honor to everyone
who assists in driving the cattle away from the sacred precincts of scholarship. But the ethical is and remains the highest task for every human
being. One may ask even of the devotee of science that he should acquire
an ethical understanding of himself before he devotes himself to scholarship, and that he should continue to understand himself ethically while

immersed in his labors; because the ethical is the very breath of the eternal, and constitutes even in solitude the reconciling fellowship with all men. But when this has been said and respected, not another word, except a word of admiration for the distinguished, and a word of inspiration and encouragement for the aspiring. The modest and retiring scientist does not bring confusion into life; he is erotically absorbed in his glorious occupation. But when, on the other hand, a tumultuous scientist seeks to invade the sphere of the existential, and there proceeds to confuse the ethical, the life-principle of the whole, then he is as scientist no faithful lover, and science itself stands ready to deliver him up to a comic apprehension.

Only a restricted intelligence could assume that the objection which reminds us that the contemplation of universal history is an approximation-process, had its roots in cowardice and sluggishness, in a shrinking from the insurmountable difficulties of the task. If the highest task lies in the direction toward this goal, and it is merely that the tremendous labor involved makes us fearful, then the objection is not worth considering. But the objection is ethical, and hence also confident; in all its humility it does not fail of its goal and aim, which is the highest. The objection says: "The ethical alone is certain; to concentrate upon the ethical yields the only knowledge which may not possibly in the last moment transform itself into an hypothesis; to exist in the ethical constitutes the only secure knowledge, the knowledge being rendered secure by something else."

To have to do ethically with the world-historical is an ethical misunderstanding, of which true science is never guilty. But while the ethical is everywhere so deprecatingly spoken of, what does life itself teach us? Just as lovers are few, just as believers are few, so the genuine ethical personalities are doubtless also few. Falstaff says somewhere[5] that he once had an honest face, but the year and date of its existence have been erased. Now this "once" may be said in innumerably different ways, all according to the manner of the erasure; but "once" is nevertheless a decisive word. Perhaps the poet wishes to teach us that it is rare to find an individual on whom that eternal mark of the divinity which expresses itself in the ethical, stands out pure and clear and distinct as once it did; that it is rare to find a personality for whom time does not lie like an eternity between him and this remembered eternal impression, but for whom the longest life is but a yesterday with respect to this mighty eternal presence; a personality (for let us not speak aesthetically, as if the ethical were a happy geniality) who day by day strives to reinstate the primitiveness which was his eternal origin! How rare it is, perhaps, to find a personality for whom the ethical preserves this sacred chastity, infinitely inaccessible to even the most distant hint of every foreign admixture; a personality that preserves, yet no, let us speak ethically, that *acquires,* that in his life acquires this virgin purity of ethical passion, in comparison with which the purity of childhood is but an amiable jest! For aesthetically a man may have a primitiveness, a wealth, a little of which he may even endure to lose in life; but ethically understood he has possessed it, and if he does not acquire anything, all is lost!

If anyone were to say that this is mere declamation, that all I have at my disposal is a little irony, a little pathos, a little dialectics, my reply would be: "What else should anyone have who proposes to set forth the ethical?" Should he perhaps set it objectively in a framework of paragraphs and get it smoothly by rote, so as to contradict himself by his form? In my opinion irony, pathos, and dialectics are precisely *quod desideratur,* when the ethical is *quod erat demonstrandum.* Yet I do not by any means consider that I have by my scribblings exhausted the ethical, since it is infinite. But it is all the more remarkable that the ethical is held to be so insignificant that we give up the certain for the sake of the uncertain, give up the most certain of all things in exchange for the various alluring tasks of approximation-knowledge. Let universal history be a mirror, let the observer sit and see himself reflected therein; but let us not forget the dog who looked at himself in a mirrored reflection[6]—and lost what he had. The ethical is also a mirror, and whoever sees himself therein doubtless loses something, and the more he looks at his reflection, the more he loses—all the uncertain, namely, in order to gain the certain. Only in the ethical is there immortality and an eternal life; otherwise understood, the world-historical is perhaps a spectacle, a spectacle which perhaps endures—but the spectator dies, and his contemplation of the spectacle was perhaps a highly significant way of . . . killing time.

(c) If we agree to overlook this objection, and concede that we need not give up the world-historical merely because intercourse with it is hazardous, or because we are cowards and fear the toil and trouble of the approximation-process: let us then consider the world-historical, not indeed *in concreto,* lest we become too voluminous, which may happen even to one who knows only what is contained in Kofod's history,[1] but *in abstracto*—let us consider *what there is to see in the world-historical.*

If the world-historical is something definite, and not a most indeterminate classification, where in spite of all one learns about China and Monomotapa, it remains in the last analysis uncertain what the limit is which separates the individual from the world-historical, so that the confusion repeatedly arises that a king is included because he is a king, and a hermit because he is in his isolation a significant personality; uncertain whether there is any limit at all, or whether everything is speculatively fused indistinguishably together, so that world-history is simply the history of the individuals; whether the limit is accidental, and relative to what the historian happens at the moment to know; whether the limit is subject to an arbitrary dialectic in relation to what the esteemed Herr Professor who is doing the arranging, has last read, or must, in view of his literary connections, take in tow—well, then: if the world-historical is something definite, it must be the history of the race. Here we confront a problem which in my opinion is one of the most difficult of all problems: in what manner and to what extent the race is a resultant of the individuals, and what the relationship is between the individual and the race. I shall make no attempt to answer this question, and if I did I might not succeed; but I propose rather to amuse myself by reflecting upon the curious circumstances that the survey of universal history has been almost completed, or is at any rate in full course of completion, without this difficulty having been removed.

If world-history is the history of the human race, it follows, as a matter of course, that it does not show forth the ethical. What it lets us see must be something that corresponds to the abstraction which the race is, and therefore to something equally abstract. The ethical is, on the contrary, a correlative to individuality, and that to such a degree that each individual apprehends the ethical essentially only in himself, because the ethical is his complicity with God. While the ethical is, in a certain sense, infinitely abstract, it is in another sense infinitely concrete, and there is indeed nothing more concrete, because it is subject to a dialectic that is individual to each human being precisely as this particular human being.

The dispassionate spectator apprehends the world-historical in terms of purely metaphysical categories, and views it speculatively as an immanent system of relationships between cause and effect, ground and consequent. Whether he is able to glimpse a *telos* for the race I shall not attempt to say; but this *telos* is not the ethical *telos* that exists for the individual, but a metaphysical *telos*. In so far as the individuals participate in the history of the race through their deeds, the dispassionate spectator does not view these deeds as reflected back into the individual and the ethical, but he views them as connected with the totality. What makes the deed ethically the property of the individual is the purpose; but this purpose is precisely something that never gets included in the world-historical, for here it is the world-historical purpose that counts. World-historically I see the effect, ethically, I see the purpose; but when I apprehend the purpose ethically and understand the ethical, I see also that every effect is infinitely indifferent, that it is indifferent what the effect was; but in that case I do not see the world-historical.

In so far as the categories of cause and effect sometimes also take on a reflected color of guilt and punishment, this is merely a consequence of the fact that the spectator does not maintain himself in a purely world-historical attitude, that he cannot quite divest himself of the ethical which is within him. But in this there is nothing at all meritorious in relation to the world-historical, and when the spectator becomes aware of this, he ought precisely to pause in his contemplative activity, in order to achieve clarity with respect to whether it is not the ethical which he ought first and last to develop within himself to its maximum, instead of using a little of it with which to deck out the world-historical. From the world-historical point of view the spectator does not see the guilt of the individual, as this makes itself evident in the intention, but sees the external action swallowed up in the totality, and within this totality bringing down upon itself the consequences of the deed. He sees therefore, what is wholly confusing and nonsensical, that the well-meant, quite as often as the ill-meant, deed brings the same consequence in its train; the best of kings and a tyrant bring about the same misfortune. Or rather, he does not see even this, for this is an ethical reminiscence; no, but he sees what is ethically scandalous, namely, that he is compelled world-historically to ignore the true distinction between good and evil, as this exists only in the individual, and in the last analysis only in each individual in his God-relationship.

Seen world-historically, one principle becomes invalid which is ethically true, and constitutes the vital principle in the ethical: the possibility-relationship which every individual has to God. This is entirely ignored world-historically, because everything is understood behindhand, and so it is forgotten that the dead were once alive. In the world-historical process as this is viewed by human beings, God does not play the rôle of sovereign; just as the ethical fails to appear in it, so God also fails to appear, for if he is not seen as sovereign he is not seen at all. In the ethical he does play this rôle, through the said possibility-relationship; and the ethical is for existing individuals, for the living, and God is the God of the living. In the world-historical process the dead are not recalled to life, but only summoned to a fantastic-objective life, and God becomes in a fantastic sense the soul in a process. In the world-historical process God is metaphysically imprisoned in a conventional straitjacket, half metaphysical and half aesthetic-dramatic, that is, the immanential system. It must be the very devil to be God in that manner.

The dramatic critic insists that the poet must make use of all the persons he has listed in his cast of characters, and bring out of them everything that there is in them; if they are unmarried young women, for example, they must be married before the play is over, or else there is something the matter with the play. When we contemplate the past, it seems to us quite natural that God must have used such and such characters; but while they lived, how many were rejected, and as for those who were used, how often were they made to understand in ethical humility that for God there is no immanential privilege, that God is not embarrassed by theatrical conventions. They were indeed made to understand the same thing that our enthusiastic ethicist (whom we have here and there introduced as speaking) found his enthusiasm in understanding: that God does not need him. We do not say that God would contradict Himself, that He would create and then refuse to use; there will always be enough ethically for everyone to do. And the possibility-relationship which is the inspiration of the ethicist in his joy over God, is God's freedom, which when properly understood can never in all eternity become identical with the systematic immanence of the world-historical process, either before or after.

The world-historical immanence is always confusing for the ethical, and yet apprehension of the world-historical is rooted in the principle of immanence. If an individual happens to see something ethical, then it is the ethical in himself, a reflex of which misleads him, so that he thinks he sees what he nevertheless does not see. In this experience on the other hand, he has, or has had, an occasion offered him to seek an ethical clarification of himself in his own consciousness. It would be incorrect to reason as follows: the more the individual is ethically developed, the more he will be able to see the ethical in world-history; no, quite the opposite: the more developed he becomes ethically, the less will he concern himself with the world-historical.

Let me here resort to an image for the purpose of giving a more intuitive notion of the difference between the ethical and the world-historical, the difference between the ethical relationship which the individual has to God, and the relationship of the world-historical to God. A king sometimes has a royal theater reserved for himself, but the difference which here excludes the ordinary citizen is accidental. It is otherwise when we speak of God and the royal theater He has for Himself. The ethical development of the individual constitutes the little private theater where God is indeed a spectator, but where the individual is also a spectator from time to time, although essentially he is an actor, whose task is not to deceive but to reveal, just as all ethical development consists in becoming apparent before God. But world-history is the royal stage where God is spectator, where He is not accidentally but essentially the only spectator, because He is the only one who *can* be. To this theater no existing spirit has access. If he imagines himself a spectator here, he merely forgets that he is himself an actor on the stage of the little theater, who must leave it to the royal spectator and actor how He will use him in this royal drama, *drama dramatum*.

This holds for the living, and only the living can be told how they ought to live; only by understanding this for oneself can one be led to reconstruct the life of one who is dead, if it really must be done, and if there is time for it. But it is certainly a topsy-turvy notion, instead of learning by living how to recall the life of the dead, to go and try to learn from the dead, apprehended as if they had never lived, how one should (aye, it is inconceivable how topsy-turvy it is) live—as if one were already dead.

(d) If it were not true that becoming subjective is the task proposed to every human being, and his highest task, one which suffices for the longest life, since it has the remarkable trait that it ceases only when life ceases—if this were not the case, there is one difficulty remaining, which must, it seems to me, press with an intolerable weight upon every human being's troubled conscience, so that he might wish himself dead today rather than tomorrow. This objection is not even mentioned in our objective and yet liberal age, which is much too deeply engrossed in forms and the System, to care anything about human lives. The objection is: *If one posits only the evolution of the race, the generations of men, how does one explain the divine wastefulness which uses the infinite host of individuals one generation after the other merely for the purpose of setting the world-historical process going?* The world-histori-

cal drama is infinitely dilatory: why does not God hasten, if that is all
He wants? What an undramatic exhibition of patience, or, rather, what
a prosaic and tiresome procrastination! And if that is all God wants,
how terrible tyrannically to waste upon it myriads of human lives! But
what does the spectator care about that? He catches world-historically
a glimpse of this play of colors, produced by the succession of generations, like the glint of a shoal of herring in the sea: the individual
herring have little worth. The spectator sits benumbed in the tremendous forest of the race, and just as one may fail to see the forest because
he sees only the individual trees, so he sees nothing but forest and not a
single tree. He hangs up draperies systematically, and uses nations and
races of men for the purpose; individual human beings are nothing to
him. Even eternity is draped with systematic synopses and with ethical
meaninglessness. Poetry indulges itself poetically in extravagant waste,
and far from fasting, it dares not aspire to the divine parsimony which
does not need, ethico-psychologically, many human beings, but all the
greater wealth of thought. What wonder that we even admire the historical spectator who is so lofty and heroic as to forget that he, too, is
a particular man, an individual existing human being. He stares at the
historical spectacle until he is lost in it; he dies and leaves the scene, and
nothing of him remains; or rather, he himself remains like a ticket in
the hands of the usher, an indication that the spectator has gone.

But if the task of becoming subjective is the highest that is proposed
to a human being, everything is beautifully arranged. First it follows
that world-history is no concern of his, but that everything in this connection is to be left to the royal poet. In the next place, there is no waste
of human lives; for even if the individuals were as numberless as the
sand of the sea, the task of becoming subjective is given to each. And
finally, the reality of the world-historical evolution is not denied, but
reserved for God and eternity, having its own time and place.

(e) First then the ethical, the task of becoming subjective, and afterwards the world-historical. I do not doubt that even the most objective
of men is at bottom in tacit agreement with what has here been set
forth, that it is right and proper for the wise man first to understand the
same thing that the plain man understands, and to feel himself obli-
gated by the same considerations that obligate the simple—so that only
after this has been done may he pass over to the study of world-history.
First then the simple. But this is naturally so easy for the wise man to
understand (or else why is he called wise?) that the task of comprehen-

sion is but the work of a moment, and he is instantly in full activity, occupied with universal history. And so also with my simple remarks: he has understood them instantly, and is at once far beyond them. Now if I could only contrive an opportunity to speak with the wise man for still another moment, I should gladly be content to be the plain man who asks him to pause a moment over the following simple remark: *Is it not the case that what is most difficult of all for the wise man to understand, is precisely the simple?* The plain man understands the simple directly, but when the wise man sets himself to understand it, it becomes infinitely difficult. Is this an indignity visited upon the wise man, that his person is so emphasized that the simplest things become the most difficult things, because it is he who is concerned with them? By no means. When a servant-girl weds a day-laborer everything passes off quietly, but when a king weds a princess it becomes an event. Is it derogatory to the king to say this about him? When a child talks away freely, it is perhaps simple enough, and when the wise man says the same thing it has perhaps become the most genial profundity. It is thus that the wise man stands related to the simple. The more the wise man thinks about the simple (and the fact that a prolonged occupation with it is conceivable, shows already that it is not so easy), the more difficult it becomes for him. And yet he feels himself gripped by a profound humanity, which reconciles him with the whole of life: that the difference between the wise man and the simplest human being is merely this vanishing little distinction, that *the simple man knows the essential,* while the wise man little by little learns *to know that he knows it,* or learns *to know that he does not know it.* But what they both know is the same. Little by little—and so also the wise man's life comes to an end: when was there then time for the world-historical interest?

But the ethical is not merely a knowing; it is also a doing that is related to a knowing, and a doing such that the repetition may in more than one way become more difficult than the first doing. Here again we meet with new delay—if we must *partout* pass on to the world-historical. However, I owe to everyone who desires to occupy himself with universal history the duty of admitting something about myself, something deplorable, which perhaps is the cause of my glimpsing tasks sufficient for an entire human life, while others are possibly able to finish them before this period expires. Most people are by nature such nice people; first, they are nice children, then nice youths and maidens, then nice men and women. This is naturally something quite different. When one has reached the pitch of having not only one's wife but also all one's sisters-in-law *en masse* say about one: he is verily an exceptionally nice man—well, then one may of course find time to take up universal history. This, I am sorry to say, is not my situation. Alas, it is only too well understood by the few who know me, and, I must admit, also known to myself: I am a depraved and corrupt individual. It is only too true; while all the nice men are without further ado, quite ready to take upon themselves the responsibility for the future of the history of mankind, I must many a time sit at home and grieve over myself. Although my father is dead and I no longer go to school, although I have not been remanded by the authorities to the discipline of a public institution, I have nevertheless perceived the necessity of doing a little something for myself, although I should undeniably rather disport myself at Frederiksberg and have to do with universal history. To be sure, I have no wife who could tell me that I am verily a good man; I am left entirely to my own devices. The only comfort I have is Socrates. He discovered in himself, so it is related,[1] a disposition to all sorts of evil; perhaps even it was this discovery that caused him to give up the study of astronomy, which the age now demands.[2] I willingly admit how little I otherwise resemble Socrates. In his case it was presumably his ethical insight that helped him make this discovery. With me it is another matter; in strong passions and the like I have sufficient material, and therefore find great difficulty in forming anything good out of it with the help of the reason.*

Let us then, so as not to introduce a disturbing element by the reference to myself, keep our attention fixed upon Socrates, to whom also the *Fragments* had resort. Because of his ethical insight, accordingly, he discovered in himself a disposition to all sorts of evil. Now indeed it is no longer so easy, so much a matter of one, two, three, to pass over to the world-historical. On the contrary, the way of the ethical becomes a very long one, for it begins with first making this discovery. The more profoundly the discovery is made, the more will one have to do; the more profoundly one makes it, the more ethical one becomes; the more ethical one becomes, the less time there is for the world-historical.

It is a strange circumstance in connection with the simple, that it can be so complicated. Let us take an example from the religious sphere, which lies so close to the ethical that they are in constant communica-

* With these words I would recall Plutarch's admirable definition of virtue: "Ethical virtue has the passions for its material, and reason as its form." See his little work *On the Ethical Virtues*.[3]

tion with one another. Prayer would seem to be something extremely simple, one might think it to be as easy as buttoning one's suspenders; and if there were no other hindrance, one ought soon to be free to take on world-historical problems. And yet, how difficult! Intellectually I need to have an entirely clear conception of God, of myself, of my relation to God, and of the dialectics of the particular relationship which is that of prayer, lest I confuse God with something else, so that I do not pray to God; lest I confuse myself with something else, so that it is not I who pray; and in order that I may be able to preserve, in the relationship of prayer, the distinction and the relationship. Sensible wedded folk admit that they need months and years of daily intercourse really to get acquainted with one another; and yet God is far more difficult to know. For God is not an externality as a wife is, whom I can ask whether she is now satisfied with me; whenever it seems to me in my God-relationship that what I do is good, and omit to bring to consciousness the self-distrust of the infinite, then it is as if God were also content with me, because God is not an externality but the infinite itself, not an externality that scolds me when I do wrong, but the infinite itself which has no need to scold, but whose vengeance is terrible—that God does not exist for me at all, in spite of the fact that I pray.

And prayer is also a deed. Alas, Luther was surely in this respect an experienced man, and yet he is reported to have said[4] that never once in his life had he prayed with such inwardness as not during prayer to have had one or another disturbing thought. So that it might also seem that prayer was as difficult an art as playing the rôle of Hamlet, of which one of the greatest of actors is said to have remarked that he had once in his life come near to playing it well. And yet he intended to devote all his power and his entire life to the continued study of this rôle. Is it not conceivable that prayer might be almost as important and significant an art?

But so it would appear that the attainment of subjectivity is a very praiseworthy goal, a task that may well be a *quantum satis* for a human life. Though I am myself under the sad necessity of making all possible haste, like Lot's wife: even the best of men will have enough to do. If with respect to this matter I should in any way be in a position to help one or another of my contemporaries, my service will be of such a nature as to carry a suggestion of the parable of the trees[5] that wanted to make the cedar their king, in order to rest in its shade. In a similar manner it is the desire of our age to have a systematic Christmas tree raised, so that we may rest and enjoy a holiday; but the trees had to be content with the bramble. If I were to compare myself with this, I should have to say: I am unfruitful, like the bramble; there is very little shade, and the thorns are sharp.

The task of becoming subjective, then, may be presumed to be the highest task, and one that is proposed to every human being; just as, correspondingly, the highest reward, an eternal happiness, exists only for those who are subjective; or rather, comes into being for the individual who becomes subjective. Furthermore, it is the presumption that the task of becoming subjective furnishes a human being with enough to do to suffice him for his entire life; so that it is not the zealous individual but only the restless one who manages to get through with life before life gets through with him. And such an individual is scarcely justified in speaking lightly of life, but is rather under obligations to understand that he has doubtless not rightly apprehended the task of life; for otherwise it would follow as a matter of course that this task lasts as long as life does, since it is the task of living. And when the individual apprehends it as his highest task to become subjective, under the progressive execution of this task, problems will reveal themselves which again might prove to be as sufficient for the subjective thinker as the objective problems that the objective thinker has before him—this man who goes on and on, never repeating himself, disdaining the repetition which immerses him more and more profoundly in the one thought, but astonishing the age first as systematician, then as philosopher of world-history, then as astronomer, as veterinarian, as water-inspector, as geographer, and so forth.[6]

How strange! But why should the task not suffice, when from the Socratic wisdom which discovers the inner propensity towards all sorts of evil before beginning to be finished as a good man, one learns to make a similar discovery: that it is the most dangerous of all experiences to have finished one's task too quickly. This is a very edifying observation, and has an extraordinary virtue to stretch the task out, and at the same time to make it really strenuous. Let us consider the curious fact that what is otherwise praised and admired, the speed, the haste, that this is in some connections so evaluated that the praise stands in a converse relationship to the haste. In general we praise quickness, and in certain circumstances it is a matter of indifference, but here it is even objectionable. When in a written examination the youth are allotted four hours to develop a theme, then it is neither here nor there if an individual student happens to finish before the time is up, or uses the entire time. Here, therefore, the task is one thing, the time another. But when the time itself is the task, it becomes a fault to finish before the time has transpired. Suppose a man were assigned the task of entertaining himself for an entire day, and he finishes this task of self-entertainment as early as noon: then his celerity would not be meritorious. So also when life constitutes the task. To be finished with life before life has finished with one, is precisely not to have finished the task.

And so the matter stands. Believe me, I, too, am a man of power, even if I do say it myself, while people in general may perhaps be disposed to put me in a class with theologues and village schoolmasters. I am a man of power; but my power is not that of a ruler or a conqueror, for the only power I have is the power to hold in check. Nor is my power of wide extent, for I have power only over myself, and I do not even have this power unless I exercise it every moment. I have not the time directly to hold my contemporaries in check, and besides I think that trying to restrain an entire contemporary age is like a passenger in a carriage holding on to the seat in front of him in order to stop the carriage: he determines himself in continuity with the age, and yet he wishes to hold it in check. No, the only thing to do is to get out of the carriage, and so hold oneself in check.

When a man thus steps out of the carriage (and being in continuity with the age is, especially in our age, equivalent to constantly riding on the railway), and never forgets that the task is to hold himself in check, since the temptation is to be finished too quickly, then nothing is more certain than that the task suffices for the whole of life. It is impossible that the task should fail to suffice, since the task is precisely that the task should be made to suffice. To be regarded as a theologue and a laggard is precisely a good sign, for theologues and laggards have the reputation of being slow.

Here follow a few examples, which in all brevity show how persistence avails to transform the simplest problem into the most difficult one; so that there is no reason for hastily choosing astronomy, the veterinary sciences, and the kind, as long as one has not understood the simple. The brevity of our exposition cannot here be a hindrance, since the problems are not finished.

For example, the problem of *what it means to die*. I know concerning this what people in general know about it; I know that I shall die if I take a dose of sulphuric acid, and also if I drown myself, or go to sleep in an atmosphere of coal gas, and so forth. I know that Napoleon always went about with poison ready to hand, and that Juliet in Shakespeare poisoned herself. I know that the Stoics regarded suicide as a courageous deed, and that others consider it a cowardly act. I know that death may result from so ridiculous and trivial a circumstance that even the most serious-minded of men cannot help laughing at death; I know that it is possible to escape what appears to be certain death, and so forth. I know that the tragic hero dies in the fifth act of the drama, and that death here has an infinite significance in pathos; but that when a bartender dies, death does not have this significance. I know that the poet can interpret death in a diversity of moods, even to the limit of the comical; I pledge myself to produce the same diversity of effects in prose. I know furthermore what the clergy are accustomed to say on this subject, and I am familiar with the general run of themes treated at funerals. If nothing else stands in the way of my passing over to world-history, I am ready; I need only purchase black cloth for a ministerial gown, and I shall engage to preach funeral sermons as well as any ordinary clergyman. I freely admit that those who wear a velvet inset[7] in their gowns do it more elegantly; but this distinction is not essential any more than the difference between five dollars and ten dollars for the hearse.

Nevertheless, in spite of this almost extraordinary knowledge or facility in knowledge, I can by no means regard death as something I have understood. Before I pass over to universal history—of which I must always say: "God knows whether it is any concern of yours"—it seems to me that I had better think about this, lest existence mock me, because I had become so learned and highfalutin that I had forgotten to understand what will some time happen to me as to every human being—sometime, nay, what am I saying: suppose death were so treacherous as to come tomorrow! Merely this one uncertainty, when it is to be understood and held fast by an existing individual, and hence enter into every thought, precisely because it is an uncertainty entering into my beginning upon universal history even, so that I make it clear to myself whether if death comes tomorrow, I am beginning upon something that is worth beginning—merely this one uncertainty generates inconceivable difficulties, difficulties that not even the speaker who treats of death is always aware of, in that he thinks that he apprehends the uncertainty of death, while nevertheless forgetting to think it into what he says about it, so that he speaks movingly and with emotion about the uncertainty of death, and yet ends by encouraging his hearers to make a resolution for the whole of life. This is essentially to forget the uncertainty of death, since otherwise the enthusiastic resolve for the whole of life must be made commensurable with the uncertainty of death. To think about it once for all, or once a year at matins on New Year's morning, is of course nonsense, and is the same as not thinking about it at all. If someone who thinks the thought in this manner also assumes to explain universal history, then it may well be that what he says about universal history is glorious, but what he says about death is stupid. If death is always uncertain, if I am a mortal creature, then it is impossible to understand this uncertainty in terms of a mere generality unless indeed I, too, happen to be merely a human being in general. But this is surely not the case, and it is only the absent-minded, like Soldin the bookseller for example, who are merely human beings in general. And if initially my human nature is merely an abstract something, it is at any rate the task which life sets me to become subjective; and in the same degree that I become subjective, the uncertainty of death comes more and more to interpenetrate my subjectivity dialectically. It thus becomes more and more important for me to think it in connection with every factor and phase of my life; for since the uncertainty is there in every moment, it can be overcome only by overcoming it in every moment.

If, on the other hand, the uncertainty of death is merely something in general, then my own death is itself only something in general. Perhaps this is also the case for systematic philosophers, for absent-minded people. For the late Herr Soldin,[8] his own death is supposed to have been such a something in general: "when he was about to get up in the morning he was not aware that he was dead." But the fact of my own death is not for me by any means such a something in general, although for others, the fact of my death may indeed be something of that sort. Nor am I for myself such a something in general, although perhaps for others I may be a mere generality. But if the task of life is to become subjective, then every subject will *for himself* become the very opposite of such a something in general. And it would seem to be a somewhat embarrassing thing to be so significant for universal history, and then at home, in company with oneself, to be merely a something in general. It is already embarrassing enough for a man who is an extraordinarily important figure in the public assembly to come home to his wife, and then to be for her only such a something in general; or to be a world-historical Diedrich Menschenschreck,[9] and then at home to be—aye, I do not care to say anything more. But it is still more embarrassing to have so low a standing with oneself, and it is most embarrassing of all to remain unaware of the fact that this is so.

The lofty thinker who concerns himself with universal history can scarcely refuse me a reply to the question of what it means to die, and the instant he makes answer the dialectical process begins. Let him cite whatever reason he likes for not wishing to dwell at length upon such thoughts, it will not help him; for this reason will again be subjected to a dialectical inquiry to determine what it essentially means. I would thus have to ask whether it is in general possible to have an idea of death, whether death can be apprehended and experienced in an anticipatory conception, or whether its only being is its actual being. And since the actual being of death is a non-being, I should have to ask whether it follows as a consequence that death is only when it is not; or whether, in other words, the ideality of thought can overcome death by thinking it, or whether the material is victor in death, so that a human being dies like a dog, death being capable of being conquered only by the dying individual's apprehension of it in the very moment of death.

This difficulty can also be expressed as follows: Is it the case that the living individual is absolutely excluded from the possibility of approaching death in any sense whatever, since he cannot experimentally come near enough without comically sacrificing himself upon the altar of his own experiment, and since he cannot experientially restrain the experiment, and so learns nothing from it, being incapable of taking himself out of the experience so as to profit from it subsequently, but sticks fast in the experience. If the answer is given that one cannot apprehend death by means of any conception of it, the case is by no means closed. A negative answer is dialectically just as much in need of development and further determination as a positive answer, and only children and naïve people are satisfied with a *"dass weiss man nicht."* The thinker demands to know more, not indeed positively about what by supposition can be answered only negatively; but he demands to have it made dialectically clear that the answer must be negative; and this dialectical clarification sets this negative answer into relationship with all other existential problems, so that there will be difficulties no end.

If the answer to our question is affirmative, the question then arises as to what death is, and especially as to what it is for the living individual. We wish to know how the conception of death will transform a man's entire life, when in order to think its uncertainty he has to think it in every moment, so as to prepare himself for it. We wish to know what it means to prepare for death, since here again one must distinguish between its actual presence and the thought of it. This distinction appears to make all my preparation insignificant, if that which really comes is not that for which I prepared myself; and if it is the same, then my preparation is in its perfection identical with death itself. And I must take into account the fact that death may come in the very moment that I begin my preparation. The question must be raised of the possibility of finding an ethical expression for the significance of death, and a religious expression for the victory over death; one needs a solving word which explains its mystery, and a binding word by which the living individual defends himself against the ever recurrent conception; for surely we dare scarcely recommend mere thoughtlessness and forgetfulness as wisdom.

And furthermore, it is evident that when the subject thinks his own death, this is a deed. For a man in general, for an absent-minded individual like Soldin or a systematic philosopher, to think death in general is indeed no act or deed; it is only a something in general, and what such a something in general really is, is at bottom a very difficult thing to say. But if the task of life is to become subjective, then the thought of death is not, for the individual subject, something in general, but is verily a deed. For the development of the subject consists precisely in his active interpenetration of himself by reflection concerning his own existence, so that he really thinks what he thinks through making a reality of it. He does not for example think, for the space of a passing moment: "Now you must attend to this thought every moment"; but he really does attend to it every moment. Here then everything becomes more and more subjective, as is quite natural when the task is to develop the subjectivity of the individual. In so far it might seem as if communication between man and man were abandoned to an unhampered freedom in lying and deception, if anyone so desires; for one need only say: "I have done so and so," and we can get no further with him. Well, what of it? But suppose he has not really done it? What business is that of mine? Such a deception would be worst for himself. When we speak about something objective it is easier to exercise a control over what is said; when, for example, a man says that Frederick the Sixth was an Emperor of China, we answer that this is a lie. But when a man speaks about death, and of how he has thought it and conceived its uncertainty, and so forth, it does not follow that he has really done it. Quite so. But there is a more artistic way of finding out whether he lies or not. Merely let him speak: if he is a deceiver, he will contradict himself precisely when he is engaged in offering the most solemn assurances. The contradiction will not be a direct one, but consists in the failure of the speech to include a consciousness of what the speech professes directly to assert. Objectively the assertion may be quite straight-forward; the man's only fault is that he speaks by rote.* That he also perspires and pounds the table with his fists, is not proof that he does not merely patter; it only goes to show that he is very stupid, or else that he has a secret consciousness that he is guilty of ranting. For it is exceedingly stupid to think that reciting something by rote could properly stir the emotions; since the emotional is the internal, while ranting is something external, like making water. And to imagine it possible to conceal the lack of inwardness by pounding the table, is a very mediocre notion of deception.

When death thus becomes something to be related to the entire life of the subject, I must confess I am very far indeed from having understood it, even if it were to cost me my life to make this confession. Still less have I realized the task existentially. And yet I have thought about this subject again and again; I have sought for guidance in books—and I have found none.†

For example, what does it mean to be immortal? In this respect, I know what people generally know. I know that some hold a belief in immortality, that others say they do not hold it; whether they actually do not hold it I know not; it does not occur to me therefore to want to combat them, for such an undertaking is so dialectically difficult

---

* The reduplicated presence of the thought in every word, in every parenthetical expression, in the moment of digression, in the unguarded moment of unfolding a simile or portraying an image: this is what must be watched for if anyone wishes to take the trouble to find out whether a man is lying or not—provided one first watches oneself. For the ability to observe in this manner is the by-product of exercising a watchful restraint upon oneself; in that case, one receives as a free gift the capacity to notice such things, and will not in general be very eager to use it against others.

† Although I have said this often, I wish here again to repeat it: What is developed in these pages does not concern the simple-minded, who bear feelingly the burdens of life, and whom God wishes to preserve in their lovable simplicity, which feels no great need of any other sort of understanding. Or in so far as such need is felt, it tends to reduce itself to a sigh over the ills of life, the sigh humbly finding solace in the thought that the real happiness of life does not consist in having knowledge. On the other hand it does concern those who deem themselves possessed of leisure and talent for a deeper inquiry. And it concerns such an one in the following manner: it seeks to estop him from thoughtlessly taking on universal history, without first considering in self-reflection that being an existing human individual is so strenuous and yet so natural a task for everyone, that one tends first as a matter of courage to apply himself to this task, and reasonably finds in the exertion thereto requisite, a sufficiency for his entire life.

that I should need a year and a day before it could become dialectically clear to me whether there is any reality in such a contest; whether the dialectic of communication, when it is properly understood, would approve of such a proceeding or transform it into a mere beating of the air; whether the consciousness of immortality is a doctrinal topic which is appropriate as a subject for instruction, and how the dialectic of instruction must be determined with relation to the learner's presuppositions; whether these presuppositions are not so essential that the instruction becomes a deception in case one is not at once aware of them, and in that event the instruction is transformed into non-instruction. Moreover, I know that some have found immortality in Hegel,[10] others have not; I know that I have not found it in the System, where indeed it is also unreasonable to seek it; for, in a fantastic sense, all systematic thinking is *sub specie aeterni,* and to that extent immortality is there in the sense of eternity, but this immortality is not at all the one about which the question is asked, since the question is about the immortality of a mortal, which is not answered by showing that the eternal is immortal, and the immortality of the eternal is a tautology and a misuse of words. I have read Professor Heiberg's *Soul after Death,* indeed I have read it with the commentary of Dean Tryde.[11] Would I had not done so; for one rejoices aesthetically in a poetic word and does not require the utmost dialectical precision which is appropriate in the case of a learner who would direct his life in accordance with such guidance. If a commentator compels me to seek for something of that sort in the poem, he has done no service to the poem. From the commentator I could perhaps hope to learn what I have not learnt from the commentary, if Dean Tryde with catechetical instruction were to take pity on me and show how one constructs a life-view upon the profundities he has propounded by paraphrasing the poem. For honor be to Dean Tryde—merely from that little article it would surely be possible to construct several different life-views— but I cannot make *one* out of it, and that, alas, is precisely the misfortune, for it is one I need, no more, since I am not a learned man. I know, moreover, that the late Professor Poul Møller, who was well acquainted after all with the newest philosophy, became aware only in his latest period, of the infinite difficulty of the question of immortality,[12] when the question is simply put, when one does not ask about a new proof and about the opinions of Tom, Dick and Harry strung upon a thread. I know also that in a treatise he sought to explain

himself, and that this treatise clearly bears the mark of his aversion
to speculation. The difficulty of the question arises precisely when it
is simply put, not as the well-trained *Privatdocent* enquires about the
immortality of man, the abstractly understood man in general, man
being understood fantastically as the race, and so about the immortality
of the human race. Such a well-trained *Privatdocent* raises and answers
the question in such a way as the well-trained reader conceives that it
ought to be done. A poor untrained reader is only made a fool of by
such reflections, like one who overhears an examination in which the
questions and answers have been agreed upon beforehand, or like one
who enters a family circle which has its own language, using words
of the mother tongue, but understanding something different by them.
It follows from this, generally speaking, that the answer is very easy,
owing to the fact that they have altered the question, wherefore one
cannot deny that they answer the question, but one can indeed affirm
that the question is not what it seems to be. When, in an examination,
the teacher is to test the knowledge of Danish history, and, seeing that
the pupil can make nothing of it, gives the examination a different
turn, as by asking about the relationship of another country to Denmark, and thereupon asking about the history of this other land—can
one say that there was an examination on the history of Denmark?
When school children write a word in their books with a reference
to p. 101 and p. 101, see p. 216 and p. 216, see p. 314, and then finally,
April Fool—can one justly say that one profits by this guidance . . .
to be made a fool of? A book raises[13] the question of the immortality of
the soul. The contents of the book constitute the answer. But the contents of the book, as the reader can convince himself by reading it
through, are the opinions of the wisest and best men about immortality, all neatly strung on a thread. Oh! thou great Chinese god! Is
this immortality? So then the question about immortality is a learned
question. All honor to learning! All honor to him who can handle
learnedly the learned question of immortality! But the question of
immortality is essentially not a learned question, rather it is a question
of inwardness, which the subject by becoming subjective must put
to himself. Objectively the question cannot be answered, because objectively it cannot be put, since immortality precisely is the potentiation
and highest development of the developed subjectivity. Only by really
willing to become subjective can the question properly emerge, therefore how could it be answered objectively? The question cannot be

answered in social terms, for in social terms it cannot be expressed, inasmuch as only the subject who wills to become subjective can conceive the question and ask rightly, "Do *I* become immortal, or am *I* immortal?" Of course, people can combine for many things; thus several families can combine for a box at the theater, and three single gentlemen can combine for a riding horse, so that each of them rides every third day. But it is not so with immortality; the consciousness of my immortality belongs to me alone, precisely at the moment when I am conscious of my immortality I am absolutely subjective, and I cannot become immortal in partnership with three single gentlemen in turn. People who go about with a paper soliciting the endorsement of numerous men and women, who feel a need in general to become immortal, get no reward for their pains, for immortality is not a possession which can be extorted by a list of endorsements. Systematically, immortality cannot be proved at all. The fault does not lie in the proofs, but in the fact that people will not understand that viewed systematically the whole question is nonsense, so that instead of seeking outward proofs, one had better seek to become a little subjective. Immortality is the most passionate interest of subjectivity; precisely in the interest lies the proof. When for the sake of objectivity (quite consistently from the systematic point of view), one systematically ignores the interest, God only knows in this case what immortality is, or even what is the sense of wishing to prove it, or how one could get into one's head the fixed idea of bothering about it. If one were systematically to hang up immortality on the wall, like Gessler's hat,[14] before which we take off our hats as we pass by, that would not be equivalent to being immortal or to being conscious of one's immortality. The incredible pains the System takes to prove immortality is labor lost and a ludicrous contradiction—to want to answer systematically a question which possesses the remarkable trait that systematically it cannot be put. This is like wanting to paint Mars in the armor which rendered him invisible. The very point lies in the invisibility; and in the case of immortality, the point lies in the subjectivity and in the subjective development of the subjectivity.

Quite simply therefore the existing subject asks, not about immortality in general, for such a phantom has no existence, but about his immortality, about what it means to become immortal, whether he is able to contribute anything to the accomplishment of this end, or whether he becomes immortal as a matter of course, or whether he is that and can become it. In the first case, he asks what significance it may have, if any, that he has let time pass unutilized, whether there is perhaps a greater and a lesser immortality. In the second case, he asks what significance it may have for the whole of his human existence that the highest thing in life becomes something like a prank, so that the passion of freedom within him is relegated to lower tasks but has nothing to do with the highest, not even negatively, for a negative employment with relation to the highest thing would in a way be the most extenuating—when one wanted to do everything enthusiastically with all one's might, and then to ascertain that the utmost one can do is to maintain a receptive attitude towards that thing which one would more than gladly do everything to earn. The question is raised, how he is to comport himself in talking about his immortality, how he can at one and the same time talk from the standpoint of infinity and of finiteness and think these two together in one single instant, so that he does not say now the one and now the other; how language and all modes of communication are related thereto, when all depends upon being consistent in every word, lest the little heedless supplementary word, the chatty subordinate phrase, might intervene and mock the whole thing; where may be the place, so to speak, for talking about immortality, where such a place exists, since he well knows how many pulpits there are in Copenhagen, and that there are two chairs of philosophy, but where the place is which is the unity of infinitude and finiteness, where he, who is at one and the same time infinite and finite, can talk in one breath of his infinitude and his finiteness, whether it is possible to find a place so dialectically difficult, which nevertheless is so necessary to find. The question is raised, how he, while he exists, can hold fast his consciousness of immortality, lest the metaphysical conception of immortality proceed to confuse the ethical and reduce it to an illusion; for ethically, everything culminates in immortality, without which the ethical is merely use and wont, and metaphysically, immortality swallows up existence, yea, the seventy years of existence, as a thing of naught, and yet ethically this naught must be of infinite importance. The question is raised, how immortality practically transforms his life; in what sense he must have the consciousness of it always present to him, or whether perhaps it is enough to think this thought once for all, whether it is not true that, if the answer is to this effect, the answer shows that the problem has not been stated, inasmuch as to such a consciousness of immortality once for all there would correspond the notion of being a subject as it were in general, whereby the question about immortality is made fantastically ludicrous, just as the converse is ludicrous, when people who have fantastically made a mess of everything and have been every possible sort of thing, one day ask the clergyman with deep concern whether in the beyond they will then really be the same—after never having been able in their lifetime to be the same for a fortnight, and hence have undergone all sorts of transformations. Thus immortality would be indeed an extraordinary metamorphosis if it could transform such an inhuman centipede into an eternal identity with itself, which this "being the same" amounts to. He asks about whether it is now definitely determined that he is immortal, about what this determinateness of immortality is; whether this determinateness, when he lets it pass for something once for all determined (employing his life to attend to his fields, to take to himself a wife, to arrange world-history) is not precisely indeterminateness, so that in spite of all determinateness he has not got any further, because the problem is not even conceived, but since he has not employed his life to become subjective, his subjectivity has become some sort of an indeterminate something in general, and that abstract determinateness has become therefore precisely indeterminateness; whether this determinateness (if he employs his life to become subjective) is not rendered so dialectically difficult, by the constant effort to adapt himself to the alternation which is characteristic of existence, that it becomes indeterminateness; whether, if this is the highest he attains to (namely, that the determinateness becomes indeterminateness), it were not better to give the whole thing up; or whether he is to fix his whole passion upon the indeterminateness, and with infinite passionateness embrace the indeterminateness of the determinate; and whether this might be the only way by which he can attain knowledge of his immortality so long as he is existing, because as exister he is marvelously compounded, so that the determinateness of immortality can only be possessed determinately by the Eternal, but by an exister can be possessed only in indeterminateness.

And the fact of asking about his immortality is at the same time for the existing subject who raises the question a deed—as it is not, to be sure, for absent-minded people who once in a while ask about the matter of being immortal quite in general, as if immortality were something one has once in a while, and the question were some sort of thing in general. So he asks how he is to behave in order to express in existence his immortality, whether he is really expressing it; and for the time being, he is satisfied with this task, which surely must be enough to last a man a lifetime since it is to last for an eternity. And then? Well, then, when he has completed this task, then comes the turn for world-history. In these days, to be sure, it is just the other way round: now people apply themselves first to world-history, and therefore there comes out of this the ludicrous result (as another author has remarked),[15] that while people are proving and proving immortality quite in general, faith in immortality is more and more diminishing.

For example, what does it mean that I am to thank God for the good He bestows upon me? This, says the parson, we ought to do; and if we merely discharge this obligation, then he who is not disposed to be satisfied with the humble tasks in life which engage the simple man, will have time to employ himself with world-history. To make everything as easy as possible I will not even object that, after all, this does take some time. No, to humor the parson I assume that I am even infinitely willing to do it, so that I do not need to calculate the time I employ in passing from a state of disinclination, which the parson assumes, to the state of inclination which the parson admonishes us to attain. I assume therefore that I am infinitely eager to thank God, more than this I do not say; I do not say that I actually know this determinately about myself, for over against God I always speak indeterminately about myself, since He is the only one who knows determinately about my relationship to Him. This cautiousness in expressing oneself about one's God-relationship involves a multiplicity of determinants, and apart from that it may well happen to one as it happens to many writers of universal history, that they contradict themselves in every third line. So I am bound to thank God, says the parson. And what for? For the good He bestows upon me. But for what good? Why, surely, for that good which I perceive is a good. Halt! If I thank God for the good which I know is a good, I make a fool of God; for instead of my relationship to God signifying that I am reformed into His likeness, I form God in my likeness. I thank Him for that good which I know is a good; but what I know is the finite, and so I proceed to thank God for the fact that He has humored my whim. And yet I am bound to thank God for that good which I know is a good, which, however, I am not able to know. What then? Am I then to cease to give thanks when that befalls me which, according to my poor finite understanding, is a good, for which perhaps I have very earnestly wished, and by which when I obtain it I am so overwhelmed that I must necessarily thank God? No, not exactly

that; but I have to reflect that the fact of having earnestly wished it is
no merit, and that it does not become meritorious for the fact that I
obtain it. So I have to preface my thanksgiving with an apology, in
order to make sure that it is God I have the honor to address, not my
friend and boon companion Privy Councillor Andersen; I have to
acknowledge with confusion of face that it seems to me so good that
I have to pray for forgiveness in giving thanks for it because I can't
help it. So then I have to pray for forgiveness for giving thanks. That is
not what the parson said. So the parson must either be wanting to make
a fool of me, or he doesn't know what he himself says or maybe this
parson is one of those who are also preoccupied with world-history. In
my God-relationship I have to learn precisely to give up my finite
understanding, and therewith the custom of discrimination which is
natural to me, that I may be able with divine madness to give thanks
always. To give thanks always—is that something in general, some sort
of a thing one does once for all? Does this "thanking God always" mean
that once a year, on the Second Sunday in Lent at evensong,[16] I reflect
that I always ought to thank God?—and perhaps not even so much as
this, for if it chances strangely that upon that Sunday I am in a peculiar
mood, I do not understand it even on that day. So then this thing of
thanking God, this simple thing, suddenly presents to me one of the
most laborious tasks, one which is enough to last my whole life. So
perhaps a little time passes before I attain this, and in case I were to
attain it, what then would be the highest thing I should grasp after in
letting this go? So then while his friend and his beloved wife look at
him with concern and say almost despairingly, "Unhappy man, what
thou must be suffering!" the God-fearing man will have the courage to
say, and in action to give expression to what he says, "My dears, you
are mistaken, it is the good which befalls me, I feel disposed to give
thanks, and, oh, if only my thanksgiving might be well-pleasing to
Him." And ere I have attained this, then when I give thanks for the
good about which the parson talks, I shall do it shamefacedly. The
difficulty which here (and so likewise at every point in the God-relationship—hence at innumerable points) proves to be the transition to
the true liberation from finitude in God who is always to be thanked
(whereas the parson's speech was spurious finery)—this difficulty I
might didactically express as follows: what the simple religious man
does directly, the simple man of knowledge does only through humor.
The humorous point would in this case consist in the fact that upon

closer inspection I must even make an apology for doing that which the authority of the first instance commands and recommends as the highest thing. Not as though this man's religiosity were humor, but humor is the boundary from which he determines his religiosity when he has to let it appear, the boundary which discriminates between him and the immediate. It is a point of transition which already is difficult enough to reach, but the true religious liberation from the finite has again forgotten this. However, it is not my intention to lecture, lest I habituate myself or prompt others to patter.

For example, what does it mean to get married? About this I know what people generally know; I have access to the garden where the erotic authors pluck flowers for their bouquets, mine shall be as fragrant as the most of them; I know where the storehouse is whence the parsons fetch their discourses. If there is nothing else to hinder one from becoming a universal historian, well then, let us now begin. But—ah, yes, but . . . After all, what is the mean which marriage expresses between the pneumatic and the psycho-somatic? How is it that this is not a hindrance? How is it that spiritually understood it is a blessing?— for to say what the erotic is, answers in fact only one part of the question. How is it that the ethical becomes a task at the same time that the erotic expects the miracle? How is it that the perfect culmination of existence is not precisely so perfect after all, that it gives a satisfaction (apart from anxiety about the necessities of life and other such things which contribute to disturb it, and which here can be left out of the account) which suspiciously suggests that the spirit within me is darkened and does not conceive clearly the contradiction involved in the fact that an immortal spirit has become existing, suspiciously raises the question whether marital happiness is not a dubious thing, whereas an unhappy marriage is hardly to be recommended, and its suffering is by no means identical with the suffering of the spirit, which in existence is the sure sign that I exist *qua* spirit; whether the ghost of paganism does not still haunt the institution of marriage; and whether the paragraphs in theology which have to do with it, along with the reverend asseverations of the parsons (be the price of them one or one hundred dollars), are not a confused multifariousness of knowledge, which now does not notice the difficulty involved in the erotic, now does not dare to utter it, now does not notice the difficulty in the religious sphere, now does not dare to utter it? Oh, yes, when a servant-maid is married to a serving-man, and if she were to wish it, I should gladly pay the musi-

cians if I am permitted to do so, and if I have time for it, I will be glad
to dance with her on the wedding day, rejoicing in the jollity—she
presumably feels no need of a deeper understanding. That I might be
better than she because I feel this need is nonsense and is very remote
from the toilsome train of my thought. Even if I were to find what I
sought, I should perhaps not be half so good. But I feel the need of
knowing what I do, the need which in its maximum triumph is rewarded with that ludicrous little difference between the simple man's
and the wise man's knowledge of the simple thing, namely, that the
simple man knows it, and the wise man knows of it that he knows it, or
knows that he does not know it. Yes, every one who simply and honestly can say that he feels no need of such an understanding is indeed
blameless, woe to the man who disturbs him and will not leave to God
what God will require of each man severally. Yea, he who humbly
rejoices in his good fortune, being honestly and modestly of the opinion
that the race does not begin with him, and trustfully follows the
impressa vestigia of the race because of the prompting of love, "humble
before God, obedient to the royal majesty of love,"[17] not assuming to
have understood that which with contentment is his earthly good fortune, yea, that man is worthy of honor, woe to him who dares to
desire to bring down the dangers and terrors of the war of thought upon
his blessed security in the enclosure of marriage. But when one everywhere employs great words, would world-historically and systematically
lead God by the nose, when even the parson would in a trice turn outward the lining of his preaching-robe so that it might almost look like
a professor's gown, when one everywhere announces that the immediate
is abolished, then it is no offense to the Deity if one enquires of these
men of exalted wisdom what they know concerning this simple matter.
I have read what the Judge has written about marriage in *Either-Or* and
in the *Stages on Life's Way*. I have read it carefully. It has not surprised
me to learn that many who are fully informed about world-history and
the future of the human race have censured a solution which first makes
the matter as difficult as it is before it attempts an explanation. For this
I cannot blame the Judge, nor for his enthusiastic zeal in behalf of
marriage; but nevertheless I think that the Judge, supposing I could
get hold of him and whisper a little secret in his ear, will concede that
there are difficulties he did not take into account.[18]

These few examples may suffice; I have indeed no lack of examples, I
can keep on indefinitely; there is enough of this for my lifetime, so I do

not need to go on to astronomy and veterinary science. These examples are of the easier sort. The thing becomes far more difficult when one would ask about the religious in the strictest sense of the word, in which case the explanation cannot consist in infinitizing man through immanence, but in becoming aware of the paradox and holding the paradox fast every moment, fearing most of all an explanation which would take away the paradox, because the paradox is not a transitory form of the relation of the religious in its stricter sense to the existing subject, but is essentially conditioned by the fact that a man is in existence, so that the explanation which takes away the paradox fantastically transforms at the same time the exister into a fantastic something or another which belongs neither to time nor to eternity—but such a something or another is not a man. So these few examples may suffice. And what then follows? Nothing, nothing at all. It is in fact my constant affirmation that between the simple man's and the wise man's knowledge of the simple there is merely this ridiculous little difference, that the simple man knows it, the wise man knows regarding it that he knows it, or knows that he does not know it. But on the other hand there does follow from this a certain consequence, namely, the query whether it would not be best to check oneself a little in the matter of world-history when such is the situation with respect to one's knowledge of the simple. More I do not say; the men of exalted wisdom perhaps know all this well enough, they have finished perhaps once for all the task in which the very point is that it should last for a whole life. Oh, that these precious thinkers who do so much for world-history would also have in mind us common people, who are not entirely simple, inasmuch as we feel a need of understanding, but yet are so narrow-minded that we especially feel the need of understanding the simple.

Thus it is I have sought to understand myself. If the understanding I have reached is meager and the outcome slight, at any rate, to make up for that deficiency, I have resolved to act with all my passion in virtue of what I have understood. In the long run perhaps it is also a more wholesome diet to understand little but to possess this little with the endless responsibility of passion in the framework of infinity, rather than to know more and possess nothing because fantastically I have myself become a fantastic "subjective-objective" something or other. I count it unworthy that I should blush before men and their judgment more than before the Deity and His judgment, as cowardly and base to ask what shamefacedness before men might tempt me to do, rather than what shamefacedness before the Deity might prompt me to do. And what are the men I have to fear? A few geniuses perhaps, a bunch of reviewers, and the type of man one sees on the street. Or have there been no men before 1845? Or what are those men in comparison with the Deity? What refreshment do we get from all their busy bustle in comparison with the delicious quickening of that lonely wellspring which exists in every man, that wellspring in which the Deity dwells in the profound stillness where everything is silent? And what is the hour and a half I have to live with men, what but a brief instant compared with eternity? Might they perhaps pursue me in all eternities? The parson says indeed that we must meet again, but does this apply to every street acquaintance? I do not think so. Suppose there were a separation, suppose I had been in the wrong—then surely I must be excluded from their society. Suppose I had been in the right—then surely I would get into another class. Suppose eternity were so roomy that I could not catch a glimpse of his reverence who was so kind as to vouch for it that we shall meet again! But woe unto me if the Deity were to condemn me in my most inward man for the fact that I wanted mendaciously to be systematic and world-historical, and to forget what it is to be a man, and therewith forget what it means that He is the Deity. Woe unto me. Woe unto me in time, and still more dreadfully when He gets hold of me in eternity! His sentence is the last, is the only one, from His cognizance none can flee, since it is woven into and works through the slightest movement of my consciousness in its solitary communion with itself—and that I should have ventured to be ashamed of Him!

This sounds almost like seriousness. If only I dared now to appeal to visions and revelations, and to the fact that I was red in the face, many (instead of regarding this as a congestion of the blood) would regard it as seriousness. For just as at the time when Socrates lived it was the requirement of the age that one should snivel and wail before the tribunal[19] (in which case he would have been acquitted), so it is the requirement of this age that one must bawl systematically and crow world-historically. But I have no miracle I can appeal to—alas, this was the fortunate lot of Dr. Hartspring![20] According to his own singularly well-written account it was at Streit's Hotel in Hamburg, on Easter morning, that by a miracle (of which the waiters were unaware) he became an adherent of the Hegelian philosophy which assumes that there are no miracles. Marvelous sign of the times! If this man is not the long-expected philosopher, who is then? Who like him knows what the age requires? Marvelous sign of the times, more glorious and significant than the conversion of Paul. For the fact that Paul was converted by a miracle to the doctrine which proclaims itself to be a miracle is more obvious; but by a miracle to be converted to a doctrine which assumes that there is no miracle,[21] is more preposterous. The miracle occurred Easter morning. The year and the day of the month, as comports well with such a poetical hero and such a poetical Easter morning, are entirely indifferent; it may well have been the same Easter morning as that we read of in Goethe's *Faust*,[22] although the two contemporaries, Dr. Hartspring and Faust, came to a different conclusion! Who is bold enough to venture an explanation of that miracle? The whole thing remains infinitely. enigmatical, even if one were to assume that Easter of that year fell upon a very early date, i.e. the first of April, so that the doctor at the same time he became a Hegelian became an April Fool— an appropriate poetic requital for wanting to embellish the transition to the Hegelian philosophy, the value of which consists in the method, and so protests against the romantic.

No, with a miracle, or with anything infinitely significant, I cannot serve you. No, I really cannot. I must beg all men of feeling, be they near or far, town dwellers or suburbanites, to be well assured that I should be more than willing to satisfy in this way the requirement of the age, but for me the truth is the thing most precious, and in this instance the truth is as far as possible from being a miracle, and hence the narrative must not be a miraculous and marvelous narrative of an exceedingly significant event, which accordingly did not take place in that remote unknown town in the West, the Hanseatic Hamburg, where a traveller rarely arrives.

It is now about four years ago that I got the notion of wanting to try my luck as an author. I remember it quite clearly; it was on a Sunday, yes, that's it, a Sunday afternoon. I was seated as usual, out-of-doors at the café in the Frederiksberg Garden, that wonderful garden which for the child was fairyland, where the King dwelt with his Queen, that delightful garden which for the youth was his happy diversion in the joyful merriment of the people, where now for the man of riper years there is such a homely feeling of sad exaltation above the world and all that is of the world, where even the envied glory of the royal dignity has faded to what it is indeed out there, a queen's remembrance of her deceased lord.[23] There I sat as usual and smoked my cigar. Unfortunately, the only resemblance I have been able to discover between the beginning of my bit of philosophic effort and the miraculous beginning of that poetical hero is the fact that it was in a public resort. For the rest there is no resemblance whatever, and notwithstanding I am the author of the *Fragments,* I am so insignificant that I stand outside of literature, have not even contributed to increase literature on the subscription plan,[24] nor can with truth affirm that I occupy an important place in it.

I had been a student for half a score of years. Although never lazy, all my activity nevertheless was like a glittering inactivity, a kind of occupation for which I still have a great partiality, and for which perhaps I even have a little genius. I read much, spent the remainder of the day idling and thinking, or thinking and idling, but that was all it came to; the earliest sproutings of my productivity barely sufficed for my daily use and were consumed in their first greening. An inexplicable persuasive power constantly held me back, by strength as well as by artifice. This power was my indolence. It is not like the impetuous inspiration of love, nor like the strong prompting of enthusiasm, it is rather like a housekeeper who holds one back, with whom one is very well off, so well off that it never occurs to one to get married. So much at least is certain, that although I am not unacquainted with the comforts and conveniences of life, of all conveniences indolence is the most comfortable.

So there I sat and smoked my cigar until I lapsed into thought. Among other thoughts I remember these: "You are going on," I said to myself, "to become an old man, without being anything, and without really undertaking to do anything. On the other hand, wherever you look about you, in literature and in life, you see the celebrated names and figures, the precious and much heralded men who are coming into prominence and are much talked about, the many benefactors of the age who know how to benefit mankind by making life easier and easier, some by railways, others by omnibusses and steamboats, others by the telegraph, others by easily apprehended compendiums and short recitals of everything worth knowing, and finally the true benefactors of the age who make spiritual existence in virtue of thought easier and easier, yet more and more significant. And what are you doing?" Here my soliloquy was interrupted, for my cigar was smoked out and a new one had to be lit. So I smoked again, and then suddenly this thought flashed through my mind: "You must do something, but inasmuch as with your limited capacities it will be impossible to make anything easier than it has become, you must, with the same humanitarian enthusiasm as the others, undertake to make something harder." This notion pleased me immensely, and at the same time it flattered me to think that I, like the rest of them, would be loved and esteemed by the whole community. For when all combine in every way to make everything easier, there remains only one possible danger, namely, that the ease becomes so great that it becomes altogether too great; then there is only one want left, though it is not yet a felt want, when people will want difficulty. Out of love for mankind, and out of despair at my embarrassing situation, seeing that I had accomplished nothing and was unable to make anything easier than it had already been made, and moved by a genuine interest in those who make everything easy, I conceived it as my task to create difficulties everywhere. I was struck also with the strange reflection, whether it was not really my indolence I had to thank for the fact that this task became mine. For far from having found it, as Aladdin did the lamp, I must rather suppose that my indolence, by hindering me from intervening at an opportune time to make things easy, has forced upon me the only task that was left over.

So then I am striving towards the exalted goal of being hailed with acclamation—unless possibly I am derided, or maybe crucified; for it is quite certain that every man who shouts *bravo* shouts also *pereat,* if not crucify, and that even without being untrue to his character, since on the contrary he remains true to himself . . . *qua* shouter. But even though my effort be misunderstood, I am convinced nevertheless that it is just as noble as that of the others. When at a banquet, where the guests have already overeaten, one person is concerned about bringing on new courses, another about having a vomitive at hand, it is perfectly true that only the first has interpreted correctly the requirement of the guests, but I wonder whether the other might not also say that he is concerned about what their requirement might be.

From that moment I have found my entertainment in this labor. I do not mean that this labor, this labor of preparation and self-development,[25] has been my material support, for till now the achievement has consisted only in the bit of a *Fragment,* and in that I have not found material support, for I have laid out money on it. However, I cannot require that people should contribute money for having something made difficult, that in fact would be to increase the difficulty by a new difficulty, and when one takes medicine, one is accustomed rather to getting a *douceur* along with it. I am so far from failing to understand this, that if I were (as I being a *subjective* author am not) objectively convinced of the efficacy of the medicine I offer, and believed that it did not depend simply and solely upon the way in which it is used, so that the way is really the medicine, I should be the first to promise every single one of my readers a reasonable *douceur,* or to open to all of my readers collectively the prospect of taking part in a lottery of tasteful gifts, in order in this way to instill into them the strength and courage required for reading my books. If then it should happen that they who make everything easy were to perceive that they truly might profit by my bit of difficulty, lest the easiness become a dead calm; if in their profound emotion at having thus understood my effort, they should resolve to support me on the sly with financial contributions, this would be gladly accepted, and I would make an inviolable promise to keep it silent, lest humankind, from whom we unitedly derive gain and profit, should learn to know the true situation.

What is here propounded one will find quite natural on the part of a subjective author. It is more extraordinary when a systematic thinker entertains us with the report that by means of a miracle he became an adherent of the System, which seems to indicate that his systematic life and career does not share with the System the characteristic that it begins with nothing.

CHAPTER II

THE SUBJECTIVE TRUTH, INWARDNESS; TRUTH IS SUBJECTIVITY

WHETHER truth is defined more empirically, as the conformity of thought and being, or more idealistically, as the conformity of being with thought, it is, in either case, important carefully to note what is meant by being. And in formulating the answer to this question it is likewise important to take heed lest the knowing spirit be tricked into losing itself in the indeterminate, so that it fantastically becomes a something that no existing human being ever was or can be, a sort of phantom with which the individual occupies himself upon occasion, but without making it clear to himself in terms of dialectical intermediaries how he happens to get into this fantastic realm, what significance being there has for him, and whether the entire activity that goes on out there does not resolve itself into a tautology within a recklessly fantastic venture of thought.

If being, in the two indicated definitions, is understood as empirical being, truth is at once transformed into a *desideratum*, and everything must be understood in terms of becoming; for the empirical object is unfinished and the existing cognitive spirit is itself in process of becoming. Thus the truth becomes an approximation whose beginning cannot be posited absolutely, precisely because the conclusion is lacking, the effect of which is retroactive. Whenever a beginning is *made,* on the other hand, unless through being unaware of this the procedure stamps itself as arbitrary, such a beginning is not the consequence of an immanent movement of thought, but is effected through a resolution of the will, essentially in the strength of faith. That the knowing spirit is an existing individual spirit, and that every human being is such an entity existing for himself, is a truth I cannot too often repeat; for the fantastic neglect of this is responsible for much confusion. Let no one misunderstand me. I happen to be a poor existing spirit like all other men; but if there is any lawful and honest manner in which I could be helped into becoming something extraordinary, like the pure I-am-I[1] for example, I always stand ready gratefully to accept the gift and the benefaction. But if it can only be done in the manner indicated, by saying *ein zwei drei kokolorum,* or by tying a string around the little finger, and then when the moon is full, hiding it in some secret place—in that case I prefer to remain what I am, a poor existing human being.

The term "being," as used in the above definitions, must therefore be understood (from the systematic standpoint) much more abstractly, presumably as the abstract reflection of, or the abstract prototype for, what being is as concrete empirical being. When so understood there is nothing to prevent us from abstractly determining the truth as abstractly finished and complete; for the correspondence between thought and being is, from the abstract point of view, always finished. Only with the concrete does becoming enter in, and it is from the concrete that abstract thought abstracts.

But if being is understood in this manner, the formula becomes a tautology. Thought and being mean one and the same thing, and the correspondence spoken of is merely an abstract self-identity. Neither formula says anything more than that the truth is, so understood as to accentuate the copula: the truth *is*, i.e. the truth is a reduplication. Truth is the subject of the assertion, but the assertion that it is, is the same as the subject; for this being that the truth is said to have is never its own abstract form. In this manner we give expression to the fact that truth is not something simple, but is in a wholly abstract sense a reduplication, a reduplication which is nevertheless instantly revoked.

Abstract thought may continue as long as it likes to rewrite this thought in varying phraseology, it will never get any farther. As soon as the being which corresponds to the truth comes to be empirically concrete, the truth is put in process of becoming, and is again by way of anticipation the conformity of thought with being. This conformity is actually realized for God, but it is not realized for any existing spirit, who is himself existentially in process of becoming.

For an existing spirit *qua* existing spirit, the question of the truth will again exist. The abstract answer has significance only for the abstraction into which an existing spirit is transformed when he abstracts from himself *qua* existing individual. This can be done only momentarily, and even in such moments of abstraction the abstract thinker pays his debt to existence by existing in spite of all abstraction. It is therefore an existing spirit who is now conceived as raising the question of truth, presumably in order that he may exist in it; but in any case the question is raised by someone who is conscious of being a particular existing human being. In this way I believe I can render myself intelligible to every Greek, as well as to every reasonable human being. If a German philosopher wishes to indulge a passion for making himself over, and, just as alchemists and necromancers were wont to garb themselves fantastically, first makes himself over into a superrational something for the purpose of answering this question of the truth in an extremely satisfactory manner, the affair is no concern of mine; nor is his extremely satisfactory answer, which is no doubt very satisfactory indeed—when you are fantastically transformed. On the other hand, whether it is or is not the case that a German professor behaves in this manner, can be readily determined by anyone who will concentrate enthusiastically upon seeking guidance at the hands of such a sage, without criticism but seeking merely to assimilate the wisdom in a docile spirit by proposing to shape his own life in accordance with it. Precisely when thus enthusiastically attempting to learn from such a German professor, one would realize the most apt of epigrams upon him. For such a speculative philosopher could hardly be more embarrassed than by the sincere and enthusiastic zeal of a learner who proposes to express and to realize his wisdom by appropriating it existentially. For this wisdom is something that the Herr Professor has merely imagined, and written books about, but never himself tried. Aye, it has never even occurred to him that this should be done. Like the custom clerk who writes what he could not himself read, satisfied that his responsibilities ended with the writing, so there are speculative philosophers who write what, when it is to be read in the light of action, shows itself to be nonsense, unless it is, perhaps, intended only for fantastic beings.

In that the question of truth is thus raised by an existing spirit *qua* existing, the above abstract reduplication that is involved in it again confronts him. But existence itself, namely, existence as it is in the individual who raises the question and himself exists, keeps the two moments of thought and being apart, so that reflection presents him with two alternatives. For an objective reflection the truth becomes an object, something objective, and thought must be pointed away from the subject. For a subjective reflection the truth becomes a matter of appropriation, of inwardness, of subjectivity, and thought must probe more and more deeply into the subject and his subjectivity.

But then what? Shall we be compelled to remain in this disjunction, or may we not here accept the offer of benevolent assistance from the principle of mediation, so that the truth becomes an identity of subject and object?[2] Well, why not? But can the principle of mediation also help the existing individual while still remaining in existence himself to become the mediating principle, which is *sub specie aeterni,* whereas the poor existing individual is confined to the strait-jacket of existence? Surely it cannot do any good to mock a man, luring him on by dangling before his eyes the identity of subject and object, when his situation prevents him from making use of this identity, since he is in process of becoming in consequence of being an existing individual. How can it help to explain to a man how the eternal truth is to be understood eternally, when the supposed user of the explanation is prevented from so understanding it through being an existing individual, and merely becomes fantastic when he imagines himself to be *sub specie aeterni?* What such a man needs instead is precisely an explanation of how the eternal truth is to be understood in determinations of time by one who as existing is himself in time, which even the worshipful Herr Professor concedes, if not always, at least once a quarter when he draws his salary.

The identity of subject and object posited through an application of the principle of mediation merely carries us back to where we were before, to the abstract definition of the truth as an identity of thought and being; for to determine the truth as an identity of thought and object is precisely the same thing as saying that the truth *is,* i.e. that the truth is a reduplication. The lofty wisdom has thus again merely been absent-minded enough to forget that it was an existing spirit who asked about the truth. Or is the existing spirit himself the identity of subject and object, the subject-object? In that case I must press the question of where such an existing human being is, when he is thus at the same time also a subject-object? Or shall we perhaps here again first transform the existing spirit into something in general, and thereupon explain everything except the question asked, namely, how an existing subject is related to the truth *in concreto*; explain everything except the question that must in the next instance be asked, namely, how a particular existing spirit is related to this something in general, which seems to have not a little in common with a paper kite, or with the lump of sugar which the Dutch used to hang up under the loft for all to lick at.

So we return to the two ways of reflection; and we have not forgotten that it is an existing spirit who asks the question, a wholly individual human being. Nor can we forget that the fact that he exists is precisely what will make it impossible for him to proceed along both ways at once, while his earnest concern will prevent him from frivolously and fantastically becoming subject-object. Which of these two ways is now the way of truth for an existing spirit? For only the fantastic I-am-I is at once finished with both ways, or proceeds methodically along both ways simultaneously, a mode of ambulation which for an existing human is so inhuman that I dare not recommend it.

Since the inquirer stresses precisely the fact that he is an existing individual, then one of the above two ways which especially accentuates existence would seem to be especially worthy of commendation.

The way of objective reflection makes the subject accidental, and thereby transforms existence into something indifferent, something vanishing. Away from the subject the objective way of reflection leads to the objective truth, and while the subject and his subjectivity become indifferent, the truth also becomes indifferent, and this indifference is precisely its objective validity; for all interest, like all decisiveness, is rooted in subjectivity. The way of objective reflection leads to abstract thought, to mathematics, to historical knowledge of different kinds; and always it leads away from the subject, whose existence or non-existence, and from the objective point of view quite rightly, becomes infinitely indifferent. Quite rightly, since as Hamlet says,[3] existence and non-existence have only subjective significance. At its maximum this way will arrive at a contradiction, and in so far as the subject does not become wholly indifferent to himself, this merely constitutes a sign that his objective striving is not objective enough. At its maximum this way will lead to the contradiction that only the objective has come into being, while the subjective has gone out; that is to say, the existing subjectivity has vanished, in that it has made an attempt to become what in the abstract sense is called subjectivity, the mere abstract form of an abstract objectivity. And yet, the objectivity which has thus come into being is, from the subjective point of view at the most, either an hypothesis or an approximation, because all eternal decisiveness is rooted in subjectivity.

However, the objective way deems itself to have a security which the subjective way does not have (and, of course, existence and existing cannot be thought in combination with objective security); it thinks to escape a danger which threatens the subjective way, and this danger is at its maximum: madness. In a merely subjective determination of

the truth, madness and truth become in the last analysis indistinguishable, since they may both have inwardness.* Nevertheless, perhaps I
may here venture to offer a little remark, one which would seem to
be not wholly superfluous in an objective age. The absence of inwardness is also madness. The objective truth as such, is by no means adequate to determine that whoever utters it is sane; on the contrary, it
may even betray the fact that he is mad, although what he says may
be entirely true, and especially objectively true. I shall here permit
myself to tell a story, which without any sort of adaptation on my part
comes direct from an asylum. A patient in such an institution seeks
to escape, and actually succeeds in effecting his purpose by leaping out
of a window, and prepares to start on the road to freedom, when the
thought strikes him (shall I say sanely enough or madly enough?):
"When you come to town you will be recognized, and you will at
once be brought back here again; hence you need to prepare yourself
fully to convince everyone by the objective truth of what you say, that
all is in order as far as your sanity is concerned." As he walks along
and thinks about this, he sees a ball lying on the ground, picks it up,
and puts it into the tail pocket of his coat. Every step he takes the ball
strikes him, politely speaking, on his hinder parts, and every time it
thus strikes him he says: "Bang, the earth is round." He comes to the
city, and at once calls on one of his friends; he wants to convince him
that he is not crazy, and therefore walks back and forth, saying continually: "Bang, the earth is round!" But is not the earth round? Does
the asylum still crave yet another sacrifice for this opinion, as in the
time when all men believed it to be flat as a pancake? Or is a man who
hopes to prove that he is sane, by uttering a generally accepted and
generally respected objective truth, insane? And yet it was clear to
the physician that the patient was not yet cured; though it is not to be
thought that the cure would consist in getting him to accept the opinion
that the earth is flat. But all men are not physicians, and what the age
demands seems to have a considerable influence upon the question of
what madness is. Aye, one could almost be tempted sometimes to believe that the modern age, which has modernized Christianity, has also
modernized the question of Pontius Pilate, and that its urge to find

* Even this is not really true, however, for madness never has the specific inwardness of the
infinite. Its fixed idea is precisely some sort of objectivity, and the contradiction of madness
consists in embracing this with passion. The critical point in such madness is thus again not the
subjective, but the little finitude which has become a fixed idea, which is something that can
never happen to the infinite.

something in which it can rest proclaims itself in the question: What is madness? When a *Privatdocent,* every time his scholastic gown reminds him that he ought to say something, says *de omnibus dubitandum est,* and at the same time writes away at a system which offers abundant internal evidence in every other sentence that the man has never doubted anything at all: he is not regarded as mad.

Don Quixote is the prototype for a subjective madness, in which the passion of inwardness embraces a particular finite fixed idea. But the absence of inwardness gives us on the other hand the prating madness, which is quite as comical; and it might be a very desirable thing if an experimental psychologist would delineate it by taking a handful of such philosophers and bringing them together. In the type of madness which manifests itself as an aberrant inwardness, the tragic and the comic is that the something which is of such infinite concern to the unfortunate individual is a particular fixation which does not really concern anybody. In the type of madness which consists in the absence of inwardness, the comic is that though the something which the happy individual knows really is the truth, the truth which concerns all men, it does not in the slightest degree concern the much respected prater. This type of madness is more inhuman than the other. One shrinks from looking into the eyes of a madman of the former type lest one be compelled to plumb there the depths of his delirium; but one dares not look at a madman of the latter type at all, from fear of discovering that he has eyes of glass and hair made from carpet-rags; that he is, in short, an artificial product. If you meet someone who suffers from such a derangement of feeling, the derangement consisting in his not having any, you listen to what he says in a cold and awful dread, scarcely knowing whether it is a human being who speaks, or a cunningly contrived walking stick in which a talking machine has been concealed. It is always unpleasant for a proud man to find himself unwittingly drinking a toast of brotherhood with the public hangman;[4] but to find oneself engaged in rational and philosophical conversation with a walking stick is almost enough to make a man lose his mind.

The subjective reflection turns its attention inwardly to the subject, and desires in this intensification of inwardness to realize the truth. And it proceeds in such fashion that, just as in the preceding objective reflection, when the objectivity had come into being, the subjectivity had vanished, so here the subjectivity of the subject becomes the final stage, and objectivity a vanishing factor. Not for a single moment is it forgotten that the subject is an existing individual, and that existence is a process of becoming, and that therefore the notion of the truth as identity of thought and being is a chimera of abstraction, in its truth only an expectation of the creature; not because the truth is not such an identity, but because the knower is an existing individual for whom the truth cannot be such an identity as long as he lives in time. Unless we hold fast to this, speculative philosophy will immediately transport us into the fantastic realism of the I-am-I, which modern speculative thought has not hesitated to use without explaining how a particular individual is related to it; and God knows, no human being is more than such a particular individual.

If an existing individual were really able to transcend himself, the truth would be for him something final and complete; but where is the point at which he is outside himself? The I-am-I is a mathematical point which does not exist, and in so far there is nothing to prevent everyone from occupying this standpoint; the one will not be in the way of the other. It is only momentarily that the particular individual is able to realize existentially a unity of the infinite and the finite which transcends existence. This unity is realized in the moment of passion. Modern philosophy has tried anything and everything in the effort to help the individual to transcend himself objectively, which is a wholly impossible feat; existence exercises its restraining influence, and if philosophers nowadays had not become mere scribblers in the service of a fantastic thinking and its preoccupation, they would long ago have perceived that suicide was the only tolerable practical interpretation of its striving. But the scribbling modern philosophy holds passion in contempt; and yet passion is the culmination of existence for an existing individual—and we are all of us existing individuals. In passion the existing subject is rendered infinite in the eternity of the imaginative representation, and yet he is at the same time most definitely himself. The fantastic I-am-I is not an identity of the infinite and the finite, since neither the one nor the other is real; it is a fantastic rendezvous in the clouds,[5] an unfruitful embrace, and the relationship of the individual self to this mirage is never indicated.

All essential knowledge relates to existence, or only such knowledge as has an essential relationship to existence is essential knowledge. All knowledge which does not inwardly relate itself to existence, in the reflection of inwardness, is, essentially viewed, accidental knowledge;

its degree and scope is essentially indifferent. That essential knowledge is essentially related to existence does not mean the above-mentioned identity which abstract thought postulates between thought and being; nor does it signify, objectively, that knowledge corresponds to something existent as its object. But it means that knowledge has a relationship to the knower, who is essentially an existing individual, and that for this reason all essential knowledge is essentially related to existence. Only ethical and ethico-religious knowledge has an essential relationship to the existence of the knower.

Mediation is a mirage, like the I-am-I. From the abstract point of view everything is and nothing comes into being. Mediation can therefore have no place in abstract thought, because it presupposes *movement*. Objective knowledge may indeed have the existent for its object; but since the knowing subject is an existing individual, and through the fact of his existence in process of becoming, philosophy must first explain how a particular existing subject is related to a knowledge of mediation. It must explain what he is in such a moment, if not pretty nearly *distrait*; where he is, if not in the moon? There is constant talk of mediation and mediation; is mediation then a man, as Peter Deacon[6] believes that *Imprimatur* is a man? How does a human being manage to become something of this kind? Is this dignity, this great *philosophicum*, the fruit of study, or does the magistrate give it away, like the office of deacon or grave-digger? Try merely to enter into these and other such plain questions of a plain man, who would gladly become mediation if it could be done in some lawful and honest manner, and not either by saying *ein zwei drei kokolorum,* or by forgetting that he is himself an existing human being, for whom existence is therefore something essential, and an ethico-religious existence a suitable *quantum satis.* A speculative philosopher may perhaps find it in bad taste to ask such questions. But it is important not to direct the polemic to the wrong point, and hence not to begin in a fantastic objective manner to discuss *pro* and *contra* whether there is a mediation or not, but to hold fast what it means to be a human being.

In an attempt to make clear the difference of way that exists between an objective and a subjective reflection, I shall now proceed to show how a subjective reflection makes its way inwardly in inwardness. Inwardness in an existing subject culminates in passion; corresponding to passion in the subject the truth becomes a paradox; and the fact that the truth becomes a paradox is rooted precisely in its having a relationship to an existing subject. Thus the one corresponds to the other. By forgetting that one is an existing subject, passion goes by the board and the truth is no longer a paradox; the knowing subject becomes a fantastic entity rather than a human being, and the truth becomes a fantastic object for the knowledge of this fantastic entity.

*When the question of truth is raised in an objective manner, reflection is directed objectively to the truth, as an object to which the knower is related. Reflection is not focussed upon the relationship, however, but upon the question of whether it is the truth to which the knower is related. If only the object to which he is related is the truth, the subject is accounted to be in the truth. When the question of the truth is raised subjectively, reflection is directed subjectively to the nature of the individual's relationship; if only the mode of this relationship is in the truth, the individual is in the truth even if he should happen to be thus related to what is not true.** Let us take as an example the knowledge of God. Objectively, reflection is directed to the problem of whether this object is the true God; subjectively, reflection is directed to the question whether the individual is related to a something *in such a manner* that his relationship is in truth a God-relationship. On which side is the truth now to be found? Ah, may we not here resort to a mediation, and say: It is on neither side, but in the mediation of both? Excellently well said, provided we might have it explained how an existing individual manages to be in a state of mediation. For to be in a state of mediation is to be finished, while to exist is to become. Nor can an existing individual be in two places at the same time—he cannot be an identity of subject and object. When he is nearest to being in two places at the same time he is in passion; but passion is momentary, and passion is also the highest expression of subjectivity.

The existing individual who chooses to pursue the objective way enters upon the entire approximation-process by which it is proposed to bring God to light objectively. But this is in all eternity impossible, because God is a subject, and therefore exists only for subjectivity in inwardness. The existing individual who chooses the subjective way apprehends instantly the entire dialectical difficulty involved in having to use some time, perhaps a long time, in finding God objectively; and he feels this dialectical difficulty in all its painfulness, because every

---

* The reader will observe that the question here is about essential truth, or about the truth which is essentially related to existence, and that it is precisely for the sake of clarifying it as inwardness or as subjectivity that this contrast is drawn.

moment is wasted in which he does not have God.* That very instant he has God, not by virtue of any objective deliberation, but by virtue of the infinite passion of inwardness. The objective inquirer, on the other hand, is not embarrassed by such dialectical difficulties as are involved in devoting an entire period of investigation to finding God— since it is possible that the inquirer may die tomorrow; and if he lives he can scarcely regard God as something to be taken along if convenient, since God is precisely that which one takes *a tout prix,* which in the understanding of passion constitutes the true inward relationship to God.

It is at this point, so difficult dialectically, that the way swings off for everyone who knows what it means to think, and to think existentially; which is something very different from sitting at a desk and writing about what one has never done, something very different from writing *de omnibus dubitandum* and at the same time being as credulous existentially as the most sensuous of men. Here is where the way swings off, and the change is marked by the fact that while objective knowledge rambles comfortably on by way of the long road of approximation without being impelled by the urge of passion, subjective knowledge counts every delay a deadly peril, and the decision so infinitely important and so instantly pressing that it is as if the opportunity had already passed.

Now when the problem is to reckon up on which side there is most truth, whether on the side of one who seeks the true God objectively, and pursues the approximate truth of the God-idea; or on the side of one who, driven by the infinite passion of his need of God, feels an infinite concern for his own relationship to God in truth (and to be at one and the same time on both sides equally, is as we have noted not possible for an existing individual, but is merely the happy delusion of an imaginary I-am-I): the answer cannot be in doubt for anyone who has not been demoralized with the aid of science. If one who lives in the midst of Christendom goes up to the house of God, the house of the true God, with the true conception of God in his

---

* In this manner God certainly becomes a postulate, but not in the otiose manner in which this word is commonly understood. It becomes clear rather that the only way in which an existing individual comes into relation with God, is when the dialectical contradiction brings his passion to the point of despair, and helps him to embrace God with the "category of despair" (faith). Then the postulate is so far from being arbitrary that it is precisely a life-necessity. It is then not so much that God is a postulate, as that the existing individual's postulation of God is a necessity.

knowledge, and prays, but prays in a false spirit; and one who lives in an idolatrous community prays with the entire passion of the infinite, although his eyes rest upon the image of an idol: where is there most truth? The one prays in truth to God though he worships an idol; the other prays falsely to the true God, and hence worships in fact an idol.

When one man investigates objectively the problem of immortality, and another embraces an uncertainty with the passion of the infinite: where is there most truth, and who has the greater certainty? The one has entered upon a never-ending approximation, for the certainty of immortality lies precisely in the subjectivity of the individual; the other is immortal, and fights for his immortality by struggling with the uncertainty. Let us consider Socrates.[7] Nowadays everyone dabbles in a few proofs; some have several such proofs, others fewer. But Socrates! He puts the question objectively in a problematic manner: *if* there is an immortality. He must therefore be accounted a doubter in comparison with one of our modern thinkers with the three proofs? By no means. On this "if" he risks his entire life, he has the courage to meet death, and he has with the passion of the infinite so determined the pattern of his life that it must be found acceptable—*if* there is an immortality. Is any better proof capable of being given for the immortality of the soul? But those who have the three proofs do not at all determine their lives in conformity therewith; if there is an immortality it must feel disgust over their manner of life: can any better refutation be given of the three proofs? The bit of uncertainty that Socrates had, helped him because he himself contributed the passion of the infinite; the three proofs that the others have do not profit them at all, because they are dead to spirit and enthusiasm, and their three proofs, in lieu of proving anything else, prove just this. A young girl may enjoy all the sweetness of love on the basis of what is merely a weak hope that she is beloved, because she rests everything on this weak hope; but many a wedded matron more than once subjected to the strongest expressions of love, has in so far indeed had proofs, but strangely enough has not enjoyed *quod erat demonstrandum*. The Socratic ignorance, which Socrates held fast with the entire passion of his inwardness, was thus an expression for the principle that the eternal truth is related to an existing individual, and that this truth must therefore be a paradox for him as long as he exists; and yet it is possible that there was more truth in the Socratic ignorance as it was in him, than in the entire objective truth of the System, which flirts with what the times demand and accommodates itself to *Privatdocents*.

The objective accent falls on WHAT is said, the subjective accent on HOW it is said. This distinction holds even in the aesthetic realm, and receives definite expression in the principle that what is in itself true may in the mouth of such and such a person become untrue. In these times this distinction is particularly worthy of notice, for if we wish to express in a single sentence the difference between ancient times and our own, we should doubtless have to say: "In ancient times only an individual here and there knew the truth; now all know it, except that the inwardness of its appropriation stands in an inverse relationship to the extent of its dissemination.* Aesthetically the contradiction that truth becomes untruth in this or that person's mouth, is best construed comically: In the ethico-religious sphere, accent is again on the "how." But this is not to be understood as referring to demeanor, expression, or the like; rather it refers to the relationship sustained by the existing individual, in his own existence, to the content of his utterance. Objectively the interest is focussed merely on the thought-content, subjectively on the inwardness. At its maximum this inward "how" is the passion of the infinite, and the passion of the infinite is the truth. But the passion of the infinite is precisely subjectivity, and thus subjectivity becomes the truth. Objectively there is no infinite decisiveness, and hence it is objectively in order to annul the difference between good and evil, together with the principle of contradiction, and therewith also the infinite difference between the true and the false. Only in subjectivity is there decisiveness, to seek objectivity is to be in error. It is the passion of the infinite that is the decisive factor and not its content, for its content is precisely itself. In this manner subjectivity and the subjective "how" constitute the truth.

* *Stages on Life's Way*, Note on p. 426. Though ordinarily not wishing an expression of opinion on the part of reviewers, I might at this point almost desire it, provided such opinions, so far from flattering me, amounted to an assertion of the daring truth that what I say is something that everybody knows, even every child, and that the cultured know infinitely much better. If it only stands fast that everyone knows it, my standpoint is in order, and I shall doubtless make shift to manage with the unity of the comic and the tragic. If there were anyone who did not know it I might perhaps be in danger of being dislodged from my position of equilibrium by the thought that I might be in a position to communicate to someone the needful preliminary knowledge. It is just this which engages my interest so much, this that the cultured are accustomed to say: that everyone knows what the highest is. This was not the case in paganism, nor in Judaism, nor in the seventeen centuries of Christianity. Hail to the nineteenth century! Everyone knows it. What progress has been made since the time when only a few knew it. To make up for this, perhaps, we must assume that no one nowadays does it.

But the "how" which is thus subjectively accentuated precisely because the subject is an existing individual, is also subject to a dialectic with respect to time. In the passionate moment of decision, where the road swings away from objective knowledge, it seems as if the infinite decision were thereby realized. But in the same moment the existing individual finds himself in the temporal order, and the subjective "how" is transformed into a striving, a striving which receives indeed its impulse and a repeated renewal from the decisive passion of the infinite, but is nevertheless a striving.

When subjectivity is the truth, the conceptual determination of the truth must include an expression for the antithesis to objectivity, a memento of the fork in the road where the way swings off; this expression will at the same time serve as an indication of the tension of the subjective inwardness. Here is such a definition of truth: *An objective uncertainty held fast in an appropriation-process of the most passionate inwardness is the truth,* the highest truth attainable for an *existing* individual. At the point where the way swings off (and where this is cannot be specified objectively, since it is a matter of subjectivity), there objective knowledge is placed in abeyance. Thus the subject merely has, objectively, the uncertainty; but it is this which precisely increases the tension of that infinite passion which constitutes his inwardness. The truth is precisely the venture which chooses an objective uncertainty with the passion of the infinite. I contemplate the order of nature in the hope of finding God, and I see omnipotence and wisdom; but I also see much else that disturbs my mind and excites anxiety. The sum of all this is an objective uncertainty. But it is for this very reason that the inwardness becomes as intense as it is, for it embraces this objective uncertainty with the entire passion of the infinite. In the case of a mathematical proposition the objectivity is given, but for this reason the truth of such a proposition is also an indifferent truth.

But the above definition of truth is an equivalent expression for faith. Without risk there is no faith. Faith is precisely the contradiction between the infinite passion of the individual's inwardness and the objective uncertainty. If I am capable of grasping God objectively, I do not believe, but precisely because I cannot do this I must believe. If I wish to preserve myself in faith I must constantly be intent upon holding fast the objective uncertainty, so as to remain out upon the deep, over seventy thousand fathoms of water, still preserving my faith.

In the principle that subjectivity, inwardness, is the truth, there is comprehended the Socratic wisdom, whose everlasting merit it was to have become aware of the essential significance of existence, of the fact that the knower is an existing individual. For this reason Socrates was in the truth by virtue of his ignorance, in the highest sense in which this was possible within paganism. To attain to an understanding of this, to comprehend that the misfortune of speculative philosophy is again and again to have forgotten that the knower is an existing individual, is in our objective age difficult enough. "But to have made an advance upon Socrates without even having understood what, he understood, is at any rate not "Socratic." Compare the "Moral" of the *Fragments*.[8]

Let us now start from this point, and as was attempted in the *Fragments,* seek a determination of thought which will really carry us further. I have nothing here to do with the question of whether this proposed thought-determination is true or not, since I am merely experimenting; but it must at any rate be clearly manifest that the Socratic thought is understood within the new proposal, so that at least I do not come out behind Socrates.

When subjectivity, inwardness, is the truth, the truth becomes objectively a paradox; and the fact that the truth is objectively a paradox shows in its turn that subjectivity is the truth. For the objective situation is repellent; and the expression for the objective repulsion constitutes the tension and the measure of the corresponding inwardness. The paradoxical character of the truth is its objective uncertainty; this uncertainty is an expression for the passionate inwardness, and this passion is precisely the truth. So far the Socratic principle. The eternal and essential truth, the truth which has an essential relationship to an existing individual because it pertains essentially to existence (all other knowledge being from the Socratic point of view accidental, its scope and degree a matter of indifference), is a paradox. But the eternal essential truth is by no means in itself a paradox; but it becomes paradoxical by virtue of its relationship to an existing individual. The Socratic ignorance gives expression to the objective uncertainty attaching to the truth, while his inwardness in existing is the truth. To anticipate here what will be developed later, let me make the following remark. The Socratic ignorance is an analogue to the category of the absurd, only that there is still less of objective certainty in the absurd, and in the repellent effect that the absurd exercises.

It is certain only that it is absurd, and precisely on that account it incites to an infinitely greater tension in the corresponding inwardness. The Socratic inwardness in existing is an analogue to faith; only that the inwardness of faith, corresponding as it does, not to the repulsion of the Socratic ignorance, but to the repulsion exerted by the absurd, is infinitely more profound.

Socratically the eternal essential truth is by no means in its own nature paradoxical, but only in its relationship to an existing individual. This finds expression in another Socratic proposition, namely, that all knowledge is recollection. This proposition is not for Socrates a cue to the speculative enterprise, and hence he does not follow it up; essentially it becomes a Platonic principle. Here the way swings off; Socrates concentrates essentially upon accentuating existence, while Plato forgets this and loses himself in speculation. Socrates' infinite merit is to have been an *existing* thinker, not a speculative philosopher who forgets what it means to exist. For Socrates therefore the principle that all knowledge is recollection has at the moment of his leave-taking and as the constantly rejected possibility of engaging in speculation, the following two-fold significance: (1) that the knower is essentially *integer*, and that with respect to the knowledge of the eternal truth he is confronted with no other difficulty than the circumstance that he exists; which difficulty, however, is so essential and decisive for him that it means that existing, the process of transformation to inwardness in and by existing, is the truth; (2) that existence in time does not have any decisive significance, because the possibility of taking oneself back into eternity through recollection is always there, though this possibility is constantly nullified by utilizing the time, not for speculation, but for the transformation to inwardness in existing.*

* This will perhaps be the proper place to offer an explanation with respect to a difficulty in the plan of the *Fragments,* which had its ground in the fact that I did not wish at once to make the case as difficult dialectically as it is, because in our age terminologies and the like are turned so topsy-turvy that it is almost impossible to secure oneself against confusion. In order if possible clearly to exhibit the difference between the Socratic position (which was supposed to be the philosophical, the pagan-philosophical position) and the experimentally evoked thought-determination which really makes an advance beyond the Socratic, I carried the Socratic back to the principle that all knowledge is recollection.[9] This is, in a way, commonly assumed, and only one who with a specialized interest concerns himself with the Socratic, returning again and again to the sources, only for him would it be of importance on this point to distinguish between Socrates and Plato. The proposition does indeed belong to both, only that Socrates is always departing from it, in order to exist. By holding Socrates down to the proposition that all knowledge is recollection, he becomes a speculative philosopher instead of an existential thinker, for whom existence is the essential thing. The recollection-principle belongs to speculative philosophy, and recollection is immanence, and speculatively and eternally there is no paradox. But the difficulty

The infinite merit of the Socratic position was precisely to accentuate the fact that the knower is an existing individual, and that the task of existing is his essential task. Making an advance upon Socrates by failing to understand this, is quite a mediocre achievement. This Socratic principle we must therefore bear in mind, and then inquire whether the formula may not be so altered as really to make an advance beyond the Socratic position.

Subjectivity, inwardness, has been posited as the truth; can any expression for the truth be found which has a still higher degree of inwardness? Aye, there is such an expression, provided the principle that subjectivity or inwardness is the truth begins by positing the opposite principle: that subjectivity is untruth. Let us not at this point succumb to such haste as to fail in making the necessary distinctions. Speculative philosophy also says that subjectivity is untruth, but says it in order to stimulate a movement in precisely the opposite direction, namely, in the direction of the principle that objectivity is the truth. Speculative philosophy determines subjectivity negatively as tending toward objectivity. This second determination of ours, however, places a hindrance in its own way while proposing to begin, which has the effect of making the inwardness far more intensive. Socratically speaking, subjectivity is untruth if it refuses to understand that subjectivity is truth, but, for example, desires to become objective. Here, on the other hand, subjectivity in beginning upon the task of becoming the

is that no human being is speculative philosophy; the speculative philosopher himself is an existing individual, subject to the claims that existence makes upon him. There is no merit in forgetting this, but a great merit in holding it fast, and this is precisely what Socrates did. To accentuate existence, which also involves the qualification of inwardness, is the Socratic position; the Platonic tendency, on the other hand, is to pursue the lure of recollection and immanence. This puts Socrates fundamentally in advance of speculative philosophy; he does not have a fantastic beginning, in which the speculative philosopher first disguises himself, and then goes on and on to speculate, forgetting the most important thing of all, which is to exist. But precisely because Socrates is thus in advance of speculation, he presents, when properly delineated, a certain analogous resemblance to that which the experiment described as in truth going beyond the Socratic. The truth as paradox in the Socratic sense becomes analogous to the paradox *sensu eminentiori*, the passion of inwardness in existing becomes an analogue to faith *sensu eminentiori*. That the difference is none the less infinite, that the characterization which the *Fragments* made of that which in truth goes beyond the Socratic remains unchanged, it will be easy to show; but by using at once apparently the same determinations, or at any rate the same words, about these two different things, I feared to cause a misunderstanding. Now I think there can be no objection to speaking of the paradoxical and of faith in reference to Socrates, since it is quite correct to do so when properly understood. Besides, the old Greeks also used the word πίστις, though not by any means in the sense of the experiment; and they used it in such a manner that, especially with reference to a work of Aristotle[10] where the term is employed, it would be possible to set forth some very enlightening considerations bearing upon its difference from faith *sensu eminentiori*.

truth through a subjectifying process, is in the difficulty that it is already untruth. Thus, the labor of the task is thrust backward, backward, that is, in inwardness. So far is it from being the case that the way tends in the direction of objectivity, that the beginning merely lies still deeper in subjectivity.

But the subject cannot be untruth eternally, or eternally be presupposed as having been untruth; it must have been brought to this condition in time, or here become untruth in time. The Socratic paradox consisted in the fact that the eternal was related to an existing individual, but now existence has stamped itself upon the existing individual a second time. There has taken place so essential an alteration in him that he cannot now possibly take himself back into the eternal by way of recollection. To do this is to speculate; to be able to do this, but to reject the possibility by apprehending the task of life as a realization of inwardness in existing, is the Socratic position. But now the difficulty is that what followed Socrates on his way as a rejected possibility, has become an impossibility. If engaging in speculation was a dubious merit even from the point of view of the Socratic, it is now neither more nor less than confusion.

The paradox emerges when the eternal truth and existence are placed in juxtaposition with one another; each time the stamp of existence is brought to bear, the paradox becomes more clearly evident. Viewed Socratically the knower was simply an existing individual, but now the existing individual bears the stamp of having been essentially altered by existence.

Let us now call the untruth of the individual *Sin*. Viewed eternally he cannot be sin, nor can he be eternally presupposed as having been in sin. By coming into existence therefore (for the beginning was that subjectivity is untruth), he becomes a sinner. He is not born as a sinner in the sense that he is presupposed as being a sinner before he is born, but he is born in sin and as a sinner. This we might call *Original Sin*. But if existence has in this manner acquired a power over him, he is prevented from taking himself back into the eternal by way of recollection. If it was paradoxical to posit the eternal truth in relationship to an existing individual, it is now absolutely paradoxical to posit it in relationship to such an individual as we have here defined. But the more difficult it is made for him to take himself out of existence by way of recollection, the more profound is the inwardness that his existence may have in existence; and when it is made impossible for him, when he is held so fast in existence that the back door of recollection is forever closed to him, then his inwardness will be the most profound possible. But let us never forget that the Socratic merit was to stress the fact that the knower is an existing individual; for the more difficult the matter becomes, the greater the temptation to hasten along the easy road of speculation, away from fearful dangers and crucial decisions, to the winning of renown and honors and property, and so forth. If even Socrates understood the dubiety of taking himself speculatively out of existence back into the eternal, although no other difficulty confronted the existing individual except that he existed, and that existing was his essential task, now it is impossible. Forward he must, backward he cannot go.

Subjectivity is the truth. By virtue of the relationship subsisting between the eternal truth and the existing individual, the paradox came into being. Let us now go further, let us suppose that the eternal essential truth is itself a paradox. How does the paradox come into being? By putting the eternal essential truth into juxtaposition with existence. Hence when we posit such a conjunction within the truth itself, the truth becomes a paradox. The eternal truth has come into being in time: this is the paradox. If in accordance with the determinations just posited, the subject is prevented by sin from taking himself back into the eternal, now he need not trouble himself about this; for now the eternal essential truth is not behind him but in front of him, through its being in existence or having existed, so that if the individual does not existentially and in existence lay hold of the truth, he will never lay hold of it.

Existence can never be more sharply accentuated than by means of these determinations. The evasion by which speculative philosophy attempts to recollect itself out of existence has been made impossible. With reference to this, there is nothing for speculation to do except to arrive at an understanding of this impossibility; every speculative attempt which insists on being speculative shows *eo ipso* that it has not understood it. The individual may thrust all this away from him, and take refuge in speculation; but it is impossible first to accept it, and then to revoke it by means of speculation, since it is definitely calculated to prevent speculation.

When the eternal truth is related to an existing individual it becomes a paradox. The paradox repels in the inwardness of the existing individual, through the objective uncertainty and the corresponding

Socratic ignorance. But since the paradox is not in the first instance itself paradoxical (but only in its relationship to the existing individual), it does not repel with a sufficient intensive inwardness. For without risk there is no faith, and the greater the risk the greater the faith; the more objective security the less inwardness (for inwardness is precisely subjectivity), and the less objective security the more profound the possible inwardness. When the paradox is paradoxical in itself, it repels the individual by virtue of its absurdity, and the corresponding passion of inwardness is faith. But subjectivity, inwardness, is the truth; for otherwise we have forgotten what the merit of the Socratic position is. But there can be no stronger expression for inwardness than when the retreat out of existence into the eternal by way of recollection is impossible; and when, with truth confronting the individual as a paradox, gripped in the anguish and pain of sin, facing the tremendous risk of the objective insecurity, the individual believes. But without risk no faith, not even the Socratic form of faith, much less the form of which we here speak.

When Socrates believed that there was a God, he held fast to the objective uncertainty with the whole passion of his inwardness, and it is precisely in this contradiction and in this risk, that faith is rooted. Now it is otherwise. Instead of the objective uncertainty, there is here a certainty, namely, that objectively it is absurd; and this absurdity, held fast in the passion of inwardness, is faith. The Socratic ignorance is as a witty jest in comparison with the earnestness of facing the absurd; and the Socratic existential inwardness is as Greek light-mindedness in comparison with the grave strenuosity of faith.

What now is the absurd? The absurd is—that the eternal truth has come into being in time, that God has come into being, has been born, has grown up, and so forth, precisely like any other individual human being, quite indistinguishable from other individuals. For every assumption of immediate recognizability is pre-Socratic paganism, and from the Jewish point of view, idolatry; and every determination of what really makes an advance beyond the Socratic must essentially bear the stamp of having a relationship to God's having come into being; for faith *sensu strictissimo,* as was developed in the *Fragments,*[11] refers to becoming. When Socrates believed that there was a God, he saw very well that where the way swings off there is also an objective way of approximation, for example by the contemplation of nature and human history, and so forth. His merit was precisely to shun this way, where the quantitative siren song enchants the mind and deceives the existing individual.

In relation to the absurd, the objective approximation-process is like the comedy, *Misunderstanding upon Misunderstanding*,[12] which is generally played by *Privatdocents* and speculative philosophers. The absurd is precisely by its objective repulsion the measure of the intensity of faith in inwardness. Suppose a man who wishes to acquire faith; let the comedy begin. He wishes to have faith, but he wishes also to safeguard himself by means of an objective inquiry and its approximation-process. What happens? With the help of the approximation-process the absurd becomes something different; it becomes probable, it becomes increasingly probable, it becomes extremely and emphatically probable. Now he is ready to believe it, and he ventures to claim for himself that he does not believe as shoemakers and tailors and simple folk believe, but only after long deliberation. Now he is ready to believe it; and lo, now it has become precisely impossible to believe it. Anything that is almost probable, or probable, or extremely and emphatically probable, is something he can almost know, or as good as know, or extremely and emphatically almost *know*—but it is impossible to *believe*. For the absurd is the object of faith, and the only object that can be believed.

Or suppose a man who says that he has faith, but desires to make his faith clear to himself, so as to understand himself in his faith. Now the comedy again begins. The object of faith becomes almost probable, as good as probable, extremely and emphatically probable. He has completed his investigations, and he ventures to claim for himself that he does not believe as shoemakers and tailors and other simple folk believe, but that he has also understood himself in his believing. Strange understanding! On the contrary, he has in fact learned something else about faith than when he believed; and he has learned that he no longer believes, since he almost knows, or as good as knows, or extremely and emphatically almost knows.

In so far as the absurd comprehends within itself the factor of becoming, one way of approximation will be that which confuses the absurd fact of such a becoming (which is the object of faith) with a simple historical fact, and hence seeks historical certainty for that which is absurd, because it involves the contradiction that something which can become historical only in direct opposition to all human reason, has become historical. It is this contradiction which constitutes the absurd, and which can only be believed. If historical certainty with respect to it is assumed, the certainty attained is merely that the something which is thus assumed as certain is not the thing in question. A witness can testify that he has believed it, and hence that so far from being an historical certainty it is directly contrary to his own reason; but such a witness thrusts the individual away in precisely the same sense that the absurd itself does. And a witness who does not so repel is *eo ipso* a deceiver, or a man who talks about something quite different, and can help only to obtain certainty about something quite different. A hundred thousand individual witnesses, who are individual witnesses precisely on account of the peculiar character of their testimony (that they have believed the absurd), cannot *en masse* become anything else, so as to make the absurd less absurd—and why less absurd? Because a hundred thousand human beings have separately, each one for himself, believed that it was absurd? On the contrary, these hundred thousand witnesses again exercise a repellent influence in nearly the same way that the absurd itself exercises it.

But this I need not here expound in greater detail. In the *Fragments* (especially where the distinction between the disciple at first-hand and at second-hand is shown to be illusory),[13] and in the first part of this book, I have already carefully enough expounded the thesis that all approximation is useless, since on the contrary it behooves us to get rid of introductory guarantees of security, proofs from consequences, and the whole mob of public pawnbrokers and guarantors, so as to permit the absurd to stand out in all its clarity—in order that the individual may believe if he wills it; I merely say that it must be strenuous in the highest degree so to believe.

If speculative philosophy wishes to take cognizance of this, and say as always, that there is no paradox when the matter is viewed eternally, divinely, theocentrically—then I admit that I am not in a position to determine whether the speculative philosopher is right, for I am only a poor existing human being, not competent to contemplate the eternal either eternally or divinely or theocentrically, but compelled to content myself with existing. So much is certain, however, that speculative philosophy carries everything back, back past the Socratic position, which at least comprehended that for an existing individual existence is essential; to say nothing of the failure of speculative philosophy to take time to grasp what it means to be so critically situated in existence as the existing individual in the experiment.

The difference between the Socratic position as here described and the position which goes beyond it is clear enough, and essentially the same as in the *Fragments*. For nothing is altered in the latter, and the former is made only a little more difficult, though not more difficult than it is. The difficulty has also been a little increased by the fact that while in the *Fragments* I merely brought out the thought-determinations of the paradox experimentally, I have here at the same time subjoined an attempt latently to make the necessity of the paradox evident. Even if this attempt is somewhat weak, it is at any rate rather different from the speculative annulment of the paradox.

Christianity has declared itself to be the eternal essential truth which has come into being in time. It has proclaimed itself as the *Paradox*, and it has required of the individual the inwardness of faith in relation to that which stamps itself as an offense to the Jews and a folly to the Greeks—and an absurdity to the understanding. It is impossible more strongly to express the fact that subjectivity is truth, and that the objectivity is repellent, repellent even by virtue of its absurdity. And indeed it would seem very strange that Christianity should have come into the world merely to receive an explanation; as if it had been somewhat bewildered about itself, and hence entered the world to consult that wise man, the speculative philosopher, who can come to its assistance by furnishing the explanation. It is impossible to express with more intensive inwardness the principle that subjectivity is truth, than when subjectivity is in the first instance untruth, and yet subjectivity is the truth.

Suppose Christianity to be a mystery and intentionally so, a genuine and not a theatrical mystery, which is revealed in the fifth act of the drama, while a clever spectator sees through it in the course of the exposition. Suppose that a revelation *sensu strictissimo* must be a mystery, and that its sole and sufficient mark is precisely that it is a mystery; while a revelation *sensu laxiori,* the withdrawal by way of recollection into the eternal, is a revelation in the direct sense. Suppose that the degree of intellectual talent in relation to the misunderstanding was marked by the varying ability of the individual to make it seem more and more deceptively plausible that he had understood the mystery. Suppose it were after all a blessed thing, critically situated in the extreme press of existence, to sustain a relation to this mystery without understanding it, merely as a believer. Suppose Christianity never intended to be understood; suppose that, in order to express this, and to prevent anyone from misguidedly entering upon the objective way, it has declared itself to be the paradox. Suppose it wished to have significance only for existing individuals, and essentially for existing individuals in inwardness, in the inwardness of faith; which cannot be expressed more definitely than in the proposition that Christianity is the absurd, held fast in the passion of the infinite. Suppose it refuses to be understood, and that the maximum of understanding which could come in question is to understand that it cannot be understood. Suppose it therefore accentuates existence so decisively that the individual becomes a sinner, Christianity the paradox, existence the period of decision. Suppose that speculation were a temptation, the most dubious of all. Suppose that the speculative philosopher is, not indeed the prodigal son, for so the anxious divinity would characterize only the offended individual whom he nevertheless continues to love, but is the naughty child who refuses to remain where existing individuals belong, namely, in the existential training school where one becomes mature only through inwardness in existing, but instead demands a place in the divine council chamber, constantly shouting that viewed eternally, divinely, theocentrically, there is no paradox. Suppose the speculative philosopher were the restless tenant, who though it is notorious that he is merely a tenant, in view of the abstract truth that all property is from the standpoint of the eternal and the divine, in common, insists on playing the owner, so that there is nothing else to do than to send for an officer to say to him what the policemen said to Geert Westphaler:[14] "It hurts us to have to come on such an errand."

Has the thing of being human now become somewhat different from what it was in older times, are the conditions not still the same, namely, to be a particular existing being, for whom existing is essential as long as he continues in existence? But men have now so much more knowledge than formerly. Quite true, but suppose Christianity is not a matter of knowledge, so that the increased knowledge is of no avail, except to make it easier to fall into the confusion of considering Christianity as a matter of knowledge. And if men do have more knowledge, and we are not speaking about the knowledge of railroads, machines, and kaleidoscopes, but knowledge about the religious, how have they acquired it? Surely with the aid of Christianity. So this is the way men show their gratitude. They learn something from Christianity, misunderstand it, and by way of additional misunderstanding use it against Christianity. If in olden times the fearful thing was that one might be offended, now the fearful thing is that there is nothing fearful any more, that in a trice, before the individual has time to look around, he becomes a philosopher who speculates over faith. And over what faith does he speculate? Is it over the faith that he has, and especially over whether he has it or not? Ah, no, such a subject is too trifling for an objective speculative philosopher. What he speculates about is the objective faith. The objective faith, what does that mean? It means a sum of doctrinal propositions. But suppose Christianity were nothing of the kind; suppose on the contrary it were inwardness, and hence also the paradox, so as to thrust the individual away objectively, in order to obtain significance for the existing individual in the inwardness of his existence, in order to place him as decisively as no judge can place an accused person, between time and eternity in time, between heaven and hell in the time of salvation. The objective faith—it is as if Christianity also had been promulgated as a little system, if not quite so good as the Hegelian; it is as if Christ—aye, I speak without offense—it is as if Christ were a professor, and as if the Apostles had formed a little scientific society. Verily, if it was once difficult to become a Christian, now I believe it becomes increasingly difficult year by year, because it has now become so easy that the only ambition which stirs any competition is that of becoming a speculative philosopher. And yet the speculative philosopher is perhaps at the farthest possible remove from Christianity, and it is perhaps far preferable to be an offended individual who nevertheless sustains a relation to Christianity than a speculative philosopher who assumes to have understood it. In so far there is hope that there will be some resemblance left between a Christian now and in the earliest days, so that it will again be regarded as folly for anyone to entertain the notion of becoming a Christian. In the earliest days the Christian was a fool in the eyes of the world, and to Jews and pagans alike it seemed folly for anyone to seek to become one. Now we are Christians as a matter of course, but if anyone desires to be a Christian with infinite passion he is judged to be a fool, just as it is always folly to put forth an infinite passionate exertion for the sake of becoming what one already is; as if a man were to sacrifice all his wealth to buy a jewel—which he already owned. Formerly a Christian was a fool in the eyes of the world, and now that all men are Christians he nevertheless becomes a fool—in the eyes of Christians.

Suppose this were so; I only say suppose, and restrict myself to the supposition. But now that we are soon grown weary of speculative philosophers who rehearse each other in print in the systematic rigmarole, it may at any rate prove diverting to ask the question, though in another manner.

"But viewed eternally and from the divine standpoint, and especially theocentrically, there is no paradox; true speculative philosophy does not therefore remain at the standpoint of the paradox, but takes a step in advance and explains it." "May I ask to be permitted a little piece; I beseech the gentlemen not to begin again in this style, for I have already said that I cannot enter into a discussion with over-earthly and under-earthly beings." "The beginning and the end of the explanation is with me, and it is for this explanation that the eternal truth has waited. For it did indeed appear in time, but the first edition was merely an imperfect and tentative attempt. The eternal truth made its appearance in the world because it felt the need of an explanation, and hoped to find this by giving rise to a discussion. In the same way a professor makes public the outlines of a system, in the expectation that as a result of being reviewed and discussed, the book may after a longer or shorter interval be published in a new and wholly revised form. This second edition, after it has had the benefit of the advice and criticism of competent authorities, is alone the truth; and similarly it is speculative philosophy which is the true and only satisfactory edition of the preliminary truth of Christianity."

Let us now proceed to show by a few examples how speculative philosophy, precisely because it refuses to understand that subjectivity is truth, has maltreated Christianity, which is once for all the paradox, and paradoxical at every point. Speculative philosophy remains in the sphere of the immanent, where recollection takes itself out of existence, and at every point in the Christian thought-structure brings about an emasculation, simply by not thinking anything decisive in connection with the most decisive categories, which precisely by means of their decisiveness are calculated to prevent the individual from taking refuge in the immanent. It uses the decisive expressions merely as phraseology, and thus becomes a pagan reminiscence against which there is nothing to object to if it straightforwardly breaks with Christianity, but much to object to if it assumes to be Christianity.

That God has existed in human form, has been born, grown up, and so forth, is surely the paradox *sensu strictissimo,* the absolute paradox. As such it cannot relate itself to a relative difference between men. A relative paradox relates itself to the relative difference between more or less cleverness and brains; but the absolute paradox, just because it is absolute, can be relevant only to the absolute difference that distinguishes man from God, and has nothing to do with the relative wrangling between man and man with respect to the fact that one man has a little more brains than another. But the absolute difference between God and man consists precisely in this, that man is a particular existing being (which is just as much true of the most gifted human being as it is of the most stupid), whose essential task cannot be to think *sub specie aeterni,* since as long as he exists he is, though eternal, essentially an existing individual, whose essential task it is to concentrate upon inwardness in existing; while God is infinite and eternal. As soon as I make the understanding of the paradox commensurable for the difference between more or less of intellectual talent (a difference which cannot take us beyond being human, unless a man were to become so gifted that he was not merely a man but also God), my words show *eo ipso* that what I have understood is not the absolute paradox but a relative one, for in connection with the absolute paradox the only understanding possible is that it cannot be understood. "But if such is the case, speculative philosophy cannot get hold of it at all." "Quite right, this is precisely what the paradox says; it merely thrusts the understanding away in the interests of inwardness in existing." This may possibly have its ground in the circumstance that there is objectively no truth for existing beings, but only approximations; while subjectively the truth exists for them in inwardness, because the decisiveness of the truth is rooted in the subjectivity of the individual.

The modern mythical allegorizing tendency declares out and out that the whole of Christianity is a myth. This at least is open and aboveboard, and everyone can readily make up his mind about it for himself. But the friendship of speculative philosophy is of a different character. For safety's sake, speculative philosophy declares its opposition to the ungodly mythical-allegorizing tendency, and then continues: "Speculative philosophy accepts, on the contrary, the paradox, but does not stand still at this position." "Nor is there any need of standing still, for when a man persists in holding the paradox fast as a believer, more and more profoundly exploring existentially the inwardness of faith, he does not stand still." Speculative philosophy does not remain standing at the standpoint of the paradox—what does this mean? Does it mean that speculative philosophers cease to be human beings, particular existing human beings, and become *en famille* I know not what? Otherwise there is no escape from remaining at the standpoint of the paradox, which is grounded in and expresses the fact that the eternal essential truth is related to existing individuals, bringing home to them the requirement of advancing further into the inwardness of faith.

What does it mean in general to explain anything? Does it consist in showing that the obscure something in question is not this but something else? This would be a strange sort of an explanation; I thought it was the function of an explanation to render it evident that the something in question was this definite thing, so that the explanation took the obscurity away but not the object. Otherwise the explanation would not be an explanation, but something quite different, namely, a correction. An explanation of the paradox makes it clear what the paradox is, removing any obscurity remaining; a correction takes the paradox away, and makes it clear that there is no paradox. But if the paradox arises from putting the eternal and an existing particular human being into relation with one another, when the speculative explanation takes the paradox away, does the explanation also take existence away from the existing individual? And when an existing individual, with or without assistance from another, has arrived at or been brought to the point where it seems to him as nearly as possible that he does not exist, what is he then? Why, then he is absent-minded. So that the explanation of the absolute paradox which concludes that there is no paradox except to a certain degree, which means that there are only relative paradoxes, is an explanation not for existing individuals, but for absent-minded persons. Thus everything is in order. The explanation is that the paradox is the paradox only to a certain degree, and it is quite in order that such an explanation should be valid for an existing individual who is an existing individual only to a certain degree, since he forgets it every other moment. Such an existing individual is precisely a person who suffers from absent-mindedness.

When one ventures to speak of the absolute paradox, characterizing it as a stumblingblock to the Jews, foolishness to the Greeks, and an absurdity to the understanding, and in this connection addresses himself to speculative philosophy, philosophy is not so impolite as to tell him directly that he is a fool. But it offers him an explanation which contains a correction, thus indirectly giving him to understand that he is in error; so a humane and superior mind always deals with an individual of more limited intelligence. The procedure is strictly Socratic; the only thing that might be un-Socratic in this connection would be if the speaker were after all much nearer the truth than the speculative explanation, in which case the difference would be that while Socrates politely and indirectly took away an error from the learner and gave him the truth, speculative philosophy takes the truth away politely and indirectly, and presents the learner with an error. But the politeness remains as the common feature. And when Christianity itself declares that it is a paradox, the speculative explanation is not an explanation but a correction, a polite and indirect correction to be sure, as befits a superior intelligence over against a more limited understanding.

To *explain* the paradox: is that tantamount to reducing the term paradox to a *rhetorical expression,* to something which the worshipful speculative philosopher asserts to have indeed a certain validity—but then again also not to have validity? In that case it remains true after all *summa summarum* that there is no paradox. All honor to the Herr Professor! It is not to take his honor away from him that I say this, as if I, too, could revoke the paradox—by no means. But when the professor has abrogated the paradox it is of course abrogated, and so I may venture to say that it is abrogated—unless the abrogation concerned the professor more than the paradox, so that he, instead of abrogating the paradox, himself became a sort of dubious fantastic abrogation. In other cases it is assumed that explaining something means to make it clear in its significance, that it is this and not something else. To explain the paradox would then mean to understand more and more profoundly what a paradox is, and that the paradox is the paradox.

God is a highest conception, not to be explained in terms of other things, but explainable only by exploring more and more profoundly the conception itself. The highest principles for all thought can be demonstrated only indirectly (negatively). Suppose then that the paradox were the limit for an existing individual's relationship to an eternal essential truth; in that case the paradox would also not be explainable in terms of anything else, when the explanation is to be an explanation for existing individuals. But in the speculative interpretation even the absolute paradox (for speculative philosophy is not afraid to use decisive expressions, the only thing it is afraid of is thinking anything decisive in connection with them) expresses only the relative difference between more and less gifted and cultured men. In this manner the face of the world will gradually be changed. When Christianity came into the world there were no professors and *Privatdocents* at all; then it was a paradox for everyone. In the present generation it may be assumed that one out of every ten is a *Privatdocent;* hence Christianity is a paradox for nine out of ten. And when finally the fullness of time arrives, that extraordinary future when an entire generation of male and female *Privatdocents* peoples the earth, then Christianity will have ceased to be a paradox.

Whoever, on the other hand, takes it upon himself to explain the paradox, under the supposition that he knows his own mind in the matter, will precisely concentrate his energies upon making it clear that it must be a paradox. To explain an unutterable joy, for example, what does that mean? Does it mean to explain that it is this or that? In that case the predicate "unutterable" becomes merely a rhetorical predicate, a strong expression, and the like. The explaining prestidigitator has everything in readiness for the performance, and now it begins. He dupes the hearer, he calls the joy unutterable—and then comes the surprise, a truly surprising surprise: he gives it utterance! But suppose the inexpressible joy had its ground in the contradiction that an existing human being is a synthesis of the infinite and the finite situated in time, so that the joy of the eternal in him becomes inexpressible because he is an existing individual, becomes a highest breath of the spirit which is nevertheless incapable of finding embodiment, because the existing individual exists: then the explanation would be that it is unutterable, that it cannot be otherwise; no nonsense please. But when a man of profundity first condemns one or another for denying that there is an inexpressible joy, and then goes on to say: "No, I assume the existence of an inexpressible joy, but I do not stop there, I go further and express it,"—he merely turns himself into a fool, and differs from the other whom he condemns only in so far that the other is more honest and straightforward, and says what the man of profundity also says, since both say essentially the same thing.

An explanation of the decisive—does such an explanation consist in transforming this expression into a rhetorical phrase, so that while one does not emulate the frivolous in denying the decisive, one yields it acknowledgment, but only to a certain degree? What does it mean to acknowledge the decisive to a certain degree? It means that one denies the decisive. The decisive is precisely what puts an end to all this everlasting prating that attaches to a certain degree; so then the speculative philosopher assumes the existence of the decisive—but only to a certain degree. For speculative philosophy is not afraid to make use of decisive expressions; the only thing it fears is meaning anything decisive by them. And when Christianity proposes to offer itself to the existing subject as the eternal decision, and speculative philosophy thereupon explains that the decisiveness is only relative, then it is clear that philosophy does not explain Christianity but corrects it. Whether speculative philosophy may not be right is an entirely different question; here we are engaged only in inquiring how its explanation of Christianity is related to the Christianity which it purports to explain.

To explain something, does this mean to abrogate it? I am well aware that the German word *aufheben* has various and even contradictory meanings;[15] it has often enough been noted that it can mean both *tollere* and *conservare*. I do not know that the corresponding Danish word (*ophaeve*) permits of any such ambiguity, but I do know that our German-Danish philosophers use it like the German word. Whether it is a good trait in a word to admit of contrary meanings, I do not know, but anyone who desires to express himself with precision will be disposed to avoid the use of such a word in the crucial passages of his exposition. We have a simple phrase current among the people, used humoristically to indicate the impossible: "To talk with one's mouth full of hot mush." This is just about the trick that speculative philosophy contrives to perform, in thus using a word with opposite meanings. To make it perfectly clear that speculative philosophy knows nothing of any decisiveness, it employs a word as ambiguous as the one cited above, to signify the kind of explanation which constitutes speculative explanation. And if we look into it a little more closely, the confusion becomes still more evident. *Aufheben* in the sense of *tollere* means to do away with, to remove; in the sense of *conservare* it means to preserve unaltered, not to do anything at all to that which is preserved. If the government abrogates or abolishes a political organization it gets rid of it; if anyone keeps or preserves something for me, it is implied that he makes no change in it at all. Neither of these meanings is the meaning assigned to the philosophical *aufheben*. Speculative philosophy removes every difficulty, and then leaves me the difficulty of trying to determine what it really accomplishes by this so-called removal (*auf-*

heben). But suppose we let the word *aufheben* mean reduction, the status of a relative moment,[16] as is also usually said when the decisive, the paradoxical, is reduced to a relativity; this will then mean that there is no paradox and nothing decisive, for the paradox and the decisive are what they are precisely through their irreconcilable resistance to such reduction. Whether speculative philosophy is right or not is another question; here the only question raised is how the speculative explanation of Christianity is related to the Christianity which it purports to explain.

Speculative philosophy does not by any means say that Christianity is false; on the contrary, it says that speculative philosophy grasps the truth of Christianity. Surely one could not demand anything more; has Christianity ever claimed to be more than the truth? And when speculative philosophy apprehends its truth, everything is in order. And yet, no, it is not so; in relation to Christianity, systematic philosophy is merely skilled in the use of all sorts of diplomatic phraseology, which deceives the unsuspicious. Christianity as understood by the speculative philosopher is something different from Christianity as expounded for the simple. For them it is a paradox; but the speculative philosopher knows how to abrogate the paradox. So that it is not Christianity which is and was and remains the truth, and what the speculative philosopher understands is not that Christianity is the truth; no, it is the philosopher's understanding of Christianity that constitutes the truth of Christianity. The understanding is thus to be distinguished from the truth it understands; here it is not the case that only when the understanding has understood everything contained in the truth, is the truth understood. Here rather it is the case that when the potential truth has been understood as the philosopher understands it, then—aye, then it is not the case that speculative philosophy has arrived at a true understanding, but that the truth which it understands has come into being. The truth is not first given, and the understanding of it awaited afterwards, but we look for the completion of the speculative understanding as that which alone can bring the truth into being. The knowledge that speculative philosophy represents is thus different from knowledge generally, where the knowledge as such is assumed to be indifferent to the object known, so that the latter is not altered by being known, but remains the same. No, the knowledge of speculative philosophy is itself the object known, and the latter is no longer the same as it was before becoming known; it has come into being at the same time with speculative philosophy and its truth.

Whether speculative philosophy is right is another question. Here we merely inquire how its explanation of Christianity is related to the Christianity which it purports to explain. And what would this relation be, in accordance with what one might naturally expect? Speculative philosophy is objective, and objectively there is no truth for existing individuals, but only approximations; for the existing individual is precluded from becoming altogether objective by the fact that he exists. Christianity on the contrary is subjective; the inwardness of faith in the believer constitutes the truth's eternal decision. And objectively there is no truth; for an objective knowledge of the truth of Christianity, or of its truths, is precisely untruth. To know a confession of faith by rote is paganism, because Christianity is inwardness.

Let us take the paradox of the forgiveness of sins. Forgiveness is a paradox in the Socratic sense, in so far as it involves a relationship between the eternal truth and an existing individual; it is a paradox *sensu strictiori,* because the existing individual is stamped as a sinner, by which existence is accentuated a second time, and because it purports to be an eternal decision in time with retroactive power to annul the past, and because it is linked with the existence of God in time. The individual existing human being must feel himself a sinner; not objectively, which is nonsense, but subjectively, which is the most profound suffering. With all the strength of his mind, to the last thought (and if one human being has a little more intelligence than another it makes no essential difference; to appeal to the greatness of one's intelligence is to betray the defectiveness of one's inwardness, for otherwise the understanding will doubtless be tested beyond its strength), he must try to understand the forgiveness of sins, and then despair of the understanding. With the understanding directly opposed to it, the inwardness of faith must lay hold of the paradox; and precisely this struggle on the part of faith, fighting as the Romans once fought, dazzled by the fierce light of the sun,[17] constitutes the tension of its inwardness.* If

* That it is possible to fight thus, dazzled by the sun, and yet see to fight, the Romans demonstrated at Zama; that it is possible to fight thus dazzled, and yet see to conquer, the Romans demonstrated at Zama. And now the warfare of faith! Is this struggle perhaps a foolish little trick, a mock combat of gallantry, this strife that is more persistent than a thirty years' war, because the task is not merely to acquire but still more hotly to preserve, where every day the heat is as burning as the one day of the battle of Zama! While the understanding despairs, faith presses on to victory in the passion of its inwardness. But when the believer uses all his understanding, every last desperate resource of thought, merely to discover the difficulty that the paradox pre-

ever any other sort of understanding threatens to come to power within him, the believer perceives that he is in the way of losing his faith; just as a young woman, when she discovers after the wedding that it is easy to understand how she became her husband's choice, ought to be able to understand that this is because she no longer loves.

But the speculative philosopher takes up the matter differently. He makes his appearance before a distinguished public and says: "Ladies and gentlemen, for so I must address you; before a community of believers the paradox may be proclaimed only by a believer, but before a distinguished public the truth may be expounded by a speculative philosopher. The forgiveness of sins," he goes on to say, "is a paradox (general tension in the audience); the pantheistic tendency is an error which speculative philosophy refutes. But speculative philosophy does not remain at the standpoint of the paradox, it explains it and abrogates it." It appears from this that the very honorable speculative philosopher did not make use of all his understanding in the effort to understand, at the same time when he despaired of the understanding; his despair was despair only to a certain degree, a feigned movement; he retained a part of his understanding—for the explanation. This is certainly to make a profit out of one's understanding. The believer has absolutely no profit from his, he loses it all in his despair; but the speculative philosopher knows how to stretch his out to make it suffice. He makes use of half of it with which to despair (as if it were not nonsense to despair by half), and uses the other half to achieve the insight that there was no reason for the understanding to despair. Aye, that makes it all quite different, and where is the error? Why, naturally in the fact that the first movement was illusory, and hence not so much in his failure to remain at the standpoint of faith, as rather in his having reached this standpoint. Suppose the paradox of forgiveness of sins

sents, then there is indeed no part of his understanding left with which to explain the paradox—but for all that, there may still be a rich faith-content in the passion of his inwardness. Sitting quietly in a ship while the weather is calm is not a picture of faith; but when the ship has sprung a leak, enthusiastically to keep the ship afloat by pumping while yet not seeking the harbor: this is the picture. And if the picture involves an impossibility in the long run, that is but the imperfection of the picture; faith persists. While the understanding, like a despairing passenger, stretches out its arms toward the shore, but in vain, faith works with all its energy in the depths of the soul: glad and victorious it saves the soul against the understanding. Has anyone done this, is there anyone who is engaged in doing it? What business is that of mine, provided this is what it means to believe. And though I am still far from having fully understood the difficulty of Christianity (and an explanation which renders the difficulty easy must be regarded as an evil temptation), I can none the less understand that the struggle of faith is not a subject for vaudeville poets, and that its strenuosity is not a diversion for *Privatdocents*.

had its ground in the circumstances that the poor existing human individual is in existence, that he is half God-forsaken even when he strives victoriously against the understanding in the inwardness of faith; suppose that only eternity can give an eternal certainty, while existence must rest content with a militant certainty, a certainty not achieved by the struggle becoming weaker, and in fact illusory, but only by its becoming stronger. In that case the explanation is that it is and remains a paradox; and only when it becomes understood that there is no paradox, or that the paradox is only paradoxical to a certain degree, only then is all lost. "But," says perhaps a respectable public, "if this is what the forgiveness of sins is, how then can anyone believe it?" The answer is: "If this is not what the forgiveness of sins is, how could it be *believed*?"

Whether Christianity is right is another question; here .we merely ask how the explanation of speculative philosophy is related to the Christianity which it explains. But if Christianity is possibly wrong, so much at least is certain: that speculative philosophy is definitely and decidedly wrong. For the only consistent position outside Christianity is that of pantheism, the taking of oneself out of existence by way of recollection into the eternal, whereby all existential decisions become a mere shadow-play beside what is eternally decided from behind. The fictitious decisiveness of speculative philosophy is, like all *fictitious* decisiveness, a piece of nonsense; for decisiveness is precisely the eternal protest against all fictions. The pantheist is eternally set at rest from behind; the moment of existence, the seventy years, is a vanishing entity. The speculative philosopher, however, desires to be an existing individual; but he wants to be an existing individual who is not subjective, who is not in passion, aye, who exists *sub specie aeterni*; in short, he is absent-minded. But what is explained in absent-mindedness is not absolutely to be depended on—such an explanation, and at this point I am at one with speculative philosophy, such an explanation is only to a certain degree.

If the speculative philosopher explains the paradox so as to remove it, and now in his knowledge knows that it is removed, that the paradox is not the essential relationship that the eternal essential truth bears to an existing individual in the extremity of his existence, but only an accidental relative-relationship to those of limited intelligence: in that case there is established an essential difference between the speculative philosopher and the plain man, which confounds existence from the foundations. God is affronted by getting a group of hangers-on, an intermediary staff of clever brains; and humanity is affronted because the relationship to God is not identical for all men. The godly formula set up above for the difference between the plain man's knowledge of the simple, and the simple wise man's knowledge of the same, that the difference consists in the insignificant trifle that the wise man knows that he knows, or knows that he does not know, what the plain man knows—this formula is by no means respected by speculative philosophy, nor does it respect the likeness involved in this distinction between the plain man and the wise man, namely, that both know the same thing. For the speculative philosopher and the plain man do not by any means know the same thing, when the plain man believes the paradox, and the speculative philosopher knows it to be abrogated. According to the above-mentioned formula, however, which honors God and loves men, the difference is that the wise man also knows that it must be a paradox, this paradox that he himself believes. Hence they both know essentially the same thing; the wise man does not know everything else about the paradox, but knows that he knows this about the paradox. The simple wise man will thus seek to apprehend the paradox more and more profoundly as a paradox, and will not engage in the business of explaining the paradox by understanding that there is none.

Thus when a simple wise man talks with a simple man about the forgiveness of sins, the simple man will doubtless say: "But I cannot understand the divine mercy which is able to forgive sins; the more vividly I believe it, the less am I able to understand it." (So it does not seem to be the case that the probability increases as faith is intensified in inwardness; rather the reverse.) But the simple wise man will say: "Such is also my experience; you know that I have had the opportunity to devote much time to investigation and reflection, and yet the sum total of all my researches amounts at most to this, that I understand that it cannot be otherwise, that it must be impossible to understand. This distinction can scarcely grieve you, or make you think sadly of your own toilsome life, and your perhaps humbler talents, as if I had any advantage over you. My advantage is something both to laugh at and to weep over, considered as the fruit of a period of study. And yet, you must not hold this study in contempt, just as I do not myself regret it; on the contrary, it pleases me most of all when I smile at it, and then again enthusiastically take hold of the strenuous labor of thought."

Such an admission is in all sincerity, and is not present merely once in a while, but essentially present in the wise man every time he engages in the task of thought. Once a year to consider that one ought always to give thanks to God, is scarcely a right understanding of the words; so also once in a while, on an extraordinary occasion, to be moved to reflect that before God all men are essentially equal, is not in truth to understand this equality, especially if one's daily work and striving tends in more than one way to bring it into forgetfulness. But precisely when most strongly entrenched in one's difference, then strongly to apprehend the equality, that is the simple wise man's noble piety.

There has been said much that is strange, much that is deplorable, much that is revolting about Christianity; but the most stupid thing ever said about it is, that it is to a certain degree true. There has been said much that is strange, much that is deplorable, much that is revolting about enthusiasm; but the most stupid thing ever said about it is, that it is to a certain degree. There has been said much that is strange, much that is deplorable, much that is revolting about love, but the most stupid thing ever said about it is, that it is to a certain degree. And when a man has prostituted himself by speaking in this manner about enthusiasm and love, he has betrayed his stupidity, which in this case is not in the direction of intelligence, however, since it has its ground rather in the fact that the understanding has become too large, in the same sense as when a disease of the liver is caused by an enlargement of the liver, and hence, as another author has remarked,[18] "is the flatness that salt takes on when it loses its savor": then there is still one phenomenon left, Christianity. If the sight of enthusiasm has not sufficed to help him break with the understanding, if love has not been able to emancipate him from his slavery: then let him consider Christianity. Let him be offended, he is still human; let him despair of ever himself becoming a Christian, he is yet perhaps nearer than he believes; let him fight to the last drop of blood for the extermination of Christianity, he is still human—but if he is able here to say: it is true to a certain degree, then he is stupid.

Perhaps someone will think that I tremble to say this, that I must be prepared for a terrible castigation at the hands of speculative philosophy. By no means. The speculative philosopher will here again be quite consistent with himself, and say: "There is a certain degree of truth in what the man says, only we cannot stop there, but must advance beyond it." It would also be strange if my insignificance should succeed where even Christianity had failed, namely, in bringing the speculative philosopher to the point of passion; if so, then my little fragment of philosophy would suddenly take on a significance I had least of all dreamed of.

But whoever is neither cold nor hot is nauseating; and just as the hunter is ill-served by a weapon that misses fire at the crucial moment, so God is ill-served by misfiring individuals. Had not Pilate asked objectively what truth is, he would never have condemned Christ to be crucified. Had he asked subjectively, the passion of his inwardness respecting what in the decision facing him he had *in truth to do,* would have prevented him from doing wrong. It would then not have been merely his wife who was made anxious by the dreadful dream, but Pilate himself would have become sleepless. But when a man has something so infinitely great before his eyes as the objective truth, he can afford to set at naught his little bit of subjectivity, and what he as subject has to do. And the approximation-process of the objective truth is figuratively expressed in washing the hands, for objectively there is no decision, and the subjective decision shows that one was in error nevertheless, through not understanding that the decision inheres precisely in subjectivity.

Suppose, on the other hand, that subjectivity is the truth, and that subjectivity is an existing subjectivity, then, if I may so express myself, Christianity fits perfectly into the picture. Subjectivity culminates in passion, Christianity is the paradox, paradox and passion are a mutual fit, and the paradox is altogether suited to one whose situation is, to be in the extremity of existence. Aye, never in all the world could there be found two lovers so wholly suited to one another as paradox and passion, and the strife between them is like the strife between lovers, when the dispute is about whether he first aroused her passion, or she his. And so it is here; the existing individual has by means of the paradox itself come to be placed in the extremity of existence. And what can be more splendid for lovers than that they are permitted a long time together without any alteration in the relationship between them, except that it becomes more intensive in inwardness? And this is indeed granted to the highly unspeculative understanding between passion and the paradox, since the whole of life in time is vouchsafed, and the change comes first in eternity.

But the speculative philosopher is of another kidney, he believes only to a certain degree; he sets his hand to the plow, and looks about him to find something to know. From the Christian point of view it can scarcely be said that it is anything good he finds to know. Even if it were not the case, as a simple wise man who seeks to apprehend the paradox would strive to show, that it cannot be otherwise; even if the paradox held a little remnant of divine arbitrariness within it, God might seem justified in laying some stress upon His person, scarcely needing to lower the price of the God-relationship on account of the dullness prevailing in the religious market (and this expression seems even more suitable here than in connection with the stock-market). And even if God could be imagined willing, no man with passion in his heart could desire it. To a maiden genuinely in love it could never occur that she bought her happiness too dear, but rather that she had not bought it dear enough. And just as the passion of the infinite was itself the truth, so in the case of the highest value it holds true that the price is the value, that a low price means a poor value; while even the highest possible price in relation to God has in it no meritoriousness, since the highest price is to be willing to do everything and still to know that this is nothing (for if it is something, the price is lower), and nevertheless to will it. Since I am not wholly unacquainted with what has been said and written about Christianity, I might also say one or two things. But here I do not choose to do so; I merely repeat that there is one thing I shall take care not to say about it: that it is to a certain degree true. It is just possible that Christianity is the truth; it is possible that there will sometime come a judgment, where the separation will turn on the relationship of inwardness to Christianity. Suppose then there came a man who had to say: "I have not indeed believed, but so much have I honored Christianity that I have employed every hour of my life in pondering it." Or suppose there came one of whom the accuser had to say: "He has persecuted the Christians," and the accused replied: "Aye, I admit it; Christianity has set my soul aflame, and I have had no other ambition than to root it from the earth, precisely because I perceived its tremendous power." Or suppose there came another, of whom the accuser would have to say: "He has abjured Christianity," and the accused replied: "Aye, it is true; for I saw that Christianity was such a power that if I gave it a little finger it would take the whole man, and I felt that I could not belong to it wholly." But then suppose there finally came a dapper *Privatdocent* with light and nimble steps, who spoke as follows: "I am not like these three; I have not only be- lieved, but I have even explained Christianity, and shown that as it was expounded by the Apostles and appropriated in the early centuries it was only to a certain degree true; but that now, through the interpretation of speculative philosophy it has become the true truth, whence I must ask for a suitable reward on account of my services to Christianity." Which of these four must be regarded as in the most terrible position? It is just possible that Christianity is the truth; suppose that now when its ungrateful children desire to have it declared incompetent, and placed under the guardianship of speculative philosophy, like the Greek poet[19] whose children also demanded that the aged parent be placed under a guardian, but who astonished the judges and the people by writing one of his most beautiful tragedies as a sign that he was still in the full possession of his faculties—suppose that Christianity thus arose with renewed vigor: there would be no one else whose position would become as embarrassing as the position of the *Privat-docents*.

I do not deny that it is a lordly thing to stand so high above Christianity. I do not deny that it is comfortable to be a Christian, and at the same time be exempted from the martyrdom which is always present, even if no persecution menaces from without, even if the Christian is as unnoticed in life as if he had not lived, and is spared the martyrdom of believing against the understanding, the peril of lying upon the deep, the seventy thousand fathoms, in order there to find God. The wader feels his way with his foot, lest he get beyond his depth; and so the shrewd and prudent man feels his way with the understanding in the realm of the probable, and finds God where the probabilities are favorable, and gives thanks on the great holidays of probability, when he has acquired a good livelihood, and there is probability besides for an early advancement; when he has got himself a pretty and attractive wife, and even Councillor Marcussen says that it will be a happy marriage, and that the young woman is of the type of beauty that will in all probability last a long time, and that her physique is such that she will in all probability give birth to strong and healthy children. To believe against the understanding is something different, and to believe with the understanding cannot be done at all; for he who believes with the understanding speaks only of livelihood and wife and fields and oxen and the like, which things are not the object of faith. Faith *always* gives thanks, is *always* in peril of life, in this collision of finite and infinite which is precisely a mortal danger for him who is a composite of both. The probable is therefore so little to the taste of a believer that he fears it most of all, since he well knows that when he clings to probabilities it is because he is beginning to lose his faith.

Faith has in fact two tasks: to take care in every moment to discover the improbable, the paradox; and then to hold it fast with the passion of inwardness. The common conception is that the improbable, the paradoxical, is something to which faith is related only passively; it must provisionally be content with this relationship, but little by little things will become better, as indeed seems probable. O miraculous creation of confusions in speaking about faith! One is to begin believing, in reliance upon the probability that things will soon become better. In this way probability is after all smuggled in, and one is prevented from believing; so that it is easy to understand that the fruit of having been for a long time a believer is, that one no longer believes, instead of, as one might think, that the fruit is a more intensive inwardness in faith. No, faith is self-active in its relation to the improbable and the paradoxical, self-active in the discovery, and self-active in every moment holding it fast—in order to believe. Merely to lay hold of the improbable requires all the passion of the infinite and its concentration in itself; for the improbable and the paradoxical are not to be reached by the understanding's quantitative calculation of the more and more difficult. Where the understanding despairs, faith is already present in order to make the despair properly decisive, in order that the movement of faith may not become a mere exchange within the bargaining sphere of the understanding. But to believe against the understanding is martyrdom; to begin to get the understanding a little in one's favor, is temptation and retrogression. This martyrdom is something that the speculative philosopher is free from. That he must pursue his studies, and especially that he must read many modern books, I admit is burdensome; but the martyrdom of faith is not the same thing. What I therefore fear and shrink from, more than I fear to die and to lose my sweetheart, is to say about Christianity that it is to a certain degree true. If I lived to be seventy years old, if I shortened the night's sleep and increased the day's work from year to year, inquiring into Christianity—how insignificant such a little period of study, viewed as entitling me to judge in so lofty a fashion about Christianity! For to be so embittered against Christianity after a casual acquaintance with it, that I declared it to be false: that would be far more pardonable, far more human. But this lordly superiority seems to me the true corruption, making every saving relationship impossible—and it may possibly be the case, that Christianity is the truth.

This sounds almost as if I were in earnest. If I now dared loudly to proclaim that I had come into the world for the purpose of opposing speculative philosophy, and had received a call to that effect; that this was my mission of judgment, while my prophetic mission was to divine the coming of a matchless future, for which reason men might safely rely on what I said because I had a loud voice and had received a call—then doubtless there would be many who, in lieu of considering the whole to be a fantastic reminiscence in the head of a fool, would regard it as earnest. But I can say nothing of this kind about myself. The resolve with which I began must rather be regarded as a notion that occurred to me; and in any case, it is so far from being true that any call came to me, that contrariwise the call, which, if I may so speak, I followed, did not issue to me but to another; and in relation to him was very far from being something that could in the strictest sense be described as a call. But even if a call did issue to him, I am without a call when I follow it.

The story is quite a simple one. It was about five years ago, on a Sunday—aye, now perhaps the reader will be disposed not to believe me, because it was again on a Sunday, but it is none the less quite certain that it was a Sunday, about two months after the one previously mentioned. It was late in the day, evening was approaching. And the evening's farewell to the day, and to him who has lived the day, is a speech of mysterious meanings. Its reminder is like the watchful mother's admonition to her child, to come home betimes; but its invitation, even if the farewell is without guilt in being so misunderstood, is an inexplicable beckoning, as if rest could be found only by remaining for the tryst of the night, not with a woman, but femininely with the infinite; persuaded by the night wind, when it monotonously repeats itself, when it breathes through forest and dale, sighing as if it sought for something; persuaded by the distant echo in one's own soul of the night's stillness, as if it had a premonition of something to come; persuaded by the lofty calm of the heavens above, as if this something had been found; persuaded by the audible soundlessness of the dew, as if this were the explanation and the refreshment of the infinite, like the half-understood fruitfulness of the quiet night, like the semi-transparency of the night mist.

Contrary to my usual custom I had come into the garden which is called the garden of the dead, where again the visitor's farewell is rendered doubly difficult, since it is meaningless to say: yet once more, when the last time is already past, and since there is no reason for ceasing to say farewell, when the beginning is made after the last time is past. Most of the visitors had already gone home, only an individual here and there vanished among the trees; not glad to meet anyone, he avoided the contact, seeking the dead and not the living. And always in this garden there prevails a beautiful understanding among the visitors, that one does not come here to see and to be seen, but each visitor avoids the other. Nor does one need company, least of all a gossipy friend, here where all is eloquence, where the dead man calls out the brief word engraved upon his tombstone. He does not expound and expand like a clergyman, but is like a silent man who says only this one word, but says it with a passion as if to burst the tomb—or is it not strange to have inscribed upon his tombstone: "We shall meet again"; and then to remain in the grave? And yet what inwardness in the word precisely because of the contradiction; for if one who may come again tomorrow says, "We shall meet again," this is not particularly moving. To have everything against you, not to have a single direct expression for your inwardness, and yet to stand by your words: that is true inwardness. For inwardness is false precisely in the degree that the outward expression in mien and visage, in words and assurances, is at once ready to hand; not precisely because the expression itself is untrue, but the falsity consists in the fact that the inwardness is merely a phase. The dead man is silent while time goes by; on the renowned warrior's grave they have laid his sword, and insolence has torn the paling about it to pieces, but the warrior does not rise to seize his sword to defend himself and his resting-place; he does not gesticulate, he gives no assurances, he does not flare up in momentary inwardness; but silent as the tomb, and still as death, he stands by his word. All honor to the living who outwardly conduct themselves as a dead man in relation to his inwardness, and precisely thereby preserve it. Such inwardness is not as a moment's excitement, or as a woman's beguilement, but as the eternal which has been won through death. Such an one is a man; for that a woman bubbles over in momentary inwardness is not unbeautiful, nor is it unbeautiful that she soon forgets it again; the one corresponds to the other, and both to the feminine and to that which in daily life is usually understood by inwardness.

Weary from walking I sat down on a bench, a wondering witness to how that proud ruler, the sun, now for thousands of years the hero of the day, and destined to remain such until the final day, how the sun in its flaming departure cast a glorifying radiance over the entire landscape; over the top of the wall which surrounds the yard, my eyes looked into that eternal symbol of eternity: the infinite horizon. What sleep is for the body, such rest is for the soul, an opportunity to breathe in peace. Suddenly I discovered to my astonishment that the trees which concealed me from the eyes of others, had concealed others from mine; for I heard a voice almost at my side. It has always wounded my sensibilities to witness another person's expression of feeling, as he gives himself up to it only when he believes himself unobserved; for there is an emotional inwardness which is properly hidden, and revealed only to God, just as a woman's beauty desires to be concealed from all, and revealed only to the beloved: hence I resolved to remove myself. But the first words I heard gripped me strongly; and since I feared that the noise of my departure might be more embarrassing than if I remained sitting, I chose the latter course, and thus remained a witness to a situation which however solemn, suffered no violation by my presence.

Through the leaves I saw that there were two: an elderly man with snow-white hair, and a child, a boy of about ten. They were both dressed in mourning, and sat before a freshly dug grave, from which it was natural to conclude that it was a recent loss in which they were engrossed. The aged man's venerable figure was clothed in increased solemnity by the glory of the setting sun; and his voice, calm and yet thrilled with feeling, enunciated each word clearly, reflecting the inwardness that possessed the speaker, who now and then ceased speaking when his voice choked with tears, or his mood ended in a sigh. For feeling is like the river Niger in Africa: its source is not known, nor its outlet, but only its course. From the conversation I learned that the little boy was the old man's grandson, and he whose grave was being visited, the boy's father. In all probability the rest of the family must already have been removed by death, since no other name was mentioned, a circumstance which I also verified upon a later visit, when I read upon the tablet the name, and the names of the many dead.

The old man talked with the child about his no longer having a father, of his having no one to cling to except an old man who was too old for him, and who himself longed to leave the world; but that there was a God in heaven, from whom all fatherhood in heaven and on the earth is named, and that there was one name in which alone there was salvation, the name of the Lord Jesus Christ. He ceased speaking for a moment, and then said half aloud to himself: "That this solace should have become my fear, that he, my son, now buried there in the grave, should have relinquished it. To what end then all my hope, my care, to what end his wisdom, when as now his death in the midst of his error must make a believer's soul uncertain of his salvation, must bring my gray hairs in sorrow to the grave, must cause a believer to leave the world in anxiety, an old man to hasten like a doubter after a certainty, and to look despondently about him upon those he leaves behind!"

Then he again addressed himself to the boy. He told him that there was a wisdom which tried to fly beyond faith, that on the other side of faith there was a wide stretch of country like the blue mountains, an illusory land, which to a mortal eye might appear to yield a certainty higher than that of faith; but the believer feared this mirage, as the sailor fears a similar appearance on the sea; that it was an illusion of eternity in which a mortal cannot live, but only lose his faith when he permits his gaze to be fascinated by the sight. He fell silent, and then once more spoke half aloud to himself: "Alas, that my unhappy son should have permitted himself to be deceived! To what end all his learning, which made it impossible for him to explain himself to me, so that I could not even speak to him about his error, because it was too high for me!" Then he arose and brought the child over to the grave, and said with a voice whose impressiveness I shall never forget: "Poor boy, you are only a child, and yet you will soon be alone in the world! Do you promise me by the memory of your dead father, who, if he could speak to you now, would speak thus, and speaks to you with my voice; do you promise me by the sight of my old age and my gray hairs; do you promise me by the solemnity of this sacred ground, by the God whose name you have learned to call upon, by the name of Jesus Christ, in whom alone there is salvation; do you promise me that you will hold fast to this faith in life and in death, that you will not permit yourself to be deceived by any illusion, however the face of the world changes—do you promise this?" Overwhelmed by the impression, the little one threw himself down upon his knees, but the old man lifted him up and pressed him to his heart.

I must in deference to the truth admit that this was the most moving scene I had ever witnessed. What may perhaps for a moment dispose one or another reader to assume that the whole story is fictitious, namely, that an old man should talk thus to a child, was precisely what moved me most of all: the unhappy old man who had been left alone in the world with a child; who had no one to talk with about his anxiety except the child; who had but one to save, the child, not able to pre-suppose sufficient maturity on the child's part to understand him, and yet not daring to wait for the coming of maturity because he himself is an old man. It is beautiful to be old, beautiful to see the new genera-tion grow up about one, a happy reckoning, to add the sum each time the number is increased; but if it comes to reckon in reverse, to subtract instead of to add, each time death takes its toll—until the end is come, and only an old man is left to strike the balance: what then is so heavy as to be old! Just as need can force a man to extreme measures, so it seemed to me that the old man's sufferings found their strongest ex-pression in what poetically must be called an improbability: that an old man has in a child his only confidant, and that a sacred promise, an oath, is demanded of a child.

Although merely a spectator and witness, I was myself deeply moved. At one moment it seemed to me that I was myself the young man whom his father had buried in so great fear; the next, it seemed to me that I was the child, bound by the sacred promise. However, I felt no impulse to rush forward, to express to the old man my sympathy, assuring him with tears and trembling voice that I should never forget the scene, or even begging him to pledge me in an oath. For only over-precipitate people, clouds without water and storm-driven mists, are quick to take an oath; because the fact is that they are unable to keep it, and there-fore must perpetually be taking it. I, for my part, am of the opinion that "never to forget this impression," is something quite different from saying once in a solemn moment: "I will never forget it." The first is inwardness, the second is perhaps only a momentary inwardness. And if one never does forget it, it does not seem that the solemnity with which it was said is so particularly important, since the continuing solemnity with which one, day by day, prevents the forgetfulness, is the truer solemnity. The womanish is always dangerous. A tender pressure of the hand, a passionate embrace, a tear in the eye: these things are not quite the same as the silent consecration of a resolve. The inwardness of the spirit is, after all, always a stranger and a foreigner in the body: why, then, gesticulations? Shakespeare makes Brutus say so truly, when the conspirators bind themselves by an oath to their enterprise:[20]

"No, not an oath: . . .
   Swear priests, and cowards, and men cautelous,
   Old feeble carrions, and such suffering souls
   That welcome wrongs; . . . but do not stain
   The even virtue of our enterprise,
   Nor the insuppressive mettle of our spirits,
   To think that, or our cause, or our performance
   Did need an oath."

The momentary outpouring of inwardness most often leaves behind a
lassitude which is dangerous. And besides, a very simple observation has
in still another way taught me caution in connection with the making
of oaths or promises, so that the true inwardness is even compelled to
express itself contrariwise. Flighty and easily excitable souls are more
prone to nothing than to the taking of a sacred promise, because the
inner weakness needs the strong stimulus of the moment. To administer
a sacred pledge to such a person is a very dubious thing, and it is far
better to prevent the solemn episode from taking place, while still binding oneself by a little *reservatio mentalis,* providing the giving of the
pledge seems at all or moderately justified. This is to the other's advantage, prevents a profanation of the holy, and frees him from being
bound by an oath that he would eventually break. Thus if Brutus, in
view of the fact that the conspirators, with a possible exception or two,
were flighty fellows, and hence precipitate to take oaths and to give
and require sacred pledges, had thrust them away from him, had for
this reason prohibited the taking of a pledge; while in view of the fact
that he considered the cause just, and also thought it just that they
should turn to him for assistance, if he had in all quietness dedicated
himself—in that case it seems to me that his inwardness would have
been greater. Now he is somewhat declamatory, and though there is
truth in what he says, there is a strain of falsity in his saying it to the
conspirators, without being quite clear in his own mind to what sort
of men he is speaking.

   And so I, too, went home. Fundamentally I had understood the old
gentleman at once, for my studies had in many ways led me to take
note of a dubious relationship between a modern Christian speculation
and Christianity, but the matter had not in any decisive manner enlisted
my interest. Now it was invested with its own proper significance. The
venerable old man with his faith seemed to be an individual with an

absolutely justified grievance, a man whom existence had mistreated, because a modern speculation, like a change in the currency, had made property values in the realm of faith insecure. His sorrow over the loss of his son, not only by death, but as he understood it, still more terribly through speculative philosophy, moved me profoundly; while the contradiction in his position, that he could not even explain how the enemy had conducted the campaign, became for me a decisive challenge to trace out a definite clue. The entire matter appealed to me as a very complicated criminal case, where the crisscrossing of many trails made it difficult to find the truth. This was something for me. And I thought to myself: "You are now tired of life's diversions, you are tired of the maidens, whom you love only in passing; you must have something fully to occupy your time. Here it is: to discover where the misunderstanding lies between speculative philosophy and Christianity." This therefore became my resolve. I have certainly never spoken to any human being about my plan, and I am sure my landlady has not seen any change in me, either the same evening or the day after.

"But," said I to myself, "since you are not a genius, and have by no means a call to bestow a beatific happiness upon all mankind, and since you have not promised anyone anything, you can address yourself to your enterprise *con amore,* and methodically, as if a poet and a dialectician watched over your every step, now that you have reached a more specific understanding of your own notion that you must try to make something difficult." My studies, which had already in a manner brought me to my goal, were now systematically organized; but whenever I was tempted to transform my investigations into an erudite learning, there always came before my mind the venerable figure of the old man. But chiefly I sought by reflection to trace the misunderstanding to its roots. My many failures I need not here recite, but finally it became clear to me that the misdirection of speculative philosophy, and its consequent assumed justification for reducing faith to the status of a relative moment, could not be anything accidental, but must be rooted deeply in the entire tendency of the age. It must, in short, doubtless be rooted in the fact that on account of our vastly increased knowledge, men had forgotten what it means to EXIST, and what INWARDNESS signifies.

When I understood this, it also became clear to me that if I desired to communicate anything on this point, it would first of all be necessary to give my exposition an *indirect* form. For if inwardness is the truth, results are only rubbish with which we should not trouble each other.

The communication of results is an unnatural form of intercourse between man and man, in so far as every man is a spiritual being, for
whom the truth consists in nothing else than the self-activity of personal
appropriation, which the communication of a result tends to prevent.
Let a teacher in relation to the essential truth (for otherwise a direct
relationship between teacher and pupil is quite in order) have, as we
say, much inwardness of feeling, and be willing to publish his doctrines
day in and day out; if he assumes the existence of a direct relationship
between the learner and himself, his inwardness is not inwardness, but
a direct outpouring of feeling; the respect for the learner which recognizes that he is in himself the inwardness of truth, is precisely the teacher's inwardness. Let a learner be enthusiastic, and publish his teacher's
praises abroad in the strongest expressions, thus, as we say, giving
evidence of his inwardness; this inwardness is not inwardness, but an
immediate devotedness; the devout and silent accord, in which the
learner by himself assimilates what he has learned, keeping the teacher
at a distance because he turns his attention within himself, this is precisely inwardness. Pathos is indeed inwardness, but it is an immediate
inwardness, when it is expressed; but pathos in a contrary form is an
inwardness which remains with the maker of the communication in
spite of being expressed, and cannot be directly appropriated by another
except through that other's self-activity: the contrast of the form is the
measure of the inwardness. The more complete the contrast of the
form, the greater the inwardness, and the less contrast, up to the point
of direct communication, the less the inwardness. It may be difficult
enough for an enthusiastic genius, who would so gladly make all men
happy and bring them to a knowledge of the truth, to learn in this
manner to restrain himself, and to give heed to the *nota bene* of reduplication, the truth not being a circular with signatures affixed, but the
valore intrinseco of inwardness; for an idler and frivolous person this
understanding comes more easily. As soon as the truth, the essential
truth, may be assumed to be known by everyone, the objective becomes
appropriation and inwardness, and here only an indirect form is applicable. The position of an apostle is different, for he has to preach an
unknown truth, whence a direct form of communication may in his
case have provisional validity.

It is strange that while there is such universal insistence on the positive, and on the direct form of communication, it occurs to no one to
register a complaint against God, who as the eternal spirit from whom

all spirits are derived, might in communicating the truth, seem to be justified in sustaining a direct relationship to the derivative spirits, in quite a different sense from that in which the relationship is one between derived spirits, who having a common derivation from God, are *essentially* equal. For no anonymous author can more cunningly conceal himself, no practitioner of the maieutic art can more carefully withdraw himself from the direct relationship, than God. He is in the creation, and present everywhere in it, but directly He is not there; and only when the individual turns to his inner self, and hence only in the inwardness of self-activity, does he have his attention aroused, and is enabled to see God.

The immediate relationship to God is paganism, and only after the breach has taken place can there be any question of a true God-relationship. But this breach is precisely the first act of inwardness in the direction of determining the truth as inwardness. Nature is, indeed, the work of God, but only the handiwork is directly present, not God. Is not this to behave, in His relationship to the individual, like an elusive author who nowhere sets down his result in large type, or gives it to the reader beforehand in a preface? And why is God elusive? Precisely because He is the truth, and by being elusive desires to keep men from error. The observer of nature does not have a result immediately set before him, but must by himself be at pains to find it, and thereby the direct relationship is broken. But this breach is precisely the act of self-activity, the irruption of inwardness, the first determination of the truth as inwardness.

Or is not God so unnoticeable, so secretly present in His works, that a man might very well live his entire life, be married, become known and respected as citizen, father, and captain of the hunt, without ever having discovered God in His works, and without ever having received any impression of the infinitude of the ethical, because he helped himself out with what constitutes an analogy to the speculative confusion of the ethical with the historical process, in that he helped himself out by having recourse to the customs and traditions prevailing in the town where he happened to live? As a mother admonishes her child when it sets off for a party: "Now be sure to behave yourself, and do as you see the other well-behaved children do,"—so he might manage to live by conducting himself as he sees others do. He would never do anything first, and he would never have any opinion which he did not first know that others had; for this "others" would be for him the first. Upon extraordinary occasions he would behave as when at a banquet a dish is served, and one does not know how it should be eaten: he would look around until he saw how the others did it, and so forth. Such a man might perhaps know many things, perhaps even know the System by rote; he might be an inhabitant of a Christian country, and bow his head whenever the name of God was mentioned; he would perhaps also see God in nature when in company with others who saw God; he would be a pleasant society man—and yet he would have been deceived by the direct nature of his relationship to the truth, to the ethical, and to God.

If one were to delineate such a man experimentally, he would be a satire upon the human. Essentially it is the God-relationship that makes a man a man, and yet he lacked this. No one would hesitate, however, to regard him as a real man (for the absence of inwardness is not directly apparent); in reality he would constitute a sort of marionette, very deceptively imitating everything human—even to the extent of having children by his wife. At the end of his life, one would have to say that one thing had escaped him: his consciousness had taken no note of God. If God could have permitted a direct relationship, he would doubtless have taken notice. If God, for example, had taken on the figure of a very rare and tremendously large green bird, with a red beak, sitting in a tree on the mound, and perhaps even whistling in an unheard of manner—then the society man would have been able to get his eyes open, and for the first time in his life would be first.

All paganism consists in this, that God is related to man directly, as the obviously extraordinary to the astonished observer. But the spiritual relationship to God in the truth, i.e. in inwardness, is conditioned by a prior irruption of inwardness, which corresponds to the divine elusiveness that God has absolutely nothing obvious about Him, that God is so far from being obvious that He is invisible. It cannot immediately occur to anyone that He exists, although His invisibility is again His omnipresence. An omnipresent person is one that is everywhere to be seen, like a policeman, for example: how deceptive then, that an omnipresent being should be recognizable precisely by being invisible,* only

* To point out how deceptive the rhetorical can be, I shall here show how one might rhetorically perhaps produce an effect upon a listener, in spite of the fact that what was said was dialectically a regress. Let a pagan religious speaker say that here on earth, God's temples are really empty, but (and now begins the rhetorical) in heaven, where all is more perfect, where water is air and air is ether, there are also temples and sanctuaries for the gods, but the difference is that the gods really dwell in these temples: then we have here a dialectical regress in the proposition

and alone recognizable by this trait, since his visibility would annul his omnipresence. The relationship between omnipresence and invisibility is like the relation between mystery and revelation. The mystery is the expression for the fact that the revelation is a revelation in the stricter sense, so that the mystery is the only trait by which it is known; for otherwise a revelation would be something very like a policeman's omnipresence.

If God were to reveal Himself in human form and grant a direct relationship, by giving Himself, for example, the figure of a man six yards tall, then our hypothetical society man and captain of the hunt would doubtless have his attention aroused. But the spiritual relationship to God in truth, when God refuses to deceive, requires precisely that there be nothing remarkable about the figure, so that the society man would have to say: "There is nothing whatever to see." When God has nothing obviously remarkable about Him, the society man is perhaps deceived by not having his attention at all aroused. But this is not God's fault, and the actuality of such a deception is at the same time the constant possibility of the truth. But if God has anything obviously remarkable, He deceives men because they have their attention called to what is untrue, and this direction of attention is at the same time the impossibility of the truth. In paganism the direct relationship is idolatry; in Christendom, everyone knows that God cannot so reveal Himself. But this knowledge is by no means inwardness, and in Christendom it may well happen to one who knows everything by rote that he is left altogether "without God in the world,"[21] in a sense impossible in paganism, which did have the untrue relationship of paganism. Idolatry is indeed a sorry substitute, but that the item *God* should be entirely omitted is still worse.

Not even God, then, enters into a direct relationship with derivative spirits. And this is the miracle of creation, not the creation of something which is nothing over against the Creator, but the creation of something which is something, and which in true worship of God can use this something in order by its true self to become nothing before God. Much less can a human being sustain such a direct relationship to another *in the truth*. Nature, the totality of created things, is the work of God. And yet God is not there; but within the individual man there is a

---

that God really dwells in the temple. for the fact that He does not so dwell is an expression for the spiritual relationship to the invisible. But rhetorically it produces an effect. I have as a matter of fact, had in view a definite passage by a Greek author,[22] whom I do not, however, wish to cite.

potentiality (man is potentially spirit) which is awakened in inwardness to become a God-relationship, and then it becomes possible to see God everywhere. The sensuous distinctions of the great, the astonishing, the shrieking superlatives of a southern people, constitute a retreat to idolatry, in comparison with the spiritual relationship of inwardness. Is this not as if an author wrote one hundred and sixty-six folio volumes, and a reader read and read, just as people look and look at nature, but did not discover that the meaning of this tremendous literature lay in himself; for astonishment over the many volumes, and the number of lines to a page, which is like the astonishment over the vastness of nature and the countless forms of animal life, is not the true understanding.

A direct relationship between one spiritual being and another, with respect to the essential truth, is unthinkable. If such a relationship is assumed, it means that one of the parties has ceased to be spirit. This is something that many a genius omits to consider, both when he helps people into the truth *en masse,* and when he is complaisant enough to think that acclamation, willingness to listen, the affixing of signatures, and so forth, is identical with the acceptance of the truth. Precisely as important as the truth, and if one of the two is to be emphasized, still more important, is the manner in which the truth is accepted. It would help very little if one persuaded millions of men to accept the truth, if precisely by the method of their acceptance they were transferred into error. Hence it is that all complaisance, all persuasiveness, all bargaining, all direct attraction by means of one's own person, reference to one's suffering for the cause, one's weeping over humanity, one's enthusiasm —all this is sheer misunderstanding, a false note in relation to the truth, by which, in proportion to one's ability, one may help a job-lot of human beings to get an illusion of truth.

Socrates was an ethical teacher, but he took cognizance of the non-existence of any direct relationship between teacher and pupil, because the truth is inwardness, and because this inwardness in each is precisely the road which leads them away from one another. It was presumably because he understood this, that he was so happy about his favorable outward appearance. What sort of an appearance did he have? Aye, just venture a guess! In our day we also say of a clergyman that he has a favorable appearance, and rejoice in this, understanding thereby that he is a handsome man, that the ministerial gown becomes him, that he has a resonant and musical voice, and a figure that every tailor, or, what am I saying? a figure that every hearer must be pleased with. Ah, yes, when a man is so endowed by nature, and so clothed by the tailor, he is surely fitted to be a teacher of religion, and fitted to perform his task with success! For teachers of religion have to meet a variety of circumstances, more so, perhaps, than is held in mind when there is complaint that some livings are so fat while others are so meager; the difference is even greater: some teachers of religion are crucified—but the religion is quite the same. The reduplicated repetition of the content of the doctrine in the conception of the teacher's life and person, is something that no one cares much about. Orthodox doctrine is expounded, and at the same time the teacher is decked out in pagan-aesthetic categories. Christ is delineated in Biblical terms. That he bore the sins of the world does not seem adequately to move the audience, yet the preacher says it; and in order to make the contrast vivid, he describes the beauty of Christ (for the contrast between innocence and sin is not strong enough), and the believing community is moved by this altogether pagan determination of God in human form: beauty.

But back to Socrates. He did not have quite so favorable an appearance as that described; he was very ugly, had clumsy feet, and, above all, a number of growths on the forehead and elsewhere, which would suffice to persuade anyone that he was a demoralized subject. This was what Socrates understood by his favorable appearance[23] in which he was so thoroughly happy that he would have considered it a chicane of the divinity to prevent him from becoming a teacher of morals, had he been given an attractive appearance like an effeminate cithara player, a melting glance like a shepherd lad, small feet like a dancing master in the Friendly Society,[24] and *in toto* as favorable an appearance as could have been desired by any applicant for a job through the newspapers, or any theologue who has pinned his hope on a private call. Why was this old teacher so happy over his favorable appearance, unless it was because he understood that it must help to keep the learner at a distance, so that the latter might not stick fast in a direct relationship to the teacher, perhaps admire him, perhaps have his clothes cut in the same manner. Through the repellent effect exerted by the contrast, which on a higher plane was also the rôle played by his irony, the learner would be compelled to understand that he had essentially to do with himself, and that the inwardness of the truth is not the comradely inwardness with which two bosom friends walk arm in arm, but the separation with which each for himself exists in the truth.

This then I was quite clear in my own mind about, that every direct communication in relation to the truth as inwardness, is a misunderstanding, though its nature may be varied in relation to the varied character of him who is guilty of it: perhaps an amiable obtuseness, an unclarified sympathy, a secret vanity, stupidity, insolence, and other things. But because I had made clear to myself the form of such communication, it did not follow that I had anything to communicate; but it was quite in order that the form should first become clear, since the form is the inwardness.

My principal thought was that in our age, because of the great increase of knowledge, we had forgotten what it means to *exist,* and what *inwardness* signifies, and that the misunderstanding between speculative philosophy and Christianity was explicable on that ground. I now resolved to go back as far as possible, in order not to reach the religious mode of existence too soon, to say nothing of the specifically Christian mode of religious existence, in order not to leave difficulties unexplored behind me. If men had forgotten what it means to exist religiously, they had doubtless also forgotten what it means to exist as human beings; this must therefore be set forth. But above all it must not be done in a dogmatizing manner, for then the misunderstanding would instantly take the explanatory effort to itself in a new misunderstanding, as if existing consisted in getting to know something about this or that. If communicated in the form of knowledge, the recipient is led to adopt the misunderstanding that it is knowledge he is to receive, and then we are again in the sphere of knowledge. Only one who has some conception of the enduring capacity of a misunderstanding to assimilate even the most strenuous effort of explanation and still remain the same misunderstanding, will be able to appreciate the difficulties of an authorship where every word must be watched, and every sentence pass through the process of a double reflection.

By adopting a direct form of communication in matters concerning existence and inwardness, one would only attain that the speculative philosopher benevolently took notice of it, and included it with the rest. The System is hospitable. Like an underbred burgher who, when he makes a holiday excursion to the woods, in view of the fact that there is plenty of room in the four-seated Holstein carriage, invites Tom, Dick, and Harry, without regard for their mutual compatibility, so the System is also generously hospitable—there is plenty of room. I do not wish to deny that I admire Hamann,[25] though I am free to admit that the elasticity of his thought lacks balance, and his supernatural tension, self-control, assuming that he proposed to work more connectedly. But the primitivity of genius is in his brief sentences, and the pregnant form is in entire correspondence with the desultory flinging out of a thought. With all his life and soul, to the last drop of blood, he is concentrated in a single word, the passionate protest of a highly gifted genius against an existential system. But the System is hospitable; poor Hamann, you have been reduced to a paragraph by Michelet.[26] Whether any monument has ever marked your grave, I do not know, whether it is now trodden under foot, I do not know; but this I know, that you have been with satanic might and main forced into the paragraph-uniform, and stuck into the ranks. I do not deny that Jacobi has often inspired me, though I readily perceive that his dialectical skill is disproportionate to his noble enthusiasm; but his is the eloquent protest of a noble, uncorrupted, lovable, richly gifted mind against putting existence into a systematic strait-jacket; a victorious consciousness and an enthusiastic championship of the conviction that existence has larger and deeper significance than the couple of years one spends in forgetting oneself in order to read the System. Poor Jacobi! Whether anyone visits your grave I do not know, but I know that the paragraph-machine plows all your eloquence, all your inwardness under, while a few scant words are registered in the System as your significance. It is said of him that he represents feeling with enthusiasm; such a reference makes game of both feeling and enthusiasm, whose secret precisely is that they cannot be reported at second-hand, and therefore cannot in so comfortable a manner, as a result through a *satisfactio vicaria,* yield bliss to a prater.

So I resolved to begin; and my first act, in order to begin from the beginning, would be *to exhibit the existential relationship between the aesthetic and the ethical within an existing individual.* The task was thus set, and I foresaw that the labor would be voluminous enough, and especially that I would have to be prepared sometimes to remain inactive, when the spirit refused to support me with an access of pathos. But what happened then I shall tell in an appendix to this chapter.

APPENDIX

A GLANCE AT A CONTEMPORARY EFFORT IN DANISH LITERATURE[1]

WHAT happens? Just as I sit there, out comes *Either-Or*. Here was realized precisely what I had proposed to myself to do. It made me feel quite unhappy to think of my solemn resolution, but then again I thought: you have at any rate not promised anyone anything, and as long as the work is done, all is well. But things went from bad to worse; for step by step, just as I was about to realize my resolve in action, out came a pseudonymous book which accomplished what I had intended. There was something curiously ironical in the entire situation; it was fortunate that I had never talked to anyone about my resolve, that not even my landlady had noticed anything, for otherwise people would doubtless have laughed at my comic predicament, as it is indeed droll enough that the cause to which I had devoted myself prospered, though not through me. And that the cause did prosper I convinced myself from the fact that every time I read through such a pseudonymous work, it became clearer to me what I had intended to do. In this manner I became a tragi-comically interested witness of the productions of Victor Eremita and the other pseudonyms. Whether my interpretation is the same as that of the authors, I can of course not know with certainty, since I am only a reader; on the other hand, it gives me pleasure to see that the pseudonyms, presumably aware of the relation subsisting between the method of indirect communication and the truth as inwardness, have themselves said nothing, nor misused a preface to assume an official attitude toward the production, as if an author were in a purely legal sense the best interpreter of his own words; or as if it could help a reader that an author had intended this or that, if it was not realized; or as if it were certain that it was realized because the author himself says so in the preface; or as if an existential misdirection could be corrected by being brought to a finite decision, in the form of madness, suicide, and the like, which feminine authors are especially prone to, and that so quickly that they almost begin with it; or as if an author were served by having a reader who precisely because of the author's clumsiness knew all about the book.

Either-Or, whose very title is suggestive, exhibits the existential relationship between the aesthetic and the ethical in existing individualities. This is for me the book's indirect polemic against speculative philosophy, which is indifferent to the existential. The fact that there is no result and no finite decision, is an indirect expression for the truth as inwardness, and thus perhaps a polemic against the truth as knowledge. The preface itself says something about it, but not didactically, for then I could know with certainty, but in the merry form of jest and hypothesis. The fact that there is no author is a means of keeping the reader at a distance.

The first of the Diapsalmata posits a rift in existence, in the form of a poet's suffering, in such a way as this might have persisted in a poet-existence, which "B" uses against "A." The last sentence in the entire work is as follows: Only the truth which *edifies* is truth *for you.* This is an essential predicate relating to the truth as inwardness; its decisive characterization as edifying *for you,* i.e. for the subject, constitutes its essential difference from all objective knowledge, in that the subjectivity itself becomes the mark of the truth.

The *first* part represents an existential possibility which cannot win through to existence, a melancholy that needs to be ethically worked up. Melancholy is its essential character, and this so deep, that though autopathic it deceptively occupies itself with the sufferings of others (Shadowgraphs), and for the rest deceives by concealing itself under the cloak of pleasure, rationality, demoralization; the deception and the concealment being at one and the same time its strength and its weakness, its strength in imagination and its weakness in winning through to existence. It is an imagination-existence in aesthetic passion, and therefore paradoxical, colliding with time; it is in its maximum despair; it is therefore not existence; but an existential possibility tending toward existence, and brought so close to it that you feel how every moment is wasted as long as it has not yet come to a decision. But the existential possibility in the existing "A" refuses to become aware of this, and keeps existence away by the most subtle of all deceptions, by thinking; he has thought everything possible, and yet he has not existed at all. The consequence of this is that only the Diapsalmata are pure lyrical effusions; the rest has abundant thought-content, which may easily deceive, as if having thought about something were identical with existing. Had a poet planned the work, he would scarcely have thought about this, and would perhaps by the work itself have set the old misunderstanding on its feet again. The relation is not to be conceived as that between an immature and a mature thought, but between not existing and existing. "A" is therefore a developed thinker, he is far superior to "B" as a dialectician, he has been endowed with all the seductive gifts of soul and understanding; thereby it becomes clearer by what characteristic it is that "B" differs from him.

The *second* part represents an ethical individual existing by virtue of the ethical. It is also the second part which brings the first part into the open; for "A" would again have conceived of the possibility of being an author, actually have realized the writing, and then let it lie. The ethicist has *despaired* (the first part *was* despair); in this despair he has *chosen himself*; in and by this choice he *reveals himself* ("the expression which sharply differentiates between the ethical and the aesthetic is this: it is every man's duty to reveal himself"—the first part was concealment); he is a husband ("A" was familiar with every possibility within the erotic sphere, and yet not actually in love, for then he would instantly, in a way, have been in course of consolidating himself), and concentrates himself, precisely in opposition to the concealment of the aesthetic, upon marriage as the deepest form of life's revelation, by which *time* is taken into the service of the ethically existing individual, and the possibility of *gaining a history* becomes the ethical victory of continuity over concealment, melancholy, illusory passion, and despair. Through phantom-like images of the mist, through the distractions of an abundant thought-content, whose elaboration, if it has any value, is absolutely the merit of the author, we win through to an entirely individual human being, existing in the strength of the ethical. This then constitutes the change of scene; or rather, now the scene is there: instead of a world of possibilities, glowing with imagination and dialectically organized, we have an individual—and only the truth which edifies is truth for you; that is, the truth is inwardness, but please to note, existential inwardness, here qualified as ethical.

And so this brush is over. The merit of the book, if it has any, is not my concern. If it has any merit, this will essentially consist in not giving any result, but in transforming everything into inwardness: in the first part, an imaginative inwardness which evokes the possibilities with intensified passion, with sufficient dialectical power to transform all into nothing in despair; in the second part, an ethical pathos, which with a quiet, incorruptible, and yet infinite passion of resolve embraces the modest ethical task, and edified thereby stands self-revealed before God and man.

There is no didacticism in the book, but from this it does not follow that there is no thought-content; thus it is one thing to think, and another thing to exist in what has been thought. Existence is in its relation to thought just as little something following of itself as it is something thoughtless. There is not even a conviction that is communicated and expounded, perhaps as we say with inwardness; for a conviction can be held also in the idea merely, and thus readily becomes dialectical in the direction of being more or less true. No, we have here presented to us an existence in thought, and the book or the work has no finite relation to anybody. This sort of transparency in existence realized for the thought, is precisely inwardness. If thus for example speculative philosophy, instead of objectively expounding *de omnibus dubitandum* and getting a swearing chorus to take its oath upon *de omnibus dubitandum,* had made an attempt to represent such a doubter in his existential inwardness, so that one could see to the smallest detail how he made shift to do it—had it done this, that is, had it begun upon it, it would have given it up, and perceived with shame that the great phrase which every spouter has sworn that he has realized, is not only an infinitely difficult task, but an impossibility for an existing individual. And precisely this is one of the saddening aspects of all communication, that a good man, sometimes to win men, sometimes from vanity, sometimes in thoughtlessness, fills his mouth so full that he has in a trice done not merely all that an eminent existing spirit could do in a long lifetime, but even what is impossible. It is forgotten that existence makes the understanding of the simplest truth for the common man in existential transparency very difficult and very strenuous. With the assistance of a result, people lyingly credit themselves with everything (I have heard people, stupid enough to run their heads against a stone wall, say that it is impossible to remain at the standpoint of the Socratic ignorance), and finally they wind up, like all windbags, with having done the impossible. Inwardness has become a matter of knowledge, existing, a waste of time. Hence it comes that the most mediocre sort of person who in our day scribbles something together speaks as if he had experienced everything, and merely by taking note of his secondary propositions you see that the man is a jesting rogue. A man in our day who exists with as much energy as a mediocre Greek philosopher, is regarded as a demon. The formulas for pain and suffering are recited by rote, also the glorious law of steadfastness. Everyone patters. If there exists a man who exposes himself to a little unpleasantness for the sake of an opinion, he is regarded as a demon, or else as stupid; for we know everything, and in order not to stop there, we also know that we ought not to do the least part of it. The external knowledge lifts us to the seventh heaven; but when a man begins to do any of it, he becomes a poor existing individual human being who stumbles again and again, and from year to year makes very little progress. If one can sometimes remember with a certain sense of relief that Caesar burned the entire Alexandrian library,[2] one could also in all good will wish that our superfluity of knowledge could be taken away, in order that we might again learn what it means to live as a human being.

It struck me as significant that *Either-Or* ends precisely in the edifying truth (but without so much as italicizing the words, much less dogmatizingly). I could have wished to see this principle more definitely emphasized, in order that the individual stages on the way toward a Christian religious existence might be clearly set out. For the Christian truth as inwardness is also edifying, but from this it does not follow that every edifying truth is Christian; the edifying is a wider category. Again I gathered myself together with reference to this point, but what happened? Just as I was about to begin, out comes *Two Discourses of Edification,* by Magister Kierkegaard, 1843. Thereupon followed three more, and the preface reiterated the assertion that they were not sermons. This was something which I, too, would have protested against, if no one else, since they employ only ethical categories of immanence, not the doubly reflected religious categories in the paradox. Unless we are to have a confusion of tongues, the sermon must be reserved for the Christian-religious type of existence. Nowadays we sometimes hear sermons which resemble nothing less than sermons, because the categories are immanent. Perhaps the Magister has wished indirectly to make this evident, by attempting to see how far it is possible to explore the realm of the edifying in a purely philosophical manner; so that the edifying discourse has its own validity, but that also by indirectly calling attention to this, the author came to the assistance of the cause which in a ludicrous sense I call my own, since I always come too late to do anything. But so curiously did things turn out, according to what Magister Kierkegaard has told me, that some unhesitatingly called the edifying discourses sermons,[3] and even meant to honor them by giving

them this title. This is as if edifying discourse and sermon were related
to one another like counsellor of the chancery to counsellor of justice,
and as if one honored the former by calling him the latter. Others on
the contrary objected to the edifying discourses that they were not really
sermons, which is like objecting to an opera because it is not a tragedy.*

The ethicist in *Either-Or* had saved himself through despair, abolishing concealment in self-revelation; but here was in my opinion a difficulty. In order to determine himself in the inwardness of the truth as
distinct from speculative philosophy, he had used the term despair
instead of doubt; but still he had made it appear that by despairing in
the very act of despair itself, as if *uno tenore,* he had been able to win
himself. Had *Either-Or* proposed to make it clear where the difficulty
lies, the entire work would have had to have a religious orientation; but
in that case it would have been necessary to say in the beginning what,
according to my ideas, should be said only successively. The difficulty
was now not at all touched upon, and this was quite in accordance with
my own plan. Whether this has been clear to the author, of course I
cannot tell. The difficulty is, that the ethical self is supposed to be found
immanently in the despair, so that the individual by persisting in his
despair at last wins himself. He has indeed used a determination of
freedom: to choose himself, which seems to lessen the difficulty, a
difficulty which presumably has not attracted the attention of many,
since it is possible *philosophice* to doubt everything in a trice, and so to
find the true beginning. But this avails nothing. When I despair, I use
myself to despair, and therefore I can indeed by myself despair of
everything; but when I do this, I cannot by myself come back. In this
moment of decision it is that the individual needs divine assistance,

---

* It is possible that in making this objection some may have had in mind, not so much the
fact that the edifying discourses were philosophical, and did not use the Christian categories, as
that they have included an aesthetic element after a larger measure than is customary in the
religious address. The more pronounced and detailed delineation of states of mind with a
psychological coloring is something that the religious address usually abstains from, tending to
leave this task to the poet and the poetic *impetus,* whatever the reason may be, whether the
individual speaker is unable or is unwilling. However, this may readily have the effect of creating
a rift in the mind of the listener, in that the religious address leaves him unsatisfied, and leads
him to seek elsewhere for what is lacking. In so far I do not understand why it might not be quite
in order to include the poetic description. Only there will always remain a decisive difference
between the poet and the religious speaker, in that the poet has no other *telos* than the psychological truth of his description and the art of his presentation, while the speaker has at the same
time the *principal* aim of transforming everything into edification. The poet loses himself in the
delineation of passion, but for the religious speaker this is but the first step; the next step is for
him the decisive one, namely, to force the obstreperous individual to lay down his arms, to
soften, to clear up; in short to translate everything into terms of edification.

while it is quite right to say that one must first have understood the existential relationship between the aesthetic and the ethical in order to be at this point; that is to say, by being there in passion and inwardness one will doubtless become aware of the religious—and of the *leap*.

Furthermore. The determination of the truth as inwardness in terms of the edifying must also be more specifically interpreted before it is religious, to say nothing of being Christian. It is true of all edification that it must first and foremost produce the necessary adequate fear, for otherwise the edification is reduced to an illusion. The ethicist had with the passion of the infinite in the moment of despair chosen himself out of the fearful plight of having his self, his life, his reality in aesthetic dreams, in melancholy, in concealment. Fear from this side can therefore no more be in question; the scene is now the ethical inwardness in an ethical individual. The new fear must be a new determination of inwardness, whereby the individual in a higher sphere comes back again to the point where revelation, which is the very life of the ethical, again becomes impossible; but so that the relations are reversed, and the ethical, which formerly helped to bring about a revelation (while the aesthetic hindered), is now the hindrance, and that which helps the individual to a higher revelation beyond the ethical is something else.

Whoever has had inwardness enough to lay hold of the ethical with infinite passion, and to understand the eternal validity of duty and the universal, for him there can neither in heaven or on earth or in hell be found so fearful a plight, as when he faces a collision where the ethical becomes the temptation. And yet this collision confronts everyone, if not otherwise, then through the fact that he is religiously referred to the religious paradigm; that is to say, through the fact that the religious paradigm is an irregularity and yet is supposed to be the paradigm (which is like God's omnipresence being evidenced by His invisibility, and a revelation through being a mystery). The religious paradigm expresses not the universal but the particular (the irregular, the exceptional, as for example by appealing to dreams, visions, and so forth), and yet it is assumed to be paradigmatical. But to be a paradigm is precisely to be for all, and one can surely be a pattern for all only by being that which all are or ought to be, i.e. the universal; and yet the *religious paradigm* is precisely the opposite (the irregular and the exceptional), while the *tragic hero* expresses the regular conformity of the universal in his mode of declension.

This had become clear to me, and I waited only for the spirit to come to my assistance with pathos, in order to give it representation in existing individualities; for an objectively dogmatic mode of presentation was to be avoided, since in my view the misfortune of the age was precisely that it had too much knowledge, had forgotten what existence means, and what inwardness signifies. The form therefore had to be indirect. I will here again say the same thing in another manner, as is fitting when the subject dealt with is inwardness; for he who is lucky enough to have to do with the manifold can easily be entertaining. When he has finished China he can take up Persia; when he has studied French he can begin Italian; and then go on to astronomy, the veterinary sciences, and so forth, and always be sure of a reputation as a tremendous fellow. Inwardness has no such compass, and cannot arouse the astonishment of the sensuous man; inwardness in love does not consist in consummating seven marriages with Danish maidens, and then cutting loose on the French, the Italian, and so forth, but consists in loving one and the same woman, and yet being constantly renewed in the same love, making it always new in the luxuriant flowering of the mood. In its application to communication, this means the inexhaustible renewal of the expression and its fruitfulness. Inwardness cannot be directly communicated, for its direct expression is precisely externality, its direction being outward, not inward. The direct expression of inwardness is no proof of its presence; the direct effusion of feeling does not prove its possession, but the tension of the contrasting form is the measure of the intensity of inwardness. The reception of inwardness does not consist in a direct reflection of the content communicated, for this is echo. But the reproduction of inwardness in the recipient constitutes the resonance by reason of which the thing said remains absent, like Mary when she *hid* the words in her heart. And not even this is the true expression for the reproduction of inwardness in the relation between man and man; for she *hid* the words as a treasure in the beautiful setting of a comely heart, but inwardness is when the thing said belongs to the recipient as if it were his own—and now it is his own. To communicate in this manner constitutes the most beautiful triumph of the resigned inwardness. And therefore no one is so resigned as God; for He communicates in creating, so as by creating to *give* independence over against Himself. The highest degree of resignation that a human being can reach is to acknowledge the given independence in every man, and after the measure of his ability do

all that can in truth be done to help someone preserve it. But such things
are not thought needful to speak of in our age. Is it permissible, for
example, as we say, to win a man for the truth? If he who has any
truth to communicate also has some persuasive art, some knowledge of
the human heart, some subtlety in catching unawares, some calculating
foresight in catching men slowly, is it permissible for him to use this
in order to gain adherents for the truth? Or ought he not rather, in
humility before God, loving men in the feeling that God does not
need him,* convinced that every human being is essentially spirit, use
these gifts precisely to prevent the establishment of a direct relationship,
and instead of comfortably having a group of adherents, dutifully reconcile himself to being accused of frivolity, of lacking earnestness, and
so forth, because he disciplines himself in the truth, and saves his life
out of the most terrible of all falsehoods—the having an adherent.

As was said above, I had understood this most fearful of all the
collisions of inwardness, and waited only for the spirit to come to my
assistance—when what happens? Aye indeed, Magister Kierkegaard
and I, each in his own way, cut a somewhat ridiculous figure with
respect to the pseudonymous books. The fact that I sit here in all
quietness and purpose to do what the pseudonymous authors actually
realize, is known to no one; Magister Kierkegaard, on the other hand,
is for it every time such a book comes out. And so much is certain, that
if all the many things said in learned tea-circles and other friendly
companies for this man's improvement and edification, if the fearsome
thunderings and the stern voices of accusation and the condemnatory
judgments could properly be turned to his advantage, he must in a
very short time become an exceptionally good man. While ordinarily
one teacher has several disciples to improve, he is in the enviable position
of having an entire contemporary society of respectabilities, men and
women, learned and unlearned, and chimney sweeps, all together
taking upon themselves the task of his improvement. Unfortunately,
the chastisement and all the rest of it, directed to the improvement of

* For God is not like a king in difficulties, who says to the trusted Minister of the Interior:
"You must try everything possible, you must induce a favorable attitude toward our proposals,
and win public opinion for our side; you can do it, use your shrewdness, for if I cannot depend
on you I have no one." But in relation to God there are for no human being any secret instructions, as little as there are any back stairs. Even the most eminent spirit who meets to present a
report had best do it with fear and trembling. For God is not embarrassed for lack of geniuses,
He can if need be create a couple of legions of them; and in the service of God to begin to think
oneself indispensable to God is *eo ipso* to be discharged. Every man is created in the image of
God; this is the absolute, and the little he has to learn from Peter or Paul is not worth so much.

his heart and understanding, takes place and is spoken only in his absence, never when he is present; otherwise something would surely come of it.

What happens? A book is published, entitled *Fear and Trembling*. The impossibility of a self-revelation, secrecy, is here given as something so fearful that aesthetic secrecy becomes child's play by comparison.

It would have been impossible to represent this existential collision in an existing individuality, since the difficulty of the collision, while lyrically it extorts the extreme limit of passion, dialectically keeps its expression back in absolute silence. Johannes *de silentio* is therefore not himself such an existing individual; he is a reflective consciousness, who with the *tragic hero* as *terminus a quo,* with *the interesting* as *confinium,* and the religious paradigmatic irregularity as *terminus ad quem,* repeatedly runs himself into a collision with the understanding, while the lyricism of the book results from the reaction. This is the way in which Johannes has described himself. To call this book *"eine erhabene Lüge,"* as the signature Kts⁴ did, recalling Jacobi and Desdemona, is in my opinion significant, in so far as the expression itself involves a contradiction. The contrasting nature of the form is absolutely necessary for every production in this and similar spheres. In the form of direct communication, in the form of a shriek, "fear and trembling" is of no great moment; for the direct form of communication shows that the direction is outward, culminating in the shriek, not inward into the abyss of inwardness, where alone fear and trembling are really fearsome, while if expressed, the fearsomeness remains only if the expression is given a deceptive form. How things really are with Johannes *de silentio* I cannot of course tell with certainty, since I do not know him personally; and even if I did, I am not precisely disposed to believe that he would wish to make a fool of himself by giving a direct communication.

The ethical constitutes the temptation; the God-relationship has come into being; the immanence of ethical despair has been broken through; *the leap is posited*; *the absurd constitutes the notification.*

When I had understood this, I thought that for safety's sake it might be well to make sure that what had been reached should not be nullified by a *coup de mains*; so that secrecy became what is called secrecy: a little aestheticism; faith became any sort of immediacy: *vapeurs* for example; and the religious paradigm any sort of pattern: a tragic hero for example. What happens? Just at that time I receive a book from

Reitzel,[5] called *Repetition*. In this book there is no dogmatizing, far from it; this was precisely what I had wished, since it was in my view the misfortune of the age to have too much knowledge, to have forgotten to exist, and what inwardness is. Under such circumstances it is desirable that an author should know how to withdraw himself, and for this purpose a confusing contrast-form is always usable. And Constantine Constantius wrote, as he calls it, "a whimsical book."[6] The category of repetition is at bottom an expression for immanence, so that persistence in despair gives possession of the self, persistence in doubt, possession of the truth. Constantine Constantius, the clever aesthetic intriguing mind, who otherwise despairs of nothing, despairs of realizing repetition; the young man has the intuition that if repetition is to come into being it must be as a new immediacy, so that the repetition itself is a movement *in virtue of the absurd,* and the teleological suspension *a trial*. The concept of a "trial" corresponds again to the fact that the religious paradigm is an irregularity. From the ethical point of view a trial is unthinkable, since it is precisely by always being valid that the ethical is the universally valid. For the religious paradigm a trial is the highest earnest; from the merely ethical point of view a trial is a jest, and the notion of *existing on trial* is so far from being earnest that it is a comic *motif* which inconceivably enough no poet has yet used to represent want of will in an almost insane maximum, as if a man proposed to marry on trial, and so forth. But the fact that the highest earnestness of the religious life is recognizable by the jest, is like the paradigm being an irregularity or particularity, and God's omnipresence His invisibility, and revelation a mystery.

Repetition was called "a psychological experiment" on the title-page. That this was a doubly reflected communication-form soon became clear to me. By taking place in the form of an experiment, the communication creates opposition for itself, and the experiment establishes a yawning chasm between reader and author, posits the separation of inwardness between them, so that an immediate understanding is rendered impossible. The experiment constitutes the conscious, challenging recall of the communication, which is always of importance for an existing individual who writes for existing individuals, to prevent the situation being altered so as to become that of a prater writing for praters. If a man were to stand on one leg, or pose in a queer dancing attitude swinging his hat, and in this attitude propound something true, his few auditors would divide themselves into two groups; and many

listeners he would not have, since most men would give him up at
once. The one class would say: "How can what he says be true, when
he gesticulates in that fashion?" The other class would say: "Well,
whether he cuts capers or stands on his head, even if he were to throw
handsprings, what he says is true and I propose to appropriate it, letting
him go." So also with the experiment. If the utterance is earnest in the
writer, he preserves the earnestness essentially for himself; if the recipient apprehends it as earnest, he does it essentially by himself, and
this is precisely the earnestness. Even in connection with the instruction
of children in school, we make the distinction between "learning by
heart" and "intelligence-training," which distinction is striking enough
in connection with the systematic "learning by heart." The interposi-
tion of the experiment is favorable to the inwardness of the two in its
tendency *away from one another in inwardness*. This form completely
gained my approval, and I thought also to discover therein that the
pseudonymous authors constantly had *existence* in view, and thus maintained an indirect polemic against speculative philosophy. When
a man knows everything, but knows it by rote, the experimental form
is a good instrument of exploration; one may tell him even what he
knows in this form, and he will not recognize it. Later a new pseudonym, Frater Taciturnus, has indicated the rôle of the experiment in relation to aesthetic, ethical, and religious productions. Compare *Stages
on Life's Way*.

If otherwise *Fear and Trembling* and *Repetition* have any value, I
shall not attempt to decide. If they have value, the standard of evalua-
tion will not be dogmatizing paragraphic importance. If it is the misfortune of the age to have forgotten what inwardness is, it is of course
not the task to write for "paragraph-eaters"; but existing individuals
must be represented in their distress, when their existence presents
itself to them as a confusion, which is something different from sitting
safely in the chimney corner and reciting *de omnibus dubitandum*. If
the production is to be significant, it should always have passion. Constantine Constantius has even used a love story, which is always a
usable motive in relation to existence; though philosophically, in relation to prating, it is but folly. He has used an engagement. This I
wholly approve, and only superannuated novel-readers are accustomed
to understand, and find the understanding to their taste, when it is said
of two people that they love each other, what the lowest rabble profanely
understands by this word. An engagement is a promise, a broken

engagement is a broken promise; but there is no secret note underneath which could cause a woman's face to change color. It does not follow that an engagement presents a more frivolous aspect, but that its earnestness, and the fearful character of the breach, become purer. To call it a promise, a broken promise, when a man seduces the heroine of the novel and then abandons her, is thoughtless and immoral; above all, such a situation forbids any further exercise of dialectics. Such behavior cannot become subject to dialectical inquiry, since sound common sense suffices to make it clear that here there have been committed at least four crimes: the seduction of the heroine (even if one afterwards married her, it still remains a crime); making the child an illegitimate child (even if one afterwards remedied this, it would still remain a crime); abandoning the mother and abandoning the child; and then as the hero of the novel entering upon a new love affair, by which, even if this new relationship were a proper marriage, one commits adultery according to the Scriptures, and reduces to fornication the marriage of the abandoned heroine if she enters into one, again according to the words of Scripture.

In so far I can understand why an engagement was chosen, later also by Frater Taciturnus.* The purer the broken relationship, while a fear of first-rate quality arises and increases, the more will dialectics be able to discover. But to use dialectics in connection with what is most suitably treated under the second protocol of the criminal courts,[7] and even to employ one's wretched little bit of dialectical skill for the purpose of letting the hero get away from it quite comfortably, that is something that must be left to novel-writers. A novel-writer would consider an engagement as something so insignificant that he could not undertake to interpret such a broken promise. The pseudonymous authors employ their dialectical powers precisely to make the situation as terrible as possible. The hero becomes a hero precisely through the passion with which he apprehends in himself the terrible, and its decisiveness for his life. The purity of the situation is preserved by the fact that the broken promise is conceived in the light of a teleological suspension, and the hero's purity consists in the fact that it is his highest

* Similarly, I can also readily understand why the pseudonymous author or authors repeatedly bring up the subject of marriage. Where the difficulties begin, there most people leave off. Poetry follows the ancient custom in taking love as its domain, leaving marriage to get along as best it can. But in modern poetry (the drama and the novel) things have even reached the point where it is common to use adultery as a refined background for a new love affair. The innocent poesy explains nothing about marriage; the guilty poesy explains it as adultery.

passion to desire to make all well again; the hero's martyrdom consists among other things in his understanding that his life will become meaningless for most men, who in general understand the ethical and the religious about as well as most novel-writers. Ethically and religiously one does not become a hero by being a flippant fellow who is able to take everything easily, but by taking life on the contrary infinitely hard; not however in the womanish sense of a half hour's shrieking, but in the sense of persistence in inwardness.

But a trial is a transitional phase (compare for its dialectic *Repetition*), the individual who has undergone such a trial returns to an existence in the ethical, though retaining an everlasting impression of its fearfulness, an impression of greater inwardness than that in which the experienced person is reminded by his gray hairs of the moment of fear and peril in which his hair turned gray. The teleological suspension of the ethical must be given a more distinctively religious expression. The ethical will then be present every moment with its infinite requirement, but the individual is not capable of realizing this requirement. This impotence of the individual must not be understood as the imperfection of a persistent striving toward the attainment of an ideal; for in that case no suspension is posited; just as an official is not suspended from his office if he performs its duties only moderately well. The suspension in question consists in the individual's finding himself in a state precisely the opposite of that which the ethical requires, so that far from being able to begin, each moment he remains in this state he is more and more prevented from beginning. He is not related to the task as possibility to actuality, but as impossibility. Thus the individual is suspended from the requirements of the ethical in the most terrible manner, being in the suspension heterogeneous with the ethical, which nevertheless has an infinite claim upon him; each moment it requires itself of the individual, and each moment it thereby only more definitely determines the heterogeneity as heterogeneity. Abraham was not heterogeneous with the ethical in his temptation, the temptation in which God tempts a man, as the story in Genesis says of Abraham; he was quite completely capable of realizing it, but was prevented by something higher, which through accentuating itself *absolutely* transformed the voice of duty into a temptation. As soon as this something higher sets the tempted individual free, all is again in order, though the fearful memory that this could happen, even if only for the tenth of a second, still remains. For the length of time the suspension lasts is less important, the decisive thing is that it is there. But these things nobody thinks about; the sermon uses the category of a "trial" quite unceremoniously (the ethical being the temptation); though this is a category which absolutely confuses the ethical, and in general all immediately direct human thought. But it is as if it were nothing—and doubtless that is what it is.

Now the situation is different. Duty is the absolute, its requirement an absolute requirement, and yet the individual is prevented from realizing it; aye, in a desperate ironical manner he is as if set free (in the same sense that the Scriptures speak of being set free from the law of God) through having become heterogeneous with it; and the more profoundly its requirement is made known to him, the clearer becomes his fearful freedom. The terrible emancipation from the requirement of realizing the ethical, the heterogeneity of the individual with the ethical, this suspension from the ethical, is *Sin,* considered as the state in which a human being is.

Sin is a decisive expression for the religious mode of existence. As long as sin is not yet posited, the suspension from the ethical becomes a transitory phase which again vanishes, or remains outside life as something altogether irregular. But sin is the decisive expression for the religious mode of existence; it is not a moment within something else, within another order of things, but is itself the beginning of the religious order of things. In none of the pseudonymous books had sin been brought to the attention. It is indeed true that the ethicist in *Either-Or* had given the ethical category of choosing oneself a religious color by accompanying the act of despair with an act of repentance, repenting himself out of continuity with the race; but this was an emasculation which presumably had its ground in the plan of keeping the work within ethical categories—quite in accordance with my wishes, in order, namely, that each phase might be made clear by itself. The edifying reflection at the close of *Either-Or,* "that over against God we are always in the wrong," constitutes no determination of sin as a fundamental condition, but is merely the discrepancy of the finite and the infinite brought to rest in an enthusiastic reconciliation in the infinite. It is the last enthusiastic cry in which the finite spirit appeals to God, within the sphere of freedom: "I cannot understand Thee, but still I will love Thee, Thou art always right; even if it seemed to me as if Thou didst not love me, I will nevertheless love Thee." Hence it was that the theme was so worded: the edification that lies in the thought, etc.; the edifying is not sought in the annulment of the mis-understanding, but in the enthusiastic endurance of it, and in this final act of courage as if bringing about its annulment. In *Fear and Trembling* sin was used incidentally to illuminate the nature of Abra-ham's ethical suspension, but not further.

So the matter stood when there was published a book, *The Concept of Dread,* described as a simple indicational psychological inquiry, tend-ing toward the dogmatic problem of original sin. Just as *Either-Or* had made sure that the teleological suspension should not be mistaken for aesthetic secrecy, so the three pseudonymous books had together made sure that sin, when it came to be brought forward, should not be mistaken for this or that weakness and imperfection; sorrow over it not be confounded with sighs and tears and blubbering over ourselves and this vale of tears; the suffering involved in it not confounded with a *quodlibet*. Sin is decisive for an entire existential sphere, the religious taken in the strictest sense. Precisely because in our age knowledge is much too abundant, it is a very easy matter to mix everything up together in a confusion of tongues, where aestheticists use the most decisive Christian terminology in the spirit of genial wit, and clergy-men use it as an official formulary independent of content.

But if it is the misfortune of our age that it has too much knowledge, that it has forgotten what it means to exist, and what inwardness signi-fies, then it was of importance not to apprehend sin in abstract terms, in which indeed it cannot be apprehended at all, or at least decisively, because it has an essential relationship to existence. In so far it was a good thing that the book was a psychological inquiry, which itself explains that sin has no place in the system, presumably like immor-tality, faith, the paradox, and other similar concepts having an essential relationship to existence, from which the systematic thought abstracts. The term "dread" does not suggest paragraph-importance, but rather existential inwardness. Just as fear and trembling represent the state of mind of the individual while under teleological suspension, so dread represents his state of mind in the desperate emancipation from the task of realizing the ethical. The inwardness of sin, as dread in the existing individual, is the greatest possible and most painful possible distance from the truth, when truth is subjectivity.

With the content of the work I shall not here further concern myself; I mention these books only in so far as they constitute stages in the realization of an idea I had conceived, but which I was ironically absolved from realizing. And now when I look back upon them from this point of view, a new and curious consideration emerges, recalling the prophecy concerning Esau and Jacob, that the greater was destined to serve the less: in this way the great pseudonymous books serve my *Fragments*. Yet I do not wish to be so presuming as to say this; rather I will say, that while the books have their own significance, they also have significance for my little piece of production.

The Concept of Dread differs essentially from the other pseudonymous writings in having a direct form, and in being even a little bit objectively dogmatic. Perhaps the author has thought that on this point a communication of knowledge might be needful, before going on to engender inwardness; which latter task is relative to one who may be presumed essentially to have knowledge, and hence not in need of having this conveyed to him, but rather needing to be personally affected. The slightly dogmatic form of the book was undoubtedly the reason why it found a little favor in the eyes of the *Docents,* as compared with the other pseudonyms. I will not deny that I consider this favor a misunderstanding, and in so far it pleased me that there came simultaneously a merry little book by Nicolaus Notabene. The pseudonymous books are generally ascribed to a single origin, and now everyone who had hoped for a dogmatizing author would at once give it up upon seeing light literature from the same hand.

And so finally came my *Fragments;* the subject of existential inwardness had by this time been so specifically described that the Christian-religious mode of it could be brought forward without danger of immediate confusion with this or that. Yet one more thing. Magister Kierkegaard's edifying discourses had steadily followed suit, which was for me a hint that he had kept track of the movement; and it was to me a striking and significant thing that the four last discourses took on a carefully modulated humoristic tone. This is doubtless the sum of what can be reached within the sphere of the immanent. While the ethical requirement is maintained, while life and existence is accentuated as a toilsome way, the decision is not posited in a paradox, and the metaphysical retirement by way of recollection into the eternal is always possible, and gives to this immanent sphere the color of humor, in the form of an infinitude's recall of the whole in the eternal decisiveness from behind.* The paradoxical expression for existence as sin,

---

* The humoristic makes its appearance when the problem of the *Fragments,* "Can there be an historical point of departure for an eternal happiness?" is answered not with the yes or no of

the eternal truth as the paradox through having come into being in time, in short, whatever is decisive for the Christian-religious mode of existence is not to be found in the Edifying Discourses, concerning which some said, as the Magister told me, that one could very well call them sermons, while others objected that they were not really sermons. When humor uses the Christian terminology it is a false reflection of the Christian truth, since humor is not essentially different from irony, but essentially different from Christianity, and essentially not otherwise different from Christianity than irony is. It is only apparently different from irony through apparently having assimilated the entire Christian position, but without having appropriated it in a *decisive* manner (while the Christian position inheres in the decision and the decisiveness). On the other hand, that which is essential for irony, namely, the retirement out of the temporal into the eternal by way of recollection, is again the essential for humor. Apparently, humor gives to existence a greater significance than irony does, but the immanent is predominant, and the more or less is a vanishing quantitative de-

decision, but with a smile of sadness (this is the lyrical in humor), which means that both the aged individual's seventy years, and the almost stillborn child's half an hour of life, are too little to become decisive for an eternity. Just as one might voluptuously tuck one's head under the pillow and not give a fig for the whole world, so the humorist tucks himself away, with the aid of immanence, into the eternity of recollection behind him, and smiles with sadness at existence in time with its breathless haste and illusory decision. The humorist does not indoctrinate immorality, far from it; he holds the moral in all honor, and does for his part all he can, and then again smiles at himself. But he is femininely in love with immanence, and recollection is his happy marriage, as recollection is also his happy longing. A humorist might very well conceive the notion, and also actually realize it, of working with greater zeal than anyone, of being as miserly with his time as a laborer on duty. But if this labor were to have the least significance in relation to the decision of an eternal happiness, he would smile. The temporal life is for him a fugitive episode having a very dubious significance; and in time it is only a foretaste of his happiness that he has his eternity assured behind him, by way of a recollection that takes him out of the temporal. Eternally only an eternal happiness is thinkable; the paradoxical consists, therefore, fully as much as in the case of trying to think an eternal unhappiness, in the fact that life in time is a point of departure, as if the existing individual had lost the eternity of recollection behind him, as if he were to receive an eternal happiness in a specific moment of time, although an eternal happiness precisely presupposes itself. Whether humor and speculation be in the right is another question, but it can never be right to declare this sort of thing identical with Christianity. When the essential decision of eternity is reached backward by way of recollection, it is quite consistent that the highest spiritual relationship with God be that God dissuades and holds in check, because existence in time never can be commensurable for an eternal decision. Thus the genius of Socrates, as is well known, was active only in dissuading, and the humorist must understand his God-relationship in the same manner. The metaphysical power and authority of the eternal recollection to solve and resolve soars above the disjunction, which the humorist does not reject, but acknowledges; and yet, and yet, in spite of all acknowledgment, he resolves it in the decisiveness of eternity from behind. In the paradox the reverse is the case, there the spirit gives an impulse forward; but this is again the paradoxical expression for how paradoxically time, and existence in time, have been accentuated.

termination over against the qualitative decisiveness of the Christian position. Humor therefore becomes the last *terminus a quo* in connection with the problem of determining the Christian. When humor uses the Christian terminology (sin, the forgiveness of sins, atonement, God in time, etc.) it is not Christianity, but a pagan speculation which has acquired a *knowledge* of the Christian ideas. It can come deceptively close to the Christian position; but where decisiveness takes hold; where existence captures the existing individual so that he must remain in existence, while the bridge of immanence and recollection is burned behind him; where the decision comes to be in the moment, and the movement is forward toward a relationship with the eternal truth which came into being in time: there humor does not follow. Modern speculative philosophy deceives in the same manner; indeed, one cannot say that it deceives, for there is soon no one to be deceived, and speculative philosophy does it *bona fide*. Speculative philosophy achieves the triumph of understanding Christianity entire; but it is to be noted that it does not understand it in a Christian manner, but speculatively, which is precisely a misunderstanding, since Christianity is the very opposite of speculation.

Magister Kierkegaard doubtless knew what he was doing when he called the edifying discourses Edifying Discourses, and abstained from the use of a Christian-dogmatic terminology, from mentioning the name of Christ, and so forth; all of which is in our day commonly indulged in without hesitation, although the categories, the thoughts, the dialectical element in the exposition, are entirely those of immanence. Just as the pseudonyms, in addition to what they are directly, indirectly constitute a polemic against speculative philosophy, so these addresses also constitute such a polemic; not because they are not speculative, for they are precisely speculative,* but because they are

---

* The signature Kts⁸ (in Professor Heiberg's *Intelligencer*) was thus fully justified in excepting the one address: "The Lord gave and the Lord took away, blessed be the name of the Lord," and saying about the others that they were too philosophical to be sermons. But he was not justified in overlooking the fact that the author himself has said the same thing by calling them edifying discourses, and by expressly calling attention in the Preface to the fact that they were not sermons. There can be no doubt that speculative philosophy in our age is engaged in confusing the sermon. One may call attention to this directly, for example, by writing a little article about it in a periodical; but this can also be done indirectly, and with a greater expenditure of effort, as by writing edifying discourses which are philosophical, and not sermons. Then when people say about these latter that they might very well deserve to be called sermons, this will show that the confusion is present; but it also shows that the author who does it, and openly brings the misunderstanding to the attention, does not precisely need to be told that the misunderstanding is there.

not sermons. Had the author called them sermons he would have been a blunderer. They are edifying discourses; the author repeats in the preface the stereotyped formula "that he is not a teacher," and that the addresses are not "unto edification," by which their teleological significance is humoristically revoked in the very preface. They are "not sermons"; the sermon corresponds in fact to the Christian categories, and to the sermon there corresponds a priest, and a priest is essentially what he is through ordination, and ordination is a teacher's paradoxical transformation in time, by which he becomes, in time, something else than what is involved in the immanent development of genius, talents, gifts, and so forth. Surely no one is ordained from eternity, or able to remember himself as ordained as soon as he is born. On the other hand, ordination constitutes a *character indelebilis*. What can this mean but that here again time becomes decisive for the eternal, so that the immanential retirement into the eternal by way of recollection is rendered impossible. Ordination again has affixed to it the Christian *nota bene*. Whether this be right, whether speculative philosophy and humor may not be the truth, is an entirely different question; but even if speculative philosophy were ever so much in the right, it can never be right in representing itself as Christianity.

So then I came with my *Fragments*. Whether I succeeded, in this little piece, in the task of indirectly connecting Christianity with existence, and by the use of an indirect form was enabled to bring it to the attention of an informed reader, whose misfortune perhaps it was that he was too well informed, I shall not attempt to decide. A direct mode of communication would not have permitted it, since such a method is relevant only to a recipient of knowledge, not essentially to an existing individual. By the use of a direct method some little sensation might have been achieved, but sensation is not relevant to existence, rather to gossip. Existence in what has been understood cannot be directly communicated to any existing spirit, not even by God, much less by a human being. As was said above, I shall not attempt to decide whether this was successfully accomplished in the piece; nor do I care to take the trouble to review it, which again would consistently have to be done in the indirect form of double reflection. What seldom happens to me is here the case; I am in agreement with all. If no one else has cared to review the book, neither do

I care to do so.* If the task was successfully achieved, so much the better; if not, well, the misfortune is not serious, such a book I do not need a long time to write, and if it became clear to me that not even by making something difficult could I serve any of my contemporaries, this depressing consciousness at least relieves me of the labor of writing.

* However, only within these last few days I have learned that it has been reviewed, and strangely enough, in a German periodical: *Allgemeines Repertorium für Theologie und kirchliche Statistik*.[9] The reviewer displays one excellent quality: he is brief, and refrains almost entirely from the otherwise customary examination-festiveness at the beginning and at the end, which consists of naming the author with praise, conferring distinction upon him, or even both conferring distinction and extending congratulations. This I appreciate so much the more, as the reviewer's first sentence (*"diese Schrift eines der produktivsten Schriftsteller Dänemarks ist wegen der Eigentümlichkeit ihres Verfahrens einer kurzer Besprechung nicht unwert"*) with the word *"Besprechung"* and so *"nicht unwert"* made me quite fearful. The reviewer describes the content of the book as a development of the positive Christian presuppositions, and then goes on to remark that this is accomplished in such a manner, *"dass unsere Zeit, die Alles nivelliert, neutralisiert und vermittelt, sie kaum widererkennen wird."* Without making any use of the hint of irony contained in what he himself says, about presenting the Christian presuppositions for our age in such a manner that although it has got through with them and advanced beyond them, it cannot even recognize them, he proceeds to furnish an abstract of the book. The abstract is accurate, and as a whole dialectically reliable, but here is the point: in spite of the accuracy of the abstract, everyone who reads that only is bound to get an entirely false impression of the book. To be sure, this misfortune is not so terrible; but on the other hand, when a book is reviewed especially on account of its peculiarity, it becomes a little unfortunate not to give any impression of this. The abstract is doctrinizing, pure and unadulterated doctrination; the reader will get the impression that the book is also doctrinizing. Now this is in my view the most distorted impression of the book it is possible to have. The contrast of the form; the challenging opposition between the experiment and the content; the impudence of the invention (which even invents Christianity), the only attempt made to go beyond, namely, beyond the so-called specula-tive construction; the unwearied incessant activity of the irony; the parody on speculative philosophy involved in the entire plan of the work; the satirical in making exertions as if *"was ganz Ausserordentliches und zwar Neues"* were to issue, and then coming out with nothing but old-fashioned orthodoxy in a suitable degree of severity: of all this the reader of the review gets not the slightest intimation. And yet the book is so far from being written for the unin-formed, to give them something to know, that the one I introduce into the book as my inter-locutor is precisely a well-informed person, which seems to indicate that the book is written for informed readers whose misfortune is that they know too much. Because everybody knows it, the Christian truth has gradually become a triviality, of which it is difficult to secure a primitive impression. This being the case, the art of *communication* at last becomes the art of *taking away,* of luring something away from someone. This seems very strange and ironical, and yet I believe that I have succeeded in expressing precisely what I mean. When a man has his mouth so full of food that he is prevented from eating, and is like to starve in consequence, does giving him food consist in stuffing still more of it in his mouth, or does it consist in taking some of it away, so that he can begin to eat? And so also when a man has much knowledge, and his knowledge has little or no significance for him, does a rational communication consist in giving him more knowledge, even supposing that he is loud in his insistence that this is what he needs, or does it not rather consist in taking some of it away? When an author communicates a portion of the knowledge that such a well-informed man has, in a form which makes it seem strange to him, it is as if he took his knowledge away from him, at least provisionally, until by having overcome the opposition of the form he succeeds in assimilating it. Suppose now the well-informed man's misfortune was that he was accustomed to a certain form, "that he could demonstrate the

Nevertheless, it has really occurred to me to ask myself whether I may not have involved myself in a misunderstanding; whether I do not presuppose something in the reader, and err in presupposing it. I will be quite frank about it; my conception of communication by means of books is very different from what I generally see put forward respecting it, and from what seems silently to be taken for granted. The indirect mode of communication makes communication an art in quite a different sense than when it is conceived in the usual manner: that the

mathematical proposition when the letters were in the order ABC, but not when they were in the order ACB," then the changed form takes his knowledge away from him, and yet this taking away is precisely the communication. When an age has systematically and rote-recitingly finished the understanding of Christianity and of all difficulties, so that it jubilantly exclaims how easy it is to understand the difficulty, it is impossible not to entertain a suspicion. For it is better to understand that something is so difficult that it cannot be understood than that a difficulty is so very easy to understand; for if it is so very easy, then perhaps it is not a difficulty at all; since a difficulty is precisely recognizable by the fact that it is hard to understand. When a communication, recognizing the existence of such an order of things, does not aim to make the difficulty any easier, then it becomes a process of taking away. The difficulty is clothed in a new form, in which it really is difficult. This then becomes a real communication—to one who has already found the difficulty easy to understand. And if it happens, as the review suggests, that a reader is scarcely able to recognize that which he has long finished with in what is thus presented to him, then the communication will give him pause, not by way of adding to his knowledge but by way of taking something from him.

Concerning the rest of the review there is nothing further to be said, except that the last four lines again show how everything in our doctrinizing age is understood in a doctrinizing manner. *"Wir enthalten uns jeder Gegenbemerkung, denn es lag uns, wie gesagt, bloss daran das eigen-tümliche Verfahren des Verfassers zur Anschauung zu bringen. Im Uebrigen stellen wir es dem Ermessen Jeden anheim, ob er in dieser apologetischen Dialektik Ernst oder etwa Ironie suchen will."* But my peculiar procedure, if it is this that is to be commented upon, and especially if it is to be brought to intuition, consists precisely in the contrast of the form, and by no means in the perhaps new dialectical combinations through which the problems are made clearer. It consists first and foremost and decisively in this contrast of the form, and only when this has been adequately emphasized can there be room for a moment's mention, if need be, of a bit of doctrinizing originality. When the reviewer leaves it to everyone to determine for himself whether he will seek earnest or irony in the piece, this is misleading. In general, it is customary to say something of the kind when one does not know what else to say; and when a book is pure and unadulterated doctrinizing earnest there might be point in saying such a thing, in so far as one then says something the book itself does not directly say. The book itself is pure earnest; now comes the critic and says: God knows whether it is irony or earnest, in which case he has said something; and he would also be saying something if he left it to the reader to determine whether to seek—what is not directly to be found in the book. But it is otherwise when it is merely a question of finding what is there. But the book was far from being pure and un-adulterated earnest, it was only the review that became unmixed earnest. In so far the concluding remark might have some meaning in relation to the review, as a satire upon it, for example; but in relation to the book it is silly. Suppose a man to have been present at one of the ironical Socratic conversations; if he relates it to another with omission of the irony, and then says: God knows whether such a way of speaking is irony or earnest, he satirises himself. But from the fact that the irony is present it does not follow that the earnestness is excluded. This is something that only *Docents* assume. While they are otherwise ready to abolish the disjunctive *aut,* fearing neither God nor the devil, since they mediate everything—they make an exception of irony, that they cannot mediate.

maker of the communication has to present something to the attention of one who knows, that he may judge it, or to the attention of one who does not know, that he may learn something. But no one bothers himself about the next consideration, that which makes communication dialectically so difficult, namely, that the recipient is an existing individual, and that this is essential. To stop a man on the street and stand still while talking to him, is not so difficult as to say something to a passer-by in passing, without standing still and without delaying the other, without attempting to persuade him to go the same way, but giving him instead an impulse to go precisely his own way. Such is the relation between one existing individual and another, when the communication concerns the truth as existential inwardness.

Relative to this, my dissentient opinion regarding communication, it has sometimes occurred to me whether this about indirect communication might not be communicable directly. Thus I see that Socrates, who otherwise holds so strictly to the method of question and answer (which is an indirect method), because the long speech, the dogmatizing lecture, the recitation by rote, only causes confusion, sometimes himself speaks more at length, and cites as a reason for this that his interlocutor needs some item of information before the conversation can get going. This he does for example in the Gorgias. But this procedure seems to me to be an inconsistency, an impatience that fears it will take too long before a mutual understanding can be reached. The indirect method would reach the same goal, only more slowly. But speed is of no value whatever in connection with a form of understanding in which the inwardness is the understanding. To me it seems better to reach a true mutual understanding in inwardness separately, though this might take place slowly. Indeed, even if this never happened, because the time passed and the author was forgotten without anyone having understood him, to me it seems more consistent not to have made the slightest accommodation in order to get anyone to understand him, first and last so tending to his own self as not to make himself important in relation to others, which is so far from being inwardness that it is noisy externality. If he acts in this manner he will have the solace in the day of judgment, when God is the judge, that he has indulged himself in nothing for the sake of winning someone, but with the utmost exertion has labored in vain, leaving it to God to determine whether it was to have any significance or not. And this will doubtless please God better than to have a busy man say to

Him: "I have won ten thousand adherents for you; some of them I won by weeping over the world's wretchedness and prophesying its early destruction, some by envisaging bright and smiling prospects for those who accepted my doctrine, others in other ways, here subtracting a little, here adding a little. They all became adherents of the truth, that is to say, moderately loyal adherents. If while I lived, you had stepped down on earth to inspect, I would have enchanted your eyes with the sight of the many adherents, just as Potemkin enchanted Catherine"[10]. . . aye, precisely as Potemkin enchanted Catherine, namely, by means of stage properties; and the ten thousand adherents to the truth were also only a theatrical diversion.

That subjectivity, inwardness, is the truth, was my thesis. I have sought to show how the pseudonymous authors in my view move in the direction of this principle, which in its maximum is Christianity. That it is possible to exist with inwardness also outside Christianity has among other things been sufficiently demonstrated by the Greeks. In our own age we seem really to have reached the point that while we are all Christians, it is a very rare thing to find a man who has even as much inwardness as a pagan philosopher. What wonder that one so quickly gets through with Christianity, when one begins by bringing oneself to a state of mind in which it is quite out of the question to get even the slightest impression of Christianity. One becomes objective, objectively one sits down to contemplate, that God was crucified, which when it happened did not permit even the temple to remain objective, for its veil was rent in twain, nor the dead, for they rose up from their graves: that is to say, what suffices to make even the lifeless and the dead subjective, that is now studied objectively by objective gentlemen. One becomes objective, objectively one proposes to contemplate Christianity, which to begin with takes the liberty to make the objective gentleman a sinner, if there can be any question of getting anything at all to see. And that most terrible of all sufferings of subjectivity, that of being a sinner, that, too, one proposes to be . . . objectively. Then again we help ourselves out with long systematic introductions, and outlines of universal history: in this connection, pure nonsense, and in relation to the decision for Christianity, a sheer waste of time. One becomes more and more objective, the earlier the better, subjectivity is held in contempt, the category of the individual is despised, and comfort is sought in the category of the race; we fail to grasp what cowardice and despair there is in the individual's reaching out after a glittering somewhat, and himself as subject becoming nothing. We are Christians without more ado, on festival occasions we still consider the question, which was becoming to the stern forebears, whether pagans can enjoy eternal bliss; and do not notice the satire, that paganism is much nearer Christianity than such an objective Christendom, where Christ has become yea and nay, while in Corinth, as preached by Paul, he was not yea and nay (2 Cor. 1:19). Existing subjectively with passion (and objectively it is possible to exist only in distraction) is in general an absolute condition for presuming to have any opinion about Christianity. Everyone who does not wish to exist so, but who nevertheless desires to concern himself with Christianity, whoever he may be, however great he may be in other respects, is in this matter essentially a fool.

Whether my conception of the pseudonymous authors corresponds to what they themselves have had in mind, I cannot of course say, since I am only a reader; but it is clear enough that they bear a relationship to my thesis. If in nothing else, this can be seen from the fact that they abstain from dogmatizing. Not to dogmatize is in my opinion the true interpretation of the confusion of the age, which consists precisely in the constant dogmatizing. *Docents* of high standing have belittled the pseudonymous books, including my own little piece, because they were not objectively dogmatic; many have from this unquestioningly concluded that the reason was that the authors, including myself, were not able to raise themselves to the lofty height necessary for objective discourse, were incapable of the objectivity which is the standpoint of the *Docents*. This may be so; but suppose subjectivity to be the truth, then there would always be something dubious about the lofty height reached by the *Docents*. It has surprised me to note, that while every theologue almost is supposed to be able to write in the objective dogmatic manner, nevertheless people could not persuade themselves that the pseudonymous authors, including myself, Johannes Climacus, might be able to write in this manner about as well as most of those who do, but on the contrary find themselves readily disposed to believe that we are such poor stuff that we cannot do what now, when an entire German literature has been developed solely in that direction, is about as easy for a studious reader who wants to make abstracts of German books, as it is nowadays to write verse, an accomplishment that may soon be required of housemaids. Be this as it may, it is always good to be distinguished by something, and I ask nothing better than to be pointed out as the only one who *cannot* doctrinize, and hence also as the only one who does not understand what the age demands.

That subjectivity, inwardness, is the truth was my thesis, and that the pseudonymous authors sustain a relationship to it is readily perceived, if from nothing else than from their sensitiveness to the comical. The comical is always the mark of maturity; but it is important that the new shoot should be ready to appear under this maturity, and that the *vis comica* should not stifle the pathetic, but rather serve an indication that a new pathos is beginning. The power to wield the weapon of the comic I regard as an indispensable legitimation for everyone who in our age is to have any authority in the world of the spirit. When an age is so thoroughly reflective as our age is, or is said to be, the comical must in so far as this is true have been discovered by everyone, and primitively discovered by everyone who proposes to have anything to say. But the *Docents* are so wanting in comic sense that it is terrifying; even Hegel, according to the assertion of a zealous Hegelian, is totally wanting in a sense for the comical. A ludicrous stiff solemnity and air of paragraph-importance that gives a *Docent* a striking resemblance to a bookkeeper out of Holberg,[11] is what the *Docents* call seriousness. Everyone who does not have this terrible solemnity is frivolous. Perhaps. But what does it mean when a man says that he has actually reflected himself out of the sphere of the immediate, without attaining mastery in the realm of the comic: what does that mean? Why, it means that the man lies. What does it mean for a man to affirm that he has reflected his way out of the immediate, and then communicates this as information in direct form? Why, it means that the man is talking through his hat. In the world of the spirit the various stages are not like towns on a route of travel, which it is quite in order for the traveller to tell about directly: as for example, "we left Pekin and came to Canton, on the 14th of the month we were in Canton." Such a traveller changes places but not himself, and hence it is in order that he tells about it in the direct unaltered form, and thus *relates* the change. But in the world of the spirit a change of place means a change in oneself, for which reason all direct assurances about having reached this or that stage are attempts *à la* Munchhausen. That a man has arrived at this or that distant place in the world of the spirit is proved by the mode of presentation itself; if this testifies to the contrary, all direct assurances become merely a contribution to the comical. The power to wield the weapon of the comic is the policeman's shield, the badge of authority, which every agent who in our time really is an agent must carry. But this comic spirit is not wild or vehement, its laughter is not shrill; on the contrary, it is careful of the immediacy that it sets aside. The scythe of the harvest hand is equipped with a cradle, some wooden rods that run parallel with the sharp blade; and while the scythe cuts the standing grain it sinks almost voluptuously down upon the supporting cradle, to be laid neatly and beautifully on the stubble. Such is also the legitimate comic spirit in relation to the immediacy that is ripe for the cutting. The task of cutting is a festive deed, the cutter is not a surly harvest hand, and though it is the sharp blade of the comical and its biting edge that compels the immediate to yield, its yielding is not unbeautiful, and even in falling it is supported by the cutter. This comic spirit is essentially humor. When the comic is cold and comfortless it is a sign that there is no new immediacy in the shoot, and then the comical does not function as a harvest, but as the contentless passion of an unfruitful wind raging over the naked ground.

It is always good to be distinguished by something; I ask nothing better than to be pointed out as the only one in our serious age who is not serious. Far from hoping for any modification of this judgment, it is rather my wish that the honorable *Docents,* both those who gesticulate *ex cathedra* and those whose voices ring loud about the tea tables, would stand by their judgment and not suddenly have forgotten the frequent private declamations of earnest phrases directed against the pseudonymous authors, but on the contrary clearly remember that it was these authors who proposed to make the comical a determination in earnestness, and to find in the jest a release from the sorriest of all tyrannies: the tyranny of moroseness, stupidity, and inflexibility of spirit. The pseudonymous authors including myself are all subjective; I ask nothing better than to be distinguished as the only one in our objective age who is incapable of being objective.

That subjectivity, inwardness, is the truth; that existence is the decisive thing; that this was the path along which it was necessary to move in order to approach Christianity, which is precisely inwardness, though not any and every type of inwardness, whence it was necessary also to fix definitely and clearly the prior stages: this was my idea. In the pseudonymous books I thought I perceived such a movement, and I have sought to make my interpretation of it clear, as well as its relationship to my *Fragments.* Whether I have found the meaning of the authors I cannot know with certainty; but in any case I wish to offer them excuses, in so far as I have in a manner reviewed them, although by abstaining from entering into a discussion of the content, I have really not written a review. It has never been a mystery to me why the pseudonymous authors have again and again asked to be excused from being reviewed. Since the contrasting form of the presentation makes it impossible to report the content in an abstract, because the abstract takes away the feature of greatest importance and falsely transforms the book into a doctrinizing treatise, the authors are fully justified in contenting themselves with a few actual readers, rather than in being misunderstood by the many who by means of a review have found something they can run with. This is also my opinion *qua* author; and I am here reminded of a remark ascribed to Zeno, who in connection with Theophrastus having so many disciples said: "His chorus is larger, mine is more harmonious." This I have just these days read again in Plutarch, in a little essay on "How a man may praise himself in a lawful manner."

My *Fragments* approached the problem of Christianity in a decisive manner, but without mentioning its name, nor the name of Christ. In an age of knowledge, when all men are Christians and know what Christianity is, it is only too easy to use the sacred names without attaching any thought to them, to recite the Christian truth by rote without having the slightest impression of it. If anyone wishes to assume that the reason for the omission of the names was my ignorance, that I did not know that the founder of Christianity was Christ, and that His doctrine is called Christianity, he is welcome to assume it. It is always good to be distinguished by something; and I for my part ask nothing better than in the midst of Christendom to be the only one who does not know that the founder of Christianity was Christ: to be ignorant is at any rate better than to be informed about it as about a hundred other trivialities.

When my *Philosophical Fragments* had thus been issued, and I was considering the matter of writing a postscript to "invest the problem in its historical costume," there came from the press still another pseudonymous book: *Stages on Life's Way.* This book has attracted the attention of only a few (as it prognosticates about itself); perhaps, among other things, for the reason that there was here no "Diary of a Seducer" as in *Either-Or,* which was the most widely read portion of that book, and naturally helped to create a sensation. Its relationship to *Either-Or* is apparent enough, and is decisively shown by the use in its first two sections of the familiar names from that work. Had the author of the *Stages* consulted me, I should for aesthetic reasons have advised him against recalling a preceding work by the use of familiar names.* In relation to everything that is venturesome, and venturesome because it requires good fortune, it is always a dubious thing to stimulate a recollection. To avoid this is easy; to do it is to risk oneself and one's good fortune in a venture whose perilousness is enunciated in several passages in the work.† There is a story about a sailor who fell down from the top of the mast without coming to any harm; when he picked himself up he said: "Do that after me." But he presumably also himself abstained from attempting to do it over again. A repetition relative to things that require good fortune and inspiration is always venturesome. There is set up, through the comparison thus engendered, an absolute standard for fruitfulness in the expression; for to repeat one's own words, or to repeat happily chosen expressions literally, is not difficult. To repeat the same, means therefore to make changes under conditions made more difficult because of the preceding effort. The merely curious reader is repelled by the fact that it is the same, for the curious reader demands external changes in names, decorations, clothes, style of dressing the hair, and so forth. The attentive reader is rendered more strict in his requirements, because there is nothing seductive, nothing distractive, no mere filling, no information about the outward appearance of unknown characters, or about the climatic conditions of distant regions, and so forth.

However, the venture was made, and the unknown author was presumably not ignorant of the danger, just as he can scarcely have been ignorant of the reason why Socrates[12] held it his honor and his pride

---

* For still another reason (assuming, as is generally done, that the pseudonymous books derive from a single author), I would have dissuaded him from the strenuous labor involved. For prudence forbids one to work too zealously or too continuously: these stupid people believe that it is botchery. No, much noise and fuss, and so little production: then the *plebs* believe that it is something. Perhaps I should still not have made any impression; for it is not unthinkable that the author himself has understood this, but thought it contemptible to act prudently, and regarded the winning of certain people's admiration as a dubious thing.

† "How easy it is to arrange a banquet, and yet Constantine has insisted that he will never risk it again. How easy it is to admire, and yet Victor Eremita has asserted that he will never again clothe his admiration (for Mozart namely) in words, because a defeat is more terrible than to become an invalid in the war!" As ethicist the Judge avows the opposite with ethical passion: "This may suffice about marriage; in this moment it does not occur to me to wish to say more; another time, perhaps tomorrow, I may say more, but always the same and about the same, for only gypsies and thieves have the motto: Never return to the same place again."

always to say the same things about the same things.* The pseudonymous author has by making this venture won an indirect triumph over a curious reading public. When such a curious reader† peeps into the book and sees the familiar names: Victor Eremita, Constantine Constantius, etc., he throws the book away and says in boredom: "It is just the same." And when such a reader says it aloud, perhaps the pseudonymous author will think to himself: "If it only were as you say, really; for this judgment is a compliment, since it cannot be understood to mean that it is word for word the same; but I feel indeed that I do not possess this vegetative luxuriance in inwardness in so great a measure, and that I have dared to repeat, therefore, only by the use of a considerable degree of abbreviation, and with important changes in the points of departure. I have one advantage, however, over the editor of *Either-Or,* for the interest of novelty, and the size of the book, and the "Diary of the Seducer" caused almost a riot, so that the book was bought, and is even supposed to be sold out; which is, alas, a very dubious argument for its merit—one is almost tempted to think that it was a New Year's present.[13] I, on the contrary, am free from the smelling explorations of the curious."

In connection with Tivoli[14] entertainments and literary New Year's presents it holds true for the catch-penny artists and those who are caught by them, that variety is the highest law of life. But in connection with the truth as inwardness in existence, in connection with a more incorruptible joy of life, which has nothing in common with the craving of the life-weary for diversion, the opposite holds true; the

---

* It is possible in general to acquire a deep insight into a man's soul, to determine whether he is a spirit or only sensually determined, by taking note of what he understands by the wealth of an author, and what by his poverty. If a clergyman could continue for a whole year to preach on one and the same text, constantly renewing himself in the vegetative luxuriance of the expression, he would in my eyes be matchless; but a sensuous auditor would find him tiresome. If Oehlenschlager the moment he had finished writing his *Valborg* could have written it over again, then he would in my eyes have been still greater than he is. To write *Signe* is already easier, because the circumstance, the scene, the surroundings, etc., are different. But to write *Valborg,* let the reader read it, and then write the same Valborg over again; the same, that is to say, all the externals being the same and familiar, only the vividness of love's expression upon Valborg's lips new, new as a new bouquet of flowers; however many might find it tiresome, I should allow myself to find it astonishing. One of the things I have most admired in Shakespeare is his Falstaff, and among other things also because he is repeated. To be sure, Falstaff does not have many scenes each time he appears, but if Shakespeare could have held Falstaff unchanged in five whole acts, and so again in five acts, no matter how many would find it tiresome, I should allow myself to find it divine.

† It is undoubtedly with respect to such a curious reader, that the first third of the book has for its motto Lichtenberg's words: *"Solche Werke sind Spiegel; wenn ein Affe hinein guckt, kann kein Apostel heraus sehen."*

law is: the same, and yet changed, and still the same. That is why lovers of Tivoli are so little interested in eternity, for it is the nature of eternity always to be the same, and the sobriety of the spirit is recognizable in the knowledge that a change in externalities is mere diversion, while a change in the same is inwardness. But so curious, by and large, is the reading public, that an author who desires to get rid of it has merely to give a little hint, just a name, and it will say: it is the same. For otherwise the differences between the *Stages* and *Either-Or* are obvious enough. Not to speak of the fact that two-thirds of it is about as different as is categorically possible.* In the first third of the book, Victor Eremita, who was before simply an editor, is now transformed into an existing individual; Constantine and Johannes the Seducer have received a more pronounced characterization; the Judge is occupied with marriage from quite a different point of view than in *Either-Or;* while scarcely the most attentive reader will find a single expression, a single turn of thought or phrase, precisely as it was in *Either-Or.*

I have intentionally lingered more at length over this, because, although it may be a matter of convenience for an author who stands thus alone, precisely loving his isolation, it means something else for me, since it is connected with what I have constantly emphasized, namely, that the age has forgotten what it means to exist, and what inwardness is. It has lost faith in the truth that inwardness makes the apparently scanty content richer, while a change in externals is merely a diversion sought by the life-weary and the life-empty. It is for this reason that the existential tasks are rejected. One learns to know in passing what faith is, and so that is known. Then one reaches out for a speculative result, and is no further along. Another day astronomy is brought up, and so we gad our way through all the sciences and all the spheres, without ever living. The poets, merely to amuse the reader, roam about in Africa and America, in Trebizond and in R—, and soon it will be necessary to discover a new continent, if poetry is not to go into the discard. And why? Because inwardness is more and more on the wane.

Let us then begin with the final two-thirds of the book, whose content is a story of suffering. Suffering may indeed be present in all

* But also in relation to the two-thirds of the book, it is prophesied that the reader will find it tiresome. A love story is a love story, says such a reading public; if we are to read about it a second time the scene must be in Africa, for it is the scenery that gives variety, and such a reading public needs "events, landscapes, many people—and also cows."

the various stages of existence; but when a book is so planned as to include an aesthetic stage, and then an ethical stage, and so finally a religious stage, and the word suffering is employed here for the first time, it would seem to be indicated that suffering is differently related to the religious than to the ethical or the aesthetic. The phrase, "Story of Suffering," seems therefore to be used pregnantly, as a category, as if suffering had a decisive significance in connection with the religious. A "Story of Suffering," viewed as a title, would here seem to mean something different from Goethe's *Leiden des jungen Werthers,* or Hoffmann's *Leiden eines armen Theaterdirectors.* In connection with aesthetic or ethical existence, suffering plays an accidental rôle; it may be absent, and the mode of existence may still be aesthetic or ethical, or if it gains here a deeper significance, it is as a transitional phase. Not so here, where suffering is posited as something decisive for a religious existence, and precisely as a characteristic of the religious inwardness: the more the suffering, the more the religious existence—and the suffering persists. The author has therefore not chosen this title for his work because he did not know what else to call it; he has had a definite thought in mind, and has enunciated it himself. While aesthetic existence is essentially enjoyment, and ethical existence, essentially struggle and victory, religious existence is essentially suffering, and that not as a transitional moment, but as persisting. The suffering is, to recall the Frater's words, the seventy thousand fathoms deep on which the religious man constantly lies. But suffering is precisely inwardness; and it is an inwardness which marks itself off from the aesthetic and the ethical types of existential inwardness. Even in the speech of daily life, when someone says of a man that he must have suffered much, we are wont to attach thereto immediately a sense of inwardness.

The title of the story of suffering is "Guilty?—Not guilty?" The question marks clearly constitute a reference to a trial. A novel-writer would presumably have telescoped the two parts of the title together, and a reading public which wishes for a result would be glad to have seen it done in that manner. The title would then have become: "Faithless, and yet a man of honor," "A broken promise, and yet an eternal loyalty," *ad modum* "A Hussar officer, and yet a good husband," and so forth. Which is which, is at once decided on the title-page, and the reader can feel secure. The reader is not troubled either by the existential, or by the dialectical precision of the categories; the story is an amiable hodge-podge of a little aestheticism, a little of the ethical, a little of the religious. But what essentially interests a thinker is not to be presented with some information afterwards, but to become contemporary with the existing individual in his existence. The Quidam of the experiment exists in the tension between the two probing questions, tortured by the sharp examination of the inquiry. If it is the misfortune of the age to have forgotten what inwardness is, and what it means to exist, it becomes all the more necessary to get as close to existence as possible. Hence the experiment does not take its point of departure at a later moment, telling of the remarkable conflict as of something past; it does not relax the tension of the conflict in a reassuring result; by means of its challenging form it makes the reader still more completely a contemporary than he could be with an actual contemporary event, and leaves him in the lurch by not allowing him any result. There have doubtless been books written before without an ending; the author died perhaps, or did not care to finish it, etc. But this is not the case here; the absence of an ending, a result, is like suffering in the preceding case, apprehended as a categorical determination of the religious existence. Frater Taciturnus develops this himself (§3). But the absence of a result is precisely a determination of inwardness; for a result is something external, and a communication of results is an external relation between a knower and a non-knower.

The "Story of Suffering" was called an experiment, and the Frater himself develops the meaning of this.

The "Story of Suffering" stands in a relationship to *Repetition*. However, the difference is obvious if we consider the categories, which alone can have an interest for thought. Differences in the masquerade costumes is what interests the gallery, which presumably also believes that the greatest actress is one that plays not only in a variety of fantastic costumes, but also in trousers and jacket, with collars. The compass of the player's art is measured by the costumes, so that the poorest actress is the one who plays particularly the parts in which she wears her own clothes. In *Repetition,* rationality on the one hand, and the higher immediacy of youth on the other, were kept separate; in Constantine, as rationality, and the young man, as being in love. In the *Stages* these two factors are put together in one individual, the Quidam of the experiment, by which the double movement becomes both necessary and evident, and even *earnestness* is constituted as a composite of

jest and earnest.* In *Repetition,* irony on the one hand, and sentimentality on the other, are brought into relationship; in the "Story of Suffering"
it is humor which is brought to light. Constantine himself takes part,
but Frater Taciturnus stands wholly aside, as an inspector; for Quidam
has enough understanding, which is precisely why humor is attained,
because he is himself in both of the discrete phases. If we leave the
feminine figure outside of the reckoning, she being in both *Repetition*
and in the "Story of Suffering" present only indirectly, *Repetition* has
two characters, while the "Story of Suffering" has only one. "It becomes
more and more tiresome; there is not even so much as a suicide, or a
case of madness, or a clandestine childbirth, or the like; besides, when
the author has already written a love story he ought to make an attempt
in a new direction, write a tale of robbers, for example."

Frater Taciturnus determines himself as occupying a lower plane
of existence than Quidam, in so far as the latter has a new immediacy.
Constantine was not indisposed to do the like in relation to the young
man, but nevertheless had a rationality and an irony lacking to the
young man. In general it is customary to think the relations conversely,
assuming that the experimenter, the observer, stands higher or is higher
than that which he produces. Hence the ease with which results are
arrived at. Here the opposite is the case; the experimenter discovers
and points out the higher, higher not in the direction of understanding
and thought, but in the direction of inwardness. Quidam's inwardness
is marked precisely by the inclusion of the opposite within himself, that
he sees the comic in that which nevertheless rules within him with
the whole passion of his inwardness. A feminine inwardness in the form
of devotion is a lesser degree of inwardness, because the tendency is
obviously outward, toward, while here the presence of the contrasting
precisely indicates the inward direction. Quidam is himself a unity of
the comic and the tragic; and yet he is more than this unity, since he is
the passion arising after the unity (the comi-tragic of §2). The Frater
is essentially a humorist, and precisely through being a humorist does
he serve to point out the new immediacy, though he thrusts it away
from him.

So now we have humor advanced to the point of being the last
terminus a quo in relation to the Christian type of the religious. In
modern philosophy humor has become the highest stage after faith.

* A little motto by Quidam is at once significant of the humorous double mood, while a Latin
motto *periissem nisi periissem* is a suffering humoristic revocation of the whole.

Faith is in this case the immediate, and through speculative philosophy, which makes an advance upon faith, we reach humor. This is the fundamental confusion inherent in the entire systematic speculative tendency, in so far as it proposes to include Christianity within itself. No, humor is the concluding stage of the immanent within the immanent; it is still essentially a retirement out of existence into the eternal by way of recollection, and only after humor do we come upon faith and the paradoxes. Humor is the last stage of existential inwardness before faith. Hence it was, according to my ideas, necessary to bring this stage to view, lest any stage be left behind that afterwards might cause confusion. This has now been done through the "Story of Suffering." Humor is not faith but comes before faith—it is not after faith or a development of faith. From the Christian point of view there is no advance beyond faith, because faith is the highest stage—for an existing individual—as has been sufficiently developed in the preceding. Even when humor makes an attempt at the paradoxes, it is not faith. Humor does not absorb the suffering side of the paradox, nor the ethical side of faith, but merely the amusing aspect. For it is a species of suffering, a martyrdom even in peaceful times, to have the happiness of the soul tied to that which the understanding despairs about.

The immature type of humor, on the other hand, which lies still further back, and which I call humor in an equilibrium between the comic and the tragic—this immature humor is a sort of brash frivolity which has even slipped away from reflection too soon. Weary of time and its infinite succession, the humorist runs away, and finds a humorous relief in positing the absurd; just as it may be a relief to parody the significance of life by paradoxically accentuating the insignificant, by giving everything up, and concentrating on playing billiards or riding horses. But this is an immature humor, falsifying the paradox, using it as a stimulus for the arbitrary whims of a melancholy passion. This immature humor is so far from being religiosity, that it is an aesthetic refinement which has overleaped the ethical.

The fact that faith and the Christian-religious mode of existence have humor as the precedent stage, shows besides what a tremendous existential compass is possible outside Christianity; and on the other side what an experience of life is required as a pre-condition for properly entering upon Christianity. But in our age we do not exist at all, and so it is quite natural that everyone is a Christian as a matter of course. One becomes a Christian as a child, which may be beautiful and well-meant on the part of Christian parents, but ridiculous when the person in question himself assumes that so the matter is decided. Stupid clergymen appeal quite directly to a Bible passage directly understood: that no one can enter the kingdom of heaven unless he comes in as a little child. Aye, indeed, what a sweet little thing Christianity becomes with the assistance of the childishness of such clergymen. In this manner the Apostles must have been excluded, for I do not know that they came in as little children. To say to the most mature spirit: "My friend, if you will take care to become a child again, then you may become a Christian"—that is a hard saying, as befits the doctrine which was an offense to the Jews and a folly to the Greeks. But to understand this dark saying, so that all difficulties are removed by being baptized as a little child and then dying, the sooner the better, is a stupidity which is directly contrary to the category of Christianity (which paradoxically accentuates temporal existence), and has not even understood the pagan feeling, expressed in imagining small children weeping in Elysium because they died so soon, which is always to concede some significance to time. Upon its entrance into the world, Christianity was not proclaimed to children, but to a superannuated Jewish religiosity, a decadent world of science and art. First the first and then the next. If the age only had as much existential inwardness as a Jew, or as a Greek, there could at least be some question of a relationship to Christianity. But if it was once terribly difficult to become a Christian, it will soon surely be impossible, because the whole matter becomes one of no significance A Greek philosopher was certainly a man who could think, and it therefore means something when Christianity determines itself as the doctrine which is an offense to the Jews and a folly to the Greeks; for the Jew had still religious inwardness enough to be capable of taking offense. But all this is gone out of use in the slack generation now living, which on the average has undoubtedly much more culture than was previously the case, but has neither the passion of thought nor of religiosity. It is possible both to enjoy life and give it significance and content outside of Christianity, as is indeed evident, since the most famous poets and artists, the most eminent of thinkers, even devout men, have lived outside Christianity. This is something of which Christianity itself has doubtless not been unaware, and yet it has not found itself warranted in changing the conditions; and the more spiritual maturity in the subject, the more terrible the paradox, which remains the unaltered condition imposed by Christianity, the signal for the offense and the folly. But let us not in its old age transform Christianity into something like an innkeeper in reduced circumstances, who must hit upon something and anything to attract customers, or into an adventurer intent upon making his fortune in the world. To be sure, at the time when Christianity came into the world it can hardly be said to have made its fortune, since it was met with crucifixions, floggings and the like. But God knows whether it has really ever desired to make its fortune here in this world. I think rather perhaps it feels a sense of shame, like an old man who sees himself decked out in the latest fashions; or rather, I think it gathers wrath over the heads of men, when it sees this parody which is supposed to be Christianity, a scented and systematically accommodated scientific figure, introduced into the soirées, whose entire secret is half-truths, and so truth to a certain degree: a radical cure, and only as such being what it is, now transformed into a vaccination treatment, and the relation to it the same as in the case of vaccination—having a certificate. No, the Christian paradox is not this or that, something wonderful and yet not so wonderful; its truth is not like Solomon Goldkalb's[15] opinion: much before and behind, and yes and no at the same time. Nor is faith something that everyone has and which no man of culture can afford to be without. Though it can be grasped and held by the simplest person, it is all the more difficult for men of culture. O wonderful, inspiring Christian humanity: the highest is the common possession of all men, and the most happily gifted are merely those who are most strictly taken to task!

But back to the *Stages*. It is obviously differentiated from *Either-Or* by its tripartite division. There are three stages: an aesthetic, an ethical, and a religious. But these are not distinguished abstractly, as the immediate, the mediate and the synthesis of the two, but rather concretely, in existential determinations, as enjoyment-perdition; action-victory; suffering. But in spite of this triple division the book is nevertheless an either-or. The ethical and the religious stages have in fact an essential relationship to one another. The difficulty with *Either-Or* is that it was rounded out to a conclusion ethically, as was shown above. In the *Stages* this is clarified, and the religious is thus assigned to its proper place.

The aesthetic and the ethical stages are again brought forward, in a certain sense as recapitulation, but then again as something new. It would also be a poor testimony to existential inwardness if every such stage were not capable of a renewal in the presentation, though it may be venturesome to reject the apparent assistance of externals in calling attention to the difference, as by choosing new names, and the like. The ethicist again concentrates on marriage as the most dialectically complex of the revelations that reality affords. Nevertheless he brings forward a new aspect, and emphasizes particularly the category of time and its significance, as the medium for the beauty that increases with age; while from the aesthetic point of view, time and existence in time is more or less a regress.

On account of the triple division, the existential situation as between the stages has been subjected to a rearrangement. In *Either-Or* the aesthetic standpoint is represented by means of an existential possibility, while the ethicist is existing. Now the aesthetic is existential; the ethicist is militant, fighting *ancipito proelio* against the aesthetic, over which he again readily gains the victory, not by means of the seductive gifts of the intellect, but with ethical passion and pathos; he seeks also to defend himself against the religious. In rounding out his position as an ethicist, he does his utmost to defend himself against the decisive form of a higher standpoint. That he should thus defend himself is quite in order, since he is not a standpoint but an existing individual. It is a fundamental confusion in recent philosophy to mistake the abstract consideration of a standpoint with existence, so that when a man has knowledge of this or that standpoint he supposes himself to exist in it; every existing individuality must precisely as existing be more or less one-sided. From the abstract point of view there is no decisive conflict between the standpoints, because abstraction precisely removes that in which the decision inheres: *the existing subject*. But in spite of this consideration, the immanent transition of speculative philosophy is still a chimera, an illusion, as if it were possible for the one standpoint necessarily to determine itself into the other; for the category of transition is itself a breach of immanence, a *leap*.

The aestheticist in *Either-Or* was an existential possibility, a young, richly gifted, partly hopeful human being, experimenting with himself and with life; one "with whom it was impossible to grow angry, because the evil that was in him, like the conceptions of evil in the Middle Ages, had something of the childlike in it"; he was not really an actuality, but "a possibility of everything": thus the aestheticist so to speak walked about in the Judge's living room.* The Judge's relation to him was one of open-hearted geniality; he was ethically sure of himself and essentially admonitory, like a somewhat older and more mature person in relation to a younger man, whose talents, whose intellectual superiority he in a manner recognizes, though unconditionally having the ascendancy over him through sureness, experience, and inwardness in living. In the *Stages* the aesthetic receives a more pronounced existential character; and hence there comes to revelation latently, in the presentation itself, the fact that an aesthetic existence, even when a milder light falls upon it, is perdition. But it is not a foreign standpoint that makes this clear, as when the Judge admonishes a young man whose life is not in the deepest sense yet decided. It is too late to admonish a decisively aesthetic existence; to assume to warn Victor Eremita, Constantine Constantius, The Fashion Tailor, or a Johannes the Seducer is to make oneself ridiculous, and to produce an effect quite as comical as a situation I once experienced: a man in an instant of danger catches up a little stick from a child—to beat a huge bandit who had forced his way into the room. Though myself sharing in the danger I was involuntarily moved to laughter, because it looked as if the man were beating clothes. The relationship between the Judge and the aestheticist in *Either-Or* made it natural and psychologically correct for the Judge to admonish. However, even in that work there was no decision in the finite sense (see the Preface), so that the reader could say: "Well, that settles it." A reader who needs the reassurance of a warning lecture in order to see that a standpoint is erroneous, or needs an unfortunate consequence, like madness, suicide, poverty and the like, does not really see anything, but only imagines that he sees; and when an author conducts himself in that manner he only shows that he writes in a womanish fashion for childish readers.† Take such a figure as Johannes the Seducer. Whoever

* Even the "Diary of the Seducer" was only a terrible possibility, which the aestheticist had in his fumbling mode of existence evoked, precisely because he had to try himself in everything, though without really having been anything.

† Here I would recall something to which *Frater Taciturnus* has called attention. The Hegelian philosophy culminates in the proposition that the outward is the inward and the inward is the outward. With this Hegel virtually finishes. But this principle is essentially an aesthetic-metaphysical one, and in this way the Hegelian philosophy is happily finished, or it is fraudulently finished by lumping everything (including the ethical and the religious) indiscriminately in the aesthetic-metaphysical. Even the ethical posits opposition of a sort between the inward and the outward, inasmuch as it regards the outward as neutral. Outwardness, as the material

needs that he should become mad or shoot himself in order to be enabled to see that his standpoint is perdition, does not see it, notwithstanding, but merely imagines it. Whoever understands it, understands it the instant the Seducer opens his mouth to speak; he hears in every word the perdition and the condemnation. The reader who needs an outer infliction of punishment merely exposes himself to be made a fool of, for an author can take a very decent man and have him become mad, and then such a reader will believe that it was an illegitimate standpoint.

The aesthetic stage is represented by "In vino veritas." Those who make their appearance here are indeed aestheticists, but are by no means ignorant of the ethical. Hence they are not merely delineated, but speak for themselves as persons fully qualified to give an account of their mode of existence. In our age it is believed that knowledge settles everything, and that if a man only acquires a knowledge of the truth, the more briefly and the more quickly the better, he is helped. But to exist and to know are two very different things.

The Young Man comes closest to being merely a possibility, and therefore he is still a hopeful case. He is essentially melancholy of thought. Constantine Constantius is case-hardened understanding. Victor Eremita is sympathetic irony. The Fashion Tailor is demoniac despair in passion. Johannes the Seducer is perdition in cold blood, a "marked" individuality in whom life is extinct. All are consistent to the point of despair.

Just as the second part of *Either-Or* answers and corrects every misdirection in the first part, so one will here find an explanation in what the ethicist has to say, only that he expresses himself essentially, and nowhere takes direct cognizance of what according to the plan of the work he cannot be supposed to know. It is thus left to the reader him-

of action, is neutral, for what the ethical accentuates is the purpose; the result, as the outwardness of action, is indifferent, for what the ethical accentuates is the purpose, and it is simply immoral to be concerned about the result; outwardness proves nothing at all ethically; outward victory proves nothing at all ethically, for ethically question is raised only about the inward; outward punishment is of little significance, and the ethical, so far from requiring with aesthetic fussiness the visibility of punishment, says proudly, "I shall punish sure enough, i.e. inwardly; and it is simply immoral to rate outward punishment as of any account in comparison with inward."—The religious posits decisively an opposition between the outward and the inward, posits it decisively as opposition, and therein lies suffering as an existence-category for the religious life, but therein lies also the inner infinity of inwardness inwardly directed. If our age had not the distinction of simply ignoring the duty of existing, it would be inconceivable that such wisdom as the Hegelian could be regarded as the highest, as maybe it is for aesthetic contemplators, but not either for ethical or for religious existers.

self to put two and two together, if he so desires; but nothing is done
to minister to a reader's indolence. To be sure, it is just this that readers
want; they want to read books in the royal fashion in which a king
reads a petition, where a marginal outline relieves him from the petitioner's prolixity. In relation to the pseudonymous authors this expectation is doubtless a misunderstanding from the side of the reader; from
the impression I have of them I do not know that they seek any sort of
favors from the lofty majority-majesty of the reading public. That
would also seem to me a very strange thing to do. I have always conceived of an author as a man who knows something more, or knows
the same thing otherwise, than the reader; that is the reason he is an
author, and otherwise he has no reason to be one. But it has never
occurred to me to think of the author as a supplicant, a beggar knock-
ing at the door of the reading public, a peddler who with the aid of a
devil of a ready tongue and a little fancy gold stuff on the cover,[16] which
quite catches the eyes of the daughters in the family, succeeds in foist-
ing his books upon them.

Johannes the Seducer ends with the proposition that *woman is only
the moment*. This is in its generality the essential aesthetic principle,
namely, that the moment is everything, and in so far again essentially
nothing; just as the sophistic proposition that everything is true means
that nothing is true. The significance attached to time is in general
decisive for every standpoint up to that of the paradox, which paradoxically accentuates time. In the same degree that time is accentuated, in
the same degree we go forward from the aesthetic, the metaphysical, to
the ethical, the religious, and the Christian-religious.

Where Johannes the Seducer ends, there the Judge begins: that
woman's beauty increases with the years. Here time is accentuated
ethically, but not otherwise than that a retirement out of existence into
the eternal, by way of recollection, is still possible.

The aesthetic stage is very briefly indicated, and it is presumably in
order to lay the accent quite emphatically upon the religious that the
author has called the first part *A Recollection*. By pressing the aesthetic
back, the ethical and particularly the religious are brought to the front.

As far as the detailed content is concerned, I shall not further pursue
it. Its significance, if it has any, will consist in the existential inwardness with which the various stages are exhibited to the intuition, in
passion, irony, pathos, humor, and dialectics. This sort of thing will
of course have no interest for *Docents*. It is perhaps not unthinkable

that a *Docent* might finally carry his politeness so far as to say *en passant,* in an intermediary proposition, in a remark affixed to a paragraph of the System: "This author represents inwardness." In this way the author and an uninformed circle of readers have been told all about it. Passion, pathos, irony, dialectics, humor, enthusiasm, and so forth— these are things that *Docents* view as something subordinate, as something everybody has. When therefore it is said of an author that he represents inwardness, everything has been said by means of this brief word that everybody can say, and much more indeed than the author himself has said. Everybody now knows what to think about it, and every *Docent* could have produced everything in this genre, but has left it to reduced subjects. Whether everyone really does know concretely what inwardness is, and would be able in the capacity of an author to produce something in that direction, I shall not attempt to decide. Of everyone who is silent, I am prepared to assume that this is the case; but the *Docents* are not silent.

   Still, as I have said, I have nothing to do with the content of the book. My thesis was that subjectivity, inwardness, is the truth. This principle was for me decisive with respect to the problem of Christianity, and the same consideration has led me to pursue a certain tendency in the pseudonymous books, which to the very last have honestly abstained from doctrination. Particularly I thought I ought to take cognizance of the last of these books, because it was published after my *Fragments,* recalling the earlier publications by means of a free reproduction, and determining the religious stage through humor as *confinium.*

CHAPTER III

REAL OR ETHICAL SUBJECTIVITY—
THE SUBJECTIVE THINKER

§ I. EXISTENCE AND REALITY

THE difficulty that inheres in existence, with which the existing individual is confronted, is one that never really comes to expression in the language of abstract thought, much less receives an explanation. Because abstract thought is *sub specie aeterni* it ignores the concrete and the temporal, the existential process, the predicament of the existing individual arising from his being a synthesis of the temporal and the eternal situated in existence.* Now if we assume that abstract thought is the highest manifestation of human activity, it follows that philosophy and the philosophers proudly desert existence, leaving the rest of us to face the worst. And something else, too, follows for the abstract thinker himself, namely, that since he is an existing individual he must in one way or another be suffering from absent-mindedness.

The abstract problem of reality (if it is permissible to treat this problem abstractly, the particular and the accidental being constituents of the real, and directly opposed to abstraction) is not nearly so difficult a problem as it is to raise and to answer the question of what it means that this definite something is a reality. This definite something is just what abstract thought abstracts from. But the difficulty lies in bringing this definite something and the ideality of thought together, by penetrating the concrete particularity with thought. Abstract thought cannot even take cognizance of this contradiction, since the very process of abstraction prevents the contradiction from arising.

This questionable character of abstract thought becomes apparent especially in connection with all existential problems, where abstract

---

* That Hegel in his *Logic* nevertheless permits himself to utilize a consciousness that is only too well informed about the concrete, and what it is that the professor needs next in spite of the necessary transition, is of course a fault, which Trendelenburg[1] has very effectively called to our attention. To cite an example from the field of the subject immediately before us, how is the transition effected by which *die Existenz* becomes a plurality of existences? *"Die Existenz ist die unmittelbare Einheit der Reflexion-in-sich und der Reflexion-in-anders. Sie ist daher* (?) *die unbestimmte Menge von Existierenden."* How does the purely abstract determination of existence come to be split up in this manner?

thought gets rid of the difficulty by leaving it out, and then proceeds
to boast of having explained everything. It explains immortality in
general, and all goes quite smoothly, in that immortality is identified
with eternity, with the eternity which is essentially the medium of all
thought. But whether an existing individual human being is immortal,
which is the difficulty, abstract thought does not trouble to inquire. It
is disinterested; but the difficulty inherent in existence constitutes the
interest of the existing individual, who is infinitely interested in existing. Abstract thought thus helps me with respect to my immortality by
first annihilating me as a particular existing individual and then
making me immortal, about as when the doctor in Holberg killed the
patient with his medicine—but also expelled the fever.[2] Such an abstract
thinker, one who neglects to take into account the relationship between
his abstract thought and his own existence as an individual, not careful
to clarify this relationship to himself, makes a comical impression
upon the mind even if he is ever so distinguished, because he is in
process of ceasing to be a human being. While a genuine human being,
as a synthesis of the finite and the infinite, finds his reality in holding
these two factors together, infinitely interested in existing—such an
abstract thinker is a duplex being: a fantastic creature who moves in
the pure being of abstract thought, and on the other hand, a sometimes
pitiful professorial figure which the former deposits, about as when
one sets down a walking stick. When one reads the story of such a
thinker's life (for his writings are perhaps excellent), one trembles to
think of what it means to be a man.* If a lacemaker were to produce
ever so beautiful laces, it nevertheless makes one sad to contemplate
such a poor stunted creature. And so it is a comical sight to see a
thinker who in spite of all pretensions, personally existed like a
nincompoop; who did indeed marry, but without knowing love or its
power, and whose marriage must therefore have been as impersonal
as his thought; whose personal life was devoid of pathos or pathological
struggles, concerned only with the question of which university offered
the best livelihood. Such an anomaly one would think impossible in
the case of a thinker, to be met with only in the external world and its
wretchedness, where one human being is the slave of another, and it is
impossible to admire the laces without shedding tears for the lacemakers.

* And when you read in his writings that thought and being are one, it is impossible not to
think, in view of his own life and mode of existence, that the being which is thus identical with
thought can scarcely be the being of a man.

But one would suppose that a thinker lived the richest human life—so at least it was in Greece.

It is different with the abstract thinker who without having understood himself, or the relationship that abstract thought bears to existence, simply follows the promptings of his talent or is made by training to become something of this sort. I am very well aware that one tends to admire an artistic career where the artist simply pursues his talent without at all making himself clear over what it means to be a human being, and that our admiration tends to forget the person of the artist over his artistry. But I also know that such a life has its tragedy in being a differential type of existence not personally reflected in the ethical; and I know that in Greece, at least, a thinker was not a stunted, crippled creature who produced works of art, but was himself a work of art in his existence. One would suppose that being a thinker was the last thing in the world to constitute a differential trait with respect to being human. If it is the case that an abstract thinker is devoid of a sensitiveness for the comical, this circumstance is in itself a proof that while his thought may be the product of a distinguished talent, it is not the thought of one who has in any eminent sense existed as a human being. We are told that thought is the highest stage of human life, that it includes everything else as subordinated to itself; and at the same time no objection is urged against the thinker failing to exist essentially *qua* human being, but only as a differential talent. That the pronouncement made concerning thought fails to be reduplicated in the concept of the thinker, that the thinker's existence contradicts his thought, shows that we are here dealing merely with professions. It is professed that thought is higher than feeling and imagination, and this is professed by a thinker who lacks pathos and passion. Thought is higher than irony and humor—this is professed by a thinker who is wholly lacking in a sense for the comical. How comical! Just as the whole enterprise of abstract thought in dealing with Christianity and with existential problems is an essay in the comical, so the so-called pure thought is in general a psychological curiosity, a remarkable species of combining and construing in a fantastic medium, the medium of pure being. The facile deification of this pure thought as the highest stage in life shows that the thinker who does it has never existed *qua* human being. It is evidence among other things that he has never willed in any eminent sense of the word; I do not mean willing in the sense of exploit, but from the standpoint of inwardness. But to have willed in this eminent sense is an absolute condition for having existed as a human being. Through having willed in this manner, through having ventured to take a decisive step in the utmost intensity of subjective passion and with full consciousness of one's eternal responsibility (which is within the capacity of every human being), one learns something else about life, and learns that it is quite a different thing from being engaged, year in and year out, in piecing together something for a system. And through thus existing essentially *qua* human being, one also acquires a sensitiveness for the comical. I do not mean that everyone who so exists is therefore a comic poet or a comic actor, but he will have a receptivity for the comical.

That the difficulty inherent in existence and confronting the existing individual never really comes to expression in the language of abstraction, I shall proceed to illustrate by reference to a decisive problem, about which so much has been said and written. Everyone is familiar with the fact that the Hegelian philosophy has rejected the principle of contradiction. Hegel himself has more than once sat in solemn judgment upon those thinkers who remain in the sphere of reflection and understanding, and therefore insist that there is an either-or. Since his time it has become a favorite sport for some Hegelian, as soon as anyone lets fall a hint about an *aut-aut,* to come riding *trip trap trap,* like a gamekeeper in *Kallundsborgs-Krøniken,*[3] and after gaining a victory to ride home again. Here in Denmark the Hegelians[4] have several times been on the warpath, especially after Bishop Mynster, to gain the brilliant victory of speculative thought. Bishop Mynster has more than once become a vanquished standpoint, though as such he seems to be doing very well, and it is rather to be feared that the tremendous exertion incident to the winning of the victory has been too much for the unvanquished victors. And yet there is perhaps a misunderstanding at the root of the controversy and the victory. Hegel is utterly and absolutely right in asserting that viewed eternally, *sub specie aeterni,* in the language of abstraction, in pure thought and pure being, there is no either-or. How in the world could there be, when abstract thought has taken away the contradiction, so that Hegel and the Hegelians ought rather be asked to explain what they mean by the hocus-pocus of introducing contradiction, movement, transition, and so forth, into the domain of logic. If the champions of an either-or invade the sphere of pure thought and there seek to defend their cause, they are quite without justification. Like the giant who wrestled with

Hercules, and who lost strength as soon as he was lifted from the ground, the either-or of contradiction is *ipso facto* nullified when it is lifted out of the sphere of the existential and introduced into the eternity of abstract thought. On the other hand, Hegel is equally wrong when, forgetting the abstraction of his thought, he plunges down into the realm of existence to annul the double *aut* with might and main. It is impossible to do this in existence, for in so doing the thinker abrogates existence as well. When I take existence away, i.e. when I abstract, there is no *aut-aut*; when I take this *aut-aut* away from existence I also take existence away, and hence I do not abrogate the *aut-aut* in existence. If it is an error to say that there is something that is true in theology which is not true in philosophy, it is at any rate quite correct to say that something is true for an existing individual which is not true in abstract thought. And it is also true that from the ethical point of view, pure being is a fantastic medium, and that it is forbidden to an existing individual to forget that he exists.

One must therefore be very careful in dealing with a philosopher of the Hegelian school, and, above all, to make certain of the identity of the being with whom one has the honor to discourse. Is he a human being, an existing human being? Is he himself *sub specie aeterni,* even when he sleeps, eats, blows his nose, or whatever else a human being does? Is he himself the pure "I am I"? This is an idea that has surely never occurred to any philosopher; but if not, how does he stand existentially related to this entity, and through what intermediate determinations is the ethical responsibility resting upon him as an existing individual suitably respected? Does he in fact exist? And if he does, is he then not in process of becoming? And if he is in process of becoming, does he not face the future? And does he ever face the future by way of action? And if he never does, will he not forgive an ethical individuality for saying in passion and with dramatic truth, that he is an ass? But if he ever acts *sensu eminenti,* does he not in that case face the future with infinite passion? Is there not then for him an either-or? Is it not the case that eternity is for an existing individual not eternity, but the future, and that eternity is eternity only for the Eternal, who is not in process of becoming? Let him state whether he can answer the following question, i.e. if such a question can be addressed to him: "Is ceasing to exist so far as possible, in order to be *sub specie aeterni,* something that happens to him, or is it subject to a decision of the will, perhaps even something one ought to do?" For if I ought to do it, an *aut-aut* is established even with respect to being *sub specie aeterni*. Was he born *sub specie aeterni,* and has he lived *sub specie aeterni* ever since, so that he cannot even understand what I am asking about, never having had anything to do with the future, and never having experienced any decision? In that case I readily understand that it is not a human being I have the honor to address. But this does not quite end the matter; for it seems to me a very strange circumstance that such mysterious beings begin to make their appearance. An epidemic of cholera is usually signalized by the appearance of a certain kind of fly not otherwise observable; may it not be the case that the appearance of these fabulous pure thinkers is a sign that some misfortune threatens humanity, as for instance the loss of the ethical and the religious?

It is necessary to be thus careful in dealing with an abstract thinker who not only desires for himself to remain in the pure being of abstract thought, but insists that this is the highest goal for human life, and that a type of thought which leads to the ignoring of the ethical and a misunderstanding of the religious is the highest human thinking. But let us not on the other hand say that an *aut-aut* exists *sub specie aeterni,* where according to the Eleatic doctrine "everything is and nothing comes into being."* But where everything is in process of becoming, and only so much of eternity is present as to be a restraining influence in the passionate decision, where *eternity* is related as *futurity* to the individual in process of becoming, there the absolute disjunction belongs. When I put eternity and *becoming* together I do not get rest, but coming into being and futurity. It is undoubtedly for this reason that

* Misled by the constant reference to a continued process in which opposites are combined into a higher unity, and so again in a higher unity and so forth, a parallel has been drawn between Hegel's doctrine and that of Heraclitus, which asserts that everything is in a state of flux and nothing remains constant. But this is a misunderstanding, because everything said in Hegel's philosophy about process and becoming is illusory. This is why the System lacks an Ethic, and is the reason why it has no answer for the living when the question of becoming is raised in earnest, in the interest of action. In spite of all that Hegel says about process, he does not understand history from the point of view of becoming, but with the help of the illusion attaching to pastness understands it from the point of view of a finality that excludes all becoming. It is therefore impossible for a Hegelian to understand himself by means of his philosophy, for his philosophy helps him to understand only that which is past and finished, and a living person is surely not dead. He probably finds compensation in the thought that in comparison with an understanding of China and Persia and six thousand years of the world's history, a single individual does not much matter, even if that individual be himself. But it seems otherwise to me, and I understand it better conversely: when a man cannot understand himself, his understanding of China and Persia and the rest must surely be of a very peculiar kind.

Christianity has announced eternity as the future life, namely, because it addresses itself to existing individuals, and it is for this reason also that it assumes an absolute either-or.

All logical thinking employs the language of abstraction, and is *sub specie aeterni*. To think existence logically is thus to ignore the difficulty, the difficulty, that is, of thinking the eternal as in process of becoming. But this difficulty is unavoidable, since the thinker himself is in process of becoming. It is easier to indulge in abstract thought than it is to exist, unless we understand by this latter term what is loosely called existing, in analogy with what is loosely called being a subject. Here we have again an example of the fact that the simplest tasks are the most difficult. Existing is ordinarily regarded as no very complex matter, much less an art, since we all exist; but abstract thinking takes rank as an accomplishment. But really to exist, so as to interpenetrate one's existence with consciousness, at one and the same time eternal and as if far removed from existence, and yet also present in existence and in the process of becoming: that is truly difficult. If philosophical reflection had not in our time become something queer, highly artificial, and capable of being learned by rote, thinkers would make quite a different impression upon people, as was the case in Greece, where a thinker was an existing individual stimulated by his reflection to a passionate enthusiasm; and as was also once the case in Christendom, when a thinker was a believer who strove enthusiastically to understand himself in the existence of faith. If anything of this sort held true of the thinkers of our own age, the enterprise of pure thought would have led to one suicide after the other. For suicide is the only tolerable existential consequence of pure thought, when this type of abstraction is not conceived as something merely partial in relation to being human, willing to strike an agreement with an ethical and religious form of personal existence, but assumes to be all and highest. This is not to praise the suicide, but to respect the passion. Nowadays a thinker is a curious creature who during certain hours of the day exhibits a very remarkable ingenuity, but has otherwise nothing in common with a human being.

To think existence *sub specie aeterni* and in abstract terms is essentially to abrogate it, and the merit of the proceeding is like the much trumpeted merit of abrogating the principle of contradiction. It is impossible to conceive existence without movement, and movement cannot be conceived *sub specie aeterni*. To leave movement out is not precisely a distinguished achievement, and to import it into logic in the form of the transition-category, and with it time and space, is only a new confusion. But inasmuch as all thought is eternal, there is here created a difficulty for the existing individual. Existence, like movement, is a difficult category to deal with; for if I think it, I abrogate it, and then I do not think it. It might therefore seem to be the proper thing to say that there is something which cannot be thought, namely, existence. But the difficulty persists, in that existence itself combines thinking with existing, in so far as the thinker exists.

Because Greek philosophy was not absent-minded, movement is perennially an object for its dialectical exertions. The Greek philosopher was an existing individual, and did not permit himself to forget that fact. In order that he might devote himself wholly to thought, he therefore sought refuge in suicide, or in a Pythagorean dying from the world, or in a Socratic form of philosopher's death. He was conscious of being a thinker, but he was also aware that existence as his medium prevented him from thinking continuously, since existence involved him in a process of becoming. In order to be able to think in very truth, therefore, he took his own life. Modern philosophy from its lofty height smiles at such childishness; for just as surely as every modern thinker knows that thought and being are one, so he also knows that it is not worth while to be what one thinks.

It is on this point about existence, and the demand which the ethical makes upon each existing individual, that one must insist when an abstract philosophy and a pure thought assume to explain everything by explaining away what is decisive. It is necessary only to have the courage to be human, and to refuse to be terrified or tricked into becoming a phantom merely to save embarrassment. It would be an altogether different thing if pure thought would accept the responsibility of explaining its own relation to the ethical, and to the ethically existing individual. But this it never does, nor does it even pretend; for in that case it would have to make terms with an entirely different dialectic, namely, the Greek or existential dialectic. The stamp of the ethical is what every existing individual has the right to expect of all that calls itself wisdom. If a beginning has already been made, if an unnoticed transition permits a man gradually to forget that he exists in order to think *sub specie aeterni,* the objection is of a different order. It is not impossible that within the sphere of pure thought many, many objections may be urged against the Hegelian philosophy; but this would leave everything essentially unaltered. Willing as I am to admire Hegel's *Logic* in the capacity of a humble reader, by no means aspiring to a critical judgment; willing as I am to admit that there may be much for me to learn when I return to a further reading of it, I shall be equally proud, insistent, fearless, and even defiant in standing by my thesis: that the Hegelian philosophy, by failing to define its relation to the existing individual, and by ignoring the ethical, confounds existence.

The most dangerous form of scepticism is always that which least looks like it. The notion that pure thought is the positive truth for an existing individual, is sheer scepticism, for this positiveness is chimerical. It is a glorious thing to be able to explain the past, the whole of human history; but if the ability to understand the past is to be the summit of attainment for a living individual, this positiveness is scepticism, and a dangerous form of it, because of the deceptive quantity of things understood. Hence the terrible thing can happen to Hegel's philosophy, that an indirect attack is most dangerous. Let a doubting youth, an existing doubter, imbued with a lovable and unlimited youthful confidence in a hero of thought, confidingly seek in Hegel's positive philosophy the truth, the truth for existence: he will write a formidable epigram over Hegel. Please do not misunderstand me. I do not mean that every youth can vanquish Hegel, far from it; if the youth is conceited and foolish enough to attempt it, his attack will be without significance. No, the youth must not even think of attacking Hegel. On the contrary, let him submit himself unconditionally, in feminine devotion, but with sufficient vigor of determination to hold fast to his problem: he will become a satirist without suspecting it. The youth is an existing doubter. Hovering in doubt and without a foothold for his life, he reaches out for the truth—in order to exist in it. He is negative and the philosophy of Hegel is positive—what wonder then that he seeks anchorage in Hegel. But a philosophy of pure thought is for an existing individual a chimera, if the truth that is sought is something to exist in. To exist under the guidance of pure thought is like travelling in Denmark with the help of a small map of Europe, on which Denmark shows no larger than a steel pen-point—aye, it is still more impossible. The admiration and enthusiasm of the youth, his boundless confidence in Hegel, is precisely the satire upon Hegel. This is something that would long ago have been perceived, if the prestige of pure thought had not been bolstered by an over-awing opinion, so that people have not dared to say that it is anything but excellent, and to avow that they have understood it—though this last is in a certain sense impossible, since this philosophy cannot help anyone to an understanding of himself, which is surely an absolute condition for all other kinds of understanding. Socrates said quite ironically that he did not know whether he was a human being or something else, but an Hegelian can say with due solemnity in the confessional: "I do not know whether I am a human being—but I have understood the System." I for my part would rather say: "I know that I am a human being, and I know that I have not understood the System." And having said so much quite simply, I will add that if any of our Hegelians will take pity on me and help me to an understanding of the System, there will be nothing in the way of hindrances interposed from my side. I shall strive to make myself as stupid as possible, so as not to have a single presupposition except my ignorance, only in order to be in a position to learn the more; and I shall strive to be as indifferent as possible over against every accusation directed against my lack of scientific training, merely to make sure of learning something.

It is impossible to exist without passion, unless we understand the word "exist" in the loose sense of a so-called existence. Every Greek thinker was therefore essentially a passionate thinker. I have often reflected how one might bring a man into a state of passion. I have thought in this connection that if I could get him seated on a horse and the horse made to take fright and gallop wildly, or better still, for the sake of bringing the passion out, if I could take a man who wanted to arrive at a certain place as quickly as possible, and hence already had some passion, and could set him astride a horse that can scarcely walk— and yet this is what existence is like if one is to become consciously aware of it. Or if a driver were otherwise not especially inclined toward passion, if someone hitched a team of horses to a wagon for him, one of them a Pegasus and the other a worn-out jade, and told him to drive— I think one might succeed. And it is just this that it means to exist, if one is to become conscious of it. Eternity is the winged horse, infinitely fast, and time is a worn-out jade; the existing individual is the driver. That is to say, he is such a driver when his mode of existence is not an existence loosely so called; for then he is no driver, but a drunken peasant who lies asleep in the wagon and lets the horses take care of themselves. To be sure, he also drives and is a driver; and so there are perhaps many who—also exist.

In so far as existence consists in movement there must be something which can give continuity to the movement and hold it together, for otherwise there is no movement. Just as the assertion that everything is true means that nothing is true, so the assertion that everything is in motion means that there is no motion.* The unmoved is therefore a constituent of the motion as its measure and its end. Otherwise the assertion that everything is in motion, and, if one also wishes to take time away, that everything is always in motion, is *ipso facto* the assertion of a state of rest. Aristotle, who emphasizes movement in so many ways, therefore says that God, Himself unmoved, moves all. Now while pure thought either abrogates motion altogether, or meaninglessly imports it into logic, the difficulty facing an existing individual is how to give his existence the continuity without which everything simply vanishes. An abstract continuity is no continuity, and the very existence of the existing individual is sufficient to prevent his continuity from having essential stability; while passion gives him a momentary continuity, a continuity which at one and the same time is a restraining influence and a moving impulse. The goal of movement for an existing individual is to arrive at a decision, and to renew it. The eternal is the factor of continuity; but an abstract eternity is extraneous to the movement of life, and a concrete eternity within the existing individual is the maximum degree of his passion. All idealizing passion† is an anticipation of the eternal in existence functioning so as to help the individual to exist.‡ The eternity of abstract thought is arrived at by abstracting from existence. The realm of pure thought is a sphere in which the existing individual finds himself only by virtue of a mistaken beginning; and this error revenges itself by making the existence of the individual insignificant, and giving his language a flavor of lunacy. This seems to be the case with almost the entire mass of men in our day, when you rarely or never hear a person speak as if he were an existing individual human being, but rather as one who sees everything in a dizzy pantheistic haze, forever talking about millions and

* This was undoubtedly what the disciple of Heraclitus meant when he said that one could not pass through the same river even once. Johannes *de silentio* made a reference in *Fear and Trembling* to the remark of this disciple, but more with a rhetorical flourish than with truth.

† Earthly passion tends to prevent existence by transforming it into something merely momentary.

‡ Art and poetry have been called anticipations of the external. If one desires to speak in this fashion, one must nevertheless note that art and poetry are not essentially related to an existing individual; for their contemplative enjoyment, the joy over what is beautiful, is disinterested, and the spectator of the work of art is contemplatively outside himself *qua* existing individual.

whole nations and the historical evolution. But the passionate anticipation of the eternal is nevertheless not an absolute continuity for the
existing individual; but it is the possibility of an approximation to the
only true continuity that he can have. Here we are again reminded of
my thesis that subjectivity is truth; for an objective truth is like the
eternity of abstract thought, extraneous to the movement of existence.

Abstract thought is disinterested, but for an existing individual,
existence is the highest interest. An existing individual therefore has
always a *telos,* and it is of this *telos* that Aristotle .speaks when he
says (*De Anima,* III, 10, 2) that νοῦς θεωρέτικος differs from νοῦς
πράκτικος τῷ τέλει. But pure thought is altogether detached, and not
like the abstract thought which does indeed abstract from existence,
but nevertheless preserves a relationship to it. This pure thought, hovering in mystic suspension between heaven and earth and emancipated
from every relation to an existing individual, explains everything in
its own terms but fails to explain itself. It explains everything in such
fashion that no decisive explanation of the essential question becomes
possible. Thus when an existing individual asks about the relationship
between pure thought and an existing individual, pure thought makes
no reply, but merely explains existence within pure thought and so
confuses everything. It assigns to existence, the category upon which
pure thought must suffer shipwreck, a place within pure thought itself;
in this fashion everything that is said about existence is essentially
revoked. When pure thought speaks of the immediate unity of reflec-
tion-in-self and reflection-in-other, and says that this immediate unity
is abrogated, something must of course intervene so as to divide the
two phases of this immediate unity. What can this something be? It
is time. But time cannot find a place within pure thought. What then
is the meaning of the talk about abrogation and transition and the new
unity? And in general, what does it mean to think in such a manner
as merely to pretend to think, because everything that is said is absolutely revoked? And what is the meaning of the refusal to admit that
one thinks in this manner, constantly blazoning forth this pure thought
as positive truth?

Just as existence has combined thought and existence by making the
existing individual a thinker, so there are two media: the medium of
abstract thought, and the medium of reality. But pure thought is still
a third medium, quite recently discovered. It therefore begins, as the
saying is, after the most exhaustive abstraction. The relation which

abstract thought still sustains to that from which it abstracts, is something which pure thought innocently or thoughtlessly ignores. Here
is rest for every doubt, here is the eternal positive truth, and whatever
else one may be pleased to say. That is, pure thought is a phantom. If
the Hegelian philosophy has emancipated itself from every presupposition, it has won this freedom by means of one lunatic postulate: the
initial transition to pure thought.

Existence constitutes the highest interest of the existing individual,
and his interest in his existence constitutes his reality. What reality is,
cannot be expressed in the language of abstraction. Reality is an *inter-esse*
between the moments of that hypothetical unity of thought and being
which abstract thought presupposes. Abstract thought considers both
possibility and reality, but its concept of reality is a false reflection,
since the medium within which the concept is thought is not reality,
but possibility. Abstract thought can get hold of reality only by nullify-
ing it, and this nullification of reality consists in transforming it into
possibility. All that is said about reality in the language of abstraction
and within the sphere of abstract thought, is really said within the
sphere of the possible. The entire realm of abstract thought, speaking
in the language of reality, sustains the relation of possibility to the
realm of reality; but this latter reality is not one which is included
within abstract thought and the realm of the possible. Reality or existence is the dialectical moment in a trilogy, whose beginning and whose
end cannot be for the existing individual, since *qua* existing individual
he is himself in the dialectical moment. Abstract thought closes up the
trilogy. Just so. But how does it close the trilogy? Is abstract thought a
mystic something, or is it not the act of the abstracting individual? But
the abstracting individual is the existing individual, who is as such
in the dialectical moment, which he cannot close or mediate, least
of all absolutely, as long as he remains in existence. So that when he
closes the trilogy, this closure must be related as a possibility to the
reality or existence in which he remains. And he is bound to explain
how he manages to do it, i.e. how he manages to do it as an existing
individual; or else he must explain whether he ceases to be an existing
individual, and whether he has any right to do this.

The moment we begin to ask this sort of question, we ask ethically,
and assert the claim which the ethical has upon the existing individual.
This claim is not that he should abstract from existence, but rather that
he should exist; and this is at the same time his highest interest.

It is not possible for an existing individual, least of all *as* an existing individual, to hold fast absolutely a suspension of the dialeçtical moment, namely, existence. This would require another medium than existence, which is the dialectical moment. If an existing individual can become conscious of such a suspension, it can be only as a possibility. But this possibility cannot maintain itself when the existential interest is posited, for which reason the awareness of it can exist only in a state of disinterestedness. But the existing individual can never wholly attain this state *qua* existing individual; and ethically he is not justified even in trying to attain it *approximando,* since the ethical seeks contrariwise to make the existential interest infinite, so infinite that the principle of contradiction becomes absolutely valid.

Here again it appears, as was shown above, that the difficulty inherent in existence and confronting the existing individual is one which abstract thought does not recognize or treat. To think about the real in the medium of the possible does not involve the same difficulty as attempting to think it in the medium of existence, where existence and its process of becoming tend to prevent the individual from thinking, just as if existence could not be thought, although the existing individual is a thinker. In pure thought we are over our ears in profundity, and yet there is something rather absent-minded about it all, because the pure thinker is not clear about what it means to be a human being.

All knowledge about reality is possibility. The only reality to which an existing individual may have a relation that is more than cognitive, is his own reality, the fact that he exists; this reality constitutes his absolute interest. Abstract thought requires him to become disinterested in order to acquire knowledge; the ethical demand is that he become infinitely interested in existing.

The only reality that exists for an existing individual is his own ethical reality. To every other reality he stands in a cognitive relation; but true knowledge consists in translating the real into the possible.

The apparent trustworthiness of sense is an illusion. This was shown adequately as early as in Greek scepticism, and modern idealism has likewise demonstrated it. The trustworthiness claimed by a knowledge of the historical is also a deception, in so far as it assumes to be the very trustworthiness of reality; for the knower cannot know an historical reality until he has resolved it into a possibility. (On this point, more in what follows.) Abstract thought embraces the possible, either the preceding or the subsequent possibility; pure thought is a phantom.

The real subject is not the cognitive subject, since in knowing he moves in the sphere of the possible; the real subject is the ethically existing subject. An abstract thinker exists to be sure, but this fact is rather a satire on him than otherwise. For an abstract thinker to try to prove his existence by the fact that he thinks, is a curious contradiction; for in the degree that he thinks abstractly he abstracts from his own existence. In so far his existence is revealed as a presupposition from which he seeks emancipation; but the act of abstraction nevertheless becomes a strange sort of proof for his existence, since if it succeeded entirely his existence would cease. The Cartesian *cogito ergo sum* has often been repeated. If the "I" which is the subject of *cogito* means an individual human being, the proposition proves nothing: "I am thinking, *ergo* I am; but if I *am* thinking what wonder that I *am*:" the assertion has already been made, and the first proposition says even more than the second. But if the "I" in *cogito* is interpreted as meaning a particular existing human being, philosophy cries: "How silly; here there is no question of your self or my self, but solely of the pure ego." But this pure ego cannot very well have any other than a purely conceptual existence; what then does the *ergo* mean? There is no conclusion here, for the proposition is a tautology.

It has been said above that the abstract thinker, so far from proving his existence by his thought, rather makes it evident that his thought does not wholly succeed in proving the opposite. From this to draw the conclusion that an existing individual who really exists does not think at all, is an arbitrary misunderstanding. He certainly thinks, but he thinks everything in relation to himself, being infinitely interested in existing. Socrates was thus a man whose energies were devoted to thinking; but he reduced all other knowledge to indifference in that he infinitely accentuated ethical knowledge. This type of knowledge bears a relation to the existing subject who is infinitely interested in existing.

The attempt to infer existence from thought is thus a contradiction. For thought takes existence away from the real and thinks it by abrogating its actuality, by translating it into the sphere of the possible. (Of this more in the following.) With respect to every reality other than the individual's own reality, the principle obtains that he can come to know it only by thinking it. With respect to his own reality, it is a question whether his thought can succeed in abstracting from it completely. This is what the abstract thinker aims at. But it avails him nothing, since he still exists; and this existential persistence, this sometimes pitiful professorial figure, is an epigram upon the abstract thinker, to say nothing of the insistent objection of the ethical.

In Greece, the philosopher was at any rate aware of what it means to exist. The so-called ataraxy of the sceptics was therefore an existential attempt to abstract from existence. In our time the process of abstracting from existence has been relegated to the printed page, just as the task of doubting everything is disposed of once for all on paper. One of the things that has given rise to so much confusion in modern philosophy is that the philosophers have so many brief sayings about infinite tasks, and respect this paper money among themselves, while it almost never occurs to anyone to try to realize the posited task. In this way everything is easily finished, and it becomes possible to begin without presuppositions. The presupposition of a universal doubt, for example, would require an entire human life; now, it is no sooner said than done.

§ 2. POSSIBILITY AS HIGHER THAN REALITY—REALITY AS HIGHER THAN POSSIBILITY—
POETIC AND INTELLECTUAL IDEALITY—ETHICAL IDEALITY

Aristotle remarks in his *Poetics* that poetry is higher than history, because history merely tells us what has happened, while poetry tells us what might have happened and ought to have happened, i.e. poetry commands the possible. From the poetic and intellectual standpoint, possibility is higher than reality, the aesthetic and the intellectual being disinterested. There is only one interest, the interest in existence; disinterestedness is therefore an expression for indifference to reality. This indifference is forgotten in the Cartesian *cogito ergo sum,* which injects a disturbing element into the disinterestedness of the intellectual and affronts speculative thought, as if it were instrumental to something else. I think, *ergo* I think; but whether I exist or it exists in the sense of an actuality, so that "I" means an individually existing human being and "it" means a definite particular something, is a matter of infinite indifference. That the content of my thought exists in the conceptual sense needs no proof, or needs no argument to prove it, since it is proved by my thinking it. But as soon as I proceed to impose a teleology upon my thought, and bring it into relation with something else, interest begins to play a rôle in the matter. The instant this happens the 'ethical is present, and absolves me from any further responsibility in proving my own existence. It forbids me to draw a conclusion that is ethically deceitful and metaphysically unclear, by imposing upon me the duty of existing.

In our own day the ethical tends more and more to be ignored. This has had among other things the harmful consequence that poetry and speculative thought have become unsettled, and have deserted the lofty disinterestedness of the possible in order to reach out for reality. Instead of assigning to each sphere its own proper scale of values, a double confusion has been introduced. Poetry makes one' attempt after the other to play the rôle of reality, which is entirely unpoetical. Speculative thought repeatedly attempts to reach reality within its own domain, assuring us that whatever is thought is real, that thought is not only capable of thinking reality but of bestowing it, while the truth is the direct opposite; and simultaneously a forgetfulness of what it means to exist, extends itself more and more. The age becomes increasingly unreal, and the people in it; hence these substitutes to make up for what is lacking. The ethical tends more and more to be abandoned; the life of the individual not only becomes poetic, but is unsettled by an abnormal historical consciousness that prevents him from existing ethically. It follows that reality must be provided in other ways. But this spurious reality resembles what would happen if a generation and its members had become prematurely old, and sought to obtain an artificial youth. Instead of recognizing that ethical existence is reality, the age has grown overwhelmingly contemplative, so that not only is everyone engrossed in contemplation, but this has finally become falsified as if it were reality. We smile at the life of the cloister, and yet no hermit ever lived so unreal a life as is common nowadays. For the hermit abstracted from the entire world, but he did not abstract from himself. We know how to describe the fantastic situation of the cloister, far from the haunts of men, in the solitude of the forest, in the distant blue of the horizon; but we take no notice of the fantastic situation of pure thought. And yet, the pathetic unreality of the hermit is far preferable to the comic unreality of the pure thinker; and the passionate forgetfulness of the hermit, which takes from him the entire world, is much to be preferred to the comical distraction of the philosopher engrossed in the contemplation of universal history, which leads him to forget himself.

Ethically regarded, reality is higher than possibility. The ethical proposes to do away with the disinterestedness of the possible, by making existence the infinite interest. It therefore opposes every confusing attempt, like that of proposing ethically to *contemplate* humanity and the world. Such ethical contemplation is impossible, since there is only one kind of ethical contemplation, namely, self-contemplation. Ethics closes immediately about the individual, and demands that he exist ethically; it does not make a parade of millions, or of generations of men; it does not take humanity in the lump, any more than the police arrest humanity at large. The ethical is concerned with particular human beings, and with each and every one of them by himself. If God knows how many hairs there are on a man's head, the ethical knows how many human beings there are; and its enumeration is not in the interest of a total sum, but for the sake of each individual. The ethical requirement is imposed upon each individual, and when it judges, it judges each individual by himself; only a tyrant or an impotent man is content to decimate. The ethical lays hold of each individual and demands that he refrain from all contemplation, especially of humanity and the world; for the ethical, as being the internal, cannot be observed by an outsider. It can be realized only by the individual subject, who alone can know what it is that moves within him. This ethical reality is the only reality which does not become a mere possibility through being known, and which can be known only through being thought; for it is the individual's own reality. Before it became a reality it was known by him in the form of a conceived reality, and hence as a possibility. But in the case of another person's reality he could have no knowledge about it until he conceived it in coming to know it, which means that he transformed it from a reality into a possibility.

With respect to every reality external to myself, I can get hold of it only through thinking it. In order to get hold of it really, I should have to be able to make myself into the other, the acting individual, and make the foreign reality my own reality, which is impossible. For if I make the foreign reality my own, this does not mean that I become the other through knowing his reality, but it means that I acquire a new reality, which belongs to me as opposed to him.

When I think something which I propose to do but have not yet done, the content of this conception, no matter how exact it may be, if it be ever so much entitled to be called a conceived reality, is a possibility. Conversely, when I think about something that another has done, and so conceive a reality, I lift this given reality out of the real and set it into the possible; for a conceived reality is a possibility, and is higher than reality from the standpoint of thought, but not from the standpoint of reality. This implies that there is no immediate relationship, ethically, between subject and subject. When I understand another person, his reality is for me a possibility, and in its aspect of possibility this conceived reality is related to me precisely as the thought of something I have not done is related to the doing of it.

Frater Taciturnus, in *Stages on Life's Way,* says that one who cannot understand, with reference to the same matter, the conclusion *ab posse ad esse* as well as he can understand the conclusion *ab esse ad posse,* does not lay hold of the ideality involved; that is, he does not understand it, does not think it. (The question concerns, that is, the understanding of a foreign reality.) If the thinker with a resolving *posse* comes upon an *esse* that he cannot resolve, he must say: this is something I cannot think. He thus suspends his thinking with respect to it; and if he nevertheless persists in trying to establish a relationship to this reality as a reality, he does not do so by way of thought, but paradoxically. (The reader is asked to remember from the preceding the definition there given of faith in the Socratic sense, *sensu laxiori* and not *sensu strictissimo*: an objective uncertainty, uncertain because the resolving *posse* has come upon a refractory *esse,* held fast in passionate inwardness.)

In connection with the aesthetic and the intellectual, to ask whether this or that is real, whether it really has happened, is a misunderstanding. So to ask betrays a failure to conceive the aesthetic and the intellectual ideality as a possibility, and forgets that to determine a scale of values for the aesthetic and the intellectual in this manner, is like ranking sensation higher than thought. Ethically it is correct to put the question: "Is it real?" But it is important to note that this holds true only when the individual subject asks this question of himself, and concerning his own reality. He can apprehend the ethical reality of another only by thinking it, and hence as a possibility.

The Scriptures teach: "Judge not that ye be not judged." This is expressed in the form of a warning, an admonition, but it is at the same time an impossibility. One human being cannot judge another ethically, because he cannot understand him except as a possibility. When therefore anyone attempts to judge another, the expression for his impotence is that he merely judges himself.

In *Stages on Life's Way* occurs the following: "It is intelligent to ask two questions: (1) Is it possible? (2) Can I do it? But it is unintelligent to ask these two questions: (1) Is it real? (2) Has my neighbor Christopherson done it?" In this passage reality is accentuated ethically. It is fatuous from the aesthetic and the intellectual point of view to raise the question of reality; and the same holds true from the ethical point of view if the question is raised in the interest of contemplation. But when the ethical question is raised in connection with my own reality, I ask about possibility; only that this possibility is not an aesthetically and intellectually disinterested possibility, but as being a conceived reality it is related as a possibility to my own reality, so that I may be able to realize it.

The mode of apprehension of the truth is precisely the truth. It is therefore untrue to answer a question in a medium in which the question cannot arise. So for example, to explain reality within the medium of the possible, or to distinguish between possibility and reality within possibility. By refraining from raising the question of reality from the aesthetic or intellectual point of view, but asking this question only ethically, and here again only in the interest of one's own reality, each individual will be isolated and compelled to exist for himself. Irony and hypocrisy as opposite forms, but both expressing the contradiction that the internal is not the external, irony by seeming to be bad, hypocrisy by seeming to be good, emphasize the principle anent the contemplative inquiry concerning ethical inwardness, that reality and deceit are equally possible, and that deceit can clothe itself in the same appearance as reality. It is unethical even to ask at all about another person's ethical inwardness, in so far as such inquiry constitutes a diversion of attention. But if the question is asked nevertheless, the difficulty remains that I can lay hold of the other's reality only by conceiving it, and hence by translating it into a possibility; and in this sphere the possibility of a deception is equally conceivable. This is profitable preliminary training for an ethical mode of existence: to learn that the individual stands alone.

It is a misunderstanding to be concerned about reality from the aesthetic or intellectual point of view. And to be concerned ethically about another's reality is also a misunderstanding, since the only question of reality that is ethically pertinent, is the question of one's own reality. Here we may clearly note the difference that exists between faith *sensu strictissimo* on the one hand (referring as it does to the historical, and the realms of the aesthetic, the intellectual) and the ethical on the other. To ask with infinite interest about a reality which is not one's own, is faith, and this constitutes a paradoxical relationship to the paradoxical. Aesthetically it is impossible to raise such a question except in thoughtlessness, since possibility is aesthetically higher than reality. Nor is it possible to raise such a question ethically, since the sole ethical interest is the interest in one's own reality. The analogy between faith and the ethical is found in the infinite interest, which suffices to distinguish the believer absolutely from an aesthetician or a thinker. But the believer differs from the ethicist in being infinitely interested in the reality of another (in the fact, for example, that God has existed in time).

The aesthetic and intellectual principle is that no reality is thought or understood until its *esse* has been resolved into its *posse*. The ethical principle is that no possibility is understood until each *posse* has really become an *esse*. An aesthetic and intellectual scrutiny protests every *esse* which is not a *posse*; the ethical scrutiny results in the condemnation of every *posse* which is not an *esse,* but this refers only to a *posse* in the individual himself, since the ethical has nothing to do with the possibilities of other individuals. In our own age everything is mixed up together: the aesthetic is treated ethically, faith is dealt with intellectually, and so forth. Philosophy has answered every question; but no adequate consideration has been given the question concerning what sphere it is within which each question finds its answer. This creates a greater confusion in the world of the spirit than when in the civic life an ecclesiastical question, let us say, is handled by the bridge commission.

Is the real then the same as the external? By no means. Aesthetically and intellectually it is usual and proper to stress the principle that the external is merely a deception for one who does not grasp the ideality involved. Frater Taciturnus says: "Mere knowledge of the historical helps simply to produce an illusion, in which the mind is beguiled by the raw material of the externality. What is it that I can know historically? The external detail. The ideality I can know only by myself, and if I do not know it by myself I do not know it at all; mere historical

knowledge avails nothing. Ideality is not a chattel which can be transported from one person to another, nor is it something to be had
gratis when buying in large quantities. If I know that Caesar was a
great man, I know what greatness is, and it is on this knowledge that
I base my judgment of Caesar; otherwise I do not know that Caesar
was great. The testimony of history, the assurances of responsible
people that no risk is involved in accepting this opinion, the certainty
of the conclusion that he was great because the results of his life demonstrate it—all this helps not a jot. To believe an ideality on the word of
another is like laughing at a joke because someone has said that it was
funny, not because one has understood it. In such case the witticism
might as well be left unsaid; for anyone who laughs at it because of
the respect he entertains for some guarantor, and on the ground of his
faith in him, could laugh with the same emphasis notwithstanding."
What then is the real? It is the ideality. But aesthetically and intellectually the ideality is the possible (the translation from *esse ad posse*).
Ethically the ideality is the real within the individual himself. The real
is an inwardness that is infinitely interested in existing; this is exemplified in the ethical individual.

Precisely in the degree to which I understand a thinker I become
indifferent to his reality; that is, to his existence as a particular individual, to his having really understood this or that so and so, to his actually
having realized his teaching, and so forth. Aesthetic and speculative
thought is quite justified in insisting on this point, and it is important
not to lose sight of it. But this does not suffice for a defense of pure
thought as a medium of communication between man and man.
Because the reality of the teacher is properly indifferent to me as his
pupil, and my reality conversely to him, it does not by any means
follow that the teacher is justified in being indifferent to his own reality.
His communication should bear the stamp of this consciousness, but
not directly, since the ethical reality of an individual is not directly
communicable (such a direct relationship is exemplified in the paradoxical relation of a believer to the object of his faith), and cannot be
understood immediately, but must be understood indirectly through
indirect signs.

When the different spheres are not decisively distinguished from one another, confusion reigns everywhere. When people are curious about a thinker's reality and find it interesting to know something about it, and so forth, this interest is intellectually reprehensible. The maximum of attainment in the sphere of the intellectual is to become altogether indifferent to the thinker's reality. But by being thus muddle-headed in the intellectual sphere, one acquires a certain resemblance to a believer. A believer is one who is infinitely interested in another's reality. This is a decisive criterion for faith, and the interest in question is not just a little curiosity, but an absolute dependence upon faith's object.

The object of faith is the reality of another, and the relationship is one of infinite interest. The object of faith is not a doctrine, for then the relationship would be intellectual, and it would be of importance not to botch it, but to realize the maximum intellectual relationship. The object of faith is not a teacher with a doctrine; for when a teacher has a doctrine, the doctrine is *eo ipso* more important than the teacher, and the relationship is again intellectual, and it again becomes important not to botch it, but to realize the maximum intellectual relationship. The object of faith is the reality of the teacher, that the teacher really exists. The answer of faith is therefore unconditionally yes or no. For it does not concern a doctrine, as to whether the doctrine is true or not; it is the answer to a question concerning a fact: "Do you or do you not suppose that he has really existed?" And the answer, it must be noted, is with infinite passion. In the case of a human being, it is thoughtlessness to lay so great and infinite a stress on the question whether he has existed or not. If the object of faith is a human being, therefore, the whole proposal is the vagary of a stupid person, who has not even understood the spirit of the intellectual and the aesthetic. The object of faith is hence the reality of the God-man in the sense of his existence. But existence involves first and foremost particularity, and this is why thought must abstract from existence, because the particular cannot be thought, but only the universal. The object of faith is thus God's reality in existence as a particular individual, the fact that God has existed as an individual human being.

Christianity is no doctrine concerning the unity of the divine and the human, or concerning the identity of subject and object; nor is it any other of the logical transcriptions of Christianity. If Christianity were a doctrine, the relationship to it would not be one of faith, for only an intellectual type of relationship can correspond to a doctrine. Christianity is therefore not a doctrine, but the fact that God has existed.

The realm of faith is thus not a class for numskulls in the sphere of the intellectual, or an asylum for the feeble-minded. Faith constitutes a sphere all by itself, and every misunderstanding of Christianity may at once be recognized by its transforming it into a doctrine, transferring it to the sphere of the intellectual. The maximum of attainment within the sphere of the intellectual, namely, to realize an entire indifference as to the reality of the teacher, is in the sphere of faith at the opposite end of the scale. The maximum of attainment within the sphere of faith is to become infinitely interested in the reality of the teacher.

The ethical reality of the individual is the only reality. That this should seem strange to many does not seem strange to me. To me it rather seems strange that the System, aye, even systems in the plural, have been completed without raising a question concerning the ethical. If we could only get the dialogue introduced again in the Greek manner, for the purpose of testing what we know and what we do not know, the entire ingenious affectation that clusters about recent philosophy, its artificiality and unnaturalness, would soon disappear. It is not by any means my opinion that Hegel should be asked to talk with a day-laborer, and that it would prove anything if the latter could not be made to understand him; though it will always remain a beautiful eulogy upon Socrates, these simple words of Diogenes,[1] that he philosophized in the workshops and in the market-place. But this is not what I mean, and my proposal does not in the slightest resemble an idler's attack on science. But let a philosopher of the Hegelian school or Hegel himself enter into conversation with a cultivated person, who has made himself competent dialectically through having existed, and from the very beginning all that is affected and chimerical will be frustrated. When a man writes or dictates paragraphs in a running stream, promising that everything will be made clear at the end, it becomes increasingly difficult to discover just where the confusion begins, and to find a fixed point of departure. By means of "Everything will be made clear at the end," and intermittently by means of the category, "This is not the proper place to discuss this question," the very cornerstone of the

System, often used as ludicrously as if one were to cite under the heading of misprints a single example, and then add, "There are indeed other misprints in the book, but this is not the proper place to deal with them,"—by means of these two phrases the reader is constantly defrauded, one of them cheating him definitely, the other intermediately. In the situation of the dialogue, however, this whole fantastic business of pure thought would lose all its plausibility. Instead of conceding the contention of Idealism, but in such a manner as to dismiss as a temptation the entire problem of a reality in the sense of a thing-in-itself eluding thought, which like other temptations cannot be vanquished by giving way to it; instead of putting an end to Kant's misleading reflection which brings reality into connection with thought; instead of relegating reality to the ethical—Hegel scored a veritable advance; for he became fantastic and vanquished idealistic scepticism by means of pure thought, which is merely an hypothesis, and even if it does not so declare itself, a fantastic hypothesis. The triumphant victory of pure thought, that in it being and thought are one, is something both to laugh at and to weep over, since in the realm of pure thought it is not even possible to distinguish them. That thought has validity was assumed by Greek philosophy without question. By reflecting over the matter one would have to arrive at the same result; but why confuse the validity of thought with reality? A valid thought is a possibility, and every further question as to whether it is real or not should be dismissed as irrelevant.

The questionableness of the "Method" becomes apparent already in Hegel's relation to Kant. A scepticism which attacks thought itself cannot be vanquished by thinking it through, since the very instrument by which this would have to be done is in revolt. There is only one thing to do with such a scepticism, and that is to break with it. To answer Kant within the fantastic shadow-play of pure thought is precisely not to answer him. The only thing-in-itself which cannot be thought is existence, and this does not come within the province of thought to think. But how could pure thought possibly vanquish this difficulty, when it is abstract? And what does pure thought abstract from? Why from existence, to be sure, and hence from that which it purports to explain.

When it is impossible to think existence, and the existing individual nevertheless thinks, what does this signify? It signifies that he thinks intermittently, that he thinks before and after. His thought cannot attain to absolute continuity. It is only in a fantastic sense that an existing individual can be constantly *sub specie aeterni*.

Is thinking identical with creation, with giving existence? I am well aware of what has been said[2] by way of reply to a stupid attack on the philosophical principle of the identity of thought and being, and am entirely willing to concede its correctness. It has been insisted quite properly[3] that this identity must not be understood as applying to existence of an imperfect order, as if, for example, I could produce a rose by thinking it. In the same spirit it has been pointed out, over against the defenders of the principle of contradiction, that the latter principle seems most valid in connection with existence of a lower order: before and behind, right and left, up and down, and so forth. But now in connection with existences of a higher order, does it hold true that thought and being are one? Does it hold, for example, in the case of the Ideas? Aye, Hegel is quite right, and yet we have not advanced a single step. The good, the beautiful, and the other Ideas are in themselves so abstract that they are indifferent to existence, indifferent to any other than a conceptual existence. The reason why the principle of identity holds in this connection is because being means in this case the same thing as thought. But since this is so, the answer offered by pure thought is an answer to a question which cannot be raised in the sphere of the answer. A particular existing human being is surely not an Idea, and his existence is surely something quite different from the conceptual existence of the Idea. An existence as a particular human being is doubtless an imperfection in comparison with the eternal life of the Idea, but it is a perfection in comparison with not existing at all. An intermediary state like existence would seem suitable for an intermediary being like man. How is it then with the supposed identity of thought and being in connection with the kind of existence that belongs to particular human beings? Am I the good because I think the good, or am I good because I think the good? The champions of the philosophical principle of identity said themselves that it did not hold of the more imperfect existences: "Is existence as a particular human being, which is what the question is about, the same with a perfect ideal existence?" Here it is the converse principle that holds: "Because I exist and because I think, therefore I think that I exist." Existence here separates thought from being, and breaks up their ideal unity. I must exist in order to think, and I must be able to think, for example the good, in order to exist in it.

Existence as a particular human being is not so imperfect an existence as the being of a rose, for example. Hence it is that we human beings are accustomed to say that however great our unhappiness, our existence is nevertheless a good: and I remember a melancholy individual who once in the midst of his sufferings, when he wished himself dead, asked himself upon seeing a basket of potatoes if he did not after all find more happiness in existence than a potato. But existence as a particular human being is not a pure ideal existence; it is only man in general who exists in that manner, which means that this entity does not exist at all. Existence is always something particular, the abstract does not exist. From this to draw the conclusion that the abstract is without validity is a misunderstanding; but it is also a misunderstanding to confound discourse by even raising the question of existence, or of reality in the sense of existence, in connection with the abstract. When an existing individual raises the question of the relation between thought and being, thinking and existing, and philosophy explains that it is one of identity, the answer does not reply to the question because it does not reply to the questioner. Philosophy explains: "Thought and being are one; but not in connection with things that are what they are solely by virtue of existing, as for example a rose, which has no Idea within itself; and hence not in connection with things that make it most clearly evident what it means to exist, as opposed to what it means to think. But thought and being are one in connection with things whose existence is essentially indifferent, because they are so abstract as to have only conceptual existence." To answer the question in this manner is to evade it; for the question had reference to existence as a particular human being. An existence of this sort is of a different order from the existence of a potato, but neither is it the kind of existence that attaches to an Idea. Human existence has Idea in it, but it is not a purely ideal existence. Plato[4] placed the Idea in the second rank of existence, as intermediary between God and matter; an existing human being does indeed participate in the Idea, but he is not himself an Idea.

In Greece, as in the youth of philosophy generally, it was found difficult to win through to the abstract and to leave existence, which always gives the particular; in modern times, on the other hand, it has become difficult to reach existence. The process of abstraction is easy enough for us, but we also desert existence more and more, and the realm of pure thought is the extreme limit of such desertion.

In Greece, philosophizing was a mode of action, and the philosopher was therefore an existing individual. He may not have possessed a great amount of knowledge, but what he did know he knew to some profit, because he busied himself early and late with the same thing. But nowadays, just what is it to philosophize, and what does a philosopher really know? For of course I do not deny that he knows everything.

The philosophical principle of identity is precisely the opposite of what it seems to be; it is the expression for the fact that thought has deserted existence altogether, that it has emigrated to a sixth continent where it is wholly sufficient to itself in the absolute identity of thought and being. We may finally reach the stage of identifying existence with evil, taken in a certain emasculated metaphysical sense; in the humorous sense, existence will become an extremely long dragging out of things, a ludicrous delay. But even so there remains a possibility that the ethical may impose some restraint, since it accentuates existence, and abstract thought and humor still retain a relationship to existence. But pure thought has won through to a perfect victory, and has nothing, nothing to do with existence.

If thought could give reality in the sense of actuality, and not merely validity in the sense of possibility, it would also have the power to take away existence, and so to take away from the existing individual the only reality to which he sustains a real relationship, namely, his own. (To the reality of another he stands related only by way of thought, as was shown above.) That is to say, the individual would have to be able to think himself out of existence, so that he would really cease to be. I venture to think that no one will wish to accept this supposition, which would betray as superstitious a faith in the power of pure thought as is conversely illustrated by the remark of a lunatic in a comedy, that he proposed to go down in the depths of Dovrefjeld and blow up the entire world with a syllogism. A man may be absent-minded by nature, or may become absent-minded through continuous absorption in pure thought. But the success is never complete, or rather, the failure is complete; and one becomes, by way of the "sometimes pitiful professorial figure," what the Jews feared so much to become, namely, a proverb. I can abstract from myself; but the fact that I abstract from myself means precisely that I exist.

God does not think, he creates; God does not exist, He is eternal. Man thinks and exists, and existence separates thought and being, holding them apart from one another in succession.

What is abstract thought? It is thought without a thinker. Abstract thought ignores everything except the thought, and only the thought is, and is in its own medium. Existence is not devoid of thought, but in existence thought is in a foreign medium. What can it then mean to ask in the language of abstraction about reality in the sense of existence, seeing that abstract thought abstracts precisely from existence? What is concrete thought? It is thought with a relation to a thinker, and to a definite particular something which is thought, existence giving to the existing thinker thought, time, and place.

If Hegel had published his *Logic* under the title of Pure Thought, without indication of authorship or date of publication, without preface or notes or didactic self-contradictions, without confusing explanations of things that might better have been allowed to explain themselves; if he had published it as a sort of analogy to the nature sounds heard on the island of Ceylon,[5] as the immanent movements of pure thought itself,—the act would have been in the spirit of a Greek philosopher. Had a Greek conceived such an idea, this is what he would have done. The reduplication of the content in the form is essential to all artistry, and it is particularly important to refrain from referring to the same content in an inadequate form. But as it now is, the *Logic* with its collection of notes makes as droll an impression on the mind as if a man were to show a letter purporting to have come from heaven,[6] but having a blotter enclosed which only too clearly reveals its mundane origin. In such a work to indulge in polemics against this or that person designated by name, to communicate hints for the guidance of the reader, and so forth, is to betray the fact that there is a thinker who thinks the pure thought, a thinker whose speech mingles with its immanent movements, and who even speaks with another thinker, thus establishing relations with him. But if there is a thinker who thinks the pure thought, the entire apparatus of Greek dialectic as well as the safety police of the existential dialectic instantly lays hold of his person, seizing him by the coat-tails not as a disciple, but in order to find out about his relationship to pure thought. In that same instant the whole enchantment vanishes. Imagine Socrates in conversation with Hegel. With the help of the notes he will soon have Hegel on the hip; and as he was not accustomed to being put off by the assurance that everything will be made clear at the end, not even permitting a continuous speech lasting for five minutes, to say nothing of a continuous development lasting through seventeen volumes of print, he would put on the brakes with all his might—merely to tease Hegel.

What does it mean to say that being is higher than thought? If this is a principle of thought, thought is *ipso facto* again higher than being. If it is capable of being thought, thought is higher; if it is not capable of being thought, no existential system is possible. It makes not the slightest difference whether you treat being roughly or politely; whether you recognize it as something higher that nevertheless follows syllogistically from thought, or regard it as something so low that it follows from thought as a matter of course. Thus when it is argued that God must possess all perfections, or that the highest being must have all perfections, existence is a perfection; *ergo,* God or the highest being must exist: this entire movement of thought is deceptive.* For if God is not really conceived as existing in the first part of the argument, the argument cannot even get started. It would then read about as follows: "A supreme being who does not exist must possess all perfections, including that of existence; *ergo,* a supreme being who does not exist does exist." This would be a strange conclusion. Either the supreme being was non-existent in the premises, and came into existence in the conclusion, which is quite impossible; or he was existent in the premises, in which case he cannot come into existence in the conclusion. For in the latter case we have in the conclusion merely a deceptive form for the logical development of a concept, a deceptive circumlocution for a presupposition. Otherwise the argument must remain purely hypothetical. If a supreme being is assumed to exist, he must also be assumed in possession of all perfections; *ergo,* a supreme being must exist—if he exists. By drawing a conclusion within an hypothesis we can surely never make the conclusion independent of the hypothesis. As for example: "If this or that man is a hypocrite he will behave like a hypocrite; a hypocrite would do this or that; *ergo,* this man had done this or that." Likewise in the argument about God. When the argument is finished, the existence of God is as hypothetical as it was before, but within the hypothesis we have made the advance of establishing a logical connection between the notion of a supreme being and being as itself a perfection; just as in the argument about the hypocrite, we established a connection between being a hypocrite and a particular expression of hypocrisy. The confusion is the same as that involved in explaining reality within the realm of pure thought. The explanatory paragraph is entitled Reality, and the explanatory paragraph deals with reality; but it has been forgotten that the entire explanation belongs in that sphere of the possible which is the sphere of pure thought. If a man begins upon a parenthesis which becomes so long that he himself forgets that it is a parenthesis, this does not avail to cancel its parenthetical character; as soon as it is read in its context, it becomes manifest

---

* However, Hegel does not speak in this fashion; with the help of the principle of identity of thought and being, he is emancipated from a more childlike manner of philosophizing, something which he himself calls attention to, for example in connection with Descartes.[7]

that to permit the parenthetical insertion to play the rôle of the main assertion is meaningless.

When thought becomes self-reflexive and seeks to think itself, there arises a familiar form of scepticism. How may this scepticism be overcome, rooted as it is in thought's refusal to pursue its proper task of thinking other things, and its selfish immersion in an attempt to think itself? When a horse bolts and runs away, we might simply say, if we disregard the damage he may do in the meanwhile, "Let him run, he will soon tire." But of the self-reflexive scepticism of thought this cannot be said, since it can continue indefinitely. Schelling put a stop to the self-reflexive process, understanding his "intellectual intuition" not as a result reached by going on with the process of self-reflection, but as a new point of departure. Hegel[8] regarded this as a fault. He speaks contemptuously of Schelling's intellectual intuition—and then came the Method. The sceptical process of self-reflection continues until it finally abrogates itself, thought struggles through to a victory and becomes again valid, the identity of thought and being is realized in pure thought.* But what does it mean to say that self-reflection continues until it abrogates itself? It need not long continue to make it apparent that there is something wrong with it; but as long as it does continue, it is precisely the same dubious process of self-reflection. What does it mean to say of it that it continues *so long—until*? Such

---

* That there is an abstract certainty tacitly presupposed in all scepticism as its ultimate ground, which gives a foothold to doubt, like the base-line on which the figure is drawn; that even the most strenuous attempts of the Greek sceptics to free the sceptical position from this latent assumption, as for example by explaining that the sceptical assertion must not be taken categorically (θητικως), fail to accomplish anything, is quite certain. But it does not follow that doubt overcomes itself. The basic certainty that supports doubt cannot hypostatize itself as long as I doubt, because doubt consists precisely in departing from this certainty in order to doubt. If I continue to doubt I shall forever be unable to transcend it, since doubt consists in a false interpretation of the basic certainty. If for a single moment I hold fast to this latent certainty as certainty, I must for that moment cease to doubt. A doubter of very mediocre caliber will therefore soonest find certainty; and next to him a doubter who merely puts the categories together to see how they combine, without making the slightest attempt to realize anything of it. I cannot refrain from returning to this point again and again, because it is so decisive. If doubt is capable of overcoming itself, if one may find the truth in doubt simply by doubting everything, without breach of continuity, and without an absolutely new point of departure, not a single Christian category can be sustained, and Christianity is *ipso facto* abolished.

speech is nothing more than deceptive phraseology, which by the introduction of a quantitative reflection seeks to corrupt the integrity of the reader's thought, trying to make it seem easier to understand how self-reflection can annul itself if it only takes a long time before it happens. This quantitative reflection is like the infinitesimally small angles of the astronomers, which finally become so small, though still remaining angles, that their sides are parallel.[9] The fairy tale about the self-reflection that continues *so long—until* distracts the attention from the dialectical issue, the question, namely, of how self-reflection comes to be abrogated. When we say that a man continued telling a lie for so long a time in jest that he finally came to believe it himself, the ethical accent is on the transition. But there is something softening and distracting in the phrase, so long, so that we almost forget the decisiveness of the transition because it takes so long. In narrative and descriptive passages, in the rhetorical address, the abstract *so long— until* produces a strong effect of illusion. The illusion may have an optical form, as in the Book of Judith: "And Judith went out, she and her maid-servant with her. But the men of the city gazed after her until she came down the mountain, until she came through the valley, and they were unable to see her any more." The maiden sat at the seashore and gazed after her beloved—until she could no longer see him. The illusion may take the form of a fantastic vanishing of time, because there is no measure and no standard of measure in this abstract *so long—until.* Then his passion overcame him and he deserted the way of truth, *until* the bitterness of remorse caught up with him and stopped him in his wild career—it would require a master of psychological delineation to produce concretely the effect induced by this abstract *until,* which leads the imagination on and on, indefinitely. But dialectically, this fantastic length is of no significance whatever. When a Greek philosopher[10] was asked to define religion, he asked for time to prepare an answer; when the agreed period had elapsed, he asked for another postponement, and so on. In this way he wished to express symbolically that he regarded the question as unanswerable. This was genuinely in the Greek spirit, beautiful and ingenious. But if he had argued with himself, that since it was so long that he had left the question unanswered, he must now have come nearer to the answer, this would have been a misunderstanding; just as when a debtor remains in debt so long that the debt is finally paid—through having remained so long unpaid. The *so long—until* has something strangely seductive about it. If a man were to say outright that the process of self-reflection abrogates itself, and then go on to explain how, nobody would be able to understand the explanation. But when he says that the process of self-reflection continues so long until it finally abrogates itself, one may perhaps be induced to think: "Ah, that is a different story altogether, there must be something in that." One feels a little anxious and afraid when confronting so great a lapse of time; one loses one's patience, and thinks: "Very well, let it then be so"—and so pure thought gets its beginning. In so far it may be true, as pure thought claims, that it does not begin as the older, more mediocre philosophers did, by begging or postulating its beginning; for the reader is so fearfully impressed by this terrible length of time, this *so long—until,* that he is ready to thank God for any kind of a beginning.

The sceptical process of self-reflection is consequently abrogated by the Method, and further speculative progress is assured in two ways. First and foremost by means of the magic phrase *so long—until.* Every time a transition is needed, the opposite continues so long until it finally passes over into its opposite—and so the Method marches. And, good heavens, we are all weak mortals and dearly love variety, as the proverb says; and since it cannot be otherwise, and since it would be extremely tiresome if the opposite were to continue until it passes over into its opposite, and hence were to continue forever—very well, then, let it pass; the transition is effected. And so the Method marches on—*with necessity.* But should it meet with a stubborn and extremely tiresome person who dares to make objection, saying: "It is as if the Method were a human being who had to be placated, and for whose sake something had to be done; it is as if instead of speculating methodically for the sake of the truth, one speculated for the sake of the Method, which is so great a good in itself that one must not be altogether too scrupulous—if only one gets the Method and the System"—if there is any such person let him beware, for what he represents is the *bad* infinite.[11] The Method has all sorts of resources at its disposal, and as far as the bad infinite is concerned, the Method is stern, and will tolerate no jesting. The stubborn objector is stamped as a blockhead, presumably so long—until. And good heavens, we are all weak mortals and like to be considered intelligent by our respected contemporaries; and since it cannot be otherwise—very well, let it pass. And so the Method proceeds—with necessity. "What is that you are saying; is the Method not necessary?" Why, to be sure, that is precisely what I am saying; it proceeds with necessity, that I am willing to swear, for since it cannot be otherwise, it must be with necessity. The bad infinite is the Method's hereditary enemy; it is the Kobold that moves whenever a transition is about to take place, and prevents it from taking place. The bad infinite is infinitely tenacious of life; it can be vanquished only by a breach of continuity, a qualitative leap. But then it is all over with the Method, the facile nimbleness of its immanence, and the necessity of the transition. This is why the Method is so severe and stern; it intimidates people to the point of being as afraid to represent the bad infinite as to be Black Peter. If the System lacks an ethic otherwise, it is absolutely moral through its use of the category of the *bad* infinite; and it is so extravagantly moral that it uses this category even in logic.

If the content of thought were reality, the most perfect possible anticipation of an action in thought before I had yet acted, would be the action. In that manner no action would ever take place, and the intellectual would swallow the ethical. It would be stupid for anyone to suppose that I mean by this to make the external the test of action. And on the other hand, to show how ethical is intellectualism, seeing that it interprets even thought as action, is a sophism exploiting an ambiguity in the meaning of the word "to think." The only possible way of drawing a distinction between thought and action is to relegate thought to the sphere of the possible, the disinterested, the objective, and to assign action to the sphere of the subjective. But along this boundary there appears a twilight zone. Thus when I think that I will do this or that, this thought is not yet an action, and in all eternity it is qualitatively distinct from action; nevertheless, it is a possibility in which the interest of action and of reality already reflects itself. The disinterestedness and the objectivity of thought are on the way to being disturbed, because reality and responsibility reach out to lay hold of it. There is thus a sin in thought.

The real action is not the external act, but an internal decision in which the individual puts an end to the mere possibility and identifies himself with the content of his thought in order to exist in it. This is the action. Intellectualism seems rigoristic in making thought itself a kind of action, but this rigorism is a false alarm, because the fundamental annulment of action in general which intellectualism permits itself, is sheer laxity. Just as in analogies mentioned in the preceding, the being rigorous within a total laxity is an illusion, the supposed rigor being essentially laxity. If someone were to interpret sin as ignorance, and then within this total determination were to conceive individual sins with rigor, the rigor would be altogether illusory. For within the total determination of sin as ignorance, every particular qualification becomes essentially frivolous, because the total determination is frivolous.

There is a certain plausible confusion between thought and action in connection with evil; but if we examine the matter more closely we shall see that the reason is to be sought in the jealous watchfulness of the good, which requires itself of the individual to such a degree that it determines even an evil thought as sin. But let us rather take the good by way of illustration. When I think of something good that I intend to do, is this identical with having done it? By no means. But neither is it the external that constitutes the criterion of action; for the human being who does not own a penny can be as charitable as one who gives away a kingdom. When the Levite journeyed along the road traversed by the unfortunate man who, between Jericho and Jerusalem, had fallen among thieves, it may well have occurred to him while he was still some distance away, how beautiful a deed it is to help a sufferer in his distress. He may perhaps even have thought, by way of anticipation, that a good deed of this sort has its reward in itself; and perhaps he rode more slowly because of his absorption in this thought. But as he came nearer the place where the victim was, the difficulties began to heap themselves up before his mind—and he rode past. Now he doubtless began to make haste, in order to get away quickly from the thought of the insecurity of the road, from the thought of the possible presence of the robbers near by, from the thought of how readily the victim might be led to confuse him with the robbers who had left him there to die. He failed to act. But now suppose that he was seized by remorse, that he turned quickly about, fearing neither the robbers nor other difficulties, but fearing only lest he arrive too late. Let us suppose that he did arrive too late, the good Samaritan having already managed to get the sufferer into the shelter of the inn. Had he not then acted? Certainly he had acted, and that in spite of the fact that he had no opportunity to act in the external sense.

Let us take a religious action. Is believing God identical with considering how glorious a thing faith is, and what peace and safety it can give? By no means. Even wishing to believe, where the interest of the subject is much more definitely involved, is not believing, is not action. The relationship of the individual to the action represented in his thought, is still merely a possibility, subject to repudiation. That there are cases, particularly in connection with evil actions, where the transition from thought to action is scarcely noticeable, is not denied; but these cases have a special explanation. They show what happens when the individual is in the power of a habit, that through often having made the transition from thought to action he has lost the power to keep this transition under the control of will. It is a state of slavery to a habit which makes the transition on his behalf ever more quickly.

Between the action as represented in thought on the one hand, and the real action on the other, between the possibility and the reality, there may in respect of content be no difference at all. But in respect of form, the difference is essential. Reality is the interest in action, in existence.

That the real action often tends to be confused with all sorts of notions, intentions, approximations to a decision, and so forth, and that it is seldom that anyone really acts, is not denied. On the contrary, it is assumed that just this state of affairs has contributed to the confusion with which we are here dealing. But let us take an act *sensu eminenti,* where everything stands out quite clearly. The external element in Luther's action consists in his appearance before the Diet of Worms; but from the moment that he had committed himself with entire subjective passion to his decision, so that every mere relationship of possibility to this action was interpreted by him as a temptation —from that moment he had acted.* When Dion[12] went aboard the

* In general, the difference between the action as conceived and the action as inwardly real, consists in the fact that while in the case of the former every additional consideration is welcome, in connection with the latter it is to be regarded as a temptation. If in spite of this, some additional consideration reveals itself as of sufficient importance to command respect, this means that the way to a new resolve goes through repentance. When I am deliberating, it is my task to think every possibility; but when I have decided, and consequently acted inwardly, a change takes place so that it is now my task to ward against further deliberation, except in

ship which carried the expedition to overthrow the tyrant Dionysius, he is said to have remarked that even if he died on the way he would still have performed a glorious deed; that is, he had acted. To assume that the external decision is higher than the internal decision is only an example of the contemptible notions concerning the highest human experience entertained by weak and cowardly and shifty men. To suppose that the external action can decide something forever and make it irrevocable, while the internal decision is not thus decisive, is to entertain a contempt for what is sacred.

To assert the supremacy of thought is Gnosticism; to make the ethical reality of the subject the only reality might seem to be acosmism. The circumstance that it will seem so to a busy thinker who explains everything, a nimble mind that quickly surveys the entire universe, merely proves that such a thinker has a very humble notion of what the ethical means to the subject. If Ethics were to take away the entire world from such a thinker, letting him keep his own self, he would probably regard such a trifle as not worth keeping, and would let it go with the rest— and so it becomes acosmism. But why does he think so slightingly of his own self? If it were our meaning that he should give up the whole world in order to content himself with another person's ethical reality, he would be justified in regarding the exchange as a dead loss. But his own ethical reality, on the other hand, ought to mean more to him than "heaven and earth and all that therein is,"[13] more than the six thousand years of human history, more than both astrology and the veterinary sciences or whatever it is that the age demands, all of which is aesthetically and intellectually a huge vulgarity. And if it is not so, it is worse for the individual himself, for in that case he has absolutely nothing, no reality at all, since to all other things the maximum relationship attainable is a possibility.

so far as something requires to be undone. The external decision is but a jest; but the more sluggishly an individual lives, the more does the external decision become the only one he knows anything about. Often people have no notion of the eternal decision that the individual may make inwardly; but they believe that when a decision has been registered on a piece of stamped paper it is really decided, but not before.

The transition from possibility to actuality is, as Aristotle rightly says, a κίνησις, a movement. This cannot be expressed or understood in the language of abstraction; for in the sphere of the abstract, movement cannot have assigned to it either time or space which presuppose movement or are presupposed by it. Here then there is a pause, and a leap. If someone were to say that this seems to be so only because I think about some definite thing and fail to abstract; that if I did abstract I would perceive that there is no breach of continuity,—my reiterated answer would be that this is quite correct, that from the abstract point of view there is no breach of continuity. But neither is there any movement, since from this point of view everything *is*. But when existence gives to the movement the requisite time, and I reflect this in my representation, the leap stands revealed in the only way possible: either that it must come, or that it has been. Let us take an example from the sphere of the ethical. It has often enough been said the good is its own reward, and that it is in so far not only right but prudent to will the good. A prudent eudaemonist may be capable of understanding this quite well. In thought, in the form of a possibility, he may approach very near to the good; because within the sphere of the possible, as within the sphere of the abstract, the possible constitutes a mere appearance. But when the transition is about to become actual, prudence finds it impossible to meet the test. The actual interval of time separates the good and its reward so long, so everlastingly, that prudence cannot bring them together, and the eudaemonist begs to be excused. It is certain indeed that to will the good is the height of prudence, but not in the sense in which the merely prudent man understands it, but in the sense in which the good man understands it. The transition thus reveals itself clearly as a breach of continuity, even as suffering. In the sermonic discourse, the illusion that transforms the transition to becoming a Christian into a mere appearance, is often evoked; in this way the hearer is deceived, and prevented from realizing the transition.

Subjectivity is truth, subjectivity is reality.

N.B. Necessity must be dealt with by itself. The fact that modern speculative thought has imported necessity into the historical process has caused much confusion; the categories of possibility, of actuality, and of necessity have all been compromised. In the *Philosophical Fragments*[14] I have sought to indicate this briefly.

§ 3. THE SIMULTANEITY OF THE INDIVIDUAL FACTORS OF SUBJECTIVITY IN THE EXISTING SUBJECT—THE CONTRAST BETWEEN THIS SIMULTANEITY AND THE SPECULATIVE PROCESS

Granted that speculative thought is justified in pooh-poohing such a tri-partite division as that of man into spirit, soul, and body; granted that its merit is to have determined man as spirit, distinguishing soul, consciousness, and spirit as three developmental stages within one and the same developing subject*—it is quite another question whether the immediate transfer of this scientific consideration to the existential, which can only too readily take place, may not be the cause of much confusion. The scientific movement of thought is from lower to higher, and thought is designated as the highest stage. In the interpretation of the historical process there is similarly a movement from lower to higher; the stages of imagination and feeling have been left behind, and thought as the highest stage is also the last. Everywhere it is decisively concluded that thought is the highest stage of human development; philosophy moves farther and farther away from contact with primitive existential impressions, and there is nothing left to explore, nothing to experience. Everything has been finished, and speculative thought has now to rubricate, classify, and methodically arrange the various concepts. One does not live any more, one does not act, one does not believe; but one knows what love and faith are, and it only remains to determine their place in the System. In the same way the domino-player has his pieces lying before him, and the game con-

---

* What is this same subject? Surely not an individual existing human being, but rather the abstract concept of man in general. There is nothing else for science to deal with, and in dealing with it science is of course fully within its rights; but here, too, we are often put off with a mere game of words. It is asserted again and again that thought becomes concrete. But in what sense does it become concrete? Surely not in the sense that it becomes a definite concrete something? That is to say then, thought becomes concrete within the general determination that it is abstract, which means that it remains essentially abstract; for the concrete is the existing, and existence corresponds to particularity, from which thought abstracts. For a thinker as such it may be quite in order to think man in general; but *qua* existing individual, he is ethically forbidden to forget himself, or to forget that he is an existing individual. The ethical is so far from celebrating the advent of each new thinker with a paean of joy that it makes the thinker morally responsible for the use he makes of his existence in order to think, and asks him for a justification of such devotion of his energies, in precisely the same sense that it makes everyone else responsible for the use to which he puts his life, without permitting itself to be blinded by appearances.

sists in putting them together. For six thousand years human beings
have loved and poets have sung the praises of love, so that now in
the nineteenth century we ought surely to know what love is; our
task is to assign love, and especially marriage, its proper place in the
System—for the professor gets himself married in distraction of mind.
The politicians have pointed out that wars will ultimately cease,
everything being decided in the cabinets of the diplomats, where the
statesmen sit and direct the military forces, and so forth. If only the
same sort of thing does not happen also in the daily life, so that we
cease to live, while professors and *Privatdocents* speculatively determine
the relationship of the different factors to man in general. It seems to
me that there is something human in the horrors of even the bloodiest
war in comparison with this diplomatic stillness; and likewise there
seems to me something horrible, something bewitched, in the dead
insensibility by which the actual life is reduced to a shadow existence.

It may be all very well from a scientific point of view to make
thought the highest stage, and it may be quite plausible from the standpoint of world-history to say that the earlier stages have been left
behind. But does our age bring forth a generation of individuals who
are born without capacity for imagination and feeling? Are we born
to begin with paragraph 14 in the System? Let us above all not confuse
the historical development of the human spirit at large with particular individuals.

In the animal world the particular specimen is directly related to the
species as an example of it, and participates immediately in whatever
development the species may have. When a breed of sheep is improved,
for example, the consequence is that improved sheep are born to the
breed, because the particular specimen merely expresses the kind. But
it is surely otherwise when an individual who is qualified as spirit
stands in a relation to the generative process. Or may we assume that
Christian parents give birth to Christian children? Christianity at least
does not; on the contrary it assumes that children born of Christian
parents are no less sinful than those born of pagan parents. Does
anyone believe that being born of Christian parents brings the child
by a single step nearer to Christianity than if born of pagan parents,
provided that in the latter case also the child receives a Christian upbringing? And yet it is a confusion of this kind which speculative
thought often indirectly occasions, even if it does not directly make
itself guilty of it. The individual is without further ado supposed to be

related to the development of the human spirit as a particular specimen to its kind, just as if spiritual development were something that one generation could bequeath to another; and as if spirit were a character belonging to the race and not to the individual, a supposition which is self-contradictory, and ethically abominable. Spiritual development is self-activity; the spiritually developed individual takes his development with him when he dies. If an individual of a subsequent generation is to reach the same development he will have to attain it by means of his own activity, and he cannot be permitted to omit anything. But it is, of course, easier, cheaper and more comfortable to bluster about being born in the nineteenth century.

If the single individual were immediately related to the development of the human spirit at large, it would follow that only defective examples of humanity would be born in each generation. But there is surely a difference between a generation of human beings and a shoal of fish, although it has now become so fashionable to seek entertainment in the shifting play of colors presented by the human shoal, and to speak with contempt of the individuals, who are worth no more than herring. Science and world-history may perhaps be indifferent to such an objection; but Ethics ought surely to have a voice in every view of life. But Ethics has been crowded out of the System, and as a substitute for it there has been included a something which confuses the historical with the individual, the bewildering and noisy demands of the age with the eternal demand that conscience makes upon the individual. Ethics concentrates upon the individual, and ethically it is the task of every individual to become an entire man; just as it is the ethical presupposition that every man is born in such a condition that he can become one. Whether anyone realizes this task or not makes no difference, the fact that the requirement is there is the important thing. And if ever so many blind and mediocre and cowardly individuals renounce their own selves in order to become something *en masse* with the help of the generative process, Ethics does not bargain with them.

As a matter of scientific principle it may be quite proper and perhaps even masterly (I am far from pretending to any critical judgment) to rise in abstract-dialectical psychological determinations from the psycho-somatic to the psychic, and from the psychic to the pneumatic; but this scientific arrangement of the concepts must not be permitted to confound existence. In existence the abstract-scientific category of being human may perhaps be something higher than a particular existing human being, and perhaps something lower; but in any case existence has only individual human beings. In respect of existence it will not do to organize the various differences so as to make them tend toward a culmination in thought, for the progressive method has no relevance to what is involved in existing as a human being. In existence all the factors must be co-present. In existence thought is by no means higher than imagination and feeling, but coordinate. In existence the supremacy of thought becomes confusing. When it is urged, for example, that the expectation of an eternal happiness here-after is an idea based upon a finite reflection of the understanding, and cannot maintain itself before the bar of thought; when it is further asserted that this notion may perhaps properly be used in the popular address, for plain people who never rise above the sphere of representa-tive thought, but that the distinction between "here" and "hereafter" does not hold for thinkers,—the answer is that this is quite correct. For thought, abstract thought, the distinction does not hold; but then again it must be remembered that for existence, abstract thought does not hold. The moment I really exist, the separation between "here" and "hereafter" is there, and the existential consequence of annulling the distinctions is suicide, as was said in the preceding. On behalf of specu-lative thought, it is usual to say that the absoluteness of the principle of contradiction is an illusion of the understanding, and that it vanishes for thought. Just so. But then again it must be remembered that the abstraction as a result of which the principle vanishes, is itself a phantom that vanishes before the reality of existence. For the abroga-tion of the principle of contradiction, if it really means anything, and is not merely a literary conceit born of an adventurous imagination, means for an existing individual that he has ceased to exist. Faith is said to be an immediacy, and it is asserted that the immediate is abrogated by thought.* This looks plausible enough from the abstract point of view; but I should like to know how an existing individual manages to exist, after thought has abrogated his entire immediacy. It is not without reason that Frater Taciturnus[1] complains that all men write books in which immediacy is abrogated, while no one breathes a single word about how they then manage to exist.

* That this is one of the most confusing propositions advanced by recent speculation has often been pointed out by the pseudonymous authors. If one wishes to speak of an abrogated im-mediacy it must be an aesthetic-ethical immediacy; faith then becomes the new immediacy, and one which can never be abrogated in existence, since it is the highest immediacy, and its abrogation would reduce a man to null and nothing.

Science organizes the moments of subjectivity within a knowledge of them, and this knowledge is assumed to be the highest stage, and all knowledge is an abstraction which annuls existence, a taking of the objects of knowledge out of existence. In existence, however, such a principle does not hold. If thought speaks deprecatingly of the imagination, imagination in its turn speaks deprecatingly of thought; and likewise with feeling. The task is not to exalt the one at the expense of the other, but to give them an equal status, to unify them in simultaneity; the medium in which they are unified is *existence*.

By positing as a task the scientific process instead of the existential simultaneity, life is confused. Even where the succession is obvious, as in the case of the different ages in the individual's life, the task is to achieve simultaneity. It may be a genial observation that the world and the human race have grown older; but is not everyone still born in infancy? In the life of the individual the task is to achieve an ennoblement of the successive within the simultaneous. To have been young, and then to grow older, and finally to die, is a very mediocre form of human existence; this merit belongs to every animal. But the unification of the different stages of life in simultaneity is the task set for human beings. And just as it is an evidence of mediocrity when a human being cuts away all communication with childhood, so as to be a man merely fragmentarily, so it is also a miserable mode of existence for a thinker who is also an existing individual to lose imagination and feeling, which is quite as bad as losing his reason.

And yet, this seems to be the goal toward which the contemporary generation tends. Poetry is crowded aside and dismissed as a transcended phase, because it is closely connected with the imagination. In a scientific arrangement of the categories, there may be no valid objection to assigning poetry a place as a transcended phase. But in existence itself, the principle holds that as long as a human being makes claim to a human form of existence, he must preserve the poetic in his life, and all his thinking must not be permitted to disturb for him its magic, but rather to enhance and beautify it. So also with religion. Religion is not childlike in the sense that it is to be put aside with the coming of the years; this notion is, on the contrary, a childish and superstitious over-valuation of thought. The true is not higher than the good and the beautiful, but the true and the good and the beautiful belong essentially to every human existence, and are unified for an existing individual not in thought but in existence.

But just as one generation affects round hats, and another prefers them three-cornered, so a fashion of the age promotes forgetfulness of the ethical requirement. I am well aware that every human being is more or less one-sided, and I do not regard it as a fault. But it is a fault when a fashion selects a certain form of one-sidedness and magnifies it into a total norm. *Non omnes omnia possumus* is a maxim that holds true everywhere in life; but the ideal task should not on that account be forgotten. The one-sidedness should partly be apprehended, not without a certain sadness, and partly it should represent a vigorous resolution of the will, preferring to be something definite in a manner worth while, rather than to be a dabbler in everything. Every distinguished individual always has something one-sided about him, and this one-sidedness may be an indirect indication of his real greatness, but it is not that greatness itself. So far are we human beings from realizing the ideal, that the second rank, the powerful one-sidedness, is pretty much the highest ever attained; but it must never be forgotten that it is only the second rank. It might be urged that the present generation is, from this point of view, praiseworthy, in so one-sidedly aiming to express the intellectual and the scientific. My answer would be that the misfortune of the present age is not that it is one-sided, but that it is abstractly all-sided. A one-sided individual rejects, clearly and definitely, what he does not wish to include; but the abstractly all-sided individual imagines that he has everything through the one-sidedness of the intellectual. A one-sided believer refuses to have anything to do with thought, and a one-sided man of action will have nothing to do with science; but the one-sidedness of the intellectual creates the illusion of having everything. A one-sided individual of this type has faith and passion as transcended phases of his life, or so he says—and nothing is easier to say.

§ 4. THE SUBJECTIVE THINKER—HIS TASK, HIS FORM, HIS STYLE

If an excursion into the realm of pure thought is to determine whether a man is a thinker or not, the subjective thinker is *ipso facto* excluded from consideration. But in and with his exclusion every existential problem also goes by the board; and the melancholy consequences are audible as an undertone of warning accompanying the jubilant cries with which modern speculative thought has hailed the System.

There is an old saying that *oratio, tentatio, meditatio faciunt theologum*. Similarly there is required for a subjective thinker imagination and feeling, dialectics in existential inwardness, together with passion. But passion first and last; for it is impossible to think about existence in existence without passion. Existence involves a tremendous contradiction, from which the subjective thinker does not have to abstract, though he can if he will, but in which it is his business to remain. For a dialectic of world-history the individuals vanish in humanity; you and I, any particular existing individual, cannot become visible to such a dialectic, even by the invention of new and more powerful magnifying instruments for the concrete.

The subjective thinker is a dialectitian dealing with the existential, and he has the passion of thought requisite for holding fast to the qualitative disjunction. But on the other hand, if the qualitative disjunction is applied in empty isolation, if it is applied to the individual in an altogether abstract fashion, one may risk saying something infinitely decisive and be quite correct in what one says, and yet, ludicrously enough, say nothing at all. Hence it is a psychologically noteworthy phenomenon that the absolute disjunction may be used quite disingenuously, precisely for the purpose of evasion. When the death-penalty is affixed to every crime, it ends in no crime being punished at all. So also in the case of the absolute disjunction. Applied abstractly it becomes an unpronounceable mute letter, or if pronounced, it says nothing. The subjective thinker has the absolute disjunction ready to hand; therefore, as an essential existential moment he holds it fast with a thinker's passion, but he holds it as a last decisive resort, to prevent everything from being reduced to merely quantitative differences. He holds it in reserve, but does not apply it so as by recurring to it abstractly to inhibit existence. Hence the subjective thinker adds to his equipment aesthetic and ethical passion, which gives him the necessary concreteness.

All existential problems are passionate problems, for when existence is interpenetrated with reflection it generates passion. To think about existential problems in such a way as to leave out the passion, is tantamount to not thinking about them at all, since it is to forget the point, which is that the thinker is himself an existing individual. But the subjective thinker is not a poet, though he may also be a poet; he is not an ethicist, though he may also be an ethicist; he is not a dialectician, though he may also be a dialectician. He is essentially an existing individual, while the existence of the poet is non-essential in relation to the poem, the existence of the ethicist, in relation to his doctrine, the existence of the dialectician, in relation to his thought. The subjective thinker is not a man of science, but an artist. Existing is an art. The subjective thinker is aesthetic enough to give his life aesthetic content, ethical enough to regulate it, and dialectical enough to interpenetrate it with thought.

The subjective thinker has the task of understanding himself in his existence. Abstract thought is wont to speak of contradiction, and of its immanent propulsive power, although by abstracting from existence and from existing it removes the difficulty and the contradiction. The subjective thinker is an existing individual and a thinker at one and the same time; he does not abstract from the contradiction and from existence, but lives in it while at the same time thinking. In all his thinking he therefore has to think the fact that he is an existing individual. For this reason he always has enough to think about. Humanity in the abstract is a subject soon disposed of, and likewise world-history; even such tremendous portions as China, Persia, and so forth, are as nothing to the hungry monster of the historical process. The abstract concept of faith is soon disposed of; but the subjective thinker who in all his thinking remains at home in his existence, will find an inexhaustible subject for thought in his faith, when he seeks to follow its declension in all the manifold *casibus* of life. Such subjective reflection is by no means a light matter; for existence is the most difficult of all subjects to penetrate when the thinker has to remain in it, because the moment is commensurable for the highest decision, and yet again a vanishing instant in the possible seventy years of a human life. Poul Møller[1] has rightly remarked that a court jester uses more wit in a single year than many a witty author in his entire lifetime. And why? Because the former is an existing individual who must have his wit at his disposal every moment of the day, while the latter is a man who is witty at intervals.

If anyone is disposed to doubt that there are difficulties connected with understanding oneself in existence in terms of thought, I shall be more than willing to try this experiment: let one of our systematic philosophers undertake to explain merely one of the simplest of existential problems. I am ready to admit that I am not worthy even to be mentioned in the same breath with such thinkers, and that I count for less than nothing in systematic bookkeeping; I am willing also to concede that the tasks of systematic thought are much greater, and that such thinkers rank far higher than the subjective thinker. But if this

THE SUBJECTIVE THINKER 4 315

is really so, then they should be able to explain also the more simple problems.

While abstract thought seeks to understand the concrete abstractly, the subjective thinker has conversely to understand the abstract concretely. Abstract thought turns from concrete men to consider man in general; the subjective thinker seeks to understand the abstract determination of being human in terms of this particular existing human being.

To understand oneself in existence was the Greek principle. However little content the doctrine of a Greek philosopher sometimes represented, the philosopher had nevertheless one advantage: he was never comical. I am well aware that if someone were nowadays to live like a Greek philosopher, existentially expressing and existentially probing the depths of what he must call his view of life, he would be regarded as a lunatic. Let it be so. But for an honored philosopher to be extremely profound and ingenious, to the point of never remembering, although he speculates upon existential problems like Christianity, to ask himself who in all the world his speculation concerns, much less to think that it concerns himself: that I find to be ridiculous.

All scepticism is a kind of idealism. Hence when the sceptic Zeno[2] pursued the study of scepticism by endeavoring existentially to keep himself unaffected by whatever happened, so that when once he had gone out of his way to avoid a mad dog, he shamefacedly admitted that even a sceptical philosopher is also sometimes a man, I find nothing ridiculous in this. There is no contradiction, and the comical always lies in a contradiction. On the other hand, when one thinks of all the miserable idealistic lecture-witticisms, the jesting and coquetry in connection with playing the idealist while in the professorial chair, so that the lecturer is not really an idealist, but only plays the fashionable game of being an idealist; when one remembers the lecture-phrase about doubting everything, while occupying the lecture platform, aye, then it is impossible not to write a satire merely by recounting the facts. Through an existential attempt to be an idealist, one would learn in the course of half a year something very different from this game of hide-and-seek on the lecture platform. There is no special difficulty connected with being an idealist in the imagination; but to *exist* as an idealist is an extremely strenuous task, because existence itself constitutes a hindrance and an objection. To express existentially what one has understood about oneself, and in this manner to understand oneself, is in no way comical. But to understand everything except one's own self is very comical.

There is a sense in which the subjective thinker speaks quite as abstractly as the abstract thinker; for the latter speaks of man in general and of subjectivity in general, while the former speaks of the one man (*unum noris, omnes*). But this one human being is an existing human being, and the difficulty is not evaded.

To understand oneself in existence is also the Christian principle, except that this "self" has received far richer and deeper determination, still more difficult to understand, in conjunction with existence. The believer is a subjective thinker, and the difference that obtains, as was shown above, is only that between the simple man and the simple wise man. Here again the "self" is not humanity in general, or subjectivity in general, in which case everything becomes easy because the difficulty is removed, and the whole task transferred to the realm of abstract thought with its shadow-boxing. The difficulty is greater than it was for the Greek, because still greater contradictions are conjoined, existence being accentuated paradoxically as sin, and eternity accentuated paradoxically as God in time. The difficulty consists in existing in such categories, not in abstractly thinking oneself out of them; abstractly thinking, for example, about an eternal God-becoming[3] and the like, all of which ideas emerge as soon as the difficulty is taken away. As a consequence, the believer's existence is still more passionate than the existence of the Greek philosopher, who needed a · high degree of passion even in relation to his *ataraxy*; for existence generates passion, but existence paradoxically accentuated generates the maximum of passion.

To abstract from existence is to remove the difficulty. To remain in existence so as to understand one thing in one moment and another thing in another moment, is not to understand oneself. But to understand the greatest oppositions together, and to understand oneself existing in them, is very difficult. Let anyone merely observe himself, and take note of how men speak, and he will perceive how rarely this task is successfully realized.

One man is good and another is shrewd, or the same man acts as a good man at one time, and shrewdly at another time; but at one and the same time to perceive in connection with the same thing what is shrewd, and to perceive this merely in order to will the good, is very difficult. One man has a predilection for laughter and another for tears, or the same man is disposed variously at different times; but at one and the same time to see the comic and the tragic in the same thing, is difficult. To be crushed under a burden of remorse, and again to be a devil of a fellow, is not difficult; but at one and the same time to be crushed in spirit and yet free from care, is difficult. To think one thought and to have forgotten all others is not difficult; but to think one and simultaneously have the opposite in mind, uniting these opposites in existence, is difficult. In a life of seventy years to have had all possible moods, and to leave behind a collection of samples from which to choose at pleasure, is not so very difficult; but to have one mood rich and full, and also to have the opposite mood, so that in giving the one mood its pathos and expression, the opposite mood is slipped in as an undertone, that is a difficult thing to do. And so forth.

In spite of all his exertion the subjective thinker enjoys only a meager reward. The more the collective idea comes to dominate even the ordinary consciousness, the more forbidding seems the transition to becoming a particular existing human being instead of losing oneself in the race, and saying "we," "our age," "the nineteenth century." That it is a little thing merely to be a particular existing human being is not to be denied; but for this very reason it requires considerable resignation not to make light of it. For what does a mere individual count for? Our age knows only too well how little it is, but here also lies the specific immorality of the age. Each age has its own characteristic depravity. Ours is perhaps not pleasure or indulgence or sensuality, but rather a dissolute pantheistic contempt for the individual man. In the midst of all our exultation over the achievements of the age and the nineteenth century, there sounds a note of poorly conceived contempt for the individual man; in the midst of the self-importance of the contemporary generation there is revealed a sense of despair over being human. Everything must attach itself so as to be a part of some movement; men are determined to lose themselves in the totality of things, in world-history, fascinated and deceived by a magic witchery; no one wants to be an individual human being. Hence perhaps the many attempts to continue clinging to Hegel, even by men who have reached an insight into the questionable character of his philosophy. It is a fear that if they were to become particular existing human beings, they would vanish tracelessly, so that not even the daily press would be able to discover them, still less critical journals, to say nothing at all of speculative philosophers immersed in world-history. As particular

human beings they fear that they will be doomed to a more isolated
and forgotten existence than that of a man in the country; for if a man
lets go of Hegel he will not even be in a position to have a letter
addressed to him.

It cannot be denied that when a man lacks ethical and religious
enthusiasm, being a mere individual is a matter for despair—but not
otherwise. When Napoleon led his army into Africa, he reminded the
soldiers that the memories of forty centuries looked down upon them
from the pyramids. It stirs the blood merely to read about it; when
confronted with such a challenge, what wonder that even the most
cowardly soldier was transformed into a hero! But if we suppose that
the world has been in existence for six thousand years, and consider
that God must have existed at least as long as the world, the memories
of six thousand years look down upon the individual existing human
being; is not this quite as inspiring? But in the midst of the brave
show of the generations, one easily perceives the despondency and
cowardice of the individuals. Just as desert travellers combine into great
caravans from fear of robbers and wild beasts, so the individuals of the
contemporary generation are fearful of existence, because it is God-
forsaken; only in great masses do they dare to live, and they cluster
together *en masse* in order to feel that they amount to something.

Every human being must be assumed in essential possession of what
essentially belongs to being a man. The task of the subjective thinker
is to transform himself into an instrument that clearly and definitely
expresses in existence whatever is essentially human. To rely on a
differential trait in this connection is a misunderstanding, for to have
a little more brain and the like is insignificant. That our age has
forsaken the individuals in order to take refuge in the collective idea,
has its natural explanation in an aesthetic despair which has not yet
found the ethical. Men have perceived that it avails nothing to be ever
so distinguished an individual man, since no difference avails anything.
A new difference has consequently been hit upon: the difference of
being born in the nineteenth century. Everyone tries to determine his
bit of existence in relation to the age as quickly as possible and so
consoles himself. But it avails nothing, being only a higher and more
glittering illusion. And just as there have lived fools in ancient times,
as well as in every generation, who have confounded themselves, in
the vanity of their delusion, with one or another distinguished man,
pretending to be this or that individual, so the peculiarity of our age is

that the fools are not even content to confuse themselves with some great man, but identify themselves with the age, with the century, with the contemporary generation, with humanity at large. To wish to live as a particular human being (which is what everyone undoubtedly is), relying upon a difference, is the weakness of cowardice; to will to live as a particular human being (which everyone undoubtedly is) in the same sense as is open to every other human being, is the ethical victory over life and all its illusions. And this victory is perhaps the hardest of all to win in the theocentric nineteenth century.

The subjective thinker has a form, a form for his communication with other men, and this form constitutes his style. It must be as manifold as the opposites he holds in combination. The systematic *ein, zwei, drei* is an abstract form, and must therefore fail when applied to the concrete. In the same degree that the subjective thinker himself is concrete, his form will become concretely dialectical. As he is not himself either poet or ethicist or dialectician, his form cannot be that of either directly. His form must first and last relate itself to existence, and in this connection he will have at his disposal the poetic, the ethical, the dialectical, and the religious. In comparison with a poet, his form will be abbreviated, while in comparison with a dialectician, his form will be broad. Regarded abstractly, concreteness in the existential is breadth. In comparison with abstract thought, the humorous, for example, is broad; but it is by no means broad when it is relative to a concrete existential communication, unless the humor is broad in itself. The person of an abstract thinker is irrelevant to his thought. An existential thinker must be pictured as essentially thinking, but so that in presenting his thought he sketches himself. In relation to abstract thought all jesting is broad, but not in relation to a concrete existential communication, unless the jest is broad in itself. But the subjective thinker does not have the poetic leisure to create in the medium of the imagination, nor does he have the time for aesthetically disinterested elaboration. He is essentially an existing individual in the existential medium, and does not have at his disposal the imaginative medium which would permit him to create the illusion characteristic of all aesthetic production. Poetic leisure is broad, in comparison with the existential communication of the subjective thinker. Secondary personalities, a scenic environment and the like, all of which help to maintain the self-sufficiency of the aesthetic production, constitute breadth. The subjective thinker has only a single scene, existence, and he has nothing to do with beautiful valleys and the like. His scene is not the fairyland of the imagination, where the poet's love evokes the perfect; nor is the scene in England, and the task to make sure of local color and historical exactness. His scene is—inwardness in existing as a human being; concreteness is attained through bringing the existential categories into relationship with one another. In comparison with the existential categories, historical actuality and accuracy constitute breadth.

But existential reality is incommunicable, and the subjective thinker finds his reality in his own ethical existence. When reality is apprehended by an outsider it can be understood only as possibility. Everyone who makes a communication, in so far as he becomes conscious of this fact, will therefore be careful to give his existential communication the form of a possibility, precisely in order that it may have a relationship to existence. A communication in the form of a possibility compels the recipient to face the problem of existing in it, so far as this is possible between man and man. Let me illustrate this point once more. By relating how this or that man *really* has done so and so, something very great and distinguished, it might be imagined that a reader would be brought nearer to the forming of a resolution to do the same, than if the account is offered merely as a possibility. Abstracting from the fact that the reader can understand such a communication only by resolving the *esse* of its reality into a *posse,* since otherwise he merely *imagines* that he understands it, the knowledge that this or that person has actually done so and so, may just as well constitute a hindrance to action as a stimulus. By means of the consideration that he is an *actual* person the reader transforms the doer of the deed into a rare exception. He admires him and says: "But I am too humble to do anything like that." Admiration has its very proper place in connection with differential achievements, but it is a misunderstanding when brought into relation with what is universally human. That a man can swim the Channel, that another is proficient in twenty-four languages, that a third man can walk on his hands, may be admired *si placet.* But if anyone is supposed to be great in connection with what is universal, by his virtue, by his faith, by his high-mindedness, by his loyalty, by his pertinacity, and so forth, admiration is a deceitful relationship, or may readily become such. Whatever is great in the sphere of the universally human must therefore not be communicated as a subject for admiration, but as an ethical *requirement.* In the form of a possibility it becomes a requirement. Instead of presenting an account of the good in the form of actuality, as is usually done, instead of insisting that such and such a person has actually lived, and has really done this or that, by which the reader is transformed into an admiring spectator, a critical connoisseur, the good should be presented in the form of a possibility. This will bring home to the reader, as closely as is possible, whether he will resolve to exist in it. A communication in the form of the possible, operates in terms of the ideal man (not the differential ideal, but the universal ideal), whose relationship to every individual man is that of a requirement. In the same degree as it is urged that it was this particular man who did the deed, it becomes easier for others to make him out an exceptional case.

One need not be a psychologist to know that there is a certain disingenuousness of spirit, which seeks to protect itself against the ethical impression precisely by means of admiration. Instead of using the ethical and the religious example to turn the spectator's eye in upon himself, and thus repel him through placing the possibility between the example and the spectator as something they both have in common, the form of presentation which appeals to actuality attracts the attention of the many to itself, aesthetically. As a consequence it degenerates into a matter for discussion, and critical examination *pro* and *con;* the communication is twisted and turned on every side, to see whether, now really, etc. and people admire and blubber over the fact that now really, etc. The example of Job's faith should be so presented that it becomes a challenge, a question directed to me, as to whether I too desire to acquire a believing mind. By no means should it be permitted to signify that I have an invitation to become a spectator at a comedy, or to play the rôle of a member of a public investigating whether now actually, or applauding that now really. The concern which a sensitive congregation and its individual members sometimes feel for the appointed curate, desiring to know whether he really . . . is a matter of very low comedy; the joy and admiration sometimes felt over having a pastor of whom it is certain that he really . . . and so forth, is equally comical. It is everlastingly untrue that anyone was ever helped to do the good by the fact that someone else really did it; for if he ever comes to the point of really doing it himself, it will be by apprehending the reality of the other as a possibility. When Themistocles was rendered sleepless by thinking about the exploits of Miltiades, it was his apprehension of their reality as a possibility that made him sleepless. Had he plunged into inquiries as to whether Miltiades really had accomplished the great things attributed to him, had he contented himself with knowing that Miltiades had actually done them, he would scarcely have been rendered sleepless. In that case he would probably have become a sleepy, or at the most a noisy admirer, but scarcely a second Miltiades. Ethically speaking there is nothing so conducive to sound sleep as admiration of another person's ethical reality. And again ethically speaking, if there is anything that can stir and rouse a man, it is a possibility ideally requiring itself of a human being.

CHAPTER IV

THE PROBLEM OF THE *FRAGMENTS*: HOW CAN AN ETERNAL HAPPINESS BE BASED UPON HISTORICAL KNOWLEDGE?

SECTION I. FOR ORIENTATION IN THE PLAN OF THE *FRAGMENTS*

§ I. THAT THE POINT OF DEPARTURE WAS TAKEN IN THE PAGAN CONSCIOUSNESS, AND WHY

THE reader of the bit of philosophy presented in the *Fragments* will remember that the piece was not doctrinal but experimental. It took its point of departure in the pagan consciousness, in order to seek out experimentally an interpretation of existence which might truly be said to go *further* than paganism. Modern speculation seems almost to have done the trick of going *further* than Christianity, *on the other side,* or of understanding that Christianity had gone so far that it had about got back to paganism. For a man to prefer paganism to Christianity is by no means confusing, but to discover paganism as a highest development within Christianity is to work injustice both to paganism and to Christianity; to Christianity, because it becomes something other than it is, and to paganism, which doesn't become anything at all, though it really was something. The speculative movement which plumes itself on having completely understood Christianity, and explains itself at the same time as the highest development within Christianity, has strangely enough made the discovery that there is no "beyond." The notions of a future life, of another world, and similar ideas, are described as arising out of the dialectical limitations of the finite understanding. The conception of a future life has become a jest, a claim so precarious that no one honors it, nay, no one even any longer issues it; it tickles our sense of humor to consider that there was once a time when this conception transformed the whole of life.

It is clear at once what may be expected from this quarter by way of an answer to the problem of the *Fragments*. The problem itself is an expression of dialectical immaturity, since in the heavenly *sub specie aeterni* of pure thought the distinction between "here" and "beyond" is abrogated. But it so happens that the problem is not at all a logical problem—what could logical thinking have in common with the most profoundly pathetic of all problems, the problem of an eternal happiness? It is an existential problem, and existence is not identical with being *sub specie aeterni.* In this connection it will perhaps again appear how necessary it is to take special precautions before entering into discussion with a philosophy of this sort: first to separate the philosopher from the philosophy, and then as in cases of black magic, witchcraft, and possession by the devil, to use a powerful formula of incantation to get the bewitched philosopher transformed into a particular existing human being, and thus restored back to his true state.

That Christianity was the content of the hypothesis experimentally developed in the *Fragments,* the piece did not say. This silence was an attempt to gain a breathing-spell, a freedom from immediate entanglement with all sorts of historical, historico-dogmatic, introductory, and ecclesiastical questions concerning what Christianity really is. For no human being can ever have been in such a situation of distress as Christianity is of late. On the one side it is furnished with a speculative explanation which finds its essential content to be paganism; on the other side it is not yet known precisely what Christianity is. One need only read through a current book catalogue to see what kind of an age we live in. In daily life, when we hear shrimps cried on the streets we naturally think it must be midsummer; when greens are cried we assume it to be spring; and when oysters, that it must be winter. But when, as happened last winter, shrimps and greens and oysters are all cried on one and the same day, one is tempted to think that the world has become confused and cannot last until Easter. A still more confusing impression, however, is gained from a moment's inspection of a book catalogue and what is said there about the books listed, both by the authors themselves and by the publishers; for the latter have become very significant voices in the literary chorus. *Summa summarum*: it is a very stirring age in which we live, or at least a very confused one.

Hence in order to obtain a little peace for the weary Christian terminology, a rest of which it may stand greatly in need, unfathomable and calmly profound as it is in itself, but made breathless and almost unmeaning in current usage; and in order to avoid if possible being entangled in the crush, I chose to suppress the name of Christianity, and to refrain from using the expressions which repeatedly find themselves tossed about and perplexed in current speech. The entire Christian terminology has been appropriated by speculative thought to its own purposes, under the assumption that speculative thought and Christianity are identical. Even newspapers use the highest dogmatic expressions as genial ingredients in the journalistic *pot-pourri.* While the statesmen look forward with apprehension to a threatened general bankruptcy of the governments, we face perhaps a far more serious bankruptcy in the world of the spirit; for the concepts have gradually been emasculated, and the words have been made to mean anything and everything, so that the disputes are sometimes as ridiculous as the agreements. For it is always ludicrous to engage in controversy on the basis of loose words, and to come to agreement on the basis of loose words. But when even the most stable and fixed of meanings have become loose and vacillating, what portends? Just as a toothless old man is reduced to mumbling through the gums, so modern discourse about Christianity has lost the vigor that can come only from an energetically sustained terminology, and the whole is reduced to a toothless twaddle.

It seems quite clear to me that the confusion in which Christianity has become involved derives from the fact that it has been set back an entire stage in human life. The circumstance that we have all become Christians as children, has led to the assumption that we are, without further qualification, that which we have merely anticipated as a possibility. The baptism of children may for all that be both justifiable and praiseworthy, partly as an expression for the well-meaning interest of the Church, partly as a defense against fanaticism, and partly as expressing the beautiful care and forethought of devout parents; the responsibility rests with the individual himself in later life. But it is and always will be ridiculous to see people who are Christians solely by virtue of a baptismal certificate assuming on solemn occasions a set of postures *à la* Christians; for the most ludicrous thing that can ever happen to Christianity is to be identified with trivial use and wont. To be persecuted and abhorred and mocked and derided, or on the other hand to be blessed and praised: this is a fate entirely suited to the mightiest of all forces. But for Christianity to become a conventional costume, *bon ton,* and the like, is to suffer the fate of becoming its own absolute opposite. It is fitting for a king to be loved by his people and honored in his majesty; or if worst comes to worst, let him be hurled from the throne in a revolution, let him fall in battle, let him languish as a prisoner of state far removed from everything that could remind him of his royal dignity. But a king transformed into an obsequious servant extremely well content with his lot: this is a transformation more absolute than his being put to death.

The converse transformation may also be ridiculous, namely, that Christians sometimes have recourse, for example at funerals, to pagan conceptions of Elysium and the like. But it is no less ridiculous that upon the death of a man to whom Christianity has meant absolutely nothing, not even so much that he has cared to renounce it, a clergyman will introduce him into a state of eternal happiness in the sense in which this concept is understood in the Christian ideology. I must ask not to be reminded in this connection of the difference that must always remain between the visible and the invisible Church, and of the truth that no one may presume to judge the secrets of the heart. Far from it indeed, very far from it. But in times when people became Christians as adults, and were baptized in mature years, one might with some assurance speak as if Christianity had some significance for the baptized. By all means, let God alone judge the secrets of the heart. But when the rite of baptism is relegated to the second week after birth, and when it must be regarded as a convenience to remain nominally a Christian, when to renounce Christianity would bring only trouble and inconvenience in its train, when the judgment of the environment would be, as noted above, that it is flat and stupid and in bad taste to make so much fuss about it: then it is impossible to deny that membership in the visible Church constitutes a very doubtful proof that this member is really a Christian.

The visible Church has suffered so broad an expansion that all the original relationships have been reversed. Just as it once required energy and determination to become a Christian, so now, though the renunciation be not praiseworthy, it requires courage and energy to renounce the Christian religion, while it needs only thoughtlessness to remain a nominal Christian. The baptism of children may nevertheless be defensible; no new custom needs to be introduced. But since the circumstances are so radically changed, the clergy should themselves be able to perceive that if it was once their duty, when only a very few were Christians, to win men for Christianity, their present task must rather be to win men by deterring them—for their misfortune is that they are already Christians of a sort. When Christianity came into the world, men were not Christians, and the difficulty was to become a Christian. At the present time the difficulty of becoming a Christian involves actively transforming an initial being-a-Christian into a possibility, in order to become a Christian in reality. And the present difficulty is so much the greater, as this change must and should take place quietly, within the individual, and without any decisive external action to signalize it, to avoid running into an Anabaptist heresy or the like.

But everyone knows that the most difficult leap, even in the physical realm, is when a man leaps into the air from a standing position and comes down again on the same spot. The leap becomes easier in the degree to which some distance intervenes between the initial position and the place where the leap takes off. And so it is also with respect to a decisive movement in the realm of spirit. The most difficult decisive action is not that in which the individual is far removed from the decision (as when a non-Christian is about to decide to become one), but when it is as if the matter were already decided. Here the difficulty is two-fold: *first,* that the earlier decision is a mere appearance, the potentiality of a decision; *second,* the difficulty of the decision itself. When I am not a Christian and confront the decision of becoming one, Christianity helps me to an acute awareness of the decision, and the distance between us is also a help, just as the preliminary running start helps to make the leap easier. But when it is as if the matter were already decided, when I am a Christian in the sense of being baptized in childhood, there is nothing in the external situation to arouse in me an awareness of the decision. On the contrary, there is something that tends to prevent me from having my attention called to it (and this is the factor that increases the difficulty), namely, that the decision has apparently already been made. In brief, *it is easier to become a Christian when I am not a Christian than to become a Christian when I am one;* and this more difficult decision is reserved for one who has been baptized in childhood.

What is baptism without personal appropriation? It is an expression for the possibility that the baptized child may become a Christian, neither more nor less. A parallel is, that one must be born and must exist in order to become a human being (for a child is not yet a human being); so one must also be baptized in order to become a Christian. An adult who was not baptized as a child may become a Christian in baptism, because he may supplement the rite by the appropriation of the believer. Take away from the Christian determinations the factor of personal appropriation, and what becomes of Luther's merit? But open to any page of his writings, and note in every line the strong pulse-beat of personal appropriation. Note it in the entire trembling propulsive movement of his style, which is as if it were driven from behind by the terrible thunderstorm that killed Alexius and created Luther.[1] Did not the papacy have objectivity enough, objective determinations to the point of superfluity? What then did it lack? It lacked appropriation, inwardness. "But these hair-splitting Sophists say nothing about faith when discussing the sacraments, but merely prate industriously of the real power inherent in them (the objective), for they are always learning and never arrive at a knowledge of the truth."[2] But if objectivity is the truth, this is surely the way in which they ought to arrive at it.

Let it be ten times true that Christianity does not inhere in the differences; let it be the most blessed solace of human life that Christianity can in its sacred humanness be appropriated by all—but is this to be understood as meaning that everyone is a Christian merely by virtue of being baptized at the tender age of two weeks?* To be a Christian is as far as possible from being a convenience, since both the wise and the simple face the necessity of existing in it. And when this task is attempted it will certainly be something different from having a baptismal certificate tucked away somewhere, from being able to produce it when matriculating as a student or applying for a license to marry; it will surely be something quite different from walking around with a certificate of baptism in one's pocket. But being a Christian has become something so entirely a matter of course that the responsibility for it rests rather upon the parents than upon the individual himself: the parents have in fact the responsibility of attending to having their children baptized. Hence the curious and not so infrequent phenomenon, that a man who for his own part has been quite satisfied to assume that his parents have attended to his baptism, leaving the whole matter at that, when he becomes a father develops a more or less personal concern for the baptism of his own child. The personal concern relative to becoming a Christian has been shifted from the individual himself to his guardian. In his capacity as the guardian of his child the father is concerned that it should receive the rite of baptism; and perhaps he is also influenced by the thought of the many annoyances and difficulties that will confront the child, if it is not baptized, in view of the existing police regulations.

And the future judgment, with all its solemnity and earnestness, where the question is whether I was a Christian, not whether as guard-

---

* In the *Fragments* [pp. 78ff. Eng. ed.] I expressed the incongruity by saying that men have made an attempt to naturalize Christianity, so that in the end to be a Christian and to be a man are identical, and one is born a Christian just as one is born a man, or at least birth and rebirth are brought into close conjunction within the space of fourteen days.

ian I attended to having my children baptized, is metamorphosed into a street scene or a scene in a passport office, where the dead come running with their certificates . . . from the parish clerk. Let it be ever so true that baptism is a divinely authorized passport for eternity, but is it also valid when frivolity and worldliness attempt to use it? Baptism is surely not the slip of paper that the parish clerk issues and which he frequently fills with errors of writing; it is surely not the mere external event that took place at 11 o'clock on the morning of the 7th of November? That time, or existence in time, should be sufficient to decide an eternal happiness is in general so paradoxical that paganism cannot conceive its possibility. But that the whole matter should be decided in the course of five minutes, two weeks after birth, seems almost a little too much of the paradoxical. It only remains to have a marriage arranged for the infant in his cradle, and his vocation also determined at the same time, for everything in a man's life to be decided at the tender age of fourteen days—unless a later decision takes the trouble to undo the first. And this might seem worth while in connection with the projected marriage, but scarcely with respect to the relationship to Christianity. Once it was that when everything else failed, the one thing left to a man was to become a Christian; now we are all Christians, and in manifold ways tempted to forget to become Christians.

Under such circumstances in Christendom (the misunderstanding of speculative philosophy on the one hand, and the presumption that one is a Christian as a matter of course on the other) it becomes more and more difficult to find a point of departure, when it is desired to determine what Christianity is. Speculative philosophy deduces paganism logically from Christianity, and the fact that people become Christians merely through being baptized transforms Christendom into a baptized paganism. For this reason I had recourse to paganism, and to Greece as the representative of the intellectual, and to Socrates as its greatest hero. After thus having made sure of paganism I sought to find as decisive a difference as was possible. Whether the content of the experiment really was Christianity is another question; but so much at least was gained by it, that if modern Christian speculation has its essential category in common with paganism, it is evidently impossible for modern speculation to be Christianity.

§ 2. THE IMPORTANCE OF A PRELIMINARY AGREEMENT CONCERNING WHAT CHRIS-
TIANITY IS, BEFORE THERE CAN BE ANY QUESTION OF MEDIATING BETWEEN
CHRISTIANITY AND SPECULATIVE THOUGHT. THE ABSENCE OF SUCH AN AGREEMENT
FAVORS THE PROPOSAL OF MEDIATION, WHILE ALSO MAKING ANY MEDIATION IL-
LUSORY; THE PRESENCE OF SUCH AN AGREEMENT PRECLUDES MEDIATION

That an eternal happiness is decided in time through the relationship
to something historical was the content of my experiment, and what I
now call Christianity. I scarcely suppose that anyone will deny that it is
the Christian teaching in the New Testament that the eternal happiness
of the individual is decided in time, and is decided through the relationship to Christianity as something historical. And in order not to distract
attention by evoking the thought of an eternal unhappiness, I here remark that I propose to deal merely with the positive aspect, namely, that
the believer is in time assured of his eternal happiness through his relationship to something historical. To avoid distraction again, I do not
wish to bring forward any other Christian principles; they are all contained in this one, and may be consistently derived from it, just as this
determination also offers the sharpest contrast with paganism. Only let
me again repeat: I do not attempt to decide whether Christianity is right
or wrong. I have already said in the piece what I always stand ready to
acknowledge, that my bit of merit, if any, consists solely in presenting
the problem.

However, the mere mention of Christianity and the New Testament
readily starts an endless chain of inquiries. Thus nothing will be easier
than for a speculative philosopher to find one or another Scripture passage to which he can appeal. For not even the sense in which speculative
philosophy proposes to use the New Testament has received a preliminary clarification. It is sometimes asserted without qualification that the
language of the New Testament lies wholly in the sphere of representa-
tive thought, from which it would seem to follow that one cannot argue
from it; and sometimes a great outcry is raised over having the authority
of the Bible in one's favor, whenever speculative philosophy finds a
Scripture passage to which it can appeal.

A preliminary agreement as to which is which, a determination of
what Christianity is before proceeding to explain it, lest instead of explaining Christianity we arbitrarily hit upon something and explain
this as Christianity—such a preliminary agreement is of extreme and
decisive importance. The meeting of both parties before the arbitrator
(to prevent mediation from playing both the rôle of party to the arbitra-

tion and arbiter) does not seem to interest speculative philosophy, which rather seems intent upon making a profit out of Christianity. Just as in lesser things there have been people who have not much troubled themselves to understand Hegel, but have been all the more eager for the profit of *going still further* than Hegel,[1] so it is tempting enough in connection with something so great and significant as Christianity to have gone further. One needs to have Christianity incorporated as a partial moment in one's thought, not precisely for the sake of Christianity, but for the sake of the imposing appearance made by the movement in advance.

On the other hand it is important that the reflection which is to determine what Christianity is, should not become a learned and scholarly affair; for as soon as this happens we are committed to an approximation-process which can never be completed, as was shown in Part I of this book. Any mediation between Christianity and speculative philosophy will then for still another reason become impossible, since the preliminary reflection can never come to an end.

The question of what Christianity is must therefore be raised, but not as a problem of learning or scholarship. Nor must it be formulated in a partisan manner, under the presupposition that Christianity is a philosophical doctrine, for in that case speculative thought will be more than one of the parties; it will then become both judge and litigant. The question must therefore be asked with an eye solely to the existential, and in this manner it must be possible not only to answer it, but to answer it briefly. It may seem natural enough for a learned theologian to devote his entire lifetime to a scholarly investigation of the teaching of the Scriptures and the Church. But it would surely be a ridiculous contradiction for an existing individual, in asking what Christianity is with a view to existence, to employ his entire life in considering the question—for when would he then find time to exist in it?

The question of what Christianity is must therefore not be confused with the objective problem of the truth of Christianity, the problem dealt with in Part I. It is possible thus to consider objectively what Christianity is, in that the inquirer sets this question objectively before him, leaving aside for the present the question of its truth (the truth is subjectivity). Such an inquirer asks to be excused both from the zealous haste of the reverend clergy to prove its truth, and from the speculative urge to go further; he desires rest, desires neither recommendations nor haste, but to learn what Christianity is.

Or is it perhaps impossible to find out what Christianity is without oneself being a Christian? All analogies seem to speak in favor of the possibility, and Christianity must itself consider those to be false Christians who merely know what Christianity is. Here again confusion has arisen through the fact that one gets the appearance of being a Christian by being straightway baptized as a child. But when Christianity came into the world, or when it is introduced into a pagan country, it did not and does not overleap the contemporary generation of adults in order to lay hold of the children. Then the situation was normal: it was difficult to become a Christian, and no one was concerned to understand Christianity. Now we shall soon have the complete parody of the normal, when it is as nothing to become a Christian, but a very difficult and laborious task to understand Christianity.* Hence it is that faith has been dethroned in favor of understanding, instead of being reckoned as the maximum relationship, as it really is when the difficulty is to become a Christian. Let us imagine a pagan philosopher to whom Christianity was preached, surely not as one more philosophical doctrine for him to understand, but as constituting a challenge to become a Christian: has he then not been told what Christianity is so that he could choose?

The possibility of knowing what Christianity is without being a Christian must therefore be affirmed. It is a different question whether a man can know what it is to be a Christian without being one, which must be denied. But a Christian must also know what Christianity is, and must be able to say this in so far as he has himself become a Christian. I do not think it possible to find a stronger expression for the questionable character of the custom of becoming a Christian at the age of two weeks than the fact that as a result we can find Christians who have not yet become Christians. The transition to Christianity is effected so early in life that it constitutes merely a possibility of the real transition. For anyone who really becomes a Christian there must have been

* In relation to a doctrine, understanding is the maximum of what may be attained; to become an adherent is merely an artful method of pretending to understand, practised by people who do not understand anything. In relation to an existential communication, existing in it is the maximum of attainment, and understanding it is merely an evasion of the task. It is a suspicious thing to become a Hegelian, understanding Hegel is the maximum; to become a Christian is the maximum, understanding Christianity is suspect. This corresponds entirely with what was developed in the preceding chapter about possibility and reality. Possibility is the maximum relationship to a doctrine, reality is the maximum relationship to an existential communication. To seek to understand an existential communication is to essay a transformation of one's own relationship to it into one of possibility merely.

a time when he was not a Christian; there must again have been a time when he came to know what Christianity is; and provided he has not wholly lost the memory of how he existed before he became a Christian, he must again be able for his part to say, when he compares his earlier life with his Christian life, what Christianity is.

As soon as the situation of transition is made contemporary with the coming of Christianity into the world, or with its introduction into a pagan country, everything becomes quite clear. Becoming a Christian is then the most fearful decision of a man's life, a struggle through to attain faith against despair and offense, the twin Cerberuses that guard the entrance to a Christian life. This most terrible of all tests in human life, where eternity is the examiner, cannot possibly have been solved by a child of fourteen days, even if it has ever so many certificates from the parish clerk as to its having been baptized. Hence there must also come a later moment for the baptized individual, a moment essentially corresponding to the situation of transition contemporary with the coming of Christianity into the world. There will come a moment for him, when although a Christian he will ask what Christianity is—in order to become a Christian. In baptism Christianity gives him a name, and he is *de nomine* a Christian; but in the moment of decision he becomes a Christian and gives his name to Christianity (*nomen dare aliqui*).[2]

Let us take a pagan philosopher. He surely did not become a Christian when he was two weeks old, while unaware of what he was doing—in truth the strangest explanation of the most decisive of steps, that it takes place when a man is unaware of what he is doing! On the contrary, he knew well what he did; he knew that he was resolved to maintain a relationship to Christianity until the wonder happened (if we wish to express it in this manner) that he became a Christian, or until he chose to become a Christian. Hence he must have known what Christianity was at the time when he accepted it, while he was not yet a Christian.

But while we are all engaged in learnedly determining and speculatively explaining Christianity, one never sees the problem of Christianity so treated as to make it clear that the question is put with a view to existence, in the interest of the existential. And why does no one pose the question in this manner? Why naturally because we are all Christians as a matter of course. And with the help of this splendid invention of being Christians as a matter of course, we have in Christendom reached the point of not knowing precisely what Christianity is. The explanation of what Christianity is, confused as it has been with the learned and philosophical explanation of Christianity, has been turned into so complex and voluminous an affair that the task is not yet quite finished; we all await a new work on the subject. Under the supposition that the situation of transition is contemporary with the coming of Christianity into the world, anyone who really became a Christian would of course have to know what Christianity is. And whoever really becomes a Christian will feel the need of this knowledge, an urge which I do not believe that even the most infatuated mother will discover in her child at the tender age of fourteen days. But, to be sure, we are all Christians. The learned Christians dispute among themselves about what Christianity really is, but it never occurs to them to think of anything else but that they are Christians, as if it were possible to know oneself certainly to be something without knowing definitely what that something is. The sermon addresses itself to the "Christian congregation," and yet it almost always moves in a direction *toward* Christianity. It seeks to persuade men to lay hold of faith, and hence to become Christians; it invites them to accept Christianity—and those addressed constitute a Christian congregation and ought therefore surely to be Christians. Imagine a man who was yesterday so deeply moved by the clergyman's recommendation of Christianity that he thought to himself: "It would not take very much more to make me decide to become a Christian"; if he dies tomorrow he will be buried the day after tomorrow as a Christian—for he was a Christian as a matter of course.

What therefore seems so clear in itself, namely, that a Christian ought to know what Christianity is, and know it with the concentration and decisiveness which the fact of having taken the most decisive of all steps both presupposes and gives, can no longer be understood so entirely without qualification. We are all Christians, and a speculative philosopher is also baptized at the age of two weeks. Now when a speculative philosopher says: "I am a Christian (meaning that he was baptized when two weeks old), a Christian ought to know what Christianity is; I say that Christianity is the mediation of Christianity, and I submit as warranty for the correctness of this assertion the fact that I am myself a Christian": what shall we say to this? If a man says: "I am a Christian, *ergo,* I surely ought to know what Christianity is," and stops there, one can do nothing but let it stand. It would be silly to contradict him, since he has not said anything. But if he goes on to develop what he understands by Christianity it must also be possible to know without being a Christian whether it is Christianity or not, assuming that it is possible to know what Christianity is without being a Christian. If what he explains as Christianity happens to be essentially identical with paganism, one is clearly justified in denying that it is Christianity.

The question of what Christianity is, must first and foremost be determined before there can be any question of mediation. But speculative philosophy makes no move in this direction. It does not first set forth what philosophy is, and then what Christianity is, to see whether the entities thus made to confront each other admit of a mediation; it does not make certain of the identity of the respective parties before proceeding to reconcile them. If speculative philosophy is asked what Christianity is, it replies at once: Christianity is the speculative interpretation of Christianity. It does not trouble to inquire whether there is anything in the distinction between a something and an interpretation of this something, which would here seem to be of importance for speculative philosophy itself; for if Christianity is identical with its speculative interpretation there can be no mediation, since in that case there is no opposition, and a mediation between identities is surely meaningless. But then perhaps we had better ask speculative philosophy what speculative philosophy is. But, behold, from the reply offered we learn that speculative philosophy is the atonement, is mediation, is in short, Christianity. But if Christianity and speculative philosophy are identical, what does it mean to mediate them? Moreover it follows from this reply that Christianity is essentially identical with paganism, for speculative philosophy will surely not deny that paganism possessed speculation. I am quite willing to admit that speculative philosophy speaks in a sense consistently. But this consistent speech also shows that no agreement has preceded the reconciling mediation, probably because no one has been able to find a place where the opposing parties might meet.

But even when speculative thought assumes a distinction between Christianity and speculation, if only for the satisfaction of being able to mediate them, as long as it does not mark the distinction definitely and decisively it becomes necessary to raise the question: Is not *mediation* a speculative category? When the opposites are mediated they (Christianity and speculation) are not equal before the arbiter. Christianity becomes a phase of speculative thought, and the latter obtains a preponderance because it already had the preponderance, and because the moment of equilibrium in which the opposed entities were to be weighed in relation to each other was never realized. When two opposites are mediated, and reconciled in a higher unity, they may perhaps be equal before the mediating process, because neither of the entities is an opposite of speculative thought itself. But when one of the opposites is speculative thought, and the other is an opposite to speculative thought, and a mediation is proposed, and mediation happens to be a speculative category, it is illusory to speak of an opposite to speculative thought at all, since the reconciling factor is itself speculative thought or the mediation-function which is its category. It is indeed permissible within speculative thought to assign to everything which claims the status of speculation its relative position, and thus to mediate all those opposites which have the common character of being essays in speculation. Thus when philosophy mediates between the doctrine of the Eleatics and that of Heraclitus, this may be quite in order, the Eleatic doctrine not being an opposite of speculative thought but itself speculative, and so with the doctrine of Heraclitus. But it is very different when the opposite in question is an opposite to speculative philosophy in general. If there is to be any mediation in this case (and let us not forget that mediation is a speculative category), it will mean that speculative thought judges between itself and its own opposite, and therefore plays the double rôle of litigant and judge. Or it means that speculative thought assumes that there can be no opposite to speculative philosophy, and that all opposition is merely relative, as being an opposition within speculative thought. But it was just this question which should have been dealt with in the preliminary agreement. Perhaps this is the reason why speculative philosophy is so shy of indicating what Christianity is, perhaps this is why it is in such a hurry to apply mediation and to recommend mediation: because it fears that the worst would happen if it became quite clear what Christianity is. The behavior of speculative thought in mediating Christianity is not unlike the behavior of a rebellious ministry which has seized the reins of power, and now governs in the king's name while keeping the king himself at a distance.

But the difficulties connected with the assumption that Christianity is a phase of speculative thought have doubtless caused philosophy to make something of a concession. It has assumed the qualification *Christian,* and thus it has proposed to make acknowledgement of Christianity, much as when two noble families are united by marriage and a composite name is adopted, or as when two business firms are consolidated under a joint name. Now if being a Christian is nothing to speak of, as is so readily assumed, Christianity must be regarded as happy to have made so good a match, bringing it to a level of dignity and honor almost equal to philosophy itself. But if, on the contrary, becoming a Christian is the most difficult of all human tasks, the respected philosopher seems rather to be the one to profit, in so far as the joint name yields him the honor of being a Christian. But becoming a Christian really is the most difficult of all human tasks, since although it is the same for all men it is nevertheless proportioned to the capacity of each individual. This does not hold of differential tasks. In relation to the task of understanding something, for example, the man with exceptional brains has a direct advantage over one of limited capacity; but this does not hold true of faith. When faith requires a man to give up his reason, it becomes equally difficult for the cleverest and the most stupid person to believe, or it becomes in a sense more difficult for the clever. Here again it appears how improper it is to transform Christianity into a doctrine to be understood, since this would make the power to become a Christian dependent on differential talent. What then is lacking? A preliminary agreement in which the status of each party is determined, before the new firm with the joint name is established.

But further. This Christian philosophy speculates within the framework of Christian principles. Nevertheless, it is not quite the same thing with the so-called *usus instrumentalis* of the reason, nor is it the same with that philosophy which consistently assumed, because it was speculation within Christianity, that some things were true in philosophy which were not true in theology. So understood, it is quite in order to speculate within a presupposition, as would seem to be the program of the said Christian philosophy in adopting the qualifying predicate Christian. But if this philosophy which thus begins within a presupposition finally reaches the point where it subjects its own presupposition to speculative treatment, and so speculates the presupposition away, what then? Why then the presupposition was a mere fiction, a piece of shadow-boxing. There is a story about the wise men of Gotham, that they once saw a tree leaning out over the water and thinking that the tree was thirsty were moved by sympathy to come to its assistance. To that end one of them took hold of the tree, another clung to the first man's legs, and so on until they formed a chain, all animated by the common idea of helping the tree—under the presupposition that the first man held fast. But what happens? The first man suddenly lets go in order to spit on his hands so that he can take a better hold—and what then? Why then the Gothamites fell into the water, because the presupposition was given up. To speculate within a presupposition in such manner as finally to speculate the presupposition as well, is precisely the same trick as thinking something so evident within a hypothetical "if" that it has retroactive power to transform the hypothesis, within which it has its validity, into a reality.

But what other presupposition can, generally speaking, come into question for a so-called Christian philosophy, but that Christianity is the precise opposite of speculation, that it is the miraculous, the absurd, a challenge to the individual to exist in it, and not to waste his time by trying to understand it speculatively. If we are to have speculation within this presupposition, it will be the function of this speculation more and more profoundly to grasp the impossibility of understanding Christianity, which task was above described as that which the simple wise man accepts for himself.

But perhaps here a speculative philosopher will be moved to say: "If Christianity is thus the very opposite of speculation, its absolute opposite, I cannot possibly get an opportunity to speculate upon it; for all speculation is rooted in mediation, and in the principle that only relative opposites exist." This may be so, I would reply, but why do you speak in this manner? Is it perhaps in order to intimidate me, so as to make me afraid of speculative philosophy, and of the tremendous respect it enjoys in the public mind; or is it to win me over, so that I may regard speculation as the highest good? Here I do not ask whether Christianity is right, but only what Christianity is. Speculative thought leaves out this preliminary inquiry, and that is why it succeeds in mediating. Before it mediates it has already mediated; that is to say, it has transformed Christianity into a philosophical doctrine. But as soon as a preliminary agreement posits Christianity as the opposite of speculation, mediation becomes *ipso facto* impossible, since mediation is a function of speculative thought. If Christianity is the opposite of speculation it is also the opposite of mediation, the latter being a category of speculative thought; what then can it mean to mediate them? But what is the opposite of mediation? It is the absolute paradox.

Hence let one who does not pretend to be a Christian raise the question of what Christianity is. In this way the whole matter becomes more natural, and we escape the ludicrous and yet sad confusion that Peter and Paul, who are themselves Christians *as a matter of course,* bring about a new confusion by explaining Christianity from the speculative point of view, which is almost to insult it. If Christianity were in fact a philosophical doctrine, one might hold it in honor by saying of it that it is difficult to understand (speculatively). But if Christianity itself assumes that the difficulty is to become and to be a Christian, it ought not even to be hard to understand, that is, to understand enough to be able to begin upon the difficulty: to become a Christian and to be one.

Christianity is not a doctrine* but an existential communication expressing an existential contradiction. If Christianity were a doctrine it would *eo ipso* not be an opposite to speculative thought, but rather a phase within it. Christianity has to do with existence, with the act of existing; but existence and existing constitute precisely the opposite of speculation. The Eleatic doctrine, for example, is not relevant to existing but to speculation, and it is therefore proper to assign to it a place within speculative thought. Precisely because Christianity is not a doctrine it exhibits the principle, as was noted above, that there is a tremendous difference between knowing what Christianity is and being a Christian. In connection with a doctrine such a distinction is unthinkable, because a doctrine is not relevant to existing. It is not my fault that the age in which we live has reversed the relationship, and transformed Christianity into a philosophical doctrine that asks to be understood, and turned *being* a Christian into a triviality. To assume that this denial that Christianity is a doctrine should imply that Christianity is contentless, is

* Now if only I might escape the fate of having a facile thinker explain to a reading public how stupid my entire book is, as is more than sufficiently evident from my willingness to be responsible for such an assertion as that Christianity is not a doctrine. Let us try to understand one another. Surely it is one thing for something to be a philosophical doctrine which desires to be intellectually grasped and speculatively understood, and quite another thing to be a doctrine that proposes to be realized in existence. If the question of understanding is to be raised in connection with a doctrine of the latter sort, this must consist in understanding that the task is to exist in it, in understanding the difficulty of existing in it, and what a tremendous existential task such a doctrine posits for the learner. At a time when it has come to be generally assumed in connection with such a doctrine (an existential communication) that it is very easy to be what the doctrine requires, but very hard to understand this doctrine speculatively, one may be in harmony with the doctrine (the existential communication) when he seeks to show how difficult it is existentially to submit to the doctrine. In the case of such a doctrine, it is contrariwise a misunderstanding to speculate upon it. Christianity is a doctrine of this kind. To speculate upon it is a misunderstanding, and the farther one goes in this direction the greater is the misunderstanding. When one finally reaches the stage of not only speculating about it, but of understanding it speculatively, one has reached the highest pitch of misunderstanding. This stage is reached in the mediation of Christianity and speculation, and hence it is quite correct to say that modern speculation is the most extreme possible misunderstanding of Christianity. This being the case, and when it is furthermore admitted that the nineteenth century is so dreadfully speculative, it is to be apprehended that the word "doctrine" will at once be interpreted to mean a philosophical doctrine which demands to be understood, and ought to be understood. To avoid this danger I have chosen to call Christianity an existential communication, in order definitely to indicate its heterogeneity with speculation.

merely a *chicane*. When the believer exists in his faith his existence acquires tremendous content, but not in the sense of paragraph-material.

The existential contradiction posed by Christianity is the one I have sought to formulate in the problem of an eternal happiness decided in time by a relationship to something historical. If I were to say that Christianity is a doctrine of the Incarnation, of the Atonement, and so forth, misunderstanding would at once be invited. Speculative philosophy would immediately pounce upon this doctrine, and proceed to expound the more imperfect conceptions of paganism and Judaism and so forth. Christianity would become a phase of speculative thought, perhaps a highest phase, but essentially it would become something identical with speculation.

§ 3. THE PROBLEM OF THE "FRAGMENTS" VIEWED AS AN INTRODUCTION-PROBLEM, NOT TO CHRISTIANITY, BUT TO BECOMING A CHRISTIAN

Neither here nor in the *Fragments* have I assumed to explain the problem, but only to present it. Hence my procedure consists in repeatedly approaching it, in offering an introduction to it, but by a method that gives the introduction a special character. For there is no immediate transition from the introduction to the becoming a Christian, the transition rather constituting a qualitative leap. Such an introduction is therefore in a sense repellent, precisely because the usual introduction, in view of the decisiveness of the qualitative leap, would here be a contradiction. An introduction of the present type does not make it easier to enter upon that to which it introduces, but rather makes it difficult. In view of the fact that being a Christian is thought to be the highest good, it may be beautiful and well meaning to try to help people become Christians by making it easy for them. Nevertheless, I am content to bear the responsibility for making it difficult within the limits of my capacity, as difficult as possible, though without making it more difficult than it is; such a responsibility may be cheerfully undertaken in a mere experiment. My idea is that if Christianity is the highest good, it is better for me to know definitely that I do not possess it, so that I may put forth every effort to acquire it; rather than that I should imagine that I have it, deluding myself, so that it does not even occur to me to seek it. From this point of view I do not deny that I regard the baptism of children as not only justifiable as orthodox practice, and praiseworthy as an expression for the piety of the parents, who cannot endure to be separated from their children with respect to what is for them a matter of eternal happiness,

but defensible in still another sense not usually remarked, namely, because it makes it still more difficult to become a Christian. This I have
already shown in another place; here I shall merely add a word of
further comment.

The fact that the external expression for the decision to become a
Christian is anticipated, makes the decision itself when realized a purely
inner one, so that its degree of inwardness is greater than when the decision is also an external act. The less outwardness, the more inwardness.
There is something strangely profound and wonderful in the fact that
the most passionate decision of human life can transpire in a man without anything external bearing witness to its presence: the individual
was a Christian and yet he became one. Thus when one who in childhood was baptized as a Christian really becomes a Christian, and the
same inwardness marks his transition as that when a non-Christian
passes to Christianity, the degree of inwardness becomes the greatest
possible, precisely because there is no outwardness to distract the attention. But it must also be remembered that the absence of outwardness
may be a temptation, may readily become for many a temptation to
leave the whole matter undecided, which can best be perceived from the
fact that many will undoubtedly feel it a strange thing to say that the
baptism of children has the significance of making it harder for them
to become Christians. Such is nevertheless the case, and all analogies
will tend to confirm the principle that the less outwardness, the more
inwardness—provided the inwardness is really there. But it is also true
that as the outwardness diminishes, the danger that the inwardness will
fail altogether becomes greater. The external is the watchman that
arouses the sleeper, the solicitous mother that reminds one of the task,
the bugle call that brings the soldier to his feet, the grand march that
helps to elicit the great endeavor. But the absence of externality may
mean that it is the inwardness itself that summons the individual inwardly; alas, and it may also mean that the individual has ceased to have
an inwardness.

But it is not only in this manner that what I call an introduction to
the becoming a Christian differs from what is ordinarily called an introduction. It is quite unlike any introduction which proceeds upon the
assumption that Christianity is a doctrine. An introduction of this kind
does not lead to becoming a Christian, but leads at most to the perception, historically motivated, that Christianity has certain advantages over
paganism, Judaism, and so forth. The introduction that I propose to

offer will be repellent, making it difficult to become a Christian. It will not conceive of Christianity as a doctrine, but as an existential contradiction and an existential communication. It is not historical but psychological, calling attention to how much must have been lived before the problem can have any significance for the individual, and showing how difficult it is to become aware of the difficulty of the decision involved. As I have already said often enough, but nevertheless cannot too often repeat, both for my own sake, because it concerns me in much inwardness, and for the sake of others, lest I exercise a disturbing influence upon them: It is not for the simple-minded that this introduction undertakes to make it difficult to become a Christian. That such an individual will also need to exert himself to the utmost in order to become a Christian is indeed my opinion, nor do I believe that anyone renders him a service by making it altogether too easy. But every essential existential task puts all human beings on a level with respect to it, the difficulty being precisely proportioned to the capacity of the individual. Self-control is thus equally difficult for the wise and for the simple, and perhaps more difficult for the wise, because the wise man's reflection will serve him with many evasions. To understand that a human being can do nothing of himself, this beautiful and profound expression for the God-relationship, is as difficult for a gifted king as for the poorest wretch, and perhaps more difficult for the king, because his apparent plenitude of power tempts him. So also in connection with becoming a Christian and existing as one. In an age when the progress of culture and the like has made it seem so easy to be a Christian, it is quite in order to seek to make it difficult, provided one does not make it more difficult than it is. But the greater a man's equipment of knowledge and culture, the more difficult it is for him to become a Christian.

If the dialogue *Hippias*[1] is regarded in the light of an introduction to the beautiful, it will present a sort of analogy to the kind of introduction I here have it in mind to present. After having propounded a number of explanations of the beautiful, all of which are rejected upon critical inquiry, the dialogue comes to an end by Socrates saying that he has at least profited so much from the conversation that he has learned how difficult the explanation must be. Whether Socrates is justified in such a procedure, in view of the fact that the beautiful is an idea and thus not relevant to existence, I shall not try to decide. But when in Christendom it has come to pass in so many ways, or it is sought to bring to pass that we forget what Christianity is, it seems fair to suppose that a suitable introduction (to say nothing of its being the only one relevant to becoming a Christian), instead of resembling the usual introductions, and thereby also resembling the hotel runners who visit the railroad stations to recommend the respective accommodations to incoming travellers, will end up by having made it more difficult to become a Christian, at the same time that it seeks to make clear what Christianity is. The distinction between knowing what Christianity is as the easier, and being a Christian as the harder, is not applicable to the beautiful, or to the theory of the beautiful. Had the *Hippias* succeeded in clearing up the notion of the beautiful, there would have been nothing left to cause difficulty. The dialogue would then have nothing corresponding to the twofold nature of our enterprise, which seeks to explain what Christianity is, but makes it difficult to become a Christian.

But if the real difficulty is to become a Christian, this being the absolute decision, the only possible introduction must be a repellent one, thus precisely calling attention to the absolute decision. Even the longest of introductions cannot bring the individual a single step nearer to an absolute decision. For if it could, the decision would not be absolute, would not be a qualitative leap, and the individual would be deceived instead of helped. But the fact that the introduction does not even in its maximum bring anyone a single step nearer, is again the expression for its inevitably repellent character. Philosophy offers an immediate introduction to Christianity, and so do the historical and rhetorical introductions. These introductions succeed, because they introduce to a doctrine, but not to becoming a Christian.

SECTION II. THE PROBLEM ITSELF

THE ETERNAL HAPPINESS OF THE INDIVIDUAL IS DECIDED IN TIME THROUGH THE RELATIONSHIP TO SOMETHING HISTORICAL, WHICH IS FURTHERMORE OF SUCH A CHARACTER AS TO INCLUDE IN ITS COMPOSITION THAT WHICH BY VIRTUE OF ITS ESSENCE CANNOT BECOME HISTORICAL, AND MUST THEREFORE BECOME SUCH BY VIRTUE OF AN ABSURDITY

The problem is pathetic-dialectic. The pathetic factor is represented in the first part above, for human passion culminates in the pathetic relationship to an eternal happiness. The dialectical factor comes to expression in the second part, and the difficulty of the problem consists precisely in its being thus composite. Love is a passion whose pathos is immediate; the pathos of a relationship to an eternal happiness in the sphere of reflection is also immediate. But the dialectical factor of our problem arises because the eternal happiness, to which the individual is assumed to have a pathetically correct relationship, is itself made subject to a dialectic by the addition of further determinations, which again react so as to excite passion to its highest pitch. When a man existentially expresses and has expressed for a longer time that he gives up and has given up everything for the sake of the relationship to the absolute *telos,* the circumstance that there are conditions has an absolute influence to develop in his passion the greatest possible tension. Even in the case of relative pathos, the introduction of a dialectical factor is as oil upon the flames, intensively inflaming the passion and manifoldly developing the compass of its inwardness. But since we have in our time forgotten what it means to exist *sensu eminenti,* and since pathos is usually referred to the sphere of imagination and feeling, the dialectical being permitted to abrogate and supplant it, instead of seeking the union of both in the simultaneity of existence, it has come about in our philosophical nineteenth century that pathos has been discredited, and that dialectics has lost its passion; just as it has become so easy and light-hearted a thing to think contradictions—for it is passion that gives tension to the contradiction, and when passion is taken away the contradiction becomes a mere pleasantry, a *bon mot.* An existential problem, on the other hand, is pathetic and dialectic at one and the same time. The problem here presented demands an existential inwardness adequate to an apprehension of its pathos, passion of thought sufficient to grasp the dialectical difficulty, and concentrated passion, because the task is to exist in it.

In an attempt to clarify the problem I shall first treat the pathetic factor, and thereupon the dialectical. But I beg the reader always to bear in mind that the difficulty of the problem lies ultimately in putting the two together. The existing individual who pathetically and existentially expresses the pathetic relationship to an eternal happiness in absolute passion, must now in addition bring himself to confront the dialectical decision. As great as his pathetic tension is in relation to his eternal happiness, so great also will be his Socratic fear of the danger of error. His exertion will therefore be the greatest possible, so much the more as deception is rendered easy by the absence of anything external to look at. The individual who loves has to do with another human being, whose *yes* and *no* he can hear; in connection with every enterprise of enthusiasm there is at least something external to lay hold of. But in his relation to an eternal happiness the individual has to do solely with himself in inwardness. The word he has received *gratis* with his mother tongue; a little of this or of that he can soon learn to recite by rote. In his outward life the idea of an eternal happiness will not *profit* him at all, since the idea is not actually present to him until he has learned to despise the external and to forget the earthly mind's notion of what is profitable. Externally it cannot *harm* him to lack this conception; without it he may nevertheless very well attain to the dignity of husband, father, and champion rifle-shot, and if it is something such that he desires, the conception of an eternal happiness will only stand in his way. The essential existential pathos in relation to an eternal happiness is acquired at so great a cost that it must from the finite point of view be regarded as simple madness to purchase it, which view comes to expression often enough in life, and in a variety of ways. An eternal happiness is a security for which there is no longer any market value in the speculative nineteenth century; at the very most it may be used by the gentlemen of the clerical profession to swindle rural innocents. So easy is the deception that the finite understanding must feel outright proud of having refused to risk anything in this direction. And this is the reason why it is so foolish, unless one's life has a dialectical structure *à la* an Apostle, to seek to set the minds of men at rest in the matter of their eternal happiness. The very maximum of what one human being can do for another in relation to that wherein each man has to do solely with himself, is to inspire him with concern and unrest.

A. Existential Pathos

§ 1. THE "INITIAL" EXPRESSION FOR EXISTENTIAL PATHOS: THE ABSOLUTE DIREC-
TION (RESPECT) TOWARD THE ABSOLUTE *telos*, EXPRESSED IN ACTION THROUGH
THE TRANSFORMATION OF THE INDIVIDUAL'S EXISTENCE—AESTHETIC PATHOS—THE
DECEPTIVENESS OF THE PRINCIPLE OF MEDIATION—THE MEDIEVAL MONASTIC MOVE-
MENT—THE SIMULTANEOUS MAINTENANCE OF AN ABSOLUTE RELATIONSHIP TO THE
ABSOLUTE "TELOS" AND A RELATIVE RELATIONSHIP TO RELATIVE ENDS

In relation to an eternal happiness as the absolute good, pathos is not
a matter of words, but of permitting this conception to transform the entire existence of the individual. Aesthetic pathos expresses itself in
words, and may in its truth indicate that the individual leaves his real
self in order to lose himself in the Idea; while existential pathos is present whenever the Idea is brought into relation with the existence of the
individual so as to transform it. If in relating itself to the individual's
existence the absolute *telos* fails to transform it absolutely, the relationship is not one of existential pathos, but of aesthetic pathos. The individual may for instance have a correct conception, by means of which
he is outside himself in the ideality of the possible, not with himself in
existence, having the correct conception in the ideality of the actual,
himself in process of being transformed into the ideality of this conception.

For an existing individual the concept of an eternal happiness is essentially related to his mode of existence, and hence to the ideality of
the actual; his pathos must be correspondingly qualified. If we conceive
love aesthetically, we must acknowledge the principle that the poet's
ideal of love may be higher than anything that reality presents. The poet
may possess an ideality in this connection such that what the actual life
yields in comparison is but a feeble reflection. Reality is for the poet
merely an occasion, a point of departure, from which he goes in search
of the ideality of the possible. The pathos of the poet is therefore essentially imaginative pathos. An attempt ethically to establish a poetic
relationship to reality is therefore a misunderstanding, a backward step.
Here as everywhere the different spheres must be kept clearly distinct,
and the qualitative dialectic, with its decisive mutation that changes
everything so that what was highest in one sphere is rendered in another
sphere absolutely inadmissible, must be respected. As for the religious, it
is an essential requirement that it should have passed through the ethical.
A religious poet is therefore in a peculiar position. Such a poet will seek
to establish a relation to the religious through the imagination; but for

this very reason he succeeds only in establishing an aesthetic relationship to something aesthetic. To hymn a hero of faith is quite as definitely an aesthetic task as it is to eulogize a war hero. If the religious is in truth the religious, if it has submitted itself to the discipline of the ethical and preserves it within itself, it cannot forget that religious pathos does not consist in singing and hymning and composing verses, but in existing; so that the poetic productivity, if it does not cease entirely, or if it flows as richly as before, comes to be regarded by the individual himself as something accidental, which goes to prove that he understands himself religiously. Aesthetically it is the poetic productivity which is essential, and the poet's mode of existence is accidental.

A poetic temperament, which through the influence of circumstances,. upbringing, and the like, has received a direction away from the theater to the Church, may therefore serve to bring about much confusion. Dazzled by the aesthetic in him, people believe that he is a religious personality, alas, even an *outstanding* personality, although perhaps he is not religious at all. Precisely this qualification of being *outstanding* is an aesthetic reminiscence, since from the religious point of view there is nothing validly outstanding, except an Apostle's paradoxical-dialectical authority. To be outstanding in the religious sphere constitutes precisely a step backward, by virtue of the qualitative dialectic which separates the different spheres from one another. The pathos of such an individual is poetic pathos, the pathos of the possible, with reality serving him as an occasion. Even if his pathos encompasses the entire process of human history, it is none the less a pathos belonging in the sphere of the possible, and ethically speaking immature; for ethical maturity consists in apprehending one's own ethical reality as infinitely more important than any understanding of the world-process.*

The pathos which adequately corresponds to an eternal happiness consists in the transformation by which everything in the existence of the individual is altered, in and through his mode of existence, so as to

---

* The world has often seen examples of the presumptuous religious individual who is perfectly secure in his own God-relationship, flippantly assured of his own salvation, but self-importantly engaged in doubting the salvation of others and in offering to help them. However, I believe it would be a fitting expression for a genuinely religious attitude if the individual were to say: "I do not doubt the salvation of any human being, the only one I have fears about is myself. Even when I see a man sink very low, I should never presume to doubt his salvation; but if it were myself, I should doubtless have to suffer this terrible thought." A genuine religious personality is always mild in his judgment of others, and only in his relation to himself is he cold and strict as a master inquisitor. His attitude toward others is like that of a benevolent patriarch to the younger generation; in relation to himself he is old and incorruptible.

bring it into conformity with this highest good.* With reference to possibility, the word is the highest pathos; with reference to reality, the deed is the highest pathos. That a poet, for instance, refuses to permit his own poetic production to influence his mode of existence is aesthetically quite in order, or altogether a matter of indifference; for aesthetically it is the poetic production and the possibility it expresses which embodies the highest value. But ethically on the other hand, this question of the individual's mode of existence is of infinite importance; ethically the poem is infinitely indifferent, but the poet's mode of existence ought to mean infinitely more to him than anything else. Aesthetically it would be the highest pathos for the poet to annihilate himself, for him to demoralize himself if necessary, in order to produce masterpieces. Aesthetically it would be in order for a man to sell his soul to the devil, to use a strong expression which recalls what is perhaps still done more often than is ordinarily supposed—but also to produce miracles of art. Ethically it would perhaps be the highest pathos to renounce the glittering artistic career without saying a single word.

When a so-called religious personality pleases to picture an eternal happiness in all the magic colors of the imagination, it means that he is a runaway poet, a deserter from the sphere of the aesthetic, who claims the privilege of native citizenship in the realm of the religious without even being able to speak its mother tongue. The pathos of the ethical consists in action. Hence when a man says that he has suffered hunger and cold and imprisonment, that he has been shipwrecked, that he has been despised and persecuted and scourged, and so on, all for the sake of his eternal happiness, this simple statement, in

* It is in this way that the individual plans his life also in connection with lesser matters. Whether he has to work for a livelihood or is privileged in this respect, whether he is to marry or remain unmarried, and so forth, will alter his mode of existence in the moment of choice, or when he takes over the condition in question. But since such a condition is subject to change, since he may suddenly fall in love or become poor, and so forth, it cannot rationally transform his existence absolutely. Strange to say, the wisdom that concerns this or that in life is not so very rare, and one may not infrequently see an existing individual who expresses existentially a relationship to a relative end, testifying to the fact that he has planned his life with this end in view, that he has given up whatever might prove to be an obstacle, and sets his hope upon what is to be gained by so doing. But an existing individual who expresses existentially a relationship to the absolute good is perhaps a rare exception. Such a one could say with truth: "I exist in such and such a manner, I have made such and such sacrifices in transforming my existence, so that if I hoped for this life alone, I should be the most wretched of all creatures, that is, the most terribly deceived, self-deceived in refusing to grasp what lay to my hand."

How alarmed are the financiers when interest payments on the obligations they hold suddenly cease to be made; how terrified are the ship owners when the government suddenly closes the harbors! But *posito,* I assume that an eternal happiness failed to eventuate; I wonder how many expectant gentlemen (and we all expect an eternal happiness) would find themselves embarrassed?

so far as it reports what he has suffered in action, is evidence of ethical pathos. Whenever the ethical is present, attention is directed entirely to the individual himself and his mode of life. The pathos of marriage, being ethical pathos, consists in action, while the pathos of a love affair consists in poesy.

Ethically the highest pathos is interested pathos, expressed through the active transformation of the individual's entire mode of existence in conformity with the object of his interest; aesthetically the highest pathos is disinterested. When an individual abandons himself to lay hold of something great outside him, his enthusiasm is aesthetic; when he forsakes everything to save himself, his enthusiasm is ethical.

What I here write must be viewed as elementary reading for the primer class, not in the speculative sense, but in the simple sense. Every child knows it, if not precisely with the same background of experience; everyone understands it, if not precisely with the same sharpness of definition; everyone is able to understand it. The ethical is quite consistently always very easy to understand, presumably in order that no time may be wasted, but a beginning made at once. On the other hand it is quite difficult to realize—equally difficult for the wise and for the simple, since the difficulty does not lie in understanding it. If it were a matter of understanding, the clever would have a great advantage.

Existence is a synthesis of the infinite and the finite, and the existing individual is both infinite and finite. Now if for any individual an eternal happiness is his highest good, this will mean that all finite satisfactions are volitionally relegated to the status of what may have to be renounced in favor of an eternal happiness. The pathos of an eternal happiness is that of an individual who exists essentially, not that of a speaker who is polite enough to *include* it in a list of the good things for which he supplicates. Ordinarily, people have a horror of denying that such a good exists; so they include it among the other goods of life, and show precisely by so including it that they do not lay hold of it. I do not know whether to laugh or to weep over the customary rigmarole: a good living, a pretty wife, health, a social position on a level with an alderman—and then, too, an eternal happiness; which is as if one were to suppose the kingdom of *heaven* to be one among the kingdoms of this *earth,* and to seek information about it in a textbook of geography. It is rather remarkable that one may precisely by talking about something, prove that one does not talk about that thing; for it would seem that this could be proved only by not talking about it. If the latter were the case, it would have to be admitted that there is considerable discourse about an eternal happiness—and yet it is apparent from what is said that nothing is said about it; or more precisely, that the subject does not really come before the mind.

Aesthetically it is quite in order to wish for wealth, good fortune, and the most beautiful of damsels; in short, to wish for anything that is subject to an aesthetic dialectic. But *at the same time* to *wish* for an eternal happiness is doubly nonsense. Partly because it is *at the same time,* thus transforming an eternal happiness into something like a present on the Christmas tree; and partly because it is a *wish,* an eternal happiness being essentially relevant to an essentially existing individual, not related by an aesthetic dialectic to a romantically wishful individual. However, this concept must often enough content itself with being included among other bon-bons, and it is regarded as *tres bien* for one so to include it; indeed, this is often looked upon as the maximum of what may be asked for in this connection. And more than this, for with respect to the other goods of life, it is not exactly customary to suppose that they may be acquired merely by wishing for them; but an eternal happiness is supposed to come if one merely wishes for it. Experience teaches that the goods of fortune are unequally distributed, inequality being the dialectic to which the concept of fortune is subject. But an eternal happiness, which has been transformed in this manner into a gift of fortune, is nevertheless supposed to be distributed equally to all who wish for it. Here we have a double confusion. In the first place, the confusion that an eternal happiness is put on a level with an exceptionally fat living and the like; in the second place, the supposition that it is nevertheless distributed *equally,* which is a contradiction when applied to one of the gifts of fortune. The aesthetic and the ethical have here been mixed up in an easy-going farrago of nonsense: the essence is borrowed from the aesthetic, and the equality of distribution from the ethical.

"But," says perhaps a wishful gentleman, an earnest man who would gladly do something for his eternal happiness, "could you not inform me what an eternal happiness is, briefly, clearly, and definitely? Could you not describe it 'while I shave,' as one describes a woman's beauty, the royal purple, or distant landscapes?" What a blessing that I cannot do this, that I am not a poet or a benevolent clergyman; for then I might perhaps attempt it, and perhaps also succeed—in again bringing an eternal happiness under aesthetic categories, so that the maximum of pathos became the wondrous quality of the description, though it is a desperate task to make anything aesthetically out of such an abstraction as an eternal happiness. It is quite proper aesthetically to turn me into an enchanted spectator of scenery bathed in theatrical moonlight, and send me home after having spent an exceedingly pleasant evening; but ethically the point is that there is to be no other transformation than my own. Hence it is quite consistently ethical in spirit that the highest pathos of an essentially existing human being should correspond to what is aesthetically the poorest of all conceptions, the idea of an eternal happiness. It has been said wittily, and aesthetically quite correctly, that the angels are the most tiresome of all creatures, that eternity is the longest and most wearisome of all days, even a single Sunday being sufficiently boring; and that an eternal happiness is an everlasting monotony, so that even the unhappiness of the damned is to be preferred. But this is ethically just as it should be, in order that the existing individual may not be tempted to waste his time in picturing and imagining, but rather be impelled to action.

If then an existing individual is to realize a pathetic relationship to an eternal happiness, his existence must express the relationship. Given his mode of existence, the character of his relationship to an eternal happiness will also be given. That is to say, it will be determined whether he has such a relationship or not, *tertium non datur,* precisely because the absolute *telos* cannot be put on a level with other things. Yet no one can know the facts except the individual himself, in his own consciousness of himself. There is no necessity of listening to a speech or reading a book or consulting a clergyman or going to see a comedy or hearing a comedy played by a clergyman—in order to obtain a vision of the theatrical moonlight in the realms beyond, or hear the rustling of the brook in the verdant dales of eternity. Let the individual merely take note of his own mode of existence and he will know it. If the idea of an eternal happiness does not transform his existence absolutely, he does not stand related to it; if there is anything he is not willing to give up for its sake, the relationship is not there.

Even a relative end transforms a man's existence partially. But since the speculative nineteenth century has unfortunately made existence tantamount to a thinking about everything, we rarely see an existence that devotes itself energetically even to a relative end. To concentrate energetically upon making money is sufficient to transform a human life, to say nothing of devotion to the absolute *telos,* which involves a volitional concentration in the highest sense. All relative volition is marked by willing something for the sake of something else, but the highest end must be willed for its own sake. And this highest end is not a particular something, for then it would be relative to some other particular and be finite. It is a contradiction to will something finite absolutely, since the finite must have an end, so that there comes a time when it can no longer be willed. But to will absolutely is to will the infinite, and to will an eternal happiness is to will absolutely, because this is an end which can be willed every moment. And this is the reason it is so abstract, and aesthetically the most poverty-stricken of all conceptions, because it is an absolute *telos* for an individual who proposes to strive absolutely, not indulging himself thoughtlessly in the illusion that he is finished, nor stupidly seeking to bargain, whereby he only loses the absolute *telos.* And therefore the resolved individual does not even wish to know anything more about this *telos* than that it exists, for as soon as he acquires some knowledge about it, he already begins to be retarded in his striving.

The pathos of the problem consists in expressing this existentially in the medium of existence. It does not consist in testifying about an eternal happiness, but in transforming one's existence into a testimony concerning it. Poetic pathos is differential pathos, but existential pathos is poor man's pathos, pathos for every man. Every human being can act within himself, and one sometimes finds in a servant-girl the pathos which one seeks for in vain in the existence of a poet. The individual can therefore readily determine for himself how he stands toward an eternal happiness, or whether he has any such relationship. He need only submit his entire immediacy with all its yearnings and desires to the inspection of resignation.[1] If he finds a single hard spot, a point of resistance, it means that he does not have a relationship to an eternal happiness.

This inspection of the individual's immediacy means that the individual must not have his life in his immediacy, and the significance of resignation is the consciousness of what may happen to him in life. If the individual shrinks from such an inspection, whether because he is so fortunate that he dare not risk becoming conscious of anything else, or while imagining himself the most unfortunate among mortals, nevertheless suspects that he might become still more unhappy than he is; whether the individual shrewdly calculates the probabilities, or is weak and leans upon others—in short, if the individual shrinks from this inspection, it is a sign that he lacks a relationship to an eternal happiness. But if as a result of the inspection, resignation finds nothing out of the way, it is a sign that in the moment of inspection the individual does have a relationship to an eternal happiness.

But here perhaps someone will say, one who sits snug within doors, with wife and children, enjoying a good livelihood, and a social position ranking with aldermen, an earnest man who would be glad to do something for his eternal happiness in so far as his interests and his family permit, an enthusiastic man, who in faith is not afraid to spend as much as ten dollars on the enterprise: "Very well, let this business of the inspection be conceded. But when it is over and finished as quickly as possible, we come to a mediation of the opposites, do we not? For I must say that the principle of mediation seems to me a most wonderful discovery, as if taken right out of my own heart; it is entirely in the spirit of the nineteenth century, and hence also wholly to my own mind, I who am a true child of the nineteenth century. My admiration for the great discoverer is unbounded, and it seems to me that everyone must admire him—that is, everyone who is oriented in universal history and has grasped the relative justification of every standpoint, and understands that a mediation must finally be arrived at." How one must envy the happy lot of the principle of mediation, thus to be acknowledged even by aldermen, aye, even by an alderman who has the leisure and the talent to survey universal history, and who must therefore be a very exceptional alderman! But no, I forget the age in which we live, the theocentric nineteenth century, in which we all contemplate the world-process—from the divine standpoint.

But let us forget our alderman, and the world-process, and what the two may have to do with one another. When an official of high rank, or perhaps the king himself, makes a tour of inspection to ascertain the condition of the public funds, an unfaithful servant may sometimes succeed in having his balances in order for the day of inspection. As soon as the audit is well over, he thinks, everything will again slip back into the old ruts. But resignation is not a king on a visit of inspection to examine the accounts of other people; it is in possession of the individual's own consciousness of himself. Nor is resignation a travelling inspector on a passing visit; it takes it upon itself to remain, making every day a day of inspection—unless indeed it is banished altogether, when all is lost; and even this is not mediation. But when resignation remains and never slumbers, when it is prompt to note the least misstep, when it never leaves the individual whether he goes out or whatever he does, be it great or small, when it lives next door to his most secret thoughts: what then becomes of mediation? It remains, I think, outside.

What is mediation when it intrudes itself into the ethical and the ethico-religious spheres? It is the miserable invention of a man who became false to himself, and to the authority of resignation. It is a *falsum* of sluggishness, and yet arrogant; it pretends to represent resignation, which is most dangerous of all, as when a thief masquerades as a policeman. In lesser matters the same thing happens. For six months perhaps, or for a year, a man will labor persistently and enthusiastically for one or another object without asking for any reward, or reckoning up how much he accomplishes, or demanding security and guarantees, because the uncertainty of enthusiasm is higher than everything else. But then he becomes tired and seeks certainty, desiring at least some reward for his pains. And when men became weary of the relationship to the eternal, became calculating as a higgling Jew, tender-skinned as an effeminate clergyman, sleepy as a foolish virgin; when they could no longer endure to understand existence (existing) in its truth as a period of courtship, an enthusiastic venture in uncertainty—then came mediation.

To be in love for half a year and stand ready to risk everything— that we can readily understand. But then at last, one must surely be permitted to wed the damsel, and stretch one's weary limbs in the privileged marriage-bed. And in the case of relative ends, the principle of mediation may indeed have its significance; such ends must submit to mediation because it would be irrational to yield an absolute devotion to a relative end. But the absolute *telos* exists for the individual only when he yields it an absolute devotion. And since an eternal happiness is a *telos* for existing individuals, these two (the absolute end and the existing individual) cannot be conceived as realizing a union in existence in terms of rest. This means that an eternal happiness cannot be possessed in time, as the youth and the maiden may possess one another, both being existing individuals. But what this means, namely, that they cannot be united in time, every lover readily understands. It means that the whole of time is here the period of courtship. In the case of a relative end, it is a portion of time that is devoted to striving, and then comes the period of secure possession. But since an eternal happiness is just a little higher up in the scale than a maid, it is quite in order that the period of endeavor should be a little longer— no, not a little longer, for an eternal happiness is not a little more precious than the queen, but the absolute *telos*; so that it is quite in order that the whole of time and of existence should be the period of striving.

In comparison with this direction toward the absolute *telos,* any and every result, even if it were the realization of the most glorious fancy born in a wishing individual's head, or in a poet's creative imagination, constitutes an absolute loss. The striving individual is better off if he thrusts it aside and says: "No, thanks, let me rather keep my relation-ship to the absolute *telos.*"

Who has not admired Napoleon, who has not abandoned himself in trembling devotion, as the child when listening to the fairy tale, and then again felt a tremor of resistance all the more indicative of profound admiration, because the adult tends to relegate such adven-tures to the realm of the imagination, when he considered that here the most fabulous of adventures had become stark reality! Now Thiers has taken it upon himself to tell the story. And with the greatest calm, with a statesman's experience, as if this were quite as it should be, he says more than once, in admiringly presenting the world-wide plans of Napoleon: "But here as everywhere all depended on the result." Whoever brings before his mind the greatness of Napoleon, and then remembers this sentence of Thiers's, thrown out so easily, so naturally, so much as a matter of course, will have the strongest pos-sible feeling of what human greatness really is. In truth, if the greatness of Napoleon rivals the most daring of conceptions, if his entire life is a fairy tale, then there is included in the picture, just as in the fairy tale, still another fabulous figure. It is an old wrinkled witch, gaunt and shriveled; or it is a spider with a mysterious sign on one of its feelers: this is the Result. And the superhuman hero whom nothing, nothing can withstand, is nevertheless in the power of this little animal. When this animal does not consent, the whole adventure comes to naught, or it becomes the adventure of the spider with a strange sign on one of its feelers. The humblest and most insignificant of men who absolutely devotes himself and all he has to the absolute *telos*—to be sure, it will scarcely be an adventure, but neither will it be the adventure of the little animal with a dot on one of its feelers. The most cleverly calculated and daring plan for transforming the world is subject to the principle that it becomes great or not great by virtue of the result. But the simple and loyal resolution of an obscure human being embodies the principle that the plan itself is higher than any result, that its greatness is not dependent upon the result. And this is surely a more blessed privilege than being the greatest man in the world and a slave of the result, whether the result be success or failure. It is indeed a blessed thing to be where we are all small in nothingness before God, but where the result is nothing at all, less than the least in the kingdom of heaven, while in the world it is the lord of lords and the dictator's tyrant.

Who has not admired Napoleon for the fact that he was hero and emperor, and been inclined to regard the thing of being poet as something of secondary importance. For in his mouth the word, the rejoinder—indeed, no poet who was content with being the greatest poet was able to put in his mouth a more masterly rejoinder. And yet I believe it once happened to him that he knew not what he said. It is a veracious story. In making the rounds of the advanced posts he encountered a young officer who attracted his attention. On returning to headquarters the officer at such and such a post was rewarded with a decoration. But lo, that officer had been relieved, and there is a new one in his place. No one can understand the why and wherefore of this citation. The person properly intended becomes aware of the situation and appeals to Napoleon with a petition that the mistake might be rectified. Napoleon answers: "No, of that man I can make no use, he has no luck." In case it is true that a man is sensible of it when death passes over his grave, if this is so, and thus it is in the fairy tale, and we in fact are in fairy land, when a man who stands vividly alive among other men is shivered to bits at the utterance of a word, is turned to straw, and is as if blown away—then in the spirit of the fairy tale this ought to have happened to Napoleon, for the saying applied to him more than to the officer.

In a preceding section I have tried to show the illusoriness of mediation when it is sought to mediate between thought and existence, as long as the mediator is an existing individual. All that is said in praise of mediation may be true and glorious, but becomes untrue in the mouth of an existing individual. Because he exists he is prevented from obtaining a foothold outside of existence in order to be able to mediate that which, being in process of becoming, eludes completion. It was also shown that the entire notion of mediation was for an existing individual quite deceptive. Abstract thought, to say nothing of pure thought, abstracts from existence; this is ethically so little meritorious that it must be regarded rather as reprehensible. It is indeed possible for an existing individual to be outside existence in one of two ways, but in neither of these ways will he be able to mediate. One of these is by way of abstracting from himself, so as to gain a sceptical freedom from affections which the ancients called *ataraxy,* an abstract indifference μέτριως παθεῖν; in Greece this was thought to be very difficult of attainment. The other way in which the individual may be carried outside of existence is in passion; but it is precisely in the moment of passion that he receives an impulse toward existing. To assume that the individual may little by little gradually succeed in mediating, is the customary attempt, by means of a fantastic vanishing of time and a seductive quantification, to draw attention away from the qualitative dialectic.

This was what was expounded concerning mediation in the philosophic sense. Here we are engaged in an ethical inquiry, and the application of the principle is to a mediation of the different moments of existence—provided the absolute *telos* may properly be regarded as one moment among others. Here lies the misunderstanding, and it is easy to see that mediation viewed as something higher than resignation is merely a step backward. Resignation leaves the individual facing, or makes him face, an eternal happiness as the absolute *telos.* This *telos* is thus not merely one end among many. The *both-and* of the principle of mediation, though less naïve, is therefore not much better than the complacent chatter mentioned above, which hospitably includes everything. In the moment of resignation, of deliberation, of choice, the individual is assumed to respect the principle of resignation—but afterwards comes the time for mediation. So a dog may be taught to walk on two legs for a while, but then mediation arrives, and the dog again walks on all fours, just like mediation.* In the spiritual sense man's upright stature consists in his absolute respect for the absolute *telos,* otherwise man walks on all fours. In the case of relative ends, the principle of mediation may have a valid application (signifying that they are all equal over against the mediating function), but in the

---

* The analogy is not quite correct, for one who has ever been rightly oriented in the direction of the absolute *telos* may indeed deteriorate and sink very deeply, but he can never again wholly forget it, which receives suitable expression in the principle that it requires great elevation to sink deeply. But the calculating shrewdness of mediation proves that the individual has never rightly been oriented with respect to the absolute *telos.*

case of the absolute *telos* any mediation means that it has been demoted to the rank of a relative end. Nor is it true that the absolute end becomes concrete in the relative ends, for the absolute distinction that was fixed between them in the moment of resignation will secure the absolute *telos* against fraternization every moment. The individual is in truth in the relative ends with his direction toward the absolute *telos*; but he is not so in them as to exhaust himself in them. It is true that before God and the absolute *telos* we human beings are all equal, but it is not true either for me or for any particular individual, that God or the absolute *telos* may be placed on a level with everything else.

It may be very praiseworthy of the particular individual to have attained to the dignity of an aldermanic title, to be known as a clever worker at the office, to be first ranking lover in the dramatic club, almost an expert on the violin, a champion rifle-shot, a member of the Hospital Board, a noble father carrying himself with dignity; in short, to be a devil of a fellow who can attend to *both-and,* and has time for everything. But let him beware of becoming altogether too much of a devil of a fellow, so that he can *both* do all this *and* at the same time find leisure to direct his life toward the absolute *telos*. For this *both-and* means that the absolute *telos* is on the same plane with all the rest. But the absolute *telos* has the remarkable characteristic that it demands acknowledgement as the absolute *telos* every moment. Hence if one understood this in the moment of deliberation, of resignation, of choice, it cannot be the intention to forget this the next moment. Resignation consequently remains with the individual, as I have expressed it above; and it is so far from being the task to mediate the absolute *telos* into a sort of *both-and,* that it is rather the task to realize that mode of existence which has in the long run the pathos of the great moment.

What has particularly helped to bring the principle of mediation forward, and to put it on its legs in the ethical sphere, is the forbidding manner in which the monastic movement of the Middle Ages has been utilized. An absolute respect for the absolute *telos* would lead straight to the cloister, so people were made to believe. The monastic movement itself was a tremendous abstraction, and the life of the cloister a continued abstraction, the time being spent wholly in prayer and psalm-singing—instead of in playing cards at the club; for if it is permissible to caricature the one without qualification, it must surely be permitted to describe the other as it has caricatured itself. Worldly wisdom has known how to make use of the monastic movement for its own advantage, just as even in this very moment it sometimes uses the cloister for the purpose of proclaiming indulgence from all concern for the religious. In a Protestant country, where Protestantism has been in the ascendant for three hundred years, and where a prospective candidate for the cloister would find himself in a situation of greater embarrassment than the anxious father who wrote: *"Where shall I send my boy to school?"*[2]—in the nineteenth century, where worldliness is triumphant, we still now and then hear a clergyman who, in the course of an address encouraging us to participate in the innocent pleasure of life, warns us against entering the cloister. As we listen to the speaker we see him perspire, and wipe the perspiration from his brow, so deeply does the subject move him. So that in order to stop the monastic movement, men hit upon the profane device of mediation. For just as it is profane to introduce the name of God carelessly into ordinary prattle, so it is also profane to place the absolute *telos* on a par with the dignity of being a champion rifle-shot and the like. But if the Middle Ages erred in eccentricity, it does not by any means follow that mediation is praiseworthy. The Middle Ages had something in common with the Greeks, and had what the Greeks also had, namely, passion. The monastic movement was the expression for a passionate decision, as is becoming in relation to the absolute *telos*, and in so far it is in loftiness far above the wretched middleman's wisdom of mediation.

Mediation claims to acknowledge (but only deceptively, please note; nor can it be done in any other manner) the pathetic moment of resignation, the direction toward the absolute *telos*. But then it wants to have this *telos* introduced among the others, and it desires finite advantage from the relationship to this *telos*. Let us then ask the following question: "What is the maximum that a man may gain through the relationship to the absolute *telos*?" In the finite sense there is nothing whatever to gain, and everything to lose. In the life of time the *expectation* of an eternal happiness is the highest reward, because an eternal happiness is the highest *telos*; and it is precisely a sign of the relationship to the absolute that there is not only no reward to expect, but suffering to bear. When the individual is no longer content with this, it means that he relapses into worldly wisdom, into a Jewish clinging to promises for the present life, into chiliasm, and the like. It is precisely here that the difficulty of sustaining an absolute relationship to an absolute *telos* manifests itself. Again and again men begin to look around for excuses, hoping to find some way of escape from thus having to walk on their toes, some way of evading—the relationship to the absolute.

The parson says indeed that there are two ways, and it is certainly a devout wish that he might be able to say this impressively. There are two ways, says the parson; and when this discourse begins we all know what he means. But for all that, it will do us no harm to hear him say it yet once more; for it is not an anecdote or a witticism which will not bear repetition. There are two ways: the one opens out before us smiling and carefree; it is easy to travel, inviting, flower-bestrewn, winding through charming dales, and the traveller along this road moves as lightly as if in a dance. The other is narrow, stony, and toilsome at the beginning; but little by little. . . . These two ways are the way of pleasure and the way of virtue. Thus the parson sometimes speaks; but what happens? Just as the way of virtue gradually changes, so there also comes a change over the parson's speech, and little by little the two ways begin pretty much to resemble one another.* In order to make virtue seem attractive to the listener, the description of the way of virtue becomes almost seductive. But it is a dangerous thing to indulge in allurement. The speaker abandons the ethical, and operates in an aesthetically correct manner by means of a shortened perspective, and what is the result? Why then the result is that there are no longer really two ways; or rather, there are two ways of pleasure, one of which is a little more prudent than the other, just as when climbing a mountain to enjoy the prospect, it is wisest not to turn around too soon—so as to be able to enjoy it all the more. And what then? Why then the devotee of pleasure (the eudaemonist) is not only mad because he chooses the way of pleasure instead of the way of virtue, but he is a mad devotee of pleasure, not to choose the pleasureful way of virtue. As soon as this "little by little" on the path of virtue receives an aesthetic coloring in a parson's mouth—it is "a lie in your throat, father!" For in that case it pleases his reverence to forget that he disposes of the conditions of existence as no human being has the right to do. He sets up a *telos* in time, and his entire teaching about virtue is a doctrine of prudence. But if a religious man happened to hear such

---

* I should like to know what passage in the New Testament is taken as a basis for the clergyman's edifying remarks about *little by little*. The New Testament also speaks of two ways, and it says that the way is narrow and the gate strait that leads to life, and that there are few who find it, but it says nothing at all concerning this *little by little*. But just as a committee has been established in Copenhagen for the beautification of the town,[3] so it would seem that a modern pastoral wisdom is active in beautifying the way of virtue with aesthetic decorations.

a sermon, he would doubtless say to his soul: "Do not allow yourself to be led astray by him; he is perhaps himself not aware that he is trying to deceive you and make you impatient, when this 'little by little' becomes a matter of years, perhaps of your entire life. No, let me rather know from the beginning that the road may be narrow, stony, and beset with thorns until the very end; so that I may learn to hold fast to the absolute *telos,* guided by its light in the night of my sufferings, but not led astray by calculations of probability and *interim* consolations."

Over the entrance to the temple at Delphi there was inscribed among other things the motto: *ne quid nimis.* These words constitute the sum total of all finite worldly wisdom. If this is the maximum of what there is to say about human life, then Christianity will instantly have to be recalled as an immature and juvenile conceit. Merely make the experiment of applying this *ne quid nimis* to the God who submits to be crucified, and there is instantly elicited a mockery of religion so witty as rarely to have been heard in the world; for the mockers are in general violent and stupid. It would be about the wittiest possible objection, presented with an undertone of humor, abstaining wholly from making any attack upon the historical and eternal truth of Christianity, merely emancipating oneself from the relationship to it in the words: "It is much too much, your reverence, that God should permit Himself to be crucified." In many a situation this rule of life, *ne quid nimis,* may have its valid application; but when applied to the absolute passionate relationship to the absolute *telos* it is galimatias. Here, on the contrary, it is necessary to risk everything, to invest absolutely everything in the venture, to desire absolutely the highest *telos;* but it is also necessary to prevent this absolute passion from acquiring even the color of earning or deserving an eternal happiness. The first genuine expression for the relationship to the absolute *telos* is a total renunciation. But unless the retreat is to sound at once, the true understanding of this initial step must be that this total renunciation is nothing if reckoned as a means of meriting the highest good. The error of paganism lay in the first place in not having the will to venture everything. The error of the Middle Ages lay secondly in misunderstanding the significance of venturing everything. The hodge-podge wisdom of our age mediates.

The questionable character of the monastic movement, aside from the error of its supposed meritoriousness, lay in the fact that the absolute inwardness, presumably in order to afford an energetic demonstration of its existence, created for itself a conspicuous expression in a distinct and special outwardness. As a consequence it became, in spite of all, only relatively different from every other outwardness. The principle of mediation either allows the relationship to the absolute *telos* to be mediated into the relative ends, or else lets it flow, as being abstract, exhaustively into the relative ends as its concrete predicates. The majesty of the absolute relationship thus becomes an empty phrase, a showy introduction to life which remains outside it, a title-page not bound with the book.[4] But the relationship to the absolute *telos* cannot pour itself exhaustively into the relative ends, because the absolute relationship may require the renunciation of them all. On the other hand, the individual who sustains an absolute relationship to the absolute *telos* may very well exist in relative ends, precisely in order to exercise the absolute relationship in renunciation.

Since almost everyone in our age is a mighty man on paper, apprehensions are sometimes met with which have no basis in reality. An example of this is the danger with which men of our age believe themselves threatened, namely, that every task is so quickly completed that they are embarrassed for something to do to help them pass the time. It is set down on a piece of paper that one must doubt everything—and so this universal doubt is realized. By the time a man is thirty years old he is embarrassed to know what to do with his time, especially if "he has only poorly provided for his old age by not learning how to play cards." So also with the task of resigning everything—it is no sooner said than done. It is asserted that the renunciation of everything is a tremendous abstraction—which is why it is necessary to pass over into laying hold of something. But if the ideal task is to resign everything, what if one made a beginning by resigning something? The backward pupil in a school is usually known by his habit of coming forward with his paper scarcely ten minutes after the task has been set, announcing that he has finished it—which must be extremely tiresome for the teacher. So also do all mediocrities in life come running at once with the announcement that they are through, and the greater the task the more quickly they finish it. It must be tiresome for the power that governs the world to have to do with such a generation. The Scriptures characterize God's patience in dealing with sinners as inconceivable, which indeed it is; but what an angelic strain of patience is required to have to do with people who have finished the tasks of life almost as soon as they are set.

In so far as, after having acquired the absolute direction toward the absolute *telos,* the individual does not pass out of the world (and why such outwardness; but let us not forget that inwardness without outwardness is the most difficult kind of inwardness, where self-deception is easiest), what then? Aye, then it is his task to express existentially that he constantly maintains the absolute direction toward the absolute *telos,* i.e. the absolute respect (*respicere*). He must express it existentially, for the pathos of words is aesthetic pathos. He must express it existentially, and yet there must be no distinctive outwardness as its direct expression, for then we have either the cloister or mediation. He will then live like other men, but resignation will make its inspection early and late, to see how he preserves the lofty solemnity with which he first acquired the absolute direction toward the absolute *telos.* He knows nothing of any *both-and,* refusing to have anything to do with it; it is as abhorrent to him as taking the name of God in vain, as abhorrent as it is for the lover to think of loving another. And resignation, this disciplinarian of life, must make the inspection. But if he loses his elevation so that he longs to walk again on all fours, if he has intercourse with a suspicious person named mediation, and if the latter finally prevails, then will resignation take its place outside this individual, standing there like the genius of death, bending down over a smoking torch;[5] for the absolute *telos* has vanished, and the dim sight of the individual has lost the vision. In outward things perhaps no change would be apparent. For the relationship to the absolute *telos* did not involve entering a cloister, and its cessation when the individual is weary of it does not mean the resumption of ordinary garb, so as to make the change outwardly recognizable. Nor did the relationship to the absolute *telos* signify that it was exhausted in relative ends, for then again the change would be outwardly evident.

In a certain sense there is something fearful in speaking thus of the inner life, that it may be there, and then again not be there, without the fact becoming immediately apparent in any outward manner. But it is also glorious to be able to speak so of the inner life—when it is there; for this is the expression for its inwardness. The principle of mediation really knows nothing of any relationship to the absolute *telos,* because this exhausts itself for mediation in relative ends. But what in that case happens to the inner life? The task is to exercise the absolute relationship to the absolute *telos,* striving to reach the maximum of maintaining simultaneously a relationship to the absolute *telos* and to relative ends, not by mediating them, but by making the relationship to the absolute *telos* absolute, and the relationship to the relative ends relative. The relative relationship belongs to the world, the absolute relationship to the individual himself; and it is not an easy thing to maintain an absolute relationship to the absolute *telos* and at the same time participate like other men in this and that. If a man merely entertains a great plan, it becomes difficult for him to be like others; he becomes *distrait,* he has no desire to participate in other affairs, all the hurrying and the scurrying about him is a torture to his spirit, he wants a little corner for himself where he can sit alone and ponder his great plan—and it is a task for diplomats and police agents to acquire the self-control necessary to hold fast to the great plan, and at the same time make conversation with the ladies, dance, play billiards, and whatever else you like. But the absolute *telos* is the greatest plan in human life, and that is why the Middle Ages sought a corner where a man might concern himself with the absolute. But just this was a loss for the absolute, since it became something external.

When the time of husband and wife has been absorbed in a multitude of engagements for perhaps a week, they sometimes say that they have had no time to live for one another, and that although they have both had the same engagements and have constantly seen each other. They therefore look forward to having a day when they may really live for each other, and this feeling of theirs may be a very beautiful thing. It would seem that one whose mind is occupied with his relationship to the absolute *telos* is in a similar situation, existence with its manifold detail tending to constitute a hindrance; so that it would seem to be quite in order for a man to live solely for his absolute *telos* once in a while. Yet just here lies the difficulty. Husband and wife stand in a relative relationship, and hence it is proper for them to have this day once in a while, when they live for one another. But to live for one's absolute *telos* once in a while is to have a relative relationship to it, and to be relatively related to the absolute *telos* is to be related to a relative *telos,* for it is the relationship that is decisive. The task is therefore to exercise myself in the relationship to the absolute *telos* so as always to have it with me, while remaining in the relativities of life—and let us not forget that in the schoolroom at least it was the mediocre pupil who came running ten minutes after the task had been set, claiming to have finished.

The principle of mediation thus remains outside. To exemplify this further, I will take love as a *telos*, and let an individual apprehend this through a misunderstanding as the absolute *telos*. He will not desert the world, he will conduct himself outwardly like the rest of us, he may perhaps be a titled dignitary, or a merchant, and so forth. But as he once understood absolutely that his love was for him the absolute, so it will be his absolute task always to understand it so; and as it was once dreadful for him to contemplate that his love might sometime not be the absolute, but become entangled in a nonsensical *both-and,* so he will strive with all his strength to prevent this from ever happening. What then became of the mediation principle? And what was his error? His mistake was in apprehending love as the absolute *telos*. But in the case of what is really the absolute *telos* the individual conducts himself rightly when he behaves in this manner. In everything he undertakes, whatever his situation, whether the world smiles or threatens, whether he jests or is serious, resignation will first of all look to see that the absolute respect for the absolute *telos* is absolutely preserved. But this is not mediation, any more than it is a mediation between heaven and hell to say that there is a wide gulf fixed between them. And in the respect which the individual entertains for the absolute *telos* there is a yawning chasm fixed between it and the relative ends.

But if this is so, and if the task is to exercise oneself in the absolute relationship, existence becomes exceedingly strenuous, since there is always a double movement to be executed. The cloister wishes to express inwardness by means of a specific outwardness which is supposed to be inwardness. But this is a contradiction, for being a monk is just as truly something external as being an alderman. Mediation abolishes the absolute *telos*, but an individual existing in true pathos will express for himself every moment that the absolute *telos* is the absolute *telos*. The profundity of all this lies in the inviolate stillness of the inner life; but herein lies also the possibility of deception and the temptation to say that one has done it. Now if anyone wishes to lie about this it will be his affair, and I shall be quite content to believe everything he says. For if it is something great, I might perhaps be able to do the same; and whether he has really done it or not, does not interest me at all. I will merely suggest to him that it would be prudent to abstain from adding that he *also* mediates; for then he informs against himself. The existing individual who has once received the absolute direction toward the absolute *telos,* and understands it as his task to exercise himself in this relationship, is perhaps an alderman, perhaps like any one of the other aldermen; and yet he is not like them, though when you look at him he seems wholly like them. He may possibly gain the whole world, but he is not as one who desires it. He may be a king; but every time he holds his scepter in his outstretched hand, resignation looks first to see whether he expresses existentially the absolute respect for the absolute *telos*—and the glory of his crown fades, although he wears it royally. It fades as it once faded in the great moment of resignation, though he now wears it in the third decade of his reign; it fades as it will some time fade in the hour of death, before the eyes of the witnesses standing by, and for his own failing sight. But thus it fades for him also in the hour of the fullness of his power. What then became of mediation? And yet there was no one who entered a cloister.

The individual does not cease to be a human being, nor does he divest himself of the manifold composite garment of the finite in order to clothe himself in the abstract garment of the cloister. But he does not mediate between the absolute *telos* and finite ends. In his immediacy the individual is rooted in the finite. But when resignation has convinced itself that he has acquired the absolute direction toward the absolute *telos,* all is changed, and the roots have been severed. He still lives in the finite, but he does not have his life in the finite. His life has, like that of other human beings, the various predicates of a human existence, but he is in them as one who is clothed in the borrowed garments of a stranger. He is a stranger in the world of the finite, but does not manifest his heterogeneity, his separation from *worldliness,* by a foreign mode of dress. This would be a contradiction, since he would thereby qualify himself in a worldly manner. He is incognito, but his incognito consists in having an appearance entirely like others. Just as the dentist has loosened the soft tissues about a tooth and cut the nerve, so the roots of his life in the finite have been severed. It is not his task to give the tooth an opportunity to grow fast again, which would be mediation. In the great moment of resignation he had no thought of mediation, but committed himself by a choice, and it is now similarly his task to acquire the requisite facility in the renewal of this choice, and in giving it existential expression. The individual does indeed remain in the finite, where he confronts the difficulty of maintaining himself in the absolute choice while still living in the finite;

but just as he deprived the finite of its unchecked vitality in the moment of resignation, so it remains his task to reinstate repeatedly the determination by which this was first accomplished. Let the world give him everything, it is possible that he will see fit to accept it. But he says: "Oh, well," and this "Oh, well" means the absolute respect for the absolute *telos*. If the world takes everything from him, he suffers no doubt; but he says again: "Oh, well"—and this "Oh, well" means the absolute respect for the absolute *telos*. Men do not exist in this fashion when they live immediately in the finite.

Whether for the Eternal, the Omniscient, the Omnipresent, it is as important whether a man forfeits his eternal happiness or a sparrow falls to the ground, I shall make no attempt to decide. Nor shall I say whether, when all comes to rest in eternity, it will appear that the most insignificant circumstance was absolutely important. I can truly avow that *time* will not permit me, because, in fact, I live in time. In existence at any rate, or for an existing individual, it cannot be so. An existing individual is himself in process of becoming, and a grandiose mediation (not even as in the Greek manner toilsomely acquired throughout an entire life, but merely legitimating itself on paper in the German fashion) is for an existing individual merely monkeyshines. A mortal eye cannot endure the dizzy sight, and the ethical will absolutely forbid him to make the attempt to see the most insignificant thing as equally important with that which is absolutely decisive. An *existing* individual cannot find, and dare not give himself, the *calm* needed to become fantastic; for as long as he is in existence he will never become eternal. In existence the watchword is always *forward*: and so long as the watchword is forward, it is man's task to exercise himself in making the absolute distinction, in attaining facility in making the distinction more and more easily, and in cultivating a good consciousness with himself. But it is not mediation when the greatly experienced individual confidently believes that he makes the absolute distinction with ease and joy. Or when the wife of graying years is happily convinced that her husband is absolutely loyal, of what is she convinced? Is it of his mediation, and of his mediating and divided heart? Or is it not of his steady and quiet maintenance of the absolute distinction of love; only that she is in glad confidence so convinced that he makes the distinction with ease and expertness that she needs no external proof. Only it must not be forgotten that marriage is not the absolute *telos,* and that the principle which holds true absolutely of the absolute can therefore only imperfectly apply to the relative.

If God were in the immediate sense the ideal for human beings, it would be right to endeavor to express a direct likeness. Thus when a distinguished man is an ideal for me, it is quite proper for me to attempt to express a direct resemblance to him, since we are both human beings and both within the same sphere. But as between God and a human being (for let speculative philosophy keep *humanity* to play tricks with) there is an absolute difference. In man's absolute relationship to God this absolute difference must therefore come to expression, and any attempt to express an immediate likeness becomes impertinence, frivolity, effrontery, and the like.* If God in His lofty majesty were to say to a human being: "You are of no more importance to me than a sparrow"; and if it were proper for a human being to express a direct likeness with the divine majesty, it would then become meritorious to reply: "You and your existence are likewise no more important to me than a sparrow": whether this reply is to be positively interpreted, because everything had become equally important for this exalted man, or negatively, because nothing had any importance. But this would surely be a mad blasphemy. Precisely because there is an absolute difference between God and man, man will express his own nature most adequately when he expresses this difference absolutely. *Worship* is the maximum expression for the God-relationship of a human being, and hence also for his likeness with God, because the qualities are absolutely different. But the significance of worship is, that God is absolutely all for the worshipper; and the worshipper is again one who makes the absolute distinction.

One who distinguishes absolutely has a relationship to the absolute *telos,* and *ipso facto* also a relationship to God. The absolute distinction is just the thing to clear a space about the absolute end, so as to make room for it, just as a marshal clears the way for a procession. It keeps the mob of relative ends at a distance, in order that the absolutely dis-

---

* It is something quite different when God, in a very childlike age and for the innocence of the naïve consciousness, becomes a reverend old man or the like, and lives on a friendly footing with the devout. Thus I remember having read in *"Biblische Legenden der Muselmänner"* as published by Weil, that God Himself personally attended the funeral of one of the saintly characters in the story, walking in front of the coffin, while the four angels walked behind. The innocent naïveté of this sort of thing is manifest among other things from the fact that when we now read it, it evokes a pure and innocent humorous effect. This childlike piety is of course free from any desire to affront God; it is on the contrary happy to invest Him with the best that its invention affords.

tinguishing individual may effect a relationship to the absolute. There is nothing meritorious in the attempt of an existing individual to approximate the equilibrium which possibly exists for the Eternal; for one who exists, the passionate decisiveness is precisely the maximum. Existing is in this respect something like walking. When everything is, and is at rest, it seems plausible enough to say that everything is equally important, provided I can acquire a view of it which is equally calm. But as soon as movement is introduced, and I am myself also in motion, my program in walking consists in constantly making distinctions. Only that this comparison cannot indicate the nature of the absolute distinction, since walking is a finite process.

But it does not follow from the fact that the task is to exercise the absolute distinction, that the existing individual becomes indifferent to the finite. This was an exaggeration characteristic of the Middle Ages; the medieval spirit did not have complete confidence in its inwardness until this became an outwardness. But the less outwardness, the more inwardness, and an inwardness expressed through its opposite (the outwardness of being wholly like all others, and that there is outwardly nothing to see) is the highest inwardness—provided it is there. This qualification must always be added, and also the warning that the less outwardness the easier the deception. An adult may very well whole-heartedly share in the play of children, and may even be responsible for really bringing life into the game; but he does not play as a child. One who understands it as his task to exercise himself in making the absolute distinction sustains just such a relationship to the finite. But he does not mediate. The inwardness of the Middle Ages was not sure of itself, and therefore wanted to see the external expression. It was in so far an unhappy inwardness, resembling a love-relationship in which the lovers are in sickly fashion jealous to see the outward expression of their love. In the same way the Middle Ages believed of God that He was jealously eager to see the outward expression. True inwardness demands absolutely no outward sign. The passion of the infinite pervades the exercise of the absolute distinction, but it desires to remain an inwardness, free from jealousy, envy, or suspicion. It does not wish contentiously to attract attention to itself as something outwardly remarkable, which would only be a loss instead of a gain, as when God's invisible image is made visible. It does not wish to create a disturbance in the finite, but neither does it mediate. In the midst of the finite and its manifold temptations, in order to forget the absolute distinction, it proposes to be for the individual his absolute inwardness; and as for other things, he may be an alderman, and so forth. But the maximum of attainment is simultaneously to sustain an absolute relationship to the absolute end, and a relative relationship to relative ends.

If this cannot be done, or if one is not willing to accept this as the task, analogies to the monastic movement are unconditionally to be preferred, whether this assertion provokes hissing or singing, is met with tears or with laughter in the speculative nineteenth century. The monastic movement had at any rate passion, and a respect for the absolute *telos*. But entering the cloister must not be regarded as something meritorious. On the contrary, this step must be taken in humility before God, and not without a certain self-deprecation. Just as a sick child does not regard it as any merit of its own that it is permitted to stay at home with the parents; just as a woman in love does not regard it as meritorious not to be able for a single minute to be out of sight of her beloved, and unable to win sufficient strength to have the thought of her lover with her while attending to her ordinary tasks; just as she does not regard it as meritorious to be permitted to sit with him at his work and be constantly at his side: so also must the candidate for the cloister look upon his relationship to God. And if he so understands it, there will be nothing more to say against his choice, whatever people may think of this in the nineteenth century.

But the sick child will soon discover the difficulty, not because the parents are not tender and loving, but because the constant association gives so many opportunities for conflict. And the woman in love will soon discover the difficulty, not because her lover is not a fine fellow, but because the constant sight of him, day after day and every hour of the day, brings in its train a tendency to languidness and debility. The candidate for the cloister will also soon discover the same sort of thing. For here again the clergyman often deceives us. He says on Sunday that the hallowed place breathes such an air of quiet and solemnity, and that if we could only remain there always, we should doubtless soon become holy men and women; but the trouble is that we must go out into the world's confusion. Shame on the clergyman, so to delude us into thinking that the fault is in the world and not in ourselves; teaching us pride, as if we had chosen the more difficult task, especially if out there in the world we do not have the absolute *telos* with us every moment. I thought it was the clergyman's duty to teach us humility, and that he ought therefore to say to us: "Now go to your homes, and give thanks to God, who knows all human weaknesses, that it is not required of you to stay here and to occupy yourselves solely in prayer and singing psalms and praising God, in which case you would perhaps discover trials and temptations of which God now permits you to remain ignorant." Going to church once a week, when otherwise immersed in the manifold business of life, readily produces an illusion by means of the aesthetically foreshortened perspective. But just for this reason the clergyman ought to know how to call our attention to this danger of illusion, rather than repeatedly to misuse the Middle Ages in order to insinuate seductive misconceptions into the minds of his hearers.

In our time there is really no very great reason for warning people against the cloister, and in the Middle Ages the reason was not what might perhaps first come to mind. Had I lived in the Middle Ages, I could never have chosen to enter a cloister. And why not? Because anyone who entered a cloister was in the Middle Ages accounted a saint, and that in all seriousness. Hence when I walked about the streets and met a poor fellow mortal who was perhaps a much better man than I,* he would bow in submission and regard me pathetically and in earnest as a holy man. But this seems to me the most terrible of all misunderstandings, a profanation of the holy, a betrayal of the absolute relationship to the absolute *telos*. If a cloister were set up in a modern environment the entrants would be regarded as mad. When we read nowadays a physician's program for a new asylum, it has a certain resemblance to an invitation to a cloister. This I regard as an extraordinary advantage. To be considered mad is something like; it is encouraging, it protects the inwardness of the absolute relationship. But to be considered in real earnest a holy man must make one anxious unto death. To give the cloister the color of a lunatic asylum I regard as the nearest thing to an outward appearance like that of all other men. For in that case the outwardness does not directly assume to express the inwardness, which was precisely the fault of the Middle Ages. I at least think as follows: Let me come to be whatever the world has in store for me, it will scarcely be anything that could be called greatness; and if the lot be ever so insignificant, I shall strive to put up with it. But there is one thing I pray that I may escape: to be regarded in earnest as

---

* And this perhaps is not so hypothetical after all, even if I were a quite different man than I am; for the human being who in sincerity and earnestness considers another as a holy man, shows *eo ipso* by this humility that he is better than the other.

a holy man; for if anyone were to dub me saint in a spirit of mockery that would be something quite different, not inappropriate, and rather encouraging.

But let due respect be shown for the monastic movement of the Middle Ages. The clergyman says indeed that the life of the cloister was an evasion of the danger, and that it is a greater thing to remain among the perils of life—but surely not with the assistance of mediation? Let us at any rate try to understand one another, and seek to agree as to what we mean by the danger. The candidate for the cloister saw his greatest danger in the failure to sustain each moment an absolute relationship to the absolute *telos*. The mediation principle knows nothing of any such danger. With its assistance one avoids the absolute danger and the absolute exertion, avoids the intercourse with the absolute in the stillness of solitude, where the least loss is an absolute loss and the least retreat is utter ruin; where the mind is not diverted by distractions, but the memory of ever so slight an infidelity is a fire that burns and from which there is no escape, paralyzing the individual like a sunstroke; where every weakness, every faint moment, every disinclination, is as if it were a mortal sin, and every such hour is like an eternity, because time will not pass: this is what the mediating individual escapes, and this life is what the clergyman calls an evasion of the danger. But he praises the courage of those who remain in the relative dangers, the dangers of the manifold, where the simplest experience teaches that one never loses everything (precisely because it is the sphere of the manifold), but that a loss in one place is made up for by a gain in another; where the perils are those of the job and the livelihood, and being attacked in the newspapers, and so forth. It is really saddening to see the eccentricity of the Middle Ages repeatedly misused to teach men to boast of themselves, as if they were devilish fine fellows. When such manner of speech is heard in our time, it is as much suggestive of parody as if someone in an institution for the aged were to unfold the idea that it is not the highest form of courage to commit suicide, but rather to live, thus suggesting to the inmates that they are the bravest of mankind, because they had the courage not to seek death. Or as when someone discourses in a gathering of calloused and hardened men on the theme of how great it is to bear one's sorrows like a man, omitting the intermediate dialectical determination: the greatness of feeling sorrow like a man. Let us visit the theater to be deceived, let actor and spectator cooperate in beautiful harmony to

carry away and to be carried away in illusion: it is glorious. If worst
comes to worst let me be deceived by my servant, or by one who seeks
a favor, or by my shoemaker because I am his best customer and he is
loath to lose me: but why should I be deceived and made almost to
tremble for myself in a church, provided I am a good listener! For
if I am a good listener I hear so as to assume that the clergyman preaches
constantly about me. An attitude of mind which in other situations is
mere vanity, and perhaps a very general habit in the world, is precisely
praiseworthy and yet perhaps very rare in the church. And why am I
brought almost to tremble for myself? Is it because the clergyman describes human beings (including me, in so far as I am a good listener and
assume that he preaches about me) as so debased that I shudder at the
thought, become pale and tremble, and say to myself with horror and
aversion: "No, I surely am not so bad as that?" Ah, no. His reverence
rather describes human beings (including me, in so far as I am a good
listener and assume that he preaches about me) in so glorious a fashion,
as so much more perfect than the retiring inmates of the cloister, that I
who assume that he is referring to me, become embarrassed and grow
red in the face and am driven to say: "No, no, your reverence is much
too polite," and look inquiringly up to see whether it is a clergyman who
speaks or a New Year's congratulant.*

* It will be seen that the clergyman's sermon today is somewhat different from that of last
Sunday, when he sought to inspire his *Christian* listeners with a desire to accept the *Christian*
faith and become Christians (cf. the preceding chapter). This is quite in order when baptism
proposes to make us Christians merely through being baptized as children; the error is to
acknowledge the baptism of children as decisive with respect to becoming Christians.

It is otherwise when the preacher quite simply makes great heroes of all his listeners. The
religious address has to do essentially with individuals, and its essential function is to serve
as an intermediary between the individual and the ideal. Its maximum effect is to assist the
individual in expressing the ideal. It assumes that all the human beings to whom it addresses
itself are essentially erring; it knows every bypath of error, every secret hiding place, every
pathological state on the erring way. But this sort of preaching is rare in our objective
age. The clergy preach *about* faith, and recount the exploits of faith—and are either
aesthetically indifferent as to whether we who listen are believers or not, or aesthetically
polite enough to suppose that we are. In this manner faith becomes a sort of allegorical figure,
and the clergyman a troubadour, and a sermon about faith becomes a sort of analogy to the
story of Saint George and the dragon. The scene is in the air, and faith overcomes every difficulty.
And so likewise with hope and love. The religious address becomes something in the same *genre*
with the first medieval essays in the dramatic art, the so-called Mysteries, when religious material was treated dramatically, and comedies were played precisely on Sunday and precisely in the
church. Because there is discourse about faith, hope, and love, and about God and Jesus Christ,
presented in a solemn tone (whether this be more artistic, or the coarse bass of an awakened
despiser of all art) and in a church, it does not follow that it is godly discourse by any means.
What counts in this connection is the manner in which the speaker and the listener are related
to the discourse or are presumed to be related. The speaker's relation to the discourse must not
be merely through the imagination, but as himself being what he speaks about, or striving toward

No, let us yield a due and decent respect to the monastic movement of the Middle Ages. Mediation is a rebellion of the relative ends against the majesty of the absolute, an attempt to bring the absolute down to the level of everything else, an attack upon the dignity of human life, seeking to make man a mere servant of relative ends. And in so far as it pretends to be something higher than the absolute disjunction, it is a fantastic fiction.

On paper the proposal to mediate looks plausible enough. First we posit the finite and then the infinite; thereupon we set it down on paper that there must be a mediation. And it is incontrovertible that here has been found the secure foothold outside of existence where an existing individual may mediate—on paper. The Archimedean point has been discovered; only it does not yet appear that the world has been moved. But when the scene is in existence and not on paper, the mediating individual being an existing individual (and thereby prevented from mediating), then any individual who becomes conscious of what it means to exist (that *he* exists) will instantly become an individual who distinguishes absolutely, not between the finite and the infinite, but between existing finitely and existing infinitely. For the finite and the infinite are put together in existence, in the existing individual; the

it in his own experience and continuing to have his own specific mode of experience in relation to it. The listeners must be informed and assisted in becoming that of which the discourse speaks. Essentially this situation will remain the same whether a direct or indirect relationship is presumed between speaker and listener. If an indirect relationship is assumed, the discourse will become a monologue, but a monologue about the speaker's own experience and its specific mode, through which, though speaking about himself, he indirectly speaks also of the listener. In godly discourse concerning faith, the important thing is that the question of how you and I (particular individuals) become believers is illuminated, that the speaker assists us in becoming emancipated from illusions, and knows all about the long and toilsome way, the dangers of relapse, and so forth. If it is described as easy to become a believer (as for example by being baptized in childhood) and if the discourse is merely *about* faith, then the whole underlying relationship is merely aesthetic, and we are attending a comedy—in church. For a mere bagatelle we receive admittance to the clergyman's dramatic spectacle, where we sit in contemplation of what faith can do—not as believers, but as spectators of the exploits of faith, just as in our age we do not so much have philosophers, as we have spectators of the exploits of philosophy. But of course for a theocentric and speculative and objective age it is presumably not enough to struggle with the ultimate difficulties, where the question becomes in the last analysis as acute, as searching, as disturbing, and as uncompromising as possible, in the effort to determine whether the individuals, you and I, are believers, and how we stand related to faith from day to day.

existing individual has therefore no need to trouble himself to create existence, or to imitate existence in thought, but needs all the more to concentrate upon existing. Nowadays existence is even produced, on paper, with the assistance of mediation. In existence, where the existing individual finds himself, the task is simpler, namely, whether he will be so good as to exist. As an existing individual he is not called upon to create existence out of the finite and the infinite; but as one who is himself composed of finite and infinite it is his task to *become* one of the two existentially. It is impossible to *become* both at the same time, as one *is* both by *being* an existing individual. For this is precisely the difference between being and becoming, and the chimerical facility of mediation, if it has any significance at all, is an expression for—the beginning. It is this which in several respects has happened to recent philosophy, namely, that having had the task of correcting a misdirection of reflection it has confused the end of this task, when it has finished it, with the end of all things, instead of recognizing that the end of this task is at most the beginning of the real task.

It is possible to *be both* good and bad, as we say quite simply, that a man has tendencies to both good and evil. But it is impossible *at one and the same time to become both good and bad*. Aesthetically the requirement has been imposed upon the poet not to present these abstract patterns of virtue, or satanic incarnations of evil, but to follow Goethe's example and give us characters which are both good and bad. And why is this a legitimate demand? Because the poet is supposed to describe human beings as they *are,* and every human being is *both good and bad*; and because the medium of the poet is imagination, is *being* but not *becoming*, or at most becoming in a very much foreshortened perspective. But take the individual out of the medium of the imagination, the medium of being, and place him in existence: Ethics will at once demand that he be pleased to become, and then he becomes— either good or bad. In the serious moment of self-examination, and in the sacred moment of the confessional, the individual takes himself out of the medium of becoming, and inquires in the medium of being, how it is with him; and, alas! the unfortunate result of this inquiry is that he *is both* good and bad. But as soon as he again enters the medium of becoming he becomes either good or bad. This *summa summarum,* that all men *are* both good and bad, does not concern Ethics in the least. For Ethics does not have the medium of *being,* but the medium of *becoming,* and consequently rejects every explanation of becoming which deceptively explains becoming within being, whereby the absolute decision that is rooted in becoming is essentially revoked, and all talk about it rendered essentially nothing but a false alarm.

It is for the same reason that Ethics must also condemn the exultation so characteristic of our own age over having overcome reflection. Who is it that is supposed to have overcome reflection? An existing individual. But existence is precisely the sphere where reflection is at home; an existing individual is in existence, and hence in the sphere of reflection: how does he then manage to overcome it? That the principle of identity is in a certain sense higher, in that it is basic to the principle of contradiction, it is not difficult to see. But the principle of identity is merely the limit; it is like the blue mountains in the distance, or like the line which the artist calls his base line: the figure is what is important. The principle of identity therefore determines a lower point of view than the principle of contradiction, which is more concrete. Identity is the *terminus a quo,* but it is not a *terminus ad quem* for existence. An existing individual may arrive at identity as a maximum, and may repeatedly arrive at it, but only by abstracting from existence. But since Ethics regards every existing individual as its bond servant for life, it will absolutely and in every moment forbid him to begin upon such an abstraction. Instead of identity annulling the principle of contradiction, it is contradiction that annuls identity; or as Hegel so often says, lets it "go to the bottom."[6]

The principle of mediation proposes to make existence easier for the existing individual by leaving out the absolute relationship to the absolute *telos.* The exercise of the absolute distinction makes life absolutely strenuous, precisely when the individual remains in the finite and simultaneously maintains an absolute relationship to the absolute *telos* and a relative relationship to the relative. But in this strenuous exertion there is nevertheless a tranquillity and a peace; for absolutely, or with all one's strength, and with the renunciation of everything else, to maintain a relationship to the absolute *telos* is no contradiction, but is the absolute correspondence of like to like. The tortured self-contradiction of worldly passion arises from the attempt to sustain an *absolute*

relationship to a relative *telos*. Avarice, vanity, envy, and so forth, are
thus essentially forms of madness; for it is precisely the most general
expression for madness that the individual has an absolute relationship
to what is relative. From the aesthetic point of view this condition is to
be apprehended as comical, since the comical is always rooted in the
contradictory. It is madness, and from the aesthetic standpoint comical,
that a being whose nature is dedicated to the eternal, uses all his strength
to lay hold of the perishable, clinging to what is precarious; it is madness for such a being to believe that he has gained everything when he
has gained this nothing—and is deceived; or to believe that he has lost
everything when he has lost this nothing—and is no longer deceived.
For the perishable is nothing when it is past, and it is of its essence to
pass away, quickly as the moment of sensuous enjoyment, the farthest
possible remove from the eternal: a moment in time filled with
emptiness.

Here perhaps someone, some "sober man," will say: "But can I be
sure that there really is such a good; is the expectation of an eternal
happiness a matter of definite certainty? For in that case I shall as-
suredly strive to attain it, but otherwise I would be mad to risk everything for its sake." This or a similar turn of thought frequently makes
its appearance in the clergyman's discourse, and forms the transition
to that part of the speech in which for the solace and reassurance of the
congregation it is proved that there is an eternal happiness to look
forward to—in order that the members of the listening congregation
may strive all the more earnestly for its attainment. Such a demonstration is food for the hungry, and is taken as true like the word of God
by the theologue, "the practical exercises being postponed as usual."
How fortunate that I am not a serious man, an asseverating philosopher
or a guaranteeing clergyman, for then I, too, might be moved to attempt
a demonstration. Fortunately my frivolity excuses me; and in my
capacity as a frivolous man I venture to have the opinion that anyone
who resolves to strive for an eternal happiness on the ground of his faith
in the assurances of the philosophers and the guarantees of the clergy,
will nevertheless not really strive for it, and that what will prevent him
is precisely this confidence of his in the philosophers and the clergy;
though the clergyman believes, to be sure, that it is lack of confidence.
Such confidence merely inspires him with a desire to follow, to associate
himself with others, to make a business transaction on the basis of a
calculation, an advantageous speculation in the market instead of an

absolute venture. This confidence in the assurances inspires a fictitious movement of the spirit, a gesture in the direction of the absolute, while still remaining totally within the relative; a fictitious transition, like the transition from eudaemonism to the ethical within eudaemonism. In general it is quite inconceivable how ingenious and inventive human beings can be in evading an ultimate decision. Anyone who has seen the curious antics of recruits when they are ordered into the water will often have occasion to perceive analogies in the realm of the spirit.

The fact is that the individual becomes infinite only by virtue of making the absolute venture. Hence it is not the same individual who makes this venture among others, yielding as a consequence one more predicate attaching to one and the same individual. No, but in making the absolute venture he becomes another individual. Before he has made the venture he cannot understand it as anything else than madness; and this is far better than the thoughtless galimatias which imagines that it understands the venture as wisdom—and yet omits to venture, whereby the individual directly accuses himself of being mad, while one who regards the venture as madness at any rate consistently asserts his own sanity by refusing to commit himself. And after the individual has made the venture he is no longer the same individual. Thus there is made room for the transition and its decisiveness, an intervening yawning chasm, a suitable scene for the infinite passion of the individual, a gulf which the understanding cannot bridge either forward or backward.

But since I have in no way undertaken to prove that there is an eternal happiness (partly because it is not my affair, but at most that of Christianity which proclaims it; and partly because if it could be demonstrated it would be non-existent, since the existence of the absolute ethical good can be proved only by the individual himself expressing it existentially in existence), I shall take a little time to examine what our serious citizen said above; his words will doubtless be found worthy of consideration. He demands that it should be made definitely certain that such a good exists and awaits us. But it is really too much to ask that anything subject to expectation should be made definitely certain. The present is, for example, separated from the future by a little moment, the influence of which is that it becomes possible to expect the future, but impossible to have a sure certainty about it in the present. The present gives certainty and security to whatever is comprised within it, but a present relationship to something in the future is *eo ipso* an uncertain relationship, and hence quite properly a relationship of expectation. The speculative principle is that I arrive at the eternal retrogressively through recollection, and that the eternal individual is in this manner directly related to the eternal. But an existing individual can have a relationship to the eternal only as something prospective, as something in the future.

The serious man continues: If he were able to obtain certainty with respect to such a good, so as to know that it is really there, he would venture everything for its sake. The serious man speaks like a wag; it is clear enough that he wishes to make fools of us, like the raw recruit who takes a run in preparation for jumping into the water, and actually takes the run,—but gives the leap a go-by. When the certainty is there he will venture all. But what then does it mean to venture? A venture is the precise correlative of an uncertainty; when the certainty is there the venture becomes impossible. If our serious man acquires the definite certainty that he seeks, he will be unable to venture all; for even if he gives up everything, he will under such circumstances venture nothing—and if he does not get certainty, our serious man says in all earnest that he refuses to risk anything, since that would be madness. In this way the venture of our serious man becomes merely a false alarm. If what I hope to gain by venturing is itself certain, I do not risk or venture, but make an exchange. Thus in giving an apple for a pear, I run no risk if I hold the pear in my hand while making the exchange. Rogues and pickpockets have a very clear understanding of this; they do not trust one another, and hence wish to hold in their possession the articles they seek to acquire by making the exchange. Aye, they have so precise a notion of risk that they even regard it as risky to permit the other party to turn his back for a moment to expectorate, lest this should be a cover for some hocus-pocus or other. When I give all that I have for a pearl, it is not a venture if I hold the pearl in my hand at the moment of making the exchange. If it is a false pearl, and I have been cheated, it is a poor exchange; but I cannot be said to have risked anything to get possession of the pearl. But if the pearl is in a far country, in Africa for example, in a secret place difficult of access, if I have never had the pearl in my hand, and I leave home and kindred, give everything up, and undertake the long and toilsome journey without knowing for a certainty whether my enterprise will succeed: then I venture—and it will no doubt be remarked that same evening at the club, just as the serious man put it, that it is madness on my part so to risk everything.* But whatever strange adventures the seeker for the pearl may experience on the long and dangerous journey to Africa, I do not believe that anything stranger can happen to him than falls to the lot of the serious man and his statement; for of all his earnestness, only one truth remains, and that is that the enterprise is madness.† To be sure it is madness. It is always madness to venture, but to risk everything for the expectation of an eternal happiness is the height of madness. To ask for certainty is on the other hand prudence, for it is an excuse to evade the venture and its strenuosity, and to transfer the problem into the realm of knowledge and of prattle. No, if I am in truth resolved to venture, in truth resolved to strive for the attainment of the highest good, the uncertainty must be there, and I must have room to move, so to speak. But the largest space I can obtain, where there is room for the most vehement gesture of the passion that embraces the infinite, is uncertainty of knowledge with

* I take pleasure in illustrating the same point by a nobler example. The lover may in the period of courtship "venture" everything for his love, for the possession of the beloved; but the husband, who already is in possession of the beloved, does not venture for her, even when he endures everything with her, or submits himself to everything for her sake. It would be to offend his wife if the husband used in this connection the expression which is the mark of love's highest enthusiasm in the period of courtship. The husband has possession of his beloved; and if it were possible for his eternal happiness to be likewise a present possession of the individual, he could not be said to venture. But the difficulty is that an eternal happiness cannot be so completely present, even to the individual who has ventured everything, as long as he is in existence. And please note here another qualification: he must have ventured everything, since it was impossible for him to get certainty beforehand from an asseverating philosopher or a guaranteeing clergyman. For strange to say, although an eternal happiness is the highest good, far greater than kingdoms or landed estates, the giver asks absolutely no question regarding security from a third party, and the recipient could not be helped, even if he had all men as his guarantors; the matter is decided solely between the giver and the recipient alone by themselves. This is almost as mad, I had almost said, on the part of the giver, in not looking better to his own security and advantage, as of the recipient, who might readily become suspicious and take alarm, when he sees that he stands alone, having lost sight completely of all guarantors.

† All wisdom of life is abstraction, and only the most wretched eudaemonism has no abstraction, but is sheer enjoyment of the moment. In the degree to which a eudaemonistic philosophy of life is prudent it has some abstraction; the more prudence, the more abstraction. This fact gives the eudaemonist a superficial resemblance to the ethical and the ethico-religious, and it might seem for a moment as if the two views might meet. And yet it is not so, for the very first step taken by the ethical is an infinite abstraction, and what happens? The step becomes too long for the eudaemonist, and although some abstraction is prudence, an indefinite abstraction is madness to the eudaemonist.

Perhaps a philosopher will wish to say here that I move only within the sphere of reflection. On paper, to be sure, it is easier to put things together; one risks everything (on paper), and at the same instant one has everything. But if I risk everything in the medium of existence, this is by itself a lifelong task, and when I remain with my venture in existence, I shall repeatedly have to continue to venture. The honorable philosopher, as usual, transfers the scene from existence to paper.

respect to an eternal happiness, or the certain knowledge that the choice is in the finite sense a piece of madness: now there is room, now you can venture!

And this is why an eternal happiness as the absolute good has the remarkable trait of *being definable solely in terms of the mode of acquisition*. Other goods, precisely because the mode of acquisition is accidental, or at any rate subject to a relative dialectic, must be defined in terms of the good itself. Money, for example, may be acquired both with and without effort on the part of the possessor, and both modes of acquisition are again subject to manifold variations; but money, nevertheless, remains the same good. And knowledge is also variously obtainable, in relation to talent and external circumstances, and cannot therefore be defined solely in terms of the mode of acquisition. But there is nothing to be said of an eternal happiness except that it is the good which is attained by venturing everything absolutely. Every description of the glory of this good is already as it were an attempt to make several different modes of acquisition possible, one easier for example, and one more difficult. This is enough to prove that the description does not really describe the absolute good, but only imagines itself doing so, while essentially dealing with relative goods. Hence it is so easy, in a certain sense, to talk about this good; for it is certain—when everything else is made uncertain, and because the speaker will never, as is so often the case with relative goods, be embarrassed by the revelation that what helps one to gain it will not help another. This is why discourse concerning this good may be so brief, for there is only one thing to say: venture everything! There are no anecdotes to tell how Peter became rich by hard work, and Paul by playing the lottery, and Hans by inheriting a fortune, and Matts by the change in the value of the currency, and Christopher by purchasing a piece of furniture from a dealer, and so forth. But in another sense the discourse may be very long, the longest of all discourses, because really to venture everything requires a conscious clarity with respect to oneself which is acquired only slowly. Here is the task of the religious address. Were it merely to say the brief word: "Venture everything," there would not be needed more than one speaker in an entire kingdom, while the longest discourse must not forget the venture. The religious address may deal with anything and everything, if only it constantly brings everything into relationship with the absolute category of religiosity. It must explore every path, it must know where the errors lurk, where the moods have their hiding-places, how the passions understand themselves in solitude (and every man who has passion is always to some degree solitary, it is only the slobberers who wear their hearts wholly on their sleeves); it must know where the illusions spread their temptations, where the bypaths slink away, and so forth: all for the purpose of bringing everything into relationship with the absolute categories of religiosity.

If one human being can do anything toward helping another in this respect, he need not trouble to pass over to the treatment of China and Persia. For just as religious discourse is higher than all other discourse, so all truly religious discourse knows nothing of anything beyond the absolute good, an eternal happiness. It knows that the task is not to begin with the individual and arrive at the race, but to begin with the individual and through the race arrive at the individual again. The religious address is the way to the good, i.e. it reflects the way, which is as long as life.* It reflects the way which the religious man describes, though not in the sense in which the planet describes its path or the mathematician a circle. But there is no short cut to the absolute good, and since this good can be described only by reference to the mode of acquisition, the absolute difficulty of the acquirement is the only mark by which the individual's relationship to the absolute good can be known. For anyone to stumble upon this good in some easier manner (as by being born under favorable circumstances, in the nineteenth century for example; or through being endowed with exceptional brain power, or through being the childhood playmate of a great man, or the brother-in-law of an Apostle), so as to be a favorite of fortune with respect to it, is merely evidence that the individual is deceived; for favorites of fortune do not belong in the religious sphere. The religious address has its merit in making the way difficult; for it is the way that is decisive of the relationship, otherwise we have aestheticism. But Christianity has made the way as difficult as it is possible to make it, and it is only an illusion by which many have been blinded, that Christianity has made the way easy. It has helped men solely by confronting them with a beginning that makes everything far more difficult than it was before. If a pagan has been able merely to catch a glimpse of the

* Here again we see why the religious speaker must not use a shortened perspective. Aesthetically there is no way, because the aesthetic corresponds to immediacy, and the expression for this is a foreshortened perspective. Ethically and ethico-religiously, however, reflection is concentrated precisely on the way, and hence it follows that what is true aesthetically becomes a deception from the ethical and the ethico-religious point of view.

absolute good, Christianity has helped men to a vision of it—by means of the absurd. When this last qualification is omitted, everything has indeed become much easier than it was in paganism. But if the point is held fast, everything is far more difficult; for it is easier to cling to a weak hope *in one's own strength,* than to acquire certainty by virtue of the absurd. When an aesthetic sufferer bemoans his fate and seeks solace in the ethical, the ethical really has solace for him, but first it makes him suffer more than he did before. When this consideration is omitted the ethical makes everything much too comfortable and easy; but in that case the ethical has also been taken in vain. If an aesthetic sufferer feels his pain ever so keenly, he may very well come to suffer more; when he sends for the ethical it first helps him from the frying-pan into the fire, so that he gets something to complain about in real earnest—and then only does it give him help. So it is also with Christianity. It requires that the individual should existentially venture all (the pathetic). This is something that a pagan can also do; he may, for example, venture everything on an immortality's perhaps. But Christianity also requires that the individual risk his thought, venturing to believe against the understanding (the dialectical). And while our serious man never arrived at the point of venturing because he demanded certainty, one thing is here certain, and that is that this is the absolute venture and the absolute risk. It may seem strenuous enough to struggle through life on the basis of the mere possibility of immortality, and to obtain a proof of the resurrection seems by comparison a tremendous help—if it were not for the fact that the very existence of this proof constitutes the greatest difficulty of all. To obtain everything by means of a mediator might seem easy in comparison with paganism, where the greatest exertion of the wise brought him but little gain; but now suppose that the very existence of a mediator constituted the very greatest difficulty of all! It seems comfortable enough to get everything by means of a gospel, were it not for the fact that the very existence of a gospel constituted the greatest difficulty. With God's help to be able to do everything, is also a comfortable privilege, were it not that being unable to do anything of oneself is the greatest of difficulties, so difficult that there are doubtless not many in each generation who can truthfully testify that they succeed even moderately in becoming conscious, day in and day out, that a human being can do nothing of himself.

But if we overlook the dialectical factor, what happens? Why then the whole affair becomes mere prattle and old wives' bawling; for Jews and women, as we all know, can bawl out more in a single minute than a man can accomplish in an entire lifetime. If we overleap the dialectical, the resurrection proof becomes, ironically enough, much too demonstrative, and the certainty for immortality even less than in paganism. The mediator becomes an ambiguous character, an aesthetically pompous figure with a glory nimbus and a wishing cup; the gospel becomes rumor, a little town gossip; and the individual who can do all things with God becomes a man who can do quite a little himself, and is polite enough to pretend that God helps him, living on a far lower plane than the individual who even moderately well exercises himself in the strenuous consciousness that he can do nothing. If we overleap the dialectical, Christianity as a whole becomes a comfortable delusion, a superstition, and a superstition of the most dangerous kind, because it is overbelief in the truth, if Christianity be the truth. A superstitious belief which embraces an error keeps the possibility open that the truth may come to arouse it; but when the truth is there, and the superstitious mode of apprehending it transforms it into a lie, no saving awakening is possible.

No, the help in solving the problem of life which Christianity has brought to the individual is marked by only one distinguishing feature, namely, the difficulty which it has introduced. It is in this fashion that its yoke is easy and its burden light—for him who has thrown all burdens away, those of hope, of fear, of despondency, and of despair; but this is a very difficult thing to do. And the difficulty again is absolute, not subject to a comparative dialectic (as if easier for one human being than for another); the difficulty is proportioned absolutely to each individual separately, absolutely requiring his absolute exertion, but no more. For just as there are no favorites of fortune in the religious sphere, or any lottery distributions, so there are also no individuals unjustly dealt with.

§ 2. THE "ESSENTIAL" EXPRESSION FOR EXISTENTIAL PATHOS: SUFFERING—FORTUNE
AND MISFORTUNE AS THE EXPRESSION FOR AN AESTHETIC VIEW OF LIFE, IN CONTRA-
DISTINCTION TO SUFFERING AS THE EXPRESSION OF A RELIGIOUS VIEW OF LIFE
(ILLUSTRATED BY REFERENCE TO THE RELIGIOUS DISCOURSE)—THE REALITY OF THE
SUFFERING (HUMOR)—THE REALITY OF THE SUFFERING IN THE LAST INSTANCE AS
EVIDENCE FOR THE POSSESSION BY THE EXISTING INDIVIDUAL OF A RELATIONSHIP TO
AN ETERNAL HAPPINESS—THE ILLUSION OF RELIGIOSITY[1]—THE CATEGORY OF
"ANFECHTUNG"—THE PRIMARY GROUND AND SIGNIFICANCE OF THE RELIGIOUS SUF-
FERING: THE DYING AWAY FROM THE LIFE OF IMMEDIACY WHILE STILL REMAINING
IN THE FINITE—AN EDIFYING "DIVERTISSEMENT"—HUMOR AS AN INCOGNITO FOR
RELIGIOSITY

From the preceding it must here be recalled that existential pathos
is action, the reconstruction of the individual's mode of existence. The
task was posited as consisting in the simultaneous maintenance of an
absolute relationship to the absolute *telos*, and a relative relationship
to relative ends. But this task must now be understood more closely in
its concrete difficulty, lest the category of existential pathos be revoked
by being brought within the sphere of aesthetic pathos, as if it were
existential pathos merely to *say* this once for all, or to repeat it once a
month with unchanged immediate passion. If everything were to be
decided on paper, one would at once begin upon the ideal task, but
in existence the beginning must be made by exercising oneself in the
relationship to the absolute *telos,* and by taking the power away from
immediacy. On paper the individual is an abstract entity, a facile some-
thing-or-other, instantly at beck and call. But the actual individual is
fast in the immediate, and is in so far really absolutely committed to
relative ends. Now the individual begins, not indeed by relating himself at one and the same time absolutely to the absolute *telos* and relatively to relative ends, since through being fast in the immediate he is
in precisely the opposite situation; but he begins by exercising himself
in the absolute relationship through renunciation. The task is ideal,
and has perhaps never been completely realized by anyone, for it is
only on paper that one begins without further ado, and has at once
completed the task. In order that the individual may sustain an absolute
relationship to the absolute *telos* he must first have exercised himself
in the renunciation of relative ends, and only then can there be a
question of the ideal task: the simultaneous maintenance of an absolute
relationship to the absolute, and a relative relationship to the relative.
But not before, for before this the individual is always to some degree

immediate, and in so far is involved absolutely in relative ends. And even when the individual has brought his immediacy into subjection, with his victory he is still in existence, and thereby again prevented from expressing absolutely the absolute relationship to an absolute *telos*. Aesthetic pathos keeps itself at a distance from existence, or is in existence in a state of illusion; while existential pathos dedicates itself more and more profoundly to the task of existing, and with the consciousness of what existence is, penetrates all illusions, becoming more and more concrete through reconstructing existence in action.

Now action might seem to be the precise opposite of suffering and in so far it may seem strange to say that the essential expression for existential pathos, which is the pathos of action, should be suffering. However, this is only apparently the case, and it becomes evident here again, as the constant criterion of the religious sphere, that the positive is the index of the negative* (in contradistinction to the simple directness of the immediate,† and the relative directness of the reflective): the distinguishing mark of religious action is suffering. The ambiguity consists in the fact that action may also be taken to mean outward activity. This may be quite valid as an interpretation of what action is, but such interpretation also signifies and implies that the question does not concern action in the religious sphere, but in another. Action outwardly directed may indeed transform existence (as when an emperor conquers the world and enslaves the peoples), but not the individual's own existence; and action outwardly directed may transform the individual's own existence (as when from having been a lieutenant he becomes an emperor, or from street peddler becomes a millionaire, or whatever else of the sort may fall to his lot), but not the individual's inner existence. All such action is therefore only aesthetic pathos, and its law is the law for aesthetic relationships in general; the non-dialectical individual transforms the world, but remains himself untransformed, for the aesthetic individual never has the dialectical within him but outside him, or the individual is outwardly changed, but remains in-

---

* The reader will remember: A revelation is signalized by mystery, happiness by suffering, the certainty of faith by uncertainty, the ease of the paradoxical-religious life by its difficulty, the truth by absurdity. Unless this is held fast, the aesthetic and the religious will be mixed up together to the confusion of both.

† The existential sphere of paganism is essentially the aesthetic, and hence it is quite in order for the pagan consciousness to be reflected in that conception of God which holds that He, Himself unchanged, changes all. This is the expression for outwardly directed action. The religious lies in the dialectic which governs intensification of inwardness, and hence it is sympathetic with the conception of God that He is Himself moved, changed.

wardly unchanged. The scene is external to the individual, and even the introduction of Christianity into a country may involve merely an aesthetic relationship, unless it is by an Apostle, whose existence is paradoxically dialectical; but otherwise it holds true that unless the individual is changed and steadily continues to change in himself, his introduction of Christianity is no more a religious act that any ordinary act of conquest. But essential existential pathos is essentially related to existence; and to exist essentially is inwardness, and action in inwardness is suffering, for the individual cannot make himself over, any such attempt becoming, like imitation, a mere affectation, and it is for this reason that suffering is the highest action in inwardness. And how difficult this enterprise is will be understood even by one who has merely a small share of the impatience of immediacy, which wants out, not in; to say nothing of one whose mind is almost wholly oriented outward—unless he has in that manner become entirely innocent of any knowledge that there is such a thing as inwardness.

Immediacy is fortune, for in the immediate consciousness there is no contradiction; the immediate individual is essentially seen as a fortunate individual, and *the view of life natural to immediacy* is one based on fortune. If one were to ask the immediate individual whence he has this view of life he would have to answer with virginal naïveté, "I do not myself understand it." The contradiction comes from without, and takes the form of misfortune. The immediate individual never comes to any understanding with misfortune, for he never becomes dialectical in himself; and if he does not manage to get rid of it, he finally reveals himself as lacking the poise to bear it. That is, he despairs, because he cannot grasp misfortune. Misfortune is like a narrow pass on the way; now the immediate individual is in it, but his view of life must essentially always tell him that the difficulty will soon cease to hinder, because it is a foreign element. If it does not cease, he despairs, by which his immediacy ceases to function, and the transition to another understanding of misfortune is rendered possible, that is, his despair may lead him to a comprehension of the suffering, and an understanding of it that grasps not only this or that misfortune, but essentially arrives at an understanding of the rôle of suffering in life.

Fortune, misfortune, fate, immediate enthusiasm, despair—these are the categories at the disposal of an aesthetic view of life. Misfortune is a happening in relation to the immediate consciousness (fate); viewed ideally, in the light of the view of life natural to immediacy, it is gone or it must go. This the poet expresses by investing immediacy with an ideality such as is never found in the finite world. Here the poet uses fortune. On the other side the poet, who must always operate within the compass of immediacy, causes the individual to be laid low by misfortune. This is the significance, understood quite generally, of the death of hero or heroine. But to comprehend misfortune, to come to an understanding with it, to turn everything upside down and to make suffering the point of departure for a view of life, is something that the poet cannot do; he ought not even to make a move in that direction, for then he is merely a bungler.

The inwardness that is the core of the ethical and ethico-religious individual understands suffering on the other hand as something essential. While the immediate individual involuntarily abstracts from misfortune, and fails to know that it is there as soon as it does not outwardly manifest itself, the religious individual has suffering constantly with him. He requires suffering* in the same sense that the immediate individual requires fortune, and he requires and has suffering even in the absence of external misfortune; for it is not misfortune that he requires, in which case the relationship would be aesthetic, and he would remain essentially undialectical in himself.

More seldom perhaps than a perfectly executed work of the poetic imagination does one see or hear a correct religious discourse, one which is clearly conscious of the categories that are to be used, and of how they are to be used. But just as sometimes in a poetic work one may come upon a remark made by a particular person which is so reflected that the person who utters it is thereby reflected out of the entire compass of the poetic, so also the religious discourse is often enough a sad hodge-podge of a little from every sphere. But, naturally, to be a poet one needs a call,—to become a religious speaker, one needs only to pass three examinations—when one is sure to receive a call.

* It is therefore an entirely correct religious collision, but at the same time a somewhat noteworthy aesthetic misunderstanding of the religious, when (for example in the Mohammedan Biblical legends published by Weil) the religious individual prays that he may be tried by great sufferings like those of Abraham, or some other of God's elect. Such a prayer is a bubbling over of the religious consciousness, in the same sense as an Aladdin's enthusiasm and a young woman's overweening happiness is a bubbling over of the immediate consciousness. The misunderstanding consists in the fact that the religious individual nevertheless views the suffering as coming from without, and hence aesthetically. In the stories cited it usually turns out that the religious individual proves too weak to be able to endure the suffering until the end. However, this does not explain anything, and such a result again marks a somewhat noteworthy consciousness lying on the borderline between the aesthetic and the religious.

The religious address need not, of course, always speak about suffering, but in whatsoever it may say, however it tumbles about, along whatever way it goes out to catch men, however it may testify in monologues to the speaker's own existence, it must always have its total category at hand as a standard of measurement, so that the experienced listener perceives at once the total orientation in the view of life that the discourse represents. The religious address may speak about everything, if only it always has its absolute standard directly or indirectly present. Just as it is confusing to be made to learn* geography from nothing but special maps of the different countries, never having seen on a terrestrial globe how the various countries are related to one another, so that it looks deceptively as if Denmark, for example, were as large as Germany, so also do the particularities of the religious discourse produce confusion, if the total category is not everywhere present to provide orientation, even though its presence be perhaps only indirect.

The religious address has essentially the task of *uplifting through suffering*. Just as immediacy pins its faith to fortune, so the religious man believes that it is precisely in suffering that life is to be found. Resolutely and vigorously, therefore, the religious address sets out upon the deep. As soon as the religious address squints in the direction of fortune, as soon as it seeks to give comfort by recourse to probabilities, as soon as it seeks to strengthen by means that fall short of a radical remedy, then it is false doctrine, constitutes a regress to the realm of the aesthetic, and is therefore a bungling patchwork. Poesy is for the immediate consciousness the explanation and glorification of life, but for the religious consciousness it is a beautiful and amiable jest, whose consolation religiosity nevertheless spurns, because the religious comes to life precisely in suffering. Immediacy expires in suffering; in suffering, religiosity begins to breathe. It is necessary always to hold the different spheres apart by the use of the qualitative dialectic, sharply distinguishing them lest everything come to be all of a piece, the poet becoming a bungler when he wants to take a little of the religious with him, and the religious speaker becoming a deceiver who delays and obstructs his listener by wishing to dabble a

---

* But if one assumes, as I am quite willing to admit is the case with many a religious discourse, that it is more difficult to be an auditor of such a discourse than to be the speaker, then the religious address is indeed made ironically superfluous, and serviceable only as a purifying fire in which the individual trains himself to become capable of being edified in the house of God by everything.

little in the aesthetic. As soon as the religious address divides men into the fortunate and the unfortunate, it *ipso facto* botches its job, for viewed religiously all men are sufferers, and the problem is to share fully in the suffering (not by plunging oneself into it, but by discovering that it is there), and not to get away from misfortune. Viewed religiously, the happy man to whom the entire world accommodates itself, is fully as much a sufferer if he is religious, as one upon whom misfortune externally falls. Viewed religiously, the distinction between the fortunate and the unfortunate may indeed be used, but only jestingly and ironically, so as to encourage the individual to enter into the suffering, and then from that point on to determine the religious.

But the religious discourse as one hears it nowadays is seldom correct in its categories. The much revered orator forgets that religiosity is inwardness, that inwardness is the relationship of the individual to himself before God, his reflection into himself, and that it is precisely from this that the suffering derives, this being also the ground of its essential pertinence to the religious life, so that the absence of it signifies the absence of religiosity. The speaker apprehends the individual as standing in a relation to an outer world, a greater or lesser environment; and now he dishes up something about fortune and misfortune, saying that the unfortunate individual must not lose his courage, since there are many who are still more unfortunate than he, and besides there is every probability that things will with God's help become better,* and finally it is through hardships that a man gets to be something: would Alderman Madsen ever have become an alderman if it had not been because, and so forth! And such talk pleases people, for it is tantamount to preaching indulgence in the name of religion from the task of religion—remission from the enthusiasm of religiosity in suffering.

When the religious orator forgets that his scene is inwardness and the individual's relation to himself, he has essentially the same task as the poet; and in that case it would be better for him to keep silent, for the poet can do it better. When the religious speaker refers in the above manner to misfortune, it is not only a scandal from the religious standpoint (because, namely, he pretends to be a religious speaker), but

* A great many people assume almost as a matter of course that when the name of God is mentioned in a discourse, it is a godly discourse. In that manner, cursing would become godly speech, if God's name is used. No, an aesthetic view of life, even if interlarded with both the name of God and of Christ, remains an aesthetic view of life; and when it is expounded the discourse is aesthetic, not religious.

he brings upon himself the satirical nemesis that it follows from what he says that there are favorites of fortune who do not suffer at all—which is religiously the most dubious of consequences. The invitation to a religious discourse is quite simply as follows: "Come hither all ye who labor and are heavy laden"—and the discourse presupposes that all are sufferers, aye, that all ought to be. The speaker is not to go down among his audience and pick out one, if there be such an one, and say to him: "No, you are altogether too fortunate to need my address," for when such a thing is heard from the mouth of a religious speaker it ought to be made to sound like the most biting irony. The distinction between fortunate and unfortunate human beings is merely a jest, and therefore the speaker should say: "We are all sufferers, but what we strive for is to be glad in the midst of suffering; there sits the fortunate man for whom everything, literally everything, succeeds as in a fairy tale, but woe unto him if he is not a sufferer." But the religious discourse is seldom oriented in this fashion; at most it is only when it reaches *thirdly* that the really religious view is expounded; that is, after having for two-thirds of the discourse tried every possible excuse to avoid having recourse to the religious, and having left the religious auditor in doubt as to whether he was invited to dance with the poet or to be edified with the parson. In that manner it is readily made to appear that the religious, instead of being equal for all men, and equal for all men through the equality of the equal suffering, which constitutes the victory of the religious over this jest about fortune and misfortune, is rather something only adapted to the exceptionally unfortunate—a glorious honor for the religious, to be admitted as a wretched subdivision under one section of the aesthetic! Certainly it is true that the religious is the last consolation in life, but there is one wretchedness greater still than that of being the unhappiest of all in the poetic sense of the term, and that is to be so extraordinarily fortunate as not even to have an inkling of the suffering which is the very element of the religious life.

Generally, the clergyman doubtless thinks that such extraordinarily fortunate individuals exist only in romantic tales, but that in life itself misfortune soon catches up with most people, so that the clergyman again gets them under treatment. This may perhaps be so, but the clergyman should have sufficient confidence in the religious not to thrust it upon people in this manner. He ought to indulge in carefree jesting about the case of a man being as fortunate as any hero of a romantic tale, and yet be convinced that suffering is an essential ingredient in the true life. He ought to be strict in hitting at every individual who wishes merely to grieve over misfortune, and who refuses to listen to any other consolation than the probability that the misfortune will cease to trouble, for such a man desires really to evade the religious. Just as Lafontaine[2] sat weeping and made his heroes unhappy throughout three volumes (quite a proper task for a poet), so the religious speaker will find his enjoyment, if I dare speak in this manner, in making his heroes as fortunate as they wish, making them kings and emperors and happy lovers who win the object of their affection, and millionaires, and so forth—but at the same time making sure to provide them with suffering in inwardness. For the more fortunate and favorable the outer circumstances, while there still is suffering, the clearer it becomes that this suffering is a matter of inwardness; and the more clearly will the religious stand out as of prime quality, in contradistinction to the clergyman's *mélange*.

When the religious view of life is maintained in terms of its own proper category, the religious orator should have religious elevation enough to be able to dispose of the entire compass of the poetic sphere in a spirit of comedy. Take an individual with a wish. When he goes to the poet the latter sees at once that he is usable in two ways, either in the direction of the fortunate by means of the magic of the wish, or in the direction of misfortune to the verge of despair. The poetic task is to gain imaginative expansion in fantasy, whether he makes him happy or unhappy; there must be no bungling patchwork. But let the same individual go to the clergyman, and he will in religious elevation transform the whole into a jest; in enthusiastic religious conviction of the significance of suffering for the highest life he will teach him to smile at the hot craving of his wish, and teach him to lift himself above the pain of the frustration—by proclaiming greater sufferings. For when it comes to a crisis, and the carriage sticks fast and cannot be moved, or threatens to turn over in the ruts, the driver will use the whip, not from cruelty, but convinced that it will help the horses, and only mollycoddles hesitate to strike. But no bungling!

The religious address asserts for itself the freedom to take this matter of being human quite simply and directly, pretty much like death, which also deals with men as men, whether they are emperors or justices or street-corner loafers, whether they are extraordinarily fortunate and marked by fortune with signs and symbols of distinction, or their situation is greatly unfortunate, and marked middling with question marks. If the clergyman cannot make the wishing individual religious, or rather, if it is not this that he aims at, then the clergyman is only a quack, and the thing to do is to let the poet rule, and either become fortunate or plunge into despair. For the proportions ought to be such that if the poet's discourse is ravishing, so that it makes maidens and youths glow with enthusiasm, then the enthusiasm of the religious discourse should be such as to make the poet grow pale with envy in the thought that there is such an enthusiasm, where it does not inspire to be a favorite of fortune or to cut loose in the bold reckless-ness of despair, no, but where it inspires to suffer. But worldly ration-ality will say that poesy is the hypertension of a maiden's consciousness, religiosity the fury of a man's. But the religious orator will not there-fore need to use violent words, since he will most surely show his superiority by the imperturbability with which he holds the impreg-nable position of the religious; for the religious does not strive with the aesthetic as with an equal, it does not strive with it at all, but has over-come it as a jest.

Just as the poet is known by his power to wrestle pathetically with the imaginative passion of the infinite in happiness and despair, and comically and wantonly to take all finite passions and the whole Philis-tine world by the nose, so also is the religious speaker known by his power to wrestle pathetically with the enthusiasm of suffering, and jestingly to look in upon the imaginative passion of the infinite. And just as the poet is a benevolent spirit who is instantly prepared to serve the fortunate in the enchanted realms of illusion, or a sympathetic spirit who is instantly prepared to serve the unfortunate again benevolently, by being to the despairing individual his voice and gesture, so will the religious orator, over against the imaginative passion of the infinite, be either as contrary and strict and annoying as the day is in the living-room, and the night is on the bed of sickness, and the week is amidst the cares of life—lest it should appear easier in church than in the living-room. Or he will be still more ready than the poet to make everyone as fortunate as can be desired, but ironically, please mark, in order to show that this happiness is an irrelevance and likewise the misfortune, but that suffering is an essential ingredient of the highest life.

When Juliet sinks in impotence because she has lost Romeo, when her immediacy has breathed its last, and she has lost Romeo so that even Romeo could no longer comfort her, because the possession itself would only be a sad daily reminder; and when the last friend, all unhappy lovers' last friend, the poet, is silent—then the religious orator will dare to break this silence. But perhaps for the purpose of presenting a little assortment of excellent consolations? Then indeed would the insulted Juliet turn to the poet, and the latter would by assigning with victorious aesthetic authority his reverence a place in the low comic* parts of the tragedy, defend that which in all eternity rightly belongs to the poet: the lovable, the despairing Juliet. No, the religious orator will dare to proclaim new suffering, still more fearful, and this will cause Juliet to rise again. Or when the despairing individual, at once, merely when a human being approaches him, condemns him with a proud glance as a traitor, that is, as one who wishes to console him; when the wrathful aspect of his visage sets the punishment of death upon anyone who dares to bring comfort, so that the whole collectivity of comforters and reasons for comfort run together in farcical terror, just as milk curdles before a thunderstorm, then the religious orator will understand how to make himself heard, by speaking of a suffering and a danger still more fearful.

Above all, the religious address must never use the foreshortened perspective, which corresponds as a fictitious ethical movement to the aesthetic. Aesthetically this perspective is the enchantment of illusion, and is alone correct, since poesy is relative to a contemplative individual. But the religious address ought to relate itself to an acting individual, one who when he comes home, has to work out a corresponding course of action. If then the religious address uses this foreshortened perspective, there results the woeful confusion that the task comes to seem much easier in church than at home, and then one is only harmed by going to church. Hence the speaker ought to spurn the foreshortened

* As soon as a clergyman is unsure in relation to his religious category, but confuses himself with poetic echoes bound in wordly experience, the poet is naturally greater than his superior. Anyone who understands how to calculate the relationships among the categories will readily perceive that precisely such a cure of souls would furnish pretty nearly one of the most normal of *motifs* for a comic figure in a tragedy. An ordinary man who represents the same balderdash, whose secret is that it has lost sight of the poetic point, a barber's apprentice, for example, or an undertaker, would naturally also be comical, but not so radically comic as a clergyman, whose name and black gown make pretension to the highest pathos. To use a clergyman pathetically in a tragedy is a misunderstanding, for if he represents essentially what he essentially is, the whole tragedy is broken up, and if he does not represent it essentially, he must *eo ipso* be apprehended as a comic figure. One sees often enough hypocritical and malicious monks in tragedies; I believe that such a spiritual-secular slobberer in full canonicals would be closer to the realities of our time.

perspective as a deception natural to youth—lest the individual tested in the living-room at home be compelled to reject the speaker's exposition as immaturity. When a poet uses it, and the observer sits at ease, immersed in contemplation, then it is glorious, enchanting; but when a religious speaker uses it, and the auditor is an acting individual in motion, then he merely helps him run his head against the parlor door. The religious speaker operates conversely by means of the lack of any ending, that there is no result, precisely because suffering essentially belongs to the religious life.

Hence, while people are often enough inclined foolishly to be occupied with the question of whether the clergyman really does what he himself says, it is my opinion that one should renounce and repress every presumptuous attempt at criticism in that direction. But one thing can and should be required of the speaker, namely, that his exposition be such that it is *possible* to act in accordance with it, lest the real auditor be made a fool of—precisely when he tries to do what the clergyman says, because, namely, the clergical rigmarole is nothing but hot air; either because the clergyman is occupied with magnificent world-historical visions and a matchless falcon's insight, according to which it is impossible to act; or he speaks aesthetically in riddles, according to which it is also impossible to act; or he describes imaginary psychological states, which the individual seeks for vainly in reality; or brings consolation by an appeal to illusion, which the acting individual does not find in reality; or evokes passions such as, at most, they might appear to one who does not have them; or overcomes dangers that are not to be found, leaving the real danger untouched upon; overcomes them by means of theatrical energies not found in life, leaving the energies of real life unutilized; in short he plays trumps aesthetically, speculatively, world-historically; and religiously he revokes.

But suffering as the essential expression for existential pathos means that suffering is real, or that the reality of the suffering constitutes the existential pathos; and by *the reality of the suffering is meant its persistence as essential for the pathetic relationship to an external happiness.* It follows that the suffering is not deceptively recalled, nor does the individual transcend it, which constitutes a retreat from the task, gained by managing in one way or another to get the scene shifted from existence to a fantastic medium. Just as resignation looks to see that the individual has an absolute direction toward the absolute *telos,* so does the persistence of the suffering guarantee that the individual remains in the correct position and preserves himself in it. The immediate individual cannot grasp misfortune, he is merely aware of its presence; the misfortune is thus stronger than he, and this relationship between them is immediacy's imaginative passion in despair. By means of the foreshortened perspective the poet presents this quite properly in the medium of the imagination, as if now all were lost. In existence it appears otherwise, and here the immediate individual often makes himself ridiculous by a womanish shrieking in the moment, which is forgotten the next moment. When thus the immediate in the existing individual has received a hurt, a little crippling blow, one must find some way out, since the scene is not in the medium of the imagination. Thus arises the entire company of experienced and rational helpers, of old-clothes menders and tinkers, who by means of probabilities and consolations rivet the pieces together or hold the patches on. Life proceeds; counsel is sought from the wise men of the spiritual or the worldly order, and the whole becomes botchwork; the individual renounces the poetic without grasping the religious.

Viewed religiously, it is necessary, as was said above, to comprehend the suffering and to remain in it, so that reflection is directed *upon* the suffering and not *away* from it. Thus while a poetic production lies in the sphere of the imagination, the existence of the poet himself may sometimes exemplify a mode of life that lies upon the boundary of the religious, though qualitatively different. A poet is often a sufferer in existence, but what we reflect upon is the poetic productivity which is thereby brought about. The existing poet who suffers in his existence does not really comprehend his suffering, he does not penetrate more and more deeply into it, but in his suffering he seeks away from the suffering and finds ease in poetic production, in the poetic anticipation of a more perfect, i.e. a happier, order of things. It is thus also possible that an actor, especially a comedian, may be a sufferer in existence; but he does not consciously penetrate his suffering, he seeks away from it, and finds an amelioration in the interchange of personalities which his art promotes. But back from the enchantment of the poetic productivity and the wishful imaginative order of things, back from the identification with the poetic character, the poet and the actor turn to the suffering of reality, which they cannot comprehend, because they have their lives in the aesthetic dialectic between fortune and misfortune. The poet can explain (transfigure) the whole of existence, but he cannot explain himself, because he will not become religious and so understand the secret of suffering as the form of the highest life, higher than all fortune and different from all misfortune. For herein lies the severity of the religious consciousness, that it begins by making everything more strict, and that it is not related to poesy as merely a new wishful invention, an entirely novel way of escape that poesy has not dreamed of, but as a difficulty which creates men in the same sense that war creates heroes.

The reality of the suffering is therefore not identical with the truth of its expression, although the real sufferer will always express himself truly. But it is not here a question of expression, because discourse itself, language being a more abstract medium than existence, is always to some extent abbreviated. Thus, if I represented to myself a poet-existence in its last agony, suffering both bodily and mental pain, and imagined that there were found among his papers the following expressions: "As the sick man longs to cast aside his bandages, so my sound spirit longs to cast aside the feebleness of the body; as the victorious general, when his horse is shot from under him, cries for a new horse, O that my spirit's victorious health might cry for a new body, for only the body is worn out; as one who in peril of his life in the waves thrusts away with the energy of despair another drowning person who seeks to cling to him, so my body clings fast to my spirit like a heavy weight, to drag it down to its death; like a steamship in a storm, when its machinery is too powerful for the strength of its hull—so I suffer"; in such a case one could not very well deny the truth of the expression nor the fearfulness of the suffering, but one might very well wish to deny its pathetic reality. "How so," someone will ask "is not this fearful suffering real?" No, for the existing individual apprehends it after all as something accidental to him; just as he wishes to cast his body aside, so he also wishes to cast aside his suffering as accidental, and the reality of the suffering as it is for the religious individual, would be for him a hard doctrine.

The reality of the suffering signifies its essential persistence, and is its essential relation to the religious life. Aesthetically, suffering stands in an accidental relation to existence. Such accidental suffering may indeed persist, but the persistence of that which is in itself accidental is not an essential persistence. As soon therefore as the religious orator makes use of the foreshortened perspective, whether he concentrates all the suffering in a single moment, or paints a cheerful picture of better times in prospect, he goes back to the aesthetic realm, and his interpretation of suffering becomes a fictitious religious movement. When the Scriptures say that God dwells in a contrite heart, this does not represent a transitory or momentary relationship (in that case the use of the world "dwell" would be extremely unfortunate), but expresses on the contrary the essential significance of suffering for the God-relationship. But if the religious orator is not at home and tried and tested in the religious sphere, he will understand this word as follows: From without there comes a misfortune which crushes the spirit of the individual, and then the God-relationship takes its beginning, and then, aye, then, gradually the religious man becomes happy again—stop there a moment, does he become happy by means of the God-relationship? For if so he will also find that his suffering persists. Or does he perhaps become happy through inheriting a fortune from a rich uncle, or by getting himself a new sweetheart, or with the help of the subscription which his reverence benevolently started for him in the newspaper? In that case the discourse backslides,* although it is sometimes in this last part that the speaker becomes most eloquent and gesticulates most violently, presumably because the religious category does not quite suit the taste, but it seems easier to botch the rôle of the poet.

* Thus, too, there is backsliding in the religious discourse when a man says for example: "After many errors I finally learned to keep close to God, and since that time He has not left me in the lurch; my business flourishes, my projects have success, I am now happily married, and my children are well and strong, etc." The religious man has here again fallen back into the aesthetic dialectic, for even if it pleases him to say that he thanks God for all these blessings, the question is how he thanks Him, whether he does it directly, or whether he first executes the movement of incertitude which is the mark of the God-relationship. Just as little as a man has the right in the midst of misfortune to say to God directly that it is misfortune, since he has to suspend his understanding in the movement of incertitude, so little dare he directly take all these things as evidence of the God-relationship. The direct relationship is an aesthetic one, and indicates that he is not in his thanksgiving related to God, but to his own ideas of fortune and misfortune. For if a human being cannot know with certainty whether a misfortune is an evil (the uncertainty inherent in the God-relationship as the form for always giving thanks to God), then he cannot know with certainty whether his good fortune is a good. The God-relationship has only one testimony, the God-relationship itself, everything else is ambiguous; religiously it holds true for every human being, even if he lived to ever so advanced an age, that in relation to the dialectic of external goods, we are born yesterday and know nothing. Thus the great actor Sydelmann[3] (as I see from his biography by Rotschel) on the evening of his triumph in the Opera House, where he was crowned with a laurel wreath amid applause lasting several minutes, when he came home, passionately gave thanks to God. With the same passion with which he gave thanks he would have rebelled against God if he had been hissed off the stage. Had he given thanks religiously, and hence given thanks to God, the Berlin public and the laurel wreath and the applause lasting several minutes would have become ambiguous in the dialectical uncertainty of the religious.

To botch, yes, to botch; for the worldly wisdom which such a cure of souls adds to the poetic, is precisely an offense to poesy, a nauseous and insulting attempt to treat Juliet as if she were not dead but only in a trance. For whoever after having been dead awakens to the same life was merely in a trance, and Catherine (her name is not Juliet; instead of the lovely figure of the poet there has come, as we say to the children, a peasant maid) will prove it by getting herself a new sweetheart. But whoever being dead awakens to life in a new sphere, was and is and remains truly dead. No, it is a glorious notion on the part of poesy to let Juliet die, but the worldly wisdom aforesaid is as nauseating to religiosity as it is an offense to poesy. The religious discourse honors Juliet by treating her as dead, and seeks to achieve a result verging on the miraculous by bidding her waken to a new life in a new sphere. And the religious is a new life, while the clerical prattle aforesaid has neither the aesthetic high-mindedness to slay Juliet,* nor the enthusiasm of suffering which believes in a new life.

The reality of the suffering thus means its essential persistence as essential to the religious life, while aesthetically viewed, suffering stands in an accidental relation to existence, it may indeed be there but it may also cease, while viewed religiously the cessation of suffering is also the cessation of the religious life. Since an existing humorist presents the closest approximation to the religious, he has also an essential conception of the suffering in which life is involved, in that he does not apprehend existence as one thing, and fortune or misfortune as something happening to the existing individual, but exists so that suffering is for him relevant to existence. But at that point the humorist turns deceptively aside and revokes the suffering in the form of the jest. He comprehends the significance of suffering as relevant to existence, but he does not comprehend the significance of the suffering itself; he understands that it belongs to existence, but does not understand its significance except through the principle that suffering belongs. The first thought is the pain in the humoristic consciousness, the second is the jest, and hence it comes about that one is tempted both to weep and to laugh when the humorist speaks. He touches upon the secret of existence in the pain, but then he goes home again.

* When it was said in the preceding that the religious discourse is severe, the aesthetic lenient, and it is now said that poesy has the courage to slay Juliet, this also quite hits the mark without convicting our exposition of self-contradiction. For to permit Juliet to die is the tender sympathy of the aesthetic, but to proclaim new suffering, and hence to let fall a new blow, is the severe sympathy of the religious.

The profundity lies in his apprehension of suffering in this intimate conjunction with existence, and that therefore all human beings suffer as long as they exist; for the humorist does not identify suffering with misfortune, as if an existing individual would be happy if such and such misfortunes were not there. This the humorist understands very well, and it may therefore sometimes occur to him to mention an altogether accidental little trouble, which no one else would call a misfortune, and then say that he would be happy if only this were removed. As for example when a humorist says: "If only I might live to see the day when my landlord installs a new bell-pull in the house where I live, so that it might be quickly and definitely decided for whom the bell is rung in the evening, then I would count myself the happiest of men." Everyone who understands repartee understands at once when he hears such a speech, that the speaker has annulled the distinction between fortune and misfortune in a higher madness—because all are sufferers.

The humorist comprehends the profundity of the situation, but at the same moment it occurs to him that it is doubtless not worth while to attempt an explanation. This revocation is the jest. When therefore an existing humorist converses with an immediate person, an unfortunate individual, for example, whose life lies in the distinction between fortune and misfortune, he will again introduce into the situation a humoristic effect. The expression for suffering which the humorist has at his disposal* satisfies the unfortunate individual, but then comes the profundity of his humor and takes away the distinction in which the other has his life, and thereupon comes the jest. When thus an unfortunate individual perhaps says: "For me all is over, everything is lost," the humorist might continue: "Aye, what poor wretches we human beings are, involved in all these manifold miseries of life, we all suffer; now if I could only live to see the day when my landlord installs a new bell-pull . . . I would count myself the happiest of men." And the humorist would by no means speak thus for the sake of hurting the feelings of the unfortunate sufferer. But the misunderstanding is that the unfortunate person in the last analysis believes in fortune (for immediacy cannot

* Irony would distinguish itself from humor at once by not expressing the pain, replying instead quizzically by the use of the abstract dialectic which protests the excess involved in the unfortunate individual's outcry of pain. Humor rather regards it as not enough, and the humorist's indirect expression for suffering is also far stronger than any direct expression. The ironist levels everything on the basis of humanity in the abstract, the humorist on the abstract God-relationship, for he does not enter concretely into this relationship, but it is just at this point that he parries by means of the jest.

comprehend suffering), whence it follows that misfortune is for him a particular something on which he concentrates his attention in the thought that if it were removed he would be happy; the humorist has, on the contrary, understood suffering so that he finds every form of documentation superfluous, and expresses this by mentioning the first thing that comes to mind.

The Roman says *respice finem,* and uses this expression in earnest; but the expression itself contains a kind of contradiction, in so far as *finis* viewed as the end has not yet come and thus lies before, while *respicere* means to look back: a similar contradiction is really the essence of the humoristic explanation of existence. It assumes that when existence is apprehended as a process of walking along a way, the distinctive and remarkable fact about existence is that the goal lies behind one— and yet one is compelled to walk forward, for walking forward is the image for existing. The humorist apprehends the significance of suffering as belonging to existence, but then he revokes the whole, for the goal lies behind him.

As a humorist exists, he also expresses himself; and in life one may sometimes hear a humorist speak, in books his remarks are most frequently distorted. Now let a humorist express himself, and he will speak for example as follows: "What is the meaning of life? Aye, tell me that; how should I know, we are born yesterday and know nothing. But one thing I do know, namely, that it is most comfortable to stride unknown through the world, without being known to His Majesty the King, Her Majesty the Queen, Her Majesty the Queen Mother, His Royal Highness, Prince Ferdinand; for such aristocratic acquaintanceships only make life troublesome and painful, just as it must be troublesome for a prince who lives in straitened circumstances in a country town to be recognized by his royal family." And so it also seems to me that to be known by God in time makes life so acutely strenuous. Wherever He is, there every half hour is of tremendous importance. But to live in that manner is not endurable for sixty years; it is scarcely possible to endure even for three years the severe study required for the professional examinations which is however not nearly so strenuous as such a half hour.

Everything resolves itself into contradiction. Now it is preached into us that we should live with the entire passion of the infinite, and buy the eternal. Very well, one takes hold of the task and puts the best foot of the infinite forward, one comes rushing in the most extreme and pas-

sionate haste, so that no man in a bombardment could hurry faster, not
the Jew who fell down from the gallery could come more completely
head over heels. What happens? Why then comes the announcement
that the auction is postponed, that the hammer will not fall today, but
perhaps only sixty years hence. So one begins to pack for departure;
what happens then? In the same second the speaker comes rushing up
and says: "But it is still possible that all will be decided, perhaps this very
moment, by the judgment of death."

What does this mean? In the last analysis all men get equally far. It
is with existence as it was with my doctor. I complained of feeling ill.
He replied: "You are probably drinking too much coffee and not taking
enough exercise." Three weeks later I again consult him and say I am
really not feeling well, but this time it cannot be the coffee for I do not
touch it, nor the lack of exercise for I walk all day. He replies: "Well
then, the reason must be that you do not drink coffee and take too much
exercise." There we have it; the lack of well-being was and remained
the same, but when I drink coffee it comes from the fact that I drink it,
and when I do not drink coffee it comes from the fact that I do not drink
it. And so with us human beings in general. Our whole earthly existence
is a kind of illness. If anyone inquires about the reason, one first asks
him how he has arranged his life; as soon as he has given an account of
it you answer: "That is it, there is the reason." And then one walks away
with an air of great importance, as if one had explained everything, until
one has turned the corner, when one sticks one's tail between one's legs
and skulks away. If one were to offer me ten dollars I would not undertake to explain the riddle of existence. And why should I? If life is a riddle, in the end the author of the riddle will doubtless explain it. I have
not invented the temporal life, but I have noticed that in the periodicals
which make a custom of printing riddles, the solution is generally
offered in the next number. To be sure, it does happen that some old
maid or pensioner is mentioned with honor as having solved the riddle,
i.e. has known the solution a day in advance—that difference is certainly
not very considerable.

In our age people have often enough confused the humorous with the
religious, even with the Christian type of religiosity, which is why I seek
everywhere to come back to it. Nor is there anything far-fetched in this,
for the sphere of the humoristic is very extensive, precisely as constituting the boundary of the religious; especially when expounded with an
undertone of sadness it may well take upon itself a deceptive resem-

blance to the religious in the wider sense, but only for one who is not accustomed to hold the totality-category in sight. This is something that no one can know better than I do, who am myself essentially a humorist, and while having my life in immanent categories, seek to discover and explore the Christian type of religiosity.

In order to throw light upon the reality of the religious suffering as expressed in its essential persistence, I shall here once more bring forward a last dialectical attempt to revoke it, to transform it into a constantly annulled moment. Aesthetically, misfortune is accidentally related to existence; aesthetically viewed, reflection is not directed to the suffering but away from it; in aesthetic muddle-headedness, worldly wisdom or prudence assigns significance to suffering in a finite teleology, through hardships a man is fitted to become something in the finite life; humor apprehends suffering in intimate conjunction with existence, but revokes its essential significance for the existing individual. Let us now see if it is possible to revoke suffering in terms of an infinite teleology. The suffering has significance for an eternal happiness—*ergo,* I should be able to rejoice over my suffering. Hence the problem becomes: Is it possible for an existing individual, at the same time that he expresses precisely by means of suffering his relationship to an eternal happiness as the absolute *telos,* is it possible for him at the same time, on the basis of his knowledge about this relationship, to place himself beyond the suffering? In such a case it is not the suffering which is the essential expression for the relationship, but the rejoicing, naturally not indeed a direct joy, as the religious discourse sometimes seeks to make us imagine, carrying us back to a little aesthetically unabashed song and dance; no, a joy grounded in the consciousness that the suffering signifies the relationship.

Let us now beware of setting down on paper the question, Which is the highest? and when we have thus written it down, perhaps even counting ourselves through with it; but let us rather impress upon ourselves that the question is not raised *in abstracto,* which of these two relationships is the highest, but let us ask which of them is possible for an existing individual. For to be in existence is always a somewhat embarrassing situation, and the question is whether this again is not one of the pressures exerted by existence, namely, that the existing individual cannot effect the dialectical exchange which turns the suffering into joy. In the eternal happiness itself there is no suffering, but when an existing individual establishes a relationship thereto, this relationship is quite rightly expressed through suffering. If an existing individual, through knowing that this suffering means the relationship, were capable of elevating himself above the suffering, then he would also be able to transform his status from that of an existing individual to that of an eternal being; but this he will scarcely wish to attempt. But if he cannot do this, he is again in the situation of suffering, because this knowledge must be held fast in the medium of existence. In the same moment the perfection of his joy will fail of being complete, as it must always fail when it must be had in an imperfect form. The pain of this circumstance is again the essential expression for the relationship.

But we read in the New Testament that the Apostles when they were scourged went away rejoicing, giving thanks to God that they were accounted worthy to suffer for Christ's sake. Quite so, and I do not doubt that the Apostles had sufficient strength of faith to be glad and to give thanks in the very moment of bodily pain, just as we even find in pagans examples of a strength of mind which makes them glad even in the moment of bodily suffering, like a Scaevola[4] for instance. But the suffering spoken of in this passage is not a case of religious suffering, concerning which, by and large, very little is said in the New Testament; and when a so-called religious discourse seeks to make us believe that everything which an Apostle suffers is *eo ipso* religious suffering, it only shows how confused such a discourse is about the categories, for this is analogous to the assumption that every discourse in which the name of God appears is religious discourse. No, when the individual is secure in his God-relationship and suffers only outwardly, then this is not religious suffering. Such suffering is subject to an aesthetic dialectic, like misfortune to the immediate consciousness; it may be present and it may be absent. But no one is justified in denying that a human being is religious because no blow of misfortune fell upon him. But because he is without experience of such misfortune he is not on that account without suffering, if in fact he is religious; for suffering is precisely the expression for the God-relationship, that is, the religious suffering, which signalizes the God-relationship and the fact that the individual has not arrived at happiness by emancipating himself from a religious relationship to an absolute *telos*.

At the same time then that the martyr (I say martyr because I do not wish to speak further in this place about an Apostle, since his life is subject to a paradoxical dialectic, and his situation qualitatively distinct from that of others,[5] and his mode of existence justifiable when it is as no one's else dares to be) suffers his martyrdom, he may very well in his joy transcend the bodily pain. But at the same time that an individual suffers religiously, he cannot in his joy over the significance of this suffering as a mark of the relationship transcend the suffering; for the suffering is rooted in the fact that he is separated from his happiness, but also signifies that he has a relationship to this happiness, so that to be without suffering means to be without religion. The immediate individual does not exist in an essential manner, for as immediate he is the fortunate synthesis of finitude and infinitude, to which there corresponds, as was shown above, fortune and misfortune as coming from without. The religious individual is reflected inward, is conscious of being existentially in process of becoming, and yet maintaining a relationship to an eternal happiness. As soon as the religious suffering is eliminated, and the individual gains a sense of security, so that he stands in relation only to fortune and misfortune, as is the case with the immediate consciousness, then this is a sign that he is an aesthetic personality who has by an error strayed into the religious sphere; and it is always easier to confuse the spheres than to hold them distinctly apart. Such a straying aesthetician may be either an awakened person or a speculative philosopher. The awakened person knows himself to be absolutely secure in his own God-relationship (poor fellow, this security is unfortunately the one certain sign that the individual does not stand in a relationship to God), and has now nothing to do except to keep himself busy treating the rest of the world in and with tracts; a speculative philosopher is finished on paper, and confuses this with existence.

The Apostle Paul mentions the religious suffering in one passage of his epistles, and in that connection one will also find that the suffering becomes a sign of the happiness. I refer of course to the passage in the Epistle to the Corinthians about the thorn in the flesh.[6] He states that it happened once, whether he was in the body or out of the body he does not know, that he was caught up into the third heaven. Let us now once for all remember that it is an Apostle that speaks, and let us then talk quite simply and straightforwardly about it. So then it happened once, only once; of course, in the case of an existing individual it could scarcely happen every day, since it would be rendered impossible by the very fact that he exists, aye, to such a degree impossible that it is only to an Apostle, to a man of rare and exceptional distinction, that such an experience could come once. He does not know whether he was in the body or out of the body; but such an experience can surely not happen to an existing individual every day, precisely because he is a particular existing human being. Aye, we learn from the Apostle that it happens so very seldom, that it happened to the Apostle, the exceptionally distinguished man, only once. And then, why? What evidence did the Apostle retain to assure him of the reality of the experience? A thorn in the flesh—that is, an experience of suffering.

We others must be content with lesser experiences, but the relationship remains entirely the same. The religious individual is not necessarily caught up into the third heaven, but neither does he know the suffering which constitutes the thorn in the flesh. The religious individual sustains a relationship to an eternal happiness, and the sign of this relationship is suffering, and suffering is its essential expression—for an existing individual.

Just as the highest principles of thought can for an existing individual be proved only negatively, and the attempt to furnish a positive demonstration of them immediately reveals that the proponent, in so far as he nevertheless really remains an existing individual, is about to become fantastic, so also it is the case that the existential relationship to the absolute good is for an existing individual determined only through the negative—the relation to an eternal happiness only through suffering, just as also the certainty of the faith which sustains a relationship to an eternal happiness is determined through its uncertainty. If I take the uncertainty away—in order to get a still greater certainty—then I do not get a believer in his humility, in fear and trembling, but I get an aesthetic coxcomb, a devil of a fellow, who wishes, speaking loosely, to fraternize with God, but who, speaking precisely, stands in no relationship to God whatever. The uncertainty is the criterion, and the certainty without the uncertainty is the criterion for the absence of a God-relationship.

So likewise in the time of courtship, to be absolutely certain that one is loved is the certain sign that one is not in love.* But no one will ever get a lover to believe that it is not, in spite of this, a blessed thing to be in love. So also with the uncertainty of faith; but one will never get a believer to imagine that it is not, in spite of this, a blessed thing to believe. But as a maiden is to a hero, so a lover is to a believer, and why? Because the lover's relationship is to a woman, but the believer's to God— and in relation to this distinction the Latin phrase applies absolutely:

* Since love is not the absolute *telos* the comparison must be understood *cum grano salis,* so much the more as being in love lies in the sphere of the aesthetic, and is a direct form of happiness.

interest inter et inter. For the same reason the lover is only relatively justified, but the believer absolutely justified, in refusing to listen at all to
anything presuming to offer another kind of certainty. For to love, that
is indeed beautiful, enchanting; O that I were a poet, able rightly to
proclaim the praise of love and explain its glory; O that I might at least
sit worthily as a listener when the poet praises it! But love is nevertheless
a jest. I do not mean this in the contemptible sense which would make
love merely a transitory feeling; no, even when the happiest love finds
its most lasting expression in the happiest marriage—aye, it is glorious
to be bound to and initiated into this, with all its troubles and difficulties,
so blessed pastime; O that I were a speaker able rightly to testify in
eulogy of marriage,[7] so that the unfortunate individual who sadly remains outside dares not listen to me, and the presumptuous individual
who mockingly remains outside would in listening discover with terror
what he has forfeited: but marriage is nevertheless but a jest. This I perceive from the fact that when I bring marriage into relationship with the
absolute *telos,* with an eternal happiness, and in order to be sure that it
is the absolute *telos* I am thinking about, permit death to come between
as arbiter, then I can say with truth: it is indifferent whether an individual has been married or not married, just as it is indifferent whether
one is Jew or Greek, free or slave. Marriage is but a jest, but a jest which
should be treated with all seriousness. This earnestness does not lie in
marriage itself, but is the reflection of the earnestness of the God-relationship, a reflection of the husband's relation to his absolute *telos,* and
of the wife's absolute relation to her absolute *telos.*

But let us return to suffering as the sign of happiness. If on account
of the fact that only an "awakened" person succeeds in escaping the suffering, and only a speculative philosopher in revoking it, so as to make
happiness itself the mark of happiness (just as all immanent speculation
is essentially a revocation of existence, which is indeed what eternity is,
but the speculative philosopher does not happen to be in eternity)—
hence, if because an *existing* individual cannot revoke the suffering and
make happiness itself the mark of happiness, which would mean that
the existing individual died and passed over into eternity, one wishes to
say that religiosity is an illusion: very well—but one must then please
remember that it is the illusion which comes after the understanding.
Poesy is the illusion which precedes the understanding; religiosity, the
illusion which comes after the understanding. Between poesy and religiosity, worldly wisdom presents its vaudeville performance. Every

individual who does not live either poetically or religiously is stupid. "What, stupid? All these shrewd and experienced people who know the world inside out, and can give advice for everything and everybody, are they stupid? And in what does their stupidity consist?" In that after having lost the poetic illusion, they have been wanting in the imagination and passion to pierce the illusions of probability and penetrate the apparent reliability of a finite teleology, all of which breaks down as soon as the infinite in a man begins to move. If then religiosity is an illusion, there are three kinds: the beautiful illusion of poesy, immediacy (the happiness is in the illusion, and afterwards the suffering comes with reality); the comical illusion of stupidity; the blessed illusion of religiosity (the pain is in the illusion, the happiness comes afterward). The illusion of stupidity is naturally the only one that is in itself comical, and while an entire movement in French poetry has been sufficiently active in presenting the aesthetic illusion in a comic light, which is an insult to the aesthetic and by no means a merit in the eyes of the religious (namely, that a poet undertakes to do it), it would be more serviceable if poetry were really to take up the case of worldly wisdom, which is equally comical whether it reckons right* or reckons wrong (a sign of how comical it really is), because all its calculations constitute an illusion, a vain preoccupation within the chimerical notion that there is something certain in the finite world. "But was not Socrates a wise man?" Yes, but I have already several times developed the point that his first proposition is from the standpoint of worldly wisdom a piece of lunacy, since it executes the movement of the infinite. No, poesy is youth, and worldly wisdom is the fruit of the years, and religiosity is the relation to the eternal; but the years only make a man more and more stupid if he has lost his youth and has not gained the relationship to the

* And perhaps most comic when it reckons right; for when it reckons wrong, one has a little sympathy for the poor chap. When thus, for example, a man counts upon such and such connections, by the use of his knowledge of the world, to help himself into a rich marriage, and it works and he gets the girl, and she actually has the money, then the comical is jubilant; for now he has become fearfully stupid. Suppose he got the girl, but it turned out that she did not have the money after all, then there would mingle a little sympathy in one's reaction. But most men generally recognize the comical by means of something extrinsic, by the unfortunate result (which does not however constitute the comical, but the pitiful), just as they recognize the pathetic by means of something extrinsic, the fortunate result (which however is not the pathetic, but the accidental). Thus it is not nearly so comical when a crazy man with his fixed idea brings confusion upon himself and others, incurring injury and loss, as when existence accommodates itself to the fixed idea. It is not, that is to say, fundamentally comical for existence to permit one to discover that a crazy man is crazy, but comical that it conceals the fact.

eternal. The serious man we talked about, who wanted to be assured of the definite certainty of an eternal happiness before he would risk everything for it, since otherwise it would be madness—would he not discover that it was the height of madness to risk everything when suffering becomes the certainty—the correct expression for the uncertainty.

Within the sphere of religious suffering there lies the special type of religious conflict the Germans call *Anfechtung,*[8] which category finds its determination only in this connection. Although I have in general to do with the religious address only as the organ of the religious view of life, I may incidentally have regard to its factual character in our time, here again in order to throw light upon the religiosity of the age with its pretensions of having advanced beyond medieval religiosity, in that I seek to assign its proper place to *Anfechtung,* incidentally recalling that nowadays we scarcely ever hear a word about it, or in so far as it is mentioned, we find it identified without further ado with temptation, aye, even with the ordinary troubles of life. As soon as we leave out the relationship to an absolute *telos* and let this exhaust itself in relative ends, *Anfechtung* ceases to exist. *Anfechtung* is in the sphere of the God-relationship what temptation is in the ethical sphere. When the ethical relationship to reality is the maximum for the individual, then temptation is his greatest danger. Hence it is quite in order that *Anfechtung* is left out, and it is only an instance of slovenliness that it is identified with temptation. But it is not only in the manner just described that *Anfechtung* differs from temptation, but the orientation of the individual is also different in the two cases. In temptation, it is the lower that tempts, in *Anfechtung* it is the higher; in temptation, it is the lower that allures the individual, in *Anfechtung* it is the higher that, as if jealous of the individual, tries to frighten him back. *Anfechtung* therefore originates first in the essentially religious sphere, and occurs there only in the final stage, increasing quite properly in proportion to the intensity of the religiosity, because the individual has discovered the limit, and *Anfechtung* expresses the reaction of the limit against the finite individual.

It was therefore a false alarm, as we saw in the preceding, when the clergyman said on Sunday that it was good to be in the sanctuary, and that if we could only remain there we would doubtless become holy; but we must out into the world. For if a man were to remain there, he would discover *Anfechtung,* and would perhaps come out of that experience in such bad shape that he would hardly feel disposed to thank the clergyman. In the moment of the individual's success in training himself for the absolute relationship through the renunciation of relative ends (and this may occur in particular moments, though the individual is again later drawn back into the conflict), and when he is now about to relate himself absolutely to the absolute, he discovers the limit, and the conflict of *Anfechtung* becomes an expression for this limit. The individual is indeed innocent in *Anfechtung* (as is not the case in temptation), but nevertheless the suffering involved is undoubtedly fearful, for I myself know nothing about it, and if anyone wishes to take to himself the ambiguous consolation, I will gladly furnish it, for it consists in the fact that no one who is not very religious will be exposed to *Anfechtung*, for *Anfechtung* is precisely the reaction to the absolute expression for the absolute relationship. Temptation assails the individual in his weak moments, while *Anfechtung* is the nemesis upon the strong moment in the absolute relationship. Temptation therefore stands in connection with the individual's ethical habitus, while *Anfechtung* on the contrary is without continuity, and is the opposition of the absolute itself.

That there is such a thing as *Anfechtung* cannot however be denied, and just for that reason there might arise in our age a not unremarkable psychological phenomenon. Suppose a man who had a profound religious need, were constantly to hear only such religious addresses as rounded everything out by letting the absolute *telos* exhaust itself in relative ends, what would happen to him? He would sink into the deepest despair, experiencing something else in himself; and yet, never having heard the clergyman talk about *Anfechtung*, about inward suffering, the suffering attached to the God-relationship, he would perhaps from respect for the clergyman and his dignity apprehend this suffering as a misunderstanding, or as something that other men also felt but overcame so easily that they never talked about it—until, with the same fear with which the discovery was made the first time, he discovered the category of *Anfechtung*. Let him then suddenly happen upon one of the older works of edification, and there quite correctly find *Anfechtung* described—aye, then he would doubtless rejoice as Robinson did upon meeting the man Friday, but what would he be led to judge about the Christian religious address that he was accustomed to hear? The religious address ought essentially to be of such a nature that the listener could acquire the most precise insight into the religious aberrations of the contemporary age, and into himself as belonging to the age. But what do I say? This insight may also be obtained by listening to a religious address which has nothing to say about *Anfechtung*. To be sure the insight is obtained, but the religious address is only an indirect source of the insight.

It is in this manner then that the religious suffering has its essential persistence, and its reality, so that it persists even in the most highly developed religious personality, and even though the religious individual may have succeeded in fighting his way through the suffering which is involved in the dying away from immediacy. The suffering persists as long as the individual is alive; but lest we be overhasty in recurring at once to the final suffering, we shall consider the individual as remaining in the first. For this conflict is so persistent, and the relapse into it so frequent, that it is doubtless a rare individual who succeeds in fighting his way through to the end, or in overcoming it for long.

This suffering has its ground in the fact that the individual is in his immediacy absolutely committed to relative ends; its significance lies in the transposition of the relationship, the dying away from immediacy, or in the expression existentially of the principle that the individual can do absolutely nothing of himself, but is as nothing before God; for here again the negative is the mark by which the God-relationship is recognized, and self-annihilation is the essential form for the God-relationship. And this self-annihilation must not receive an external expression, for then we have the monastic movement, and the relationship becomes after all a worldly one; and the individual must not allow himself to imagine that it can be done once for all, for this is aesthetics. And even if it could be done at a stroke, because the individual is an existing individual, he will again encounter suffering in the repetition.

In the immediate consciousness there is rooted the wish to have the power to do everything, and ideally its faith is that it can do everything, its factual inability being apprehended as due to an obstacle which comes from without, and from which it therefore essentially abstracts, just as it abstracts from misfortune; for the immediate consciousness is not dialectical in itself. Religiously it is the task of the individual to understand that he is nothing before God, or to become wholly nothing and to exist thus before God; this consciousness of impotence he requires constantly to have before him, and when it vanishes the religiosity also vanishes.

The youthful sense of power of the immediate consciousness may become comical for a third party, but the religious sense of impotence can never become comical for a third party, for there is not a trace of contradiction in it.* The religious individual does not become comical himself, but the comical may on the contrary present itself to him when it appears in the outer world that he has power to do many things. But if this jest is to be a holy jest, and if it is to continue to present itself, then it must in no single moment be allowed to disturb the earnestness in the thought that the individual is nothing before God and can do nothing; nor must it interfere with the labor of holding this thought fast, nor with the suffering connected with expressing it existentially. Thus if Napoleon had been a genuinely religious individual, he would have had a rare opportunity to enjoy the most divine of amusements; for to have the power apparently to accomplish everything, and then to understand this divinely as an illusion: verily, this is jesting in real earnest!

The comic is in general present everywhere, and every type of existence may at once be determined and relegated to its specific sphere by showing how it stands related to the comical. The religious individual has as such made the discovery of the comical in largest measure, and yet he does not regard the comical as the highest, for religiosity is the purest pathos. But if the individual regards the comical as the highest, then his own comic consciousness is *ipso facto* lower; for the comical always lies in a contradiction, and if the comical itself is the highest, there is lacking the contradiction in which the comical consists, and in which it makes its showing. Hence it is true without exception that the more thoroughly and substantially a human being exists, the more he will discover the comical.† Even one who has merely conceived a great plan toward accomplishing something in the world, will discover it. For let

* There is no contradiction in the idea that a man can do nothing before God except to become aware of this fact; for this is only another expression for the absoluteness of God, and that a human being should not even $\kappa\alpha\tau\grave{\alpha}$ $\delta\acute{\nu}\nu\alpha\mu\iota\nu$ be able to achieve this consciousness would be an expression for his non-existence. There is no contradiction here, and hence there is nothing comical either; but it is on the other hand comical, for example, that walking on one's knees should mean anything before God, just as in general the comical is most clearly evident in idolatry, in superstition, and in other things of the kind. However, one must never forget to have regard to the childlikeness which may be at the bottom of the aberration, making it more touching than comical. Just as a child who wishes much to please an old man may hit upon the strangest things, but all with the devout intention to please him, so the religious individual may also produce a touching impression when in his pious zeal he does not know what he should do to please God, and so finally hits upon something altogether absurd.

† But the highest form of the comical, like the highest form of pathos, rarely attracts the attention of men, and cannot even be presented by the poet. For it does not make a show of itself, as the saying goes, while lower forms of the pathetic and lower forms of the comical do show themselves through being recognizable by something extrinsic. The highest in life does not make a showing, because it belongs to the last sphere of inwardness, and is in a holy sense received into itself.

him have his resolve with him, living solely for its realization, and then let him go out into the world and carry on intercourse with men: the comical will present itself—provided he keeps silent. Most men have, as a matter of fact, no great plans, and speak most frequently in terms of a finite rationality, or altogether immediately. If he will now only keep silent, almost every other word that is spoken will comically affect his great resolution. But if he gives up his great resolve and his strenuous inner existence in relation to it, then the comical will vanish. If he is unable to maintain a silence with respect to his great plan, but must prematurely slobber it out, he becomes himself comical. But the resolution of the religious individual is the highest of all resolves, infinitely higher than all plans to transform the world and to create systems and works of art: therefore must the religious man, most of all men, discover the comical—when he is really religious; for otherwise he becomes himself comical. (But more of this below.)

Suffering as a dying away from immediacy is thus not flagellations and the like; it is not *self-torture*. For the self-torturer does not by any means express that he can do nothing before God, for he counts his acts of self-torture as being something. But the suffering is nevertheless there, and may continue as long as a man exists; for though one may quickly say that a man is nothing before God, it is so difficult existentially to express it. But more concretely to describe and sketch this is again difficult, because speech is after all a more abstract medium than existence, and all speech in relation to the ethical is something of a deception, because discourse, in spite of the most subtle and thoroughly thought out precautionary measures, still always retains an appearance of the foreshortened perspective. So that even when the discourse makes the most enthusiastic and desperate exertions to show how difficult it is, or attempts its utmost in an indirect form, it always remains more difficult to do it than it seems to be in the discourse.

But whether we speak about this task of existentially expressing the dying away from immediacy or not, it is still something that must be done; and religiosity is not thoughtlessness, of a sort that consists in once in a while in giving utterance to the highest, and for the rest lets odd be even through mediation. The religious does not preach indulgence, but proclaims that the greatest exertion is nothing—at the same time requiring it. Here again the negative is the sign, for the greatest exertion may be recognized by the fact that through making it, one becomes nothing; if one comes to be something, the exertion is *eo ipso* less. How ironical this seems, although even in lesser matters, in a lower sphere, the same principle already applies. For by the exertion of partial industry and a little botchwork, a man will easily come to deceive himself into thinking that he understands many different sciences and will make a success in the world and be widely read; but with the exercise of complete industry and absolute integrity he will find it difficult even to understand only a small part of what everybody knows, and will be regarded as a tiresome dawdler. But the principle that is only relatively valid in this lower sphere, is absolutely valid in the religious sphere; and among tried and tested religious personalities one will always find it cited as a last temptation, that the utmost exertion seeks to deceive one with the apparent significance of being something.

Since I am now compelled to make the sad admission that I cannot speak about China, Persia, the System, the astrological or veterinary sciences, I have, in order to hit upon something to do in my embarrassment, exercised my pen within the powers bestowed upon me, in imitating and describing as concretely as possible the affairs of daily life, which are often enough something quite different from the Sunday-go-to-meeting atmosphere. If anyone is pleased to find this sort of description, or my description, tiresome, let him do so; I do not write for any medal, and shall be quite content to admit, if this be required of me, that it is much more difficult, connected with far greater commotion and involving far more serious responsibilities novelistically, to slay a rich uncle to get money into the story, or to provide a ten-year interval, letting some time pass in which the most important things have happened, and then to begin with that which has happened; it requires a very different talent for brevity to describe the victory of faith in half an hour than to describe what an ordinary man fills out the day with in the living-room. Aye, it certainly requires speed to write a story of thirty pages or so, in which the action covers a hundred years, or a drama in which the action covers three hours, but where so much happens and the events so pile up, that such an experience does not befall a man in an entire lifetime.

But what all is not required to present a human being as he is in daily life! If only language does not embarrass one by revealing itself as insufficient, because it is so abstract in comparison with existing, in the sense which this has in reality. But the religious orator ought surely to bring himself to do it, since it is precisely with the living-room he has to do; and the speaker who does not know how the task looks in daily life and in the living-room, might just as well keep still, for Sunday glimpses into eternity lead to nothing but wind. To be sure, the religious orator is not to remain in the living-room, he must know how to hold fast the total category of his sphere, but he must also be able to begin everywhere. And it is in the living-room that the battle must be fought, lest the religious conflict degenerate into a parade of the guard once a week; in the living-room must the battle be fought, not fantastically in the church, so that the clergyman is fighting windmills and the spectators watch the show; in the living-room, the battle must be fought, for the victory consists precisely in the living-room becoming a sanctuary. Let the direct effort in the church be to give a perspective over the forces engaged in the conflict: under whose flag the struggle is to be fought; in whose name the victory is to be sought; to describe the position of the enemy; to rehearse the attack; to praise the omnipotent Ally and strengthen the confidence by arousing misgivings: strengthening the confidence in Him by arousing misgivings with respect to oneself. Let the indirect effort be through the application of a secret sympathy's ironical but therefore also most tender compassion; but the important thing is that the individual goes home from church with zeal and ambition to fight in the living-room. If the activity of the clergyman is to consist in an attempt to tow the community's freight-ship nearer to eternity, then the whole collapses and amounts to nothing, for a human life cannot, like a canal boat, remain in the same place until next Sunday. It is for this reason that the difficulty must be brought out, and especially in the church; it is better to go from church with misgivings and find the task easier than one had supposed, than to go home filled with bravado and become despondent in the living-room.

Thus the religious orator will even be careful not to put his strong moments together for a speech, or to have his strongest moment in the speech, in order, namely, not to deceive himself and others. He will rather be as one who might indeed speak in a higher key but dare not, lest the "mystery of faith" be betrayed and prostituted through too much publicity, but who feels rather that it should be "kept" (1 Tim. 3:9), being still greater and more powerful than it seems in his discourse. For since it is the speaker's chief task, like that of everyone else, to live what he professes, and not once a week to electrify the congregation, startling it galvanically, he will be careful lest he bring upon himself the disgust that comes with the realization that what seemed so glorious in the high-sounding discourse shows itself so different in the daily life. But to yield, to compromise, to bargain, is a course upon which he will not enter for anything in the world. Even when he seems farthest removed from the absolute requirement of religiosity, this requirement must nevertheless be present, determining the terms and the judgment; even when he involves himself with the most paltry fractional interest of the daily life, this absolute general measure must be there, though perhaps hidden, and must each second be ready to posit the absolute requirement.

And now what does the task look like in daily life? For I always have my favorite theme *in mente.* Is everything quite in order with the urge which our theocentric nineteenth century feels to advance beyond Christianity, to speculate, to carry the evolution further, to fashion to itself a new religion, or to abolish Christianity? As for my own humble person, the reader will please remember that it is I who find the matter and the task so extremely difficult, which would seem to indicate that I have not successfully realized it, I, who do not even profess to be a Christian; but please note that this is not to be taken in the sense that I have ceased to be a Christian in consequence of having gone further. Still, it is always something to have called attention to the difficulty, even if this is done, as here, only in the edifying *divertissement,* brought forward essentially with the aid of a spy whom I send out among men on week days, and with the additional assistance of a few dilettantes who are made to play a rôle against their wills.

Last Sunday the clergyman said: "You must not depend upon the world, and not upon men, and not upon yourself, but only and alone upon God; for a human being can of himself do nothing." And we all understood it, myself included; for the ethical and the ethico-religious are so very easy to understand, but on the other hand so very difficult to do. A child can understand it, the most simple-minded individual can understand it quite as it is said, that we can do absolutely nothing. On Sunday it is understood with such fearful ease (aye, fearful; for this ease leads often enough the same way as the good resolutions) *in abstracto,* and on Monday it is so very difficult to understand that it concerns this little particular within the relative and concrete existence in which the individual has his daily life, where the mighty man is tempted to forget humility, and the humble person is tempted to confound humility before God with a relative deference toward his superiors; and yet this little particular something is a sheer trifle in comparison with everything. Aye, even when the clergyman complains that no one acts in accordance with his admonition, this is again so easy to understand; but the next day this understanding has become so difficult that the person incurs, in the case of this particular, this insignificant trifle, his own share of the guilt. Then the clergyman added: "This is a fact we ought always to remember." And we all understood it; for *always* is a glorious word which says everything at once, and is so fearfully easy to understand; but it is on the other hand the most difficult thing in the world to do something always, and on Monday afternoon at four o'clock it is extremely difficult to understand this *always* merely for the space of half an hour. Even in the clergyman's discourse there was a hint of something which indirectly called attention to this difficulty; for there were a few matters so described as to indicate that he himself scarcely did it always; aye, that he had scarcely done it in each one of the few factors by which he mediated his sermon; aye, that he scarcely did it in each period of the brief address.[9]

Now today it is Monday, and the spy has abundant time to go out and seek contact with men; for the clergyman makes speeches for them, but the observer converses with them. So then he strikes up a conversation with a man, and the talk finally veers around to the subject that the spy wants to bring up. He says: "That is all quite true, but there is still something that you cannot do; you cannot build a palace with four wings and marble floors." The other answers: "No, you are quite right about that; how should I be able to do that when my income is just about enough for my necessities, perhaps permitting me to save a little each year, but I certainly have no capital for building palaces, and besides I do not understand the builder's trade." So then it appears that this man does not have the power. The spy leaves him, and next has the honor to meet a man of great importance; he flatters his vanity, and finally the conversation turns to the matter of the palace: "But a palace with four wings and marble floors will surely be too much for you to manage." "What," says the other, "you surely forget that I have already accomplished this, that my great residence in Palace Square is precisely the structure you describe." So this man turned out to have the power, and the spy bows himself out of his presence, heaping congratulations upon the mighty man. In going away the spy now meets a third man, to whom he recounts the conversation he has just had with the two others, and this man then gives utterance to the following reflections: "Aye, the destinies allotted to men in this world are strange indeed, their capabilities vary exceedingly, one man is able to do so much and another so very little; yet every human being would be able to accomplish something if he would learn from experience and the available knowledge of the world to remain within the sphere of his limitations." The differences then are noteworthy; but is it not still more noteworthy that these different utterances about the differences say one and the same thing, and say that all men are equally endowed with capacity for accomplishment? Number one is unable to do this or that because he does not have the money, which means that he has the power essentially; number two can do it, he is essentially endowed with the power, and this fact reveals itself accidentally through his having the money; number three is even able by virtue of his shrewdness to do without some of the conditions and still have the power—what a mighty man would he not be if he possessed the conditions!

But last Sunday, that is to say yesterday, the clergyman said that a human being can do absolutely nothing of himself, and we all understood it. When the clergyman says it in church we all understand it, and if a man tries to express it existentially during the six days of the week so that people notice it, it is not long before we all understand that he is crazy. Even the most religious man will have occasion to catch himself a dozen times a day entertaining the delusion that he can at least do something. But when the clergyman says that a man can do absolutely nothing, we all understand it with such fearful ease, and a speculative philosopher understands this ease again in such a manner as to prove from it the necessity of going further, of passing over to that which is much more difficult to understand: China, Persia, the System; because the philosopher speculatively scorns the poor trifling jest about the living-room, because instead of going from the church and the abstract Sunday conception of man, home to himself, he goes from the church direct to China, Persia, and astronomy—yes, to astronomy. Old Master Socrates did just the opposite, and gave up astronomy, choosing the higher and more difficult task of understanding himself before God.

But the speculative philosopher proves the necessity of going further with such necessity that even a clergyman loses his poise, and in the pulpit is of the professorial opinion that the understanding by which the particular individual understands himself as unable to do anything of himself, is only for simple and humble people. He even warns them *ex cathedra,* or (what was I about to say?) from the pulpit, to be content with this paltry task, and not to become impatient because it is not given them to reach the higher level of an understanding of China and Persia. And the clergyman is quite right in supposing that the task is for simple people; but the secret of it is that it is equally difficult for the most eminent talent, since the task is not comparative: a task for a simple man in comparison with a distinguished talent, but rather a task for the distinguished talent in comparison with himself before God. And the philosopher is quite right in supposing that it is something more to understand China and Persia than to understand the abstract Sunday conception of the abstract Sunday man, China and Persia being in fact something more concrete. But more concrete than all other understanding, the only absolutely concrete understanding there is, is the understanding by which the individual comprehends himself in comparison with himself before God; and this is also the most difficult kind of understanding because the difficulty cannot here be made to serve for an excuse.

So it goes. In the six days of the week we can all do something, the king more than his minister; the witty journalist says: "I will show this man or that what I can do," that is, make him appear ridiculous; the policeman says to the man in the shabby jacket: "Perhaps you do not know what I can do to you," namely, arrest him; the cook says to the poor woman who comes on Saturdays: "You may have forgotten what I can do," namely, persuade the mistress not to give her any longer the week's left-overs. We can all do something, and the king smiles at the minister's power, and the minister laughs at the journalist's power, and the journalist laughs at the policeman's, and the policeman at the man in the shabby jacket, and the shabby man at the Saturday woman—and on Sunday we all go to church (with the exception of the cook, who never has time because there are always dinner guests on Sunday at his Honor's), and hear from the lips of the clergyman that a man can do absolutely nothing of himself—that is if we are so fortunate as not to be listening to a speculative preacher. Yet, one moment: we have arrived at church; with the assistance of a very authoritative usher (for the usher is especially powerful on Sundays, and indicates with a silent glance at so and so what he can do), we are severally assigned to our seats with reference to our particular position in society. The clergyman enters the pulpit—but at the very last moment there is a very influential man who has come late, and the usher must now exercise his authority. Then the preacher begins, and we all now understand from our different positions and standpoints what the clergyman says from his lofty standpoint, namely, that a man can do nothing of himself. On Monday the clergyman is himself a mighty man, that we are all made to feel, except those who are more mighty than he. But one of the two must surely be a jest:

either what the clergyman says is a jest, a kind of social game, to indulge once in a while in the reflection that a man can do nothing of himself; or the clergyman is right after all in saying that a human being should always remember this—and we others, including the clergyman and myself too, are wrong when we so wretchedly interpret the word *always,* although a man has thirty, forty, or fifty years for the perfecting of himself in this art, so that every day is a day of preparation, but also a day of testing.

Today it is Tuesday, and the spy is paying a visit to a man who has under construction a large building just outside the town; he again leads the conversation around to touch upon what a man can do, and upon his respected host's ability to do things. But this man replied, not without a certain solemnity: "A man can do absolutely nothing of himself, and it is only with God's help that I have accumulated this great fortune, and with God's help that I . . ." Here the solemn stillness of the conversation is broken in upon by a loud noise outside the house. The man excuses himself and rushes out; he leaves the door half open, and our spy, whose ears are sharp, now hears to his great astonishment, blow upon blow to the accompaniment of these words: "I will show you what I can do to you." The spy can scarcely restrain his laughter—well, the spy, too, is a human being, who may at any moment be tempted by the delusion that he can do something, as now for example, to think that it was he who had caught the mighty man in his ludicrousness.

But if a man proposes to himself every day to bear in mind and existentially to hold fast what the clergyman says on Sunday, understanding this as the earnestness of life, and therewith again understanding all his ability and inability as a jest: does this mean that he will undertake nothing at all, because everything is empty and vain? Ah, no, for then precisely he will have no occasion to appreciate the jest, since the contradiction will not arise which brings it into juxtaposition with the earnestness of life: there is no contradiction involved in that everything is vanity in the eyes of a creature of vanity. Sloth, inactivity, the affectation of superiority over against the finite—this is poor jesting, or rather is no jest at all. But to shorten one's hours of sleep and to buy up each waking period of the day and not to spare oneself, and then to understand that the whole is a jest: aye, that is earnestness. And religiously the positive always has its criterion in the negative; its earnestness may be recognized by the jest, in order to make sure that it is a religious earnestness, not an immediate earnestness, the stupid official gravity of a man of title, the stupid self-importance of a journalist with reference to the age, an "awakened" individual's stupid importance over against God, as if God could not create a million men of genius if He were in any way embarrassed. To hold the fate of many human beings in one's hand, to transform the world, and so, constantly, to understand that this is a jest; aye, that is earnestness indeed! But in order that this should be possible all finite passions must be atrophied, all selfishness outrooted, both the selfishness which wants to have everything, and the selfishness which proudly turns its back on everything. But just herein sticks the difficulty, and here arises the suffering in the dying away from self; and while it is the specific criterion of the ethical that it is so easy to understand in its abstract expression, it is correspondingly difficult to understand *in concreto*.

We ought always to bear in mind that a human being can do nothing of himself, says the clergyman; hence also when one proposes to take an outing in the Deer Park,[10] he ought to remind himself of this, as for example, that he cannot enjoy himself; and the illusion that he surely is able to enjoy himself at the Deer Park, since he feels such a strong desire for it, is the temptation of his immediacy; and the illusion that he surely can take this outing since he can easily afford it, is the temptation of his immediacy. Now today happens to be Wednesday, and a Wednesday in the Deer Park season; let us then again send the spy out among men.

But perhaps one or another religious individual is of the opinion that it is not seemly for him to take an outing of this kind. If this is the case, then I must by virtue of the qualitative dialectic demand respect for the cloister, for mere dabbling will get us nowhere. If the religious man is to be in any way peculiar in his behavior outwardly, then the cloister is the only energetic expression therefor; the rest is only botchwork. But our age is supposed to be advanced in comparison with medieval religiosity; what then did the religiosity of the Middle Ages express? That there was something in the finite world which could not be thought together with, or existentially held together with the thought of God. The passionate expression for this was to break with the finite. If the religiosity of our age is more advanced, it follows that it can hold fast existentially to the thought of God in connection with the frailest expression of the finite, as for example with the enjoyment of an outing in the Deer Park; unless indeed the advanced character of our religiosity is betokened by its having retreated to childish forms of religiosity, in comparison with which the youthful enthusiasm of the Middle Ages is a glory.

It is a childish form of religiosity, for example, once a week to seek permission from God to indulge one's pleasure the whole of the following week, and so again the next Sunday to ask permission for the next week by going to church, and hearing the clergyman say that we should always bear in mind that a man can do absolutely nothing. The child has no reflection, and therefore feels no need to think differences together. For the child, the serious moment is when it must ask for permission from the parents; if I can only get permission, the child thinks, I shall certainly know how to enjoy myself. And when it has been to see father in the study and obtained his permission, it comes away in jubilant mood, confident that mother will of course assent; concerning the serious moment in the study, he thinks: "Thank God, that is now over" —so the child thinks, I think, because the child does not really think. If the same type of relationship repeats itself in the adult's life before God, then it is childishness, which like the child's speech, is recognizable by its partiality for abstract expressions *always, never, just this once,* and so forth. The Middle Ages made an energetic attempt existentially to think God and the finite together, but came to the conclusion it could not be done, and the expression for this is the cloister. The religiosity of our age is more advanced. But if the God-relationship and the finite world in all its smallest detail (where the difficulty becomes greatest) are to be held together existentially, the assent to the finite must find expression within the sphere of religiosity itself; and it must be of such a character that the individual does not here again make the transition from the God-relationship to a mode of existence in entirely different categories.

Lower forms of religiosity than that of the medieval monastic movement will at once be recognizable by the existence in them of the above division, whereby the God-relationship becomes something for itself, and the rest of life something separate and different. There are therefore three lower forms: (1) that in which the individual goes home from the Sunday God-relationship to exist quite immediately in the dialectic of the pleasant and the unpleasant; (2) that in which the individual turns from the Sunday God-relationship to exist in a finite ethic, and quite fails to notice the persistent claim of the God-relationship, while he attends to his business, earns money, and so forth; (3) that in which he goes home from the Sunday God-relationship to have his life in a speculative-ethical view, which permits the God-relationship to exhaust itself without further ado in relative ends, a view of life whose formula is: an efficient performance of vocational duties, as king, as carpenter, as tight-rope walker, etc., is the highest expression of the God-relation-ship, so that in so far one does not really need to go to church. For every such form of religiosity absolves itself, by going to church once a week, from the necessity of having the God-relationship present with it every day in everything; on Sunday it obtains, not precisely like the child, per-mission to enjoy itself the week through, but it obtains absolution from further thinking about God throughout the week.

The religiosity which is to be an advance upon the medieval must find an expression in its devout reflections for the principle that the religious individual exists on Monday in the same categories, and will on Mon-day actually so exist. The Middle Ages were praiseworthy in that they were earnestly concerned about this problem; but then they arrived at the conclusion that it could be done only in the cloister. The religiosity of our age goes further; on Sunday the clergyman says that we must always bear in mind the fact that we can do nothing of ourselves; but for the rest we must be as other men, we must not enter the cloister, we can take our outings in the Deer Park—but surely we must first consider the relationship to God through the religious intermediary principle that a man can do absolutely nothing of himself. And it is this that makes life so tremendously strenuous, and it is this that makes it possible that perhaps all men are in truth genuinely religious individuals; because true religiosity is the religiosity of the secret inwardness, the secret in-wardness in the religious individual, who even employs all his art in order that no one shall notice anything special in his demeanor. For just as the criterion of God's omnipresence consists in His being invis-ible, so the criterion of true religiosity is its invisibility, i.e. there is noth-ing outwardly to be seen. The god that can be pointed out is an idol, and the religiosity that makes an outward show is an imperfect form of religiosity.

But how strenuous! No singer can continuously produce trills, only once in a while a note will be in *coloratura;* but the religious individual whose religiosity consists in the secret inwardness, will, if I may so speak, produce the trills of the God-relationship in connection with everything he does; and what is most difficult of all, even when a specially desig-nated time is devoted to it, he does it so easily that no time is taken for it: the witticism comes precisely in the right place, although he first executes the religious movement quietly for himself; when responding to an invitation he comes precisely on the dot with the requisite gayety of spirits, although he first executes the religious movement. Ah, and when a man has only a little external strain put upon him, it disturbs him while dressing for an evening's company and he comes late, and one can notice something a little strange in his demeanor. But the most strenuous of all thoughts, in comparison with which even the most earnest thought about death is easier, namely, the thought of God—this thought the religious individual can handle with the same ease as is shown by you and me and Tom and Dick and Counselor Madsen—for it is quite certain that no one notices anything in us.

Now the spy goes forth. He will doubtless come upon a man who cannot take an outing in the Deer Park because he has no money, i.e. a man who can do it. If the spy were to give him the money and say, "Nevertheless, you cannot do it," he would probably think him mad, or assume that there must be some undisclosed obstacle, or that perhaps the city gates were closed and the tollgates likewise. In short, out of politeness, and in order not immediately to reward the spy's benevolence by declaring him mad, he would doubtless attempt a number of acute guesses; and when all these failed in consequence of the spy's assertion that there was nothing of that kind in the way of his going, he would regard him as mad, thank him for the gift—and proceed to go out to the Deer Park. And the same man would understand the clergyman next Sunday very well when he preaches about a man's inability to do anything of himself, and that we always ought to bear this in mind. Herein precisely lies the jest, namely, that he can well understand the clergyman; for if there were a single human being so simple-minded that he could not understand the task that the clergyman essentially has the duty to present, who could then endure to live?

So the spy meets another man, who says: "To take an outing in the Deer Park when one can well afford it, and one's engagements permit it, and when one takes wife and children and even the servants along, and returns home at a decent time, is an innocent form of enjoyment. And one ought to partake of the innocent pleasures of life, and not retire like a coward into a monastery, which is tantamount to fleeing the danger." The spy answers: "But did you not say in the beginning of our conversation that you heard the clergyman say last Sunday that a man can do absolutely nothing of himself, and that we ought always to bear this in mind; and did you not say that you understood it?" "Yes." "Then you must have forgotten what it is we are talking about. When you say that such an outing is an innocent pleasure, this is the opposite of a guilty pleasure; but this contrast belongs to morals or ethics. The clergy-

man, on the other hand, spoke of your relation to God. Because it is
ethically permissible to take an outing in the Deer Park it does not follow that it is religiously permissible; and, in any case, it is just this you
have to prove, according to the clergyman, by thinking it together with
the thought of God. And this not in general terms merely, for you are
not a clergyman who has to preach on this theme, though you and many
others seem in daily life to confuse yourselves with the parson, so that it
is clear that it cannot be the most difficult of tasks to be a clergyman. A
clergyman speaks in general terms about the innocent pleasures of life,
but you have to express existentially what the clergyman says. Hence
you are not called upon today to deliver a little lecture on the innocent
joys of life, in view of your proposing to yourself an outing in the Deer
Park, for that is the business of a speaker. But you are to consider, in
view of the fact that you propose today, Wednesday, the fourth of July,
to take an outing in the Deer Park with wife, children, and servants,
what the clergyman said last Sunday, namely, that a man can of himself
do nothing, and that he should always bear this in mind. It was about
how you manage to realize this task, that I wished for some information
from you, for if I had desired a kind of a lecture, I should have addressed myself to the clergyman." "How absurd," the man replies, "to
demand more of me than of the clergyman. I find it quite in order for
the clergyman to preach in this manner, it is for this he receives a salary
from the State; and as far as my own pastor is concerned, the Reverend
Mr. Michaelsen, I shall always be ready to testify that he preaches the
genuine evangelical doctrine, and that is why I attend the church where
he preaches. For I am no heretic, who wants to have the articles of faith
altered; even if it might seem doubtful, according to what you say,
whether I am really a believer, it is certain all the same that I am a true
orthodox believer, one who abominates the Baptists. But it never occurs
to me to bring such trifles as an outing in the Deer Park into connection with the thought of God; that seems to me to be even an affront to
God, and I know also that it does not occur to any single one of my
many acquaintances to do it." "And so you doubtless find it in order, just
as you approve of the clergyman's preaching in this manner, that he
also preaches about no one doing as he says!" "What nonsense!" the
man replies, "Of course I find it in order for such a man of God to speak
in that fashion on Sundays and at funerals and weddings; it is no longer
than two weeks ago that I publicly thanked him in the newspaper for
the glorious unsolicited address he delivered, and which I shall *never*

forget." "Say, rather, which you will *always* remember; for this expression connects itself more closely with the subject of our conversation, namely, that we ought *always* to bear in mind that a man can do nothing of himself. But let us discontinue this conversation, for we evidently do not understand one another, and I see no hope of eliciting from you the information I sought, about how you manage to do what the clergyman says; but I willingly concede you an unmistakable talent for preaching. However, you can do me one service if you will give me the assurance in writing, and if possible get me similar attestations from your many acquaintances, that it never occurs to you or to them to bring the thought of God into connection with anything like taking an outing in the Deer Park."

We will now permit the spy to retire, and merely ask him, for the sake of luring him out on thin ice, for what purpose he wants these statements, and what it is he really has in the back of his mind. He speaks as follows: "Why do I want these statements? That, I am quite ready to tell. I am informed that the clergy are accustomed to meet in conventions,[11] where the reverend brethren raise and answer the question what the age demands—naturally with respect to the religious interest, for otherwise the conventions in question would not differ from the meetings of the political representatives of the citizens. It is said that the Convention has recently arrived at the conclusion that this time it is a new hymnal the age requires.[12] And it is quite possible that the age does demand a new hymnal, but it does not therefore follow that it needs it. Why should not the same things happen to the age, as a moral personality, which happen to other moral persons, that it demands what it does not need; that all the many things it demands, even if it obtained them, would not satisfy its craving, because this consists in demanding, in harboring cravings. Perhaps the times will soon demand that the clergy wear gowns of a new style in order to edify more effectively; it is not at all impossible that the age might actually demand this, and with respect to such a demand, I am not unwilling to assume that the age actually feels the need. Well, then, it is my purpose to gather a number of written statements relating to the manner in which the clergyman's Sunday preaching is understood on Mondays and the other week days, in order, if possible, to make some contribution toward answering the question what the age demands—or, as I would prefer to express myself, what it needs; so that the question would not be worded: 'What is lacking in the religiosity of our age?' since it is always misleading to bring the answer into the question, but so: 'What is lacking to our age? Religiosity.'

"Everybody is preoccupied with what the age demands, no one seems to care about what the individual needs. Possibly no new hymnal is needed. Why does no one hit upon the idea which lies so close at hand, closer perhaps than many will believe: the idea of experimenting with the plan of having the old hymnal furnished with a new binding, to see if a different binding might not do the trick, especially if the bookbinder were to print on the cover, The New Hymnal. The objection may be made that it would be too bad to sacrifice the old binding, since strangely enough the copies of the old hymnal in the hands of the congregation are said to be in very good condition, presumably because the book is so little used, so that the binding would be a useless expense. But this objection must be met with a deep-voiced reply, a deep voice, please note: 'Every serious man in our seriously troubled age readily perceives that something must be done'—and with this reply every objection vanishes as nothing. For the fact that particular private conventicles[13] and dogmatic isolations really feel the need of a new hymnal, in order to hear their catchwords in the vaulted church reecho from the sounding-board of the 'awakened': that is no such serious matter. But when the entire age, unanimously and with many voices, demands a new hymnal, aye, almost several new hymnals, then something must be done; things cannot go on as they are now, or it will be the ruin of religion.

"How comes it that church attendance is relatively so small as it is in the country's capital? Why, quite naturally, the answer is clear as day: it comes from the aversion felt toward the old hymnal. How does it come that those who do go to church are disorderly enough to come just as the clergyman enters the pulpit, or a little later? Why, quite naturally, the answer is clear as day: because of the aversion for the old hymnal. What was it that destroyed the Assyrian Empire? Dissension, madam.[14] What is the reason for the indecent haste with which the people leave the church the moment the clergyman has said Amen? Why, naturally, the answer is clear as day: because of aversion for the old hymnal. How comes it that the practice of family worship is so rare, although at home there is freedom of choice in the use of hymnals? Why, naturally, it is clear as day, that the aversion for the old hymnal is so great that no one has any willingness as long as the old hymnal exists; its mere existence is sufficient to quench altogether the spirit of worship. How comes it that the members of the congregation unfortunately practise so little what is sung on Sunday? Why, naturally, it is clear as day, that it is because the old hymnal is so bad that it even prevents people from doing what is said in it. And how then comes it that all this was unfortunately the case long before the need of any new hymnal was mentioned? Why, naturally, it is as clear as day, that it was the deeply rooted need of the congregation, its deep need, though still unconscious, since there was yet no convention to give it utterance.

"But for this very reason it seems to me that we ought to go slow in abolishing the old hymnal, lest we experience too great a measure of embarrassment when we have to explain the same phenomenon after the new hymnal has been introduced. If the old hymnal has never before been of any service, it is now extremely valuable; for by means of it we can explain everything, everything which would otherwise be inexplicable, considering that the age is so seriously concerned, and the clergy likewise, not only each one for his own little congregation and its individual members, but for the entire age. Nevertheless, suppose that before the new hymnal is adopted something else happens, suppose that the individual resolved to lay the accent of accountability in another place, and in saddened mood sought a reconciliation with the hymnal and the confirmation day of which it constitutes a reminder; suppose the individual conscientiously attended church, arrived on time, sang the hymns, listened to the sermon, departed without indecent haste, preserved the impression on Monday, went further and preserved it on Tuesday, aye, even on Saturday—then the urge to have a new hymnal might become less urgent. The clergy on the other hand, since the individuals had little by little learned to help themselves, would find time and leisure wholly to devote themselves to conventions, where the reverend brethren raise and answer the question what the age demands, naturally with respect to the religious interest; for otherwise such a convention would not differ from an ordinary meeting of the political representatives of the citizens."

So much for the spy, who must now be left to shift for himself; and back to the dictum of the clergyman, that a man can do nothing of himself, and that we should always bear this in mind—therefore, even when we propose to take an outing in the Deer Park. Many readers have presumably long since grown weary of this process of concretion, which never ends, and which nevertheless says nothing at all in comparison with the summary statement that we can do absolutely nothing, and that we should always bear this in mind. But so it is, the ethical and the ethico-religious is in its abstract generality so quickly said and so fearfully easy to understand; in the concreteness of the daily life, however, the discourse which attempts to deal with it is so slow, and the execution of it so very difficult. Nowadays a clergyman scarcely dares to speak in church on the subject of taking an outing in the Deer Park, or even so much as mention the words: so difficult is the task, merely in a religious address to bring a pleasure outing and the thought of God together.

But on the other hand, we are all able to do it in practice. Where then do the difficult tasks arise? In the living-room and on the Shore Road leading to the Deer Park. Nowadays, although preaching against the cloister, the religious address observes the most rigid monastic abstinence, and keeps itself at a distance from reality quite as much as the cloister, thereby indirectly revealing that the existence of daily life is carried on in different categories, or that the religious does not assimilate the daily life to itself. It is in this fashion that we make an advance upon the Middle Ages. But in such a situation the religious individual is compelled by the qualitative dialectic to demand the cloister. If we are not to preach the cloister, and if our religiosity is to be an advance upon the medieval, let the clergyman be so good as to talk about the simplest of things, and let him abstain from the eternal truths *in abstracto*. For surely no one will wish to argue with me that it is so very easy to have the thought of God present with one in connection with petty trifles.

But the implication is not that the clergyman ought to sit in the living-room and talk like a vacationist about pleasure outings in the woods, for that is truly easy enough, unless his dignity should make it a little difficult for him. No, the meaning is that he is to speak religiously about it, and with the divine authority of the religious transform even such conversation into edifying discourse. If he cannot, if he thinks it cannot be done, then he ought to warn his hearers against it—and also show respect for the Middle Ages when he judges them. When on the other hand, the religious address indirectly confirms the illusion that religiosity consists in apprehending oneself in a fantastic-dignified interpretation once a week, in listening to some eternal truths presented *in abstracto,* hearing criticism of those who never go to church, and so for the rest living in other categories—what wonder that the confusion about going further gets the upper hand more and more? A competent clergy should be the moderators of the age, and if it is a clergyman's task to bring consolation, he ought also to know how, when needful, to make the religious so difficult as to force every rebellious individual to his knees. And as the gods piled mountains upon the heaven-storming Titans to bring them to book, so will the clergyman lay the heavy burden of the religious task upon every rebel (naturally, by laying it upon himself), so that no one will imagine that the religious is something light and playful, a mere trifle, or something at most for simple-minded and stupid people; or imagine that religiosity is relatively and comparatively dialectical, and identical with the conventional drill-discipline of the finite; or that the religious is to be made difficult by means of world-historical outlines and systematic results, by which it merely becomes easier.

When therefore the religious speaker, in explaining that a man can do nothing of himself, sets something wholly particular in relation to this principle, he gives the auditor occasion to secure a profound insight into his own inmost heart, helps him to penetrate the delusions and illusions, so as to lay aside at least for a moment the bourgeois, small-town sugar-coating in which he otherwise goes wrapped. Essentially, the religious orator operates by reference to the absolute relationship, that a man can do nothing of himself; but he makes the transition by means of the particulars which he brings into connection with it. If he confines himself merely to saying: *nothing, always, never, everything*— it might easily happen that the whole issues in nothing;* but if he forgets himself and the fundamental absolute, *nothing, always, never, everything*—then he transforms the temple, if not into a den of robbers, at least into a stock exchange.

If then no one else can be found willing to bring together in exposition the absoluteness of the religious and the particularities of life, which togetherness is in existence precisely the ground and significance of the religious suffering, then I propose to myself the task, though I am neither a religious orator, nor myself a religious individual, but merely a humoristic experimenting psychologist. If anyone wishes to laugh at this, it is his privilege, but I should like to see the aesthetician or the dialectician who can show the least tincture of the comical in the religious suffering. If there is anything I have studied from the ground up, and pursued into its farthest ramifications, it is the comic;

* The religious discourse must therefore always be a little teasing, just as existence is; for herein lies the teasing, that we human beings have our heads full of great imaginings, and then comes existence and offers us the commonplace.

precisely for this reason I know that the comical is excluded from the
religious suffering, which is inaccessible to the comical because this
suffering is precisely the consciousness of the contradiction, which is
pathetically and tragically incorporated in the consciousness of the
religious individual; precisely for this reason the comical is excluded.

What the conception of God or an eternal happiness is to effect in the
individual is, that he transform his entire existence in relation thereto,
and this transformation is a process of dying away from the immediate.
This is slowly brought about, but finally* he will feel himself confined
within the absolute conception of God; for the absolute conception of
God does not consist in having such a conception *en passant,* but consists in having the absolute conception at every moment. This is the
check on his immediacy, the death verdict which announces its
annihilation. Like the bird which flits carefree here and there, when it is
imprisoned; like the fish which fearlessly cleaves the waters and
makes its way among the enchanted regions of the deep, when it lies
out of its element on the dry ground—so the religious individual is
confined; for absoluteness is not directly the element of a finite creature.
And as one who is sick and cannot move because he feels pain everywhere, and as one who is sick and cannot keep from moving as long as
he lives, although he feels pain everywhere—so the religious individual lies fettered in the finite with the absolute conception of God
present to him in human frailty. Neither the bird in its cage, nor the
fish on the shore, nor the invalid on his sickbed, nor the prisoner
in the narrowest cell, is so confined as he who is imprisoned in the
conception of God; for just as God is omnipresent, so the imprisoning
conception is also everywhere and in every moment. Aye, just as it is
said to be terrible for one who is thought to be dead while he still
lives, and has the power of sensation, and can hear what those present
say about him, but is unable in any way to express that he is still alive,
so also for the religious individual is the suffering of his annihilation
a fearful thing, when he has the absolute conception present with him
in his nothingness, but no mutuality. If it has happened, and if it is
poetically true so to conceive it, that merely a great and comprehensive
plan laid down in the human mind and there held fast, has crushed the
frail vessel; if it has happened that a young woman, as a consequence
of being loved by one who is the object of her admiration, has been

* I use here a fantastic form in referring to the vanishing of time: "slowly—but finally."
Since the special interest of my present exposition has not yet begun, this is quite in order.

annihilated in the suffering of her good fortune—what wonder then
that the Jews assumed that to see God was to die, and the pagans
thought that the God-relationship was the precursor of madness![15]
Even though it be true that the conception of God is the absolute help,
it is also the only help which is absolutely capable of revealing to man
his own helplessness. The religious man lies in the finite as a helpless
child; he desires absolutely to hold fast to the conception, and precisely
this annihilates him; he desires to do all, and while he summons his
will to the task, his impotence begins, since for a finite being there is
always a meanwhile; he desires to do all, to express this religious
absoluteness, but he cannot make the finite commensurable therefor.

Is there anyone who wishes to laugh? If ever the position of the stars
in the firmament has signified something fearful, then the position of
the categories in this situation signifies something other than laughter
and jesting. Try now the proposal to take a pleasure outing in the
Deer Park. You will shrink from it, you will seek some excuse, it will
seem to you that there are higher ends for which a man can live. Just
so. And so you will turn away. But there is always a meanwhile—and
meanwhile the impotence returns. You will say to yourself: "little by
little." But there, where for the first time, the first beginning of this
little by little revealed itself as a transition from the absolute, there is
just the place where the fearfulness is. Novelistically, to let a year
intervene is naturally only to make a fool of myself and of the
religious individual.

The religious individual has lost the relativity of the immediate
consciousness, its distraction, its time-wasting activity—precisely, its
wastage of time; the absolute consciousness of God consumes him as the
burning heat of the summer sun when it will not go down, as the
burning heat of the summer sun when it will not abate. But so he is
sick; a refreshing sleep will strengthen him, and sleep is an innocent
employment of time. Aye, let one who has never had any intercourse
except with sleeping partners find it in his sleepy order to go to bed;
but one who has merely gone about with a great plan in his head, for
him the cry of the watchman is indeed a sad memento, and the approach
of sleep more saddening than the coming of death; for the sleep of
death is only a moment and a momentary check, but sleep is a long
delay.

Then let him begin some task. Perhaps taking the first that comes
to hand? No, let a nimble-fingered tradesman of the finite always have

something at hand to putter with; one who merely stands in a relationship to his beloved through the thought of love knows something different; when the will to do everything still does not seem enough, and
the exertion involved in willing all generates lassitude and weakness,
and he again stands at the beginning. But then he must come to himself,
seek to understand himself. Perhaps express himself in words? If one
who believes that to speak is to let one's tongue run on unchecked
can boast that he was never at fault for an expression, that he never
in vain sought for the right word—then one who merely lost his power
to speak in admiration of human greatness doubtless learned that at
least in such a moment he needed no admonition to keep his tongue
in check. And he that never went weeping to bed, weeping, not because
he could not sleep, but because he did not dare to remain longer awake;
and he that never endured to the end the suffering of the impotence
felt when making a beginning; and he that never was struck dumb,
he at least should never take it upon himself to talk about the religious
sphere, but remain where he belongs—in the sleeping chamber, in the
trading shop, in the tittle-tattle of the street. Nevertheless, how relative
must that be which permits a man to experience such things, how
relative in comparison with the individual's absolute relationship to the
absolute!

A man can do nothing of himself, this he should always bear in mind.
The religious individual is in this situation—he is thus among other
things also unable to take an outing in the Deer Park, and why?
Because he is in his own estimation better than other men? *Absit,*
this is the superior pose of the cloister. No, it is because he really is
a religious individual, not a fantastic clergyman who talks about
always or a fantastic listener who understands *always*—and *nothing.*
It is because he understands hour by hour that he can do nothing. In
his sickly condition, the religious individual is unable to bring the
God-idea together with such an accidental finitude as the taking a
pleasure outing in the Deer Park. He feels the pain of this, and it is
surely a deeper expression for his impotence that he understands it in
relation to something so insignificant, that the use of the pretentious
expression *nothing,* when nothing more is said, may readily become
unmeaning. The difficulty is not that he cannot do it, humanly
speaking, but the difficulty is first and foremost, to attain to a comprehension of his inability, and so to annul the illusion, since he should

always bear in mind that he can do nothing of himself—this difficulty he has conquered, and now there remains the second difficulty: with God to be able to do it.

The more critical an enterprise, a resolution, an event, the easier it is, precisely because it is more direct and natural, to bring the God-idea into relation with it—the easier it is; that is to say, this ease has its ground in the fact that one can be so easily self-deceived through resting in a delusion. In romances and novels one may frequently see at the great crises, either the entire novelistic personnel picturesquely grouped and kneeling in prayer, or the principal character kneeling by himself. However, the respected authors and authoresses are naïve enough to betray, by the content and form of the prayer, and by the attitude of the petitioner, that their heroes and heroines cannot have prayed many times before in their lives, and that, although the scene is laid in the year 1844, in a Christian country, and the persons are Christians, and both the romance and the novel have set themselves the task of describing men as they actually are, even a little better. With great inwardness the hero of the novel brings the God-idea into connection with this extremely important event—but from the religious point of view the inwardness of the prayer is not measured by its momentary impetuosity, but by its persistence. The more insignificant, on the other hand, anything is, the more difficult it is to bring the God-idea into relation with it; and yet it is precisely here that we have the touchstone of the God-relationship. In taking over a great resolution, in connection with the publication of a work that is to transform the world, in time of earthquakes, at golden-wedding festivities, in perils of the sea, when a child is born in secrecy, the name of God is perhaps used quite as often by way of ejaculation as religiously. One must not, therefore, let oneself be deceived by the fact that a clergyman ignores the petty events of life, concentrating his eloquence and gesticulation on great scenes; and then at most, half-abashed and as a tribute to decency, adds at the close of the discourse that one should also show in the daily life the same faith, the same hope, and the same courage; instead of planning his discourse conversely, as befits religious discourse, namely, with reference to the small events, the ordinary humdrum activities of life, and so at most adding a few words of warning against the illusion which may so easily be the foundation of that religiosity which manifests itself only on leap-year days.* The former is aestheticism, and aesthetically the invocation of God is neither more nor less than the loudest of ejaculations, God's manifestation of Himself in events is a theatrical tableau.

We left the religious individual in the crisis of his sickness, but this sickness is not unto death. We shall now permit him to be strengthened by precisely the same concept that annihilated him, the conception of God. I use again a foreshortened perspective, because the chief interest of my task has not yet begun; and I do not dwell upon how the ethical (which is always somewhat distant from the absolute God-relationship) must enter in regulatively, and take command. Nevertheless, I shall ask the reader to pause at this point for one or two remarks. First and foremost, that in each generation there are doubtless not many who even get so far as to exhaust the suffering connected with the beginning of the absolute God-relationship; and next, that a beginning in the medium of existence is far from being something that is decided once for all; for it is only on paper that one finishes the first state, and then has nothing further to do with it. The absolute exertion in the medium of existence is and remains merely an approximation, though this must not be understood comparatively, in relation to the more or less of others, for then the individual will have lost his ideality. This is because the eternal aims from above at the existing individual, who by existing is in process of movement, and thus at the moment when the eternal strikes, he is already a little moment away. The beginning of an absolute decision in the medium of existence is the last thing in the world that can be characterized once for all, as something left

* In general there is nothing so faithfully guarded by the comical as the religious, and its nemesis is nowhere so instantly at hand as it is in the religious sphere. When one listens to an aestheticising religious discourse in church, it is of course one's duty to be edified, even if his reverence rattles on ever so topsy-turvily; but when one calls it to mind again at a different time, the comic effect is not uninteresting, and the law for it is that where the speaker spreads every sail of eloquence to express the highest, there he satirizes without knowing it! "The praying individual arises from his prayer so strengthened, so very much strengthened, so extraordinarily strengthened." But religiously a man's true strengthening consists in being prepared to find that the struggle may begin again the next moment. "The individual binds himself to God by a promise, a sacred pledge, that he will ever and always, and so forth; and now he rises from his prayer in such peace of mind, in such great peace of mind." But religiously one is very careful about making vows (cf. Ecclesiastes),[16] and religiously the measure of the inwardness of the vow is the brevity of the posited term, and the distrust of oneself. No, the whole-souled inwardness of the individual and the consent of a heart purified from all double-mindedness to a promise for the present day, or for the forenoon—such a vow has religiously a greater degree of inwardness than this aestheticising clinking the glasses with Providence. The one procedure signifies that the maker of the vow has his life every day in the religious sphere, the other betrays satirically enough that he is a travelling member introduced by the clergyman.

behind; for the existing individual is not an abstract X, who passes through something and then goes on further, if I may so express myself, undigested through life. The existing individual becomes concrete in his experience, and in going on he still has his experience with him, and may in each moment be threatened with the loss of it; he has it with him not as something one has in a pocket, but his having it constitutes a definite something by which he is himself specifically determined, so that by losing it he loses his own specific determination. As a consequence of having made a decision in existence, the existing individual has attained a more specific determination of what he is; if he lays it aside, then it is not he who has lost something; he does not have himself while happening to have lost something, but he has lost himself and must now begin from the beginning.

The religious individual has thus got over his illness, though tomorrow perhaps it may return as the result of a little carelessness. He strengthens himself perhaps by means of the edifying consideration that God who made man must Himself know best all the many things that may seem impossible to bring into connection with the thought of God, all this earthly distress, all the confusion in which he may be involved, and the necessity of diversion, of rest, even of sleep.

It follows of itself that we do not here have reference to that indulgence which is proclaimed in the world, where one man comforts himself by appealing to another, where men console themselves mutually, and leave God out of account. Every human being is gloriously constituted, but what ruins so many is, among other things, also this wretched tittle-tattle between man and man about that which should be suffered and matured in silence, this confession before men instead of before God, this hearty communication between this man and that about what ought to be secret and exist only before God in secrecy, this impatient craving for intermediary consolation. No, in suffering the pain of his annihilation, the religious individual has learned that human indulgence profits nothing, and therefore refuses to listen to anything from that side; but he exists before God and exhausts the suffering of being human and at the same time existing before God. Therefore it cannot comfort him to know what the human crowd knows, man with man, what men know who have a shopkeeper's notion of what it means to be a man, and a facile gossipy notion at seventeenth hand of what it means to exist before God. From God he must derive his consolation, lest his entire religiosity be reduced to a rumor. That is not to say that he is to discover new truths, etc.; no, he is merely to keep a watch over himself lest the craving for gossip and the lust for preaching should prevent him from experiencing what thousands upon thousands have experienced before him. If it be true even of love, that only then does a love experience become ennobling when it teaches a man to keep his feeling within himself, how much more is this true about the religious!

Let us think about what paganism dreamed of in myths, that a god fell in love with an earthly woman. If she remained in ignorance of the fact that he was a god, this relationship would constitute the greatest possible unhappiness; for in consequence of the belief that the same standard was applicable to both, she would plunge herself into despair by requiring of herself an impossible likeness. If, on the other hand, she came to know that he was a god, she would at first be annihilated in all her lowliness, so that she would hardly dare face her inferiority; she would make one desperate attempt after the other to raise herself to his level; she would suffer the pangs of anxiety every time her lowliness made it necessary for them to be separated; she would be tortured agonizingly by the question whether it was her lack of will or lack of ability.

Let us now make the application to the religious. Where is the limit for the particular individual in his concrete existence between what is lack of will and lack of power, between what is slackness and earthly selfishness, and what is the limitation of his finitude; when is, for an existing individual, the period of preparation over, when this question cannot return with all its first anxious strenuousness, when does this moment come in existence, which in its entirety is a period of preparation? Let all the dialecticians in the world combine their exertions, they cannot decide the question for a particular existing individual *in concreto*. For dialectics is in its truth a benevolent helper, which discovers and assists in finding where the absolute object of faith and worship is—there, namely, where the difference between knowledge and ignorance collapses in absolute worship with a consciousness of ignorance, there where the resistance of an objective uncertainty tortures forth the passionate certainty of faith, there where the conflict of right and wrong collapses in absolute worship with absolute subjection. Dialectics itself does not see the absolute, but it leads, as it were, the individual up to it, and says: "Here it must be, that I guarantee; when you worship here, you worship God." But worship itself is not dialectics. A dialectic that mediates is a derelict genius.

The earthly woman who was loved by the god would then first be annihilated in her lowliness; but then she would doubtless learn to stand erect in the consciousness that he must know all this better than she. She would be annihilated through thinking divinely about him, but would stand erect again through the conception that he thought humanly about her. Aye, even when a maiden of lowly station is united with a king ruling over a foreign people, what suffering would she not endure in attempting to find assurance with respect to everything that reminded her of her lowliness, with respect to what seemed to constitute a hindrance to the relationship, striving to find peace of mind in that border warfare between being over-indulgent toward herself and requiring too much of herself!

But one ingredient in the lowliness of a human being is that he is temporal, and cannot endure to lead uninterruptedly the life of the eternal in time. And if his life is in time, then it is *eo ipso* piecemeal; and if it is piecemeal, it is sprinkled with diversions and distractions; and in the diversion the human being is absent from his God-relationship, or present in it, yet not as in the strong moment.

Men say it is a hardship when lovers are separated; should not then such separation be a heavy thing for the religious individual to bear, and is it less heavy because it is a diversion rather than a toilsome task that separates them, when the necessity for diversion is precisely the most unequivocal indication of his lowliness? For our religious individual is not so situated that the clergyman needs to admonish him to seek God; rather he is so strongly stirred that there must be diversion for him if he is not to perish. Here is the place where the monastic movement becomes tempting. Would it not become possible through superhuman exertion to approach nearer to God, to preserve the relationship without interruption, without sleep if possible! We say in another connection that love has power to make the lovers equal. Aye, and this is quite true with reference to a love-relationship between human beings, because they stand essentially on the same level, and the differences between them are accidental. Between God and man, however, there exists an absolute difference, and hence this direct equality is a presumptuous and dizzy thought, though this constitutes no comparative human indulgence from the utmost exertion. But since there is this absolute difference between God and man, how does the principle of equality in love express itself? By means of the absolute difference. And what is the form of this absolute difference? Humility. What sort of humility? The humility that frankly admits its human lowliness with humble cheerfulness before God, trusting that God knows all this better than man himself. The monastic movement is an attempt to be superhuman, an enthusiastic, perhaps even a devout attempt to resemble God. But herein lies the profound suffering of true religiosity, the deepest thinkable, namely, to stand related to God in an absolutely decisive manner, and to be unable to find any decisive external expression for this (for a happy love between human beings expresses itself externally in the union of the lovers). This inability is rooted in the necessary relativity of the most decisive external expression, in its being both too much and too little; it is too much because it involves a certain presumptuousness over against other men, and it is too little because it is after all a worldly expression.

There are thus two ways disclosed to deliberation: the way of humble diversion and the way of desperate exertion, the way to the Deer Park and the way to the cloister. To the Deer Park? Oh, yes, let me mention only this, though I might just as well name much else that comes under the same classification. A fool will doubtless laugh at this thought, and a priggish religious individual will feel offended, and both will serve as proof that the thought has its validity. But why mention such a thing as an outing in the Deer Park? It is much more elegant to talk on Sunday in very indeterminate and vague Sunday-decorous expressions about these innocent pleasures—and so on week-days to talk about them in vulgar terms. Of course it is more elegant, and I can suspect the degree of embitterment which will be aroused in the breast of a fastidious man by the word Deer Park in this connection; because in this connection it serves perhaps as an indirect reminder of the sense in which the religiosity of our time is more advanced than the medieval, and because it is unpleasant to have the religious by means of such a word brought so near home, instead of glimpsing it from afar, as when saying *nothing, always, never, daily watchfulness.*

Our religious individual chooses the way to the Deer Park, and why? Because he does not dare to choose the way to the cloister. And why does he not dare? Because it is too high-flown. So then he takes the outing. "But he does not enjoy himself," someone will say. Oh yes, he certainly does. And why does he enjoy himself? Because it is the humblest expression for his God-relationship to admit his humanity, and because it is human to enjoy oneself. If a woman can succeed in wholly transforming herself merely that she may please her husband, why should not the religious individual in his relation to God succeed in enjoying himself, when this is the humblest expression for the God-relationship?

If a poor workman were in love with a princess and thought himself to be loved by her, what would be the humblest mode of preserving the relationship? Would it not be by living exactly like other workmen, by going to his work as usual and sharing the life of the rest; and when, while at work, he fell to thinking about the relationship, by admonishing himself with the thought that humility would please the princess better than anything else as long as he constantly kept the thought of her quietly in his mind, and as long as he would more than gladly express the relationship in stronger terms if he dared? For it could never occur to the humble workman that the princess might be so foolish, and so foolishly worldly-minded, that she could find any sort of satisfaction in attracting the world's attention because of a workman's queer behavior, or the fact that she was loved by a laborer.

But there is a certain kind of religiosity which, presumably because the first beginning of its annihilation was not thorough enough and not thoroughly inward enough, entertains a notion of God that makes Him a jealous and stupid despot, driven by a sickly eagerness to have the whole world know, because of the queer gesticulations of some particular individual, that God is the object of a certain human being's love. As if God could desire any mark of distinction, or as if this were a suitable distinction for God, though everyone can see that it is no distinction at all for a princess to be loved by a laborer. Such religiosity is itself sickly, and therefore it makes God sickly in its imagination. That a tyrannically-minded human being might be imbued with the idea that the world should be brought to realize how much power he has over others by means of an ostentatious subjection on their part, surely proves nothing with respect to God. Or would the religious individual hesitate to do all this if it could occur to him to think in such a manner about God, as, namely, that God in the last analysis came to be in need of the world's admiration, and of an "awakened" individual's queer gesticulations, attracting the world's wonder and thereby directing the world's most august attention to the fact that God exists—poor God, who in His embarrassment at being invisible while still so dearly desiring that public attention should be focused upon Him, must sit there and wait for someone to do it for Him!

Up to this point I have kept my exposition still somewhat abstract, and shall now refer to my problem as if it were an occurrence of today, for today is Wednesday in the Deer Park season, and our religious individual is to take a pleasure outing, while I experimentally observe his psychological condition. It is easy enough to talk about it, to do it is something else. And yet, in a certain sense talking about it may not be quite so easy; I understand very well the risk I take, that I risk the loss of my little bit of reputation as an author, since everyone will find it extremely tiresome. It is still the same Wednesday in the Deer Park season, the whole thing is about taking an outing there, and yet so many pages have already been filled that a novelist would have had space to recount the highly interesting events of ten years, with great scenes and tense situations and assignations and clandestine childbirths; aye, so many pages have been used that half of them would have been enough for a clergyman to have finished up both time and eternity and death and the resurrection, *all* and *always* and *never* and *nothing,* and that in such a manner that one would have enough from one such sermon for the whole of life.

It is, accordingly, a Wednesday in the Deer Park season. The religious individual has understood himself in the general consideration of the significance of necessary diversion, but it does not by any means follow that diversion is necessary precisely today. Here lies the difficulty of the process of concretion, which remains as long as the religious individual is in the medium of existence, when he has to bring the general principle into connection with this particular moment on this particular day, with these particular moods and states of mind, and under these particular circumstances. When life is understood in this manner, the vain quantitative differences between human beings vanish, for the "how" of a man's inwardness determines the significance, not the quantitative "what."

Our religious individual happens to be an independent and well-to-do man who keeps a carriage and horses, and has in so far both time and means at his disposal for an outing in the Deer Park every day if he so desires. In this manner our experiment shapes up most effectively, for, as was said above, the religious address ought to be sufficiently ironical to make men more than usually fortunate in external circumstances, merely in order that the religious may thus more clearly show itself. A man who has only one Wednesday free during the season has perhaps not so many difficulties in getting away. But this ease, and the difficulty that he cannot get away on the other days, also makes it probable that the religious factor fails to become the decisive item in his motivation. It is with this as it is with seriousness. Many a man believes himself to be serious because he has a wife and children and burdensome engagements. But it does not follow from this that he has religious seriousness; his seriousness might also be moroseness and surliness. When religious seriousness is to be depicted, it therefore shows itself best in outwardly privileged circumstances; for here it cannot so easily be confused with something else.

Our individual will then first make sure that it is not a momentary craving, a whim of his immediacy, that determines him; he wishes to be conscious of the fact that he actually needs the diversion, and trusts that God doubtless also knows it. This is not the impudent self-assurance of an "awakened" individual over against God, as in general such an aesthetic coxcomb may be recognized by the fact that he has once for all secured his letter of credit from God. But though he is conscious of this, and that his search for diversion is not the craving of his immediacy, since he would more than gladly do without, nevertheless his concern of mind about this will arouse distrust of himself, the thought that perhaps he might be able to do without it a little longer. But on this point also he is conscious that as long ago as last Sunday he felt this need of diversion without giving way to the impulse, in order to prove from which side the impulse came; for he is convinced that God will not leave him in the lurch but help him to find the right, where the boundary that divides selfishness from the limitations of finitude is so difficult to find. But at the same moment when he anxiously begins to explore the possibility of doing without diversion so as to stick it out another day, almost at the same moment there awakes in him the human irritability which keenly feels the sting of being so dependent, of so constantly having to understand that a man can do nothing of himself. And this irritability is sophistical; it tries to make him think that the God-relationship is vitiated when it is applied to such insignificant matters, and that it reveals itself in its truth in great crises. And this irritability is proud; for although the religious individual has more than once convinced himself that yielding to the need for diversion is the humblest expression for the God-relationship, it is always seductive to understand what is perhaps not to be done in the same moment, seductive to understand something in the strong moment of enthusiasm when the work prospers under his hands, seductive in comparison with understanding it precisely when it is to be done in connection with a definite particularity.

But this *Anfechtung* vanishes again, for the religious individual is silent, and whoever is silent before God[17] doubtless learns to yield, but also learns that this is blessed. Had our religious individual had a gossipy friend at hand he would have reached the Deer Park easily enough, for it is a small matter when one has a carriage and horses and sufficient means, and is talkative—but in that case he would not have been our religious individual, and our religious individual also reaches the Deer Park. Now then, the resolution is made to seek diversion, and in the same moment the task is altered. If little by little the thought steals into his soul that it was a mistake, then he takes refuge in an ethical principle to defend himself against it; for over against a resolution taken after conscientious deliberation, a fugitive thought must not be permitted to play the rôle of master. He disarms this thought ethically, in order not again to be driven back into the highest relationship, whereby the significance of the diversion resolved upon would be nullified. Thus the movement of the mind is not here as when the clergyman preaches, in a direction toward the God-relationship; but the God-relationship itself bids the individual to withdraw from it temporarily; it is, as it were, an agreement entered into between God's solicitude and man's necessities. The ethical principle in question is quite simply this, that if a mistake has to be made, it is worse to become a fickle-minded waverer than resolutely to carry out what has been decided upon; for a habit of vacillation is the absolute ruin of every spiritual relationship.

We all await some great event, in order that we may have occasion to show in action what brave fellows we are; and when a crown prince takes up the reins of government in the mightiest European kingdom, taking over the responsibility for the destinies of millions, then there is occasion to conceive a resolution and to act *sensu eminenti*. Undeniably! But this is the profundity, and also the ironical feature of existence, that it is fully as possible to act *sensu eminenti* when the individual in question is a man, and the enterprise is to take an outing in the Deer Park. For the highest thing that His Imperial Highness can do is to make a resolution before God. The accent lies on this: before God; the many millions are only an illusion. But even the humblest man can conceive a resolution before God, and a man who is really so religious that he is able before God to resolve to take an outing in the Deer Park need not be put to shame when standing by the side of any imperial highness.

So much for the religious suffering, which is a dying away from immediacy; let this be sufficient. I myself feel most keenly how poor a showing it makes to prosecute inquiries in regard to such an everyday affair, one that everybody down to the simplest servant-girl and soldier-boy, is completely familiar with; how imprudent it is to admit the presence of difficulties, thus betraying one's inability to raise oneself even a little above the intellectual horizon of the lower classes; how near at hand is the satire, that after having devoted one's time and industry over a series of years, one realizes in the end no further advance than is involved in arriving at what the most stupid human being knows—alas, instead of in the same period of time and with the same industry, perhaps to have been able to produce something about China, Persia, or even astronomy. There are perhaps not ten people who have the patience to read what I have expounded above, and scarcely one man in the kingdom who would take the trouble to compose anything like it; which last, however, in one way consoles me, for if everybody can do it, if the work is mere routine, contract-writing by the sheet, then it becomes precisely my merit to have done what all can do (this is the humiliating feature of it for the weak human heart), but which no one else cares to do. Well, then, no one cares to expound it—but existentially to express it, to do it? To be sure there is one advantage that action has over description, namely, that what needs a long time to relate may be done so quickly—if one can. But before the individual has acquired this skill, what about the trouble involved in learning? Well, I merely say that I cannot do it; but since the point consists precisely in the hidden inwardness of religiosity, it is possible that they can all do it—at least there is no one who notices anything in their manner or behavior.

If, on the other hand, someone shrinks back in fear from facing the tremendous strenuosity of living in this manner (and how strenuous it is I can perceive sufficiently from the fact that even I who merely sit and experiment with it, and thus essentially keep myself outside, feel the strenuousness of this labor), well, I do not say anything to contradict him, though I admire the enterprise of inwardness which religiosity has embarked upon, admire it as the greatest of miraculous actions, but also frankly admit that I should not succeed in doing it: in passing from and with the highest conception of God and an eternal happiness to arrive at enjoying myself in the Deer Park. Miraculous it is, so I consider it; and I do not talk about it for the sake of making life still more troublesome for poor people, if it was my business to do so, far from it, since it is already troublesome enough for them; or for the sake of vexing any human being by making life more difficult for him, in so far as it is already sufficiently difficult, God forbid! On the contrary, I hope to render a service to the cultured classes, either by eulogizing the secret inwardness of their religiosity (for the point is that no one should notice anything, and there is no one who does), or else by making the matter, if possible, so difficult that it could meet their requirements, since in their going further they have left so many difficulties behind. For if anyone shrinks back in fear from facing the tremendous exertion involved in living thus, I find it still more fearful that there are those who even go further, and, moreover, go further by passing over to speculative philosophy and world-history—that I find more fearful still. Yet what am I saying—everything that has the characteristic of going further is known by its being *not only this, but also* something more; that, then, is something I find more fearful still, and also something more: fearfully stupid.

The significance of the religious suffering is that it is a dying away from immediacy; its reality consists in its essential persistence; but it belongs to the inwardness of a man, and must not express itself outwardly, as in the monastic movement. Now when we take a religious individual, as a knight of the secret inwardness, and set him down in the medium of existence, in relating himself to the environment there will emerge for him a contradiction, of which he must needs become conscious. The contradiction does not consist in his being different from all others—this self-contradiction is precisely the law for that nemesis which the ironical brings upon the monastic movement; but the contradiction is, that with all this inwardness hidden within him, with this pregnancy of suffering and blessing in his soul, his appearance is precisely like that of other men—whereby his inwardness is concealed, by the fact that he looks like other men.* Something comical is here

* Another author (in *Either-Or*) has properly carried the ethical back to the determination of self-revelation: that it is every man's duty to reveal himself.[18] Religiosity on the other hand is the secret inwardness, but not, please note, an immediacy which needs to be brought out into the open, not an unclarified inwardness, but an inwardness whose clarifying determination it is to be hidden. For the rest, it is something that surely scarcely needs to be called to mind, that when I say that the religious individual's incognito is to look just like everybody else,

present, for there is a contradiction here, and where there is a contradiction, there the comical is also present. This comical aspect, however, does not exist for others, who know nothing about it; but it exists for the religious individual himself, when humor is his incognito, as Frater Taciturnus says in *Stages on Life's Way*. And it is well worth the effort to seek a closer understanding of this; for next after the confusion pervading recent speculation, which identifies faith with immediacy, perhaps the most confusing notion prevalent among us is that humor is the highest stage; for humor is not yet religiosity, but lies on its boundary. With reference to this matter a few remarks will be found in the preceding, which I must ask the reader to bear in mind.

But is humor the incognito of the religious individual? Is it not his incognito that there is absolutely nothing that marks him off from others, absolutely nothing that could serve as a hint of his secret inwardness, not even so much as the humoristic? At the supreme maximum, if this can be obtained in existence, this would doubtless be so;* but as long as the conflict and the suffering persist in his inwardness, he will not succeed in wholly concealing it. But he will not express himself directly, and he will negatively prevent such a direct expression with the assistance of the humoristic. An observer who goes out among men to discover the religious individual, would therefore follow the rule of making everyone in whom he found the humoristic, the object of his attention. But if he has clearly understood the relation-

---

I do not thereby mean that his incognito should be the reality of a robber, a thief, or a murderer; for surely the world has not sunk to such depths that an open breach of legality can be regarded as representative of the universally human. No, the expression to look like everybody else, naturally secures for itself legality; but this may very well be present without there being any religiosity in a man.

* Such a "knight of faith" was depicted in *Fear and Trembling*. But this picture was only a daring and somewhat reckless anticipation, and the illusion created was gained by presenting this knight in a state of completeness, and hence in a false medium, instead of in the medium of existence. The beginning was made by running away from the contradiction of how an observer, generally speaking, could have his attention so aroused by him that he could now place himself admiringly outside, and admire him because there was nothing, absolutely nothing, to mark him; unless Johannes *de silentio* wishes to say that this knight of faith is his own poetic production. But then the contradiction is there again, in the fact that he takes the double standpoint of being at one and the same time both creative poet and observer in relation to the same character, and hence as poet produces a figure in the medium of the imagination (for this is the poet's medium), and then as observer, observes the same poetical figure in the medium of existence.

This dialectical difficulty seems to have attracted the attention of Frater Taciturnus, for he has avoided the difficulty by adopting the form of an experiment. Nor is he in the attitude of an observer with respect to the Quidam of the experiment, but translates his observation into a psychological-poetic production; and he makes this approach reality as nearly as possible by using, instead of the foreshortened perspective, approximately the standard of length found in existence, and also by the form of the experiment.

ships that obtain within the sphere of inwardness, he will also know that he may be deceived; for the religious individual is not a humorist, but a humorist only in his outward appearance. Thus, for example: an observer seeking a religious individual and finding me would be deceived, for he would indeed find the humoristic in me, but he would be deceived if he drew any conclusion from that alone; for I am not a religious individual, but solely a humorist.

Perhaps someone will feel that it is a fearful presumption on my part to call myself a humorist, and will avow that if I were really a humorist he would be only too ready to show me respect and honor. I shall neither dwell upon this possible criticism nor essay a reply; for the objector evidently assumes that the humoristic is the highest stage of life. I, on the contrary, say that the religious individual *stricte sic dictus* is infinitely higher than the humorist, and qualitatively different from him. And as for my critic's unwillingness to regard me as a humorist, I shall be perfectly willing to transfer the observer's attitude from myself to the objector, let the objector as observer focus his attention upon him: the result will be the same, the observer is deceived.

There are thus three spheres[19] of existence: the aesthetic, the ethical, the religious. Two boundary zones correspond to these three: irony, constituting the boundary between the aesthetic and the ethical; humor, as the boundary that separates the ethical from the religious.

Let us take irony. As soon as an observer discovers an ironist his attention will be aroused, for it is possible that the ironist is an ethicist. But he may also be deceived, for it does not necessarily follow that an ironist is an ethicist. The individual who lives in his immediacy is at once recognizable, and as soon as he is recognized it is a given fact that he is no ethicist, for he has not executed the infinite movement. The ironical response if correct (and the observer is supposed to be an experienced man who knows how to tease and trick the speaker to find out whether it is something which he has learned by rote, or whether there are adequate resources of irony behind his speech, as there always will be when the individual is an existing ironist) reveals that the speaker has exercised the infinite movement, but proves nothing more. Irony arises from the constant placing of the particularities of the finite together with the infinite ethical requirement, thus permitting the contradiction to come into being. Whoever can do this with facility, so that he does not permit himself to be caught off guard by any relativity where his skill is shy, must have executed the movement of infinitude in his soul, and in so far it is possible that he is an ethicist.* An observer will therefore not succeed in catching him out because of his inability to apprehend himself ironically; for this, too, comes within the scope of his ability, he can speak about himself as about a third party, he can place himself as a vanishing particularity in connection with the absolute requirement, aye, *set these two together;* how wonderful that the same expression which signifies the ultimate difficulty of human existence, which consists precisely in putting differences together (like the idea of God with an outing in the Deer Park), that the same expression also serves in our language to signify to set by the ears.

But although such an individual's realization of the infinite movement is given, it is not given that he is an ethicist. The latter is what he is solely and exclusively through maintaining an inner relationship to the absolute requirement. Such an ethicist uses irony as his incognito. Socrates was in this sense an ethicist, but it is well to note that he was an ethicist who tended well up toward the limit of the religious, for which reason we also gave some indication in the preceding (Chapter II, Section 2) of the analogies to faith presented by his existence. What then is irony, if we wish to call Socrates an ironist, not like Magister Kierkegaard consciously or unconsciously presenting only one side of him?[20] Irony is a synthesis of ethical passion which infinitely accentuates inwardly the person of the individual in relation to the ethical requirement—and of culture, which infinitely abstracts externally from the personal ego, as one finitude among all the other finitudes and particularities. This abstraction causes the emphasis in the first attitude to pass unnoticed, and herein lies the art of the ironist, which also insures that

* If the observer can catch him in a relativity which he does not have energy enough to apprehend ironically, then he is not really an ironist. For when irony is not taken in a decisive sense, every human being is at bottom ironical. As soon as a man who has his life in a certain relativity (and this shows precisely that he is not ironical) is placed outside of this in a relativity that he regards as lower (a nobleman, for example, in a circle of farmers; a professor in a group of rural school-teachers; a millionaire in a town together with poverty-stricken dependents; a royal coachman in a room together with peat-cutters;[21] a cook in a prominent family together with weed-pickers, etc.) he becomes ironical. That is to say, he is not really ironical, since his irony is simply that of a relative illusory superiority, but the symptoms and the phrases will have a certain resemblance to the ironical. But this is all merely a game within certain presuppositions; its inhumanity is readily recognized by the fact that the person in question cannot apprehend himself ironically; and its spuriousness is recognizable by the attitude of subjection which the same person assumes when a relativity appears which is higher than his own. Alas, this is what the world calls modesty: the ironist is proud!

the first movement shall be truly infinite.* The masses of men live in the converse manner; they are concerned to be something when somebody is looking at them; they are if possible something in their own eyes when others observe them; but inwardly, when the absolute requirement looks in upon them, there they have no taste for accentuating their own persons.

Irony is an existential determination, and nothing is more ridiculous than to suppose that it consists in the use of certain phraseology, or when an author congratulates himself upon succeeding in expressing himself ironically. Whoever has essential irony has it all day long, not bound to any specific form, because it is the infinite within him.

Irony is a specific culture of the spirit, and therefore follows next after immediacy; then comes the ethicist, then the humorist, and finally the religious individual.

But why does the ethicist use irony as his incognito? Because he grasps the contradiction there is between the manner in which he exists inwardly, and the fact that he does not outwardly express it. For the ethicist does indeed reveal himself, in so far as he pours himself forth in the tasks of the factual reality in which he lives; but this is something that the immediate individual also does, and what makes him an ethicist is the movement of the spirit† by which he sets his outward life inwardly in juxtaposition with the infinite requirement of the ethical, and this is something that is not directly apparent. In order not to be distracted by the finite, by all the relativities in the world, the ethicist places the comical between himself and the world, thereby insuring himself against

* The derelict Hegelian ethics, with its desperate attempt to make the State the court of last resort, is a most unethical attempt to reduce the individuals to finitude, an unethical flight from the category of the individual personality to the category of the race (cf. Chapter I of Section 2). The ethicist in *Either-Or* has already directly and indirectly protested against this; indirectly at the close of the essay on the equilibrium between the aesthetic and the ethical in the personality, where he himself is compelled to make concessions in the direction of the religious; and again at the close of the article on "Marriage" in the *Stages,* where even from the point of view of the ethics which he champions, which is quite the opposite of the Hegelian, he does indeed raise the price of the religious to as high a level as possible, but nevertheless makes room for it.

† When Socrates adopted a negative attitude toward the State, it is partly connected with the fact that his task was precisely to discover the ethical, partly with his dialectical position as an exception and *extraordinarius,* and finally with the fact that he is an ethicist tending toward the limits of the religious. Just as there is to be found in him an analogy to faith, so there must also be found an analogy to the hidden inwardness, only that he outwardly expressed this by means of negative action, by abstention, and in so far contributed toward helping people to become aware of him. The secret inwardness of religiosity in the incognito of humor evades attention by being like others, only that there is an echo of the humorist in the even response, and a tinge of it in the everyday mode of living, but it nevertheless requires a skilled observer to notice anything; the abstention practised by Socrates, nobody could fail to perceive.

becoming comical through a naïve misunderstanding of his ethical passion. An immediate enthusiast assails the world's ears with his twaddle early and late, always on his feet and arrayed in buskins, he plagues people with his enthusiasm, and he does not notice that what he says does not inspire them, unless they begin to beat him. He is well informed, and the orders are to effect a complete transformation—of the world; but there he has heard wrong, for the orders are to effect a complete transformation of himself. If such an enthusiast happens to be contemporary with an ironist, the latter will of course know how to utilize him profitably as comic material. The ethicist is, on the other hand, ironical enough to perceive that what interests him absolutely does not interest the others absolutely; this discrepancy he apprehends, and sets the comical between himself and them, in order to be able to hold fast to the ethical in himself with still greater inwardness. Now the comedy begins. The judgment of men upon such an individual will always be: for him there is nòthing that is important. And why not? Because for him the ethical is absolutely important, differing in this from men in general, for whom so many things are important, aye, nearly everything, but nothing absolutely important. Nevertheless, as we have said, an observer may be deceived if he accepts an ironist as an ethicist, for irony is only the possibility thereof.

So again in the case of the humorist and the religious individual, since according to the foregoing the dialectic of the religious sphere itself forbids the direct expression, forbids the outward difference by which recognition could be effected, protests against the assumed commensurability of the external, and yet honors the monastic movement, if there must be misdirection, as ranking much higher than mediation. The humorist constantly (this not in the sense of the clergyman's "always," but at every hour of the day, wherever he is, and whatever he thinks about or undertakes) sets the God-idea into conjunction with other things and evokes the contradiction—but he does not maintain a relationship to God in terms of religious passion *stricte sic dictus,* he transforms himself instead into a jesting and yet profound exchange-center for all these transactions, but he does not himself stand related to God. The religious man does the same, he sets the God-idea into juxtaposition with everything and sees the contradiction, but in his inmost conscious-ness he is related to God. An immediate religiosity rests in the pious superstition that it can see God directly in everything; the "awakened" individual has impudently made arrangements for God's presence wherever he himself happens to be, so that as soon as you catch sight of him you may be sure that God is there, because the "awakened" individual has Him in his pocket. Religiosity with humor as its incognito is there-fore a synthesis of absolute religious passion (the inwardness being dia-lectically produced) with a maturity of spirit, which withdraws the religiosity away from all externality back into inwardness, where again it is absolute religious passion.

The religious individual discovers that what occupies him absolutely seems to occupy others very little, but he draws no conclusion from this; partly because he does not have the time, and partly because he cannot know for certain whether all these people may be knights of the hidden inwardness. He feels compelled by the environment to do what the dialectical process of producing inwardness demands of him, namely, to set up a screen between himself and men, in order to safeguard and insure the inwardness of his suffering and his God-relationship.

From this it does not follow that such a religious individual becomes inactive. On the contrary, he does not leave the world but remains in it, for this is precisely his incognito. But he transforms his outward activity into an inward matter, inwardly before God, by admitting that he can do nothing of himself, by severing every teleological relation to his ac-tivity in the outward direction and cutting off every resultant in the finite world, although he labors to the limit of his powers; and this precisely is enthusiasm. An "awakened" individual always uses the name of God in an external fashion;* the certainty of faith is in him secure enough. It is certain that everything pleasing to God will prosper for the devout individual, so very certain, nothing being so certain as this. But now for the next consideration, and please note that the inquiry is not on paper but in the medium of existence, and that the believer is a particular existing individual situated in the concretion that existence brings with it. This then is an eternal certainty, that what pleases God prospers in the hands of the devout man. But now the next question: what is it that pleases God? Is it this or that, is it this occupation in life that he ought to choose, this young woman he ought to marry, this piece of work he ought to begin, this enterprise he ought to give up? Perhaps, and perhaps not. Is not this ironical enough? And yet it is an eternal certainty, and there is nothing else so certain, that what pleases God will

---

* Let me remind the reader: the life of an Apostle has a paradoxical dialectic, whence it comes that he turns himself outward; by so doing, everyone who is not an Apostle becomes only an aesthetician gone astray.

prosper for the devout. Yes, but on that account the religious man ought not so much to be concerned about external things, but rather seek the highest good, peace of mind, his soul's salvation: this always pleases God. And it is certain, as certain as that God lives, that the devout man will succeed in every undertaking that pleases God. Accordingly, it pleases God for him to seek the highest good; but when will success come? At once, or at the end of a year, or perhaps only at the end of this earthly life; may not the conflict and the trial of his faith last so long? Perhaps, and perhaps not. Is not this ironical enough? And yet it is certain, so very certain, that the devout man will succeed in whatever undertaking pleases God. If this certainty of conviction fails, then faith fails; but if the uncertainty which is the mark and form of faith ceases, we have not advanced in religiosity, but have retreated to childish forms of it. As soon as the uncertainty ceases to be the form of the certainty, as soon as the uncertainty no longer keeps the religious individual constantly on the *qui vive* to seize the certainty, as soon as certainty is permitted to weight the individual down as if with lead, that moment the religious individual is on the point of becoming a mere dead weight.

But the hidden inwardness with humor as its incognito seems to insure the individual against becoming a martyr; and this is a fate which the "awakened" individual would gladly welcome. To be sure the knight of hidden inwardness is safe, he is as a sucking infant in comparison with one who is "awakened" and cheerfully goes to meet his martyrdom—unless the martyrdom consists in that suffering of annihilation which is a dying away from immediacy, consists in the opposition encountered from the side of the divine itself against the existing individual, who is prevented from fully realizing the absolute relationship, a martyrdom, finally, which consists in his living in the world, with this inwardness in his breast without having any expression for it.

It is quite simply a psychological fact that the same energy which when directed outwardly accomplishes this or that, requires a still greater energy in order to check its outward striving. For when the energy is directed outwardly, and when the opposition comes from without, then the opposition is only in part to be reckoned as opposition, in part it is to be reckoned as help. Hidden inwardness has its martyrdom in itself. But is it not then possible that every other human being you meet is such a knight of hidden inwardness? Yes, why not? To whom could this assumption do any harm? Perhaps some individual who has a little religiosity and who thinks it unjust that this should not be openly

recognized, i.e. one who could not endure the sight, if the most passionate inwardness should outwardly deceptively resemble its opposite. But
why, then, does not such a religious individual choose the cloister, since
there is even there an opportunity for promotion to a higher rank, an
entire system of rankings for the religious individuals? The knight of
hidden inwardness would not be disturbed by such a sight, for he is
wholly occupied with being religious, and less concerned with seeming so (in so far as he must use some effort to prevent the seeming); it
would make absolutely no difference to him if all other men were held
in regard as religious.

But let us now turn from this hypothetical insight back to the observer. We have said that he may be deceived if without further ado he
accepts a humorist as a religious individual. In his own inwardness the
religious individual is anything but a humorist; on the contrary, he is
absolutely engrossed with his God-relationship. Nor does he posit the
comical between himself and others in order to make them ridiculous,
or in order to laugh at them (such an externality tends away from the
religious). But in view of the fact that true religiosity is that of the secret
inwardness, he dares not express his religiosity outwardly, because this
would infect it with worldliness. This renders it certain that he will discover the contradiction; and precisely because he has not yet wholly
succeeded into retiring into his inwardness, humor becomes his incognito, and an indication of his inner life. He does not conceal his inwardness in order to be able to apprehend others comically, but conversely:
in order that the inwardness that is within him may be inwardness in
truth, he conceals it, and in consequence of this concealment he discovers
the comical, which, however, he does not give himself time to dwell
upon. Nor does he feel himself to be better than others, for such a comparative religiosity is precisely externalism, and hence not religiosity.
Nor does he hold that others regard as a trifling jest what he regards as
the most important of all things; even if someone should say this, he has
no time to listen; but he knows that absolute passion marks the limit for
mutual understanding.

Absolute passion cannot be understood by a third party, and this holds
both for his relationship to others and for their relationship to him. In
absolute passion the individual is in the very extremity of his subjectivity, as a consequence of his having reflected himself out of every external
relativity; but a third party is precisely such a relativity. Even one who
is absolutely in love knows this. A lover who is absolutely in love does

not know whether he is more or less in love than others, for anyone who knows this is, just on that account, not absolutely in love. Nor does he know that he is the only lover who has been truly in love; for if he knows this, he knows precisely that he himself is not absolutely in love —and yet he knows that a third party cannot understand him, because a third party will understand him only generally with respect to the object of his passion, but cannot understand him in the absoluteness of his passion.

If anyone thinks that this has its explanation in the fact that the object of a lover's passion has an accidental character through being this particular object, and then offers the objection that God is not such a particular object, so that one religious individual should be able to understand the other in the absolute passion, the reply is that all understanding between man and man is always in terms of something external, something abstract, something with which neither can be identified. But in the absolute passion which is the very extreme of subjectivity, and in the inward "how" of this passion, the individual is precisely at the farthest possible distance from this externality. Nevertheless, love actually has a different dialectic from religiosity, for love is capable of outward expression while religiosity is not; that is, if the true religiosity is that of hidden inwardness, and if the monastic movement is a misdirection.

If anyone wishes to say that this hidden inwardness with humor as its incognito is pride, he merely informs against himself, that he is not religious; for otherwise he would be in precisely the same case as the person he judges, absolutely introverted. What the objector really desires to accomplish by his objection is to involve the religious individual in a relative squabble about which of the two is more religious, and so attain that neither of them becomes religious. In general, there are a great number of objections which merely contain self-accusations, and in thinking of such I often call to mind a story about an army lieutenant and a Jew, who met one another on the street. The lieutenant was angered because the Jew looked at him, and burst out: "What is the Jew staring at?" The Jew answered with a correct irony: "How do you know, lieutenant, that I am looking at you?" No, indeed, if anything is pride and presumption, and I say this without having any particular person in mind, much less presuming his awareness, then it is the direct expression for the God-relationship, every direct expression by means of which the religious individual seeks to make himself manifest.

If the God-relationship is man's highest distinction, highest, although open to everybody, the direct expression for it is presumptuous. And this holds even for the direct expression for what is called being an outcast, one rejected of God. Aye, even the transformation of the world's derision into a direct expression for one's own religiosity is presumption, for the direct expression involves indirectly an accusation against the others, an assertion that they are not religious. The humane religiosity is that of the secret inwardness in absolute passion, wherein again there lies an acknowledgement that every other human being has an equal approach to God. For whoever desires to know, in absolute inwardness, that he is one of the elect, is *eo ipso* lacking in inwardness, since his life is on a comparative basis. It is this comparative and relativising tendency which often enough seeks with unconscious self-deception an easy indulgence, under the form of a mutual heartfelt outpouring of feeling. One who is absolutely in love has absolutely nothing to do with third parties; he willingly assumes that all others are as deeply in love as he; he finds no human being ridiculous in the character of a lover. But he finds it ridiculous that he should *qua* lover stand related to a third party, just as, conversely, every other lover would find him ridiculous if he desired to play the rôle of a third party.

The religiosity of hidden inwardness does not permit the individual to regard himself as better than any other human being; nor does it permit him to be distinguished by the God-relationship in any other way than every human being can be, much less more distinguished than others. But he also knows that if there is a third party present as a witness (with his knowledge, that is, for otherwise it is the same as if there were no witness) to the fact that he humbles himself before God, then he does not humble himself before God. However, it follows from this quite consistently that he will participate in the outward worship; for partly his impulse to do so will be like that of all other men, and partly, to abstain therefrom would be a worldly attempt negatively to call attention to himself; and finally, there is no third party there, at least not with the knowledge of the religious individual, since he naturally assumes that everyone of those present is there for his own sake and not to observe others; which last is not even the case with those who according to the words of a high landed proprietor, go to church for the sake of the servants, so as to set them a good example—of how one ought not to go to church.

The comical is brought out when the hidden inwardness comes into relationship with an environment, in that the religious individual comes to hear and see that which when brought into conjunction with his inward passion, produces a comic effect. Hence even when two religious individuals converse with one another, the one will produce a comic impression on the other, for each of them will constantly have his own inwardness in mind, and will now hear what the other says in the light of this, and hear it as comical, because neither dares directly express the secret inwardness; at most they will entertain a suspicion of one another because of the humoristic undertone.

Whether there really exists or has existed such a religious person as above described, whether all are religious or no one is, I do not propose to decide, nor would it be at all possible for me to decide. Even if I really were a skilled observer, I should get no farther in relation to such a religious individual than to form a suspicion because of the humoristic —and as far as I am concerned, I know only too well that I am not religious. But surely I may be permitted the satisfaction of sitting here and experimenting, to see how such a religious individual would conduct his life, without in speculative fashion committing myself to the paralogism of inferring existence from the hypothetical, contrary to the old rule: *conditio non ponit in esse;* much less concluding from my hypothetical thinking that it is myself, by virtue of the identity of thought and being. My experiment is as innocent as possible, far, far from affronting anyone; for it is not so personal as to say about anyone that he is a religious person, and it does not offend anyone by denying that he is religious. It establishes the possibility that no one is religious and the possibility that everyone is religious—with the exception of those who cannot be offended, because they themselves say that they are not religious in this sense, either directly as I do it, or indirectly by claiming to have gone further.

Also in this category must be placed one or another "awakened" person, whom it would offend if it were asserted of him that he was a religious individual of this type—and my experiment proposes to offend no one. Hence it willingly admits that such an "awakened" person is not a knight of hidden inwardness; this is evident enough, for the "awakened" person makes himself sufficiently manifest. Just as there is an ungodliness which courts recognition, and desires to be known openly, so there is also a corresponding godliness; though in this case one must take note of whether the factor of display may not be due to the fact that the "awakened" person is sickly, being overwhelmed by the religious impression, so that the display of his religiosity is a helpless condition under which he suffers, until the religiosity within him gathers itself together more normally in inwardness. But where godliness courts recognition as godliness, the situation is different. It is a devout and, in the strictest sense, godly expression for the relationship to God, that one acknowledges oneself to be a sinner; there is an ungodliness that seeks to become known through an attitude of defiance, which loudly denies it. But now the other side of this manifestation of the religious: if three "awakened" persons carried on a dispute of honor between them concerning which of them was the greatest sinner, hence a sort of brawl about this dignity, then it is clear that the godly expression has for them become a worldly title.

A principle propounded by Lord Shaftesbury,[22] which makes laughter a test of truth, was the occasion during the last century for the appearance of one or another little inquiry[23] as to whether this is so or not. In our time the Hegelian philosophy has desired to give preponderance to the comical,[24] which might seem a particularly strange thing for the Hegelian philosophy to do, since this philosophy is surely least of all equipped to withstand an attack from that side. In ordinary life we laugh when something is made to seem ridiculous, and after having laughed we sometimes say: but one is really not justified in making such a thing ridiculous. But if the comic interpretation is well done, one cannot restrain oneself from laughingly spreading the story further—naturally accompanied by the edifying afterthought: but it is not right to make such a thing ridiculous. It goes unnoticed how ridiculous this is, that there is a contradiction in the fictitious attempt to act ethically by means of an edifying afterthought, instead of renouncing the illegitimate antecedent. Now when this is so, when the advance and wider dissemination of culture and polished manners, when the refinement of life contributes to develop a sense for the comic, so that an overwhelming partiality for the comical is characteristic of our time, which both in the correct and the incorrect sense seems to rejoice in the Aristotelian view that lays stress on a sense for the comic as a distinguishing mark of man's nature—in such circumstances the religious address must long since have taken note of how the comical stands related to the religious. For what occupies the minds of men so much, what constantly recurs in conversation, in intercourse, in books, in the modifications of the entire view of life, that is something that the religious dare not ignore; unless indeed the Sunday performances in church are meant to constitute a kind of indulgence, where at the price of a grumpy devotionalism for an hour's time, one buys immunity to laugh unchecked the whole week through. The question of the legitimacy of the comic, of its relationship to the religious, of whether it does not have a place in the religious address itself—this question is of essential significance for a religious existence in our times, where the comical everywhere runs away with the victory. To cry alas and alack over this tendency only proves how little the champions of religion respect what they fight for. It is surely an indication of far greater respect for the religious to demand that it be given its proper place in daily life, than to keep it at a Sunday-distance away from life, in high-flown eccentricity.

The matter is quite simple. The comical is present in every stage of life (only that the relative positions are different), for wherever there is life, there is contradiction, and wherever there is contradiction, the comical is present. The tragic and the comic are the same, in so far as both are based on contradiction; but *the tragic is the suffering contradiction, the comical, the painless contradiction.** That something which the

* The Aristotelian definition (Chapter V of the *Poetics*): τὸ γὰρ γελοῖόν ἐστιν ἁμάρτημά τι καὶ αἶσχος ἀνώδυνον οὐ φθαρτικόν[25] is such that it fails to leave entire families of the comical secure in their ludicrousness, and it becomes doubtful whether the definition, even in relation to the part of the comical that it covers, does not bring us into collision with the ethical. His example: that we laugh at an ugly and distorted countenance when this does not entail pain for the one who has it, is neither quite correct nor so happily chosen as to clear up at a single stroke the secret of the comical. The example lacks reflection, for even if the distorted countenance does not cause pain, it is nevertheless painful to be destined thus to arouse laughter as soon as one shows one's face. It is handsome and correct of Aristotle that he wishes to separate from the sphere of the ridiculous that which tends to arouse compassion, to which also belongs the wretched and the pitiful. Even in comic poets of high rank it is possible to find examples of the use of what is not purely ludicrous, but has an admixture of the pitiful: ("Trop," for example, is in several scenes more pitiful than ludicrous. The "Busy Man," on the contrary, exemplifies the ridiculous unmixed, precisely because he is in possession of every condition necessary to live carefree and happily). In this sense the Aristotelian example lacks reflection, but the definition also lacks it, in so far as it conceives the ludicrous as a something, instead of recognizing that the comical is a relation, the faulty relationship of contradiction, but free from pain.

I shall here tumultuously throw in a few examples, to show that the comical is present wherever there is a contradiction, and wherever one is justified in ignoring the pain, because it is non-essential.

Hamlet swears by the fire-tongs;[26] the comical lies in the contradiction between the solemnity of an oath and the attribution which annuls the oath, whatever its object. If one were to say: "I would stake my life that there is fully four shillings worth of gold in the binding of this book,"[27] it would be comical. The contradiction is that between the highest pathos (to risk one's life) and the object; it is teasingly sharpened by the word *fully,* which keeps open the prospect of perhaps four and one-half shillings worth, as if that were less contradictory. Holophernes[28] is said to be seven and one-fourth yards tall. The contradiction lies essentially in the fraction. The seven yards are fantastic, but the fantastic is not in the habit of speaking about quarter-fractions; the quarter of a yard as a measure is reminiscent of reality. Whoever laughs at the seven yards does not laugh correctly, but he who laughs at the seven yards and a quarter, knows what he laughs at. When the clergyman gesticulates most vigorously where the category is in a lower sphere, it is comical; it is as if one were to say calmly and indifferently, "I will sacrifice my life for my country," and then add with the highest pathos, with gestures and play of countenance, "Aye, I will do it for ten dollars." But when it happens in church I must not laugh, because I am not an aesthetic spectator but a religious auditor, whatever the clergyman may be.

It is genuinely comical for Pryssing to say "he" in speaking with Trop,—and why? Because the Maecenas-relativity that Pryssing thus seeks to establish over against Trop is in contradiction with the total ludicrousness within which Trop and Pryssing are equals and on a basis of equality.

When a child of four turns to a child of three and a half years and says patronizingly: "Come now, my little lamb," it is comical; although because neither of the children is ridiculous *per se,* one smiles rather than laughs, and the smile is not without its emotion. But the comic lies in the relativity that the youngster seeks to establish against the other; the moving feature lies in the childlike manner in which it is done.

When a man seeks permission to establish himself as innkeeper and is refused, it is not comical; but if the refusal is based on the fact that there are so few innkeepers, then it is comical, because a reason for is used as a reason against. Thus there is a story about a baker who said to a poor person: "No, mother, I cannot give you anything; there was another here recently whom I had to send away without giving anything: we cannot give to everybody." The comical lies in the circumstances that he seems to reach the sum and result—all, by subtracting.

When a woman seeks permission to establish herself as a public prostitute, this is comical. We properly feel that it is difficult to become something respectable (so that when a man is refused permission to become master of the hounds, for example, this is not comical), but to be refused permission to become something despicable, is a contradiction. To be sure, if she receives permission, it is also comical, but the contradiction is different, namely, that the legal authority shows its impotence precisely when it shows its power: its power by giving permission, its impotence by not being able to make it permissible.

Errors are comical, and are all to be explained by the contradiction involved, however complicated the combinations.

When something that is in itself comical has become customary, and so belongs to the order of the day, it does not arouse attention, and we laugh only when it is manifested in some higher degree. When we know that a man suffers from distraction, we become familiar with it and do not reflect upon the contradiction, until it reduplicates itself upon occasion, when the contradiction is, that what is intended to conceal the first distraction reveals one still greater. As when an absent-minded person puts his fingers in a bowl of salad served by the waiter, and when he discovers his distraction, in order to conceal it, says: "Ah, I thought it was caviar"; for caviar is not eaten with the fingers either.

A discontinuity in speech may produce a comic effect because there is a contradiction between the discontinuity and the rational conception of human speech as something connected. If it is a madman who speaks thus, we do not laugh.

When a farmer knocks at the door of a man who speaks only German, and talks with him to find out whether there is not someone in the house, whose name the farmer has forgotten, but who has ordered a load of peat, and the German, in impatience at being unable to understand what the farmer is talking about, says: "Das ist doch wunderlich," to the great joy of the farmer who says: "That is right, Wunderlich was the man's name"; then the contradiction is that the German and the farmer cannot talk together because the language is in the way, and in spite of this, the farmer gets his information with the aid of the language.

Through being involved in a contradiction, that which is not in itself ridiculous may produce laughter. When a man goes dressed in a strange manner for everyday use, but then once in a while appears elegantly dressed, we laugh at this, because we remember the other.

When a soldier stands in the street and gazes at the glorious display in the window of a fancy-goods shop, and he comes closer to see better, when he then with glowing countenance, and eyes fixed solely on the window display, fails to discover that the cellar comes dangerously far forward, so that just as he is about to see best, he pitches into the cellar—the contradiction is in his movement, the head and the eyes directed upward, and then the subterranean movement down into the cellar. If he had not been looking upward, it would not have been so ludicrous. Therefore it is also more comical when a man who walks about gazing at the stars falls into a hole in the ground, than when it happens to one who is not so uplifted above the earthly sphere.

It is for this reason that an intoxicated man can produce so comical an impression, because he expresses a contradiction in his movements. The eye requires steadiness of gait; the more there still remains some sort of reason to require it, the more comical is the contradiction (a completely intoxicated man is therefore less comical). Now if a purposeful man, for example, comes by, and the intoxicated individual, his attention drawn to him, gathers himself together and tries to steady his gait, then the comical becomes more evident; because the contradiction is clearer. He succeeds for a couple of steps, until the spirit of contradiction again runs away with him. If he succeeds entirely while passing the purposeful man, the first contradiction becomes another: that we know him to be intoxicated, and that this is, nevertheless, not apparent. In the one case we laugh at him while he sways, because the eye requires steadiness of him; in the second case we laugh at him because he holds himself steady when our knowledge of his condition requires that we should see him sway. So it also produces a comic effect when a sober man engages in sympathetic and confidential conversation with one whom he does not know is intoxicated, while the observer knows of the condition. The contradiction lies in the mutuality presupposed by the conversation, that it is not there, and that the sober man has not noticed its absence.

It is comical when in ordinary conversation a man uses the rhetorical question of the sermon (which does not demand an answer, but only forms a transition for the speaker's answering it himself); it is comical when the man he speaks to misunderstands it, and interjects the answer. The comic lies in the contradiction involved in attempting to be an orator and a conversationalist at the same time, or wishing to be an orator in a conversation; the other's error reveals this, and is a righteous nemesis; for anyone who uses such forms in talking with another says indirectly— "We do not converse with one another, but it is I who am the speaker."

A caricature is comical, and why? Because of the contradiction between likeness and unlikeness; the caricature must resemble a human being, an actual, particular person; if it resembles no one at all, it is not comical, but is a straightforward essay in the sphere of the unmeaning fantastic.

The shadow of a man on the wall, while you sit and talk with him, can produce a comic effect because it is the shadow of the man you are talking with (the contradiction is that you see at the same time that it is not he). If you were to see the same shadow on the wall, but no man was present, or if you saw the shadow and not the man, it would not be comical. The more the man's reality is accentuated, the more comical the shadow becomes. If one is impressed by the expression of the face, for example, the tone of voice, and the correctness of the remarks— and at the same moment sees the caricaturing shadow, then the comic effect is greatest, unless it wounds the sensibilities. If it is a scatterbrain who talks, the shadow does not so much impress itself as comical, but it rather satisfies one that the shadow resembles him ideally.

Contrast produces a comic effect by means of the contradiction, whether the relationship is that the in and for itself non-ridiculous is used to make ridiculous the ridiculous, or the ridiculous makes that ridiculous which is in itself non-ridiculous, or the ridiculous and the ridiculous make each other mutually ridiculous, or the in and for itself non-ridiculous and the in and for itself non-ridiculous become ridiculous through the relationship.

When a German-Danish clergyman says from the pulpit: "The word became pork (*Flaesk*, *Fleisch*) that is comical. The comical lies not merely in the general contradiction which arises when a man speaks in a foreign language with which he is unfamiliar, and produces on the mind an entirely different impression from the one he intends; but the contradiction is made sharper by the fact that he is a clergyman, and that he is preaching, since speaking in connection with a clergyman's address is used in a very specific sense, and the least that can be assumed is that he can speak the language. Besides, the contradiction tends to wander in upon the ethical sphere: that a man may innocently come to make himself guilty of blasphemy.

When in a cemetery, one reads on a gravestone verses in which a man pours his heart out in bewailing the loss of his son for three lines, until he finally exclaims in the fourth line: "Console yourself, O Reason, he shall live!" and finds this outpouring signed: Hilarius, the Execu-

comic apprehension envisages as comical may entail imaginary suffering for the comical individual, is quite irrelevant. In that case, for example, it would be incorrect to apprehend the hero of Holberg's *The
Busy Man* as comical. Satire also entails pain, but this pain has a dialectic
which gives it a teleology in the direction of a cure. The difference between the tragic and the comic lies in the relationship between the
contradiction and the controlling idea. The comic apprehension evokes
the contradiction or makes it manifest by having in mind the way out,

tioner, this will certainly produce a comic effect on everyone. First, the name itself, Hilarius, will
in this connection make a comic impression, one thinks involuntarily: "When a man's name is
Hilarius, what wonder that he knows how to console himself!" Then comes his dignity as
executioner; for it is indeed true that every man can have feeling, but there are certain situations
in life that do not seem to stand in a very close relation to tenderness of feeling. Finally the
expression: Console yourself, O Reason! That perhaps a professor of philosophy might get the
notion of confusing himself with Reason, might at any rate be plausible; but for an executioner,
this will be more difficult. If anyone were to object that it is not himself the executioner addresses
(Console yourself, O abstract being!) but Reason, the contradiction is quite as comical; for say
what you will about Reason in our time, it is still a daring assumption to suppose that it is on
the road to despair because Hilarius lost his son.

Let these examples be sufficient, and let everyone whom the note disturbs leave it unread.
It is easy to see that the examples are not carefully collected, but also that they are not odds and
ends from aestheticians. Of the comical there is certainly enough everywhere, and at every time,
if a man only has an eye for it; one could continue indefinitely, unless through being clear about
where to laugh, one also understood where not to laugh. Let the comic be brought to consciousness; it is no more immoral to laugh than it is immoral to weep. But just as it is immoral
to go around whining at all times, so it is also immoral to give oneself up to the indefinite
excitement which lies in laughing when one does not really know whether to laugh or not,
so that one does not enjoy the laughter, and makes it impossible to repent if one has laughed in
the wrong place. Hence the comical has become the tempter in our time, because it is almost
as if it desires the appearance of illegitimacy in order to acquire the enchantment of the forbidden, and again as the forbidden intimates that laughter can destroy everything. But though
I do not have much to be proud of *qua* author, I am nevertheless proud in the consciousness
that I can scarcely be accused of having exercised my pen in connection with the comical, that I
have never permitted my pen to serve the interest of the moment, that I have never applied
the comic point of view to anyone or anything, without first, by putting the categories together,
inquired from what sphere the comic came, and how it would be related to the same thing or
the same person if pathetically apprehended. Really to acquire a clear consciousness of where
the comic lies is also satisfying, and there are perhaps many who would lose their laughter if they
understood it, but such a man has really never had a sense for the comic, and yet it is on the
laughter of such people that all those reckon who muddle around with the comical. There are
also perhaps some who can be comically productive only in recklessness and abandon, who, if it
were said to them: "Remember you are ethically responsible for the way in which you use your
comic powers," would lose their *vis comica*. And yet in relation to the comical it is precisely
the opposition which gives it its vigor, and prevents a man from capsizing. Recklessness and
frivolity as productive energies produce the loud laughter of indeterminancy and sensuous
irritability, which is extremely different from the laughter that accompanies the great translucency
of the comical. If one desires to learn in a good school, one should for a time renounce laughing
at what arouses antipathetic passion, where turgid forces may easily carry a man away; exercising
oneself rather in perceiving the comical in this or that for which one has partiality, where the
sympathy and the interest, aye, the partiality, create the disciplinary opposition against incon-
siderateness.

which is why the contradiction is painless. The tragic apprehension sees the contradiction and despairs of a way out. It is a matter of course that this must be understood so that the various nuances of the comic are again kept subject to the qualitative dialectic of the different spheres, which passes judgment upon all subjective arbitrariness. Thus if one proposed to make everything comical by means of nothing, it is clear at once that his comedy is nowhere at home, since it lacks a foothold in any sphere. The discoverer of this type of comedy would himself be open to comic apprehensions from the standpoint of the ethical sphere, because as an existing individual he must himself in one way or another have a foothold in existence.

If one were to say: repentance is a contradiction, *ergo* it is comical, it would at once be apparent that this is nonsense. Repentance belongs in the ethico-religious sphere, and is hence so placed as to have only one higher sphere above it, namely, the religious in the strictest sense. But it was not the religious it was proposed to make use of in order to make repentance ridiculous; *ergo* it must have been something lower, in which case the comic is illegitimate, or something only chimerically higher, as for example the sphere of abstraction; and then our friend of laughter is himself comical, as I have frequently in the preceding sought to show over against speculative philosophers, namely, that in consequence of having made themselves fantastic, and in that manner having attained to the highest standpoint, they have made themselves comical. The lower can never make the higher comical, i.e. it cannot legitimately apprehend the higher as comical, and has not the power to make it comical. It is another thing that the lower, by being brought into conjunction with the higher, may make the relationship ridiculous. Thus it is possible for a horse to be the occasion for a man showing himself in a ridiculous light, but the horse has no power to make him ridiculous.

The different existential stages take rank in accordance with their relationship to the comical, depending on whether they have the comical within themselves or outside themselves; yet not in the sense that the comical is the highest stage. The immediate consciousness has the comical outside itself, for wherever there is life there is contradiction, but the contradiction is not represented in the immediate consciousness, which therefore has the contradiction coming from the outside. A finite worldly wisdom presumes to apprehend immediacy as comical, but thereby itself becomes comical; for the supposed justification of its comic apprehension is that it definitely knows the way out, but the way out which it knows is still more comical. This, then, is an illegitimate comic apprehension. Wherever there exists a contradiction and the way out is not known, where the contradiction is not cancelled and corrected in something higher, there the contradiction is not painless;* and where the correction is based on something only chimerically higher (from the frying-pan into the fire), it is itself still more comical, because the contradiction is greater. Thus in the relationship between immediacy and finite worldly wisdom. A comic apprehension on the basis of despair is also illegitimate, for despair is despair because it does not know the way out, does not know the contradiction cancelled, and ought therefore to apprehend the contradiction tragically, which is precisely the way to its healing.

Humor has its justification precisely in its tragic side, in the fact that it reconciles itself to the pain, which despair seeks to abstract from, although it knows no way out. Irony is justified as over against immediacy, because its state of equilibrium, not as mere abstraction but as an existential art, is higher than the immediate consciousness. Only an existential ironist is therefore justified over against immediacy; total irony once for all, like a bargain-priced notion set down on paper, is, like all abstractions, illegitimate over against every sphere of existence. Irony is indeed an abstraction, and an abstract putting together of things, but the justification of the existential ironist is that he expresses this himself existentially, that he preserves his life in it, and does not toy with the grandeurs of irony while himself having his life in Philistinism; for then his comic apprehension is illegitimate.

The immediate consciousness has the comical outside itself; irony has it *within* itself.† The ethicist who has irony as his incognito can again

* But this must be so understood as not to forget that not knowing the way out may be subject to apprehension as comical. In this way the "Busy Man" of Holberg's play is comical, because it is comical that a rational being, a well-to-do man, does not know the way out of all this bookkeeper nonsense, the way out of which quite simply consists not in taking on still another couple of scribblers to confer with, but in driving them all out through the door.

† Aristotle remarks (*Rhetoric* 3:18) ἔστιν δ' ἡ εἰρωνεία τῆς βωμολοχίας ἐλευθεριώτερον. ὁ μὲν γὰρ αὑτοῦ ἕνεκα ποιεῖ τὸ γελοῖον, ὁ δὲ βωμόλοχος ἑτέρου.[29] The ironist enjoys the comical himself, in contrast with the prankster, who serves others by making something ridiculous. An ironist, therefore, who needs assistance from friends and relatives and town criers in order to be able to enjoy the comical, is *eo ipso* a mediocre ironist and on the way to becoming a buffoon. But there is also another sense in which the ironist has the comical within him and by bringing it to consciousness has insured himself against having it outside of himself. As soon as an existential ironist falls out of his irony he becomes comical, as if, for example, Socrates had become pathetic on the day of his death sentence. It is in this that his justification is to be found, when irony is no jackanapes trick, but an existential art; for

see the comic side of irony, but assures himself of justification only through constantly holding himself to the ethical, and therefore sees the comical only as constantly vanishing.

Humor has the comical *within* itself, and is justified in the existential humorist; for humor once for all *in abstracto* is as illegitimate as everything else that is in this manner abstract; the humorist earns his justification by having his life in his humor. Against religiosity only it is not justified, but it is justified against everything that courts recognition as religiosity. The religiosity which has humor as its incognito can also see the humoristic as comical, but preserves its justification only by constantly keeping itself in religious passion with respect to the God-relationship, and hence it sees the comic aspect of humor only vanishingly.

Now we have reached the limit. The religiosity of hidden inwardness is *eo ipso* inaccessible to comic apprehension. The comical cannot be outside it, precisely because it is hidden inwardness and therefore cannot come into contradiction with anything. The sphere of contradiction which humor dominates, including as it does the highest range of the comical, is something that such religiosity has itself brought to consciousness, and it has it within itself as something lower. Thus it is absolutely secured against the comical, or is by means of the comical secured against the comical.

When the religious in church and state has sometimes sought the assistance of legislation and the police against the comical, this may be very well intentioned, but the question is whether the motivation is in the last analysis religious in character; and it is certainly unjust to the comical to regard it as an enemy of the religious. The comical is no more than the dialectical an enemy of the religious, which everything on the contrary serves and obeys. But the religiosity which essentially pretends to externality, essentially makes the external commensurable, needs to look to itself, and to fear itself more than the comical (lest it become aesthetics); the comical might indeed legitimately help it get its eyes open. Much in Catholicism may serve as an example of this. And as far as the individual is concerned, the principle holds that a religious individual who wants everybody to be serious, perhaps even serious in precisely the same manner that he is, because he is stupidly serious, is involved in a contradiction, and the religious individual who cannot endure, if it comes to that, that all others laugh at what interests him

then the ironist solves greater problems than the tragic hero, precisely by his ironic mastery over himself.

absolutely, is lacking in inwardness, and hence desires the consolation of an illusion, the knowledge that many are of the same opinion as he, aye, of the same type of countenance; and he will be edified by adding the weight of the world-historical to his own bit of reality, "since now everywhere a new life is beginning to stir, the heralded new era, with eye and heart for the cause."[30]

The hidden inwardness is inaccessible to the comical, as can also be seen from the fact that if such a religious individual could be incited suddenly to externalize his religiosity, if for example he so far forgot himself as to come into conflict with a comparative religious individual, and again so forgot himself and the absolute requirement of inwardness as to wish comparatively to be regarded as more religious than the other, then he is comical, and the contradiction consists in his wishing at one and the same time to be visible and invisible. Humor makes use of the comical over against presumptuous forms of the religious, precisely because a religious individual must know the way out if he merely wills to know it. If this cannot be presumed, such a comic apprehension of him becomes dubious in the same sense as a comic apprehension of Holberg's hero in *The Busy Man,* if it were assumed that he really was weak-minded.

The law for the comical is quite simple: it exists wherever there is contradiction, and where the contradiction is painless because it is viewed as cancelled; for the comical does not indeed cancel the contradiction, but a legitimate comic apprehension can do so, otherwise it is not legitimate. Talent in this field consists in the ability to represent the comical *in concreto.* The test of the comical is to be found in the relationship between the spheres which the comical presupposes; if this relationship is not correct, the comic apprehension is illegitimate; and a comic apprehension which has no foothold anywhere is *eo ipso* illegitimate. The sophistical in relation to the comic therefore has its foothold in nothing, in the realm of pure abstraction, and this is expressed by Gorgias[31] in the abstract proposal to annihilate seriousness by means of the comical, and the comical again by means of seriousness (cf. Aristotle's *Rhetoric* 3:18). The balance of the account here ends in bosh, and the dubiousness of the procedure is easily perceived, in the fact that an existing individual has transformed himself into a fantastic letter "X"; for it must surely be an existing individual who proposes to use this procedure, which can only serve to make him ridiculous when one uses against him the formula of exorcism against speculative philosophers proposed in an earlier passage: "May I have the honor to ask with whom I have the honor to converse; is it a human being, etc.?" For Gorgias with his invention lands in the fantastic exaggeration of pure being; for when he annihilates the one by the other there is nothing left. However, Gorgias has perhaps in the first instance wished merely to characterize the trickiness of a pettifogger, who seeks a victory by changing his weapons in relation to the weapons of his opponent. But a pettifogger has no standing in relation to the comical, he will have to whistle for his justification—and be content with the profit, which, as is well known, has always been the favorite result with all sophists: money, money, money, or whatever is on the same level with this.

In the religious sphere, when this is preserved in its purity as inwardness, the comical is a willing servant. One might say that repentance, for example, involves a contradiction, and this not from the standpoint of the aesthetic, or from that of a finite worldly wisdom, which is lower, or from the standpoint of the ethical, which has its strength in this passion, or from the standpoint of abstraction, which is fantastic and therefore lower (it was the proposal to apprehend it as comical from this standpoint, which was rejected as nonsense in the preceding), but from the religious standpoint itself, which is acquainted with a weapon against it, an expedient. But this is not so. The religious knows of no weapon against repentance which abstracts from repentance; on the contrary the religious always uses the negative* as its own essential form, so that the consciousness of sin is a definite factor in the consciousness of its forgiveness. The negative does not come upon the scene once for all, later to be replaced by the positive; but the positive is constantly wrapped up in the negative, and the negative is its criterion, so that the regulative principle *ne quid nimis* does not here find any application.

When the religious is conceived aesthetically, when in the Middle Ages indulgence is preached for four shillings, and it is assumed that this is the end of it, if one wishes to hold fast to this fiction, then repentance becomes comical and the individual who is crushed under the burden of remorse is comical, like Holberg's *The Busy Man,* provided of course that he has the four shillings; for this expedient is so easy, and

* This is also the reason why, even when the religious apprehends the aesthetic suffering with a certain comic tinge, it nevertheless does it leniently, because it is recognized that this suffering must have its period. Repentance, on the other hand, does not, from the religious point of view, wish to be allotted its duration, and then be past and over, the uncertainty of faith does not have its period, then to be relegated to the past, the consciousness of sin does not have its time, then to be past: for in that case we go back to the aesthetic.

the fiction assumes that this is the expedient. All this galimatias comes
from the fact that the religious has been transformed into farce. But in
the same degree as the negative is abolished in the religious sphere, or
treated as having presented itself once for all, and with that enough said,
in the same degree will the comical make itself felt in opposition to the
religious, and justifiably—because the religious has become aesthetics,
and yet presumes to represent the religious.

One finds, frequently enough, examples of a misdirected effort to emphasize the pathetic and the serious in a ridiculous, superstitious sense,
as if it were a bliss-bringing panacea, as if seriousness were a good in
and for itself, something to be taken without directions, so that all is
well if one is merely serious at all times, even if it happens that one is
never serious in the right place. No, everything has its dialectic, not indeed such a dialectic as makes it sophistically relative (this is mediation), but a dialectic by which the absolute becomes manifest as the
absolute by virtue of the dialectical. It is therefore quite as dubious, precisely quite as dubious, to be pathetic and serious in the wrong place,
as it is to laugh in the wrong place. One-sidedly we say that a fool laughs
all the time, one-sidedly, for it is indeed true that it is folly always to
laugh; but it is nevertheless one-sided to stamp only the misuse of laughter as folly, since the folly is quite as great and quite as ruinous when it
expresses itself by always being equally serious in stupidity.

§ 3. THE "DECISIVE" EXPRESSION FOR EXISTENTIAL PATHOS: GUILT[1]—THAT THE IN-
VESTIGATION GOES BACKWARD INSTEAD OF FORWARD—THE ETERNAL RECOLLECTION
OF GUILT IS THE HIGHEST EXPRESSION FOR THE RELATION BETWEEN THE CONSCIOUS-
NESS OF GUILT AND AN ETERNAL HAPPINESS—LOWER EXPRESSIONS FOR THE CON-
SCIOUSNESS OF GUILT, AND CORRESPONDING FORMS OF SATISFACTION—SELF-IMPOSED
PENANCE—HUMOR—THE RELIGIOUSNESS OF HIDDEN INWARDNESS

The dialectical reader will easily perceive that the investigation goes
backward instead of forward. In § 1 the task proposed was to relate
oneself at the same time absolutely to the absolute *telos* and relatively to
the relative ends. Just when a beginning ought to be made with this, it
became evident that first of all immediacy must be overcome, or the
individual must die from it, before there can be any question of realizing
the task proposed in § 1. Section 2 treated suffering as the essential expression of existential pathos, suffering regarded as dying from immediacy, suffering as the mark of the relationship of the exister to the
absolute *telos*. In § 3 guilt is treated as the decisive expression for the

existential pathos, and with this the remoteness from the task proposed in § 1 is still greater, and yet not in such a way that the task is forgotten, but in such a way that the investigation, keeping this in view, goes backward, plunging deeper into existence.

In existence the individual is a concretion, time is concrete, and even while the individual deliberates he is ethically responsible for his use of time. Existence is not an abstract spurt but steady striving and a continuous meanwhile; even at the instant when the task is clearly set there has been some waste, for meanwhile time has passed, and the beginning was not made at once. Thus things go backward: the task is presented to the individual in existence, and just as he is ready to cut at once a fine figure (which only can be done *in abstracto* and on paper, because the loose trousers of the abstractor are very different from the strait-jacket of the exister) and wants to begin, it is discovered that a new beginning is necessary, the beginning upon the immense detour of dying from immediacy, and just when the beginning is about to be made at this point, it is discovered that there, since time has meanwhile been passing, an ill beginning is made, and that the beginning must be made by becoming guilty and from that moment increasing the total capital guilt by a new guilt at a usurious rate of interest. The task appeared so lofty, and one thought, "Like for like; as the task is, so surely must he be who is to realize it." But then came existence with one "but" after another, then came suffering as a more precise determinant, and one thought, "Oh, yes, a poor exister must put up with that, since he is in existence." But then came guilt as the decisive determinant—and now the exister is in thorough distress, i.e. now he is in the medium of existence.

And yet this backward movement is a forward movement, in so far as going forward means going deeper into something. *In abstracto* and on paper the deception is to be off like Icarus, soaring up to an ideal task. But this progress, being chimerical, is sheer retrogression, and every time an exister makes a beginning at anything of that sort, the inspector of existence (the ethical) takes note of him that he is rendering himself guilty, even though the man himself takes no note of it. On the other hand, the more deeply an individual in dealing with his task plunges into existence, the more he goes forward, even if the expression, if one cares to say so, goes backward. But since all deliberation means "going back to fundamentals,"[2] so to recall the task back to a more concrete expression, means precisely a deeper absorption in existence. In comparison with the totality of the task, the fact of realizing a little of it is a retrogression, and yet it is progress in comparison with having the whole task in view and accomplishing nothing at all. I once read an account of an Indian drama—the drama I did not read. Two armies are drawn up against one another. Just as the battle should begin the leader lapses into thought. With this begins the drama, which recounts his thoughts. Thus it is the task appears to the exister; for an instant it deludes him with the notion that it is the whole thing, with the notion that he is now ready (for the beginning always has a certain resemblance to the end); but then existence comes in between, and the more deeply he is engaged with the task, in thought and in practical effort (for this is the essential characteristic of the existence-medium, a thinker being more or less inclined to abstract from existence), the further he is from the task in which he is engaged.

But how can the consciousness of guilt be the decisive expression for the pathetic relationship of an exister to an eternal happiness, and this in such a way that every exister who has not this consciousness is *eo ipso* not related to his eternal happiness? One might think that this consciousness is an expression of the fact that one is not related to it, the decisive expression of the fact that one is lost and the relationship is relinquished. The answer is not difficult. Precisely because it is an exister who is to relate himself, while guilt is at the same time the most concrete expression of existence, the consciousness of guilt is the expression for the relationship. The more abstract the individual is, the less is he related to an eternal happiness, and the more remote he is from guilt; for abstraction assumes the indifference of existence, but guilt is the expression for the strongest self-assertion of existence, and after all it is an *exister* who is to relate himself to an eternal happiness. The difficulty is really a different one; for the fact that guilt is accounted for by existence seems to make the exister guiltless, it seems as though he could throw the blame upon the one who has placed him in existence, or upon existence itself. In this case the consciousness of guilt would be nothing else but a new expression for the suffering of existence, and the investigation would have got no further than § 2, wherefore § 3 ought to fall out, or be treated as an appendix to § 2.

Accordingly, the exister should be able to cast the blame away from himself upon existence, or upon him who put him in existence, and so be without guilt. Without any ethical thunder but quite simply let us see how the matter stands. The procedure here proposed involves a contradiction. To him who is essentially innocent it can never occur to cast guilt away from him, for the innocent man has nothing to do with the determinant we call guilt. Therefore when in a particular case a person casts from him the blame and thinks that he is without guilt, at that very instant he makes the concession that on the whole he is one who is essentially guilty, only possibly in this particular he is not guilty. But here indeed we are not dealing with a particular case in which a man casts guilt from him and precisely by this denounces himself as essentially guilty, but it is a question of one's essential relation to existence. But to will essentially to throw off guilt from oneself, i.e. guilt as the total determinant, in order thereby to become innocent, is a contradiction, since this procedure is precisely self-denunciation. It is true of guilt, if it is of any other determinant, that there is a catch to it; its dialectic is so crafty that he who justifies himself totally, denounces himself, and he who justifies himself partially denounces himself totally. This, however, not in the same sense in which the old proverb says, *qui s'excuse s'accuse*. The meaning of the proverb is that he who defends or excuses himself in relation to something may do it in such a way that he accuses himself with respect to that very thing, so that the excuse and the accusation apply to the same thing. Such is not the meaning here; no, when a man really justifies himself in the particular instance, he denounces himself totally. Anyone who does not live only comparatively will easily observe this. In every-day life the total guilt, as a thing which is generally presupposed, is gradually so taken for granted that it is forgotten. And yet it is this totality of guilt which makes it possible that in the particular instance one can be guilty or not guilty. He who totally or essentially is guiltless cannot be guilty in the particular instance; but he who is totally guilty can very well be innocent in the particular instance. So then, not only by being guilty in a particular instance does a man denounce himself as essentially guilty (*totum est partibus suis prius*), but also by being innocent in the particular instance (*totum est partibus suis prius*).

The priority of the total guilt is not to be determined empirically, is no *summa summarum;* for no determination of totality ever results from numerical computation. The totality of guilt comes into being for the individual when he puts his guilt together with the relation to an eternal happiness. Hence we began as we did by affirming that the consciousness of guilt is the decisive expression for the relationship to an eternal happiness. He who has no relation to this never gets to the point of conceiving himself as totally or essentially guilty. The very least guilt—even if from that time on the individual were an angel—when it is put together with a relationship to an eternal happiness, is enough, for the composition determines the quality. And in *putting together* consists all deeper apprehension of existence. Comparatively, relatively, before a human tribunal, as apprehended by memory (instead of by the recollection of eternity), one guilt (collectively understood) is by no means sufficient to this end, nor is the sum of all. The root of the matter is, however, that it is precisely unethical to have one's life in the comparative, the relative, the outward, and to have the police-justice, the court of conciliation, a newspaper, or some of Copenhagen's notables, or the rabble of the Capital, as the court of last resort in relation with oneself.

One reads in the older works of theology a defense of eternal punishment in hell which affirms that the magnitude of sin requires such a punishment, and that the magnitude of sin is determined in turn by the fact that it is sin against God. The *naïveté* and outwardness of this is that it makes as if it were a law, a tribunal, a third party which deliberates and votes upon the cause which is between the man and God. Thus there is always something naïve and outward when a third party talks about that which essentially concerns the individual precisely in his isolation before God. The *naïveté* and outwardness disappear entirely when it is the individual himself who puts the conception of God together with the conception of guilt, be it never so small—but, halt! this the individual does not know, for this is the comparative which conducts into bypaths. By the fact that the conception of God is included, the definition of the guilt is transformed into a qualitative definition. Put together with the comparative as a standard, the guilt becomes quantitative: confronted with the absolute quality, the guilt becomes qualitative.*

* In the religious address, examples are sometimes found of the opposite tactics, in the fact that the religious orator, bringing down the thunder of guilt upon the head of the individual, would comparatively compel him to the totality of the consciousness of guilt. That is hardly feasible; and the more the orator thunders, the more odious beyond other men he makes the individual, so much the less is the end attained, and when he gesticulates most violently he is farthest from it—not to speak of the ironical glimpse he grants into the state of his reverence's own soul. The thing goes better another way, when the religious orator, "humble before God, and submissive to the royal majesty of the ethical,"³ in fear and trembling on his own account, puts guilt together with the conception of an eternal happiness, so that the hearer is not hounded on, but is affected indirectly, when it appears to him as if the parson were talking only about himself. In the tribunal it is a capital gesture to point accusingly to Cataline as he sits there; in the pulpit it is more effective to smite oneself upon the breast, especially when talking about the totality of guilt; for when the parson smites himself upon the breast he prevents any comparison; if he would point to himself, we have then the comparative again.

Childishness and the comparative consciousness of guilt are both recognizable by the fact that they do not comprehend the requirement of
existence: to *put things together*. So also in relation to thinking, childishness is recognizable by the fact that it thinks only as occasion suggests,
with reference to this or that, and then again about something else; it is
recognizable by the fact that in the long run it does not think one
thought but many thoughts. Childishness in relation to the consciousness of guilt assumes, for example, that today it is guilty in this or that,
then a week goes by when it is innocent, but then on the eighth day
something went wrong again. The comparative consciousness of guilt
is recognizable by the fact that it has its standard outside itself, and when
on Sunday the parson employs a very high standard (without, however,
employing that of eternity), it seems dreadful to the comparer to think
what he has deserved; in good company on Monday it does not seem
to him so bad, and thus the outward relationship suffices to determine
an entirely different conception, which in spite of fine variations always
misses one thing: eternity's determinant.

So the essential consciousness of guilt is the first deep plunge into existence, and at the same time it is the expression for the fact that an
exister is related to an eternal happiness (the childish and comparative
consciousness of guilt is related to itself and to the comparative), it is
the expression for the relationship by reason of the fact that it expresses
the incompatibility or disrelationship.*

Though the consciousness be ever so decisive, it is nevertheless the
relationship which always sustains the disrelationship, only the exister
cannot get a grip on the relationship because the disrelationship is constantly placing itself between as the expression for the relationship. But
on the other hand, the eternal happiness and the exister do not so repel
one another that it comes to an absolute breach; on the contrary, it is

---

* That is to say: within the total determination in which we find ourselves. The reader will
remember (in the Second Section of Chapter II, in connection with the discussion of the
Fragments) that the *paradoxical* accentuation of existence plunges deep into existence. This is
the specifically Christian characteristic, and it will come again to the fore in Section B. The
spheres are thus related: immediacy; finite common sense; irony; ethics with irony as incognito;
humor; religiousness with humor as incognito; and then finally the Christian religiousness,
recognizable by the paradoxical accentuation of existence, by the paradox, by the breach with
immanence, and by the absurd. Religiousness with humor as incognito is therefore not yet Christian religiousness. Even if this latter is the hidden inwardness, it is nevertheless related to the
paradox. It is true that humor also has to do with the paradox, but it cautiously keeps itself
within immanence, and it constantly seems as if it was aware of something different—hence
the jest.

only by holding together that the disproportion repeats itself as the decisive consciousness of guilt, not of this or the other guilt.

That is to say, the consciousness of guilt still lies essentially in immanence, in distinction from the consciousness of sin.* In the consciousness of guilt it is the selfsame subject which becomes essentially guilty by keeping guilt in relationship to an eternal happiness, but yet the identity of the subject is such that guilt does not make the subject a new man, which is the characteristic of the breach. But the breach, in which lies the paradoxical accentuation, cannot occur in the relationship between an exister and the eternal, because the eternal embraces the exister on all sides, and therefore the disrelationship or incompatibility remains within immanence. If the breach is to be effected, the eternal must determine and define itself as temporal, as in time, as historical, whereby the exister and the eternal in time get eternity as an obstacle between them. This is the paradox (to which attention is called in the foregoing Second Section of Chapter II and in B which is to follow).

In the religious sphere the positive is recognizable by the negative, the relationship to an eternal happiness, by suffering (§ 2); now the negative is decidedly stronger, the relationship being recognizable by the totality of the consciousness of guilt. In comparison with guilt-consciousness as the characteristic note, suffering might seem to be a direct relationship (of course not aesthetically direct: happiness recognizable by happiness). If one were to affirm this, then guilt-consciousness is the repellent relationship. However, it would be more correct to say that suffering is a direct reaction of a repellent relationship, guilt-consciousness a repellent reaction of a repellent relationship, but with the caution that it is still constantly within immanence, even if an exister is constantly prevented from having his life in this, or from being *sub specie aeterni,* but has this only as an annulled [*ophævet,* German *aufgehoben*] possibility—not in such a way as the concrete is annulled so as to find the abstract, but as one annuls the abstract by being in the concrete.

The consciousness of guilt is the decisive expression for existential pathos in relation to an eternal happiness. As soon as one leaves out the eternal happiness, the consciousness of guilt also drops out essentially, or it results in childish definitions which are on a par with a schoolboy's report for conduct, or it becomes a defense of civil order. Therefore the decisive expression for the consciousness of guilt is in turn the essential

* On this point compare Appendix to B.

maintenance of this consciousness, or the eternal recollection of guilt, because it is constantly put together with the relationship to an eternal happiness. So here there can be no question of the childish thing of making a fresh start, of being a good child again, but neither is there any question of the universal indulgence that all men are like that. One guilt is enough, as I have said, and with that the exister who along with this is related to an eternal happiness, is forever caught. For human justice pronounces a life sentence only for the third offense, but eternity pronounces sentence the first time forever. He is caught forever, harnessed with the yoke of guilt, and never gets out of the harness—unlike the beast of burden, from which the burden after all is sometimes taken off; unlike the day-laborer, who yet once in a while has freedom. Not even at night is he essentially out of harness. Call this recollection of guilt a fetter and say that it is never taken off the prisoner, and you indicate only the one side of it, for the thought most closely associated with the fetter is deprivation of freedom, but the eternal remembrance of guilt is at the same time a burden which is to be dragged from place to place in time; rather therefore call the eternal remembrance of guilt a harness, and say that the man never gets out of harness. For his consciousness is that he is decisively changed, whereas nevertheless the identity of the subject consists in the fact that it is he himself who becomes conscious by putting guilt together with the relationship to an eternal happiness.* But still he is related to an eternal happiness, and the consciousness of guilt is a higher expression of this than is suffering. And in the suffering of guilt-consciousness, guilt at once assuages and rankles. It assuages because it is an expression of freedom as this is found in the ethico-religious sphere, where the positive is recognizable by the negative, freedom by guilt, but not directly recognizable aesthetically: freedom recognizable by freedom.

So it is that things go backward: to suffer guiltily is a lower expression than to suffer innocently, and yet it is a higher expression because the negative is the mark of a higher positive. An exister who suffers innocently is *eo ipso* not related to an eternal happiness, unless it be that the exister himself is the Paradox, with which definition we are in another sphere. With regard to every exister pure and simple it is true that if he suffers only innocently (totally understood, of course, not in the

---

* The consciousness of sin is the paradoxical, and in turn, quite consistently with this, the paradoxical thing is that the exister does not discover this by himself, but comes to know it from without. Thereby the identity is broken.

sense that he suffers innocently in this case or that, or in many cases), he is not related to an eternal happiness and has avoided the consciousness of guilt by existing abstractly. This must be held fast lest the spheres be confounded, lest we suddenly slip back into determinants which are far lower than the religiousness of hidden inwardness. Only in the paradoxical religiousness, i.e. the Christian, can it be true also of the Paradox that to suffer innocently is a higher expression than to suffer guiltily. To determine the order of the spherical totalities, one has simply to employ humor as the terminus for defining the religiousness of hidden inwardness, and this religiousness as the terminus for defining the Christian religiousness. The Christian religiousness is also recognizable by its category, and wherever this is not present, or is pratingly used, the Christian religiousness is not present—unless one assumes that to utter the name of Christ is Christianity, even when it is taking Christ's name in vain.

The eternal recollection of guilt is the decisive expression of it; but the very strongest expression of despair in the instant is not existential pathos. To relate oneself with existential pathos to an eternal happiness is never expressed by once in a while making a great effort, but by persistence in the relationship, by the perseverance with which it is put together with everything, for therein consists the whole art of existing, and here perhaps it is that men are most lacking. What holy vows a man knows how to make at the instant of mortal danger! But when that is passed, the vow is so promptly and so completely forgotten. And why? Because the man does not know how to put things together. When the mortal danger does not come from without, he cannot by himself put it together by his own effort. When the earth quakes at the outburst of the volcano, or when the pestilence is abroad in the land, how swiftly then and how thoroughly does even the dullest scholar, even the drowsiest man comprehend the uncertainty of everything! But then when this is over, he is no longer capable of putting things together, and yet it was precisely then he ought to be employing himself about it, for when nature puts things together for him, when the fury of the elements preaches to him with more than Sunday eloquence—why then understanding comes pretty much of itself, so easily indeed that the task rather is to prevent despair by having understood earlier the same thing.

In the eternal recollection of the consciousness of guilt the exister is related to an eternal happiness, yet not in such a way that he is now directly closer to it; for now, on the contrary, he is as remote as possible, but nevertheless is related to it. The dialectical in this (though it is within immanence) sets itself in opposition so as to raise pathos to a higher power. In the relationship which underlies the disrelationship, in the immanence barely suspected which underlies the divisive dialectic, the man holds on to the happiness, suspended as it were by the finest thread, by the aid of a possibility which is constantly being annulled—precisely for this reason the pathos is stronger, if there be any.

The consciousness of guilt is the decisive expression, and one guilt put together with an eternal happiness is enough, and yet it is true of nothing so much as of guilt that it catches itself. However, it is the total guilt which is decisive; to have made oneself guilty fourteen times is child's play in comparison with this. Hence it is that childishness always sticks to the numerical. On the other hand, when the consciousness of a new guilt leads again to the absolute consciousness of guilt, the eternal recollection of guilt is thereby preserved, in case the exister should be about to forget it.

If one is inclined to say that no man can endure such an eternal recollection of guilt, that it must lead to madness or to death, then mark well who it is that says this, for finite common sense often talks this way so as to prate indulgence. And such talk seldom fails of its effect when men are gathered in three and fours, for I doubt if any one in solitude has been able to deceive himself with this talk, but when there are a number together and they hear that the others comport themselves thus, one is less troubled. Besides, how inhumane it is to want to be better than others! Once more a false pretext, for he who is alone with the ideal does not know at all whether he is better or more lowly than others. So then it is possible that this eternal recollection of guilt may lead to madness or death. Oh, well then, you know that a man cannot endure bread and water for a very long time; but then it is for a physician to estimate how things may be arranged for the particular individual, in such a way, be it noted, that he does not come to the pass of living with the rich, but that the fasting régime is so precisely reckoned for him that he can just keep alive. Just because the existential pathos is not an affair of the moment but demands persistence, the exister himself (who in fact is enthusiastic in pathos, and not so depraved by use and wont that he is on the lookout for evasions) will seek to discover the minimum of forgetfulness which is required for holding out, since he himself is aware that the instantaneous is a misapprehension. But since it is impossible in this dialectical process to find an absolute certainty, he will, in spite of the effort it involves, manage to get the consciousness of guilt again totally defined by the consideration that in relation to an eternal happiness he never would dare to say that he has done everything he could to hold fast the recollection of guilt.

The concept guilt, defined as a totality, belongs essentially to the religious sphere. As soon as the aesthetical essays to deal with it, the concept becomes dialectical like fortune and misfortune, and thereby everything is brought to confusion. Aesthetically considered, the dialectic of guilt is this: the individual is innocent, then we have innocence and guiltiness as alternating qualifications of life, at one moment the individual becomes guilty in this or that respect, at another moment he is innocent. If this or that had not been, the individual would not have become guilty; under other conditions the man who now is regarded as guilty would have been innocent. This *pro* and *contra* as the *summa summarum* (hence not a particular case of guilt or innocence within the total definition of guilt) is a subject for the attention of the tribunal, for the interest of novelists, for gossip, and for the meditation of certain parsons. The aesthetic categories are so easily recognized, and it is so easy to use God's name, the words duty, guilt, etc., without talking ethically or religiously. What constitutes the situation as aesthetical is the fact that the individual becomes undialectic in himself. One man lives sixty years, having been twice convicted and placed under special police supervision; another lives sixty years and has never been convicted of a crime, but rumor circulates a lot of ugly stories; still another lives sixty years and he was a thoroughly fine man. And what of that? Have we learnt anything from this? No—except that it gives us a notion how one after another can go on with twaddle when the exister has not in himself the inwardness which is the native land and the true home of all total determinants.

The religious address has essentially to do with total determinants. It can make use of a crime, of a weakness, of a fault of omission, in short of any particular, whatever it may be, but what distinguishes the religious address as such is that from this particular it gets at the total determinant by putting it together with the relationship to an eternal blessedness. For the religious always has to deal with total determinants, not learnedly (so that it looks away from the particular individual), but existentially, and hence it has to do with bringing the individual, by fair means or foul, directly or indirectly, in and under the totality, not in such a way as to disappear in it, but in such a way as to put him together with it. If the religious discourse expands merely upon particulars, if it dishes up now praise and now blame, if it bestows high honors upon some person *encomio publico ornatus*[4] and rejects others, it thereby confounds itself with the ceremony of conferring degrees, only without announcing the names. If the religious address supposes it a way of aiding the police by thundering against criminals who evade the arm of the law, then it is in point to say that if the religious address does not thunder by virtue of total determinants (and these are so serious that they stand in no need of violent gesticulations), his reverence is confounding himself with a sort of assistant policeman, who appropriately might go around with a stick and deserves to be rewarded by the civil magistrate. In every-day life, in business, in common intercourse, one man is accounted guilty in this respect, another in that, and there's the end of it; but a religious address has to do with inwardness, where the total determinant grips a man. The total determinant is the religious characteristic, everything else, if it is lacking in this, is essentially an illusion, according to which even the greatest criminal is after all innocent at bottom, and a good-natured man is a saint.

The eternal conservation of the recollection of guilt is the expression for existential pathos, the highest expression for it, higher than the most enthusiastic penance which would make up for the guilt.* This treasuring up of guilt cannot find its expression in any outward act, whereby it is only finitized; it belongs therefore to hidden inwardness. As usual, this way of putting the case offends nobody. It offends nobody by declaring that he is a religious man, and thus betraying what he hides. It offends nobody by denying that he is the religious man, for the point precisely is that this is hidden and no one can observe anything.

I shall now indicate briefly the conceptions of guilt, along with the corresponding conceptions of satisfaction for it, which are lower than the eternal recollection of guilt which is characteristic of the hidden inwardness. Inasmuch as in the foregoing section I have been so copious, I can express myself here the more briefly, for what was expounded

---

* It is to be remembered that the forgiveness of sin is the paradoxical satisfaction by virtue of the absurd. In order merely to observe how paradoxical it is, the eternal recollection of guilt as the highest expression must come in between, lest the spheres become confused and the Christian conception be prated into childish definitions of the forgiveness of sin which belong where the ethical is not present, still less the religious, and still less the Christian.

in the foregoing section must here recur again. Here as ever it is the
category only which is regarded, and therefore I include conceptions
which, though they are often called Christian, yet when they are confronted with the category, prove not to be such.

The fact that a clergyman, though he be a prelate, that an ecclesiastical dignitary who is ranked with real Christians as a regular baptized
Christian, concocts something or another, does not suffice to make this
something Christianity, any more than it follows directly from the
fact that a doctor writes something on a prescription blank that this
something is medicine—it may be bosh. There is nothing new in
Christianity in such a sense that it has not been in the world before,* and
yet it is all new. So in case one were to use the name of Christianity and
the name of Christ, but the categories (in spite of these expressions)
are anything but Christian, is this then Christianity? Or in case (cf.
the First Section of Chapter II) one were to maintain that a man
should not have a disciple, and another were to declare himself an
adherent and subscribe to this doctrine, is there not a misunderstanding
between them, in spite of the adherent's assertions of admiration and
of his thorough appropriation of the . . . misunderstanding? The
characteristic mark of Christianity is the paradox, the absolute paradox.
As soon as a so-called Christian speculation annuls the paradox and
reduces this characterization to a transient factor, all the spheres are
confused.

Consequently, every conception of guilt is lower which does not
by an eternal recollection put guilt together with the relation to an
eternal happiness, but by memory puts it together with something

---

* If such were the case, Christianity would be plainly recognizable aesthetically: novelty by
novelty—and again everything would be confused. Sheer novelty, for example, may be the mark
by which a mechanical discovery is recognizable, and this novelty is accidentally dialectic; but
this novelty cannot constitute a stumblingblock or offense. In the last resort, the occasion of
offense applies to an individual who is in relationship to the essential when one would make
new to him that which he essentially believes he possesses. He who has no religiousness at all
cannot possibly be offended at Christianity, and the reason why the possibility of offense lay so
close to the Jews was that they stood closest to Christianity. If Christianity had wanted merely
to add something new to the old, it could have aroused offense only relatively; but precisely
because it wanted to take all the old and make it new, the offense lay so close to it. In case the
novelty of Christianity had never entered into the heart of man, in the sense that before its
coming man had never possessed that which he imagined was the highest, it never could have
aroused offense. Precisely because its novelty is not plain but can only be apprehended by first
removing an illusion, the offense is possible. The novelty of Christianity, therefore, has behind
it the eternal religiousness of hidden inwardness; for in relation to the eternal a novelty is
indeed a paradox. Lumped at random with other novelties, or annulled by the affirmation that
among all novelties it is the most remarkable, it is aesthetic.

lower, something comparative (one's own fortuitous situation or that of another man), and allows forgetfulness to step between the particular instances of guilt. This makes life easy and untroubled, as the life of the child is, because the child has a great deal of memory (the direction of which is outward) but no recollection, and has at the utmost the inwardness of the instant. It is always a question how many men there are who, in the last resort, relate themselves absolutely to spiritual determinants. It is a question—more than that I do not say, for it is indeed possible that we all do so, inasmuch as the hidden inwardness is in fact hidden. Only so much is certain, that the question is not the same as that about talents, rank in society, skill in an art, learning, etc. The lowliest man can relate himself absolutely to spiritual determinants quite as well as the gifted man; for brilliant parts, learning, talents, are after all a "what," but the absoluteness of relationship to spirit is a "how," indicative of what one is, be it much or little.

Every conception of guilt is lower which puts guilt together momentarily with the conception of an eternal happiness—on Sunday, for example, on New Year's morning at the early sermon heard with "fasting heart" . . . being then free throughout the whole week or the whole year.

Every mediation is a lower conception of guilt; for mediation constantly dispenses a man from the absolute relationship to the absolute and lets this exhaust itself in partial predicates, in the same sense in which a hundred-dollar bill may be regarded as so many ones. But the absolute relationship is absolute precisely for the fact that one possesses it as one's own by relating oneself to the absolute, as a jewel which can be possessed as a whole and cannot be parcelled out in small change. Mediation dispenses man from absorbing himself in determinants of totality and makes him busy outwardly, his guilt being external, the suffering of his punishment external; for the solution of mediation and its indulgence is that the outward is the inward and the inward is the outward, whereby the absolute relationship of the individual to the absolute is abolished.

To every lower conception of guilt there corresponds a satisfaction for guilt which is lower than that eternal recollection which accepts therefore no satisfaction, although the underlying immanence within which the dialectical has its being is an obscurely sensed possibility of it.

One of the lower satisfactions is the civil conception of punishment. This conception corresponds to this guilt or that, and hence it is entirely outside the definition of guilt as totality.

One of the lower satisfactions for guilt is the aesthetic-metaphysical conception of nemesis. Nemesis is outwardly dialectic, it is the consequence of outwardness, or the righteousness of nature. The aesthetic is the unopened inwardness; hence that which is or should be inwardness must manifest itself as an outward perception. It is as when in a tragedy the hero of a bygone age manifests himself as spirit before the eyes of the sleeper; the spectator must behold the spirit, although its manifestation is due to the sleeper's inwardness. So it is also with the consciousness of guilt: inwardness becomes externality. Hence one could see the Furies; but precisely this visibility of theirs makes the inwardness less terrible, and precisely by reason of their visibility a limit was prescribed to them: the Furies did not dare to enter the temple. On the other hand, when one conceives the consciousness of guilt as remorse, though it were only for a single fault, this guiltiness is precisely the terrible experience, for remorse no one can see, and remorse accompanies one across every threshold. But the visibility of the Furies expresses symbolically the commensurability between the inward and the outward, whereby the consciousness of guilt is finitized and satisfaction made to consist in the suffering of temporal punishment and atonement to consist in death, wherewith everything ends in the sadly exalted feeling which is death's assuagement, that the whole thing is now over, and there was no eternal guilt.

One of the lower satisfactions for guilt is self-inflicted penance in all its forms, which are lower not merely because they are self-inflicted, but because even the most hearty penance has the effect of finitizing guilt by making it commensurable, whereas its merit consists in the sincere discovery of guilt which eludes the attention not only of the police but of nemesis. What has been said already about the monastic movement of the Middle Ages applies again here. All respect for the medieval practice of penance. At the least, it is a childlike and hearty endeavor on a grand scale; and that man must have lost all imagination, and by reason of his much understanding have become as good as completely stupid, who cannot put himself back into the situation of the Middle Ages and can actually extol forgetfulness and lack of thought and "just look at my neighbor" as something truer. For if the penance of the Middle Ages was false, it was a touching and enthusiastic falsehood, and even if forgetfulness and lack of thought are not chargeable with a false conception of God as one who finds pleasure in seeing a man scourge himself, it is surely a falsehood even more dreadful to leave God, if I may say so, out of the game, and to confide in the fact that one has never been convicted of crime, that one is even the leader of the cotillion at the club. On the other hand, the Middle Ages let God, if I may so speak, take a hand in the game. Of course the conceptions are rather childlike, but yet God is included absolutely. Let one try a thought-experiment. Take a man who puts his guilt together with the conception of an eternal happiness, who also precisely for this cause becomes alone with himself, with the guilt and with God (herein consists the truth, in contrast with all comparative busyness and thoughtlessness in the school of herring), let one imagine him desperately pondering whether after all there might not be something he could hit upon as a satisfaction for his guilt, imagine the distress which stimulates all his inventiveness with the hope that after all it might be possible to hit upon something which would make God favorable to him again—and then let a man laugh if he can at the sufferer who hits upon penance, assuming (as in the experiment one always may venture to do) that honestly it is his thought and his wish that God perhaps might be touched and appeased by all this suffering. To be sure there is something comic in this, because this conception transforms God into a fantastic figure, a Holofernes, a pasha with three horsetails, who could find pleasure in such things. But is it better to abolish God in such a way that He becomes a titulary deity who sits in heaven and cannot get near enough for any one to descry Him, because His operations affect a man only through the compact mass of intermediary causes, and the blow therefore becomes an unobservable touch? Is it better to abolish God in such a way that one has got Him tricked in the meshes of natural law and the necessary development of immanence? No, all respect for the penance of the Middle Ages, and for all that is analogous to it outside of Christianity, which contains always this much truth, that man is not related to the ideal through the medium of successive generations, through the State, through the centuries, through the market price quoted for man in the town where he lives— that is to say, is not prevented by this from relating himself to the ideal, but does actually relate himself to it, though with defective understanding. What all cannot a maiden hit upon to make her lover favorable to her again when she believes he is offended! Even if she hits upon a ludicrous device, does not her love hallow the ludicrous? And is not this the element of truth in her behavior, that she is ideally related to her love by the pristine apprehension of this passion, and therefore does not seek the society of any tattler who could relate to her how other maidens treat their lovers? Everyone who has an eye for the categories easily sees that the maiden we have imagined is comic only for a purer view of the case, which therefore benevolently smiles at her a little in order to help her to something better, though always with deferent respect for her passion; and that, on the other hand, a tattler, a gadabout, who knows something at third hand, is unconditionally comic in the capacity of lover, in which situation such studies at third hand are a sign of slovenliness in sentiment, which is worse than unfaithfulness and shows that she has nothing to be faithful with.

And so also it is true of the religious man who goes astray by reason of his pristine passion that this puts him in a kindly light, in comparison with the religious man who from what he learns on the street, from the newspapers, and at the club, knows all about how to manage God, knowing how the other Christians do it. By reason of the infiltration of the State and social groups and the congregation and society, God can no longer get a hold on the individual; even if God's wrath were ever so great, the punishment nevertheless which should overtake the guilty must be transmitted through all the authoritative instances of objectivity. In this way, by the use of the most obliging and courteous philosophic terminology, they have shown Him the door. They are busy about getting a truer and truer conception of God but seem to forget the very first step, that one should fear God. A man who in the objective mass of men is objectively religious does not fear God; in the thunder he does not hear Him (this is natural law, and perhaps he is right); he does not see Him in events (this is immanential necessity uniting cause and effect, and perhaps he is right)—but how then about the inwardness of solitude before God? Yes, that is too little for him, he does not know it, this man who is on the point of realizing the objective.

Whether our age is more immoral than other ages I shall not decide; but as a defective notion of penance was the specific immorality of a period of the Middle Ages, so that of our age might easily be a fantastic ethical weakness, a voluptuous, soft exaltation of despair, in which individuals, as in a dream, fumble after a conception of God without feeling any terror thereat, but on the contrary pluming themselves upon the superiority which in dizziness of thought, with the indefiniteness of the impersonal, possesses as it were a presentiment of God in the indefinite, fantastically encounters Him whose existence remains pretty much like that of the mermaids. And the same thing might easily be repeated in the individual's relationship to himself, that the ethical and responsibility and power of action and the nervous strength for discrimination required by repentance evaporate in a degenerate cleverness in which the individual dreams metaphysically of himself, or lets existence as a whole dream of him, confounds himself with Greece, Rome, China, world-history, our age, this century, immanently comprehends the necessity of his own development, and then again objectively allows his own *ego* to float over it all like a scum, forgetting that even though death transforms a man's body to dust and mingles it with the elements, it is after all very dreadful to be, while one lives, a scum upon the immanent development of infinity. So rather let us sin, sin out and out, seduce maidens, murder men, commit highway robbery—after all, that can be repented of, and such a criminal God can still get a hold on. But this proud superiority which has risen to such a height scarcely can be repented of, it has a semblance of profundity which deceives. So rather let us mock God, out and out, as has been done before in the world—this is always preferable to the disparaging air of importance with which one would prove God's existence. For to prove the existence of one who is present is the most shameless affront, since it is an attempt to make him ridiculous; but unfortunately people have no inkling of this and for sheer seriousness regard it as a pious undertaking. But how could it occur to anybody to prove that he exists, unless one had permitted oneself to ignore him, and now makes the thing all the worse by proving his existence before his very nose? The existence of a king, or his presence, is commonly acknowledged by an appropriate expression of subjection and submission —what if in his sublime presence one were to prove that he existed? Is that the way to prove it? No, that would be making a fool of him; for one proves his presence by an expression of submission, which may assume various forms according to the customs of the country—and thus it is also one proves God's existence by worship . . . not by proofs. A poor wretch of an author whom a later investigator drags out of the obscurity of oblivion may indeed be very glad that the investigator succeeds in proving his existence—but an omnipresent being can only by a thinker's pious blundering be brought to this ridiculous embarrassment.

But in case this might come to pass, or in case at a certain time it is so, how then does it come about, unless it be owing precisely to the fact that the consciousness of guilt is left out? Just as paper money may be important as a means of exchange between man and man, but is in itself a chimerical entity in case there is in the last resort no gold reserve to support it, so, too, the comparative, the conventional, the external, the legal conception of the ethical may be useful enough in common intercourse, but in case it is forgotten that the substantial value of the ethical must be in the inwardness of the individual, if it is to be anywhere at all, in case a whole generation could forget this, then that generation, even if one were to assume as a fact (which, however, enlightenment and culture cannot by any means be said to bring with them unconditionally) that there did not exist a single criminal but only honest folks, that generation is nevertheless ethically impoverished in an essential sense, and is essentially bankrupt. In commerce it is quite right to account every third party a third party, but in case this expertness in commercial dealings leads the single individual in his inwardness before God to account himself a third party, i.e. to think of himself outwardly, then the ethical is lost, inwardness is no more, the thought of God has become meaningless, ideality has vanished, for he whose inwardness does not reflect the ideal has no ideality. In connection with the human crowd (i.e. when the individual is looking to see how the other behaves; but this goes in fact the whole round, since every one of the "others" is in turn the individual), it is all right to apply a comparative standard, but in case this use of the comparative standard gets so much the upper hand that the individual in his inward man applies it to himself, then the ethical is done for, and the ethical which has been thus politely discarded might appropriately find its place in a commercial journal under the headline: Average price for average quality.

The respectable feature of medieval penance was that to himself the individual applied the absolute standard. If people know nothing higher than the comparative, the political gauge, the standard of the small town and of revivalistic sectarianism, they should not smile pityingly upon the Middle Ages. All agree that narrow-minded Philistinism is comic. But what then is Philistinism?[5] Philistinism always consists in the use of the relative as the absolute in connection with the essential. That many a man takes no notice when an obvious relativity is employed, merely shows the limitation of his sense for the comic. As with Philistinism, so it is with irony. Every man, right down to the lowliest, dabbles in being ironical, but at the point where irony properly begins, all of them fail, and the mass of all these people, who are relatively ironical, each man for himself, from above down, turns in exasperation against the real ironist.[6] The claim to be the best man in the town of Kjøge is laughed at in Copenhagen, but to be the best man in Copenhagen is just as laughable, for the ethical and the ethico-religious have nothing whatever to do with the comparative. Every comparative measurement, be it that of Kjøge or of Copenhagen, or of our age or century, in claiming to be the absolute, is Philistinism.

On the other hand, whenever the individual turns against himself with the absolute requirement, there will also emerge analogies to the self-inflicted penance, even though they do not express themselves so naïvely, and above all, being kept in the hiding-place of inwardness, are prevented from manifesting themselves in conspicuous outward expressions which so easily become an invitation to misunderstanding, equally injurious to the individual himself and to others, for all comparison means delay, and for this reason mediocrity lays such store by it, and in it catches everyone it can by its paltry friendship, making him virtually a captive in spite of the fact that he becomes even an object of admiration as something extraordinary . . . among mediocrities, or is tenderly embraced by his peers. It is entirely fitting that every man, even the most excellent man, as a third party in relation to another, whether it be by sympathy he is moved or by any other motive, applies a smaller standard of measurement than that which every man ought to have within himself in silent relationship with the ideal. He therefore, who makes against men the accusation that it is they who depraved him, talks nonsense and denounces himself as one who has skulked away from something and now wants to skulk back to something. For why did he not prevent it? And why does he continue in depravity instead of making up if possible for lost time by seeking the standard which is in his own inmost parts? It is perfectly true that a man can require of himself strenuous efforts which the most well-meaning friend would counsel him against if he were aware of them; but do not accuse the friend, let a man rather accuse himself for the fact that he had higgled for this alleviation. Everyone who in truth has ventured his life has had the standard of silence; for a man may and always should advise against it, simply for the reason that he who, when he is about to venture his life, has need of a confidant with whom to deliberate about it, is unfit for it. But when things begin to get hot, and the final effort is required—then one leaps aside, then one seeks alleviation from a confidant and gets the well-meant advice: Spare yourself. Then time goes by, and the need is passed. And sometime at a later moment when one is visited by a recollection, one accuses men, as a new proof that one has lost oneself and has his ideality among things which are gone. But he who keeps silent accuses no one except himself, he offends no one by his effort; for his triumphant conviction is this, that in every man there is and can and shall be this privy understanding with the ideal which demands all and comforts only with annihilation before God. Let then who will be the spokesman for mediocrity, or grunt against it, or make a loud fuss—if it is permitted to defend oneself against a robber on the highway, there is also a defense against the persecutions of mediocrity which is permissible, and above all is well-pleasing to God, namely, silence. In the relationship of silence to the ideal, there is a sentence passed upon a man —woe to him who as third party would dare to condemn a man thus! From this sentence there is no appeal to any higher instance, for this is absolutely the highest. But there is a way of evasion, and so one gets an indescribably milder sentence. And then when one day a man dreams his life over again, he is terrified and accuses men, as a new proof that his cause is still pending in the forum of mediocrity. In the relationship of silence to the ideal there is a standard which transforms even the greatest effort into an insignificance, transforms the continual struggle of year after year into a cock-stride—but in chattiness one makes a giant-stride without effort. And then when discouragement had got the better of a man, when he found it cruel of the lofty ideal that when all his efforts were put together with it they disappeared as naught, when he could not put up with it that impracticability is the path of the ideal and its standard—then he sought alleviation and found it, found it in the person who perhaps in all honesty was well-meaning, who did what one can require and ought to require of a third party, and he thanked him . . . until he ended foolishly by accusing men because he himself on the easily practicable path of mediocrity got nowhere. In the accord of silence with the ideal, one word is lacking, the loss of which is not felt, for the thing it denotes does not exist: it is the word excuse. In loud tones outside, in the whispered agreement between neighbor and neighbor, this is a root-word, and innumerable are its derivations. Let this be said in honor of the ideality of silence. He who lives thus cannot say this, for he is silent. Very well, then I say it, and it is unnecessary to add that I make no pretense of doing it.[7]

Accordingly, he who turns against himself with the absolute standard will naturally not be able to live on in the blissful confidence that if he keeps the Commandments, and has never been convicted, and is regarded by a revivalistic clique as really a man of heart, in the confidence that he is a splendid fellow who, if he does not die too soon, will in the course of time become all too perfect for this world—on the contrary he will again and again discover guilt, and again will discover it within the total definition, as guilt. But in human nature the sense is deeply implanted that guilt demands punishment. How obvious it is then to hit upon something, a toilsome labor perhaps, even if it is dialectic in such a sense that it possibly might be profitable to others, benevolence to the needy, the renunciation of a wish, etc. Is this then ludicrous? I find it childlike and pretty. And yet this is an analogue to self-inflicted penance, and after all it does finitize guilt, however well meant it may be. There is in it a childlike hope and a childlike wish that everything might be made up for, a childlikeness in comparison with which the eternal recollection of guilt in hidden inwardness is dreadful earnest. What is it that makes the child's life so easy? It is the fact that quits is called so often, and so often a fresh start is made. The childlikeness of self-inflicted penance lies in the fact that the individual is inclined to conceive that the punishment is worse than the recollection of guilt. No, the recollection is precisely the hardest punishment. Punishment is hardest for the child, because the child has no recollection, and the child thinks in this fashion: "If only I could escape the punishment, then I should be joyful and glad." But what is inwardness? It is recollection. The comparative sort of people who are to be had by the dozen, who are as people mostly are in their town, and resemble one another like tin soldiers in a box, show their lack of thought by the fact that they possess no *tertium comparationis;* the childlike inwardness in older people consists in directing their thoughts to themselves, but the fraudulent thing about it is the acquittance. But seriousness is the eternal recollection, and it is not to be confounded exactly with the seriousness of getting married, having children, having podagra, preparing for the examination in theology, becoming deputy to parliament, or even public executioner.

Humor as the border line for the religiousness of hidden inwardness comprehends guilt-consciousness as a totality. The humorist therefore talks rather rarely of this or that guilt because he comprehends guilt totally, or if occasionally he accentuates this or that particular, it is because the totality is thereby expressed. The humorous effect is produced by letting the childlike trait reflect itself in the consciousness of totality. Intellectual culture on an absolute scale put together with childishness produces humor. One often enough encounters men who are full grown, confirmed, and "men of heart," who in spite of being older in years do everything or leave undone like a child, and who even in their fortieth year would undeniably be regarded as promising children if it were the custom for every man to become two hundred and fifty years old. But childishness and loutish pranks are very different from humor. The humorist possesses the childlike quality but is not possessed by it, constantly prevents it from expressing itself directly, but lets it only shimmer through an absolute culture. Hence when one puts together an absolute culture and a child, they always in combination bring the humorous to evidence: the child utters it and does not recognize it, the humorist recognized that it was uttered. On the other hand, relative culture put together with a child discovers nothing, for it looks down upon the child and its foolishness.

I recall a rejoinder made in a definite situation which I shall recount. It was in one of the groups transitorily formed in the midst of a larger company; it was a young woman who, not without a certain appropriateness in connection with an unfortunate event which was mentioned in conversation, uttered her complaint against life, that it kept so few of its promises, and with that exclaimed, "No, there is happy childhood, or rather the child's happiness!" She fell silent, bent down to a child who fondly clung to her, and patted the little one on the cheek. One of the men present, whose voice by its emotion indicated sympathy for the woman, continued as follows: "Yes, and above all, the happiness of childhood in getting a licking."* Thereupon he turned away and talked to the lady of the house who just then was passing by.

* At this rejoinder people laughed. That was a pure misunderstanding. They took the rejoinder for irony, which it was not. If the rejoinder had been irony, the speaker would have been a pretty poor ironist; for there was a note of pain in the rejoinder, which ironically is entirely incorrect. The rejoinder was humorous and therefore made the situation ironical by the misunderstanding. This again is quite in order, for an ironical rejoinder cannot make a situation ironical. What the ironist does precisely is to assert himself and prevent situations, but the concealed pain of the humorist contains a sympathy whereby he himself takes part in creating situations, and thereby an ironical situation is made possible. But people often confound that which is said ironically with that which, when it is said, has in the situation an ironical effect. Here the situation became ironical by the fact that people laughed and took the rejoinder for a teasing jest, without detecting that the rejoinder contained much more sadness with respect to the happiness of childhood than did the saying of the young woman. His sad interpretation of childhood stands in relation to the contrast presented by her longing look at the child. But the greatest contrast is the eternal recollection of guilt, and the saddest longing is quite rightly expressed by the longing to get a licking. When the young woman was speaking, people were somewhat moved; at the humorist's rejoinder they were almost shocked, in spite of the laughter, and yet he said something far more profound. The longing for the happiness of childhood which is prompted by all the twaddle of life, the travail

Precisely because the pleasantry of humor consists in revocation (a start being made with profundity, which is revoked) it naturally is often a regression to childhood. If a man like Kant who stands at the pinnacle of scientific culture were to say regarding the proofs for God's existence, "Well, I know nothing more about it except that my father told me it was so," this would be humorous, and he would be saying more than a whole book on the proofs, in case such a book forgets this item. But because humor is always a concealed pain, it is also an instance of sympathy. In irony there is no sympathy, there is self-assurance, and therefore its sympathy is sympathetic in an entirely indirect way, not with any man in particular, but with the idea of self-assurance as the possibility of every man. Hence in woman one often finds humor but never irony. If an essay is made at it, it ill becomes her, and a purely womanly nature will regard irony as a kind of cruelty.

Humor reflects upon the consciousness of guilt as a totality, and is therefore truer than all comparative measuring and gauging. But the profound thought is revoked in jest, just as we saw earlier in the case of suffering. Humor comprehends guilt as a totality, but just as it comes

of soul and the striving after wind, by sullen seriousness, yea, even by the daily pain of an unhappy marriage, is not nearly so sad as the longing prompted by the eternal recollection of guilt, and it was upon this the humorist reflected with melancholy longing; for with consciousness of the totality of guilt, to long after an imaginary representation of the pure innocence of the child is really nonsensical, notwithstanding that this longing is often employed with touching effect . . . by superficial speakers. The rejoinder was not a discourteous and teasing jest, on the contrary, it was sympathetic. It is related of Socrates that a man came to him with the complaint that people slandered him in his absence. Socrates replied: "Is that anything to worry about? For my part it is a matter of such indifference what people do in my absence that for all I care they might beat me in my absence." This rejoinder is correct irony; it is uttered without the sympathy wherewith Socrates was capable of creating a common situation with another, and the law for this teasing irony is quite simply this: that the craftiness of irony constantly prevents a conversation from being a conversation, though it has the appearance of being a conversation, perhaps even a cordial conversation. This rejoinder was teasingly ironical, even though for all that it has a tendency towards the ethical, seeking to rouse the man to win self-assurance. Hence Socrates says less than the man did, for slander is after all something, but to get a beating in one's absence is meaningless. On the other hand, a humorous rejoinder must always contain something profound, thought it is concealed by jest, and therefore it must say more. Thus when a man has recourse to an ironist in order to confide to him a secret under pledge of silence, and he answers, "Rely upon me completely, one can be absolutely confident in confiding a secret to me, for I forget it as quickly as it is uttered"; in this case a confidential relationship is annihilated quite correctly by means of an abstract dialectic. If the other actually confides to him his secret, it is true that they converse together, but if that is taken to be a confidential conversation, it is a misunderstanding. If, on the other hand, that man who was persecuted by slander had said to a young girl, for example, the same thing he said to Socrates, complaining that this man or the other had spoken ill of him in his absence, and the young girl had replied, "Then I may count myself fortunate, for me he has completely forgotten," this rejoinder has a touch of the humorous, though it falls short of it in so far as it does not reflect upon any determinant of totality, which by its specific contrast constitutes the humorous.

to the point of giving an explanation, it becomes impatient and revokes it all, saying, "However, that would be too long drawn out and too profound, I therefore revoke it all and give back the money." "We are all of us debtors," the humorist would say, "many a time we fall and in various ways, all of us who belong to the animal species which Buffon thus describes . . ." Here might follow a definition expressed purely in terms of natural history. The contrast has here attained its highest expression: between an individual who in the eternal recollection has the totality of guilt, and a specimen of an animal species. There is therefore no analogy here to the developmental metamorphosis of a man, in so far as he has the highest experience, that of being subsumed under the absolute definition of spirit. A plant is as germ that which it becomes as developed plant, and so also the animal, but not a child. Whence also it comes that in every generation there are many who never come under the definition of spirit absolutely.* The humorous swing away from the individual to the species is also a return to aesthetic concepts, and it is by no means in this that the profundity of humor consists. The totality of guilt-consciousness in the particular individual before God in relation to an eternal happiness is religiousness. Upon this humor reflects, but revokes it again. For, religiously regarded, the species is a lower category than the individual, and to thrust oneself under the category of the species is evasion.†

Humor puts the eternal recollection of guilt together with everything, but does not by this recollection relate itself to an eternal happiness. Now we come to the hidden inwardness. The eternal recollection of guilt cannot be expressed outwardly, it is incommensurable with such expression, since every outward expression finitizes guilt. But the eternal recollection of guilt which characterizes the hidden inwardness is anything but despair; for despair is always the infinite, the eternal, the total, at the instant of impatience; and all despair is a kind of bad temper. No, the eternal recollection is the mark indicative of the relationship to an eternal hap-

---

* It is to be remembered that in this connection there is no question of differences of talent, but that the possibility of spiritual existence is available to every man, in spite of the fact that the metamorphosis involves a change so clearly qualitative that it is not to be explained in terms of the "little by little" which accounts for simple evolution, although the eternal consciousness of guilt, once it is posited, assumes itself.

† Only in the final definition of the religious as the paradox-religious does the race become higher, but then it is only in virtue of the paradox, and one must have had the intermediate definition of the religious which makes the individual higher than the species, if the spherical differences are not to coagulate and people to prate aesthetically about the paradox-religious.

piness, a mark which is as far as possible from being a plain indication, but which is always sufficient to prevent the leaping aside of despair.

Humor discovers the comic by putting the total guilt together with the relativity as between man and man. The comic lies in the fact that the total guilt is the foundation which supports the whole comedy. In case essential innocence or goodness were at the basis of the relative, the situation is not comic, for it is not comic that the more or the less is defined within the positive definition. But when relativity rests upon the total guilt, the more or the less rests upon that which is less than nothing, and this is the contradiction which the comic detects. In so far as money is a something, the relativity as between richer and poorer is not comic, but when counters are used instead of money it is comic that there should be a relativity. When men's busy activity in running around has as its reason a possibility of escaping danger, this activity is not comic; but in case, for example, it is on a ship which is sinking, there is something comic in all this running around, for the contradiction is that in spite of all this movement they do not move away from the place where destruction is.

The hidden inwardness must also discover the comic, not for the fact that the religious man is different from others, but for the fact that he, though most heavily burdened by bearing the eternal recollection of guilt, is like all others. He discovers the comic, but inasmuch as in the eternal recollection he is constantly related to an eternal happiness, the comic is constantly evanescent.

INTERMEDIATE CLAUSE BETWEEN A AND B

THE Problem presented (cf. Second Section, Chapter IV) was an existence-problem, and as such it is pathetic-dialectic. The part, A, which is the pathetic part, has been dealt with: the relationship to an eternal happiness. Now we go on to the dialectic part, B, which is the decisive part for this problem. For the religiousness which has hitherto been dealt with, and which for the sake of brevity is henceforth to be called religiousness A, is not the specifically Christian religiousness. On the other hand, the dialectical part is the decisive part only in so far as it is combined with the pathetic to create new pathos.

Generally one is not contemporaneously aware of both. The religious address is inclined to present the pathetic factor and to annul the dialectic, and therefore, however well meaning it may be, it is sometimes a confused tumultuous pathos, composed of all sorts of things, aesthetics, ethics, religiousness A, and Christianity, and hence it is sometimes self-contradictory; "but there are lovely passages in the sermon!"—lovely especially for those who are bound to act and exist according to it. The dialectical takes its revenge by slyly and ironically making a mock of gestures and big words, and above all by this ironical judgment upon the religious address, that it is very easy to hear, but not easy to do.

Learning is inclined to take charge of the dialectical, and with this intent to carry it over into the medium of abstraction, wherewith the problem is again missed, inasmuch as it is an existence-problem and the real dialectical difficulty vanishes when it is explained in the medium of abstraction which takes no account of existence. If the tumultuous religious address is for emotional people who are quick to sweat and quickly sweated out, the speculative view is for pure thinkers, but neither is for people who are acting and by virtue of acting are existers.

The distinction between the pathetic and the dialectical must, however, be more closely defined; for religiousness A is by no means undialectic, but it is not paradoxically dialectic. Religiousness A is the dialectic of inward transformation; it is the relation to an eternal happiness which is not conditioned by anything but is the dialectic inward appropriation of the relationship, and so is conditioned only by the inwardness of the appropriation and its dialectic. Religiousness B, as henceforth it is to be called, or the paradoxical religiousness, as it has hitherto been called, or the religiousness which has the dialectical in the second instance, does on the contrary posit conditions, of such a sort that they are not merely deeper dialectical apprehensions of inwardness, but are a definite something which defines more closely the eternal happiness (whereas in A the only closer definitions are the closer definitions of inward apprehension), not defining more closely the individual apprehension of it, but defining more closely the eternal happiness itself, though not as a task for thought, but paradoxically as a repellent to produce new pathos.

Religiousness A must first be present in the individual before there can be any question of becoming aware of the dialectic of B. When the individual is related to an eternal happiness by the most decisive expression of the existential pathos, then there can be question of becoming aware how the dialectic in the second instance (*secundo loco*) thrusts a man down into the pathos of the absurd. One will therefore perceive how foolish it is when a man without pathos wants to relate himself to

the Christian; for before there can be any question at all of merely being
in the situation for becoming aware of it, one must first exist in religiousness A. However, the preposterous case has often enough occurred, that
people have appropriated, as a matter of course, Christ and Christianity
and the paradox and the absurd, in short, everything that is Christian,
in an aesthetical hodge-podge, just as though Christianity were wholesome fodder for simpletons because it cannot be thought, and as though
the characteristic that it cannot be thought were not precisely the most
difficult to hold on to . . . especially for clever pates.

Religiousness A can exist in paganism, and in Christianity it can be
the religiousness of everyone who is not decisively Christian, whether he
be baptized or no. That is only natural. To become a cheap edition of
a Christian in perfect comfort, is very much easier, and at the same time
it comes to about the same as the highest attainment, the man is indeed
baptized, he has received a copy of the Bible and the Hymn Book as a
confirmation present—is he then not a Christian, an Evangelical Lutheran Christian? However, that is the affair of the party concerned. My
opinion is that religiousness A (within the boundaries of which I have
my existence) is so laborious that it is always enough of a task. My purpose is to make it difficult to become a Christian, yet not more difficult
than it is, nor to make it difficult for stupid people, and easy for clever
pates, but qualitatively difficult, and essentially difficult for every man
equally, for essentially it is equally difficult for every man to relinquish
his understanding and his thinking, and to keep his soul fixed upon the
absurd; it is comparatively more difficult for a man if he has much understanding—if one will keep in mind that not everyone who has lost
his understanding over Christianity thereby proves that he has any. This
is my purpose—in such a sense, that is to say, as an experimenter who
does everything for his own sake can be said to have a purpose. Every
man, the wisest and the simplest, can qualitatively (the comparative
produces misunderstanding, as in the case when a clever pate compares
himself with a simple man, instead of understanding that the same task
is for each one severally and not for the two in comparison) distinguish
just as essentially between what he understands and what he does not
understand (of course his laborious conclusion will be the fruit of his
utmost effort, and two thousand years lie between Socrates and Hamann,
the two upholders of this distinction), and he can discover that there is
something which is, in spite of the fact that it is against his understanding and way of thinking. When he stakes his life upon this absurd, he

makes the motion in virtue of the absurd, and he is essentially deceived in case the absurd he has chosen can be proved to be not the absurd. In case this absurd is Christianity, he is a believing* Christian; but if he understands it as not the absurd, he is *eo ipso* no longer a believing Christian (though he be baptized and confirmed and possessor of the Bible and the Hymn Book, were it even the expected New Hymnal), until he annuls understanding again as an illusion and a misunderstanding, and relates himself to the Christian absurd. For in case religiousness A does not come into the picture as *terminus a quo* for the paradoxical religiousness, religiousness A is higher than B, for then the paradox, the absurd, etc., are not to be taken *sensu eminenti* (in the sense that they absolutely cannot be understood either by clever or by stupid people), but are used aesthetically of the marvelous among other marvelous things, which are indeed marvelous, but which after all can be comprehended. Speculative philosophy (in so far as it does not desire to do away with all religiousness in order to introduce us *en masse* into the promised land of pure being) must consistently hold the opinion that religiousness A is higher than B, since it is the religiousness of immanence. But why then call it Christian? Christianity is not content to be an evolution within the total definition of human nature; such an offer is too trifling a one to propose to the Deity, who does not want to be at one moment for the believer the paradox, and then little by little to supply him with an understanding; for the martyrdom of faith (crucifixion of the understanding) is not a martyrdom of the instant but precisely the martyrdom of endurance.

Existing religiously, one can express one's relationship to an eternal happiness (immortality, eternal life) outside of Christianity, and this has surely been done; for of religiousness A one may say that, even if it has not been exemplified in paganism, it could have been, because it has only human nature in general as its assumption, whereas the religiousness which has the dialectical in the second instance cannot have been before itself, nor even after it has come, can it be said to be able to have been before it was. The specific thing in Christianity is the dialectical in the second instance, only not, be it noted, as a task for thought (as

* The definition of faith was given in Part Second, Chapter 2, also in Chapter 3, which deals with ideality and reality. Whenever one reasons in this fashion: "One cannot stop at the paradox because this is too small a task or too easy and indolent," then one must reply: "No, on the contrary, it is exactly the opposite, it is the most difficult thing of all, day in and day out, to relate oneself to something upon which one bases one's eternal happiness, holding fast to the passion with which one understands that one cannot understand, especially as it is so easy to let this go in the illusion that now one has understood it.

though Christianity were a doctrine, not an existence-communication. Cf. Part Second, Chapter 2, and Chapter 4, Section 1, § 2), but relating itself to the pathetic as an incitement to new pathos. In religiousness A an eternal happiness is something simple, and the pathetic becomes the dialectical factor in the dialectic of inward appropriation; in religiousness B it becomes dialectic in the second instance, since the communication is in the direction of existence, pathetic in inward appropriation.

In proportion as the individual expresses the existential pathos (resignation—suffering—the totality of guilt-consciousness), in that same degree does his pathetic relationship to an eternal happiness increase. So when the eternal happiness as the absolute *telos* has become for him absolutely the only comfort, and when accordingly his relationship to it is reduced to its minimum through the attainment of existential depth, by reason of the fact that guilt-consciousness is the repelling relationship and would constantly take this *telos* away from him, and yet this minimum and this possibility are absolutely more than everything else to him, then is the appropriate time to begin with the dialectical. When he is in this situation it will arouse in him a still higher pathos. But one does not prepare oneself to become attentive to Christianity by reading books, or by world-historical surveys, but by immersing oneself deeper in existence. Every other propaedeutic must *eo ipso* end in a misunderstanding, for Christianity is existence-communication, it would politely excuse itself from being understood (cf. Part Second, Chapter 2); to understand what Christianity is, is not the difficulty, but to become and to be a Christian (cf. Part Second, Chapter 4, Section 1, § 2).

Comment. Inasmuch as the edifying is essentially a predicate of all religiousness, religiousness A will also have its own particular edification. Whenever the God-relation is found by the exister in the inwardness of subjectivity, there is to be found the edifying which belongs to subjectivity, whereas by becoming objective one abandons this; for although it belongs to subjectivity it is not necessarily associated with it, any more than love is or being in love, which also may be abandoned by becoming objective. The totality of guilt-consciousness is the most edifying factor in religiousness A.* The edifying element in the sphere of religiousness A is essentially that of immanence, it is the annihilation by which the individual puts himself out of the way in order to find God, since precisely the individual himself is the hin-

* Let the reader remember that a direct God-relationship is aesthetic and is really not a God-relationship, any more than a direct relationship to the absolute is an absolute relationship, because the discrimination of the absolute has not been accomplished. In the religious sphere the positive is recognizable by the negative. The most exuberant sense of well-being in the delight of immanence, which exults in joy over God and the whole of existence, is a very lovable thing but not edifying and not essentially a God-relationship.

drance.* Quite rightly the edifying is recognizable here also by the negative, by self-annihilation, which in itself finds the God-relationship, is based upon it, because God is the basis when every obstacle is cleared away, and first and foremost the individual himself in his finiteness, in his obstinacy against God. Aesthetically, the holy resting place of edification is outside the individual, who accordingly seeks the place; in the ethico-religious sphere the individual himself is the place, when he has annihilated himself.

This is the edifying in the sphere of religiousness A. If one does not give heed to this and to the importance of having this definition of the edifying in the picture, then again everything is brought to confusion when one comes to define the paradoxical edifying, which then is confounded with an aesthetic relationship outwardly directed. In religiousness B the edifying is a something outside the individual, the individual does not find edification by finding the God-relationship within himself, but relates himself to something outside himself to find edification. The paradox consists in the fact that this apparently aesthetic relationship (the individual being related to something outside himself) is nevertheless the right relationship; for in immanence God is neither a something (He being all and infinitely all), nor is He outside the individual, since edification consists precisely in the fact that He is in the individual. The paradoxical edification corresponds therefore to the determination of God in time as the individual man; for if such be the case, the individual is related to something outside himself. The fact that it is not possible to think this, is precisely the paradox. It is another question whether the individual will not be repelled by it—that is his affair. But if the paradox is not held fast in this sense, religiousness A is higher, and Christianity as a whole is reduced to aesthetic terms, in spite of Christianity's affirmation that the paradox it talks about cannot be thought, and thus is different from a relative paradox which at the utmost presents difficulty for thought. One must give speculative philosophy credit for holding fast to immanence (even if this must be understood as something different from Hegel's pure thought), but speculative philosophy must not call itself Christian. By me therefore religiousness A has never been called Christian or Christianity.

B. The Dialectical

It was with this subject the *Fragments* essentially dealt; I can therefore refer constantly to that book, and can express myself here the more briefly. The difficulty consists merely in holding fast the qualitative dialectic of the absolute paradox and bidding defiance to the illusions. In the case of that which can and shall be and wills to be the absolute paradox, the incomprehensible, it requires passion to hold fast dialectically the definition of incomprehensibility. Ludicrous as it is therefore, in the case of something which can be understood, to hear superstitious and fanatical persons utter dark sayings about its incomprehensibility;

---

* The aesthetic always consists in the fact that the individual imagines that he is busy grasping after God and getting hold of Him, and in the conceit that the individual is pretty smart if only he can get hold of God as something external.

TIME 499

the inverse case is just as ludicrous: when it is a case of the essential paradox, to behold efforts to want to understand it, as though the task were
not the qualitative opposite, namely, to hold fast the fact that it cannot
be understood, lest non-understanding, i.e. misunderstanding, end by
confusing all the other spheres as well. When the paradoxical religious
address is not attentive to this, it puts itself at the mercy of a well-de-
served ironical interpretation; whether with revivalistic befuddlement
and spiritual intoxication it tries to get a glimpse behind the curtain,
interprets Runic inscriptions, descries explanations, and then preachifies
them in a singsong tone which is the resonance of the seer's unnatural
intercourse with the marvelous, seeing that the absolute paradox would
beg to be excused from explanations; or whether the paradoxical religious address modestly disclaims understanding, yet is willing to
concede that this is something far higher; or whether it makes an attempt at understanding and only then admits the incomprehensibility;
or finds in something else a parallel to the incomprehensibility of the
paradox. All of this which irony has to scent out and bring to light has
its ground in the fact that one does not respect the qualitative dialectic
of the spheres, does not notice that while in the case of the incomprehensible, which nevertheless is essentially comprehensible, the explanation is meritorious, it is not meritorious in the case of the essentially
incomprehensible. The misunderstanding has its ground in the fact that,
notwithstanding the use of Christ's name etc., one has managed to push
Christianity back into the aesthetic sphere (in which unwittingly the
hyper-orthodox especially are successful) where the incomprehensible is
the relatively incomprehensible (relative either with regard to the fact
that it has not yet been understood, or to the fact that in order to understand it there is requisite a seer with the eye of a hawk), which is followed by comprehensibility or understanding as a higher position in
time, whereas on the contrary Christianity is an existence-communication which makes existence paradoxical and remains paradoxical as long
as one exists, and only eternity possesses the explanation, so that it is not
in the least meritorious, as long as one is in time, to want to dabble in
explanations, that is, to want to imagine that one is in eternity, for as
long as one is in time the qualitative dialectic designates every such attempt as unwarranted dabbling. The qualitative dialectic enjoins that
one is not to fool *in abstracto* with that which is the highest, and hence
want to dabble at it, but must comprehend *in concreto* one's essential
task and essentially express it.

But there are certain things it is difficult to get into certain persons' heads, and among them the passionate definition of the incomprehensible. The religious address begins perhaps quite correctly, but in a trice nature gets the better of discipline, his reverence cannot after all resist the notion that to glimpse a thing is something higher, and then the comedy begins. Even in the case of many a relative problem, people can make themselves ridiculous by their busy air of self-importance in explaining things with a profound hint; but in the case of the absolute paradox this glimpsing and blinking with the eyes, this attentive silence of the "revived" congregation, which is only broken when one after another of the "revived" stands up in a tense attitude to catch a glimpse of that which his reverence glimpses, while the females take off their hats to catch every prophetic word—all this tension in the case of the glimpsing of his reverence is very ludicrous. And the most ludicrous thing of all is that this glimpsing is taken to be something higher than the passion of faith. If anything, it must rather be something to put up with as a weakness on the part of brethren who are weak in faith, lacking the force to accentuate passionately the incomprehensible, and therefore must do a bit of glimpsing, for all glimpsing is impatience. And the inclination to glimpse and to drop profound hints is, in general, seductive only to a certain class of narrow-minded and fanatical persons; every man who is fairly competent and serious will strive to know which is which: whether it is something which can and shall be understood, in which case he will not be content to glimpse; or something which cannot and shall not be understood, in which case he will be no more inclined to glimpse [skimte], or what in this connection is the same thing, to banter [skjemte]; for in spite of the serious air and the raised eyebrows the glimpsing is only sport, even if Mr. Knud who does it believes that it is the purest seriousness.

All of this glimpsing and all that goes with it (which in our time to be sure, whatever the reason may be, has become rather rare) is neither more nor less than pious coquetry. A Christian clergyman who does not know how, with the passion of existential effort, to keep himself and the congregation in awe by proclaiming that the paradox cannot and shall not be understood, who does not affirm precisely that the task is to hold fast to this and to endure the crucifixion of the understanding, but has understood everything speculatively—that clergyman is comic. But the more he accentuates the incomprehensibility, if after all it ends in glimpsing, the more demoralizing is his coquetry, because it amounts to complimenting himself: implying that whereas the difficulty and the incomprehensibility are an impediment to the shallow [*"de Aandløse"*], he is clever [*aandrig*] enough . . . to glimpse into the dark riddle. Christianity is an existence-communication which makes the thing of existing paradoxical and difficult to a degree it never was before and never can be outside of Christianity, but it is no short cut to becoming incomparably clever. Perhaps, however, it is chiefly among "awakened" students the phenomenon occurs that, failing to make any progress along the narrow path of science and learning and thinking, one leaps away and becomes absolutely "awakened" . . . and incomparably clever. Preferable then is the misunderstanding of speculation, where, apart from this, there is so much to learn and so much to admire in the men who combined with the force of genius an iron endurance—preferable then the misunderstanding of speculation . . . that it can explain everything. The case is much the same with faith's crucifixion of the understanding as with many another ethical determinant. One man renounces personal vanity . . . but would be admired for doing it. One gives up, as he says, the understanding in order to believe . . . but then he acquires a higher understanding, so much higher that by virtue of it he comports himself as an incomparably clever seer, etc. But it is always a questionable thing to derive profit or apparent profit out of one's religiousness. Because an individual gives up his understanding for faith and believes against the understanding, he should not think meanly of the understanding, nor suddenly arrogate to himself a glittering distinction within the total compass of the understanding; for after all a higher understanding is also an understanding. Herein consists the presumption of the religiously "awakened" man. But respectful as one should be in dealing with a Christian, and lenient with the sickliness which sometimes in a period of transition may derange one and produce a disturbing effect, one should calmly deliver up a presumptuous specimen of the "awakened" to be dealt with by irony. If in the degenerate period of the Middle Ages the inmate of the cloister would like to have profit from his life by being honored as a saint, it is quite as objectionable and only a little more ludicrous for one to want to become incomparably clever by reason of one's religiousness; and if it is a pitiable error to want to be like God by reason of virtue and holiness, instead of becoming more and more humble, it is more ludicrous to want to be that in consideration of having an exceptionally clever mind; for virtue and holiness do after all stand in an essential relation to God's nature, and the other determinant makes God Himself ridiculous as the *tertium comparationis*. He who in truth has given up his understanding and believes against the understanding (which is like rolling a burden up a mountain), such a man will be prevented from playing the genius on the score of his religiousness. The contradiction in the case of the religiously awakened man is that after he has entered by means of faith against the understanding into the last enclosure of inwardness, he would like at the same time to be out in the street and to be incomparably clever. And the farce or benefit performance is equally ludicrous whether he eagerly appropriates the world's admiration when some of it is seen to fall to his lot (a new inconsistency: that he who possesses the higher understanding should allow himself to be admired by the world which has in fact only the lower and whose admiration therefore is nonsense), or whether he condemns the world's shallowness and thunders against it when it will not admire (a strange ceremony, since he himself knows that the world has only the lower understanding), or whether he laments the fact that he is misunderstood (which is, however, quite in order, and lamentation over it is only a misunderstanding which betrays the secret communication he maintains with worldliness).

The misunderstanding is invariably due to the false notion that the incomprehensibility of the paradox must be related in some way to the difference between more or less understanding, to the comparison between clever and foolish pates. The paradox is related essentially to man as man, and qualitatively related to every man severally, whether he has much or little understanding. The most intelligent man can therefore believe just as well (against the understanding), and by his much understanding he is only to this extent hindered from believing, that he has also the advantage of knowing by experience what it is to believe against the understanding. Socrates, whose ignorance was in an earlier passage (Second Section, Chapter II) shown to be a kind of analogy to faith (remembering, however, that essentially there are no analogies to the paradox-religiousness of faith), was not a blockhead because he would not be duped into glimpsing this or that, but would be absolutely ignorant. But on the other hand it never occurred to Socrates, after he had discredited the common human knowledge, to want to be admired for a higher understanding, or to want to engage in straightforward conversation with any man, since by his ignorance he had essentially nullified communication with all.

The "awakened" religionists are often enough busied about the un-godly world which derides them—though from another point of view this is after all just what they themselves would wish, for the sake of being well assured that they are the "awakened" . . . seeing that they are derided, and then again for the sake of having the advantage of being able to complain of the world's ungodliness. It is always, however, a dubious proof of the world's ungodliness that it laughs at an "awak-ened" individual, especially when he begins to glimpse, for then he really is ridiculous. In our age, with its great tolerance or indifference, it certainly is not impossible for a real Christian, who is severe with him-self and therefore is not engaged in condemning others, to live on in peace—but of course he would have nevertheless the martyrdom within himself of believing against the understanding. But all presumptuous-ness, when in addition it is self-contradictory, is comic. Let us take an example drawn from a lowlier sphere of life, keeping constantly in mind, however, that so far as the application is concerned there is no analogy to the sphere of the paradox-religious, and that the application is revoked as soon as it is understood. A man arranges his life in a par-ticular way which according to his knowledge of himself, his capacities, his faults, etc., is the most advantageous for him and hence also the most comfortable. It very well may be that this mode of life, and more espe-cially his consistency in carrying it out, appears at the first glance or from many another viewpoint a ludicrous thing. If he is a presumptuous person, his eccentric mode of life will of course be proclaimed a higher understanding, etc. If, on the contrary, he is a serious man he will calmly listen to other people's views, and by the way he engages in conversation about it he will show that he himself can very well perceive the comic aspect it may have for a third party—and thereupon he will go home quite calmly and pursue the plan of life he had adopted as most suitable to him in view of the precise knowledge he has of himself. So it is also in the case of one who is really a Christian—if we remember that there is no analogy. He may very well have understanding (indeed he must have it in order to believe against understanding), he can use it in all other connections, use it in intercourse with other men (seeing that it is also an inconsistency to desire to converse with anyone who does not possess the higher understanding when one would for his part make use of the higher understanding, for conversation is an expression of the ordinary and mutual understanding, the relation between one who has the higher understanding and the ordinary man would be that of an apostle or absolute teacher, not that of a fellow man), he will be well able to see the point of every objection, indeed to present it himself as well as the best of them, for otherwise a higher understanding would in a suspicious way be a dubious promotion for stuff and nonsense. It is easy enough to leap away from the toilsome task of developing and sharpening the understanding, and so get a louder hurrah, and to defend oneself against every accusation by remarking that it is a higher understanding.* So the believing Christian not only possesses but uses his understanding, respects the universal-human, does not put it down to lack of understanding if somebody is not a Christian; but in relation to Christianity he believes against the understanding and in this case also uses understanding . . . to make sure that he believes against the understanding. Nonsense therefore he cannot believe against the understanding, for precisely the understanding will discern that it is nonsense and will prevent him from believing it; but he makes so much use of the understanding that he becomes aware of the incomprehensible, and then he holds to this, believing against the understanding.

An enthusiastic ethical individual uses understanding to discover what the shrewdest thing is, in order not to do it; for what we commonly call the shrewdest thing is seldom the noblest. But even this behavior (a kind of analogy to that of the believer, only that to understand the application is to revoke it) is very seldom understood; and when one sees a man sacrifice himself with enthusiasm, choose with enthusiasm exertion instead of an easy life which would be rewarded by admiration and promotion, many a man will think it a kind of narrow-mindedness, will smile at him pityingly, and perhaps go so far that in a fit of good nature he would help the poor man to see what the shrewdest course is—though he only helps the poor fellow to get a little ironical insight into the soul of his counselor. Such counsel is a misunderstanding which has its ground not so much in lack of understanding as in lack of enthusiasm. The enthusiastic ethicist therefore will not resent the objections or the ridicule; long before this befalls him he will have realized that it would befall him, he will be as ready as the best of them to construe his effort as comic—and then with calm resolve he will choose to use the understanding to see what the shrewdest thing is . . . in order not to do it. The analogy is not complete, since there is no suffering for such an ethicist in this opposition to the understanding; after all, his enthusiastic

* Hence it was said above that it is always rather awkward to represent anything as the absurd, the incomprehensible, about which another can declare that it is easy to understand.

action is an understanding for the infinite, and he breaks only with the deplorable misery of shrewdness; in him there is no breach, nor the suffering involved in the breach. But a believer who believes, i.e. believes against the understanding,* takes the mystery of faith seriously and is not duped by the pretense of understanding, but is aware that the curiosity which leads to glimpsing is infidelity and betrayal of the task.

The dialectical aspect of the problem requires thought-passion—not to want to understand it, but to understand what it means to break thus with the understanding and with thinking and with immanence, in order to lose the last foothold of immanence, eternity behind one,[1] and to exist constantly on the extremest verge of existence by virtue of the absurd.

As I have said, this dialectic is what the *Fragments* dealt with especially. I will be briefer here, and being able to refer to that work I will merely endeavor so far as I can to express the same thing more definitely and succinctly.

§ I. THE DIALECTICAL CONTRADICTION WHICH IS THE BREACH: TO EXPECT AN ETERNAL HAPPINESS IN TIME THROUGH A RELATIONSHIP TO SOMETHING ELSE IN TIME

By this contradiction, existence is paradoxically accentuated, and the distinction of "here" and "hereafter" is absolutely defined by the fact that existence is paradoxically accentuated for the reason that the eternal itself came into the world at a moment of time. Let it be constantly remembered that I do not undertake to explain the problem but merely to state it.

The apprehension of the distinction "here" and "hereafter" is decisive for every existence-communication. *Speculative philosophy* resolves it absolutely into pure being, as it does the principle of contradiction of which it is an example; and this in turn is an expression for the fact that speculative philosophy is not an existence-communication, and this is a doubtful recommendation, seeing that it would like to explain existence. *Religiousness A,* which is not speculative philosophy, but yet is speculative, reflects upon this distinction when it reflects upon what it is to exist; but even the decisive definition of guilt-consciousness is within the sphere of immanence after all. *The paradoxical religiousness* defines the distinction absolutely by accentuating paradoxically what it is to

---

* And faith belongs essentially in the sphere of the paradox-religious, as has constantly been asserted (cf. among other passages, Second Section, Chapters 2 and 3); all other faith is only an analogy, which is no faith, an analogy, which may serve to call attention, but nothing more, and the understanding of which therefore is revocation.

exist. For as the eternal came into the world at a moment of time, the existing individual does not in the course of time come into relation with the eternal and think about it (this is A), but *in time* it comes into relation with the eternal *in time;* so that the relation is within time, and this relationship conflicts equally with all thinking, whether one reflect upon the individual or upon the Deity.

The apprehension of the distinction "here" and "hereafter" is at bottom the apprehension of what it is to *exist,* and the other distinctions converge about this—if one is careful to notice that Christianity is not a doctrine but an existence-communication. *Speculative philosophy* discounts existence; in its eyes the fact of existing amounts to having existed (the past), existence is a transitory factor resolved into the pure being of the eternal. Speculative philosophy as the abstract can never be contemporary with existence as existing but can only see it in retrospect. This explains why speculative philosophy prudently holds itself aloof from ethics, and why it becomes ridiculous when it makes a trial at it. *Religiousness A* accentuates existence as actuality, and eternity (which nevertheless sustains everything by the immanence which lies at the base of it) disappears in such a way that the positive becomes recognizable by the negative. To the eyes of speculative philosophy, existence has vanished and only pure being is, and yet the eternal is constantly concealed in it and as concealed is present. *The paradoxical religiousness* places the contradiction absolutely between existence and the eternal; for precisely the thought that the eternal *is* at a definite moment of time, is an expression for the fact that existence is abandoned by the concealed immanence of the eternal. In the religiousness A the eternal is *ubique et nusquam,* but concealed by the actuality of existence; in the paradoxical religiousness the eternal is at a definite place, and precisely this is the breach with immanence.

In the Second Section, Chapter II it was said that what our age has forgotten, and what explains the misunderstanding of Christianity on the part of speculative philosophy, is "what it is to exist, and what inwardness is." Religiousness is indeed inwardness in existing, and everything which serves to deepen this determinant heightens the religiousness, and the paradox-religiousness is the ultimate.

All interpretations of existence rank in accordance with the degree of the individual's dialectical apprehension of inwardness. Taking for granted what has been said in this work, I will now merely recapitulate, with the warning that speculative philosophy has of course no part to play here, since, being objective and abstract, it is indifferent to the concretion of the existing subject and at the most has to do with the pure idea of mankind, whereas existence-communications understand something else by *unum* in the saying *unum noris omnes,* understand something else by "thyself" in the saying "Know thyself," understand thereby an actual man, and thereby indicate that these words are not concerned with the anecdotal differences between Dick and Harry.

If the individual is in himself undialectical and has his dialectic outside himself, then we have the *aesthetic interpretation.* If the individual is dialectical in himself inwardly in self-assertion, hence in such a way that the ultimate basis is not dialectic in itself, inasmuch as the self which is at the basis is used to overcome and assert itself, then we have the *ethical interpretation.* If the individual is inwardly defined by self-annihilation before God, then we have *religiousness A.* If the individual is paradoxically dialectic, every vestige of original immanence being annihilated and all connection cut off, the individual being brought to the utmost verge of existence, then we have the *paradoxical religiousness.* This paradoxical inwardness is the greatest possible, for even the most paradoxical determinant, if after all it is within immanence, leaves as it were a possibility of escape, of a leaping away, of a retreat into the eternal behind it; it is as though everything had not been staked after all. But the breach makes the inwardness the greatest possible.

Again, the various existence-communications rank in accordance with the interpretation of what it is to exist. (Speculative philosophy, as abstract and objective, entirely ignores the fact of existence and inwardness; and inasmuch as Christianity accentuates this fact paradoxically, speculation is the greatest possible misunderstanding of Christianity.) *Immediacy, the aesthetic,* finds no contradiction in the fact of existing: to exist is one thing, and the contradiction is something else which comes from without. *The ethical* finds the contradiction, but within self-assertion. *The religiousness A* comprehends the contradiction as suffering in self-annihilation, although within immanence, but by ethically accentuating the fact of existing it prevents the exister from becoming abstract in immanence, or from becoming abstract by wishing to remain in immanence. *The paradoxical religiousness* breaks with immanence and makes the fact of existing the absolute contradiction, not within immanence, but against immanence. There is no longer any immanent fundamental kinship between the temporal and the eternal, because the eternal itself has entered time and would constitute there the kinship.

Comment. One may compare with this the first two chapters of the *Fragments,* which deal with teaching the truth, with the instant, and with the Deity in time as teacher. In the *aesthetic view* one is master, the other, apprentice or pupil, and then in turn, master, etc., in short, the relation is that of relativity. *Religiously* viewed, there is no disciple and no teacher ("the teacher is merely an occasion," cf. the *Fragments*), every individual is in essence equally adapted for eternity and essentially related to the eternal, the human teacher is a vanishing transition. As seen from the *paradox-religious* standpoint the teacher is the Deity in time, the disciple a new creature ("the Deity as the teacher in time provides the condition," cf. the *Fragments*). Within the paradox-religious sphere, religiousness A holds good in the relation between man and man. When therefore within Christianity a Christian (who as such is paradoxically a disciple of the Deity in time in the sense of being a new creature) becomes in turn a disciple of this man or that, it awakens an indirect suspicion that all his Christianity is nothing but a bit ol aesthetic galimatias.

The problem constantly dealt with here is this: how there can be an historical starting-point, etc. In religiousness A there is no historical starting-point. The individual merely discovers in time that he must assume he is eternal. The moment in time is therefore *eo ipso* swallowed up by eternity. In time the individual recollects that he is eternal. This contradiction lies exclusively within immanence. It is another thing when the historical is outside and remains outside, and the individual who was not eternal now becomes such, and so does not recollect what he is but becomes what he was not, becomes, be it observed, something which possesses the dialectic that as soon as it is, it must have been, for this is the dialectic of the eternal. This proposition inaccessible to thought is: that one can become eternal although one was not such.

In A, the fact of existing, my existence, is a moment within my eternal consciousness (note that it is the moment which is, not the moment which is passed, for in this way speculative philosophy explains it away), and is thus a lowlier thing which prevents me from being the infinitely higher thing I am. Conversely, in B the fact of existing, although it is a still lowlier thing as it is paradoxically accentuated, is yet so much higher that only in existing do I become eternal, and consequently the thing of existing gives rise to a determinant which is infinitely higher than existence.

§ 2. THE DIALECTICAL CONTRADICTION THAT AN ETERNAL HAPPINESS IS BASED UPON
SOMETHING HISTORICAL

It holds good of all thinking that the eternal is higher than anything historical since it is at the basis of everything. In the religiousness of immanence therefore the individual does not base his relation to the eternal upon his existence in time, but the individual's relation to the eternal, by the dialectic of inward appropriation, determines him in transforming his existence in accordance with this relation and expresses the relation by the transformation.

The confusion of speculative philosophy, here as everywhere, is due to the fact it loses itself in pure being. Irreligious and immoral views of life reduce existence to a naught, a mere prank. Religiousness A makes the thing of existing as strenuous as possible (outside the paradox-religious sphere), but it does not base the relation to an eternal happiness upon one's existence but lets the relation to an eternal happiness serve as basis for the transformation of existence. From the individual's relation to the eternal, there results the how of his existence, not the converse, and thereby infinitely more comes out of it than was put into it.

In this case, however, the dialectical contradiction lies essentially in the fact that the historical comes in the second place. For it is true of all historical knowledge and learning that it is only an approximation, even at its maximum. The contradiction is: to base one's eternal happiness upon an approximation, a thing which can be done only when one has in oneself no eternal determinant (and that again is no more possible to think than how such a notion could occur to any one, since the Deity must provide the condition for it), and hence this again is connected with the paradoxical accentuation of existence.

In relation to the historical, all knowledge of it is at its maximum only an approximation, even with respect to the individual's own knowledge of his own historical externality. The reason for this is in part the impossibility of being able to identify oneself absolutely with the objective, and in part it is the consideration that everything historical, in the fact of being known, is *eo ipso* past and has the ideality of recollection. In the Second Section, Chapter III, the thesis is advanced that the individual's own ethical reality is the only reality—but the ethical reality is not the individual's externality. That my purpose was such and such I can absolutely know to all eternity, for this precisely is the expression of the eternal in me, my very self; but the historical externality a moment later is to be attained only *approximando*.

The historian seeks to attain the greatest possible certainty, and the historian is in no contradiction with himself, for he is not in passion, at the utmost he has the objective passion of the investigator, but he has no subjective passion. As investigator he takes part in a great endeavor carried on from generation to generation, to him it is always objective, scientifically it is important to come as near as possible to certainty, but it is not subjectively important. If, to suppose, for example, a case which would be accounted a fault on the part of an investigator, it were suddenly to become for him quite personally a question of honor to acquire absolute certainty upon such and such a point—then, having incurred a righteous nemesis, he would discover that all historical knowledge is only an approximation. This is no disparagement of historical investigation, but it illuminates precisely the contradiction involved in bringing the utmost passion of subjectivity into relation with something historical, and that is the dialectical contradiction in the problem, which does not talk, however, of any unwarranted passion, but of the profoundest of all. The philosopher seeks to permeate the historical reality with thought, he is objectively employed in this labor, and in proportion as it succeeds the historical detail becomes less important to him. In this again there is no contradiction.

The contradiction first emerges in the fact that the subject in the extremity of such subjective passion (in the concern for an eternal happiness) has to base this upon an historical knowledge which at its maximum remains an approximation. The investigator lives calmly on; in his subjective being and existing he is entirely unconcerned about that which occupies him objectively and scientifically. In case it is supposed that a person is in one way or another absorbed by a subjective passion and that his task is to give this up, then with this the contradiction will also vanish. But to require the greatest possible subjective passion, to the point of hating father and mother, and then to put this together with an historical knowledge, which at its maximum can only be an approximation—that is the contradiction. And again the contradiction is a new expression for the fact that existence is paradoxically accentuated; for if there is any vestige of immanence, an eternal determinant left in the exister—then it is not possible. The exister must have lost continuity with himself, must have become another (not different from himself within himself), and then, by receiving the condition from the Deity, he must have become a new creature. The contradiction is that this thing of becoming a Christian begins with the miracle of creation, and that this occurs to one who already is created, in spite of which Christianity is preached to all men, implying that they are nonexistent, seeing that the miracle whereby they come into being must intervene either as actual or as an expression of the breach with immanence and of the opposition which absolutely makes the passion of faith paradoxical as long as one exists in faith, that is, for the whole of life; for one constantly has one's eternal happiness based upon something historical.

He who with the greatest possible passionateness, in distressful concern for his eternal happiness, is or should be interested in the fact that somebody or another existed, must be interested in the least detail, and yet he cannot attain more than an approximate certainty, and is absolutely in contradiction. Conceding that the historical account of Christianity is true—then, though all the historians of the world were to unite in investigating for the sake of attaining certainty—it would be impossible nevertheless to attain more than an approximation. From the standpoint of the historian there are therefore no objections; but the difficulty is a different one, and that comes when the subjective passion has to be put together with something historical, the task being not to give up the subjective passion. If a woman who is in love were to receive at second hand the assurance that the man she loved (who was dead and from whose mouth she had never heard the assurance) had affirmed that he loved her—let the witness or witnesses be the most reliable of men, let the case be so plain that a captious and incredulous lawyer would say it is certain—the lover will at once detect the precariousness of this report; it is hardly a compliment to the woman to suppose that she would not, for objectivity is no crown of honor for a lover. In case a man had to find out from historical documents with absolute certainty whether he was a legitimate or an illegitimate child, and his whole passion was involved in this question of honor, and the situation was such that there was no tribunal or other external juridical authority to decide the question in a way which might possibly put his fears at rest—do you suppose he would be able to find the certainty which would satisfy his passion, even if the certainty were found which would satisfy the captious and incredulous lawyer and an objective person? However, the woman in love and the man who was concerned for his honor would surely strive to give up this passion, consoling themselves with the eternal, which is more blessed than the most legitimate birth and is the very blessedness of love, be one loved or not loved. But concern for an eternal blessedness cannot be given up, for in that case a man would have nothing eternal to console him, and yet he has to base his eternal happiness upon something historical, knowledge of which at its maximum is an approximation.

Comment. One may compare with this the *Fragments,* Chapters III, IV, and V *passim.* The objective interpretation of Christianity is misleading or misled when it

conceives that by learning to know objectively what Christianity is (as an investigator learns it by the way of research, scholarship, learning) one thereby becomes
a Christian (who bases his blessedness upon this historical witness). One thus
leaves out the difficulty, or one assumes, as at bottom the Bible-theory and
the Church-theory assume, that in a way we are all what one calls Christians
of a sort, and then subsequently (for at the time when we became Christians this was not necessary) we have to know objectively what Christianity
properly is (presumably in order to cease to be Christians, which we became so
easily that we did not need to know what Christianity is—so then in order to cease
to be Christians and to become investigators). The difficulty (and note that it is
essentially the same in every generation, so that now and in 1700, etc., it is just
as difficult to become a Christian as in the first generation and in every generation
when Christianity was first introduced into a country)—the difficulty consists in
willing subjectively to aspire to knowledge about the historical in the interest of
one's own blessedness; and he who does not possess this highest subjective passion
is not a Christian; for, as was said somewhere above, an objective Christian is
precisely a pagan.

In the case of religiousness A it may be said: let the six thousand years of history be true or not be true, to the exister, as concerning the question of his blessedness, it makes no difference, for in the last resort he reposes in the consciousness of
eternity.

Objectively it is no more difficult to ascertain what Christianity is than what
Mohammedanism is or any other historical religion, except in so far as Christianity
is not a simple historical fact; but the difficulty is to become a Christian, because
every Christian is such only by being nailed to the paradox of having based his
eternal happiness upon the relation to something historical. To transform Christianity speculatively into an eternal history, and the Deity in time into an eternal
becoming of the divine, etc., is only an evasion and a play upon words. Once more:
the difficulty is that I can ascertain nothing historical in such a way that I (who
objectively can well be satisfied with scholarship) can subjectively base an eternal
happiness upon it, not that of another man, but my own—that is to say, in such a
way that I can think it. In case I do so, I break with all thinking and should not
then be so foolish as to want to understand it afterwards, since I, if I am to understand anything, cannot, either before or afterwards, get to understand anything
else but that it conflicts with all thinking.

§ 3. THE DIALECTICAL CONTRADICTION THAT THE HISTORICAL FACT HERE IN QUES-
TION IS NOT A SIMPLE HISTORICAL FACT, BUT IS CONSTITUTED BY THAT WHICH
ONLY AGAINST ITS NATURE CAN BECOME HISTORICAL, HENCE BY VIRTUE OF THE
ABSURD

The historical assertion is that the Deity, the Eternal, came into being
at a definite moment in time as an individual man. The peculiar characteristic of this historical datum (that it is not something simply historical, but the historical which only against its nature can become such)

has assisted speculative philosophy to accept a pleasant illusion. Such an historical fact, an eternal historical fact as they call it, one can easily understand, yea, even can understand it eternally. Thanks for the climax; it has the remarkable trait of going backwards; for to understand this eternally is precisely the easier thing—if only one is not embarrassed by the fact that this is a misunderstanding. If the contradiction is this: to base an eternal happiness upon the relation to something historical—then this contradiction is not resolved by the consideration that the historical fact in question is constituted out of a contradiction, when nevertheless one is to hold fast that it is historical; and if this is not to be held fast, then indeed the eternal has not become historical; and even though it were to be held fast, the climax becomes ludicrous, since if it is to be formed it must be formed conversely.

An eternal historical fact is a play on words, and it amounts to transforming the historical fact into a myth, even though in the same paragraph one contends against the mythical tendency. Instead of noticing that there are two dialectical contradictions, first, the basing of one's eternal happiness upon the relation to something historical, and then the fact that this historical datum is compounded in a way contradictory to all thinking, they leave out the first and explain the second away. A man in accordance with his possibility is eternal and becomes conscious of this in time. This is the contradiction within immanence. But that that which in accordance with its nature is eternal comes into existence in time, is born, grows up, and dies—this is a breach with all thinking. If on the other hand the becoming of the eternal in time is to be an eternal becoming—then religiousness A is done away with, "all theology is anthropology,"[1] Christianity is transformed from an existence-communication into a metaphysical doctrine appropriate to professors, religiousness A is bedizened with an aesthetic-metaphysical embellishment which from a categorical standpoint makes no difference at all.

One may compare with this Chapters IV and V of the *Fragments,* where stress is laid upon the peculiar paradox-historical dialectic. For this reason also the difference between the disciple at first and at second hand is done away with, because in relation to the paradox and the absurd we are all equally close. Cf. in this book Chapter II in the Second Section.

Comment. This is the paradox-religious sphere, the sphere of faith. It can be believed altogether—against the understanding. If anyone imagines that he understands it, he can be sure that he misunderstands it. He who understands it plainly (in contrast to understanding that it cannot be understood) will confound Christianity with one or another pagan analogy (analogies which lead away from factual reality); or with the possibility which underlies all the illusory analogies drawn from paganism, which do not possess God's essential invisibility as a higher though intermediate dialectical determinant, but are deluded by the aesthetic-direct criteria of recognition (cf. Second Section, Appendix to Chapter II). Or else he will confound Christianity with something which has indeed entered into the heart of man to believe (that is, into the heart of humanity), he will confound it with human nature's own idea and will forget the qualitative distinction which accentuates the absolutely different point of departure: what comes from God, and what comes from man. Instead of employing the analogy in order to define the paradox in contrast with it (the novelty of Christianity is not the outright novelty, and for this reason precisely it is the paradoxical novelty), he will, through a misunderstanding, revoke the paradox by the aid of the analogy, which is however only the analogy of illusion, and the application of it therefore the revocation of the analogy not of the paradox. In his misunderstanding he will understand Christianity as a possibility and forget that what is possible in the fantasy-medium of possibility (and this it is that underlies all speculative talk about an eternal divine becoming which shifts the scene to the medium of possibility) must in the medium of reality become the absolute paradox. In his misunderstanding he will forget that understanding applies only in case the possibility is higher than the actuality, whereas here, on the contrary, the actuality is the highest, the paradox; for Christianity as a thought-project is not difficult to understand; the difficulty, the paradox, is that it is real. Hence it was shown in the Second Section, Chapter III, that faith is a sphere for itself which, paradoxically distinguished from the aesthetic and metaphysical, accentuates existence, and paradoxically distinguished from the ethical, accentuates the existence of another person, not one's own existence. Hence a religious poet is a questionable figure in relation to the paradoxically religious, because from the aesthetic point of view, possibility is higher than actuality and the poetical consists precisely in the ideality of imaginative intuition, and hence one often sees hymns which, though they are touching and childlike, with a tinge of fancy bordering on the fantastic, when regarded categorically are not Christian, when regarded categorically do far more to encourage the mythical view by what poetically viewed is so lovely—the pale azure, the sound of ding-dong bells—than does any free-thinker; for the free-thinker asserts that Christianity is myth, the naïve orthodox poet abhors this and maintains the historical reality of Christianity . . . in fantastic verse. He who understands the paradox (in the sense of understanding it directly) will in his misunderstanding of it forget that what at one time he apprehended with the decisive passion of faith as the absolute paradox (not the relative, for the appropriation of that would not be faith), as that therefore which absolutely was not his own thought—he will forget that this never can become his own thought (in a direct sense) without transforming faith into an illusion, whereby also at a later moment he reaches the perception that he was deluded when he absolutely believed that it was not his own thought. On the other hand, he can very well by faith maintain his relation to the absolute paradox. But within the sphere of faith the moment can never arrive when he understands the paradox (in a direct sense); for if that occurs, then the whole sphere of faith passes away as a misunderstanding. Actuality, i.e. the fact that this or that actually occurred, is the subject of faith, and this surely is not any thought of man or of mankind, for thought at its highest is possibility, but possibility as the medium of understanding is precisely the understanding whereby the backward step is taken of ceasing to believe. He who understands the paradox will in his misunderstanding forget that Christianity is the absolute paradox (just as its novelty is the paradoxical novelty) precisely because it nullifies a possibility (the analogy of paganism, an eternal divine becoming) as an illusion and turns it into actuality, and precisely this is the paradox—not the strange and unusual in a direct (aesthetic) sense, but the apparently well known, and yet the absolutely strange, which precisely as actuality turns the apparent into a deception. He who understands the paradox will forget that by understanding it (as a possibility) he has gone back to the old notions and lost touch with Christianity. In the fantasy-medium of possibility God can perfectly well for the imagination be fused with a man, but that this should occur in reality with an individual man, this precisely is the paradox.

However, to confuse things, and to go further by going backwards, or to condemn and to roar in defense of Christianity, when after all these same people with their racket and self-importance employ the categories of misunderstanding, is easier than to keep a strict dialectical diet, and it is generally better rewarded, if one accounts it a reward (and not a suspicious *nota bene*) to acquire adherents, accounts it a reward (and not a suspicious *nota bene*) to have satisfied the requirements of the times.

Appendix To B

THE RETROACTIVE EFFECT OF THE DIALECTICAL UPON THE PATHETIC, AND THE FACTORS SIMULTANEOUSLY PRESENT IN THIS PATHOS

The religiousness which has nothing dialectical in the second instance (that is, religiousness A, which is the individual's own pathetic transformation of existence, not the paradoxical transformation of existence by faith through the relation to an historic fact) has to do with the pure man, in such a way that it can be assumed that every man as he is viewed essentially has a share in this blessedness and finally becomes blessed. The difference between a religious man and a man who does not transform his existence religiously thus becomes a humorous distinction: that whereas the religious man employs his whole life in becoming sensible of a relation to an eternal blessedness, and the other does not trouble himself about it, they then both of them, eternally viewed, get just as far along. (Note that the religious man has his satisfaction in himself, and being introspective he is not busied with senseless complaints that others acquire easily what he with difficulty and with the utmost effort aspires after.) In this consists the sympathetic humor, and the seriousness consists in the fact that the religious man does not let himself be put out by comparing himself with others. So in religiousness A there is constantly a possibility of revoking existence into the eternity behind.

Religiousness B is discriminative, selective, and polemical: only upon a definite condition do I become blessed, and as I absolutely bind myself to this condition, so do I exclude every other man who does not thus bind himself. This is the incentive of particularism in universal pathos. Every Christian possesses the pathos of religiousness A, and then this pathos of discrimination. This discrimination imparts to the Christian a certain resemblance to one who is fortunate through favor, and when it is so conceived selfishly by a Christian we have the desperate presumption of predestination. The fortunate man cannot essentially sympathize with others who are not in possession of the favor or cannot come into possession of it. Hence the fortunate man must either remain ignorant that the others exist, or he himself becomes unhappy through this consciousness. To have one's own eternal happiness based upon an historical fact makes the Christian's happiness or good fortune recognizable by suffering, so that the religious determinant of being God's elect is as paradoxically contrary as possible to being a Pamphilius of fortune, precisely because the elect, though he is not the unfortunate man, is not in the plain understanding of the word the fortunate; no, it is a thing so difficult to understand that for everybody but the elect it must be enough to drive one to despair. Hence the notion of being the elect is so disgusting when one aesthetically wishes to be, for example, in the place of an Apostle.[1] The blessedness which is contingent upon an historical situation excludes all who are not in this situation, and of them there are countless numbers who are not excluded by their own fault but by the accidental circumstances that Christianity has not yet been preached to them.

More closely defined, the sharpened pathos is:

(a). *Sin-consciousness*.* This consciousness is the expression for the paradoxical transformation of existence. Sin is the new existence-medium. Apart from this, to exist means merely that the individual

---

* With this one may compare what was said about guilt-consciousness under A §3. Cf. also Second Section, Chapter 2.

having come into the world is present and is in the process of becoming; now it means that having come into the world he has become a sinner; apart from this, "to exist" is not a more sharply defining predicate, but is merely the form of all the more sharply defining predicates: one does not become anything in particular by coming into being, but now, to come into being is to become a sinner. In the totality of guilt-consciousness, existence asserts itself as strongly as it can within immanence; but sin-consciousness is the breach with immanence; by coming into being the individual becomes another, or the instant he must come into being he becomes another, for otherwise the determinant sin is placed within immanence. From eternity the individual is not a sinner; so when the being who is planned on the scale of eternity comes into the world by birth, he becomes a sinner at birth or is born a sinner, and then it is that existence, by surrounding this being on all sides so that every communication with the eternal by way of recollection is cut off, and the predicate "sinner" which is then first applied but applied at once at the moment of coming into the world—then it is that existence acquires such overwhelming power that the act of coming into the world makes this being another. This is the consequence of the Deity's presence in time, which prevents the individual from relating himself backwards to the eternal, since now he comes forwards into being in order to become eternal by relationship to the Deity in time.

Hence the individual is unable to acquire Sin-Consciousness by himself, as he can guilt-consciousness; for in guilt-consciousness the identity of the subject with himself is preserved, and guilt-consciousness is an alteration of the subject within the subject himself; sin-consciousness, on the other hand, is an alteration of the very subject himself, which shows that outside of the individual that power must be which makes clear to him the fact that in coming into life he has become another than that he was, has become a sinner. This power is the Deity in time. (With this one may compare the *Fragments,* Chapter 2, on the Moment.)

In sin-consciousness the individual becomes conscious of his difference from the humane in general which becomes by itself conscious of what it is to exist *qua* man. For since the relation to that historical fact (the Deity in time) is the condition for sin-consciousness, sin-consciousness could not have been during all that time when the historical fact had not been. On the other hand, in so far as the believer would also in the consciousness of sin become conscious of the sin of the whole race, another isolation presents itself. The believer extends sin-consciousness to the whole race, and at the same time does not know the whole race as saved, inasmuch as the salvation of the particular individual will depend upon his being brought into relation with the historical fact, which, precisely because it is historical, cannot be everywhere at once but requires time to become known to men, during which time whole generations die one after the other. In religiousness A there is fellow-feeling for all men, because this religiousness is related to the eternal which every man is assumed essentially to be able to be, and because the eternal is in every place, so that no time is involved in awaiting or in summoning that which being historical cannot be everywhere at once, and concerning which countless races can remain in ignorance that it ever was.

To have one's existence in this determinant is sharpened pathos, both because it cannot be thought, and because it is isolating. Sin, that is to say, is not a dogma or a doctrine for thinkers (in that case the whole thing comes to nothing), it is an existence-determinant, and precisely one which cannot be thought.

(b). *The possibility of offense,* or the autopathic collision. In religiousness A the offense is not possible, for even the most decisive definition is within immanence. But the paradox, which requires faith against the understanding, at once brings to evidence the offense, whether this be more closely defined as the offense which suffers, or as the offense which mocks at the paradox as foolishness. As soon as the man who has had the passion of faith loses it, he is *eo ipso* offended.

But this again is the sharpened pathos: to have constantly a possibility which, if it comes to pass, is a fall just so much the deeper as faith is higher than all the religiousness of immanence.

In our age Christianity has become so naturalized and so accommodated to the world that nobody dreams of the offense. Well, that is quite natural, for no one takes offense at an insignificance, and that is what Christianity is about to become. Otherwise, to be sure, it is the only power which is able truly to arouse offense, and the strait entrance to the narrow way is the offense, and the dreadful opposition to the beginning of faith is the offense, and when things proceed as they should in the matter of becoming a Christian the offense must in every generation take its percentage as it did in the first generation. Christianity is the only power which is able truly to arouse offense; for hysterical and sentimental fits of offense at this or that can be simply dismissed and explained as lack of ethical seriousness which is coquettishly busy about complaining of the whole world instead of itself. For the believer, the offense is at the beginning, and the possibility of it is the perpetual fear and trembling in his existence.

(c). *The smart of sympathy,* because the believer cannot, like religiousness A, have a latent sympathy or fellow-feeling with every man *qua* man, but only with Christians. He who with the whole passion of his soul bases his blessedness upon terms which involve a relation to something historical, naturally cannot at the same time regard these terms as tomfoolery. Such a thing is only possible for a dogmatic philosopher, who finds it easy to do the latter since he lacks pathos for the former. For the believer it holds good that apart from these terms there is no blessedness, and to him it applies or may apply that he must hate father and mother. For is not this hating them as it were when he possesses his blessedness upon terms which they do not accept? And is not this a dreadful sharpening of pathos with regard to an eternal happiness? And suppose that this father or this mother or this loved one had died without having the blessedness based upon these terms! Or if they were living, but he could not win them over! He can unto the very last desire to do everything for them with the greatest enthusiasm (Christianity does not exclude such behavior when it bids us hate), and yet when these terms separate them, they separate them forever—is not this as though he hated them?[2]

Such experiences have been known in the world. Nowadays they are not known; we all of us indeed are Christians. But with this what have we all become, I wonder; and what has Christianity become by the fact that we all of us as a matter of course are Christians of a sort?

CHAPTER V

CONCLUSION

THIS work has made it difficult to become a Christian, so difficult that among people of culture in Christendom the number of Christians will perhaps not be very great;[1] I say "perhaps" for I can have no certain knowledge of such things. Whether this attitude is Christian I do not decide. But to go further than Christianity and to fumble with determinants with which the pagans were familiar, to go further and then, so far as concerns existence-efficiency, not to be able by far to compete with the pagans—this, to say the least, is not Christian. The difficulty is not raised here (in the experiment, I mean, for the book has no *telos*) in order to make it difficult for laymen to become Christians. First of all, everybody can become a Christian; and, in the second place, it is assumed that everyone who says he is a Christian and has done the highest things, is actually a Christian and has done the highest things—if in putting himself forward with self-importance he does not give one occasion (in a purely psychological interest and to learn something for oneself) to look into the matter more closely. Woe unto him who would be a judge of hearts. But when a whole generation, though in various ways, seems to want to unite *en masse* in going further; when a whole generation, though in various senses, aspires to objectivity as the highest thing (by which one ceases to be a Christian . . . if one was such), this may well prompt an individual to take notice of the difficulties. On the other hand, what it must not prompt him to, is the new confusion: by the statement of the difficulties to want to be important in the sight of anybody, not to say of the whole human race, for with that he also begins to become objective.

In times when one resolved to become a Christian in mature years, perhaps having been knocked about in life and tempted, perhaps with the pain of having to break the tenderest relationship with parents and kindred, perhaps with the fiancée, then one felt no urge to go further, because one comprehended what effort was required every day to maintain oneself in this passion, comprehended in what terrors one passed one's life. In our days, on the contrary, since it has come to look as though one already were a Christian as a child a week old, whereby again they have managed to transform Christ into "a friend of tiny tots" *à la* Uncle Franz, or Godman,[2] or a charity school-teacher— it seems that after all as a man one ought to do something, and so one must go further. The pity is that one does not go further by really becoming a Christian, but by speculative philosophy and universal history goes back to lower and in part fantastic views of existence. Since we are accustomed to be Christians as a matter of course and to be called Christians, the incongruity emerges that views of life which are much lower than Christianity are propagated within Christianity and have proved more pleasing to men (i.e. to Christians), as naturally is the case, because Christianity is the more difficult, and these views have been acclaimed as higher discoveries which surpass Christianity pure and simple.

Rather than hold on to the name of Christian lukewarmly, it doubtless would be better, for it would be a sign of life, if some people in our time were to admit bluntly to themselves that they could wish that Christianity never had come into the world or that they themselves had never become Christians. But let the admission be made without scorn and mockery and wrath. What is the use of that? One can well have reverence for that which one cannot compel oneself to accept. Christ himself says that He was attracted to the young man who nevertheless could not make up his mind to give all his possessions to the poor. The young man did not become a Christian, and yet Christ "loved" him. So then, better frank sincerity than lukewarmness. For Christianity is a fine belief to die in, the only true comfort, and the moment of death is the appropriate situation for Christianity. Perhaps it is for this reason that even the lukewarm will not give it up; for just as one deposits something in a burial society so as to be able when one's time comes to be able to defray the costs, so does one keep Christianity treasured up until the last: one is a Christian, but becomes such only at the moment of death.

Peradventure there was one who, if he understood himself in sincerity, might admit that he could wish rather he had never been brought up in Christianity than to turn away from it with indifference. Better frank sincerity than lukewarmness. But let the admission be made without anger, without defiance, with a quiet reverence for the power which, as he thinks, has upset his life perhaps, for the power which indeed might have bettered him but has not.[3] If it has happened that a father, even the most loving and tender of fathers, precisely at the moment when he wished to do the best for his child has done the worst, has done that very worst thing which perhaps upset the child's whole life—shall the son for this cause suppress filial piety in the oblivion of indifference, or transform it to anger if he remembers the relationship? Yea, let paltry souls who only love God and men when everything is according to their liking, let them hate and defy ill-temperedly—a faithful son loves unchangeably; and it is always a sign of a mediocre man that when he is convinced that he who made him unhappy did it with the intention of doing the best for him, separates from him in wrath and bitterness. Thus a strict upbringing in Christianity may perhaps have made life too hard for a man without helping him in turn; in his heart he may perhaps feel a desire like that of the people who besought Christ to depart from their country because He made them afraid. But the son whom the father made unfortunate, if he is high-minded, will continue to love the father, and when he suffers from the consequences he sometimes maybe will sigh despondently, "Would this had never happened to me," but he will not abandon himself to despair, he will labor against the suffering by laboring through it. And as he labors the sorrow will be assuaged; he soon will be more sorry for the father than for himself, he will forget his own pain in the profound sympathetic sorrow of the reflection how hard it must be for the father if he understood it—so he will strive more and more mightily, his salvation will be important to him for his own sake, and now almost more precious for the father's sake—thus he will labor, and it will succeed surely. And if it succeeds, he will be, as it were, out of his wits with the joy of enthusiasm; for after all what father has done so much for his son, what son can be so much indebted to his father! And so it is with Christianity. Even if it has made him unhappy, he does not for this cause give it up; for it never occurs to him that Christianity might have come into the world to do men harm; it constantly remains venerable to him. He does not let it go, and even if he sighs despondently, "Would I had never been brought up in this doctrine," he does not let it go. And despondency becomes sadness, as though almost it must be hard on Christianity that such a thing could occur; but he does not let it go, in the end Christianity must make it good to him. In the end—yea, that is not little by little, it is much less, and yet infinitely much more. But only slatternly men let go of that which once has made an absolute impression upon them, and only paltry souls practise despicable usury with their own suffering by seeking to get out of it the miserable profit of being able to unsettle others, and by becoming self-important with the basest presumption which wants to prohibit others from finding comfort because one has not found it himself. If there be any man in our time whom Christianity has unsettled (as I have no doubt is the case, and as can be proved factually), one thing can be required of him, that he keep silent. For his talk, ethically regarded, is a thievish assault, and in its consequences still worse than that, for it ends with neither of them having anything, neither the robber nor the victim.

Just as Christianity did not come into the world during the childhood of mankind but in the fullness of time, so, too, in its decisive form it is not equally appropriate to every age in a man's life. There are periods in a man's life which require something which Christianity wants, as it were, to leave out altogether, something which at a certain age seems to be the absolute, although the same man at a later period of life sees the vanity of it. To cram Christianity into a child is something that cannot be done, for it is a general rule that everyone comprehends only what he has use for, and the child has no decisive use for Christianity. As indicated by the coming of Christianity into the world after a foregoing preparation, the invariable law is this: *No one starts by being a Christian, every one becomes such in the fullness of time . . . if he does become such.* A strict Christian upbringing in the most decisive definitions of Christianity is a very risky undertaking; for Christianity makes men whose strength is in their weakness, but if one cows a child into Christianity in its most decisive form, it generally makes an exceedingly unhappy youth. The rare exceptions are a stroke of luck.

The Christianity which is taught to a child, or rather which the child pieces together for itself when no violence is used to force the little exister into the most decisive Christian determinants, is not properly Christianity but idyllic mythology. It is childishness in the second power, and sometimes the relationship is so inverted that it is rather the parents who learn from the child than the child from the parents, that the child's lovable misunderstanding of Christianity transfigures mother- and father-love into a piety which nevertheless is not properly Christianity. There are not lacking instances of people who previously were not religiously moved and first became so through the child. But this piety is not properly the religiousness which should belong to older people, and it is no more reasonable that the mother should be nourished by the milk which nature provides for the babe than that the religiousness of the parents should find decisive expression in this piety. Father- and mother-love clings so tightly to the child, embraces it so tenderly, that the piety of the relationship discovers by itself that which in fact is taught us: that there must be a God who receives little children. But if this mood is the whole religiousness of the parents, they lack the real religiousness and are refreshed only by a sad sympathy for what it is to be a child. Gracious and lovable is this piety of the parents and the willingness of the child to learn and the ease with which it understands this blessedness; but Christianity it properly is not, it is Christianity in the medium of fantasy, it is a Christianity from which the terror has been taken away. They bring the *innocent* child to God or Christ. Is this Christianity, the point of which precisely is that it is a sinner who has recourse to the paradox? It is pretty and touching and becoming that an older person at the sight of a child feels his guilt and sadly conceives of the child's innocence; but this mood is not decisively Christian. For the sentimental conception of the child's innocence forgets that Christianity recognizes no such thing in the fallen race, and that the qualitative dialectic defines sin-consciousness as an advance upon innocence. The strict Christian conception of the child as a sinner does not put the child in a position of advantage, for sin-consciousness the child does not possess, and thus is a sinner without sin-consciousness.

But they have in fact a Biblical passage they can appeal to, and that passage is sometimes understood in such a way (perhaps without consciousness of it) that the interpretation contains the deepest satire upon Christianity and represents Christianity as the most comfortless view of life, since it makes it indescribably easy for a child to enter into the kingdom of heaven, but impossible for an adult, and the consequence is that it would be the best and the most proper wish that the child should die, the sooner the better.

This is in the nineteenth chapter of Matthew, where Christ says, "Suffer the little children to come unto me and forbid them not, for of such is the kingdom of heaven." The whole chapter deals with the difficulty of entering the kingdom of heaven, and the expressions are as strong as possible. Verse 12, "There are eunuchs who have castrated themselves for the kingdom of heaven's sake." Verse 24, "It is easier for a camel to go through a needle's eye than for a rich man to enter into the kingdom of God." The disciples were so dismayed that they said, "Who then can be saved?" And after Christ had replied to this, there is in turn (verse 29) talk of those who have forsaken houses, or brethren, or sisters, or father, or mother, or children, or lands, for the sake of Christ's name—altogether a dreadful expression of the collisions wherein a Christian may be tempted. So then, entrance into the kingdom of heaven is made as difficult as possible, so difficult that even teleological suspensions of the ethical[4] are mentioned. In the same chapter there is then related quite briefly the little incident that small children were brought to Christ and that He uttered the words quoted above. However, be it observed that there is a little intermediate clause, an intermediate occurrence, which comes in between: the fact that the disciples rebuked the children, or rather those who carried them (cf. Mark 10:13). Now if Christ's saying about being a child is to be understood simply and directly, the confusion arises that whereas for adults it is made as difficult as possible to enter into the kingdom of heaven, the only difficulty for the child is that the mother carries it to Christ and that the child is carried thither—and so we can at once reach the climax of despair: Better to die as an infant. But the meaning is not difficult in Matthew. Christ utters the words to the disciples who rebuked the children—and the disciples indeed were not children. In Matthew 18:22 it is related that "Jesus called a little child and set him in the midst of them and said, 'Except ye turn and become as little children, ye shall in no wise enter into the kingdom of heaven.' " He does not enter into conversation with the child, but He uses the child against the disciples. If on the other hand this means a direct affirmation about how lovely it is to be a little child, a regular little angel (and not even for angels does Christianity seem to have partiality, since it stands in relation to sinners), then it would be cruel to utter these words in the presence of the Apostles, who in that case were in fact in the sorry plight of being full-grown men; and then with that explanation the whole of Christianity is explained away. Why then did Christ, I wonder, want to have disciples who were full-grown before they became disciples? Why did He not say: Go out and baptize little children? If it is distressing to behold an arrogant speculation which would understand everything, it is always equally distressing that anyone pretending to speak in the light of orthodoxy would turn Christianity into moonlight and charity-school sentimentality. But to say to men, precisely at the moment when perhaps they were too forward with Christ and would require finite reward for the close relationship, or at least lay emphasis upon the close relationship—to say to them that "of *such*"* (namely, little children) is the kingdom of heaven, and thus to

---

*τοιοῦτοι. Precisely this word indicates sufficiently that Christ is not talking about the children or to the children directly, but that He is talking to the disciples. A child simply understood is not τοιοῦτος, for τοιοῦτος contains a comparison which implies a distinction. So here nothing

put the disciples a little way off from Him by means of a paradox; yes, that is a dark saying; for, humanly speaking, it is possible to castrate oneself and to forsake father and children and wife, but to become a little child when one has become a man—that is a way of securing oneself against all forwardness by putting the distance of the paradox between. The Apostles rebuked the little children, but Christ does not rebuke in turn, He does not even reprove the Apostles; He turns to the little children, but He speaks to the Apostles, and like that look He gave to Peter, so is this turning towards the children understood as an address to the Apostles, as a judgment upon them, and in the nineteenth chapter of Matthew, which deals with the difficulty of entering into the kingdom of heaven, this is the strongest expression of it. The paradox consists in making the child a paradigm. This is a paradox because, *in the first place*, a child (humanly speaking), cannot be a paradigm, since it is "immediate" and explains nothing (for the same reason that a genius cannot be a paradigm—this is the sad feature in the distinction of genius), explains nothing even in relation to other children, for every child is simply itself immediately; and *in the second place,* because it is made a paradigm for full-grown men who in the humility of sin-consciousness are to resemble the humility of innocence.

Enough of this, however. Such a childish conception of Christianity only makes it ridiculous. If this thing of being a child is understood simply and directly, then it is nonsense to preach Christianity to adults. And yet in this way Christianity is defended by orthodox champions. But, of course, if anybody wants something to laugh at, there is hardly to be found more copious material than in the way Christianity in these times is defended and attacked. An orthodox preacher thunders against the egoism of freethinkers "who will not enter into the kingdom of God as little children but want to be something." Here the category is correct; but now comes the moment for giving emphasis to his discourse and for appealing to that Biblical passage, simply understood, about being a little child (simply understood). Can one take it amiss of the freethinker for taking his reverence to be a bit cracked (quite simply understood)? The talk of difficulty with which the orthodox preacher began has become galimatias; for it is not difficult in the least for the

is said about children directly, nothing about the fact that a little child (simply understood) has free entrance; but it is said that only he who is as a child can enter into the kingdom of heaven. But as for the adult it is the most impossible thing of all to become a little child (simply understood), so too for a little child (simply understood) it is the most impossible thing of all to become *as* a child, precisely for the reason that he *is* a child.

little child, and for an adult it is impossible. To be something and to want to be something is in a certain sense the condition (the negative condition) for entering into the kingdom of heaven as a little child—if this is supposed to be difficult—and lacking this condition, it is no wonder that a man remains outside when he is forty years old. So the freethinker will perhaps mock at Christianity, and yet there is no one who makes it so ridiculous as does the orthodox defender.

Psychologically viewed, this misunderstanding is due to the comfortable security attained by identifying Christianity simply with being a man, is due to the light-minded and heavy-hearted dread of making decisions, which puts off and puts off and so gets the thing of becoming a Christian shoved so far back that it is decided before one knows anything about it. One accentuates the sacrament of baptism with such exorbitant orthodoxy that one actually becomes heterodox on the dogma of regeneration, forgetting the objection raised by Nicodemus and the reply to it, because with hyper-orthodoxy one decrees that a little child has actually become a Christian by being baptized.

Childish Christianity, which is lovable on the part of a little child, is in the case of an adult the childish orthodoxy which has been rendered blissful in the medium of fantasy and has contrived to introduce the name of Christ into it. Such an orthodoxy brings everything to confusion. When it remarks that the determinant faith is beginning to fall in price, that all want to go further and regard faith as something for stupid people, then it has to screw up the price. What happens? Faith becomes something so extraordinary and rare, "not the affair of every man," in short, faith becomes a differential endowment of genius. If such be the case, by this one definition the whole of Christianity is revoked—by an orthodox teacher. It is quite right of the orthodox teacher to want to screw the price up, but differential valuations can bring everything to confusion, for a differential endowment of genius is not difficult for the genius and is impossible for others. Faith is rightly made the most difficult thing of all, but with a qualitative dialectic, i.e. equally difficult for all; and it is the ethical determinant in faith which is of assistance here, for this quite simply prohibits the one believer from being curious and comparative, it forbids all comparison between man and man, and so becomes the thing which is equally difficult for all.

Such a childish orthodoxy has also managed to direct decisive attention to the fact that Christ at His birth was swaddled in rags and laid in a manger, in short, to the humiliation of coming in the lowly form of a servant, and it believes that this is the paradox, in contrast to coming in glory. Confusion. The paradox consists principally in the fact that God, the Eternal, came into existence in time as a particular man. Whether this particular man is a servant or an emperor is neither here nor there, it is no more adequate for God to be king than to be beggar; it is not a greater humiliation for God to become a beggar than to become an emperor. One recognizes the childishness at once; for precisely because the child has no developed conception of God or no real conception (but only imaginative inwardness), he cannot become aware of the absolute paradox, but has a touching understanding of the humorous touch, that the mightiest of all, the Almighty (though without decisive definition in thought and only in a romantic sense different from that which is on a line with it, this thing of being king or emperor), at his birth was laid in a manger and swaddled in rags. On the other hand, if the childish orthodoxy insists upon this humiliation as the paradox, it shows *eo ipso* that it is not aware of the paradox. Of what avail then all its effort to defend? If it is postulated and granted that it is easy to understand that God becomes a particular man, so that the difficulty first emerges in the next fact, that He becomes a lowly and despised man— then in *summa summarum* Christianity is humor. Humor distracts attention from the first, the determinant God, and then accentuates the fact that the greatest, the mightiest one, who is greater than all kings and emperors, became the lowliest. But the definition, "the greatest, the mightiest one, who is greater than all kings and emperors," is a very indefinite definition, it is fantasy, and not a qualitative definition like that of being God. On the whole it is observable that orthodoxy, when it comes to the pinch, employs fantasy—and thus produces the greatest effect. But, as I have said, "the greatest, the mightiest one, who is greater than all kings and emperors," is not God for all that. If one would talk about God, let him say, God. That is the quality. If the priest would say eternity, let him say, eternity—yet sometimes he says, when he would really say something, "unto all the eternities of eternity, world without end." But if Christianity is humor, everything is brought to confusion, and so it ends with my becoming the best Christian, for regarded as a humorist I am not so bad, but bad enough to regard this in as humorous a light as possible, in comparison with being a Christian, which I am not.

A childish orthodoxy accentuates Christ's suffering erroneously. By the most romantic definitions, which are anything but apt to enjoin silence upon the human understanding (for it is easy enough for it to perceive that this is galimatias), it accentuates the frightfulness of the suffering, Christ's delicate body which suffers so prodigiously; or it accentuates, qualitatively and comparatively, the fact that He who was holy, the purest and most innocent of all, had to suffer. The paradox is that Christ came into the world *in order to suffer*. Take this away, and then an army of analogies takes by storm the impregnable fortress of the paradox. That in the world the innocent have to suffer (heroes of intellectuality and art, the martyrs of the truth, the quiet martyrs of womanhood, etc.) is not absolutely paradoxical but humorous. But the purpose of the martyrs when they came into the world was not to suffer; their purpose was this or that, and to accomplish it they had to suffer, to bear suffering, to go to their death. But suffering is not their *telos*. Religiousness comprehends suffering, defines it teleologically for the sufferer, but suffering is not *telos*. If therefore the suffering of the martyrs in general is no analogy to Christ's suffering, no more is the suffering of the believer; and the absolute paradox is recognizable by the fact that every analogy is a fallacy. Thus it might rather seem to be an analogy if, in accordance with a fantastic view (the transmigration of souls), one were to assume that a man who had once been in the world came again *in order to suffer*. But as the analogy belongs to a fantastic view of life, it is *eo ipso* a fallacy, and even apart from this consideration, the "in order" of the suffering is precisely the opposite: it is a guilty man who again comes to the world *in order* to suffer his punishment. There is a fatality as it were which hangs over the childish orthodoxy. It is often well meaning, but as it is not well oriented, it often is led into exaggeration.

So when one hears an orthodox preacher perpetually talking about childish faith, childish wisdom, a womanly heart, etc., possibly it may be only a humorous character who has contrived to confuse Christianity with childishness (simply understood), and now is longing after childhood, with a longing which is characterized more particularly as a longing for the loving tenderness of a pious mother. (I, however, as a humorist protest against any fellowship with him, since he emphasizes erroneously.) It may also be a fraudulent fellow who tries to shun the terror when he has to face the serious question of becoming truly a child instead of combining humorously the childish and the adult traits. For so much is certain, that if a little child (simply understood) is to provide the definition of what Christianity is, this will be without terror, for it will not contain that factor which was to the Jews a stumblingblock and to the Greeks foolishness.

When one talks to a child about Christianity, and the child is not violently ill-treated (in a figurative sense), the child will appropriate everything that is gentle, childish, lovable, heavenly; he will live in companionship with the little child Jesus, and with the angels, and with the Three Kings of Orient, he sees their star in the dark night, he travels the long road, now he is in the stable, one amazement after another, he is always seeing the heavens opened, with all the inwardness of fantasy he yearns for these pictures—and now . . . let us not forget the gingernuts and all the other splendid things which are the perquisites of this festival. For above all let us not be old curmudgeons who lie about childhood, who lyingly affect its extravagances, and belie the reality of childhood. Truly he must be a blackguard who does not find childhood touching and charming and blissful. One should certainly not suspect a failure to appreciate the reality of childhood on the part of a humorist, that unhappy-happy lover of recollection. But certainly he also is a blind leader who would say in any way whatsoever that this is the interpretation of Christianity which was to the Jews a stumblingblock and to the Greeks foolishness. Christ becomes the divine Child, or for an older stage, the kindly figure with gentle countenance (the mythological commensurability), not the paradox in whom the Jews could see nothing (directly understood), not John the Baptist even (cf. John 3:31, 33), nor even the disciples until they were made to take notice (John 1:36, 42), just as Isaiah had prophesied (53:2-4, especially verse 4). The childish construction of Christianity is essentially that of fantasy-intuition, and the idea of fantasy-intuition is commensurability, and commensurability is paganism, whether it is power, glory, beauty, or it is hidden within a little humoristic contradiction which, however, is not concealment but an incognito easily discerned. The form of a servant is the incognito, but the gentle countenance is the direct means of recognition. Here as everywhere there is a certain orthodoxy which, when it is a question of cutting a really fine figure upon greater festivals and important occasions, calls to its aid in *bona fide* a little paganism—and then the thing succeeds best of all. A parson perhaps on ordinary occasions holds steadily to the strict and correct definitions of orthodoxy. But what happens? One Sunday he has to make a special effort. To show how vividly Christ stands before him he has to afford a glimpse into his own soul. Well, it is perfectly true that Christ is the object of faith, but faith is very far from being fantasy-intuition, and fantasy-intuition is not precisely a higher thing than faith. Now he is off: the gentle countenance, the kindly look, grief in his eye, etc. There is nothing at all comic in the fact that a man teaches paganism instead of Christianity, but there is something comic in the fact that an orthodox preacher when he uses all the registers on an occasion of great solemnity, pulls out by mistake the stop of paganism without noticing it. In case the organist were ordinarily to play a waltz, he would be dismissed; but in case an organist who commonly played the hymn-tunes decorously should want to play a waltz on the great festivals, in order to celebrate the day thoroughly, and because he had an accompaniment of trumpets—that would indeed be comic. And yet in the orthodox preachers there is to be found a little of this sentimental and effeminate paganism, not for ordinary use, but precisely upon the high festivals when they have to open their hearts; and one finds this more particularly in the concluding part of the discourse. Direct recognition is paganism; all solemn protestations that this is indeed the Christ and that He is the true God are of no avail when after all the thing ends with direct recognition. A mythological figure is recognizable directly. If one makes this objection to an orthodox, he becomes furious and blazes out: "Yes, but Christ is indeed the true God, and therefore He is no mythological figure . . . one can see that in his mild countenance." But if one can see this in Him, then He is *eo ipso* a mythological figure. One will easily see that room is left for faith; for once direct recognition is taken away, faith is in its right place. The place is indicated precisely by the crucifixion of the understanding and of fantasy-intuition, which hinders direct recognition. But it is easier to slink away from the terror and to slink into a little paganism which is rendered unrecognizable by the strange connection, by the fact, namely, that it serves as the last and loftiest explanation in an address which began perhaps with perfectly correct orthodox determinants. In case an orthodox minister were to confide to one that he really had no faith—well, in that there is nothing ludicrous. But when an orthodox minister, carried away by blissful enthusiasm, and himself almost astonished at the lofty flight of his discourse, thoroughly opens his heart in confidence and unhappily makes a mistake in the direction so that he *ascends* from the higher to the lower—then it is more difficult to suppress a smile.

The age of childhood (directly understood) is therefore not the true age for becoming a Christian. On the contrary, the more advanced age, the age of maturity, is the time when it is to be decided whether a man will be a Christian or not. The religiousness of childhood is the universal, the abstract, and yet it is the foundation in fantasy-inwardness of all subsequent religiousness. Becoming a Christian involves a decision which belongs to a much later age. The child's receptivity is so completely without decision that it is said proverbially, "One can make a child believe anything." The elders of course bear responsibility for what they venture to make the child believe, but the fact is perfectly certain. And the fact that the child is baptized cannot therefore make it older in understanding or riper for decision. A Jewish child, a pagan child, brought up from the start by tender Christian foster-parents who treat it as lovingly as parents treat their own children, will appropriate the same Christianity as the baptized child.

If on the other hand a child is not permitted as it should be to play with the holiest things, if its existence is forced into the decisive Christian determinants, such a child will have to suffer a great deal. Such an upbringing will either precipitate the child into despondency and dread, or provoke lust and the dread of lust[5] in a measure with which even paganism was unacquainted.

It is a beautiful and lovable thing (and the opposite is indefensible) that parents, who are careful in other ways for the child, should also be careful with regard to its notions of religion. Infant baptism, as I have frequently said above, is entirely defensible as an anticipation of the possibility, as an attempt to prevent the dreadful laceration that the parents might have their blessedness attached to one thing, and the children not to the same. Only a stupid misunderstanding, both sentimental and churlish, a misunderstanding not so much of infant baptism as of the age of childhood, is reprehensible; but sectarian externality also is equally reprehensible, since the decision properly belongs to inwardness. It is a rape—be it never so well meant—to force the child's existence into the decisive Christian categories, but it is a great stupidity to say that childhood (simply and directly understood) is properly the decisive age for becoming a Christian. As people have wanted deceitfully to construct a direct transition from eudaemonism to the ethical through shrewdness, so too it is a deceitful invention to identify as nearly as possible the thing of becoming a Christian with that of becoming a human being and to make any man believe that he becomes such decisively in childhood. And in so far as this tendency and inclination to shove the thing of becoming a Christian back to childhood becomes universal, it will be precisely a proof that Christianity is on the point of dying out. For what one desires to do is to transform the thing of becoming a Christian into a beautiful recollection, whereas in fact it is the most decisive thing a man becomes. One would embellish the endearing innocence of childhood fantastically by the further definition that this innocence is equivalent to becoming a Christian, and thus one would have sadness take the place of decision. For the sadness in legitimate humor consists in the fact that honestly and without deceit it reflects in a purely human way upon what it is to be a child (directly understood), and it is eternally certain that this cannot return: childhood, when it is past, remains only a recollection. But humor (in its genuine form) does not concern itself with the decisive Christian conception of becoming a Christian, nor identify becoming a Christian with being a child (simply understood); for with that, being a Christian becomes in exactly the same sense a recollection. At this point it will be quite clear how perverse it is to make humor the highest thing within Christianity, since humor, or rather the humorist, if he be within Christianity, does not deal with the decisive Christian determinant of becoming a Christian. Humor is always a recalling (existence within the eternal by means of recollecting what is behind, manhood's recollection of childhood, etc.), it is the backward perspective; Christianity is the forward direction towards becoming a Christian, and towards becoming such by continuing to be such. Without a standstill no humor; for the humorist always has time in abundance, because he has the abundant time of eternity behind him. Christianity has no room for sadness: it is salvation or perdition. Salvation lies ahead; perdition behind—for everyone who turns back, whatever it is he sees. For Lot's wife was turned to stone when she looked back, because she saw the abomination of desolation; but, Christianly understood, to look back—even though one were to get a sight of childhood's charming, enchanting landscape—is perdition.

When one makes a single concession to speculative philosophy with respect to beginning with pure being, all is lost, and it is impossible to put a stop to the confusion, since it has to be stopped within pure being. When one makes to childish orthodoxy a single concession with respect to the specific superiority of the age of childhood for becoming a Christian, everything is brought to confusion.

But then that Biblical passage—it is after all in the Bible! In the foregoing I have already made myself sufficiently ridiculous by being obliged for my part also to engage in the pusillanimous and timorous interpretation of the Bible. I shall make no further attempt at it. If a childish orthodoxy has cast a comic light upon Christianity, so also has such Bible interpretation, which by its deferential timidity inverts the proper relationship without being aware of it, and is not so anxious to understand the Bible as to be understood by it, not so anxious to understand a Biblical text as to get a Biblical text to appeal to—just such a contradiction as when one who is engaged in affairs would ask counsel of a man (thus expressing the relationship of dependence), but asks it in such a way that he requires his counselor to answer thus and so, and ventures to use every means to get him to answer precisely thus. Deference to the authority of the counselor becomes a sly way of deriving advantage from his authority. But is that to seek counsel? It is in fact a cowardly way of shoving off all responsibility from oneself by never acting with independence—as though one had no responsibility for the way one gets a Bible text for one's support. Psychologically it is very remarkable how ingenious, how inventive, how sophistical, how persevering in learned investigations certain men may be, merely to get a Bible text to appeal to. On the other hand, they do not seem to observe that this precisely is to make a fool of God, to treat Him as a poor devil who has been foolish enough to commit something to writing and now must put up with what the lawyers will make of it. Thus it is a cunning little child will behave towards a severe father who has not known how to win the child's love. He reasons thus: If only I can get his permission, then it's all right, although I have to employ a little guile. But such a relation is not a tender and hearty one between father and son. And neither is it a hearty relationship between God and a human being when they are so remote from one another that there is place and use for all this anxiousness and sophistry and rumination of a dispirited deference. Examples of such behavior one finds most readily among talented men whose enthusiasm is not proportionate to their intellectuality. Whereas narrow and busy men fancy that they are acting and acting and acting, the mark of a certain type of intellectuals is the virtuosity they display in avoiding action. It is pathetic that Cromwell, who indeed was a practised Bible-reader, had sophistry enough to find Biblical texts for his justification, or at least to find in a *vox populi* a *vox dei* to the effect that it was by an act or dispensation of providence he became Protector of England, not by any act of his, for indeed the people had elected him. As one rarely sees a real hypocrite, so, too, a man entirely without conscience is rare, but a sophistical conscience is not rare, whether it be the agonizing self-contradiction of having to explain away a responsibility and being at the same time unconscious of what one is doing, or morbidity in a man who is perhaps well meaning, a morbidity which involves great suffering and makes the unhappy man's breathing more straitened and painful than the most troubled conscience when it is able to breathe out in sincerity.

A childish orthodoxy, a pusillanimous Bible interpretation, a foolish and unchristian defense of Christianity, a bad conscience on the part of the defenders with respect to their own relation to it, all this has in our time its share in occasioning passionate and frantic attacks upon Christianity. One should not chaffer, should not want to alter Christianity, should not overdo the thing by putting up resistance at the wrong place, but should simply take care that it remains what it was, to the Jews a stumblingblock, to the Greeks foolishness—not just any sort of a foolish thing in which Jews and Greeks find no offense but smile at it, and are only incited against it by the defense advanced for it.

But about the labor of inwardness in becoming and continuing to be a Christian very little is heard. And yet surely this is what remains to be experienced and by means of experience to be expounded after Christianity has been introduced into a land, and in the Christian lands where the ordinary Christians are not all required to go out into the world as missionaries to spread Christianity. In the first ages it was different. The Apostles became Christians at an adult age; therefore after they had passed a part of their life in other categories (consequently the Scripture has nothing to say about all the collisions which may arise from having been brought up from childhood in Christianity), they became Christians by a miracle* (here analogies with ordinary men are lacking), or at any rate so suddenly that there is no further explanation of it. There-

* In the foregoing it has frequently been said that the existence of an Apostle is paradoxically dialectical. I will now show how. The Apostle's *direct* relationship to God is paradoxically dialectical, because a direct one is lower (the intermediate determinant is the religiousness of immanence, religiousness A) than the indirect relationship of the general congregation, since the indirect relationship is one between spirit and spirit, the direct relationship is aesthetic—and yet in this instance the direct relationship is higher. So the Apostle's relationship is not plainly higher than that of the general congregation, as a chatty parson makes a gaping congregation believe—wherewith the whole thing returns to the aesthetic. Also the Apostle's *direct* relationship to other men is paradoxically dialectical for the fact that the Apostle's life is turned outward, employed in spreading Christianity throughout kingdoms and lands, for this relationship is lower than the indirect relationship of the private person to others, which is grounded in the fact that he has to do essentially with himself. The direct relation is an aesthetic relation (oriented outward), and to that extent lower—and yet as an exception it is higher for the Apostle. This is the paradoxically dialectical aspect. It is not plainly higher, for with that we get the world-historical bustle of this man and everybody. The paradox consists precisely in the fact that what counts as higher for an Apostle does not so count for others.

upon they turn their attention outward in order to convert others; but here again analogies are lacking with a poor simple man who has only the task of existing as a Christian. Hence, when one is not attentive to the labor of inwardness, the urge to go further is easily explained. One lives in Christendom; one is a Christian, at least is like all the others; since Christianity has now subsisted for so many centuries and permeated all relationships, it is so easy to become a Christian; one has not the task of the missionary—well then, naturally, the task is to go further and to speculate upon Christianity. But to speculate upon Christianity is not the labor of inwardness. Thus one disdains the daily tasks concerned with the practice of faith, the task of maintaining oneself in one's paradoxical passion, overcoming all illusions; one inverts the situation and forgets that in proportion as understanding and civilization and culture increase, it becomes more and more difficult to preserve the passion of faith. Oh, yes, if Christianity were a subtle doctrine (in the plain sense of the word), culture would help directly; but in relation to an existence-communication which paradoxically accentuates what it is to exist, the only way culture helps is . . . by making the difficulties greater. Thus the cultured classes have only a very ironical superiority over the simple with respect to becoming and continuing to be a Christian: the superiority that it is more difficult. But here again people have forgotten the qualitative dialectic; comparatively and quantitatively they have wanted to construct a plain transition from culture to Christianity. Hence the labor of inwardness will increase with the years and give the Christian who is not a missionary plenty to do, not in the way of speculating, but in the way of becoming and continuing to be a Christian. In the nineteenth century it is not easier to be a Christian than it was in the first age, on the contrary, it has become more difficult, especially for the cultured, and it will become more difficult from year to year. The predominance of intellect in the man of culture and the direction towards the objective will in his case constantly cause resistance against becoming a Christian, and this resistance is the sin of intellect: lukewarmness. If Christianity once changed the face of the world by overcoming the crude passions of immediacy and ennobling the State, it will find in culture a resistance just as great. But if the strife is to be carried on, it naturally must be carried on within the sharpest definitions of reflection. The absolute paradox will maintain itself well enough, for in relation to the absolute, more intellect gets no farther than less intellect; on the contrary they get equally far, the man of distinguished talents slowly, the simple man swiftly. Let others extol culture unreservedly—let it then be extolled, but I would rather extol it because it makes it so difficult to become a Christian. For I am a friend of difficulties, especially of such as possess the humoristic quality that the most cultured person, after having endured the greatest exertions, has got no farther than the simplest man can get.

For, after all, the simplest man can become a Christian and continue to be such; but, in the first place, because he does not possess intellect on any great scale, and, in the second place, because the simple man's circumstances in life turn his attention outward, he is exempted from the laborious effort with which the cultured man maintains his faith, striving with more and more effort in proportion as his culture increases. Since it is in fact the highest attainment to become and continue to be a Christian, the point of it cannot be to reflect upon Christianity, but only by reflection to intensify the pathos with which one continues to be a Christian.

And it was about this the whole work has turned, the first part having to do with the objective conception of what it is to become or to be a Christian, the second having to do with the subjective conception.

OBJECTIVELY, WHAT IT IS TO BECOME OR TO BE A CHRISTIAN IS DEFINED IN THE FOLLOWING WAY:

1. A Christian is one who accepts the doctrine of Christianity. But if it is the doctrine which is to decide in the last resort whether one is a Christian, then instantly attention is directed outward, in order to learn to know in the minutest detail what the doctrine of Christianity is, because this indeed is to decide, not what Christianity is, but whether I am a Christian. That same instant begins the erudite, the anxious, the timorous effort at approximation. Approximation can be protracted as long as you please, and in the end the decision whereby one becomes a Christian is relegated to oblivion.

This incongruity has been remedied by the assumption that everyone in Christendom is a Christian, we are all of us what one in a way calls Christians. With this assumption things go better with the objective theories. We are all Christians. The Bible-theory has now to investigate quite objectively what Christianity is (and yet we are in fact Christians, and the objective information is assumed to make us Christians, the objective information which we who are Christians shall now for the first time learn to know—for if we are not Christians, the road here taken will never lead us to become such). The Church theory assumes that we are Christians, but now we have to be assured in a purely objective way what Christianity is, in order that we may defend ourselves against the Turk and the Russian and the Roman yoke,[6] and gallantly fight out the battle of Christianity so that we may make our age, as it were, a bridge to the peerless future which already is glimpsed. This is sheer aesthetics. Christianity is an existence-communication, the task is to become a Christian and continue to be such, and the most dangerous of all illusions is to be so sure of being such that one has to defend the whole of Christendom against the Turk—instead of being alert to defend our own faith against the illusion about the Turk.

2. One says, No, not every acceptance of the Christian doctrine makes one a Christian; what it principally depends upon is appropriation, that one appropriates and holds fast this doctrine quite differently from anything else, that one is ready to live in it and to die in it, to venture one's life for it, etc.

This seems as if it were something. However, the category "quite differently" is a mediocre category, and the whole formula, which makes an attempt to define more subjectively what it is to be a Christian, is neither one thing nor the other, in a way it avoids the difficulty involved in the distraction and deceit of approximation, but it lacks categorical definition. The pathos of approximation which is talked of here is that of immanence; one can just as well say that an enthusiastic lover is so related to his love: he holds fast to it and appropriates it quite differently from anything else, he is ready to live in it and die in it, he will venture everything for it. To this extent there is no difference between a lover and a Christian with respect to inwardness, and one must again recur to the *what,* which is the doctrine—and with that we again come under No. 1.

The pathos of appropriation needs to be so defined that it cannot be confused with any other pathos. The more subjective interpretation is right in insisting that it is appropriation which decides the matter, but it is wrong in its definition of appropriation, which does not distinguish it from every other immediate pathos.

Neither is this distinction made when one defines appropriation as faith, but at once imparts to faith headway and direction towards reaching an understanding, so that faith becomes a provisional function whereby one holds what essentially is to be an object for understanding, a provisional function wherewith poor people and stupid men have to be content, whereas *Privatdocents* and clever heads go further. The mark of being a Christian (i.e. faith) is appropriated, but in such a way that it is not specifically different from other intellectual appropriation where a preliminary assumption serves as a provisional function looking forward to understanding. Faith is not in this case the specific mark of the relationship to Christianity, and again it will be the *what* of faith which decides whether one is a Christian or not. But therewith the thing is again brought back under No. 1.

That is to say, the appropriation by which a Christian is a Christian must be so specific that it cannot be confused with anything else.

3. One defines the thing of becoming and being a Christian, not objectively by the *what* of the doctrine, nor subjectively by appropriation, not by what has gone on in the individual, but by what the individual has undergone: that he was baptized. Though one adjoins to baptism the assumption of a confession of faith, nothing decisive will be gained, but the definition will waver between accentuating the *what* (the path of approximation) and talking indefinitely about acceptance and acceptance and appropriation, etc., without any specific determination.

If being baptized is to be the definition, attention will instantly turn outward towards the reflection, whether I have really been baptized. Then begins the approximation with respect to a historical fact.

If, on the other hand, one were to say that he did indeed receive the Spirit in baptism and by the witness it bears together with his spirit, he knows that he was baptized—then the inference is inverted, he argues from the witness of the Spirit within him to the fact that he was baptized, not from the fact of being baptized to the possession of the Spirit. But if the inference is to be drawn in this way, baptism is quite rightly not regarded as the mark of the Christian, but inwardness is, and so here in turn there is needed a specific definition of inwardness and appropriation whereby the witness of the Spirit in the individual is distinguished from all other (universally defined) activity of spirit in man.

It is noteworthy moreover that the orthodoxy which especially has made baptism the decisive mark is continually complaining that among the baptized there are so few Christians, that almost all, except for an immortal little band, are spiritless baptized pagans—which seems to indicate that baptism cannot be the decisive factor with respect to becoming a Christian, not even according to the latter view of those who in the first form insist upon it as decisive with respect to becoming a Christian.

SUBJECTIVELY, WHAT IT IS TO BECOME A CHRISTIAN IS DEFINED THUS:

The decision lies in the subject. The appropriation is the paradoxical inwardness which is specifically different from all other inwardness. The thing of being a Christian is not determined by the *what* of Christianity but by the *how* of the Christian. This *how* can only correspond with one thing, the absolute paradox. There is therefore no vague talk to the effect that being a Christian is to accept, and to accept, and to accept quite differently, to appropriate, to believe, to appropriate by faith quite differently (all of them purely rhetorical and fictitious definitions); but *to believe* is specifically different from all other appropriation and inwardness. Faith is the objective uncertainty due to the repulsion of the absurd held fast by the passion of inwardness, which in this instance is intensified to the utmost degree. This formula fits only the believer, no one else, not a lover, not an enthusiast, not a thinker, but simply and solely the believer who is related to the absolute paradox.

Faith therefore cannot be any sort of provisional function. He who from the vantage point of a higher knowledge would know his faith as a factor resolved in a higher idea has *eo ipso* ceased to believe. Faith *must* not *rest content* with unintelligibility; for precisely the relation to or the repulsion from the unintelligible, the absurd, is the expression for the passion of faith.

This definition of what it is to be a Christian prevents the erudite or anxious deliberation of approximation from enticing the individual into byways so that he becomes erudite instead of becoming a Christian, and in most cases a smatterer instead of becoming a Christian; for the decision lies in the subject. But inwardness has again found its specific mark whereby it is differentiated from all other inwardness and is not disposed of by the chatty category "quite differently" which fits the case of every passion at the moment of passion.

The psychologist generally regards it as a sure sign that a man is beginning to give up a passion when he wishes to treat the object of it objectively. Passion and reflection are generally exclusive of one another. Becoming objective in this way is always retrogression, for passion is man's perdition, but it is his exaltation as well. In case dialectic and reflection are not used to intensify passion, it is a retrogression to become objective; and even he who is lost through passion has not lost so much as he who lost passion, for the former had the possibility.

Thus it is that people in our age have wanted to become objective with relation to Christianity; the passion by which every man is a Christian has become too small a thing for them, and by becoming objective we all of us have the prospect of becoming . . . a *Privatdocent*.

But this situation in turn has made the strife in Christendom so comic, because in so many ways the strife consists merely in exchanging weapons, and because the strife about Christianity is waged in Christendom by Christians or between Christians who, all of them by being objective and going further, are about to give up being Christians. At the time when the Danish Government transferred the English three per cent loan from Wilson to Rothschild[7] there was an outcry raised in the papers, there was held a general assembly of people who did not possess the bonds but had borrowed one in order to take part in the meeting as bondholders. It was resolved that a protest should be made against the action of the government by refusing to accept the new bonds. And the meeting was made up of people who owned no bonds and therefore would hardly incur the embarrassment of being compelled by the government to accept the new bonds. The thing of being a Christian is on the point of losing the interest of passion, yet the strife is waged *pro* and *contra,* one argues from himself as a postulate: "If this is not Christianity, then I am no Christian, which nevertheless I surely am"; and the situation has been so inverted that one is interested in Christianity in order to know what Christianity is, not interested in knowing what Christianity is in order to be a Christian. The name of Christ is used as those people used the borrowed bonds—in order to take part in the general assembly where the fate of the Christians is decided by Christians who for their own sake do not care a fig about being Christians. For whose sake then do they do all this?

Precisely because people in our age and in the Christendom of our time do not appear to be sufficiently aware of the dialectic of inward appropriation, or of the fact that the "how" of the individual is an expression just as precise and more decisive for what he has, than is the "what" to which he appeals—precisely for this reason there crop up the strangest and (if one is in the humor and has time for it) the most laughable confusions, more comic than even the confusions of paganism, because in them there was not so much at stake, and because the contradictions were not so strident.

But tit for tat, if friendship is to be maintained and if one is to continue to be an optimist. He who, experimenting in the domain of passion, excludes himself from all the bright and smiling prospects of becoming *Privatdocent* and from what that brings in, ought at least to have a little humoristic compensation because he takes so much to heart what others, aiming at something higher, regard as a bagatelle—the little humoristic compensation that his passion sharpens his sense for the comical. He who, though he is a friend of humanity, exposes himself to be abhorred as an egoist, seeing he does not concern himself with Christianity for the sake of other people, ought on the score that he is a friend of laughter to have a little subsidy from the State. It really does not do at all to have the reproach of being an egoist and have no advantage from it—in this way indeed one is not an egoist.

An orthodox champion fights in defense of Christianity with the most frightful passion, he protests with the sweat of his brow and with the most concerned demeanor that he accepts Christianity pure and simple, he will live and die in it—and he forgets that such acceptance is an all too general expression for the relation to Christianity. He does everything in Jesus' name and uses Christ's name on every occasion as a sure sign that he is a Christian and is called to fight in defense of Christendom in our age—and he has no inkling of the little ironical secret that a man merely by describing the "how" of his inwardness can show indirectly that he is a Christian without mentioning God's name.* A man becomes converted New Year's Eve precisely at six o'clock. With that he is fully prepared. Fantastically decked out with the fact of conversion, he now must run out and proclaim Christianity . . . in a Christian land. Well, of course, even though we are all baptized, every man may well need to become a Christian in another sense. But here is the distinction: there is no lack of information in a Christian land, something else is lacking, and this is a something which the one man cannot directly communicate to the other. And in such fantastic categories would a converted man work for Christianity; and yet he proves (just in proportion as he is the more busy in spreading and spreading) that he himself is not a Christian. For to be a Christian is something so deeply

---

* In relation to love (by which I would illustrate again the same thing) it does not hold good in the same sense that a man merely by defining his "how" indicates what or whom it is he loves. All lovers have the "how" of love in common, the particular person must supply the name of his beloved. But with respect to believing (*sensu strictissimo*) it holds good that this "how" is appropriate only to one as its object. If anybody would say, "Yes, but then one can also learn the 'how' of faith by rote and patter"; to this one must reply that it cannot be done, for he who declares it directly contradicts himself, because the content of the assertion must constantly be reduplicated in the form of expression, and the isolation contained in the definition must reduplicate itself in the form.

reflected that it does not admit of the aesthetical dialectic which allows one man to be for others something he is not for himself. On the other hand, a scoffer attacks Christianity[8] and at the same time expounds it so reliably that it is a pleasure to read him, and one who is in perplexity about finding it distinctly set forth may almost have recourse to him.

All ironical observations depend upon paying attention to the "how," whereas the gentleman with whom the ironist has the honor to converse is attentive only to the "what." A man protests loudly and solemnly, "This is my opinion." However, he does not confine himself to delivering this formula verbatim, he explains himself further, he ventures to vary the expressions. Yes, for it is not so easy to vary as one thinks it is. More than one student would have got *laudabilis* for style if he had not varied his expressions, and a great multitude of men possess the talent which Socrates so much admired in Polos: they never say the same thing —about the same. The ironist then is on the watch, he of course is not looking out for what is printed in large letters or for that which by the speaker's diction betrays itself as a formula (our gentleman's "what"), but he is looking out for a little subordinate clause which escapes the gentleman's haughty attention, a little beckoning predicate, etc., and now he beholds with astonishment (glad of the variation—*in variatione voluptas*) that the gentleman *has not* that opinion—not that he is a hypocrite, God forbid! that is too serious a matter for an ironist—but that the good man has concentrated his force in bawling it out instead of possessing it within him. To that extent the gentleman may be right in asserting that he has that opinion which with all his vital force he persuades himself he has, he may do everything for it in the quality of talebearer, he may risk his life for it, in very much troubled times he may carry the thing so far as to lose his life for this opinion*—with that, how the deuce can I doubt that the man had this opinion; and yet there may have been living contemporaneously with him an ironist who even in the hour when the unfortunate gentleman is executed cannot resist laughing, because he knows by the circumstantial evidence he has gathered that the man had never been clear about the thing himself. Laughable it is, nor is it disheartening that such a thing can occur; for he who with quiet introspection is honest before God and concerned for himself, the Deity saves from being in error, though he be never so simple, him

* In turbulent times when the government must defend its existence by the penalty of death, it would not be unthinkable that a man might be executed for an opinion which indeed in a juridical and civil sense he had, but hardly in an intellectual sense.

the Deity leads by the suffering of inwardness to the truth. But meddle-
someness and noise is the sign of error, the sign of an abnormal condition, like wind in the stomach, and this thing of stumbling by chance
upon getting executed in a tumultuous turn of affairs is not the sort of
suffering which essentially characterizes inwardness.

It is said to have chanced in England that a man was attacked on the
highway by a robber who had made himself unrecognizable by wearing
a big wig. He falls upon the traveller, seizes him by the throat and
shouts, "Your purse!" He gets the purse and keeps it, but the wig he
throws away. A poor man comes along the same road, puts it on and
arrives at the next town where the traveller had already denounced the
crime, he is arrested, is recognized by the traveller, who takes his oath
that he is the man. By chance, the robber is present in the court-room,
sees the misunderstanding, turns to the judge and says, "It seems to me
that the traveller has regard rather to the wig than to the man," and he
asks permission to make a trial. He puts on the wig, seizes the traveller
by the throat, crying, "Your purse!"—and the traveller recognizes the
robber and offers to swear to it—the only trouble is that already he has
taken an oath. So it is, in one way or another, with every man who has
a "what" and is not attentive to the "how": he swears, he takes his oath,
he runs errands, he ventures life and blood, he is executed—all on account of the wig.

If my memory is not very bad, I have already recounted this story once
in this work; yet I desire to end the whole book with it. I believe that
no one can with truth accuse me of having varied it so that it has not
remained the same.

APPENDIX

THE undersigned, Johannes Climacus, who has written this book, does not give himself out to be a Christian; he is completely taken up with the thought how difficult it must be to be a Christian; but still less is he one who, having been a Christian, has ceased to be such by going further. He is a humorist; content with his situation at this moment, hoping that something higher may be granted him, he feels himself singularly fortunate, if the worse must come to worst, in being born precisely in the speculative, theocentric century. Yea, our age is the age of speculative philosophers and great men with peerless discoveries; and yet I believe that none of these gentlemen is as well off as, in all quietness, is a humorist in private practice, whether apart by himself he smites upon his breast or laughs right heartily. He very well therefore can be an author, if only he takes care to do it for his own diversion, not to get into the crush, not to perish in self-importance, not to be like a spectator at a fire who is set to work at the pump, or is merely embarrassed by the thought that he may be getting in the way of the distinguished men who are and shall be and must be and will be important.

In the aloofness of the experiment the whole work has to do with me myself, solely and simply with me. "I, Johannes Climacus, now thirty years of age, born in Copenhagen, a plain man like the common run of them, have heard tell of a highest good in prospect, which is called an eternal blessedness, and that Christianity will bestow this upon me on condition of adhering to it—now I ask how I am to become a Christian" (cf. the Introduction). I ask only for my own sake, yes, certainly that I do, or rather I have asked this question, for that indeed is the content of the whole work. Let no one put himself out to say that the book is entirely superfluous and quite irrelevant to the times—unless in the end he has to say something, for in that case he pronounces the wished-for judgment, which indeed I have already passed upon the author. He comprehends very well what an ignominious task it is to write such a book, if anyone pays attention to it. As soon as someone merely . . . but what am I saying? Whither wouldst thou entice me, O vain heart? No, no, it is not well to be led into temptation. Otherwise I would say: as soon merely as someone could inform me where and to whom one is to address a suit for permission as a single individual to dare to write or to establish myself as an author in the name of mankind, of the century, of our age, of the public, of the many, of the majority, or what may be regarded as a still rarer favor, to dare as a single man to write against the public in the name of "the many," against the majority in the name of another majority on the same issue, even when acknowledging oneself to be in the minority to dare to write in the name of the many; and also to have at the same time as a single man the polemical elasticity of being in the minority and favor in the eyes of the world by being in the majority; in case anyone could inform me what expenses are connected with the favorable acceptance of such a suit (for even if the costs are not paid in cash, they might for all that be exorbitant)—then, on the assumption that the costs do not exceed my means, I might not be able to resist the temptation of writing an exceedingly important book which speaks in the name of millions and millions and millions. Till then no one (in consistency with his standpoint—and from my standpoint the reproach has a different sense) can bring against my book the reproach of being superfluous, if he cannot elucidate the inquiry it raises.

So then the book is superfluous; let no one therefore take the pains to appeal to it as an authority; for he who thus appeals to it has *eo ipso* misunderstood it. To be an authority is far too burdensome an existence for a humorist who regards it precisely as one of the conveniences of life that there are men of a sort who can and will be authorities, from whom one has the profit that one can without ado accept their opinions —if one is not foolish enough to pull these great men down, for in that there is no profit. Above all, may heaven preserve the book and me from every appreciative violence which might be done it—that a bellowing partisan might quote it appreciatively and enroll me in the census. If it escapes his notice that no party can be well served by an experimental humorist, he himself can all the better perceive his ineptness for the employment which in every way he tries to escape. I have no qualification for being a partisan, for I have no opinion except the one, that it must be the most difficult of all things to become a Christian, which opinion is no opinion and possesses none of the qualities which usually characterize an "opinion"; for it does not flatter me, since I do not give myself out to be a Christian; it does not affront the Christian, since he cannot object if I regard as the most difficult thing that which he did and is doing; it does not affront the adversary of Christianity, since his triumph becomes all the greater, seeing that he goes further . . . than that which is the most difficult thing of all. I am consistent in desiring no factual proof that I really have an opinion—no adherent, no hurrah, no public execution, etc.—for I have no opinion and wish to have none, being content and delighted with things as they are. As in Catholic books, especially those of an earlier age, one finds at the back of the volume a note which informs the reader that everything is to be understood conformably with the doctrine of the Holy Catholic Mother Church—so what I write contains also a piece of information to the effect that everything is so to be understood that it is understood to be revoked, and the book has not only a Conclusion but a Revocation. More than that no one can require, either before or after.

To write and edit a book, when one has not a publisher,[1] who might be put to embarrassment by the fact that it doesn't sell, is indeed an innocent pastime and diversion, a lawful private enterprise in a well-ordered state which tolerates luxury and where everyone is permitted to spend his time and his money as he will, whether it be in building houses, buying horses, going to the theatre, or writing superfluous books and having them printed. But if this view may be held, it is still more reasonable to reckon that it may be regarded in turn as one of the innocent and lawful joys of a quiet life which neither disturbs the Sunday ordinance nor any other precept of duty and morality, to imagine a reader, whom from time to time one might address in the book, when one does not, be it noted, in the remotest way make an attempt or seem to wish to oblige a single real person to be the reader. "Only the positive is an encroachment upon another man's personal freedom" (cf. the Preface); the negative is the courtesy which not even in this case can be said to cost money, for it is only the publication that costs, and even if one were discourteous enough to want to palm the book off on people, it is not implied in this that anybody would buy it. In a well-ordered state it is indeed lawful to be in love quietly, and the more profound the quiet of love, so much the more lawful. On the other hand, it is not lawful for a man to assault all girls and assure each one severally that she is his only love. And he who has a real ladylove is prohibited by fidelity and morality from dangling after an imaginary one, even if he does it ever so quietly. But he who has none—yea, he is at liberty to do it—and the author who has no real reader is at liberty to have a fancied one, he is even at liberty to admit it, for there is no one whom he offends. All praise to the well-ordered state! How can anybody be so busy wanting to reform the state and to get the government changed! Of all forms of government the monarchical is the best, more than any other it favors and protects the private gentleman's quiet conceits and innocent pranks. Only democracy, the most tyrannical form of government, obliges everyone to take a positive part, as the societies and general assemblies of our time often enough remind one. Is this tyranny, that one man wants to rule and so leave the rest of us free? No, but it is tyranny that all want to rule, and in addition to that would oblige everybody to take part in the government, even the man who most insistently declines to have a share in governing.

For an author, therefore, to have an imagined reader as a quiet fiction and a purely personal diversion, is a thing that concerns no third party. Let this be said as a political apology and defense for what stands in need of no defense, since by the quietness it is screened from attack: the innocent and lawful, and yet perhaps disdained and unappreciated diversion of having an imaginary reader is a pleasure of infinity, the purest expression of freedom of thought, precisely because it renounces freedom of utterance. In praise and honor of such a reader I do not count myself capable of speaking worthily. Everyone who has had intercourse with him will certainly not deny that he is absolutely the most agreeable of all readers. He understands one at once and line by line; he has the patience not to skip over subordinate clauses or to hasten from the woof of the episode to the warp of the table of contents; he can hold out as long as the author; he can understand that understanding is revocation; he can understand that to write a book and revoke it is something else than not writing it at all; that to write a book which does not claim importance for anybody is something else than leaving it unwritten, and although he always complies with one's humor and never sets himself in opposition, one can nevertheless have more respect for him than for the noisy contradictions of a whole lecture room; but then, too, one can talk to him in perfect confidence.

My dear reader! If I have to say it myself, I am anything but a devilish good fellow at philosophy, one who is called to direct it into new paths. I am a poor, individual, existing man, with sound natural capacities, not without a certain dialectical dexterity, nor entirely destitute of education. But I have been tried in life's *casibus* and cheerfully appeal to my sufferings, not in an apostolic sense as a title of honor, for they have only too often been self-deserved punishments, but yet I appeal to them as my teachers, and that with more pathos than when Stygotius[2] boasted of all the universities in which he had studied or held disputations. I am confident of having a certain sincerity which forbids me to repeat like a parrot what I cannot understand, and bids me (and this has long caused me pain in my desertion of Hegel) to refrain from appealing to Hegel except in particular instances—which is the same thing as having to renounce one's claim to the recognition one gains by having connections, whereas I remain what I myself concede is infinitely little, a vanishing unobservable atom, as every individual man is; a sincerity which then in turn comforts and arms me with an uncommon sense for the comic and a certain talent for making ludicrous what is ludicrous; for, strangely enough what is not ludicrous I cannot make ludicrous, presumably other talents are required for that. I am (so it is I understand myself) precisely so much developed by self-thinking, so much enlightened by reading, so much oriented within myself by existing, that I am prepared for being an apprentice, a learner, which in itself is no small task. I do not give myself out to be more than this: fit to be able to begin in a higher sense to learn. If only among us there were to be found teachers! I am not speaking of the teacher of classical learning, for such a one we have;[3] if it were this I had to learn, I should be helped so soon as I had acquired knowledge of the preliminary disciplines in order to be able to begin to learn. I am not speaking of the teacher of the philosophy of history, wherein it is true I lack the preliminary discipline, if only we had a teacher. I am not speaking of the teacher in the difficult art of the religious address, for such a distinguished teacher we have, and I know that I have striven to profit by his serious leadership (though not from profit derived from appropriation, lest I attribute anything to myself or measure his importance by my accidental attainments), I know it by the reverence I conserve for the Most Reverend man. I am not speaking of the teacher in the fine art of poetry along with its secrets of language and style, for such an initiate we have, that I know, and I hope I shall never forget either him or what I owe him. No, the teacher of whom I speak and speak in a different manner, ambiguously and doubtingly, is the teacher of the ambiguous art of thinking about existence and existing. So then, in case he were to be found— I vouch that something, by Jove, would come out of it if he definitely were to undertake my instruction, and to that end would go forward slowly, line by line, permitting me, as becomes a good teacher, to put questions and to make sure nothing is passed over before I have completely understood it. For I cannot suppose that such a teacher could believe he had nothing else to do but what a mediocre teacher of religion in the common school does: set a paragraph for me to learn every day and to recite the next day by rote.

But since no such teacher, who precisely offers what I seek, has as yet come under my eyes (be this a joyful or a sorrowful sign), my attempt is *eo ipso* without importance and only for my own diversion— as must be the case when a learner in the art of existence, who thus cannot want to teach others (and far be from me the vain and empty thought of wanting to be such a teacher!), propounds something which one might in a way expect of a learner who essentially knows neither more nor less than what pretty much every man knows, only that he knows something about it more definitely and, as a set-off, with regard to much that every man knows or thinks he knows, knows definitely that he does not know it. Perhaps I should not be believed if I were to say this to anybody but thee, my dear reader. For in our time, when one says, "I know all," he is believed; but he who says, "There is much I do not know," is suspected of a propensity to lie. Thou wilt remember that in a play by Scribe[4] a man experienced in wanton love affairs relates that he employed this method when he was tired of a girl. He writes to her: "I know all!"—and he adds that this device has hitherto never failed. Neither in our time do I believe that it has ever failed for any speculative philosopher who says, "I know all." Ah, but the ungodly and mendacious men who say, "There is much that I do not know"—they get their just deserts in this best of worlds, yea, the best of worlds for all who get the best of it by knowing all . . . or by knowing nothing.

J. C.

A FIRST AND LAST DECLARATION

Formally and for the sake of regularity I acknowledge herewith (what in fact hardly anyone can be interested in *knowing*) that I am the author, as people would call it, of *Either-Or* (Victor Eremita), Copenhagen, February 1843; *Fear and Trembling* (Johannes de silentio) 1843; *Repetition* (Constantine Constantius) 1843; *The Concept of Dread* (Vigilius Haufniensis) 1844; *Prefaces* (Nicholaus Notabene) 1844; *Philosophical Fragments* (Johannes Climacus) 1844; *Stages on Life's Way* (Hilarius Bookbinder: William Afham, the Judge, Frater Taciturnus) 1845; *Concluding Postscript to the Philosophical Fragments* (Johannes Climacus) 1846; an article in *The Fatherland,* 1843, No. 1168 (Victor Eremita); two articles in *The Fatherland,* January 1846 (Frater Taciturnus).

My pseudonymity or polynymity has not had a casual ground in my *person* (certainly it was not for fear of a legal penalty, for in this respect I am confident that I have committed no misdemeanor, and at the time the books were published, not only the printer but the Censor, as a public functionary, was officially informed who the author was), but it has an *essential* ground in the character of the *production,* which for the sake of the lines ascribed to the authors and the psychologically varied distinctions of the individualities poetically required complete regardlessness in the direction of good and evil, of contrition and high spirits, of despair and presumption, of suffering and exultation, etc., which is bounded only ideally by psychological consistency, and which real actual persons in the actual moral limitations of reality dare not permit themselves to indulge in, nor could wish to. What is written therefore is in fact mine, but only in so far as I put into the mouth of the poetically actual individuality whom I *produced,* his life-view expressed in audible lines. For my relation is even more external than that of a poet, who poetizes characters, and yet in the preface is himself the author. For I am impersonal, or am personal in the second person, a *souffleur* who has poetically produced the *authors,* whose preface in turn is their own production, as are even their own names. So in the pseudonymous works there is not a single word which is mine, I have no opinion about these works except as third person, no knowledge of their meaning except as a reader, not the remotest private relation to them, since such a thing is impossible in the case of a doubly reflected communication. One single word of mine uttered personally in my own name would be an instance of presumptuous self-forgetfulness, and dialectically viewed it would incur with one word the guilt of annihilating the pseudonyms. Just so far as I am from being the Seducer or the Judge in *Either-Or,* just so far am I from being the editor Victor Eremita, precisely as far. He is a poetically actual subjective thinker, whom one encounters again in "In Vino Veritas." I am just as far from being Johannes *de silentio* in *Fear and Trembling* as I am from being the Knight of Faith whom he depicts, precisely as far; and again just as far from being the author of the Preface, which is the individual production of a poetically actual subjective thinker. In the passion story (Guilty?/Not Guilty) I am just as far from being the Quidam of the Experiment as I am from being the Experimenter, precisely as far, since the Experimenter is a poetically actual subjective thinker, and the object of the Experiment is his own production with psychological consistency. So I am in a position of indifference: that is to say, it is a matter of indifference what and how I am, precisely because in its turn the question whether in my inmost man it is indifferent to me what and how I am, is for this production absolutely irrelevant. What therefore, in relation to a non-reduplicated undertaking, may have its proper and happy significance in beauteous accord with the distinguished man who is responsible for it, could here, in relation to the foster father of a production which is perhaps not insignificant, have only a disturbing effect. My facsimile with portrait, etc., like the question whether I go abroad with hat or with cap, could be the object of attention only for those to whom the indifferent has become important—perhaps as compensation for the fact that the important has become indifferent. In a juridical and a literary sense the responsibility is mine;* but, as it is dialectically easy to understand, it is I that have occasioned the audibility of the production in the world of reality, which of course cannot deal with poetically actual persons and therefore consistently and with absolute right holds me responsible in a juridical and literary sense. In a juridical and literary sense, I say, for all poetic production would *eo ipso* be rendered impossible and unendurable if the lines must be the very words of the producer, literally understood. My wish, my prayer, is that, if it might occur to anyone to quote a particular saying from the books, he would do me the favor to cite the name of the respective pseudonymous author, i.e. divide between us in such a way that in the sense of woman's juridical right the saying belongs to the pseudonym, and in a civil sense is my responsibility. From the beginning I perceived very clearly and do still perceive that my personal reality is an embarrassment which the pseudonyms with pathetic self-assertion might wish to be rid of, the sooner the better, or to have reduced to the least possible significance, and yet again with ironic courtesy might wish to have in their company as a repellent contrast. For my relationship combines in a unity the function of being secretary and (ironically enough) that of being the author of the author or authors. Therefore, whereas surely everyone who has felt the least concern about such things has as a matter of course hitherto regarded me as the author of the pseudonymous books before this declaration was made, the declaration will perhaps in the first instance make the strange impression that I, who after all must know best, am the only one that very doubtfully and ambiguously regards me as the author, for the reason that I am figuratively the author, whereas on the contrary I am quite literally the author of the Edifying Discourses, and of every word in them. The poetized author has his definite life-view, and the lines attributed to him, which with this understanding of the case might possibly be significant, witty, arousing, would perhaps if put in the mouth of a definite factual individual man sound strange, ludicrous, disgusting. If in this way anybody who

* For this reason my name as editor was promptly placed on the title-page of the *Fragments* (1844), because the absolute importance of the subject for reality required the expression of dutiful observance, that there should be named a responsible person to accept what reality might propose.

is unacquainted with the educative effect of companionship with an ideality which imposes distance, has perverted for himself the impression of the pseudonymous books by an ill-conceived intrusion upon my factual personality, if he has made a fool of himself, *really* made a fool of himself by having to drag the weight of my personal reality instead of having the doubly reflected, light ideality of a poetically actual author to dance with, if with paralogistic insolence he has deceived himself by senselessly extracting my private singularity out of the dialectic duplicity of the qualitative contrast—then this surely is not my fault, who becomingly and in the interest of the purity of the relationship have for my part decidedly done all that I could to prevent what a curious portion of the reading world (God knows in the interest of whom) has done everything to attain.

Opportunity seems to offer itself, yea, almost to require this of me if I were reluctant—so then I will take advantage of it to make an open and direct statement, not as author, for that I am not in the ordinary sense, but as the one who has contributed to bring it about that the pseudonyms could become authors. First I would render thanks to Governance which in such manifold ways has favored my effort, favored it without perhaps a single day's interruption of the labor throughout four and a half years, and granted me more than ever I could have expected, although I dare attest truthfully on my own behalf that with the utmost expenditure of strength I have staked my very life—more than I at least could have expected, even if to others the production may appear a prolix insignificance. And so with hearty gratitude to Governance I do not find it disturbing that I cannot exactly be said to have accomplished anything, or (what is more indifferent to me) accomplished anything in the outward world. I find it ironically appropriate, considering the character of the production and my ambiguous authorship, that the honorarium has, to say the least, been rather Socratic.[1] In the next place, after beseeching in advance indulgence and forgiveness if anyone should think it unseemly that I speak thus, though he might again think it unseemly were I to omit it—I would with the thankfulness of recollection call to mind my deceased father, the man to whom I owe most, with respect also to my work as an author. Herewith I part from the pseudonyms with doubtful good wishes for their future fate, that, if this should be favorable to them, it may be so precisely in the way they could wish. I am acquainted with them indeed through familiar intercourse, and I know that they could neither expect nor desire to have many readers. Oh, that they may find the single individuals they desire! From my reader (if I dare speak of such) I would request the favor of a forgetful remembrance accorded me in passing, a token that it is me he remembers, because he remembers me as irrelevant to the books, as the relationship requires, just as the expression of appreciation is sincerely offered here at the moment of leave-taking, when moreover I thank heartily everyone who has kept silent, and thank with profound reverence the signature Kts[1]. . . that it has spoken.

In so far as the pseudonyms may have offended in any way whatsoever any respectable person, or indeed any man whom I admire, in so far as the pseudonyms in any way whatsoever may have disturbed or made questionable anything that is really good in the Establishment, there is no one more willing to make apology than I, who in fact have responsibility for the employment of the niggardly pen. What I know after a sort about the pseudonyms does not of course justify me in making any assertion, but neither does it justify any doubt of their assent, since their importance (be it *in reality* what it may) absolutely does not consist in making any new proposal, any unheard-of discovery, or in forming a new party, or wanting to go further, but, precisely on the contrary, consists in wanting to have no importance, in wanting (at a distance which is the remoteness of double reflection) to read solo the original text of the individual, human existence-relationship, the old text, well known, handed down from the fathers—to read it through yet once more, if possible in a more heartfelt way.

And, oh, that no half-learned man would lay a dialectic hand upon this work, but would let it stand as now it stands!

S. KIERKEGAARD

Copenhagen. February 1846.

EDITOR'S NOTES

EDITOR'S NOTES

PAGE	NOTE	
3	1	In my *Kierkegaard*, note 1 to p. 308, I remarked that in a long drawn out correspondence with Professor Swenson about what title would be most appropriate for this book I had consented for the sake of uniformity to use any of the five words proposed —except the word "Fragments." When at last his choice fell upon this word I could not conform because my book was already in the press. Now, of course, I must use the name which has been given to the only English translation of this book, although in several of my translations, which were written before I was informed of Swenson's decision, I could not easily eliminate the name "Scraps" for which I had a preference. Fate is exceedingly ironical in compelling me now to use more than a hundred times the word I do not like. I have scant comfort in the fact that Professor Hirsch applauded my choice. What prompted S. K. to use the word *Smuler* is revealed in the quotation from *Hippias Major* which is printed on the back of the title-page of this book.
	2	The motto printed on the back of the title-page of the *Fragments*. It is the German improvement upon Shakespeare's "Many a good hanging has prevented a bad marriage," *Twelfth Night*, Act I, Scene 5.
	3	Alluding to the title of one of Holberg's comedies.
4	4	In his *Thomas More, or the Triumph of Friendship over Love*. Danske Wærke, 1845, I, p. 218.
5	5	Introduced into the American prison discipline in 1823.
	6	A saying found in the Preface to the *Fragments*.
16	1	By "the System" S. K. always means Hegel's system of philosophy. What follows in this paragraph is an account of his youthful preoccupation with it. This book contains his most express and complete polemic against the System.
18	2	This was printed on the title-page of the *Fragments*.
	3	Page 92 of the English translation.
26	1	A work begun in 1825 but owing to many disasters not finished till 1845.
28	2	Luther's *Werke*, Erlangen edition, Vol. 63, pp. 114 *f.*, 156 *f.*
32	3	In Holberg's *Den Stundesløse*, Act III, Scene 5.
34	4	Inasmuch as S. K. was constantly combating Hegel, and especially in this book, it is well that the reader should be made

acquainted with some expression of his admiration. The following was designed as a foot-note to the *Postscript* (VI B 54, 12).

"I here would beg the reader's attention to a remark I have often desired to make. Let no one misunderstand me, as though I imagined I were the devil of a thinker who might transform everything. Such thinkers are as remote from me as possible. I cherish a respect for Hegel which is sometimes an enigma to me; I have learnt much from him, and I know that on returning again to him I could still learn much more. The only things I credit myself with are sound capacities, and then a certain honesty which is armed with a sharp sight for the comic. I have lived and have been perhaps unusually tried in life's *cassibus;* trusting that there might be paths left for thought to find, I have had recourse to the writings of the philosophers, of Hegel among others. But it is precisely here he leaves one in the lurch. His philosophical knowledge, his astonishing learning, the sharpsightedness of his genius, and whatever else can be alleged to the advantage of a philosopher, I am as ready as any disciple to concede—but no, not to concede, that is too proud an expression; I would say rather, willing to admire, willing to let myself be taught. But for all that, one who is thoroughly tried in life's vicissitudes and has recourse in his need to the aid of thoughts will find him comic—in spite of the great qualities which are no less certain."

Somewhere in the Journal (I have lost the reference) S. K. says: "If he had written his whole *Logic* and declared in the Preface that it was only a thought-experiment (in which, however, at many points he had shirked some things), he would have been the greatest thinker that ever lived. Now he is comic."

34   5   See Holberg's *Erasmus Montanus,* Act III, Scene 3.

        6   Reported by Herodotus 1.32 as a saying of Solon.

        7   "Man is the measure of all things." In S. K.'s time this was generally understood to mean that there is no universally valid truth, but that truth is dependent upon the make-up of the individual. See Hegel, *Geschichte der Philosophie,* II. 28.

        8   Plutarch's *Morals,* The Apothegms of Eudamidas.

        9   A saying found in Plato's *Apology.*

      10   By F. C. Olsen. Cf. *Efterladte Skrifter* of Poul Møller (2nd ed., Vol. VI, p. 151), who was the teacher S. K. most admired,

to whom he dedicated *The Concept of Dread.* See Lowrie, *Kierkegaard,* pp. 78, 143 *f.*

36   1   Grundtvig's *Maanedskrift,* Vol. I (1831), p. 609. In a note (VI B 33) which was not published with the *Postscript* (VI B 33) and which was not on the whole flattering to Grundtvig, S. K. expressed his appreciation of the man's talents: "As poet, as hymn-writer, as a forceful nature who, strongly moved by 'immediate' passion, has worked day and night, as a man of much learning in many fields, though without being exactly a master in them, Grundtvig will have his importance—as a thinker his importance is very dubious."

       2   Delbrück, *Philip Melanchton, der Glaubenslehrer,* 1826. Cf. Grundtvig's *Maanedskrift,* Vol. X (1827), and S. K.'s *E. P.* VI B 21, 7.

       3   He is doubtless thinking of the conclusion of the 7th of Lessing's *Axiomata* (*Werke,* ed. Maltzahn, Vol. X, p. 142).

       4   "Hiatus" is to be understood here in the original sense of a yawn, suggesting that Grundtvig opened his mouth wide to bawl. In Denmark today the adherents of Grundtvig are ready to forgive S. K. for his many cruel jibes at their master. They may well be magnanimous, for they are absolutely predominant in the Church of Denmark.

38   5   Grundtvig's *Handbook of Universal History,* 1833, p. 321.
40   6   *Nordisk Kirkentidende,* 1834, pp. 289 *ff.*
41   7   H. N. Clausen, *Theological Party-Spirit,* 1830.
       8   *Nordisk Kirkentidende,* 1834, pp. 828 *ff.;* 1836, pp. 305 *ff.*
42   9   Since 1840 the small Baptist congregations had been in conflict with the State Church, which enforced the baptism of infants. S. K.'s brother Peter, supported by other Grundtvigian partisans, defied Bishop Mynster by refusing to give baptism to a child whose parents were opposed to it. Professor Martensen wrote a booklet in defense of the position of the Danish Church against the Baptists. In the end the Baptists were exempted from the exactions of the law. S. K., though he opposes the Lutheran doctrine as expounded by Martensen, holds to the custom of infant baptism as a natural expression of parental piety, and he expresses as usual his antipathy to sectarian movements.

46   1   Cf. S. K.'s *E. P.* VI B 25. This citation has not been found.
50   1   A free rendering of a passage in Plato's *Apology.*
51   2   Whatever is known, is known in the mode of the knower.

52   3   Hegel's *Logic,* Book II, Section 2, Chapter C, note. In the *Werke,* pp. 180 *ff.*

54   4   *Nicomachean Ethics,* Book X, Chapter 7.

60   1   In Holberg's *Erasmus Montanus,* Act I, Scene 2.

65   2   Alluding to a phrase used by Constantine Constantius in the Letter which accompanies the *Repetition.*

        3   Cf. p. 94.

66   4   This must refer to the passage in Plutarch's *Apothegmata* where it is reported of Cato (but not Cato the Elder) that he said of people who take serious things humorously, that they would be ridiculous in a serious situation.

        5   The sly Ulysses.

75   1   The Danish editors remark that this phrase is "derived from Spinoza." Doubtless it is, but Spinoza's word in the *Ethica* (where it occurs 14 times) is *aeternitatis.* By this phrase he describes the *tertium cognitionis genus,* which is intuition of God, leading to the true knowledge and to *amorem Dei intellectualem.* The manuscript delivered to me made an attempt to correct S. K. and to conform this phrase to Spinoza's usage; but since S. K. was a good Latinist and the form he uses is an agreeable one (whether it is supported by precedent I do not know), and since friends in the faculties of Classics and Philosophy at Princeton unite in counselling me not to alter it, I do not presume to do so.

76   2   Diogenes Laertius, II.5, 21.

77   3   As related by Plato in the *Symposium.*

        4   S. K.'s manuscript indicates that the reference is to an article by Fr. Helweg in Vol. III (1845), pp. 55 *ff.*

        5   Plato's *Gorgias,* where, however, Socrates represents the skipper as content with a modest remuneration.

        6   In the *Symposium* and the *Alcibiades.*

78   7   The *Privatdocent* was a German invention which had not yet been accepted in Denmark, and therefore, as S. K. remarks, his constant allusions to this personage could not be taken to imply disparagement of any particular individual. Later, however, he dropped the *Privatdocent* in favor of "the professor," which evidently enough meant Martensen in particular, though his name was never mentioned in any of the works which he published before the diatribe of his last year. S. K.'s appreciation of Martensen's talents is expressed in an unpublished article written to repudiate a review of the *Postscript* by an over-

enthusiastic admirer (VII B 88, p. 291): "What if this reviewer in an idle moment were to think over the problem where anyone is to be got in Professor Martensen's place. I say, in an idle moment, for so long as he is tirelessly active in getting Professor Martensen deposed, there can be no question of an idle moment, or of thinking things over. First of all, it is now a simple fact in Denmark that there can be no question of many candidates for a professorial post. Secondly, it is absolutely certain that Professor Martensen at the time he was installed was absolutely the best qualified, and not only this, for there was no one else at all who could be taken into consideration, but he was absolutely qualified and in the possession of talents and learning. It is also well known what a sensation he aroused in his time. Oh, well, perhaps there was a little exaggeration in that, such things can readily happen, but it is certain all the same, that he is a distinguished *Docent,* and that he has no rival now, any more than he could be said to have one in his time. Taking it all in all, the admiring reviewer would likely be of the opinion that Magister Kierkegaard is the man for it. This I regard as an extremely foolish, indeed, a stupid opinion. Magister Kierkegaard is neither more nor less than what he gives himself out to be: a self-thinker. In this respect one may concede to him whatever one will, perhaps also one thing and another which people would gladly refuse to concede, one may also concede to him learning and 'rich culture.' But certain it is that he is not capable of being a *Docent,* and least of all in the sense in which Professor Martensen is an eminent *Docent,* so eminent that absolutely any instant he would be able to get an appointment in the most celebrated university in Germany." "In his time" is here a significant phrase, when we reflect that Martensen's works were translated into English and highly acclaimed when Kierkegaard was unknown. But his time was by no means past when S. K. wrote this, for he was still to become the Bishop Primate of Denmark.

80   8   Lucian's *Charon,* Cap. 6.
81   9   Already referred to on p. 77.
83   10   See Plutarch, *De Pythiae oraculis,* Cap. 19.
       11   *The Concept of Irony,* the notable work of S. K.'s youth by which he won the degree of *Magister Artium* in 1841. He here takes occasion to criticize his earlier conception of Socrates.

PAGE	NOTE	
84	12	Lessing's opponents in the dispute about the Wolfenbüttler Fragments. See Lessing's *Werke*, Maltzahn's ed., Vol. X.
86	1	*Ueber den Beweis des Geistes und der Kraft*, Vol. X.
	2	Reciting the lesson in unison, some boys would deceive the teacher by murmuring, "I pretend to read my lesson, but I do not read at all."
88	3	*Fragments*, Chapters IV and V.
89	4	*Fragments*, "Interlude."
90	5	It means passing to another realm of thought. Aristotle (Analyt. post. 1.7) remarks that proofs applicable in one realm cannot be transferred as a matter of course to another.
	6	Act V, Scene 1.
91	7	Like Socrates in Plato's *Gorgias*.
94	8	Cf. Plato's *Gorgias*.
95	9	Cf. Hegel, *Ueber Friederich Heinrich Jacobis Werke*, in his *Werke*, Vol. XVII, p. 33.
	10	Like the writer Th. C. Bruun, who after the publication of his book *Mine Fritimer* had to have a meeting with Bishop Balle in order to be instructed in Christianity.
	11	In the first instance Jacobi had recounted his conversation with Lessing in a letter to Moses Mendelssohn, sending it by the hand of Elsie Reimarus, their common friend. Jacobi published this letter in a brief work entitled *Ueber die Lehre Spinozas*, and here he gives Elsie the name of Emilie.
	12	Chapter III.
97	1	*Werke*, Vol. X, p. 53.
99	2	Israel Joachim Behrend, a broker in Copenhagen about whom many amusing anecdotes were told. He died in 1821. Cf. S. K.'s *E. P.* II A 571.
101	3	See Hegel's *Logik*, I. (*Werke*, Vol. III, p. 68.)
	4	*Werke*, Vol. III, pp. 59 *ff*.
102	5	Hegel's *Logik*, in Vol. III of the *Werke*, pp. 147 *ff*., 263 *ff*. The following passage doubtless has in view Heiberg's review of Rothe's "Doctrine of the Trinity." In *Perseus* I, pp. 21 *ff*.
105	6	In Heiberg's comedy, *The Reviewer and the Beast*, Scene 2: "I can take my oath at any moment that I came near passing my Latin examination in Law."
	7	*Aristophanes und sein Zeitalter*, Berlin, 1837, especially Chapter 5, pp. 31 *ff*., on the concept of tragedy and the transition to comedy.
	8	*Cyclus dramatische Caraktere*, Berlin, 1844, pp. 99-132.

PAGE	NOTE	
106	9	Referring generally to the controversy between Schelling and Hegel, which in fact turned chiefly upon the question of the starting-point of philosophy. Cf. Hegel's *Logik,* in the *Werke,* Vol. III, p. 60. S. K. had in mind Sibbern's criticism of Hegel in *Maanedskrift for Litteratur,* Vol. XIX (1838). He could think of this as "a big *book,*" for he possessed it as a separate pamphlet.
108	1	I.e. S. K.'s pseudonym Frater Taciturnus in the *Stages,* cf. Quidam's Diary, entry for February 2, midnight.
	2	This is S. K.'s constant complaint.
110	3	In the *Symposium.*
	4	Solon said: "I grow old constantly learning many things."
119	1	A reference to Hegel's "Philosophy of History," which begins with a description of China and Persia. See the *Fragments,* The Interlude, §2.
	2	Cf. Plato's *Phaedrus.*
123	3	Cf. Plato's *Phaedrus.*
	4	Hegel's *Logik* II, *Werke,* Vol. IV, pp. 178 *ff.*
126	5	Frater Taciturnus in the *Stages.*
	6	In Schiller's poem "Resignation."
127	1	Schiller, in *Die Götter Griechenlands.*
128	2	"Fast from evil"—the advice of Empedocles, reported by Plutarch in *De cohibenda ira,* Cap. 16.
130	3	Henry IV of France proposed that every peasant should have a fowl in the pot on Sundays.
131	4	See Plutarch *De genio Socratis,* Cap. 20.
132	5	Reference to the title of a play by Scribe founded upon an anecdote which ascribed the fall of Marlborough to the accident that his wife spilt a glass of water upon the gown of Queen Anne.
	6	According to one reading of the text, he was condemned by only three votes; more likely it was thirty.
	7	A slip of memory, for it was in Plato's *Gorgias* Socrates said jestingly that he did not understand about letting people cast a vote.
134	1	Cf. Hegel's *Logik,* I (*Werke,* Vol. III, p. 60): *"die jenige ... die aus der Pistole, aus ihrer innern Offenbarung, aus Glauben, intellectueller Anschauung u.s.w. anfangen, und der Methode und Logik überhoben wolten."*
	2	Doubtless the reference is to Hegel's *Geschichte der Philosophie,* I (*Werke,* Vol. XIII, pp. 137 *ff.*)—mention is made there of *three* Chinese.

564   NOTES

PAGE	NOTE	
134	3	A negro kingdom in South West Africa which played a rôle in the 17th and 18th centuries.
	4	Scene 12.
	5	It seems that such an utterance is not to be found in Shakespeare.
137	6	See *Phaedrus Fabler*, No. 5.
	1	"Universal History in Abridgement," first published in Copenhagen in 1813 and many times reprinted.
144	1	In Plato's *Phaedrus*. S. did not know whether he was like Typhon (a mythical monster which breathed out fire and fought with Zeus) or a gentler and more innocent being.
	2	A dig at Heiberg.
	3	*De virtute morali*, Cap. 1.
145	4	Similar utterances are to be found in Luther's works, e.g. in Walch's ed., Vol. VIII, p. 609.
	5	Judges 9:7-15.
146	6	Another dig at Heiberg.
	7	Worn by bishops and doctors of theology.
148	8	A book-dealer in Copenhagen about whose absent-mindedness many humorous stories were current.
149	9	The hero of Holberg's comedy by that name, Scene 20.
153	10	See Poul Møller's *Værke*, Vol. V, 2nd ed., p. 39.
	11	In *Tidskrift for Literatur og Kritik*, 1841, pp. 174-95.
	12	See his "Essay on Immortality," *Efterladte Skrifter*, Vol. V, pp. 38-140.
	13	Cf. Poul Møller's essay mentioned above.
155	14	See Schiller's *William Tell*, Act I, Scene 3.
158	15	Vigilius Haufniensis, the pseudonym to whom S. K. attributed *The Concept of Dread*.
159	16	For which there was a special prayer of thanksgiving prescribed at evensong.
161	17	Quoted from the Judge's paper in the *Stages* (Danish ed., p. 117, English ed., p. 111).
	18	Proof that S. K. did not share the simple optimism of the Judge. But already in the *Stages*, Quidam's Diary reveals difficulties which were not dreamt of in the Judge's philosophy.
163	19	Cf. Plato's *Apology*.
	20	Meaning J. L. Heiberg. See his *Prosaiske Skrifter*, Vol. II, p. 500, according to which the "miracle" occurred in Hotel König von England.
164	21	See Hegel's *Religionsphilosophie, Werke*, Vol. XII, pp. 323 ff.

PAGE	NOTE	
164	22	Part I, lines 384 *ff.*
	23	Referring to the widow of Frederik VI, who continued to reside there a great part of the year.
165	24	A sly reference to Heiberg's *Perseus.* Cf. *Prefaces* VIII.
166	25	A pun on the word *Underholdning,* which means material support as well as entertainment. S. K. frequently complains that he had to "lay out money" on his books, and from this it has commonly been inferred that he received from the sales less than he laid out. But Professor Frithiof Brandt's recent book, *S. K. og Pengnene,* 1935, proves that he actually made money, though he might justly complain that it was not enough to support the author.
169	1	Referring to Fichte's philosophy.
171	2	As in Fichte's philosophy, *Werke,* Vol. I, p. 98. The "pure I" equals "subject-object."
173	3	Act III, Scene 1.
175	4	Like Geert Westphaler in Scene 8 of the comedy of that name.
176	5	As when Axion sought to embrace Juno and found that he was embracing a cloud.
177	6	As in Holberg's comedy *Erasmus Montanus,* Act III, Scene 3.
180	7	The reference is doubtless to Plato's *Apology* and to his *Phaedrus,* though in neither is to be found exactly what S. K. says here.
183	8	P. 93 in the English ed.
184	9	Beginning of Chapter I.
185	10	In the *Rhetoric,* where this word is used in the sense of a means of producing conviction. Cf. S. K.'s *E. P.* VI A 1 and C 2.
188	11	The Interlude, §4, pp. 64 *ff.* in the English ed.
189	12	The title of a comedy by Overskou.
	13	Pp. 44 *ff.*
192	14	In the comedy of that name, Act IV, Scene 2.
199	15	Hegel, *Logik,* I, *Werke,* Vol. III, p. 110.
200	16	Hegel, *Logik,* I, *Werke,* Vol. III, pp. 108 and 111.
201	17	At Canae the Romans fought with dust and wind in their face—not with the sun.
205	18	Vigilius Haufniensis, in *The Concept of Dread,* Chapter II, §2.
208	19	Sophocles.
214	20	*Julius Caesar,* Act II, Scene 1.

PAGE	NOTE	
261	15	Heiberg's *Salomon Goldkalbs and Jørgen the Hatter*, Scene 26.
264	16	Alluding to Heiberg's *Urania*. Cf. *Prefaces* IV.
	1	*Logische Untersuchungen*, II, Chapter on the Dialectical Method.
	2	*Barselstuen*, Act III, Scene 5.
	3	Baggesen, *Danske Wærke* (1189), Vol. I, p. 169.
	4	S. K.'s manuscript reads: "Martensen and Heiberg."
291	1	Diogenes Laertius, "The Lives of Famous Philosophers."
293	2	Hegel's *Encyclopädie*, *Werke*, Vol. VI, p. 12.
	3	Hegel's *Logik*, *Werke*, Vol. IV, p. 70.
295	4	In *The Republic*, X.
297	5	According to Schubert, *Ansichten von der Nachtseite der Naturwissenschaft*, 2nd ed., p. 376, there was to be heard in the island of Ceylon a threatening sound at night which could not be accounted for.
	6	There was in vogue a type of religious book which purported to be letters from heaven.
298	7	In the *Geschichte der Philosophie*, III (*Werke*, Vol. XV, p. 320). The argument for the existence of God which S. K. here derides is substantially the famous ontological argument of Anselm.
299	8	*Logik*, *Werke*, Vol. III, p. 60.
	9	As in measuring the distance of the stars by their parallaxes.
300	10	It was the poet Simonides. See Cicero, *De natura deorum*, I. 60.
301	11	See p. 175 and a note about the "bad eternity."
304	12	An instance adduced by Aristotle, *Politics*, V. 10.
305	13	Quoted from Balle's *Lesson Book*, Cap. I, 1. §2—the schoolbook out of which S. K. had been instructed as a child, and to which he often refers humorously.
307	14	In the Interlude.
310	1	In the *Stages*, a note immediately before the Conclusion.
314	1	*Strøtanker* I., *Værke*, Vol. III, 2nd ed., pp. 9 f.
315	2	A slip of memory, for this is related of Pyrrho by Diogenes Laertius, IX. 11, 66.
316	3	A notion characteristic of ancient Gnosticism, but not remote from Hegelianism.
327	1	On July 2, 1505, a thunderstorm prompted Luther to enter a monastery. According to a later tradition, his friend Alexius was killed by lightning. At all events the death of his friend is said to have influenced him in forming this resolution.

PAGE	NOTE	
327	2	Quoted from Gerlach's small edition of Luther's works, Berlin 1840-41, p. 195. In Walch's ed., Vol. XIX, p. 149.
330	1	Referring particularly to Prof. Martensen.
333	2	In Roman military language, it means to report for duty.
342	1	*Hippias Major,* a dialogue attributed to Plato which deals with the idea of the beautiful.
353	1	The word "resignation" crops up here unexpectedly. This may puzzle a reader who is not aware of the part played by "infinite resignation" in *Fear and Trembling,* where it is illustrated by the example of Abraham.
360	2	The title of a book by R. Gad, which was much discussed in its time.
361	3	Such a committee was formed in Copenhagen by H. R. Clausen in 1841.
363	4	He means the "dust cover" (*Smutstitel*), as he calls it in other passages.
364	5	As the genius of death was represented on Roman sarcophagi.
377	6	Hegel's *Logik,* II, Second Section, Chapter I.
386	1	A word I am loath to use because inevitably it suggests disparagement. Dr. Swenson, too, sought to avoid it by various circumlocutions, but in this chapter where *Religiøsitet* occurs frequently, he deliberately chose to translate it by "religiosity," and I am not free to alter his manuscript in this respect. After all we have no word in English which exactly renders the Danish word, or the German *Religiosität,* or the French *religiosité.*
393	2	A. H. J. Lafontain, a German author of many novels.
399	3	A famous German actor, whose Life, written by Rötcher, was published in Berlin in 1845.
405	4	Mucius Scaevola is said to have thrust his right hand into the fire and let it burn up before the eyes of the Etruscan king, Porfinnas, without altering the expression of his face.
	5	The dialectic of the Apostle profoundly engrossed the attention of S. K., as is shown by the "big book on Adler" (which he did not publish), and by the essay "On the Difference between a Genius and an Apostle," which has been published in *The Present Age.*
406	6	2 Cor. 12:7 taken in relation with verse 2. What S. K. meant by his "thorn in the flesh" has been endlessly discussed without much profit. But lately a young Ukrainian scholar, Dr. George

Malantschuk, did me the favor of showing me an essay of his which very much clarifies the question by bringing it into relation with S. K.'s experience of "an indescribable joy," thus relating it to St. Paul's experience of being "caught up even to the third heaven," which was associated with his "thorn in the flesh." I have no doubt that this is an important consideration. It is illustrated in this passage. From this we can understand why S. K. was reluctant to draw out the thorn.

408   7   As in fact S. K. did in the Second Part of *Either/Or* and in the paper of Judge William in the *Stages*.

410   8   Dr. Swenson uses here the German word *Anfechtung* (to translate the kindred Danish word *Anfægtelese*) because unfortunately we make no distinction in English between temptation and temptation, between the temptation which repels and the temptation which attracts. With the word temptation, we commonly associate the enticement of pleasure, and yet in the Lord's Prayer it means the repellent force of danger, to which, for example, the Apostles were exposed when in Gethsemane Jesus bade them "pray that ye enter not into temptation, for the spirit is willing but the flesh is weak." Jesus assumed that His disciples would always be exposed to danger of one sort or another. In this passage S. K. contemplates the danger the intellect must face in accepting the paradox. I cannot assume that all readers are acquainted with the exact sense of the German word which is used here. Commonly I translate this word by "trial of temptation," but this does not quite serve to make it clear that what we are dealing with is the repellent temptation, not the enticement of pleasure.

418   9   S. K. was a regular churchgoer. It is pathetic to think how many sermons he was obliged to hear. His Journal shows that his critical faculty was not held in check. The many passages in his works which give examples of "Christian oratory" were presumably taken from life.

422   10   An extensive park including a great tract of wild woodland north of Copenhagen.

427   11   These conventions of pastors were an innovation, begun in 1841 by the adherents of Grundtvig. Bishop Mynster was hostile to them, and the congregations were generally unsympathetic. In 1843 Bishop Mynster issued for trial and approval an Appendix to the Hymnal, in which he did not include the collection of hymns published by Grundtvig in 1838. Consequently the

Convention of Copenhagen rejected the Appendix and proposed the appointment of a committee to make a new hymnal. This proposal was put into effect by the Roskilde Convention, and the New Hymnal, which is still in use, was authorized in 1855.

427   12   The new hymnal was a need so deeply felt because it was to include hymns in the rollicking manner of Grundtvig, which are now sung with unction in all the churches of Denmark.

428   13   An allusion to the partisans of Grundtvig, among whom his brother Peter was reckoned.

14   The question and answer are quoted from Holberg's comedy, *Hexerie og blind Allarm*, Act IV, Scene 4.

433   15   This has in view the argument in Plato's *Phaedrus*, Cap. 22.

436   16   Eccl. 5:4 *f*. "When thou vowest a vow unto God, defer not to pay it; for he hath no pleasure in fools. Better is it that thou shouldst not vow, than that thou shouldst vow and not pay."

444   17   Eccl. 5:2.

446   18   This is the thesis of Judge William in the Second Part of *Either/Or*. The same thought is also expressed in *Fear and Trembling*, Problem III.

448   19   This is a better expression than "stages of existence." The title of the great work, *Stages on Life's Way*, has fixed attention upon the latter term, but even in the *Stages*, S. K. speaks of "existential spheres."

449   20   As he did in his dissertation *On the Concept of Irony*, written before he had learned to know Socrates as he did later.

21   A term used in *Fear and Trembling*. The point is that, on account of their load, peat-cutters were proverbially slow drivers.

458   22   "An Essay on Freedom, Wit and Humour," 1709.

23   The reference is especially to Herder's *Andrastea*, 14.

24   E.g. Hegel's *Aesthetik, Werke*, Vol. X, 3, pp. 579 *f*.

459   25   "For the ludicrous is a sort of fault and reproach which is painless and harmless."

26   *Hamlet*, Act III, Scene 2. Schlegel translated "these pickers and stealers" by *Diebeszangen*, and evidently the word *Zangen* suggested to S. K. the notion of *Ildzangen*, fire-tongs.

27   Another jest at the expense of Heiberg's *Urania*.

28   In Holberg's *The Reviewer and the Beast*, Scene 6.

464   29   "Irony, however, is more becoming to a free man than is jest; for the ironical man evokes the ludicrous for his own

sake, the jester for the sake of others." Aristotle's *Rhetoric,*
III. 18, 7.

466   30   Although this sentence is evidently quoted from Grundtvig
or from one of his adherents, the source of it has not been
identified.

31   A Greek rhetorician of the 5th century B.C., who offered
this suggestion to orators as a shrewd way of worsting an
opponent.

468   1   It is to be noted that S. K. draws a sharp distinction between
the sense of guilt and the sense of sin. Sin is dealt with later,
in the Appendix to B, paragraph (a).

469   2   This is a frequent refrain in Hegel's works.

472   3   This is not an exact quotation, though it is printed as if it
were. It is a hint—a hint in S. K.'s most subtle manner. It
refers ultimately to a passage in the *Stages* (p. 111 in the Eng.
ed.) where Judge Williams exalts marriage by the use of an
expression which borders on paganism: "humble before God,
and submissive to the divine majesty of love." In an earlier
passage in the *Postscript* (p. 161) which warns against the
deification of life, Climacus quoted this as an instance of
ethical *naïveté,* but there he corrected it by writing "royal"
instead of "divine." Here he corrects it further by suppressing
the word "love" and writing instead of it, "the ethical." It is
worth while noting this subtlety as a hint that we have reason
to heed S. K.'s warning not to attribute to *him* anything the
pseudonyms say. In particular, we should be cautious not to
attribute to him all Judge William says about marriage. Some
passages of his sound like an ironical echo of nuptial addresses
about "holy" matrimony. To my mind, such notes as this,
pedantic as it may seem, are needed as an accompaniment to
S. K.'s works, when once they are all of them published in
English, so that cross references will be possible. But perhaps
this is asking too much, perhaps there will be no one capable
of doing it. The *Postscript* needs and deserves such a commentary more than any of the other works, but I am less able to
provide it, since I have not labored over it page by page as the
translator.

479   4   The formula employed for presenting scholars for honorary
academic degrees.

486   5   Alas, I carelessly omitted a good line here. S. K. says: "Cannot
one be a Philistine in a great city? Why not?"

487   6   Note that this was written before the attack of the *Corsair* had aroused the *plebs* of Copenhagen against S. K., "the master of irony," and made them "ironical *en masse*."

488   7   So said Johannes Climacus. S. K. said more in honor of silence and said it more eloquently in one of his discourses on "The Lilies and the Birds." Cf. *Christian Discourses*, pp. 319 *ff*.

513   1   Feuerbach, *Wesens des Christenthums*, Preface, p. vii: *"Dass das Geheimniss der Theologie Anthropologie ist."*

516   1   We see here that S. K. was already alert to the problem of apostolic authority before he became acquainted with Adler's books, which he purchased three months and a half later than the date when this work was published.

519   2   Cf. Christian Discourses, English ed., pp. 191 *f*.

520   1   Schleiermacher's "Addresses on Religion to the Cultured Classes" was published three years before the *Postscript*. Perhaps S. K. is not reflecting on it here, but at all events the contrast is striking.

521   2   Characters in two popular books for children which had been translated from German into Danish: *Uncle Franz and his Journey Round the World,* and *Godmand; or, The Friend of Tiny Tots,* 1798.

        3   Without any peradventure there actually was such a man; for here S. K. describes exactly his own situation as a youth. In what follows in this paragraph he reflects upon his relation to his father, who, as he said in his Journal, had done the worst for him, "but out of love," and whom therefore he loved above every other man. In the subsequent paragraphs, which deal with the relation of the child to Christianity, S. K. does not propound a theory but states the result of his own experience. Even through the medium of a translation the reader will hardly fail to detect here a sudden change in style corresponding to the personal theme which is suddenly introduced. Such abrupt changes in style, one can frequently observe in S. K.'s works.

525   4   "The teleological suspension of the ethical" is the problem of *Fear and Trembling,* where Abraham's readiness to kill his son is cited as the classical example.

532   5   Cf. *The Concept of Dread*.

538   6   A reference to Grundtvig; cf. his *Om Nordens historiske Forhold,* 1843, p. 19, and *Nordens Mythologie,* 1832, pp. 9, 46.

PAGE	NOTE	
541	7	The great 3 per cent. loan of 1825, which was underwritten by the banking-house of Wilson, and upon the failure of that house was taken over by Rothschild.
543	8	Feuerbach and his *Wesen des Christenthums*. Cf. the *Stages,* p. 415.
547	1	Up to this time S. K.'s works were published at his own expense, the bookseller Reitzel (and for the Discourses, Philipsen) receiving a commission.
548	2	In *Jacob von Tyboe,* Act III, Scene 5.
549	3	The reference here is to Madvig, Minister of Culture, and in the passage which follows, "the religious address" points to Bishop Mynster, "poetry" to Oehlenschlager, and "the philosophy of history" to Martensen.
550	4	*A Fetter,* Act IV, Scene 1.

INDEX OF NAMES

GENERAL INDEX